Essential Papers on the Talmud

ESSENTIAL PAPERS ON JEWISH STUDIES
General Editor: Robert M. Seltzer

ESSENTIAL PAPERS ON THE TALMUD

Edited by Michael Chernick

NEW YORK UNIVERSITY PRESS
New York and London

NEW YORK UNIVERSITY PRESS
New York and London

Library of Congress Cataloging-in-Publication Data
Essential papers on the Talmud / edited by Michael Chernick.
p.   cm. — (Essential papers on Jewish studies)
Includes bibliographical references and index.
ISBN 0-8147-1496-X. — ISBN 0-8147-1505-2 (pbk.)
1. Talmud—Criticism, interpretation, etc.   2. Talmud Yerushalmi—
—Criticism, interpretation, etc.   I. Chernick, Michael L.
II. Series.
BM504.2.E78   1994
296.1'25061—dc20   94-17490
                                   CIP

New York University Press books are printed on acid-free paper,
and their binding materials are chosen for strength and durability.

Manufactured in the United States of America

To my parents, Samuel and Sara Chernick.
May they go from strength to strength.

Contents

I

THE TRADITIONAL STUDY OF THE BABYLONIAN TALMUD

Introduction

Michael Chernick

No work has informed Jewish life and history more than the Babylonian Talmud, usually referred to simply as the Talmud. Its relative, the Palestinian Talmud—a work I shall discuss later—never achieved the same status. This gigantic collection of teachings and traditions contains the intellectual output of hundreds of Jewish sages, who considered all aspects of an entire people's life from the Hellenistic period in Palestine (c. 315 B.C.E.) until the end of the Sassanian era in Babylonia (615 C.E.). Each Talmud contains two parts, *Mishnah*, the first collection of protorabbinic and rabbinic law and lore (c. 185–220), and *gemara*, loosely, a commentary on the Mishnah or sources related to it.

The Talmud scales the heights of theological speculation and plumbs the depths of human experience. Its stance is one of "religious humanism" rooted in the view that "humanity is precious because it was created in God's image, and even more precious having been made aware that it was created in God's image."[1] Furthermore, the talmudic sages viewed themselves as the authorized interpreters of the constitution they believed God provided for the Jewish people, the written and oral Torahs. Just as the first five books of the Bible, which constituted the written Torah, contained theology, insights into the human condition, and laws covering the entire spectrum of human activity, so did the Talmud, which contained the oral Torah and the teachings of the sages.[2] Nevertheless, the Talmud stands apart from the written Torah in the intensity of its legislative and interpretational activities. What the Bible spoke about generally, the Talmud's sages discussed in minute detail, extending the concerns of the Torah to every nook and cranny of Jewish life. The Talmud thus presents views and regulations about such widely diverse issues as table etiquette and theology, business law and sexuality, ritual obligation and ethical responsibility with equal enthusiasm. It therefore became the repository of protorabbinic and rabbinic thought from the third century B.C.E. until at least the sixth century C.E., perhaps beyond. Once the Talmud was redacted, it served as the constitutional document of rabbinic Jewry and then of world Jewry, until the twentieth century. Clearly, to understand Jewish intellectual and social history and the contemporary Jewish experience one must have at least some acquaintance with the Talmud.

The Talmud's unique form of expression explains its enduring influence and its power to arouse interest perennially. Its style also provides insight into its basic values. The average talmudic page is an intellectual battleground: on it appear the disputes and conflicting views of the Talmud's sages. This indicates a will to preserve "the Tradition" in all its multifacetedness. Varying views appear to have posed no threat to rabbinic Jewry's essential unity, which was based more on shared concerns and interpretational methods than on uniform practice. The formative rabbinic world appears to have espoused considerable pluralism, albeit limited to those who were part of it.[3]

The Talmud subjects its sages' opinions to intensive scrutiny. It poses questions about them and, where possible, provides answers to those questions. The questions may focus on a detail as small as the formulation of a view or as large as its logic, source, extensions, and analogues, or its relation to other opinions expressed by the same or other sages. I believe this literary convention expresses respect mediated by an unwillingness to accept authority without challenge. No matter how revered the sage, his view must stand the test of consistency with the written Torah, logic, and practicability in order to be defensible. No authority is too great to be challenged, God included.[4] This "reverent irreverence" marks the Talmud as a work that esteems intellectual probing and restlessness. These values have left their imprint on Jewish culture, and their internalization has been the source of many individual Jews' creativity and contributions to humanity.

Occasionally the Talmud's discussion of various sages' opinions ends in a definitive decision in favor of one view over another. Usually, however, there is no clear-cut conclusion as to which sage or view wins. The Talmud's open-endedness, its commitment to process rather than product, endears it to those who love the intellectual search as much as—or perhaps more than—its results. Thus, the Talmud directly espouses learning for its own sake as one of its prime values.[5] The continued stress on learning in the Jewish community is the result of talmudic socialization, which prompted Jews to honor and reward the literate and educated.

Finally, the Talmud, for all its rich discursiveness, does not favor abstraction. It presents its theology and ethics in the form of examples, parables, and didactic tales rather than as dogmatic statements or philosophically framed arguments. It discusses legal issues in the form of cases rather than as general legal principles. This may signal a conscious rejection by rabbinic circles of the more abstract Greek and Hellenistic forms of thought, but it is just as likely to be a peculiarity of Near Eastern expression.[6] Whatever the case, it conveys the rabbis' preference for the concrete over the "ideal." The Talmud's interest is in human action and deeds rather than in statements of high principle. While the talmudic sages certainly concerned themselves with spiritual, ethical, and intellectual matters, they tried to concretize these concerns in norms and actual "programs" directed to their constituencies. Unfortunately, this has given rise to the incorrect notion that talmudic Judaism was about "deed, not creed," or legalism. In fact, the Talmud reflects the interpenetration of belief, spiritual intention, and action that characterizes rabbinic Judaism and makes it an interesting mix of the religious and the secular.[7]

Debate, questioning, open-endedness, exempla, and case law all characterize the talmudic argument and suggest what its creators valued. These characteristics do not produce the linear arguments or literary formulation we are accustomed to in Western literature. Rather, we find in the Talmud a running investigative and interpretive commentary on a variety of rabbinic sources. As the detailed inspection of these sources progresses, the talmudic argument becomes richer and more intricate. Moreover, the Talmud's penchant for terse expression begs the student to fill in words and ideas, to participate in the talmudic discussion. This makes the Talmud a special challenge to the intellect, logic, and interpretive creativity of its veteran scholars and incoming students alike. Therefore, this volume includes two excellent articles about the talmudic argument, its sources and methods.

Robert Goldenberg's "Talmud" introduces the various literary components that, together, form the Talmud. It also provides some basic terms that orient the reader to the various eras of the Talmud's sages and strata. A clear step-by-step "unpacking" and analysis of a talmudic passage follows. Louis Jacobs's "Talmudic Argument" traces the talmudic argument's origin and development and presents key rhetorical phrases that signal different kinds of questions and responses in talmudic discussions. The article concludes with a classification and description of the most common forms of talmudic arguments.

The Talmud we have described until now is the complete Babylonian work as we have it today. Unfortunately, it does not include an editors' preface explaining why and how it came to be. Questions of this sort are called redactional questions, and the proposed answers to them are quite varied and often hotly debated by contemporary talmudic historians and critics.

Jacob Neusner has questioned whether the great debates about the Talmud's redaction are important compared to uncovering the redactors' ideological agenda as expressed in the Talmud's final form. I wonder, however, if one can arrive at any conclusions about that agenda without a theory of the Talmud's redaction history. Different theories have important implications for understanding any given statement or passage in the Talmud and for comprehending the meaning of the Talmud as a whole.

For example, the Babylonian Talmud cites a tradition formulated in Hebrew that states, "The promise the Holy Blessed One made to women is greater than that to men." A biblical proof text, Isaiah 32:9, appears in support of this view. Rav, a first-generation amora, commented to his uncle, R. Hiyya, "By what means do women merit?" The passage continues, "By bringing their children to the synagogue to study Scriptures; by sending their husbands to the study-house to learn the rabbinic traditions; and by waiting patiently until their husbands return from the study-house." The entire comment unit appears in Aramaic.

Given the rise of feminist studies and the study of the history of ideas and religion, this passage is very important. It tells us something about women's position in formative rabbinic Judaism, which, in light of the Talmud's impact on Jewish life, tells us something about their social standing and role in later traditional Jewish societies. But what does the passage actually say? Depending upon how one reads it, it may say that women's appropriate role is that of "service people" or that women are more spiritually gifted than men. To a degree, each of those readings is the product of the redaction theory one applies to the passage.

Let us say that we accept the most traditional redaction theory, namely, that the Talmud is an actual record of rabbinic discussions. We could then posit that Rav's Aramaic comment was redacted together with its referent, the tradition about women and God's promise to them. This would mean that Rav, or perhaps R. Hiyya, thought that God promised women more, presumably in the world to come, because of the service role they accept during their lives in the here and now. That, then, would be the only view recorded in the Talmud about women's special merits—and their "place."

On the other hand, if we do not accept that redaction theory, Rav's comment may have been an independent unit of thought in a list of views about women and their merits. Given the biblical proof text in the first statement, women might merit more than men because their trust in God is greater. Rav's comment, rather than explaining that unit, asks independently what the source of women's merits is. After all, they are not obliged to participate in some of Judaism's major activities, especially Torah study. He responds that their position as enablers to males who study grants them merit. According to this reading, two independent opinions have been cited in order to show the breadth of rabbinic opinion about women. One views them as spiritually gifted, the other as patiently subservient "home-front" supporters of men.

Clearly, different redaction theories yield different readings and understandings of this talmudic passage. Depending on which we choose, we have two divergent views of women and their spiritual natures and social status. We would then have to decide whether formative Judaism's stance toward women was strongly divided, monolithically misogynist, or mildly sympathetic. We might look to other talmudic sources to decide the question, but they too would inevitably be read from one redactional viewpoint or another.

Obviously redaction theories are important. They are the prism through which we view the Talmud. Why and how the Talmud came to be are not merely antiquarian concerns. They influence contemporary studies of this Jewish cultural treasure.

Why the Talmud came into existence is probably the least knotty redactional question. After all, Jews had been preserving their narrative and legal traditions for centuries before the rabbinic world came into existence. The Hebrew Bible is the most obvious example of this activity. Intertestamental works like Jubilees and the Dead Sea Scrolls, the New Testament's earliest strata, and the Mishnah—the Talmud's starting point—all continued the ancient Jewish tradition of preserving great teachers' teachings.

The rabbinic world's new contribution to this endeavor is one of form. It departed from the convention of preserving traditions as if they were new revelations or scriptural works. In order to achieve this the rabbis used Mishnaic Hebrew, a dialect distinct from biblical Hebrew. They also used two literary styles for recording important teachings, midrash form and mishnah form. The first appended rabbinic comments to the biblical text;[8] the second let rabbinic teachings stand totally on their own without reference to Scripture. The latter was completely new.

Mishnah form corresponded especially to the radical rabbinic agenda that minimized prophecy. The rabbis insisted that even during the prophetic age no prophet could add anything to pentateuchal legislation (Sifra, Behukotai 13:7), and they declared the age of prophecy over. Therefore, they regarded human reason as the primary tool for interpreting the Torah's revelation and extending its parameters.[9] This, I believe, was one of rabbinic Judaism's most important contributions to Jewish culture. As a result, Jewish thought and practice stabilized and developed organically, since no new revelations were expected or, from a rabbinic standpoint, necessary. The shift in rabbinic emphasis to the sphere of human capability flowered into Jewish religious humanism, a view that proposed that serving God honored the Creator and simultaneously perfected humanity and the world.[10]

How the Talmud came to be is, however, a more complicated issue. The Talmud itself contains little clear or direct information about its own development. For example, the traditional view that the Babylonian Talmud was redacted by two early fifth-century teachers, R. Ashi and Ravina, is based on the statement, "R. Ashi and Ravina are the end of instruction" (BT Baba Meziʿa 86a). This declaration is a typical source used to reconstruct the Talmud's redaction history on the basis of "internal evidence." No wonder, then, that the question of the Talmud's origins and development remains hotly debated and open.

Given the paucity of direct, internal evidence about the Talmud's redaction, contemporary redaction theories depend on hints that can be culled from the Talmud's formulation, stylistic characteristics, and textual problems. Variant and parallel texts in the Talmud itself, in related literatures, manuscripts, original imprints, and early talmudic commentaries also play a role in various redaction theories' development.[11] Yet the great diversity of views on redaction results, I believe, from division over two major issues: (1) whether traditional material was formulated and transmitted orally or in writing; and (2) whether the paradigm for the Talmud's style and form is essentially Palestinian or independently Babylonian.

One might ask why anyone would imagine that a collection the size of the Talmud might be formulated and transmitted orally. Yet the Talmud itself records a prohibition on writing down rabbinic legal traditions.[12] This reference might have settled matters were it not for the fact that the Talmud also refers to written texts containing rabbinic views, legal and nonlegal.[13] Thus, the Talmud's "internal evidence" about oral and written traditions is ambiguous, allowing scholars, past and present, to take sides on the issue.[14]

The second issue that divides various schools' redaction theories is the question of the degree to which Palestinian models influenced the Babylonian Talmud. According to early medieval traditions the Babylonian Talmud's redactors possessed the Palestinian Talmud. These traditions' roots are in ninth- and tenth-century struggles between Babylonian and Palestinian authorities over supremacy in the Jewish community. There is little textual evidence to support this claim, and very few contemporary scholars consider it factual.[15]

Textual evidence shows, however, that Palestine and Babylonia shared and exchanged traditions from Mishnaic times until the fifth century, when the Palestinian center became dormant.[16] The major question for redaction historians and critics is whether they shared redactional methods. Those who answer the question affirmatively use the Palestinian Talmud's typical list-like presentation of traditions as the model for detecting the Babylonian Talmud's earliest strata. They also hold that the Babylonian Talmud's discursive presentation has its roots in the Palestinian Mishnaic and early post-Mishnaic periods. It differed from its Mishnaic and early post-Mishnaic forebears only in its length, richness, and prevalence. Redaction historians and critics try to explain why this form expanded in length and became predominant.

Those who negate major Palestinian influence on the Babylonian Talmud accentuate the difference between the terse Mishnaic and

Palestinian talmudic styles and the Bablyonian Talmud's extended discussions. According to them these divergent styles reflect the two centers' differing approaches to the study and analysis of Mishnaic and post-Mishnaic traditions. Palestinian sages were more interested in the application of their traditions to actual Jewish practice. They interpreted sources according to their plain meaning and extended older legal traditions to new situations using strict legal logic. The Babylonians' study methods were more flamboyant. They enjoyed comparing and contrasting traditions, harmonizing them, and testing their logic and underlying theory by application to hypothetical situations, some quite distant from everyday realities or occurrences.

The Babylonians' approach to traditions might be the result of their attempt to apply Mishnah, a Palestinian work, to the Babylonian Jewish world and its established practices. Alternatively, it may be the product of their analysis of Mishnaic material, which was often purely theoretical in Babylonian circumstances, for example, agricultural laws applicable only to the land of Israel. Whatever the case, the Babylonian Talmud's argument style reflects its creators' study patterns and is essentially independent of Palestinian influence.

The proponents of an orally formulated and transmitted talmudic tradition favor an approach to the talmudic text called source criticism, which holds that most textual problems occur because an original source was replaced by a closely related variant. According to its canons both the variant's development and the original source's replacement can best be explained by the fluidity that characterizes oral transmission. Source critics feel their theory and methodology best uncover the Talmud's original formulations and its redaction history.

David Weiss-Halivni, the leading talmudic source critic, views the redaction of the Talmud as a two-stage process. During the first stage Mishnaic and post-Mishnaic sages' teachings were summarized and received extremely brief oral formulation (c. 185–425 C.E.). The original reasoning underlying these summaries was eliminated because it was deemed insignificant. Due to the fluidity of oral transmission, the teachings' recipients often got truncated, modified, or unclear versions of original material.

During the second stage, the redactors clarified unclear traditions, completed fragmented ones, and placed them into the discursive form that characterizes the Babylonian Talmud as we have it. The discussion's function is twofold. In some cases it seeks to solve the textual problems caused when a variant replaced an original source. In those circumstances we often find forced interpretations. At other times the discussion attempts to restore the reasoning, originally discarded, that generated the Talmud's first stratum of brief dicta.

A different methodology and redaction history emerge when talmudic historians and critics believe the Talmud's sources were literary entities. Written sources come in a fixed form and may be easily arranged formally, for example by author's name, or conceptually, for example by a shared topic. If the work of collection and formulation went on continuously in a particular institution or circle, we might expect chronological lists of attributed sources arranged according to the Mishnah's paragraphs. In the case of comments on extensive Bible citations we would probably find the sages' traditions arranged by verse.

A written source allows its readers to inspect its style and formulation. They can then easily notice significant literary details and formulary oddities that arouse interest. For example, most attributed statements in the Talmud are in Hebrew. Anonymous comments on them were, however, consistently in Aramaic. This phenomenon persuaded most talmudic literary critics that the Hebrew texts' creators were not the same parties who produced the Aramaic ones.

Using linguistic and other literary criteria, talmudic literary critics like Abraham Weiss, Hyman Klein, and J. Kaplan have concluded that the Babylonian Talmud came into existence in three stages. The first stage was the collection in writing of the Mishnah and its ancillary literature, the baraitot. In the second stage, tradition collectors created lists of baraitot and later post-Mishnaic comments and teachings. They arranged their lists according to the Mishnah's paragraphs, adding to them generation after generation. This arrangement was chronological: baraitot first, first-generation amoraic teachings next, and so on until the traditions of the seventh-generation Babylonian amoraim.[17] Those who hold this view posit that Palestine provided the model for collection and preservation. They point to the Palestinian Talmud's list-like formulation as indicative of the way this second stage proceeded for all rabbinic centers, Palestinian and Babylonian.

In the Talmud's final redactional phase, the redactors' efforts went into making sense of the lists they received. They tried to determine the relationships among various independent teachings and between comments and their referents. This effort produced the talmudic argument as we know it. The talmudic argument is therefore not a record of actual discourse nor an attempted restoration of original thought processes. Rather, it is, for the most part, the final redactors' creation of a synthetic debate out of the units of tradition preserved in "traditions lists." This debate attempts to account for the presence of all the traditions in the list.

Due to the importance of redaction theories to understanding talmudic Judaism and modern academic Talmud study, I have included selections from Heinrich Graetz's *History of the Jews* and from David Weiss-Halivni's *Midrash, Mishnah, and Gemara,* Meyer S. Feldblum's description of Abraham Weiss's method and redactional theory in "The Talmud: Abraham Weiss's Views," and Baruch Micah Bokser's article, "Talmudic Form Criticism." These studies present the most widely accepted views about the Talmud's redaction, cite the evidence that supports them, and describe each view's methodological foundation. They represent the "state of the art" in traditional and contemporary talmudic academic scholarship.

In our discussion of redaction theories we noted that one of the main issues dividing scholars is Palestinian influence on the Babylonian Talmud's redactional process and final form. The main source for constructing a picture of what Palestinian redactional activity was like is the much-neglected Palestinian Talmud, mistakenly referred to as "the Yerushalmi," the Jerusalem Talmud. During the Palestinian Talmud's development there was virtually no Jewish settlement in Jerusalem, at first because the Roman authorities prohibited it, subsequently because the city's pagan and Christian atmosphere discouraged it.

Disregard of the Palestinian Talmud originates in post-talmudic Babylonian rabbinic authorities' denigrating attitudes toward Palestinian customs and rules and eventually toward the Palestinian Talmud itself.[18] Indeed, the animosity between the two centers' scholars seems to have been well entrenched early on and continued into the ninth and tenth centuries.[19] Babylonia's ultimate domination of the rabbinic enterprise could only result in the Palestinian Talmud's marginalization.

Some scholars have also "blamed the victim." They have pointed to the Palestinian Talmud's elliptical, if not fragmentary, argument structure, unanswered queries, and misplaced pericopes as examples of its exceptionally poor editing. Though these scholars pardon the editors' sloppiness by blaming it on Byzantine Roman persecution, they nevertheless agree that irreparable damage has been done: the Palestinian Talmud is barely comprehensible.[20]

Many contemporary scholars disagree with this assessment. The Palestinian Talmud's purported difficulty is more an issue of the reader's failed expectations than of any major failure of the work itself. One expects the Palestinian Talmud to be something like the Babylonian one, but it isn't. Rather, the Palestinian Talmud is probably what the Babylonian Talmud was like before its final redaction: a basically chronological list of individual teachings tightly or loosely related to the Mishnah. When we approach the Palestinian Talmud this way, it presents a simple and lucid, though somewhat disjointed, set of comments on the Mishnah or related material. While there are fragmented and misplaced sections in the Palestinian Talmud, the Babylonian Talmud contains them as well.[21] In both Talmuds' case one needs to consider whether these flaws arise from the original redaction, later copyists' errors, or our distance from the texts' intentions and mode of discourse.

A short example of a Palestinian talmudic unit should help in understanding its list-like form and commentative style. The Mishnah states: "One who says [as a prayer] 'Your mercies extend to the bird's nest.' should be silenced" (M. Berakhot 5:3). The prayer's text has as its background Deut. 22:6. The verse requires one who takes eggs or chicks from a nest to send the mother bird away. This rule might be interpreted as a sign of God's merciful concern for the mother's instinctual distress at witnessing the plunder of her nest. But why should one who prays this way be silenced? The Palestinian Talmud provides several answers:

1. R. Phineas cited R. Simon: (One who prays thus is) like a person who complains about God's attributes. (Implicitly he says) "On a bird's nest God has mercy, but not on me."

2. R. Yosi cited R. Simon: (One who prays thus is) like a person who limits God's attributes. (Implicitly he says,) "Up to a bird's nest God's mercy extends (but no further)."

2a. (Referring to the Mishnah's formulation:) There are those who teach this Mishnah using "on" (Hebrew ʿal) and there are others who teach it using "up to" (Hebrew ʿad). The one who teaches "on a bird's nest" supports R. Phineas's citation. The other, who teaches "up to a bird's nest" supports R. Yosi's citation.

3. R. Yosi, son of R. Bun, said, "They who make the sum total of God's attributes merely mercy do not act properly." (I.e., to state that God's commandment is the product of God's mercy is theologically arrogant. No one can state with certainty what motivates God's commandments.)

We might outline the Palestinian Talmud's discussion of the Mishnah thus:

Implied Question: Why does the Mishnah rule as it does?

Answer 1: The "bird's nest prayer" implies a complaint against God.

Answer 2: The prayer implies a limitation on God's mercy.

Gloss: Different Mishnaic formulations underlie these two answers.

Answer 3: The prayer suggests that one can know the reason for God's commands; those who suggest this do not act properly.

The passage comments on the Mishnah in logical and clear fashion. It answers a question that the Mishnah begs us to ask and provides a gloss that explains the the first two views' generative sources. There is no real discussion or argument here. Rather, as stated earlier, there is a list of independent amoraic views. The list of attributed sources is chronological. The first two teachers, R. Phineas and R. Yosi, are fourth-generation amoraim who cite R. Simon, a third-generation amora. The third, R. Yosi, son of R. Bun, was one of two amoraim by that name. The first was a fourth-generation amoraic sage; the other, a fifth-generation one. Either way, the Palestinian Talmud's list remains perfectly chronological.

The gloss in 2a is unattributed and refers to both the Mishnah and comments 1 and 2. Because of the commentator's anonymity the gloss cannot be dated. Furthermore, it appears in Aramaic, unlike the attributed views, which are formulated in Hebrew. Because this phenomenon occurs in both Talmuds, it suggests they shared a common format for preserving attributed and unattributed material.

Most contemporary scholars maintain that the Palestinian Talmud was completed around the mid-fifth century. They also maintain that the Babylonian Talmud's anonymous, mostly Aramaic stratum—the one most responsible for the Talmudic argument—developed late, from the early sixth century until perhaps the eighth. The presence of a similar stratum in the Palestinian Talmud presents a challenge to these views: either the Palestinian Talmud was redacted later than generally believed, or the anonymous Aramaic stratum developed earlier than commonly held. Possibly an early shared phenomenon developed to a higher degree in Babylonia after the Palestinian Talmud's completion.[22]

As we have seen, studying the Palestinian Talmud using methods appropriate to its Babylonian relative made it impenetrable. The fact that it grew in the land of Israel with its own material, social, and intellectual cultures distinct from Babylonia's also made it foreign to those whose starting point was the Babylonian Talmud. These factors make most traditional, prenineteenth-century commentaries on the Palestinian Talmud an exercise in forced interpretations.

Three factors united to create modern commentaries that elucidate the Palestinian Talmud on its own terms: the Jewish "enlightenment" movement (Hebrew *haskalah*), archeology, and Zionism. Haskalah opened the world of late-eighteenth-century and nineteenth-century Western learning to European Jewry. Some became knowledgeable in classical languages, history, the sciences, and philosophical studies and applied these to Jewish texts, thereby creating the "science of Judaism" *(Wissenschaft des Judentums)*. Archeology began to uncover the ancient Near East, including the artifacts and inscriptions of later Jewish, Hellenistic, Roman, and Byzantine cultures in the Holy Land. Finally, the Zionist movement, intent on recreating a Jewish state in the land of Israel, had a nationalistic interest in all aspects of historic Jewish creativity, life, and self-government there. The Palestinian Talmud's extensive records and legends of internally autonomous Jewish life in the land of Israel during the first through fifth centuries were, therefore, a natural focus of interest for Zionist historians, religious figures, and academics. They approached it much as Israeli archeologists approach an archeological mound today: looking for the past with an eye to the present and the future.

Modern Palestinian talmudic studies and commentaries appeared beginning in the late nineteenth century. Zechariah Frankel's *Introduction to the Palestinian Talmud*, the first modern study, set the standard for future academic research on the Palestinian Talmud. Frankel's knowledge of Jewish and Roman history, as well as of Greek and Latin, elucidated many ambiguous terms, stories, and cases in the Palestinian Talmud. He also tried to reconstruct its history and to describe its main features. Louis Ginzberg's *Commentary on the Palestinian Talmud* became the prototype for modern scientific Palestinian talmudic commentaries. Ginzberg's knowledge of Jewish and Roman Palestine's material and social cultures contributed immensely to understanding the Palestinian Talmud's world and frame of reference. Saul Lieberman's *Yerushalmi Kifeshuto* (The Palestinian Talmud according to its plain meaning) and *Talmudah shel Kisrin* (The Talmud of Caesarea) continued Ginzberg's work. Lieberman, a master philologist and an expert in rabbinic and classical languages, literature, and history, elucidated many difficult passages in which Greek and Latin terms were central or where Hellenistic or Roman mores and ideas were referred to. His keen philological observations led him to the conclusion that the Palestinian Talmud included the "talmuds" (collected traditions) of at least two schools. According to Lieberman, the Palestinian Talmud was mainly the contribution of the talmudic academy of Tiberias. The talmudic academy of Caesarea, however, was responsible for the Palestinian Talmud's civil law tractates (Hebrew *nezikin,* literally, damages). The Palestinian Talmud's final redactors appear to have favored the Caesarean talmudic academy's civil law traditions. They may have felt that proximity to Caesarea, Roman Palestine's main political, economic, and administrative center, had endowed its scholars with greater expertise and authority in civil law than their colleagues. Lieberman's views, much argued when they first appeared, are generally accepted today.

With few exceptions, works on the Palestinian Talmud have appeared in Hebrew. This is true of all the modern classics listed above. Consequently, the Palestinian Talmud has remained virtually unknown to the English-speaking public despite the fact that modern studies, introductions, and commentaries have made the work more accessible. For this reason this volume includes Ginzberg's introduction to the Palestinian Talmud from his *Jewish Law and Lore,* Abraham Goldberg's overview of the Palestinian Talmud and contemporary scholarship on it, and Neusner's taxonomy of the Palestinian Talmud in his "Talmud of the Land of Israel and the Mishnah." These three articles and the Palestinian talmudic examples they cite provide an excellent orientation to "the Yerushalmi," an ancient literary tell still being unearthed and explored.

Unceasing study of the Talmud has characterized Jewish learning for over a thousand years. Yet the modes of Talmud study have been anything but static. A subtle blend of internal Jewish communal need and cultural interaction with surrounding societies molded new approaches to the Talmud's treasure house of Jewish thought.

During the gaonic period, the first post-talmudic era in Babylonia (c. 750–1010), the Talmud became the third constitution of rabbinic Jewry, following the Bible and the Mishnah. The gaonate, the central legislative and academic institution of Babylonian Jewry, consciously used the Talmud in constitutional fashion. Among its activities were establishment of the rules for deciding the disputes that covered the Talmud's pages and production of legal codes based on the Talmud.[23] At a more advanced stage, the gaonate used the Talmud to respond to questions that were sent to it from the Jewish communities it controlled, thereby creating a genre called responsa. Responsa are still produced today by outstanding Jewish legal authorities, whose advice is sought by those seeking a reply to a contemporary legal, ethical, or religious question.

The gaonic use of the Talmud was clearly pragmatic. Having received the right to autonomy under the Islamic caliphs in Baghdad, the Jewish community had to find a means of self-governance. The Talmud provided the source for the community's legal system. Modeling itself on the caliphate's vision of an Islamic empire united by a uniform Islamic way of life, the gaonate sought to be the single authority for Jewry through its efforts at standardization of Jewish practice. We need to recognize that the gaonic agenda conflicted directly with the Talmud's open-endedness and pluralism, but it was culturally and politically appropriate to its time. While it abandoned the Talmud's implicit ethos, it used the Talmud's explicit dicta to preserve and advance Jewish life. The gaonate's model became paradigmatic for Oriental Jewish culture, whose most famous postgaonic rabbinic figures, Isaac Alfasi and Moses Maimonides, are best known for their codes and responsa.

In contrast, Jewish scholars in medieval France and Germany (c. 950 to the fifteenth century) produced Talmud commentaries. The commentaries' function was to clarify and explicate the talmudic text according to its plain meaning. The commentator's task is to grasp both the implicit and the explicit aspects of a text in order to reveal its total message.

Certainly the commentators' close association with the talmudic text and their grasp of its "internal" as well as "external" meanings created the lively debate and pluralism that characterized the medieval French and German Jewish communities. But I believe they were also influenced by the culture of the principality and the duchy, fairly small, self-governing political units that dotted the medieval map. That culture was characterized by a strong sense of local law, custom, and territorialism, features that describe well France and Germany's early Jewish settlements and the European Ashkenazic Jewry that grew from them. Franco-German Jewish intellectual and political leaders viewed themselves as "children of the King" (M. Shabbat 14:4), the Jewish analogue of the feudal sense of nobility. Their domain was the Jewish community and the Jewish text, and each scholar-"prince" held the right to rule independently in his place. Frequently a single Jewish community had many scholars. In such cases communal governance was shared by a group of elected officials from the scholarly and wealthy classes, which, in Franco-Germany, were frequently the same. This body replicated the Talmud's "seven good men of the city" (BT Megillah 26a-b).

The most famous talmudic commentator, R. Solomon b. Isaac of Troyes, is known by his acronym, Rashi (eleventh century). His work presents a running explanation of the Talmud's discussions, written in the form of short, clear glosses. His grandsons created a talmudic exegetical method that left its mark on all subsequent talmudic study. They were called the Tosafists because they viewed their work as additions (Hebrew tosafot), to Rashi's commentary. Initially they sought to critique and improve Rashi's work, but their secondary goal, the harmonization of contradictions within the Talmud, soon became the Tosafists' dominant concern. Ephraim Urbach, the eminent Israeli scholar, viewed their efforts as the Jewish adaptation of medieval scholasticism's unifying and harmonizing approach to secular and canon law and Scripture.[24] Later generations spoke of the Tosafists "rolling the Talmud into a single ball." Though this activity was probably somewhat contrary to the actual nature of the Talmud, it was consistent with the traditional view that R. Ashi and Ravina had thoroughly edited the work. If that was so, reasoned the Tosafists, contradictions in the Talmud were merely apparent, and they proceeded to "prove" that view.

The Tosafists' greatest contribution to Talmud study was starting the process of organizing and defining talmudic terms and rubrics. Further, as they brought the Talmud together into a harmonious unity, they noticed important phenomena along the way. Tosafistic phenomenology led the way to more sophisticated studies of the Talmud's characteristics and, finally, to the modern historical-critical study of the Talmud. In many instances Tosafistic explanations and analyses of talmudic phenomena have not been surpassed by modern scholars.

Most post-Tosafistic exegesis concentrated on the Tosafists' "additions," which, by the fifteenth century, had themselves become a "talmud." A return to the Talmud itself did not occur until the late eighteenth century, and even then very hesitantly. It was as if later authorities felt that the earlier sages had said all that could be said about the Talmud. Nevertheless, R. Elijah of Vilna (Lithuania, 1720–1797), traditionally called "the Vilna Gaon," an immensely creative and probing intellect, renewed direct analysis of formative rabbinic texts, foremost among them the Talmud. His students and continuators, R. Chaim of Volozhin (late eighteenth to early nineteenth century) and R. Chaim Soloveitchik of Brisk (1853–1918), renewed talmudic exegesis and gave it a remarkable new direction. Their method attempted to reduce the Talmud's detailed disputes and discussions to their underlying legal and theological principles. The test used to prove that such principles existed was twofold. The principle had to be a rubric mentioned in the Talmud, and it had to explain neatly and simply major talmudic debates and post-talmudic views derived from them. This method helped organize huge amounts of talmudic discussion into streamlined and usable categories. In sum, the Tosafists made the Talmud's textual data more manageable, and the "Gaon's school" made its range of concepts more easily accessible.

All of these premodern approaches to talmudic learning interpreted the Talmud through itself. Even responsa, which were directed toward new issues and questions, reshaped those matters to fit the Talmud's rubrics. With notable exceptions, the sense of traditional Jewry was that all necessary wisdom lay within the written and oral Torahs; hence, the talmudic tradition was self-sufficient. Borrowing from the general culture was either fully unconscious or carefully masked. For example, in the mid-tenth century the fledgling German Jewish community legally prohibited polygamy. This was a radical departure from both biblical practice and talmudic law. Yet, there is no mention whatsoever of the reason for this enactment in the Jewish texts that speak of it. Nevertheless, it seems reasonable to conclude that the Church's attitude toward polygamy and the improvement of noble women's status due to the

Marian cult's development were the social forces behind what ultimately became the norm for most of world Jewry.

All this changed with the liberalization of European attitudes toward Jewry, a process that began in some countries as early as the late seventeenth century. Finally, the nineteenth-century emancipation of Western European Jewry fully opened the ghetto to European culture, which had been renewing itself from the Renaissance on. A Jewish "enlightenment" movement began, which, at its best, consciously sought to illuminate historic Jewish culture by applying Western scientific and academic methods to it. Quickly integration of Jewish and Western learning became the norm even for the most traditionally observant Western European Jew.[25] Inevitably, interdisciplinary studies appeared, linking talmudic law and lore with the West's cultural curriculum.

Today, talmudic studies intersect comfortably with archeology, biology, economics, ethics, folklore, history, law, literary criticism, medicine, music, philosophy, political science, the academic study of religion, sociology, theology, and other disciplines. This is an important "new wave" in talmudic learning, which has generated impressive results for nearly one hundred years. Notable examples of successful disciplinary cross-fertilization are works like Julius Preuss's *Talmudic Medicine,* a classic, and Fred Rosner's works on medicine and Jewish law, which are becoming classics; Daniel Sperber's major works combining talmudic studies with archeology, the study of ancient coinage, and seafaring; Yehudah Feliks's scientific botanical and agricultural commentary on the Palestinian Talmud tractate dealing with the seventh year fallow[26] and Yonah Fraenkel's literary analyses of the talmudic short story. And the list can easily be extended.

In order to provide a taste of this interdisciplinary feast I have included Jacob Neusner and David Kraemer's debate over the Talmud as a historical source; Aaron Levine and Nahum Rakover on talmudic law, economics, and business ethics; and Geoffrey B. Levey and myself on two contemporary ethical questions, the obligation to die for one's country and the care of elderly parents. Articles by Boaz Cohen and Saul Lieberman, two great luminaries of the last generation, show the results achieved when knowledge of the classical world and the Talmud converge. Cohen's article is on the spirit of the law in Roman and Jewish sources; Lieberman's shows the relationship between the Greek rhetoricians' methods of interpreting Greek literature and rabbinic methods of biblical interpretation. The volume ends with Ari Elon's "The Torah as Love Goddess," a delightful analysis of a recurring literary theme in talmudic stories.

The Talmud is a huge storehouse of wisdom, experience, history, folklore, and wit. In this volume I have sought to add the insights of modern talmudic scholarship and criticism to the growing number of more traditionally oriented works that seek to open the talmudic heritage and tradition to contemporary readers. In doing so I have intended to build a bridge between past and present, between the familiar map of Western culture, with its disciplines and methods, and the less familiar terrain of ancient Palestinian and Babylonian Jewish learning. I hope this bridge will help those journeying toward an understanding of the Talmud and its significance for Jewry and humanity to reach their goal. Now—*zil g'mor*, go and learn!

NOTES

1. M. Avot 3:14.
2. See Maimonides' *Introduction to the Commentary on the Mishnah* (in Hebrew), pp. 4–5.
3. Examples of rabbinic pluralism appear in M. 'Eduyyot 1:5 and BT Shabbat 130a. The first source discusses preservation of minority opinions in Mishnah. The second records that individual sages' practices, though minority opinions, were observed in their locales and not suppressed. BT Hagigah 15a tells the story of Elisha B. Abuyah, who apostasized. Despite this, his teachings still appear in the Talmud (see Mo'ed Katan 20a). Nevertheless, there were parties to whom the Talmud refers as *minim*, sectarian heretics. These people were "beyond the pale" or, according to the Talmud, did not receive a share in the world to come. See M. Berakhot 5:3 and M. Sanhedrin 10:1–4, BT Megillah 24b, Sanhedrin 37a and 38b.
4. BT Baba Mezi'a 59b.
5. BT Sukkah 49b.
6. Near Eastern legal literature from Hammurabi's Code until the Quran speaks in terms of cases. The narrative and the parable were the major Near Eastern vehicles for communicating theology and ethics. This is true of the Gilgamesh story and the Ugaritic Anat epic, biblical wisdom literature, and Jesus' parables in the New Testament.
7. BT Berakhot 13a, 'Eruvin 95b, Pesahim 114a, and Sanhedrin 106b provide a sample of talmudic passages that discuss the role of intention and "the heart" in carrying out the requirements of Jewish law.

8. The midrash form may not have been original with the rabbis. The *pesher,* "interpretation," found among the Dead Sea Scrolls appended "midrashic" comments to the biblical book of Habbakuk.

9. The rabbis based their right to interpret the Torah on Deut. 17:8–11. They also proclaimed that prophecy had ended and that the sages were greater than prophets (see BT Baba Batra 12a). The equality of Scripture and logic is inherent in the talmudic phrase, "If you wish, Scripture [may serve as proof], . . . if you wish, logic [may serve as proof]." See examples of this in BT Yebamot 35b, Kiddushin 35b, and Sanhedrin 30a.

10. Bereshit Rabbah 44:1.

11. Shamma Friedman, "A Critical Study of Yebamot X with a Methodological Introduction" (in Hebrew), in *Texts and Studies: Analecta Judaica,* ed. H. Z. Dimitrovsky (New York: Jewish Theological Seminary of America, 1977), pp. 301–13.

12. BT Gittin 60b; Temurah 14b.

13. BT Shabbat 6b and 156a; Ketubot 49b, Baba Mezi'a 114a, Horayyot 13b, Temurah 14a, and Niddah 68a.

14. It should be noted that the Zoroastrian sacred scriptures, the Avesta, was preserved orally for more than a millennium prior to its being consigned to writing. The Babylonian Talmud is a product of the Sassanian Persian world in which the Avesta was written down. The following prominent traditional and modern scholars believe the Talmud was written: R. Sherira Gaon (*Epistle,* Recension I), R. Hai Gaon, Maimonides, Isaac Hirsch Weiss, Zechariah Frankel, Chanoch Albeck, and Abraham Weiss. The following believe the Talmud or aspects of it were orally transmitted: R. Sherira Gaon (*Epistle,* Recension II), Rashi, most of the Tosafists, Saul Lieberman, and David Weiss-Halivni.

15. See, however, Martin S. Jaffee, "The Babylonian Appropriation of the Talmud Yerushalmi: Redactional Studies in the Horayot Tractates," in *New Perspective on Ancient Judaism,* ed. Alan J. Avery-Peck (Lanham, MD: University Press of America, 1989) 4:3–27.

16. A class of traveling scholars linked Palestine and Babylonia. They are called *nehutei,* "those who travel[ed] down" to Babylonia and then returned to Palestine. The Talmud uses the phrase "when X came . . ." to introduce their traditions. See, for example, BT Berakhot 6b and 21a; Shabbat 7a, 'Eruvin 3a, Pesahim 60b, Rosh ha-Shanah 20a and Sanhedrin 63b.

17. See the glossary of terms for the study of Talmud and halakhic literature, p. 478.

18. "Pirkoi b. Baboi," *Genizah Studies* (in Hebrew), ed. Louis Ginzberg (New York: Jewish Theological Seminary of America, 1929), pp. 544–73; *Teshuvot ha-Geonim* ed. Simcha Assaf (Jerusalem: Darom, 1929), pp. 125–26.

19. PT Pesahim 6:1 (33a); Joshua Schwartz, "Tension between Palestinian Scholars and Babylonian Olim in Amoraic Palestine," *Journal for the Study of Judaism,* vol. 11, no . 1 (1980): 78–94.

20. Zechariah Frankel, *Mevo ha-Yerushalmi* (Breslau: Schletter, 1870; Jerusalem: Amanim, 1967), pp. 136–39; Louis Ginzberg, *A Commentary on the Palestinian Talmud* (New York: Jewish Theological Seminary of America, 1949), pp. xl–xli.

21. Abraham Weiss, *The Talmud in Its Development* (in Hebrew) (New York: Philipp Feldheim, 1954), pp. 233, 375; *Studies in the Literature of the Amoraim* (in Hebrew) (New York: Yeshiva University, 1962), p. 111; David Weiss-Halivni, *Mekorot u-Mesorot,* Shabbat, p. 263, and 'Eruvin-Pesahim (Jerusalem: Jewish Theological Seminary of America, 1982), p. 481.

22. Modern scholars are divided over the Talmud's anonymous Aramaic stratum called in Hebrew *stam* (pl. *stamot*). Chanoch Albeck favors an early, Amoraic period dating for it. See his *Introduction to the Talmud, the Babli and Yerushalmi* (in Hebrew) (Tel Aviv: Dvir 1969), pp. 576–96. Shamma Friedman favors regarding the *stam* as late unless proved otherwise. See his "Critical Study of Yebamot X," pp. 294–96 and n. 42 there. Most modern talmudic critics consider the *stam* late but keep open the possibility of early *stamot*. See also p. 300, n. 57 of "A Critical Study," where Friedman acknowledges the Palestinian talmudic *stam* as similar to, but much more limited than, the Babylonian Talmud's anonymous Aramaic stratum.

23. *Seder Tannaim ve-Amoraim* is a gaonic chronicle of "the chain of tradition." It also contains rules for deciding Talmudic disputes. Geonic legal codes include *Halakhot Gedolot* and *Halakhot Pesukot*. According to Ginzberg, *Halakhot Gedolot* was authored by R. Jehudai Gaon (c. 750), though most authorities attribute the work to R. Simeon Kayyara (c. 840).

24. Ephraim E. Urbach, *Baʿalei ha-Tosafot,* (Jerusalem: Mossad Bialik, 1957) pp. 27–29.

25. Neoorthodoxy, the creation of R. Samson Raphael Hirsch of Frankfort-am-Main, had as its motto, "Torah with worldly knowledge." This 19th century German Jewish movement produced a number of talmudic critics and historians who were rigorously orthodox and university educated. That combination was virtually unknown in Eastern European Jewish circles until the 20th century.

26. The seventh year fallow is a biblical injunction. See Ex. 23:11 and Lev. 25:1–7.

1

Talmud

Robert Goldenberg

When the persecutions of Hadrian were over, our Sages gathered at Usha: R.[1] Judah, and R. Nehemiah, and R. Meir, and R. Yose, and R. Simeon ben Yohai, and R. Eliezer the son of R. Yose the Galilean, and R. Eliezer ben Jacob. They sent a message to the elders of the Galilee, saying, "Let whoever has learned come and teach, and whoever has not learned come and learn." They gathered together, learned and taught, and did as the times required.

—Song of Songs Rabbah 2.16

Although this story appears only in a relatively late source, it reflects the central motive of the rabbinic movement from the time of its first appearance in Jewish life. Convinced that Jewish life could recover from its defeats at the hands of Rome only through renewed dedication to "Torah," rabbis organized themselves to spread their teaching, gain disciples, and achieve the largest possible role in Jewish life. Of all the books that ancient rabbis have left behind, the most revealing, the most challenging, and the most rewarding is the Talmud.

The word "Torah" was just placed in quotation marks to call attention to its special meaning. For the ancient rabbis, "Torah" meant far more than the five books attributed to Moses that Jews customarily call by that name. For them, Torah was the Divine Wisdom which had existed before the world came into being (see Prov. 8.22–31), indeed, the blueprint according to which Creation had followed its proper course. Torah included all possible knowledge of God's will, of the life

"Talmud" by Robert Goldenberg, from *Back to the Sources: Reading the Classic Jewish Texts,* edited by Barry W. Holtz, Summit Books, New York, 1984. Reprinted by permission of the author and Barry W. Holtz.

the Creator intended for the Chosen People to live. All things, from the most trivial to the most sublime, were within its realm.

Basing this notion on certain hints in the text of Scripture, ancient rabbis taught that the revelation granted to Moses had been delivered in two forms, a smaller revelation in writing and the larger one kept oral. This "Oral Torah" had been transmitted faithfully by the leaders of each generation to their successors, by Moses to Joshua, and then to the elders, then to the prophets, to the men of the Great Assembly, to the leaders of the Pharisees, and finally to the earliest rabbis. Thus only these rabbis knew the *whole* Torah—written *and* oral—and only such knowledge could qualify anyone for legitimate leadership over the people of Israel.

The earliest rabbis saw themselves, as noted, as heirs to the Pharisees. This ancient sect has acquired a terrible reputation, primarily because of the intense hostility to it expressed in a few chapters of the New Testament. What the Pharisees aimed at, however, was essentially the extension of holiness from the limits of the Jerusalem Temple to a wider range of everyday life. They sought, for example, to eat all their meals, not only sacrificial foods, in a state of Levitical purity; this concern, which will be reflected in the sample passage below, titled "Mishnah Berakhot, Chapter One," had the effect of putting much routine activity under the regulation of laws originally intended for special events. On the one hand, this tendency produced the concern for ritual detail that underlies the early Christian critique of Pharisaism, but on the other it turned life into an inexhaustible supply of opportunities to fulfill divine law and thus to sanctify life.

Associated with the Pharisees were the scribes, also attacked in the New Testament as pettifogging, self-righteous hypocrites, but also open to more charitable understanding. The scribes were men who devoted their entire lives to the study and teaching of Holy Writ and to the unending development of new techniques for interpreting it, again a religious style open to corruption, but again one founded on an unexceptionable premise. The scribes were Jews who considered the Scriptures a source of infinite wisdom, and saw no better way to spend their lives than in study.

The rabbinic movement can be understood as combining these two impulses; it sought to merge studiousness with a sense that the laws of Scripture should be expanded to cover all of life, not limited to their own originally intended contexts. Beginning in the Land of Israel, the rabbis sought to carry this conception of Jewish life to the entire Diaspora, that widespread dispersion of Jewish communities that had begun in Babylonia in the sixth century B.C.E., and had been growing ever since. Within a century of the destruction of the Temple in the year 70 C.E., rabbis had started organizing the "Oral Torah," and were preparing it for permanent transmission:

> R. Akiba [d. 135] was like a worker who took his basket and went outside. He found wheat and put it in; he found barley and put it in; he found spelt and put it in; he found lentils and put them in. When he came into his house, he set aside the wheat by itself, the barley by itself, the beans by themselves. R. Akiba did likewise, and made the whole Torah into separate rings.
> —Avot d'Rabbi Nathan, ch. 18

This rather odd story expresses the rabbis' conception of how their own literature began to grow. Rabbi Akiba, the great martyr-hero of the early second century, is described as the first compiler of "Oral Torah." Much like a gleaner who sorts the day's collection after his return home, Akiba is credited with initiating a process in which numerous miscellaneous fragments of transmitted lore were organized and collected under subject headings ("rings") of various kinds. This earliest codification of rabbinic teaching began, it is said, early in the second century; although this part of the tradition cannot be verified, it is certain that by the turn of the third century the Mishnah ("Recitation," "Recapitulation," that is, of the Oral Torah) was complete.

The Mishnah is the core document of the Talmudic tradition. Composed in very terse language and arranged topic by topic over a wide range of subjects, the Mishnah looks much like a code of Jewish law, though it probably is something other than that. Full of unresolved legal disputes and liberally sprinkled with nonlegal materials (stories, interpretations of Scripture, and so on), the Mishnah probably represents an early attempt to reduce the Oral Torah to an official compilation, to prepare some authoritative statement of the minimal amount of learning a disciple had to acquire for admittance to advanced rank in the rabbinic movement. The Mishnah is thus the earliest teaching-text, the oldest curriculum of Jewish learning in the world today.

The Mishnah is divided into six Orders, each dealing with a broad area of Jewish life. These in turn are divided into smaller topical sections called *massekhtot* ("webbings," usually translated "tractates" or "treatises"); there are sixty-three of these in all. The tractates of the Mishnah vary in length, and within each Order are generally arranged according to size. Each Order and almost every tractate is called by a one-word name that reflects its dominant theme.

The first Order of the Mishnah is called *Zera'im* (Seeds), and deals mostly with agricultural law (tithes, first-fruits, and so on). The first tractate, however, is called Berakhot (Blessings); it deals with the life of prayer in Judaism, both regular daily prayer and prayer for special occasions, and presumably was placed at the beginning of the entire work because it seemed an appropriate way to start it out. A good way to see what the Mishnah as a whole is like is to see how it begins.

MISHNAH BERAKHOT, CHAPTER ONE

1. From what time [may people] recite the evening Shema? From the hour that the priests come in to eat of their Heave-offering, until the end of the first watch; [these are] R. Eliezer's words, but the Sages say, Until midnight. R. Gamaliel says, Until the first light of dawn. There was a case when his sons came back from a feast; they said to him, "We have not recited Shema." He said to them, "If the first light of dawn has not appeared, you are obliged to recite." And not only [in] this [case], but [in] every [case where] the Sages have said "Until midnight," the commandment [applies] until the first light of dawn: the burning of fat parts and [prescribed] limbs [on the altar]—the commandment [to do so applies] until the first light of dawn; all [sacrifices] which are to be eaten for [only] one day—the commandment [to do so applies] until the first light of dawn. If so, why did the Sages say "Until midnight"? In order to keep a man away from transgression.

2. From what time [may people] recite the morning Shema? From [the time one can] distinguish between blue and white. R. Eliezer says, Between blue and green. And he [must] finish it by sunrise. R. Joshua says, Within three hours [of sunrise], since it is the way of princes to arise at the third hour. One who recites from this hour forward has not lost anything; [he is] like a man reading in the Torah.

3. The House of Shammai say, In the evening every man [must] recline and recite, and in the morning, they [must] stand, as it is said, "When you lie down and when you rise up" (Deut. 6.7). But the House of Hillel say, Every man reads in his [own] way, as it is said, "And as you go along the way" (Ibid.). If so, why does it say, "And when you lie down and when you rise up"?—At the hour that people [generally] lie down and the hour that people [generally] rise up. Said R. Tarfon, "I was once travelling and I lay down to recite according to the opinion of the House of Shammai, and I endangered myself on account of robbers."

They said to him, "You deserved to lose your life, since you violated the opinion of the House of Hillel."

4. In the morning [one] recites two blessings before [Shema] and one after it, and in the evening two before it and two after it, one long and one short. At a place where they said to lengthen, he is not permitted to shorten; [where they said] to shorten, he is not permitted to lengthen. [Where they said] to seal off [a blessing, with the words "Blessed art Thou . . ."], he is not permitted not to seal off; [where they said] not to seal off, he is not permitted to seal off.

5. [People] make mention of the Exodus from Egypt at night [as well as by day]. Said R. Eleazar b. Azariah, "Behold, I am as one seventy years old but I was never worthy [to prove] that the Exodus from Egypt should be mentioned at night, until Ben Zoma offered this interpretation, as it is said, 'In order that you remember the day of your leaving the land of Egypt all the days of your life' (Deut. 16.3): 'The days of your life' [would mean] the days; 'all the days of your life' [includes] the nights." But the Sages say, "The days of your life" [means] this world; "all the days of your life" includes the days of the Messiah.

Even without stopping to explain all the technical details of this chapter (some of that will be done below), the reader can learn much from examining it. First, the text takes very much for granted. The reader of this chapter must already know what "reciting Shema" means, and is expected to agree that the recitation must take place twice a day, since it seems that only details of hour and posture remain to be clarified. References to entirely unconnected matters of cultic ritual are added without any effort to explain them, and indeed one such reference (to the time that priests eat Heave-offering)[2] is crucial to the very first sentence in the chapter. Technical concepts like "seal off a blessing" similarly are mentioned with no effort to explain what they mean. It is of course true that the Mishnah is a large work, and that many of these phrases are explained more fully elsewhere in it. Still, the text as it stands here makes no reference to such explanations. One simply begins at the beginning, and one is expected to make one's own way.

Second, disagreements are never resolved. The text reports that the "Houses" of Shammai and Hillel do not agree concerning the proper posture for reciting Shema, but it fails to indicate how one really ought to recite it. It reveals that R. Tarfon's colleagues shared the Hillelite opinion, but not why, or whether they considered that everyone should share this preference. Similarly, the different time limits in paragraphs 1 and 2 are simply allowed to stand side by side. No single answer is ever declared authoritative, and in fact several of them are couched in extremely vague or exotic terms and never clarified at all.

Third, nonlegal materials (several stories, the Midrash of Ben Zoma) are regularly used to support or to illustrate legal opinions. Such a "proof" is quoted in full in the last paragraph but then rejected anyway. Indeed, the Sages' interpretation of Deuteronomy 16.3 implies that the Exodus from Egypt is not part of the evening Shema after all, though even that is never clearly stated, nor is the implied disagreement ever resolved. Thus the relationship between the rules and the supporting materials in this chapter remains unclear.

In other words, while the Mishnah *looks like* a code of rules for Jewish life, it apparently *is* something else. It requires more elucidation than it supplies, and it fails to tell how its contents might actually be put into practice. It is, however, a remarkably seductive text: anyone studying these chapters will almost inevitably frame a list of questions for further inquiry—What is "reciting Shema" anyway? Why evening? Why morning? Why do these authorities disagree like this, and who are they, anyway? How has each arrived at his opinion, and how are those who would be their disciples actually supposed to act?

The Mishnah serves extremely well for the training of disciples or for the education of a community. It covers the main themes of Jewish life, and it does so in a way that teaches the most important point of all: Jewish life is a life of constant study; one's Jewish learning is never complete while any part of it remains unexplained or incompletely integrated with the rest. Thus the Mishnah almost at once gave rise to a tradition of careful, detailed text-study that has continued down to the present.

FROM MISHNAH TO TALMUD

Within a generation of its first appearance toward the turn of the third century C.E., the Mishnah had become the central text of the Oral Torah.[3] In the Galilee, and increasingly in Babylonia (today part of Iraq) as well, groups of rabbis and their disciples would gather to study its tractates, clarify their meaning, and apply their instructions to situations arising in their own lives. These study groups, which apparently began as informal arrangements meeting in people's homes, are the ancestors of the academies of Talmudic study *(yeshivot)* that are still the centers of rabbinic training today.

Over succeeding generations, as rabbis continued their study of Oral Torah, a tradition of commentary and explanation began to grow. The first generation applied itself chiefly to clarifying passages of the Mishnah that seemed obscure, but this work was soon accomplished, and rabbinic attention moved on to other concerns: extracting general principles of action from the particular rules that the Mishnah supplies, or expanding the collection of recorded precedents and actual applications of Mishnah-law in functioning rabbinic courts. Soon a new body of Oral Torah began to accumulate with the Mishnah as its core: the first generation discussed the Mishnah; the second generation continued this discussion, but also discussed the comments of their predecessors; the third generation discussed the Mishnah, both sets of earlier comments, and also their relationship to one another; and so on for several hundred years.

This rapidly expanding mass eventually became an object of study in its own right, called *talmud* in Hebrew and *gemara* in Aramaic; both words mean "study," and both had had other meanings before they became the names for the post-Mishnaic rabbinic tradition. The "webbing" of the Oral Torah grew ever tighter, as traditions attached to different passages of Mishnah came to refer to one another, or to draw connections between related Mishnaic materials that do not themselves express these links. Attention came to be drawn to the various sayings attributed to a given rabbi in the hope of detecting the hidden principles that held his teachings together, or alternatively to find apparent contradictions in his rulings and then to resolve them. As new materials were produced by successive generations, it became necessary to decide where to fit them in. Thus the Talmudic tradition became more and more tightly organized, while at the same time newly created materials always threatened to dismember this organization at its seams. When, after centuries, this process of steady accumulation and slightly less steady organization finally came to a halt, the books now called the Talmud[4] remained as its monument. All modern forms of Jewish religion stand on this foundation.

There are two Talmuds. The earlier, the Jerusalem or Palestinian Talmud (it was really produced in the Galilee), dates from the first half of the fifth century. It takes the form of an extremely loose and elaborate commentary on selected tractates of the Mishnah. Proceeding paragraph by paragraph, it offers a jumble of textual elucidation, case precedents and other stories, moral instruction both general and specific, theological speculation, legends about Bible characters and later people too, and so forth. It shows signs of insufficient editing: transitions, both within arguments and also between sections, are weak, and parallel discussions appear in widely separated sections with no reference to one another, each sometimes duplicating, sometimes contradicting the others. The first English translation of the Jerusalem Talmud has just now begun to appear, and it will run to numerous volumes and thousands of pages.

Yet the Jerusalem Talmud is barely half the size of the Babylonian. Dating from a century or two later, the Babylonian Talmud shows the result of more leisurely and more skillful preparation. The arguments in the legal sections are far more elegantly presented, with points made more trenchantly and with the help of a much larger arsenal of standard technical terms and rhetorical devices. The narratives in the Babylonian Talmud also tend to be smoother and more elaborate. In general, studying the Babylonian Talmud tends to be more challenging, but also more gratifying. It is frequently difficult, but the Jerusalem Talmud is often just obscure.

The complete Babylonian Talmud was issued in English translation several decades ago by the Soncino Press. It is currently available in several different formats.

A TALMUDIC GLOSSARY

In preparation for examining a sample passage from the Talmud, it may help to explain a number of terms.

Mishnah—As already mentioned, this is the name of the earliest major rabbinic book, though the term also is used to denote a single paragraph of that collection. The Mishnah as a whole is arranged like a code: a *mishnah* (i.e., a single paragraph) is part of a chapter, a chapter part of a tractate, a tractate part of an Order. Every passage of the Talmud ostensibly belongs to the discussion of one *mishnah* or another. The central status of the Mishnah in the rabbinic tradition is reflected in the fact that the Talmud has a special set of technical terms for quoting from it, terms that ought not to be used when other rabbinic materials are cited.[5]

Tosefta (Aramaic, supplement)—A collection of older traditions similar to the Mishnah, this work concentrates on materials that the editor(s) of the Mishnah chose not to include. The Tosefta is arranged like the Mishnah into Orders and tractates, but its relationship to the Mishnah is hard to determine. Certain sections seem like commentaries on the parallel sections in the Mishnah, others seem more like alternate versions of the Mishnah itself, others seem to have almost nothing to do with the Mishnah, almost no connection at all. These different sorts of relationships can appear within one tractate, in unpredictable sequence. For scholars, therefore, the Tosefta is noteworthy because it sheds some light on the development of the materials appearing in the Mishnah itself, but there will be little further occasion to mention it here.

Baraita (Aramaic, outside)—A *baraita* is a piece of tradition appearing in one of the Talmuds but attributed to a rabbinic teacher who lived in the time of the Mishnah or even earlier. All such early traditions, though not part of the Mishnah itself, were held by later teachers to be authoritative in some way,[6] but since they often contradicted one another, and since later teachers also often felt free to disregard them, the exact nature of that authority is hard to determine. At the very least it can be said that no such tradition could simply be ignored. If a *baraita* was quoted in the course of a discussion, its meaning and its implications necessarily had to be explored. Any later teacher could strengthen the authority of his opinion by quoting a *baraita* in its support.

Tanna (Aramaic, repeater)—The Tannaim, as they are collectively known, were the authorities whose work is assembled in the Mishnah; the name reflects their characteristic mode of teaching—repeating Oral Torah. The first century or so following the destruction of Jerusalem is thus known as the Tannaitic period, and the Mishnah, the Tosefta, and certain other books are called Tannaitic literature. The shorthand for the preceding discussion of *baraita* could therefore be this: the Talmuds consider any fragment of Tannaitic tradition worthy of their most serious attention.

Amora (Aramaic, discusser)—The Amoraim are the rabbinic teachers of the post-Mishnaic era whose traditions are found in the *gemara* part of the Talmuds themselves. The Amoraic era was thus the successor to the Tannaitic. In theory, the Amoraim simply expanded on the Tannaitic foundation of Judaism, but in fact the several centuries of Amoraic activity saw the rabbinic tradition enter into a decisively new phase, as the preceding description of the Talmud tried to suggest.

Halakhah (Hebrew, law; derived from the verb *to go*)—The *halak-*

hah is the set of rules often known as "Jewish law" that governs Jewish life. It must be kept in mind, however, that the *halakhah* embraces far more than the term "law" usually suggests in English; its subject matter is much broader, and much Jewish "law" is in principle unenforceable. Who, for example, really knows which kitchens in a given community are kosher, or which members of that community secretly violate the Sabbath?

Although the Mishnah only looks like a law code, nevertheless, most of its content pertains to the *halakhah;* although the Talmud only looks like a commentary on the Mishnah, the same can be said of it. The earliest public role in the Jewish community that rabbis were able to achieve was as judges and community officials. *Halakhah* naturally became their chief concern, a concern that fit their theological conviction that Judaism essentially amounts to learning precisely what the Torah commands and then *doing* it.

Aggadah (Hebrew, discourse)—Any nonhalakhic Talmudic discussion can be labeled *aggadah.* The term sometimes has the more specific meaning of rabbinic narrative, either stories about Bible heroes or about great rabbis of earlier generations. More broadly speaking, however, *aggadah* also embraces moral exhortation, theological speculation, and a great, miscellaneous variety of folklore. Despite its primary concern for *halakhah,* the Talmud is large enough to contain great quantities of *aggadah* sprinkled seemingly at random among its pages.

Finally, a schematic drawing of a page of the Talmud, and then a sample passage. Figure 1 depicts the very first page of the Babylonian Talmud, just as the analysis that is to follow will examine the Talmud's very first discussions. As the picture and key make clear, even the layout of a page of Talmud reflects its character as discussion. In the middle of the page, set in larger type, are the oldest stages of the conversation, the Mishnah and the *gemara* themselves. The first word is enclosed in an ornate frame (this is true for every tractate), and then the first Mishnah is printed out in full. On the fourteenth line, set off by the enlarged Hebrew letters *gimmel-mem* (for *gemara*), the Mishnah ends and the Talmudic discussion begins; it will continue for fifteen pages and will include numerous and wide-ranging digressions (see below). Then *mishnah* number two is printed, and the Talmudic discussion resumes.

Surrounding the Talmudic text are the two most famous of the medieval commentaries. To the right is the commentary of Rashi (Rabbi

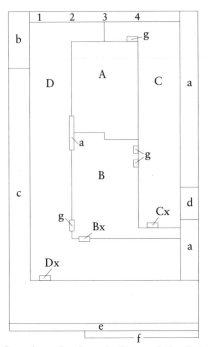

Fig. 1. Schematic Drawing of a Sample Page of the Talmud.

KEY TO SCHEMATIC DRAWING

Heading:

1. The letter *bet,* indicating page two, side one. There is no page one; see the text.
2. "Berakhot"
3. "First Chapter"
4. "From When"; most chapters of the Mishnah, and therefore of the Talmud, are named after their first words

Major blocks of print:

A. Mishnah Berakhot 1:1, with an ornate design surrounding the first word.
B. The beginning of the *gemara.* The *gemara* pertaining to this *mishnah* will continue until page 9b.
C. The commentary of Rashi (1040–1105)
D. The comments of Tosafot, (Rashi's descendants and disciples)
On Rashi and the Tosafot, see the text.
In keeping with the early custom of printers, the first word on the next page is indicated for the *gemara,* Rashi, and the Tosafot. This custom is especially helpful with the sort of complicated page layout the Talmud tends to present. These words are indicated in the small boxes Bx, Cx, and Dx.

Other blocks of print:

a. Cross-references to other passages in the Talmud
b. Cross-references to medieval codes of Jewish law. These codes include the *Mishneh Torah* of Maimonides (1135–1204), the *Great Commandment-book* of R. Moses of

continued

*Sh*lomo *Itzhaki, 1040–1105)*, the master of Jewish commentators. In the course of his life, Rashi produced commentary on almost all the Bible and almost all the Talmud, and to this day no traditional Jew will study either of those sacred texts without having Rashi at hand. Indeed, starting with the first printings of the Talmud in the late 1400s, almost every edition that has ever appeared has put Rashi right next to the central text, as he appears here. In this page, which stands to the left of the binding, Rashi is on the right, but on alternate pages he stands on the left. Thus, Rashi is always at the center of the volume, at the "heart" of the study of the Talmud.

On the right, in the outside column, are the Tosafot (Heb., supplements). Originally amplifications of Rashi's comments by his own disciples and successors, the Tosafot developed over the next few generations into a vast interconnected set of specific queries. Where Rashi tries to keep track of the discussion on any specific page, the Tosafot seek to connect it with some other discussion elsewhere. Where Rashi seeks simplicity and clarity, the Tosafot aim at complexity—but often produce obscurity. Much of the Talmud's reputation for overcomplicated, "hairsplitting" dialectic derives from the Tosafot and their attempt to combine all Talmudic literature into a single, integrated whole. This was undeniably a worthy aim, but it has sometimes turned the Talmudic conversation into a gathering where everyone is talking at once.

Beyond Rashi and the Tosafot, at the margins of the page, numerous other voices enter the discussion: cross-references to other Talmudic sources, a key to quotations from the Bible and another to the great codes of Jewish law, additional briefer commentaries from medieval and even recent centuries. Off the page altogether, at the back of every volume of Talmud, even more such materials can be found. Commentar-

KEY TO SCHEMATIC DRAWING *continued*

Coucy (13th century), the *Four Turim* (Rows) of R. Jacob b. Asher (d. 1340), and the *Shulhan Arukh* of R. Joseph Caro (1488–157.5).

c. The comments of R. Nissim Gaon (d. 1062)

d. A textual emendation by R. Joel Sirkes (1561–1640)

e. Notes by R. Akiba Eger (1761–1837)

f. An anonymous comment, possibly added by the original printers of this edition (Romm, Vilna, 1880–86)

g. Key to quotations from the Bible

ies and codifications of the Talmudic tradition have kept the Oral Torah alive up through the present.

In the upper left-hand corner of the page is the Hebrew letter *bet*, indicating that this is page two. No Talmudic tractate has a page one; the book always begins, so to speak, on the second page. An old explanation of this practice has it that by starting on page two, by not learning page one first, you know from the very beginning of your studies that you will never "know it all." More to the point, early printers assigned the number one to the very elaborate title page which they placed at the beginning of each volume, and then began the text with page two.[7] Furthermore, Hebrew books in those days numbered leaves, not pages. Thus every page number belonged to both sides of the sheet that carried it, and source references would have to cite "folio x, side a" or "side b." The standard way of citing the page just pictured therefore became "Berakhot 2a"—the first side of the second numbered sheet in tractate Berakhot. Since almost every edition of Talmud since the invention of printing has maintained a standard pagination, there is no need to specify edition or source beyond this number. "Berakhot 2a" will be the same in any edition a reader is likely to consult.

A SAMPLE PASSAGE: BERAKHOT 2A–3A

The following sample passage was taken from the Babylonian Talmud; since that one is "the" Talmud—the more authoritative, the more accessible, the more interesting—it seemed appropriate to draw our sample from it. The passage will be translated in full, without omissions, to give the full flavor of the Talmudic style of discourse. There will, however, be interruptions for explanation or elaboration; the text itself will be printed with indented margins, so any such interruptions will be easy to identify. The passage chosen is the very beginning of the Talmud, Berakhot 2a–3a; it is thus attached to the chapter of Mishnah that was translated above.

This entire section purports to be a discussion of the very first phrase in the Mishnah: "From what time may people recite the evening Shema? From the hour that the priests come in to eat of their Heave-offering. . . ." After a few introductory queries, the passage will present several definitions of the time when Shema may be recited and will raise certain questions concerning the relationship of these definitions to one another.

It may seem that this is all a practical discussion, an effort to decide when in fact the time for Shema arrives and then to produce convenient tests for determining whether that moment has come.

It is important to keep in mind that this is not at all the true purpose of the passage. Two facts make this clear: the practical question at hand (When should Shema be recited?) is never explicitly resolved, while the answer accepted by later tradition—Shema may be recited when the stars first appear—actually is provided in this passage but receives no particular attention. The Talmud both ignores the practical question and also answers it without noticing! If one may personify a text in such a way, its mind is clearly on something else.

It will be easier and more appropriate to discuss that "something else" after the sample passage has been examined.[8] For now, let it just be noted that the relationship of all these opinions to one another— which rabbi holds which view, which definition refers to an earlier hour, and so on—will turn out to be of greater interest than the practical matter of determining the law.

> Gemara. Where is the Tanna standing that he teaches "From when," and further why is it that he starts with the evening? Let him start with the morning! The Tanna "stands" on Scripture, as it is written, "When you lie down and when you rise up" (Deut. 6.7), and he teaches thus: When is the time of the Shema-recitation of lying down? From the time that the priests come in to eat of their Heave-offering.

(The "I" in the next sentence can be understood as the editor adding his own observation to the ongoing discussion. Since all this material did in fact originate as oral give-and-take, such semiparenthetical remarks could very easily be inserted as extended treatments of any particular *mishnah* continued to develop. There is usually no way to determine who any given "I" is, or when any such insertion actually found its way into the text.)

> And if you like I can say he learns [this] from [the story of] the creation of the world, as it is written. "And it was evening, and it was morning, one day." (Gen. 1.5)

The Talmud begins simply, with an attempt to fill in the gaps in the Mishnah's presentation. Assuming that the author of the Mishnah must surely have biblical warrant for his rules—a warrant the Mishnah itself makes no effort to provide, and indeed for which it seems to feel no need—the *gemara* quotes the relevant verses from the Torah. Thus, the mutual independence of Written Torah and Oral Torah, which the Mishnah so clearly establishes in its very first chapter, appears to the Talmud a weakness that it equally quickly sets out to rectify. On the other hand, the basic terms of the Mishnah's discussion—the need to recite Shema at all, the connection with Heave-offering—are once again simply taken for granted.

Having identified the Tanna's biblical warrant, the Talmud proceeds to question his consistency in applying it.

If so, later on, where he teaches "In the morning one recites two blessings before it and two after it" (Mishnah 1.4), let him teach about the evening first!

People normally live their lives from morning to night; that is the natural way to conceive a "day." Yet our *mishnah* begins with a question about the evening Shema! The *gemara* began by demanding an explanation of this odd procedure, and by way of explanation provided a pair of biblical verses that reverse the sequence and put evening or "lying down" before morning. But now it turns out that the Tanna himself goes on to disregard these same precedents, because in *mishnah* 1.4 he treats the morning before the evening! What's going on?

The answer to this question has to do with literary techniques. The biblical verses induced the Tanna to start with the evening, but he did not wish to keep skipping back and forth. Thus, once he began to speak (in 1.2) of the morning, he decided to complete that discussion before he returned to his first topic. In technical language, this is called a chiastic structure, and rabbinic literature employs this pattern in a variety of ways.

The Tanna began with the evening and then returned to teach about the morning *[in 1.2]*; as long as he was treating of the morning he explained matters pertaining to the morning, and then he turned back and explained matters pertaining to the evening.

Having thus defended the Tanna's editorial methods, the discussion turns to the substance of the law:

The Master said, "From the time the priests come in to eat of their Heave-offering." Now when do priests eat Heave-offering? From the time the stars come out. Let him teach "From the time the stars come out"! *[By proceeding as he does]* he teaches us something extra by the way: Priests eat Heave-offering from the time the stars come out.

This paragraph clearly implies that Shema may be recited from the hour of the appearance of the stars, yet as already mentioned, this crucial conclusion is left implied, as though it was not worth stating. Instead, the question about Shema is now simply forgotten, and this mention of the stars becomes the pretext for a complex digression. The editors of the Talmud apparently sensed this was odd, and expressed their discomfort in the form of a question about the *mishnah* itself: why, if the point here is that one recites Shema when the stars come out, did the Tanna proceed so obliquely? They answer once again in terms of literary technique. By answering the question so indirectly, the Tanna was able to teach two things: (1) recite Shema when the stars come out, and (2) that is also the time when priests should eat their Heave-offering.

This brief digression, however, now leads to a longer one: after showing one lesson the Tanna teaches "by the way" (namely, that priests eat their Heave-offering when the stars come out), the Talmud now goes on to point out another. It is necessary to know that certain kinds of levitical impurity could be removed simply through an act of ritual immersion, while in other cases the individual being purified was obligated as well to bring a special offering to the Temple. This purification-sacrifice was called "expiation."

And he teaches us *[as well]* that *[lack of]* expiation does not hold back *[a priest from eating Heave-offering, as impurity itself would]*, as it is taught, "And when the sun sets he shall be clean" (Lev. 22.7)—sunset holds him back from eating Heave-offering, but expiation does not hold him back from eating Heave-offering.

In other words, a defiled priest who has properly bathed himself becomes "clean" as soon as that day ends at sunset. Even if he still owes an expiation-sacrifice, his impurity has been removed. He must, of course, offer the sacrifice at the first opportunity, but he may have his share of sacred foods at once.

The formula "it is taught" used in the preceding paragraph normally introduces a *baraita*. This particular *baraita* comes from Sifra, an ancient Midrash on Leviticus.

The digression now continues. It should be noted that the Hebrew term for sunset literally means "when the sun comes," and possibly reflects the old conception that the setting sun goes home after its long day's race. Such an expression, however, could equally well be taken to mean sun*rise,* the time when the sun *leaves* its "home" and comes back into the world. This ambiguity explains the perplexing discussion that now unfolds.

And from what *[do we infer]* that "and when the sun sets" means sunset and this "he shall be clean" means at the end of the day? (*[2b]* Perhaps it refers to the appearance of *[the sun's]* light *[the next morning],* and "he shall be clean" means "he can now cleanse himself *[with the appropriate sacrifice]*." Said Rabbah the son of R. Shela, "If so, Scripture should say, 'he shall thereafter become clean.' What is the meaning of 'He shall be clean'?—With the *[new]* day, as people say, 'The sun has turned to evening, and the day is clean.' "

This *[teaching]* of Rabbah b.[9] R. Shela was not known in the West *[i.e., the schools of the land of Israel],* and they raised the question, Does this "and when the sun sets" refer to sunset, so that "he shall be clean" means with the *[new]* day? Perhaps it refers to the appearance of *[the sun's]* light and "he shall be clean" means "the man can now cleanse himself."

But then they resolved the matter from a *baraita;* as it is taught in a *baraita:* "The sign for the matter is the emergence of the stars." You can deduce that *[Scripture]* refers to sunset, so that "he shall be clean" means with the *[new]* day.

It is typical of the Talmud that a digression that really has nothing to do with the subject at hand is treated in the same thorough manner as the central theme of the discussion. The motif of "the emergence of the stars" has led to consideration of the proper sequence of acts required for a defiled person's repurification, and thus to the claim that an expiation-sacrifice, though obligatory, is not a prerequisite for the purification itself. The Talmud now supports this assertion by every means at its disposal: extremely painstaking analysis of a single biblical verse, citation of a relevant *baraita,* reference to a presumably well-known popular slogan reflecting the favored interpretation. Along the way, it becomes clear as well that not every rabbi knew all pertinent traditions. In the absence of Rabbah b. R. Shela's elegant inference—it depends on the absence of a single letter from the Hebrew text of the Bible—the rabbis of "the West" had to reach the conclusion in a much less direct way, by citing a *baraita* of no clear relevance (the sign of *what* matter? What is this *baraita* talking about?) and then simply saying that it proved their point!

The discussion now returns to the actual subject—the precise definition, for purposes of reciting Shema, of the onset of evening.

The Master said:

(This usually is a general formula for reintroducing any text previously quoted in the discussion, though the phrase appears without this meaning just a few lines above. Normally, the text thus introduced was previously incidental to the discussion, but now becomes central. In the present case, the text in question turns out to be our *mishnah* itself.)

"From the hour that the priests come in to eat of the Heave-offering." But throw these [together]:

(A standard formula for introducing a second text which seems to contradict the one already under consideration.)

From what time [may people] recite the evening Shema? From when a poor man comes in to eat his bread with salt until the hour he gets up at the end of his meal.

The final part [of this new text] certainly differs from our Mishnah [which provides a much later end-limit]; shall we say the beginning contradicts our Mishnah [as well]? No; a poor man and a priest [represent] one measure [of time].

That is, the *mishnah* speaks of priests and the *baraita* speaks of "a poor man," but these definitions of the earliest time for Shema do not conflict because the two events in question coincide: they represent the same "measure" of time. This response, however, gives rise to further complications, but note that the relevance of the *baraita* about "the sign for the matter" has now been clarified.

But throw these [together]: From what time [may people] begin to recite the evening Shema? From the hour that people come in to eat their bread on Sabbath eves; [these are] R. Meir's words, but the Sages say, From the hour that the priests have the right to eat their Heave-offering. The sign for the matter is the emergence of the stars. And even though this matter has no proof it has a [Scriptural] indication, as it is said, "And we worked at the task, while half of them held spears, from the first light of dawn until the emergence of the stars" (Neh. 4.15). And it says, "So they were for us a guard by night, and a workforce by day" (Neh. 4.16).

Before the real work of determining the mutual relationship of all these "signs" can proceed, the cited sources once more provoke a digression that must first be cleared away. If the aim is to show that night is considered to begin with the appearance of the stars, then surely verse 15 makes that clear. Why bring in verse 16 at all? The answer is that

verse 15 by itself might be taken to describe only these particular workers' personal habit; only verse 16 explicitly identifies their working hours
as "day" and their idle hours as "night."

Why "and it says"? If you say it becomes night when the sun sets, but these
[people worked] late and *[resumed work]* early, come and hear: "So they were
for us a guard by night, and a workforce by day."

(The phrase "come and hear" is a very common formula used to introduce a text intended to prove a point or resolve a dispute. This can be a
biblical citation, as here, or a rabbinic saying taken from some other
context.)
    The discussion now returns to the real, underlying question: How do
all these different definitions of the time for the evening Shema compare?

[If] you assume that a poor man and "people" *[represent]* one measure *[of
time]*, and if you say that a poor man and a priest *[represent]*
one measure *[of time, as was indeed just proposed]* then the Sages agree with R.
Meir! You must rather infer that a poor man *[represents]* one measure and a
priest *[represents]* a different measure. No; a poor man and a priest *[represent]*
one measure *[of time]*, while a poor man and "people" do not *[represent]* one
measure *[of time]*.

In the name of various authorities, different Tannaitic traditions are
cited to determine the time "night" begins. This is necessary because all
take the beginning of "night" to be the point after which the evening
Shema may be recited. These various limits, however, are expressed in
terms that have nothing to do with reciting Shema or with one another!
They speak of priests becoming cleansed and eating their Heave-offering,
poor people eating their humble daily meal, "people" in general starting
their Sabbath meal, and so on. Only one of these definitions—the appearance of the stars—directly concerns "night"; all the rest refer to
apparently familiar social and cultural arrangements which no one here
stops to clarify. For this proliferation of definitions to make any sense at
all, it must be assumed that the various authorities disagree, and that
each has found some well-known custom that illustrates his particular
opinion. Otherwise they all have indulged in a terrible game of obfusca-
tion, giving numerous unclear answers to the basic question when one
simple answer would have done. Part of the Talmud's task here, then, is
to clarify the disagreements that these traditions presumably report.
    The present complication arose because the Talmud tried to eliminate

an apparent contradiction between two such traditions by saying that a poor man and a priest (that is, the time such people begin their evening meal) represent one time limit and not two. They could be identified in this way because the two limits in question are both reported anonymously, and therefore can be taken to express the consensus of "the Sages," not some individual's divergent opinion. On the other hand, Meir's term "people," initially taken as a generality embracing all other terms (the point of his answer would then lie in its reference to the Sabbath), in the end is understood as having a specific meaning of its own. While this interpretation may seem less attractive than the first, it means that the earlier contradiction need not be resolved anew.

This extravagantly "Talmudical" discussion actually reflects a basic conflict of principles. Two assumptions have been working here — that (a) different named authorities give different answers to the same question because they in fact disagree, but that (b) all anonymous answers are consistent with one another, even when they seem to differ. The Talmudic authorities knew well that exceptions to both these principles could be found (some will presently be cited), but they preferred to uphold them whenever they could. Needless to say, these principles pull the discussion in opposite directions: one multiplies disagreements, while the other seeks to deny them. This tension is the root cause of the complicated discussion now underway.

> But *do* a poor man and a priest [*represent*] one measure? Throw these [*together*]:
> From when [*may people*] begin to recite the Shema evenings? From the hour that the day becomes holy on Sabbath eves; [*these are*] R. Eliezer's words, but R. Joshua says, From the hour that the priests become cleansed in order to eat of their Heave-offering. R. Meir says, From the hour that the priests immerse themselves in order to eat of their Heave-offering. (R. Judah said to him, "But do not priests immerse themselves while it is still day?") R. Hanina says, From the hour that a poor man comes in to eat his bread with salt. R. Ahai (some say R. Aha) says, From the hour that most people come in to sit down [*to their meal*].
> And if you say that a poor man and a priest [*represent*] one measure, then R. Hanina[*'s opinion*] and R. Joshua[*'s opinion*] are the same. Must you not rather infer that the poor man's measure is one [*thing*] and the priest's measure is another [*thing*]? You must infer [*this after all*].

Thus finally the tension between the two working principles is resolved: once both "priest" and "poor man" are identified as the opinions of specific, named authorities, it can be taken for granted that they refer to different time limits. The anonymous statements that gave rise to this extended discussion may now be allowed to differ, since each can now be traced back to a different early master—the *mishnah* to Joshua and the original *baraita* to Hanina. Why, in the course of transmission, each opinion came to be separated from the name of its author, so that both seemed anonymous statements expressing a single consensus, is apparently not a question that arouses concern. It is just assumed that such things happen.

Once the Talmud has thus resolved the technical question it found so bothersome, it moves on to another of the same kind; the substantive question of when actually to recite Shema will never receive such careful consideration. In the following question, "them" refers to the same two criteria, the priest and the poor man.

Which of them is later? It makes sense that the poor man must be later, for if you say that the poor man is earlier, R. Hanina*['s opinion]* is the same as R. Eliezer*['s]*.[10] Must you not infer that the poor man is later? You must infer *[this]*.

The Talmud's consideration of the Mishnah and its implications will go no farther, but there are a few concluding details before the discussion actually ends.

The Master said: "R. Judah said to him, 'But do not priests immerse themselves while it is still day?' " R. Judah speaks well to R. Meir! R. Meir *[can]* say to him as follows: "Do you suppose I am speaking on *[the basis of]* your *[conception of]* twilight," as R. Yose said, "Twilight is like the blink of an eye; this one comes in and this one goes out and it is impossible to grasp *[the moment]*."

As Leviticus 22.7 makes clear (see above), immersion for the removal of impurity must precede *sunset*, while Shema must be recited at the time "when you lie down," that is, after *night* has begun. Thus, it is clear that immersion comes before the time for Shema, and in fact Meir proposes that the priests' immersing themselves be the sign to onlookers that the time for Shema has arrived. Judah's objection is that between the time for immersing and the time for Shema there is an intermediate stage called twilight which is not appropriate for either activity; it is no longer day, but it is not yet night. Meir's rule for Shema will lead people to perform the recitation before the proper time.

Meir's response grants Judah's logic, but denies his premise. Judah assumes that "twilight" lasts a substantial period of time (Rashi in his commentary suggests this is the time it takes a man to walk half a mile), but Meir and their contemporary, Yose, do not agree. On their understanding, "twilight" is really only a logical concept; it is the name people give to the transition from day to night, but it has no duration of its own at all. Since priests always immerse themselves at the last possible moment before sunset, their behavior is indeed a reliable indicator that the time for Shema has arrived.

The composition of this brief exchange requires further comment. This passage, while it *may* begin with an authentic comment by R. Judah, almost certainly does not record R. Meir's actual response. Numerous details suggest this conclusion. For one thing, Judah speaks Hebrew, as does Yose in the final remark attributed to him, while Meir is made to speak Aramaic—and Babylonian Aramaic at that. Furthermore, Yose's description of twilight is introduced with the phrase "as R. Yose *said*," as though this were a saying of the master received from past generations. Yose was in fact the contemporary of Meir and Judah; if we were dealing here with a live debate between the latter two, Yose's saying would be introduced in different terms. It seems, therefore, that Yose's comment was appended by a later contributor to indicate the basis of Meir's remark,[11] and that Meir's response itself really shows how someone else thought he could have answered Judah's challenge.

This whole debate is an expansion of an earlier tradition (the introductory "the Master said" makes this clear), an expansion that grew by stages: first someone supplied a defense of Meir's position against Judah's challenge and formulated this defense as though it were Meir's own, and then Meir's defense was reinforced by showing that his contemporary, Yose, agreed with him in his basic dispute with Judah. As is often the case with such expanded traditions, the new materials appear in the language of their Aramaic-speaking inventors, while older traditions appear in Hebrew.

The fact that such a debate could have been composed in this way teaches an important feature of the Talmudic tradition. The names of Judah and Meir and Yose function here chiefly as ways of designating specific points of view. These points of view are what matter, not the names. Meir as a historical personage is of very little interest here; his name, along with the others, is used as a label and little more. No doubt these men really lived and as far as anyone knows they really held the opinions attributed to them here. But in the course of time their legal rulings took on an importance that had nothing to do with these teachers as real people, and finally overshadowed their flesh-and-blood humanity until it could hardly be seen. The fact that Judah's disagreement with Meir was continued this way by later generations shows how important the disagreement remained, while the fact that it was continued in the form of a historical fiction shows how unimportant the "reality" of these people came to be.

These considerations shed light on the Talmud's final question: can these teachers really have said the things attributed to them? In the Talmudic context, this question does not mean, is the attribution to Meir historically reliable, because after all we wish to follow the great man's teaching as he really spoke it? Instead it means, are the teachings attributed to Meir internally consistent, so that we may use them for the purpose of building a more elaborate dialectic, so that we can use the name "Meir" and expect our hearers will know the set of opinions we mean to invoke? Or are they inconsistent, so that the Talmudic technique of labeling rulings with the names of past authorities turns out to be useless?

[3a] R. Meir's [opinion creates a] difficulty for R. Meir's [other opinion]. Two Tannaim [handed down traditions] according to R. Meir.

Meir's opinion quoted earlier, that Shema may be recited from the hour that people come home to eat their Sabbath meal, conflicts with the opinion quoted just now, that Shema may be recited after the priests have had their ritual baths; the first ruling stipulates a rather later hour than the second. The Talmud concedes the difficulty and simply says that different "reciters" cited traditions in the name of R. Meir which were not in accord with one another. Thus the Talmud grants the existence of unreliable traditions, though the assumption seems to be that traditions are to be considered reliable unless specific evidence casts doubt on them, as here. No consideration is given to the question of which of these two "Tannaim" was right; evidently there is no way to tell.

In the post-Mishnaic age, the title "Tanna" was also given to a functionary in the rabbinic schools whose sole task was to memorize older traditions and then to recite them on command. Unlike the earlier

Tannaim, these later ones were figures of low prestige. It was widely recognized that the qualifications for this position were an excellent memory and a general lack of imagination; these had to be people who could be counted on simply to repeat what they had learned, without trying to "improve" it in any way. In the present case, two such Tannaim are said to have transmitted incompatible traditions in Meir's name. The Talmud makes no effort either to explain how this situation arose or to consider its wider implications.

> R. Eliezer's [opinion creates a] difficulty for R. Eliezer's [other opinion]. Two Tannaim [handed down traditions] according to R. Eliezer; or if you like I can say that the beginning [of the mishnah] is not R. Eliezer['s opinion].

Again, an inconsistency is alleged among one man's teachings; in this case, Eliezer's ruling in the last baraita authorizes reciting Shema from the onset of Sabbath holiness while the mishnah itself, apparently in the name of Eliezer, draws the line at the hour that priests eat Heave-offering. This latter has now been identified as nightfall, while the Sabbath begins with sunset, which is earlier.

At first, the Talmud offers the same solution as in the case of Meir's teachings, but here a second possibility arises. According to the Mishnah, Eliezer, "the Sages," and Gamaliel clearly disagree over the end of the time for the evening Shema. Since Eliezer's name follows hard on the first clause of the text, it is natural to take that clause as reflecting his opinion. But that initial clause treats of the beginning of the time for Shema; what if it really represents an anonymous statement of the rabbis' consensus, and not Eliezer's opinion at all? In that case, there is no inconsistency in Eliezer's position; the baraita explicitly reports his position, in his name, and the Mishnah has nothing to do with him.

This proposal once again reflects the Talmud's indifference toward the history behind these traditions. The first clause of the Mishnah may or may not reflect Eliezer's real opinion, and in the end the Talmud seems not to care. As long as the internal consistency of the set of opinions attributed to Eliezer can be maintained, the question whether these really were his teachings drops out of sight. The set of opinions must be maintained in its integrity, for it is needed as a stone in the edifice of legal tradition; as a historical record, however, it evokes no interest at all.

This brief discussion marks the end of the Talmud's treatment of the first clause of the Mishnah. As noted, the second clause is undoubtedly to be taken as Eliezer's opinion, so this way of resolving the alleged contradiction in his teaching plays a double role: it completes the first major section of the Talmud and it supplies a transition to the next. In medieval manuscripts and most printed editions, the second clause of the Mishnah is actually copied out here, providing a break in the text and calling attention to the change in subject. The Talmud does not always supply such a clear marker, and there are many passages where it is no longer clear which clause of Mishnah is the one under consideration. Here, however, there can be no such doubt, and this rather lengthy translation/commentary can therefore come to an end.

WHAT WAS THIS PASSAGE TRYING TO DO?

An outline of the first section of the Talmud would look like this:

  I. "Where does the Tanna stand?"—Inquiry into the basis of the Mishnah
     A. Biblical warrants
     B. Principles of editorial arrangement
 II. Why not just say "from the appearance of the stars"?—a long side discussion about expiation-sacrifices and priests eating their holy foods
III. The first outside source: the poor man
     Solution to problem: poor man equals priest
 IV. The second outside source: people/priests
     A. Prooftext from Nehemiah provokes second digression
     B. Solution to problem: poor man still equals priest, but "people" is different
  V. The third outside source: Sabbath/priests may eat/immersion (challenged)/poor man/most people
     A. Final proof that poor man and priest are not the same measure
     B. Which is later? . . .
 VI. Final matters
     A. Judah's challenge and Meir's response
     B. Meir *vs.* Meir
     C. Eliezer *vs.* Eliezer

Although our *mishnah* seems concerned with fixing the proper rule for reciting Shema, and although the *gemara* seems concerned with clarifying this rule, a look at this outline makes clear that the actual work of determining the proper time for Shema receives almost no attention at all. From the very beginning, and almost as a side point, it is taken for granted that the time for saying Shema begins with the appearance of the stars, but the Talmud never says this, and instead keeps adding more and more opinions to an increasingly complicated mix. In general, the Talmud seems more interested here in understanding all these opinions, and in clarifying their relationship to one another, than in actually choosing one to be the operative rule. (This is not always the case, to be sure, but this passage must be allowed to speak for itself.) Perhaps for this reason, later codes of Jewish law simply disregarded all these Talmudic complications and laid down the rule that Shema may be recited from the time that three stars of medium brightness have appeared in the sky.

If, then, the Talmud is not primarily interested in determining the law, what is it trying to do? As already hinted, and as its own name implies, the Talmud is a scholastic text. *Its chief purpose is to preserve the record of earlier generations studying their own tradition and provide materials for later generations wishing to do the same.* It is a book produced by and for people whose highest value was the life of study.

Thus, to the extent that the Talmud is concerned with law, its purpose is not really to lay down simple, hard-and-fast rules, but rather to build the law up into an elegant structure, all parts of which are interwoven with all other parts. The aims of this enterprise are clarity and consistency, but not necessarily simplicity. The clarity must be won; it is the goal, not the starting point. The elements of the desired structure are not general principles, but specific, highly detailed rules, usually, though not always, attributed to well-known teachers from previous generations. Each man's teachings must both be internally consistent and also in some way distinguishable from every other man's. The attribution of precisely the same teaching to two different authorities is a redundancy that must be explained (though this is not, on the Talmud's terms, hard to do).

This method for organizing the tradition soon made the dispute between named masters a basic form for transmitting rabbinic legal teaching. Hardly a chapter of the Mishnah is free of disputed rules. Here lies the origin of the argumentative style for which Talmudic reasoning has been famous (or infamous!) for centuries.

These accumulations of rulings attributed to past authorities took on a life of their own. Later teachers would use earlier traditions to support their own opinions. Sets of rulings became the subject matter for later generations' study; the edifice of interconnection became more and more elaborate, and the countervailing distinctions more and more subtle, as time went on. Eventually, as the sample passage above illustrated, the actual historical identity of these earlier authorities lost all relevance. "R. Meir" was simply shorthand for "the opinions attributed to R. Meir," and a rabbi centuries after Meir's time would say, "I agree with R. Meir" but mean, "I share the opinion attributed to R. Meir." As a result, new opinions could begin circulating in Meir's (or anyone's) name, even if he himself had never spoken them. All one meant by identifying an opinion as his was that such a ruling fit into the system generated and transmitted in his name and was therefore to be considered part of that system. For the purpose of later generations, it made no difference at all whether Meir had or had not actually originated the saying under discussion. The process of developing the tradition of rabbinic law could work equally well in either case.

Paradoxically, this withering away of earlier rabbis' historical reality served to liberate historical imagination about them. Parallel to these legal developments there grew legends about these men that seem to heighten our awareness of them as real people, even while the narratives have little or no actual relationship to them as historical personages. Some of the greatest rabbis (Akiba, for example, or especially the earlier Hillel) are known to us almost exclusively through the stories that grew up around them. Great rabbinic leaders thus became both disembodied bearers of an elaborate legal tradition and also heroes of a marvelously rich tradition of legend; meanwhile they had in fact disappeared behind this two-layered screen.

From the historian's point of view, the Talmud thus becomes a terribly frustrating book. It is rich with stories that may—or may not—reflect the way certain events happened, and it is full of legal discussions that may—or may not—report the actual content of early rabbinic scholarly activity. Everything is fascinating, everything is potentially an open window on the past, but nothing can be trusted. At various points in the later development of the rabbinic tradition, leaders needed techniques for overcoming this uncertainty—the present generation is no different in this respect. It will be useful to review some of those earlier techniques, and then at last to raise the question how people of the present generation can approach this remarkable tradition.

NOTES

1. The standard abbreviation for Rabbi or Rav ("Rav" was the title of ordination in the ancient Babylonian Jewish community).

2. Heave-offering (Hebrew *terumah*) was a kind of religious tax on fresh produce that people gave to the priests. It had to be kept undefiled, and could not be eaten by persons who had become impure.

3. Note that a "text" can be oral.

4. Unfortunately, the word "Talmud" has two meanings. It can refer to the *gemara*, that is, to the huge mass of rabbinic discussion of Mishnah that accumulated after that text appeared, or it can refer to the composite works—Mishnah plus *gemara*—that usually go by that name. This ambiguity sometimes became deceiving because the two meanings are so closely related.

5. This does not mean, to be sure, that the contents of the Mishnah always determined the actual law.

6. In general, the various periods in the history of the rabbinic tradition (Mishnaic, Talmudic, early medieval, late medieval, etc.) are arranged hierarchically in order of age. Though this rule was often disregarded, there was a general tendency for every age to accept as binding the texts and the decisions of its predecessors.

7. Most modern books are similar. Very few actually have a page one containing part of the body of the text.

8. For people who can't wait, an outline of the entire section appears below.

9. An abbreviation for *ben* or *bar* ("son of" in Hebrew and Aramaic, respectively). The expression is translated fully in the preceding paragraph, where this rabbi is mentioned for the first time.

10. Author's note: I do not understand the logic here myself. Tosafot suggest there is simply a limit to the number of distinctions one can make, but this seems implausible so late in a discussion where so many have already been introduced.

11. That is why the quotation marks ending the translation of Meir's response to Judah appear before "as R. Yose said."

2

The Talmudic Argument

Louis Jacobs

The Babylonian Talmud consists almost entirely of arguments having as their aim the elucidation of the law, ruling, religious teaching or ethical idea. Theories are advanced and then contradicted. They are examined from many points of view and qualified where necessary. One argument leads to another when logic demands it. The claims of conflicting theories are investigated with great thoroughness and much subtlety. Fine distinctions abound between apparently similar concepts. The whole constitutes reasoning processes which have received the most careful study on the part of generations of Jewish scholars and have contributed more to the shaping of the Jewish mind than any other factor.

No serious student of the Babylonian Talmud can be unaware that, for all the variety of topics discussed in the work, there is a formal pattern to the argumentation. Whatever the subject matter, the moves open to the debaters are comparatively few in number and these are always expressed in the same stereotyped formulae. There is much originality in Talmudic argumentation but this consists in the application to new situations of conventional responses, not in the invention of new responses. The game is always played according to the rules.

These formal methods of argumentation occur with the utmost frequency in the Babylonian Talmud yet, although there is to be observed a complete consistency in their use, nowhere in the Talmud itself is any attempt made at their enumeration and classification. Part of this task

Reprinted by permission of the author and Cambridge University Press from *The Talmudic Argument: A Study in Talmudic Reasoning and Methodology*, New York, 1984.

was left to the famous post-Talmudic methodologies, largely concerned with the classification of Talmudic method. However, in the main, the Talmudic methodologies deal with the precise definition of the terms used rather than with the actual types of argument. Of these there has been very little detailed, systematic treatment.[1]

In every complete Talmudic unit—the *sugya*—the differing views are presented in the form of a debate. The protagonists may be actual teachers expressing their opinions, Rav and Samuel, R. Johanan and Resh Lakish, Rabbah and R. Joseph, Abbaye and Rava and so forth. Very frequently, however, the thrust and parry of the debate is presented anonymously. It has long been conventional among students of the Talmud to give a kind of fictitious personality to the arguments by attributing questions to an alleged 'questioner' (the *makshan*) and answers to an alleged 'replier' *(tartzan)*. In a particular *sugya* different types of argument may be produced as the course of the debate demands, e.g. an appeal to authority, the detection of flaws in an analogy, the readmission of a rejected plea and so forth. The unit as a whole consists of all the arguments, together with any extraneous material which may arise as the discussion proceeds.[2]

The sustained argument, particularly in the form of question and answer, as presented in the Babylonian Talmud, has strong antecedents in the earlier sources. There are numerous instances in the Pentateuch and in the historical books of the Bible: Eve's debate with the serpent (Genesis 3:1–5); God's accusation of Adam (Genesis 3:9–13); God's interrogation of Cain (Genesis 4:9–15); Abraham's plea to God to spare Sodom (Genesis 18:23–33); Abimelech's upbraiding of Abraham (Genesis 20:9–17); Abraham's reproof of Abimelech (Genesis 21:22–30); Abraham's purchase of the field and bargaining with Ephron (Genesis 23:3–16); Jacob's dialogue with his wives (Genesis 31:4–16) and with Laban (Genesis 31:26–53); the arguments presented by Schechem and Hamor (Genesis 34:4–23); the arguments and counter-arguments in the Joseph saga (Genesis 42:7–38; 43:2–14; 44:6–34); Joseph's bargain with the Egyptians (Genesis 47:15–25); Pharaoh's complaint against the midwives (Exodus 1:15–19); Moses' confrontation with God (Exodus 3:4 to 4:17); Moses' dialogue with Pharaoh (Exodus 10:1–11); Jethro's plea for reforms (Exodus 18:13–23); Moses' entreaty on behalf of his people (Exodus 32:7–14 and 33:12–23); Moses' questioning of Aaron and his sons (Leviticus 10:16–20); Moses' complaint (Numbers 11:11–

23); the episode of Moses, Aaron and Miriam (Numbers 12:1–14); the debate between Caleb and the spies (Numbers 13:27 to 14:10); the rebellion of Korah (Numbers 16:1–19); Moses and the King of Edom (Numbers 20:14–21); Balaam and the ass (Numbers 22:28–35); the account of the sons of Reuben and Gad (Numbers 32:1–32); the two lawsuits concerning the daughters of Zelophehad (Numbers 27:1–7 and 36:1–10). The major portion of the book of Deuteronomy consists of a sustained argument in which Moses reminds the people of their history and their obligations in the future. Among arguments of this type in the historical books are: Rahab and the spies (Joshua 2:1–21); the debate between the other tribes and the sons of Reuben and Gad (Joshua 22:13–14); Jotham's argument (Judges 9:7–20); Jephthah and the sons of Ammon (Judges 11:12–28); Samuel against the appointment of a king (I Samuel 8:10–21); his rebuke of the people in this matter (I Samuel 12:1–24); his castigation of Saul (I Samuel 13:10–14); Eliab and David (I Samuel 17:28–37); Jonathan and Saul (I Samuel 20:21–32); David at Nob (I Samuel 21:2–7); David and Saul (I Samuel 24:9–22); David and Abigail (I Samuel 25:23–35); David and Uriah (II Samuel 11:10–12); David and the death of his child (II Samuel 12:17–23); the woman of Tekoa (II Samuel 14:4–24); Barzillai and David (II Samuel 19:32–40); Bath-sheba and David (I Kings 1:11–27); Solomon and the two harlots (I Kings 3:16–27); Obadiah and Elijah (I Kings 18:7–15); Elijah and the prophets of Baal (I Kings 18:21–7); the four lepers (II Kings 7:3–4); Rab-shakeh and Eliakim (II Kings 18:19–35).

As for the prophetic books, the whole of the prophetic message is in the form of a sustained argument. The passages especially to be noted are: Isaiah 40:12–26; 44:9–20; 49:14–26; 51:12–13; 58:2–14; 66:1–2; Jeremiah 2:4–37; 12:1–13; Ezekiel 18:1–29; Amos 3:3–8; 6:1–2; 9:7; Jonah 1:6–15; 4:2–11; Micah 6:3–8; Zechariah 4:1–7; Malachi 1:2–14; 2:10–17; 3:13–16.

The same type of sustained argument is found in the book of Psalms. Psalm 10 in its entirety is a plea for the salvation of the righteous from the hands of the wicked. In both Psalm 15 and Psalm 24 the way of righteousness is prescribed and expressed as a reply to a question. Psalm 23 draws the conclusion that man should trust in God from the premiss that the Lord is his Shepherd. Psalm 50 is an argument in favour of the view that it is righteousness that God wants, not sacrifices. Psalm 96 is a mighty plea that God be praised and Psalm 100 that He is to be thanked. These themes are repeated in Psalms 104 and 105. Psalm 112 is an argument for righteous living and Psalm 115 against idolatry. Psalm 119 exhausts the letters of the alphabet eight times in calling attention to the need for man to be loyal to God's law. In Psalm 136 there are a number of 'proofs' that God's mercy 'endureth for ever'. Psalm 139 argues that it is impossible to escape from God. Psalm 146 argues that it is better for man to put his trust in God than in princes. And the book of Psalms in general is mainly an appeal by argument to God, expressed in poetry, that He should pay heed to the cry of the poor and oppressed.

In the other books of the Hagiographa the same phenomenon is to be observed. In Proverbs we find arguments for the cultivation of wisdom (3:13–23); against harlotry (5:1–20; 7:5–23); against sloth (6:6–15); against wickedness (10:2–32); and for the worth of a good wife (31:10–31). The book of Job has the arguments of Satan (1:6 to 2:6); of Job's friends and his replies (4:1 to 37:24); of God to Job (38 to 41) and Job's reply (42:1–6). The book of Ruth contains Naomi's argument to her daughters-in-law (1:8–17) and that of Boaz with his kinsman (4:1–12). In addition to the argument for pessimism, the general theme of Ecclesiastes, there are arguments in favour of melancholia (7:2–6); of wisdom (7:10–12); of mirth (8:15); and of effort (11:1–8). Esther contains the arguments advanced by Memucan for deposing Vashti (1:16–22); Haman's arguments for destroying the Jews (3:8–11); Esther's dialogue with Mordecai (4:10–14) and Esther's plea for her people (7:3 to 8:6).

The dialectical tone of the above passages was no doubt familiar to the Babylonian Amoraím and, for that matter, to many of their fellow-Jews, from infancy. In addition, so far as we can tell, the hermeneutical principles laid down by the Tannaím were widely discussed and accepted by all the Amoraím. These principles are themselves largely ways of argumentation and references to them abound in the Babylonian Talmud.[3]

The Babylonian Amoraím thus had a long tradition behind them of skill in debate and argument. The study of the Torah was their consuming purpose in life to which they applied themselves with ruthless devotion and dedication. Over the years, the exercise of their minds in these dialectics seems to have produced an automatic response to the problems they were concerned to solve. Naturally, it is necessary to distinguish between the use of argument by the Amoraím themselves and the use by the final editors. But even if, as seems extremely probable, the final form of these arguments owes much to the redactors or compilers of the Talmud, the methods must have had a history and some were almost certainly used even by the earliest of the Babylonian Amoraím.

On the more general question of attitudes towards skill in debating matters of Torah, it is clear that such skill was highly praised. In the Mishnah (*Avot* 2:8) we find a report that Rabban Johanan b. Zakkai praised his disciple R. Eliezer b. Hyrcanus, saying that he was 'a plastered cistern which loses not a drop', i.e. he had an extraordinarily retentive memory and was able to recall everything he had been taught. He praised another disciple, R. Eleazar b. Arakh, saying that he was 'an ever-flowing spring', i.e. he had the ability to advance fresh, original arguments and theses. Two versions are then recorded. According to one of these, the master declared that if all the Sages of Israel were in one scale of the balance and Eliezer b. Hyrcanus in the other he would outweigh them all. The other version, in the name of Abba Saul, is: if all the Sages of Israel were in one scale of the balance, together with Eliezer b. Hyrcanus, and Eleazar b. Arakh was in the other scale, he would outweigh them all. A Talmudic report (*'Eruvin* 13b) about the second-century teacher R. Meir says that no one in his generation could be compared to him in brilliance but that, none the less, the law does not follow his opinions because his colleagues were incapable of penetrating to the depths of his mind and the law always follows the majority opinion. Of R. Meir it is also said that he was able to produce arguments to render the clean unclean and the unclean clean. This statement was puzzling to the *Tosafists* to the passage. 'What is so meritorious', they ask, 'in arguing against the laws of the Torah?' Is it possible that we have here an echo of an institution in which disciples were taught to test their skills in argumentation by arguing for positions known to be false because contradicted by the Torah? In the same Talmudic passage it is stated, R. Judah the Prince declared that the reason his intellect was sharper than his colleagues' was because he had had the privilege of sitting in the lecture-hall behind R. Meir. Had he sat in front of the master when he taught, his brilliance would have been even greater; no doubt a reference to the use of gestures and facial expressions by the teacher in order to convey the teachings more effectively. In support the verse is quoted: 'But thine eyes shall see thy teachers' (Isaiah 30:20). In the legend told (*Shabbat* 33b) regarding R. Meir's contemporary R. Simeon b. Yohai, it is said that this teacher spent twelve years of privation in a cave, which had the effect of heightening his intellectual powers. Before that time, when R. Simeon suggested a problem his son-in-law was able to provide 12 different solutions, but after the experience in the cave the roles were reversed: to every problem set by his son-in-law R. Simeon was able to offer 24 different solutions. It is said (*Bava Metzi'a* 84a) of the two third-century Palestinian Amoraím, R. Johanan and R. Simeon b. Lakish, that 'Resh Lakish' was able to produce 24 objections to every statement made by R. Johanan. When Resh Lakish died, the Sages sent R. Eleazar b. Pedat as a substitute for Resh Lakish, but R. Johanan found him very unsatisfactory. R. Eleazar was able to do no more than produce 24 proofs in support of R. Johanan's statements and this was of no help to the master, who preferred to be challenged, as he was by Resh Lakish.[4]

The two types of scholar referred to, as above, as 'the plastered cistern' and 'an everflowing spring' were called, in the Amoraic period (*Berakhot* 64a), 'Sinai' (one who knows the whole Torah as it was given at Sinai) and *'oker harim* ('uprooter of mountains'). In an age when teachings were transmitted orally, the scholar with vast stores of information was highly regarded but his claim to pre-eminence was hotly contested by admirers of the less knowledgeable but more original and brilliant scholar. Rabbah was such a scholar while his colleague, R. Joseph, belonged to the other type. The scholars of Palestine, when asked for their advice, sent a message that R. Joseph was to be preferred as the Sinai type (*Horayot* 14a). This same Rabbah, it is said, was fond of encouraging his disciples to cultivate sharpness of mind by appearing, on occasion, to act contrary to the law in order to see whether the disciples would be sufficiently alert to spot his mistakes (*Berakhot* 33b; *Hullin* 43b; *Niddah* 4b). This method of 'alerting the mind of the disciples' *(le-hadded et ha-talmidim)* is also said to have been practised by Samuel (*'Eruvin* 13a); by R. Akiba (see *Niddah* 45a); and by the latter's teacher, R. Joshua (*Nazir* 59b).In another passage (*Zevahim* 13a) the method is attributed to Rabbah's teacher, R. Huna. This idea of sharpening the wits of the disciples must not be confused with the demand that words of Torah should be 'sharp' in the scholar's mouth (*Kiddushin* 30a) even though the same term *(mehuddadim)* is used, since there the meaning is a sharp clear utterance ('when someone asks you a question do not stammer when you tell him the answer'; cf. *Sifre* to Deuteronomy 6:7, where the reading is *mesudarim*, 'well-ordered', see edn. Friedmann, p. 74a and Friedmann's note).

The Talmudic debate and argument reached their apogee in the work of Abbaye and Rava, Rabbah's disciples. Hundreds of debates between these two are recorded in the Babylonian Talmud. Later generations considered the work of these two to be so typical of Rabbinic learning that when they wished to list the many themes with which Rabban Johanan b. Zakki was conversant they referred, anachronistically, to his being familiar with 'the arguments of Abbaye and Rava' *(havayot de-Abbaye ve-Rava),* though these are described as a 'small thing' in comparison with the 'great thing', the mystical study of the Heavenly Chariot seen by Ezekiel *(Sukkah* 28a; *Bava Batra* 134a).[5]

Some time before the Amoraic period, the debate in Torah matters was described in military terms—*milḥamtah shel Torah (Sanhedrin* 111b). On the verse: 'And he carried away all Jerusalem, and all the princes, and all the mighty men of valour' (II Kings 24:14) the *Sifre* (to Deuteronomy 32:25) comments: 'What mighty deeds could have been accomplished by men taken into captivity and what kind of warfare could men bound in chains have engaged in? But "all the mighty men of valour" means, in the warfare of the Torah.' This enabled the Rabbis to interpret Biblical verses glorifying military prowess as referring to the battles of the mind. For instance, on the verse: 'Happy is the man that hath his quiver full of them: they shall not be ashamed, but they shall speak with the enemies in the gate' (Psalm 127:5), a Rabbi commented: even father and son, master and disciple, become enemies of one another when they are on opposing sides in the Torah debates *(Kiddushin* 30b). The debates were said to take place even in Heaven, the scholars in the Yeshivah on High having the right to disagree even with God Himself *(Bava Metzi'a* 86a). Both motifs, of military metaphor and debate in Heaven, are present in the comment *(Bava Kama* 92a) on: 'Hear, Lord, the voice of Judah, and bring him unto his people; let his hands be sufficient for him; and be thou an help to him from his enemies' (Deuteronomy 33:7). Moses prayed that Judah be admitted to the Heavenly Yeshivah but Judah was unable to understand the debates in order to participate in them. Moses' prayer for Judah to participate was granted, but a further plea by Moses was required before Judah was able to argue so convincingly that his decisions in matters of law could be followed.

In the same vein are the statements regarding King David when he rendered legal decisions (*Berakhot* 4a). R. Judah, in the name of Rav, interprets (*Sanhedrin* 93b) the verse praising David's qualities (I Samuel 16:18) as referring to his skill in debate: 'that is cunning in playing'— knowing the right questions to ask; 'a mighty valiant man'—knowing the correct answers; 'a man of war'—knowing how to give and take in the battle of the Torah; 'prudent in matters'—knowing how to deduce one thing from another; 'and a comely person'—who demonstrates the proofs for his opinions; 'and the Lord is with him'—the ruling is always in accordance with his views.

Skill in Torah debate was also compared to the skill exhibited by a competent craftsman. The 'craftsmen and smiths' carried away into captivity (II Kings 24:14) were identified with scholars gifted with great reasoning powers (*Sifre* to Deuteronomy 32:25). On the basis of this the keen debater was compared to a carpenter. Of a text presenting severe problems of interpretation it was said that neither a carpenter nor his apprentice could remove the difficulties (*'Avodah Zarah* 50b, cf. Palestinian Talmud *Yevamot* 8:2, 9b). In similar vein scholars were compared to builders (*Berakhot* 64a), possibly because scholars 'built up' their arguments, as in the very frequent *binyan av*, 'father construction', for an argument by inference where the premiss is the 'father' to the conclusion reached by a process of 'building'. The expression: 'Do you weave them all in the same web' (*Berakhot* 24a; *Shabbat* 148a; *Pesaḥim* 42a; *Ḥullin* 58b) suggests that scholars were compared to weavers, as does the use of *massekhet*, 'web', for a tractate. The purveyor of the difficult Halakhic teachings was compared to a dealer in precious stones for the connoisseur whereas the more popular but less profound Aggadic teacher was compared to the retailer of cheap tinsel goods which all can afford to buy (*Sotah* 40a).

The keen scholar was called a *ḥarif*, 'sharp one'. Thus there is a discussion as to which is the superior scholar, the *ḥarif*, capable of raising objections, or the more cautious debater who is less quick in refutation but can arrive more readily at a correct solution (*Horayot* 14a). When a particularly pungent argument was seen to solve a problem far more effectively than more learned but pedestrian attempts, it was said that one grain of sharp (*ḥarifta*) pepper is worth more than a basket-full of pumpkins (*Megillah* 7a). The acuteness of a scholar's reasoning process was spoken of as his 'sharp knife' (*Ḥullin* 77a, cf.

Yevamot 122a). The scholars of Pumbedita were especially renowned for their sharpness. Among these were Efa and Avimi, described as 'the sharp ones of Pumbedita' (*Sanhedrin* 17b; *Kiddushin* 39a; *Menaḥot* 17a). The brilliance of the Pumbeditans was, however, somewhat suspect in that it bordered on the eccentric, so that they acquired the reputation of 'causing an elephant to pass through the eye of a needle', i.e. of producing far-fetched, improbable arguments (*Bava Metzi"a* 38b, cf. *Berakhot* 55b).

There are found in the Babylonian Talmud a number of formal terms for the moves in an argument and for the argument itself, some of them of earlier usage. The earlier term for argumentation and debate is *nosē ve-noten*, 'give and take' (*Sifre* to Deuteronomy 32:25). This term is also used (e.g. in *Shabbat* 31a) for business dealings, 'buying and selling', as in the idiomatic English expression 'selling an idea'. The Aramaic equivalent is *shakla ve-taria* (*Bava Kama* 92a; *Sotah* 7b). The reasoning by means of which an argument is supported is *sevara* ('theory', 'reasoning', 'common-sense') with a root meaning of 'to think'. Very frequently in the Talmud one finds the expression: '*mar savar . . . u-mar savar . . .*', 'this master holds .. . and this master holds . . .'. The term Saboraím, for the post-Talmudic teachers is derived from this term; perhaps 'expounders'. An objection is a *kushia* (*Bava Kama* 117a; *Bava Metzi"a* 84a and very freq.), from a root meaning of 'hardness', hence, a difficulty. A stronger term, used when the difficulty is insurmountable, is *tiyuvta*, 'refutation' (*Bava Kama* 15b and freq.). The term *metevē*, 'an objection was raised' (from the same root) and similar expressions are used when the refutation is from a Tannaitic source. When the objection is based on Amoraic reasoning, the term used is *matkif,* from a root meaning 'to seize', i.e. A seized hold of B's theory and sought to refute it. The reply to an objection raised is *tirutz*, 'an answer', from a root meaning of 'to make straight' (*Gittin* 4b; *Bava Metzi'a* 14b and freq.), generally used when a difficulty is 'straightened out', e.g. by emending a text and the like. A more direct reply is *piruka*, 'a reply', from a root meaning of 'to break', i.e. to shatter the objection (*Bava Kama* 117a; *Bava Metzi"a* 84a; *"Avodah Zarah* 50b and freq.). The term for a proof advanced in support of a theory is found in the Mishnah (*'Eduyot* 2:2) and used by the Amoraím (*Pesaḥim* 15a). The term is *raáyah*, literally 'a seeing'. The Aramaic equivalent is *sa'ya*, 'a support', with a root meaning of 'to assist' (*Sanhedrin* 71b; *Ḥullin* 4a and very freq.). The unit of argument and counter argument is *shema'ta*, from a root meaning 'to hear' (*Kiddushin* 50b; *Sanhedrin* 38b). The *shema'ta* generally consists of the text, *gemara*, and its exposition, the *severa*. The bringing of an argument to a successful conclusion so that it results in a correct application of the law is *a'sukey shema'ta aliva de-hilkheta*, i.e. bringing the argument to a final ruling, to the *halakhah*, the actual ruling in practice (e.g. in *Bava Kama* 92a). An abstract problem of definition in which the two ways of looking at the matter are so equally balanced that, without proof from some authority, it is impossible to decide which is correct, is known as a *ba'ya*, from a root meaning of 'to request', i.e. to request a solution to the problem. (*Berakhot* 2b; *Pesahim* 9b and very frequently throughout the Talmud). Solutions to this kind of problem are described by terms taken from the root *pashat*, 'to make clear', 'to smooth out' a difficulty (*Berakhot* 26b; *Kiddushin* 9b and very freq.). Where no solution is forthcoming the term used is *teyku*, 'it remains standing', i.e. the two possibilities are so equally balanced and, in the absence of proof from authority, there is no solution to the problem; it is by nature insoluble (*Berakhot* 8a; 25b; and very freq.). There are over 300 instances of this phenomenon in the Babylonian Talmud but none in the Palestinian. A doubt about the facts used in an argument or about the correctness of a theory that has been advanced is *safek*, 'a doubt' (*Berakhot* 3b; *Bava Metzi'a* 83b; *Keritot* 21b and freq.).[6]

Two terms are, at times, ambiguous. These are: *ve-ha-tanya*, 'and we have learnt in a *Baraita*' and *peshita*, 'it is obvious'. In the majority of instances these are questions: 'But have we not learnt?'; 'Is it not obvious?' Occasionally, however, they are statements: 'We have learnt'; 'It is obvious that'. *Rashi* usually helps the student by pointing out when these terms are used as simple statements. There are no punctuation marks in the Talmud so that the reader has to supply these by inflections of the voice. To obtain the best results in detecting the various moves in a Talmudic *sugya* the Talmud has to be 'sung', as it is in Yeshivot today with the traditional 'Gemara *niggun*'. There can be no doubt that melody was used in Talmud study from the earliest times and it seems certain that the compilers themselves relied on melody as a means of punctuation. There is even some evidence for a system of cantillation with musical notes as in the Biblical books.

The various kinds of arguments found in the Babylonian Talmud can be classified according to a number of formal types or patterns. All the main moves will be found to belong to one or other of these categories. The *argument from authority* consists of a proof or support of the correctness of a theory by an appeal to an incontrovertible source, i.e. Scripture or a Tannaitic source; a Mishnah or a *Baraita*. Where the attempted proof is from Scripture the only way to refute it is to interpret the relevant verse or verses differently. Where the attempted proof is from a Tannaitic source two moves are open to the contestant who wishes to engage in refutation. He can either demonstrate that an alternative interpretation is possible, or, perhaps, necessary, or he can adduce another Tannaitic source which disagrees with the one quoted by his opponent and on which he can now rely. This is based on the generally accepted view, at least by the later Amoraím, that an Amora cannot disagree with a Tanna unless he can find support for so doing in the opinions of another Tanna.[7]

The *argument by comparison* is the deduction of a rule, not stated explicitly, from an accepted teaching to which it bears a strong resemblance. The refutation of this consists in demonstrating that although the two cases do appear to be analogous they are, in fact, different. This can be termed an *argument by differentiation*. The *either/or argument* seeks to demonstrate that whichever one of two possible interpretations of a given premiss is adopted, it will lead to the desired conclusion. The *on the contrary argument* seeks to demonstrate that, far from the premiss yielding the suggested conclusion, it yields the exactly opposite conclusion. The *acceptance of an argument in part* seeks to demonstrate that a particular conclusion will follow from one construction of the phenomenon under consideration but not from a different construction. The *argument based on an opponent's position* seeks to demonstrate that even if the suggested premiss is true, which, in fact, it is not, the suggested conclusion does not follow from it. The *argument exposing the flaws in an opponent's argument* is a suggestion to the opponent that if he will only examine carefully the steps in his argument he will see for himself that his case is faulty. An argument is, at times, put forward only to be rejected.[8]

In addition to arguments based on pure reason there are to be found arguments based on the facts of the case or the interpretation of the facts. An example of this is the *argument based on historical or geographical conditions,* in which an attempt is made to demonstrate that these conditions affect the law and limit its application. Another example is the *argument based on the analysis of states of mind,* in which the law is said to depend on how human beings normally react psychologically in a given situation.[9]

At times there occurs the *readmission of an argument that has been previously rejected.* An argument that has been rejected in favour of what seemed to be a more convincing argument is now reinstated as offering, after all, the best solution of the difficulty, the reason for the original rejection then being shown to be unsound. The *argument against a statement of the obvious* is presented whenever a statement is made that appears to be quite superfluous since no one would have thought otherwise. The defence is to demonstrate that what seemed so obvious is not so at all. Reasons are given why it might have been thought otherwise and the statement requires, therefore, to be stated.[10]

The *argument to resolve a contradiction between sources* occurs where two Scriptural verses or two Tannaitic sources appear to contradict one another. Where the contradiction appears to be between two Scriptural verses the only way open is to show that, rightly understood, there is no contradiction, that it is only apparent not real. Where two Tannaitic sources appear to be in contradiction this solution is open but here, on occasion, the argument may proceed to demonstrate that there is, indeed, a contradiction and we must conclude that there is a debate on the matter between Tannaím. The attempt is then made to identify the Tannaím involved by referring to other Tannaitic sources. The *argument by textual emendation* seeks to demonstrate that the text of a Mishnah or *Baraita* cannot possibly be accepted as it stands, that it is obviously corrupt. The correct text is then established by means of emendation. The *argument from the principle of literary economy* proceeds on the assumption that the earlier, classical texts have been so carefully worded that any apparently superfluous statement is not coincidental or due to mere literary style but is contrived and the text is then examined in order to discover what the apparently superfluous statement intends to teach.[11]

Frequently in the Talmudic debate a statement is presented in more than one form. The *different versions of an argument* are due to the difficulties in transmitting accurately reports of what the earlier teachers actually said. Similarly, there is the *argument presented by different teachers* where the statement itself is not in doubt but the doubt is about who made the statement. In both these instances there is generally an attempt to demonstrate the *consequences of different arguments,* i.e. the practical differences which result from looking at the matter in one way rather than another. The Talmudic debate also frequently calls attention to the *limited application of an argument.* The suggestion here is that the argument is sound so far as it goes but when examined turns out to be limited in scope.[12]

A large portion of the Talmudic debate is taken up with the posing of purely academic problems. These are either set by individual Amoraím or anonymously and the aim of the exercise is to discuss theoretically the principles upon which the law is based. As we have noted in connection with the term *ba'ya,* in this type of problem the two halves are so equally balanced that no reason exists for favouring one over the other. There are more than a thousand of these problems scattered through the Talmud. It is highly probable that such contrived problems were set consciously as an intellectual exercise, especial skill being required to see that the two halves were, in fact, equally balanced.[13]

It has to be said that there is no actual classification of the different types of argument in the Talmud itself and the names for them are our invention. Nevertheless a close study of the Talmud reveals that the patterns we have noted are there. Certain 'ploys' are always used as the occasion demands. These are strictly limited but the richness and variety of the Talmudic debate are nevertheless preserved, because these depend not on the number of the moves available but on the ingenuity of the protagonists in making the right move at the right time.

NOTES

1. For Talmudic methodology see W. Bacher, *Exegetische Terminologie der jüdischen Traditionsliteratur,* Hebrew translation by A. Z. Rabbinowitz under title *'Erkhey Midrash* (Tel-Aviv, 1924); H. Strack, *Introduction to the Talmud and Midrash* (Philadelphia, 1945), pp. 135–9; M. Meilziner, *Introduction to the Talmud,* 4th edn. with new bibliography by A. Guttmann (New York, 1968), part III: 'Talmudic terminology and methodology', pp. 190–280; and I. H. Weiss' survey of the methodological literature in *Bet Talmud,* vol. I (Vienna, 1881) and vol. II (Vienna, 1882). The most important of the methodologies are: *Mevo ha-Talmud* attributed to Samuel ha-Naggid (d. 1055), printed with commentaries in the Vilna edition of the Talmud after tractate *Berakhot; Sefer Keritut* by Samson of Chinon (end of thirteenth century), ed. J. Z. Roth with commentary (New York, 1961), and

by S. B. D. Sofer with commentary (Jerusalem, 1965); *Halikhot 'Olam* by Joshua ha-Levi of Tlemcen (compiled in Toledo *c.* 1467), edition Warsaw, 1883, with commentaries: *Kelaley ha-Gemara* by Joseph Karo (1488–1575) and *Yavin Shem'ua* by Solomon Algazi (seventeenth century); *Sheney Luḥot ha-Berit* by Isaiah Horowitz (d. *c.* 1630) (Amsterdam, 1649), section *Torah she-be-'al Peh; Yad Malakhi* by Malachi Ha-Kohen of Leghorn (early eighteenth century) (Jerusalem, 1976).

2. On the use of the terms *makshan* and *tartzan* see e.g. *Rashi, Shabbat* 104a top; *Kiddushin* 2a, s.v. *ve-khesef minalan; Tosafists* to *Berakhot* 44a s.v. *inhu* and *Yoma* 43b s.v. *amar R. Yehudah.* Cf. ben Yehudah's *Thesaurus,* vol. VII, p. 3295 and vol. XVI, p. 7923.

3. It should be noted that it is acknowledged in the Rabbinic literature itself that the argument from the minor to the major is found in the Bible; see my article: 'The "*qal va-ḥomer*" argument in the Old Testament', *BSOAS,* 35: 2 (1972), 221–7. A. Schwarz, in *Der Hermeneutische Syllogismus in der Talmudischen Litteratur* (Karlsruhe, 1901); *Die Hermeneutische Antinomie in der Talmudischen Litteratur* (Vienna, 1913); *Die Hermeneutische Quantitätsrelation in der Talmudischen Litteratur* (Vienna, 1913) and in other works, has examined the thirteen principles of R. Ishmael with the utmost attention to detail. These principles are found in *Sifra,* Introduction. The seven principles attributed to Hillel are found in *Sifra,* Introduction, end; *ARN* 37; *Tosefta Sanhedrin,* 7, end. The twelfth-century Karaite author Judah Hadassi argued for Greek influence on the hermeneutic principles and this matter has been discussed by David Daube, 'Rabbinic methods of interpretation and Hellenistic rhetoric', *HUCA,* 22 (1949), 239–64 and by Saul Lieberman, *Hellenism in Jewish Palestine* (New York, 1950), pp. 47–82. Cf. J. Z. Lauterbach, 'Talmud hermeneutics', *JE,* vol. XII, pp. 30–3; Chaim Hirschensohn, *Berurey ha-Middot* (New York, 1929–31); M. Ostrowsky, *ha-Middot she-ha-Torah Nidreshet ba-Hem* (Jerusalem, 1924); and my article 'Hermeneutics', *EJ,* vol. VIII, pp. 366–72. The Palestine Talmud uses some of the methods of argument that are found in the Babylonian Talmud but these are in a much less finished form in the Palestinian Talmud; see I. H. Taviob, '*Talmudah shel Bavel ve-Talmudah shel Eretz Yisrael*' in his *Collected Writings* (in Hebrew) (Berlin, 1923), pp. 73–88 and the Introduction, *Ḥomat Yerushalayim* by S. Feigensohn (*Shafan ha-Sofer*), based on Z. Frankel's work, in the Vilna edition of the Palestinian Talmud.

4. To be noted is the number 24, in this narrative and the one about R. Simeon b. Yohai and his son-in-law. In the latter story the number is perhaps a play on the number 12, the period of years R. Simeon spent in the cave. The number 24 is a formal number, almost certainly corresponding to the 24 books of the Bible with which the scholar is expected to be familiar; see *Exodus R.* 41: 5 and *Tanḥuma,* ed. Buber, to Exodus 31: 18 and Buber's notes. Cf. the number 48 (twice 24) in the account of Symmachus' reasoning powers in *'Eruvin* 13b and the 48 days in which the Torah is acquired, *Avot*

6: 5 (*Kinyan Torah*). Cf. *Taʿanit* 8a: 'R. Adda b. Ahavah used to arrange his lessons in proper order 24 times, corresponding to the number of books of the Torah, Prophets and Hagiographa, before he appeared in the presence of Rava.'

5. A study of Abbaye and Rava, listing every reference to them in the Talmud, is: *Abbaye ve-Rava* by J. L. Maimon (Jerusalem, 1965). In the twelfth century, Maimonides identified 'the arguments of Abbaye and Rava' with the typical approach of the whole range of Talmudic study, *Yad, Yesodey ha-Torah* 4: 13. David Kimhi remarked in a letter (*Kovetz Teshuvot ha-Rambam*, ed. A. Lichtenberg (Leipzig, 1859), part III, pp. 4c–d) that, for all his love of philosophy, he was thoroughly familiar with *havayot de-Abbaye ve-Rava*. Cf. Frank E. Talmage, *David Kimhi The Man and His Commentary* (Harvard University Press, 1975), pp. 37–8. In later ages this identification became a commonplace so that the term *havayot de-Abbaye ve-Rava* was used as a synonym for the Halakhic discussions of the Talmud.

6. On the *teyku* phenomenon see my study: (London–New York, 1981), in which all the instances are noted. The debate between scholars is called a *mahaloket*, 'division', 'controversy', e.g. the debates between the House of Shammai and the House of Hillel are described in the Mishnah (*Avot* 5: 7) as: 'controversy for the sake of Heaven', *mahaloket le-shem shamayyim*. The whole subject of the *mahaloket* is treated by B. De Friess, *Mehkarim be-Sifrut ha-Talmud* (Jerusalem, 1968), pp. 172–8. The *locus classicus* for the problem is *Tosefta Sanhedrin* 7: 1 (ed. Zuckermandel, p. 425). This reads: 'R. Jose said: "At first there was no controversy (*mahaloket*) in Israel except in the Court of the Seventy in the Chamber of Hewn Stones ... When the disciples of Hillel and Shammai who had not served (their masters) sufficiently increased, controversy increased and there were two Torot in Israel." ' In the Babylonian Talmud (*Sanhedrin* 88b) this is quoted as: 'R. Jose said: "At first they did not increase controversy in Israel ... When the disciples of Shammai and Hillel, who had not served sufficiently, increased, controversy increased and Torah became as if it were two Torot." ' Thus, according to the reading in the *Tosefta,* controversy between the Sages is said to have been completely unknown before the rise of the disciples of Shammai and Hillel, whereas according to the reading in the Babylonian Talmud it is said that controversy was known before this period, but not to any large extent. De Friess discusses how far R. Jose's view is historical. In any event, the term *mahaloket* became in our literature the normal one for the controversy or debate with its Aramaic equivalent, *pelugta*. When, for instance, the Talmud states, as it does very frequently, that A and B disagree on this or that point, it is usually expressed as: *be-mai ka-mippalgi*, 'on what point do they disagree?'

7. The terms used to introduce a proof from authority are: *minalan*, 'How do we know this?' (*Berakhot* 7a; *Pesahim* 7b; *Kiddushin* 3b and freq.); *mena hanney miley*, 'How do we know these things?' (*Hullin* 24b and very freq.);

mina ha milta, 'How do we know that?' (*Hullin* 10b; 11a); *mina amina lah?*, 'How do I know this?' (*Sanhedrin* 61b); *Mai ta'ama*, 'What is the reason?* (*Bava Batra* 173b and very freq.); *ta shema'*, 'Come and hear' (*Bava Kama* 22a and very freq.); *dikhetiv*, 'For it is written in Scripture' (*Sanhedrin* 61b and very freq.); *diténan*, 'For we have learnt in a Mishnah', *Yevamot* 57a and very freq.); *de-tono rabbanan*, 'For our Rabbis have taught' (*Hullin* 24b and very freq.) introducing a *Baraita; de-tanya*, 'For we have learnt in a *Baraita*' (*Bava Kama* 30a and very freq.); *she-neémar*, 'For it is said in Scripture' (*Berakhot* 7b and very freq.); *ve-ha-tenan*, 'But we have learnt in a Mishnah' (*Bava Batra* 30a and very freq.); *af anan nami teninan*, 'We have also been taught this' (*Berakhot* 27a and freq.); *tenituha*, 'We have learnt it in a Mishnah' (*Bava Kama* 22a and freq.); *amar kera*, 'Scripture said' (*Kiddushin* 3b and freq.); *amar rahamana* 'The All-Merciful said', used for a Scriptural proof (*Bava Metzi'a* 3b and very freq.); *de-amar R . . .*, 'For Rabbi . . . said' (*Pesahim* 7b and very freq.). This last term is sometimes used even for a proof from an Amora, provided the Amora is an established authority.

8. The following are the terms used: (a) *Argument by comparison: hainu*, 'that is', i.e. 'this is the same as that' (*Pesahim* 9b–10a and freq.); *yalfinan*, 'we learn' (this from that) (*Yevamot* 57 and freq.); *shema'minah*, 'hear from this', i.e. compare that to this (*Pesahim* 5b and very freq.). (b) *Argument by differentiation: shani hatam*, 'there it is different' (*Kiddushin* 50a and very freq.); *ve-R.*, 'and what will R . . . say in reply?' (*Kiddushin* 51a and freq.); *mi damey*, 'are the two cases alike?' (*Pesahim* 14b and freq.); *hakhi hashta*, lit. 'how now', i.e. 'what is the comparison?' (*Hagigah* 13b and freq.). (c) *Either/or argument: mi-mah nafshakh*, 'whichever way you see it' (*Hullin* 29a and freq.). (d) *On the contrary argument: ipkha mistabbera*, 'it is more plausible to see it in the opposite way' (*Pesahim* 28a and freq.); *aderabbah*, 'on the contrary' (*Pesahim* 28a and freq.). Sometimes, as in *Pesahim* here, the two terms are combined: *aderabbah ipkhah mistabbera;* sometimes they are used separately. In J. S. Roth's edition of Samson of Chinon's *Sefer Keritut*, p. 434, note 2, there is a fairly comprehensive list of the instances of *aderabbah* in the Babylonian Talmud. (c) *Acceptance of an argument in part: bishelama . . . ela . . .*, 'This is correct according to . . . but . . .' (*Pesahim* 7a and very freq.); *hanihah*, 'this is appropriate' (*Bava Kama* 12a and very freq.). (f) *Argument based on an opponent's position: u-le-ta 'amekh*, 'and according to your reasoning' (*Berakhot* 43a and very freq.); *li-devarav de-R . . .*, 'according to the opinion of R . . .' (*Kiddushin* 51a and freq.). (g) *Argument exposing a flaw in an opponent's argument: ve-tisbera*, 'and even according to your theory' (*Bava Kama* 32a and freq.); *mi sabbarit*, 'do you hold' (*Berakhot* 27a and freq.). (h) *Argument put forward only to be rejected: mahu de-tema*, 'it might have been said' ('*Arakhin* 21b and freq.); *saleka da'atekh amina*, 'I might have argued' (*Kiddushin* 34b; *Sotah* 44a and very freq.); *ka-saleka da'atekh*, 'you might have supposed' (*Pesahim* 26a and very freq.).

9. The terms are: (a) *Argument based on historical or geographical conditions:* *bimey R. nishnet . . .* , 'this was (only) taught in the days of R . . .' (e.g. *Bava Kama* 94b); *ha lan ve-ha le-hu*, 'this is according to us (the Babylonians) and that according to them (the Palestinians)' (*Berakhot* 5b; *Kiddushin* 29b and freq.). (b) *Argument based on analysis of states of mind: ḥazakah*, 'it is an established fact that' (*Bava Metzi'a* 3a; *Bava Batra* 6b and freq.). For a full treatment of this argument see *ET,* vol. XIII, s.v. *ḥazakah* 3, pp. 693–713.

10. The terms are: (a) *Readmission of an argument that has been previously rejected: le-'olam . . .* , 'in reality', 'actually' (*Berakhot* 3a–b and very freq.); *ela meḥavrata ke . . .* , 'but it is better to say' (*Pesaḥim* 55b and freq.). (b) *Argument against a statement of the obvious: mai ka-mashma' lan*, 'what does he tell us?' (*Shabbat* 108a and freq.); *peshita*, 'is it not obvious?' (*Bava Batra* 137a and freq.).

11. The terms are: (a) *Argument to resolve a contradiction between sources:* *mar amar ḥada u-mar amar ḥada ve-lo feligey*, 'this master says one thing and the other master another and they are not in disagreement' (*Hullin* 105a and freq.); *terey tannai*, 'there are two Tannaím' (i.e. who disagree on the matter (*Berakhot* 3a and freq.). (b) *Argument by textual emendation: ḥesurey meḥasara ve-hakhi ka-teni*, 'something is missing and this is how it should read' (*Pesaḥim* 10b; *Bava Kama* 16a and very freq.). The standard methodologies differ as to whether the intention in such instances is really to emend the text or is simply a way of explaining the text, i.e. the text does not really have to be read differently but this is what it means. For the first view see *Rashi* to *Berakhot* 11b, s.v. *af li-gemara; Rashi* to *Megillah* 28b, s.v. *hey tzana* and the other sources quoted by M. Higger, *Otzar ha-Baraitot,* vol. X (New York, 1948), pp. 130–1. For the opposite view see Isaiah Horowitz: *Shelah, Torah she-be-'al Peh* s.v. *be-khamah mekomot.* Other terms for the same device are: *meshabeshta hi*, 'the text is erroneous' (*Gittin* 73a); *al tinney*, 'do not learn thus' (*Sotah* 49b); *teni*, 'learn it thus' (*Bava Kama* 4a–b and freq.). (c) *Argument from the principle of literary economy: tzerikhey*, 'both are necessary', generally after *lama li le-mitney*, 'why do I have to state?' (*Gittin* 8a and very freq.).

12. The terms are: (a) *Different versions of an argument: ika de-amrey*, 'others say' (*Hullin* 3b and very freq.). (b) *Argument presented by different teachers:* 'R . . . says . . . and R . . . says' (*Berakhot* 3b–4a and very freq.); *ve-ibbayit ema*, 'and if you want I can say' (*Berakhot* 3b and very freq.). (c) *The consequences of different arguments: mai beynayhu . . . ika beynayhu . . .* , 'what is the difference between them? The difference between them is . . .' (*Kiddushin* 50a; *Bava Kama* 23a; *Bava Batra* 174b and freq.). (d) *Limited application of an argument: haney miley*, 'when are these words applied?' (*Berakhot* 15a and very freq.); *lo nitzrekha*, 'it is not necessary (to state it except in the following instance)' (*Bava Metzi'a* 30b and very freq.); *lo amaran ela*, 'we do not state it except . . .' (*Berakhot* 8b and freq.).

13. M. Guttman, '*Sheélot Akademiot ba-Talmud*' in *Dvir*, 1 (Berlin, 1923), 38–
     87; 2 (Berlin, 1924), 101–64, has assembled all the material in the Talmud
     on the purely academic question—the *ba'ya*—which he compares to math-
     ematical puzzles or philosophical conundrums such as Zeno's problem of
     Achilles and the tortoise.

II

THE MODERN STUDY OF THE BABYLONIAN TALMUD

3

The Last Amoraim

Heinrich Graetz

The period 375–500 C.E. during which the Roman empire was approaching a state of complete dissolution marks an epoch of decay and regeneration, destruction and rejuvenescence, ruin and reconstruction, in the history of the world. The storm, which burst in the north, under the wall of China, brought down a black thunder-cloud in its train, and shattered the giant tree of the Roman empire, which, sapless and leafless, had only continued to exist thus far by the force of gravity; nothing now remained but a wreck of splinters, the toy of every capricious wind. The uncouth Huns, the scourge of God, drove before them horde upon horde, tribe upon tribe, whose names the memory refuses to retain or the tongue to utter. The period of the migration of the nations confirms almost literally the words of the prophet: "The earth staggers like a drunken man, and her sins lie heavy upon her; she falls and cannot rise, and the Lord Zebaoth punishes the bands of heaven in heaven, and the kings of earth upon earth." Small wonder indeed that in the Goths, the first wave of the migration of tribes which inundated and devastated the Roman empire, the Jews did not fail to discover Gog from the land of Magog, of whom a prophet had said: "Thou shalt ascend and come like a storm, thou shalt be like a cloud to cover the land, thou and all thy bands, and many people with thee" (Ezekiel xxxviii. 9).

In this remarkable alternation of disappearance of nations and their formation, the conviction forced itself upon Jewish thinkers that the

Reprinted by permission of The Jewish Publication Society of America from *History of the Jews, volume 3*, by Heinrich Graetz, Philadelphia, 1955.

Jewish people was eternal: "A nation arises, another vanishes, but Israel alone remains forever." The barbaric tribes, the avengers of the long-enslaved nations, settled on the ruined sites of the Roman empire, wild plants only to be cultivated by the master-hand of history, uncouth savages, to be civilized by earnest teaching. In this iron time, when no man could be certain of the next day, the leaders of Judaism in Palestine and Babylonia felt deeply the necessity of placing the treasure which had been confided to their hands in safety, so that it might not be imperiled by the accidents of the day. An epoch of collection commenced, during which the harvest which had been sown, cultivated, and reaped by their forefathers was brought under shelter. The subject-matter of tradition, which had been so greatly augmented, enriched and purified by a long series of generations and the diversity of schools, was henceforward to be set in order. This tendency of compilation and arrangement was represented by Ashi.

Rabbana Ashi (born 352, died 427) was the son of Simaï, and the descendant of an ancient family. He so early gave evidence of complete maturity of mind, that while still a youth he restored the long-desolate Soranian academy to its former place of honor. He was certainly not more than twenty when he became principal of that school. Coming of a wealthy family, Ashi possessed many forests, the wood of which he had no compunction in selling to feed the holy fire for the worship of the Magi. It is remarkable that nothing is known of the history of his youth and education; there is even no indication of the reason which induced him to infuse new life into the half-decayed Soranian academy; probably Sora was his native town. He pulled down and rebuilt the school which had been erected several centuries previously by Rab, and which was already beginning to exhibit signs of decay; and in order that no delay should occur in the rebuilding, he brought his bed on the site, and remained there night and day until the gutters of the house had been put up. The Sora school was built on an elevation so that it might overlook the whole city. Ashi's splendid qualities so impressed his contemporaries that he was regarded as the supreme authority, a position to which no person had been able to attain since Raba's death. Ashi united thorough knowledge of the entire body of the Law, characteristic of Sora, with Pumbedithan dialectics, and thus satisfied all claims. His contemporaries conferred upon him the distinguishing title of Rabbana (our teacher). During the fifty-two years over which his public labors extended, seven principals succeeded each other in Pumbeditha. Nahardea, which had made no figure since its destruction by Ben-Nazar (Odenath), also began to come into some repute again on account of the academy opened there by Amemar (390–420). But none of these teachers really disputed the supremacy with Ashi, and Sora again occupied the honorable position into which it had been placed by Rab. The oldest Amoraïm, Amemar and Mar-Zutra, voluntarily subordinated themselves to Ashi's authority, and resigned to him the task of restoring unity. The most distinguished among them, even the two successive Princes of the Captivity of this period (Mar-Kahana and Mar-Zutra I), submitted to his orders. It was in Sora that the Princes of the Captivity now received the homage of the delegates of all the Babylonian communities; this ceremony had formerly taken place, first at Nahardea, and then, during the prime of its academy, at Pumbeditha. This homage was paid every year on a Sabbath, at the commencement of the month of Marcheshvan (in the autumn), and this Sabbath was known as the "Rigle" of the Prince of the Captivity. The extraordinary assemblies of the people, which met at the command of the Prince of the Captivity, were henceforward also held in Sora, and for this reason the Patriarchs were obliged to repair to that town, even though they had fixed their residence in some other place. Ashi had thus made Sora the center of Jewish life in Babylonia, and had connected it with everything of public or general interest. The splendor with which its numerous assemblies invested it, was so great that Ashi expressed surprise that the heathen Persians could be witnesses of it all, and not feel themselves moved to embrace Judaism.

In consequence of this concentration of power in his own person, Ashi was enabled to undertake a work, the consequences of which were incalculable, both as regards the fate and the development of the Jewish people. He began the gigantic task of collecting and arranging the explanations, deductions, and amplifications of the Mishna, which were included under the name "Talmud." The immediate motive which suggested this undertaking was undoubtedly the consideration that the immense accumulation of matter, the result of the labor of three generations, ought not to be allowed to vanish from memory through lack of interest. This would certainly be the case if some means were not provided of impressing it easily upon the mind. Ashi even then complained of the diminution of the power of memory in his time as compared with times gone by, without, however, taking into account that by reason of the accumulation of matter the memory was infinitely more charged than formerly. His successful treatment of this exuberant material was rendered the easier by the fact that he was permitted to work at it for more than half a century. Every year on the occasion of the assembly of all the members, disciples, and pupils during the Kalla months, certain tractates of the Mishna, together with the Talmudical explanations and corollaries, were thoroughly gone into, and thus in about thirty years more than fifty of them were completely arranged. In the latter half of his period of office Ashi went through the whole of the matter which had thus been put in order for the second time. What remained after this double process of winnowing and testing was accepted as of binding force.

This arrangement of the bulky matter of the Talmud was not committed to writing. The conservation in writing of oral tradition, the incarnation, as it were, of what is spiritual, was still regarded as a crime against religion, more especially at this period, when Christendom had taken possession of the Holy Scriptures as its own spiritual property, and considered itself as the chosen part of Israel. According to the views of the times, Judaism was now possessed of no distinguishing feature, except the Oral Law. This thought frequently found expression in a poetical form—"Moses requested permission to commit to writing the Mishna or Oral Law, but God saw in advance that the nations would one day possess a Greek translation of the Torah, and would affirm: 'We are Israel; we are the children of God,' while the Jewish people would also declare, 'We are God's children,' and He therefore gave a token for this purpose: 'He who possesses my secret (mysterion) is my son.' This secret is the Mishna and the oral exegesis of the Law. Therefore did the prophet Hosea say: 'Were I to write the fulness of the Law, Israel would be accounted as a stranger.' "

It is not at all astonishing that this multitude of ordered details could be retained by the memory, for before the time of Ashi they had been retained though not yet reduced to order. By his compilation of the Talmud, Ashi completed the work which had been begun by Judah two centuries previously. But his task was infinitely more difficult. The Mishna embraced only the plain Halacha in artistically constructed paragraphs of the Law. The Talmud, however, gave also the living part of the development of the Law and its spiritual tenor, and this with dialectic exactitude. The first impulse to the compilation of the Talmud marks one of the most important epochs in Jewish history. From this time forward the Babylonian Talmud (Talmud Babli) became an active, potent, and influential element. Ashi, however, did not entirely complete this gigantic task; for, although he directed his ardor wholly to the work of compilation, the creative power was not so completely conquered either in him or his contemporaries, that they were content to entirely restrict their energies to the work of compilation. On the contrary, Ashi solved many of the questions which had been left doubtful, or had been unsatisfactorily answered by the preceding Amoraïm, and his decisions are as forcible and ingenious as they are simple; in fact, one often wonders how they could have been overlooked by his predecessors. About this time the Jerusalem or Palestinean Talmud was compiled and concluded. The name of the compiler is not known. The latest authorities whose names have been preserved are Samuel bar Bun and Jochanan bar Moryah, contemporaries of Ashi.

The period of Ashi's activity falls within the reign of Jezdijird (400–420), a king of the Sassanian dynasty, who was favorably disposed towards the Jews. The Magians gave to this noble prince the surname of "Al Hatim" (the sinner), because he refused to surrender his own will and allow himself to be ruled by them. He was exceedingly well affected towards the Jews, and at the same time favorably disposed towards the Christians. On the days of homage there were present at his court the three representatives of the Babylonian Jews: Ashi, of Sora; Mar-Zutra, of Pumbeditha; and Amemar, of Nahardea. Huna bar Nathan, who, if he was no Prince of the Captivity, must nevertheless have been possessed of considerable influence, held frequent intercourse with Jezdijird's court. This mark of attention on the part of a Persian king, who proclaimed himself the child of the Sun, a worshiper of Ormuz, and the King of the Kings of Iran, may be regarded as a proof of high favor.

Ashi was devoid of all exaggerated enthusiasm, and seems to have attempted to suppress the hope of the coming of the Messiah, which kept the minds of the Jews in greater suspense than ever at this time of the migration of nations and of universal revolution, when sin-laden Rome was suffering the punishment of God. An ancient sibylline saying, attributed to the prophet Elijah, was current, according to which the Messiah would appear in the eighty-fifth jubilee (between 440 and 470 of the common era). Such messianic expectations were always certain of creating enthusiasts, who aimed at converting their silent belief into fact, and without exactly intending to deceive, attempted to carry away such of the crowd as were of like opinions, and to excite them to such a pitch that they would willingly sacrifice their lives. In point of fact such an enthusiast did appear during Ashi's time in Crete, and he gained as adherents all the Jewish congregations of this important island, through which he had traveled in a year. He promised them that one day he would lead them dry-footed, as Moses had formerly done, through the sea into the promised land; he is said to have adopted the name of the great lawgiver. For the rest, this Cretan Moses was able to convince his followers so thoroughly of his divine mission, that they neglected their business, abandoned all their property, and only waited for the day of the passage through the sea. On the appointed day, Moses the Messiah marched in front, and behind him came the entire Jewish population of Crete, including the women and the children. From a promontory projecting out into the sea, he commanded them to throw themselves fearlessly into the ocean, as the waters would divide themselves before them. Several of these fanatics met their death in the waves; others were rescued by sailors. The false Moses is said, however, never to have been found again. It was against such false hopes as these, whose consequences were so sad, that Ashi warned the Jews. At the same time he suggested another interpretation of the prophecy which had been set in circulation: "It is certain," said he, "that the Messiah cannot appear *before* this time, before the eighty-fifth jubilee, but after the lapse of this period the hope, although not the certainty, of his coming may be entertained." Ashi died, greatly respected by his contemporaries and the Jews of aftertimes, at a ripe old age (427), two years before the capture of Carthage by Genseric. This Prince of the Vandals, who wrested from Rome her accumulations of spoil, also carried to Africa the vessels of the Temple, which Titus had added in triumph to the plunder of so many nations. Like the sons of Judæa, the Temple vessels wandered much.

By reason of the Patriarchate, Judæa was still regarded as their head by the Jewish communities of the Roman Empire. During this period it presents an even more gloomy picture of complete decay than formerly. The oppression of hostile Christianity bore all too heavily upon the country, and stifled the impulse to study. Tanchuma bar Abba, the chief supporter of the later Agada, is the last Halachic authority of Judæa. There also, as in Babylonia, the last Amoraïm collected the traditions and planned and arranged the Jerusalem, or, more correctly, the Judæan or Western Talmud (Talmud shel Erez-Israel, Gemara di Bene Ma'araba). But so defective is the history of Judæa that not even the names of the compilers or the originators of the movement are known. Doubtless the example of Babylonia suggested the making of this collection. Only so much is certain, that Tiberias, the seat of the Patriarchate and of the School, was the birthplace of the Jerusalem Talmud.

In Babylonia, where up till now the Jews had enjoyed quiet and independence but seldom disturbed, troubles and persecutions also began to increase. It was for this reason that a dearth of prominent personages began to make itself felt. Creative power declined, and made way for the tendency to reproduce and establish what had already been produced. The Jewish history of this country moved within a narrow circle; the principals of the schools succeeded one another, taught, and died, and it was only by the appearance of persecutions that a sad variety was imparted to its course. Of Ashi's six successors at the Academy of Sora (427–456), not one accomplished anything worthy of remark.

Some small importance was possessed, however, by Ashi's son, Mar, who also bore the name Tabyome. He happened to be at Machuza at the time when he heard the news of the occurrence of a vacancy at the head of the Soranian Metibta. He hurried off to Sora, and arrived there just in the nick of time, for the members of the academy were assembled for the election. Delegates were sent to confer with him on the choice of Acha of Diphta, and were detained by him, as were also others who were sent after them, until they were ten in number; whereupon he delivered a lecture, and was hailed as Resh-Metibta by all the members present (455). Acha was exceedingly hurt by this slight, and applied to his own case the following saying, "He who is unlucky, can never attain to luck."

In the same year a persecution of the Jews broke out with unprecedented rigor in the Babylonian countries. It was the commencement of a long series of bloody attacks which the Jews had to suffer at the hands of the last of the neo-Persian kings, and which rendered their position as sad as that of their co-religionists of the Roman Empire. Jezdijird III (440–457), unlike his predecessor of the same name, instituted a religious persecution of the Jews; they were forbidden to celebrate the Sabbath (456). The reason of this sudden change in the conduct of the Persian ruler towards the Jews, who had always been sincerely attached to him, is probably to be found in the fanaticism of the Magi, whose influence over many of the Persian monarchs was not less than that of the spiritual advisers of the eastern emperors over their masters. The Magi of this period appear to have learnt their proselytism and their love of religious persecution from the Christians. Besides this, Christianity had by its proselytism provoked the Magi to resistance. The Manicheans who had compounded Jewish, Christian, and Persian religious ideas into a medley of their own, made accusations of heresy as common in Persia as in the Roman Empire. Jezdijird persecuted both Manicheans and Christians. Sooner or later the light-worship of the Persians was bound to take offense at Judaism, and to place the Jews upon the list of its enemies. The chronicles are silent concerning the conduct of the Jews with regard to the prohibition of the celebration of the Sabbath; conscientious Jews, however, cannot have failed to obtain opportunities of evading it, and for this reason the names of no martyrs have survived this persecution. The constraint was continued about after a year, as Jezdijird was killed a short time after; a civil war was carried on by his sons Chodar-Warda and Firuz for the possession of the crown.

Mar bar Ashi was the sole authority of this period; and although all his decisions, with the exception of three, received the force of law, he does not seem to have acquired any special repute in the Soranian Academy. He continued his father's work of completing the Talmudical collection, and included the latter's decisions therein. He and his contemporaries must have felt themselves all the more impelled to complete the work of compilation, as the persecution they had gone through made them feel that the future was precarious. Nothing more is known of Mar bar Ashi's character than a trait of conscientiousness, which stands out in strong contrast with Raba's partiality towards members of his own class. He relates as follows: "When an associate appears before me in court, I refuse to exercise the functions of my office, for I regard him as a near relation, and might involuntarily show partiality in his favor."

After Mar's death the Jews of the Persian Empire were the victims of a fresh persecution under Firuz (Pheroces, 457–484), which was far more terrible than that which had occurred under his father, Jezdijird. This persecution is said to have been occasioned by the desire for vengeance entertained by this monarch, who was swayed by the Magi against the whole Jewish community, because certain of them were said to have killed and flayed two Magi in Ispahan. As a punishment for this deed Firuz put to death half the Jewish population of Ispahan, and had the Jewish children forcibly brought up in the Temple of Horvan as worshipers of fire. The persecution extended also to the communities of Babylonia, and continued for several years, until the death of the tyrant. Mar-Zutra's son, Huna-Mari, Prince of the Captivity, and two teachers of the Law, Amemar bar Mar-Janka and Meshershaya bar Pacod, were thrown into prison, and afterwards executed (469–70). They were the first martyrs on Babylonian soil, and it is a significant fact that a Prince of the Captivity bled for Judaism.

A few years later the persecution was carried to a still wider extent; the schools were closed, assemblies for the purpose of teaching prohibited, the jurisdiction of the Jews abolished, and their children compelled to embrace the religion of the Magi (474).

The city of Sora seems to have been destroyed at this period. Firuz, whose system of persecution puts one in mind of Hadrian, invented a new means of torture, which had not occurred to that emperor, which was to remove the young from under the influence of Judaism, and to bring them up by force in the Persian religion. For this reason he was branded by the Jews of after times, like Hadrian, with the name of "the wicked" *(Piruz Reshia)*. The immediate result of this persecution was the emigration of Jewish colonists, who settled in the south as far as Arabia, and in the east as far as India.

This emigration of the Jews to India is expressly marked as occurring about the time of Firuz's persecution. An otherwise unknown person, Joseph Rabban by name, who is recognizable as a Babylonian by reason of this title, arrived in the year 4250 of the Jewish era (490), with many Jewish families, on the rich and busy coast of Malabar; he must accordingly have started on his journey before this date, and therefore have emigrated under Firuz. Airvi (Eravi), the Brahmin king of Cranganor, welcomed the Jewish strangers, offered them a home in his dominions, and suffered them to live according to their peculiar laws, and to be ruled by their own princes (Mardeliar). The first of these chiefs was their leader Joseph Rabban, upon whom the Indian monarch conferred special rights and princely honors, to be inherited by his descendants. He was allowed, like the Indian princes, to ride upon an elephant, to be preceded by a herald, accompanied by a musical escort of drums and cymbals, and to sit upon a carpet. Joseph Rabban is said to have been followed by a line of seventy-two successors, who ruled over the Indo-Jewish colonists, until quarrels broke out among them. Cranganor was destroyed, many of the Jews lost their lives, and the remainder settled in

Mattachery, a league from Cochin, which acquired from this fact the name of Jews'-town. The privileges accorded by Airvi to the Jewish immigrants were engraved in ancient Indian (Tamil) characters, accompanied by an obscure Hebrew translation, on a copper table, which is said to be extant at the present day.

As soon as the terrors of persecution had ceased with Firuz's death, the ancient organization was again restored in Jewish Babylonia; the academies were re-opened, principals appointed, and Sora and Pumbeditha received their last Amoraïc leaders—the former in the person of Rabina, the latter in José. These two principals and their assessors had but one end in view, the completion and termination of the work of compiling the Talmud begun by Ashi. The continual increase of affliction, the diminished interest which probably on that account was extended to study, the uncertainty of the future, all these causes forcibly suggested the completion of the Talmud. Rabina, who held office from 488 to 499, and José, who discharged the duties of principal from 471 to about 520, are expressly mentioned in the old chronicles as "the close of the period of the Amoraïm" *(Sof Horaah)*. There is no doubt, however, that the members of the two academies, whose names have been preserved, also had a part in this work, and that they therefore are to be regarded as the last of the Amoraïm. The most important among them was Achaï bar Huna of Be-Chatim, near Nahardea (died 506), whose decisions and discussions are distinguished by characteristic peculiarities, and bear witness to a clear and sober mind, and to great keenness. Achaï was known and esteemed for these qualities beyond Babylonia. An epistle received by the Babylonian academy from Judæa, which, as far as is historically known, was probably the last addressed by the deserted mother-country to its daughter colony, speaks of him in terms of greatest reverence: "Neglect not Achaï, for he is the light of the eyes of the exiles." Even Huna-Mar, the Prince of the Captivity, must have possessed Talmudical acquirements, for the chronicle, which is by no means favorable to the princes of the Captivity, numbers him among this series of teachers of the Law, and concedes to him the title of Rabbi. His history, with which certain important events are connected, belongs to the following period.

In conjunction with these men, Rabina and José accomplished the completion of the Talmud, that is to say, they sanctioned as a complete whole the collection of all previous transactions and decisions which they had caused to be compiled, and to which no additions or amplifications were henceforward to be made. The definite completion of the Babylonian Talmud (called also the Gemara) occurred in the year of Rabina's death, just at the close of the fifth century (13th Kislev or 2nd December, 499), when the Jews of the Arabian peninsula were sowing the first seeds of a new religion and laying the foundations of a new empire, and when the Gothic and Frankish kingdoms were rising in Europe from the ruins of ancient Rome. The Talmud forms a turning-point in Jewish history, and from this time forward constitutes an essential factor therein.

The Talmud must not be regarded as an ordinary work, composed of twelve volumes; it possesses absolutely no similarity to any other literary production, but forms, without any figure of speech, a world of its own, which must be judged by its peculiar laws. It is extremely difficult to give any sketch of its character because of the absence of all common standards and analogies. The most talented could, therefore, hardly hope to succeed in this task, even though he had penetrated deeply into its nature, and become intimately acquainted with its peculiarities. It might, perhaps, be compared with the literature of the Fathers of the Church, which sprang up about the same time; but on closer examination even this comparison fails to satisfy the student. It is, however, of less consequence what the Talmud is in itself, than what was its influence on history, that is to say, on the successive generations whose education it chiefly controlled. Many judgments have been passed on the Talmud at various times and on the most opposite grounds. It has been condemned, and its funeral pyre has been ignited, because only its unfavorable side has been considered, and no regard has been paid to its merits, which, however, can be rendered apparent only by a complete survey of the whole of Jewish history. It cannot be denied, however, that the Babylonian Talmud is marred by certain blemishes, such as necessarily appear in every intellectual production which pursues a single course with inflexible consistency and exclusive one-sidedness. These faults may be classed under four heads. The Talmud contains much that is immaterial and frivolous, of which it treats with great gravity and seriousness; it further reflects the various superstitious practices and views of its Persian birthplace, which presume the efficacy of demoniacal medicines, of magic, incantations, miraculous cures, and interpretations of dreams, and are thus in opposition to the spirit of Judaism. It also contains isolated instances of uncharitable judgments and decrees against the members of other nations and religions, and finally it favors an incorrect exposition of the Scriptures, accepting, as it does, tasteless misinterpretations. The whole Talmud has been made responsible for these defects, and has been condemned as a collection of trifles, a well of immorality and falsehood. No consideration has been paid to the fact that it is not the work of any one author, who must answer for every word of it, or if it be, that that author is the entire Jewish nation. More than six centuries lie petrified in the Talmud as the fullest evidence of life, clothed each in its peculiar dress and possessing its own form of thought and expression: a sort of literary Herculaneum and Pompeii, unmarred by that artificial imitation which transfers a gigantic picture on a reduced scale to a narrow canvas. Small wonder, then, that if in this world the sublime and the common, the great and the small, the grave and the ridiculous, the altar and the ashes, the Jewish and the heathenish, be discovered side by side. The expressions of ill-will, which are seized upon with such avidity by the enemies of the Jews, were often nothing but the utterance of momentary ill-humor, which escaped from the teacher, and were caught up and embodied in the Talmud by over-zealous disciples, unwilling to lose a single word let fall by the revered sages. They are amply counterbalanced, however, by the doctrines of benevolence and love of all men without distinction of race or religion, which are also preserved in the Talmud. As a counterpoise to the wild superstitions, there are severe warnings against superstitious heathen practices, to which a separate section is devoted.

The Babylonian Talmud is especially distinguished from the Jerusalem or Palestine Talmud by the flights of thought, the penetration of mind, the flashes of genius, which rise and vanish again. An infinite fulness of thought and of thought-exciting material is laid up in the mine of the Talmud, not, however, in the shape of a finished theme which one can grasp at a glance, but in all its original freshness of conception. The Talmud introduces us into the laboratory of thought, and in it may be traced the progress of ideas, from their earliest agitation to the giddy height of incomprehensibility to which at times they attain. It was for this reason that the Babylonian rather than the Jerusalem Talmud became the fundamental possession of the Jewish race, its life's breath, its very soul. It was a family history for succeeding generations, in which they felt themselves at home, in which they lived and moved, the thinker in the world of thought, the dreamer in glorious ideal pictures. For more than a thousand years the external world, nature and mankind, powers and events, were for the Jewish nation insignificant, non-essential, a mere phantom; the only true reality was the Talmud. A new truth in their eyes only received the stamp of veracity and freedom from doubt when it appeared to be foreseen and sanctioned by the Talmud. Even the knowledge of the Bible, the more ancient history of their race, the words of fire and balm of their prophets, the soul outpourings of their Psalmists, were only known to them through and in the light of the Talmud. But as Judaism, ever since its foundation, has based itself on the experiences of actual life, so that the Talmud was obliged to concern itself with concrete phenomena, with the things of *this* world; so it follows that there could not arise that dream-life, that disdain of the world, that hatred of realities, which in the Middle Ages gave birth to and sanctified the hermit life of the monks and nuns. It is true that the intellectual tendency prevailing in the Babylonian Talmud, aided by climatic influences and other accidental circumstances, degenerated not infrequently into subtilty and scholasticism; for no historical phenomenon exists without an unfavorable side. But even this abuse contributed to bring about clear conceptions, and rendered possible the movement toward science. The Babylonian Amoraïm created that dialectic, close-reasoning, Jewish spirit, which in the darkest days preserved the dispersed nation from stagnation and stupidity. It was the ether which protected them from corruption, the ever-moving force which overcame indolence and the blunting of the mental powers, the eternal spring which kept the mind ever bright and active. In a word, the Talmud was the educator of the Jewish nation; and this education can by no means have been a bad one, since, in spite of the disturbing influence of isolation, degradation and systematic demoralization, it fostered in the Jewish people a degree of morality which even their enemies cannot deny them. The Talmud preserved and promoted the religious and moral life of Judaism; it held out a banner to the communities scattered in all corners of the earth, and protected them from schism and sectarian divisions; it acquainted subsequent generations with the history of their nation; finally, it produced a deep intellectual life which preserved the enslaved and proscribed from stagnation, and which lit for them the torch of science. How the Talmud made its way into the consciousness of the Jewish people, how it became known and accessible to distant communities, and how it became a stumbling-block to the enemies of Judaism, will be told in subsequent pages.

As soon as peace was restored the representatives of the Babylonian Jews hastened to re-establish their institutions, to re-open the academies, and, as it were, to re-unite the severed links in the chain of tradition. The fugitive Giza, who had remained in hiding by the river Zab, was called to preside over the academy at Sora; the sister academy at Pumbeditha chose Semuna as its head. A third name of this period has been transmitted to posterity, that of Rabaï of Rob (near Nahardea), whose position and office are, however, not clearly known. These men, with their associates and disciples, devoted their whole activity to the Talmud. It was the sole object of the attention of all thoughtful and pious men of that period; it satisfied religious zeal, promoted tranquillity of mind, and was also the means of acquiring fame, and thus furthering both spiritual and temporal aims. The persecution of the Law endeared and sanctified it, and the Talmud was the sacred banner around which the entire nation rallied.

But the disciples of the last Amoraïm had lost all creative power, and were unable to continue the development of the Talmud. The subject-matter and the method of teaching were both so fully defined that they were incapable of extension or of amplification. The stagnation in Talmudical development was more marked than ever before. The presidents of the academies were content to adhere to the ancient custom of assembling their disciples during the months of Adar (March) and Ellul (September), giving them lectures on the traditional lore and the methodology of the Talmud, and assigning to them themes for private study. At the utmost they settled, according to certain principles, many points of practice in the ritual, the civil law and the marriage code, which had until then remained undetermined, or concerning which there was a difference of opinion in the academies. Their purpose was to render the exhaustless material of the Talmud, which discussion and controversy had deprived of all definiteness, available for practical use. In order to prevent the decay of religious living, it was necessary that all doubt and uncertainty should cease; the judges stood in need of fixed principles by which to decide the cases brought before them, and all were ignorant of authoritative precepts by which to regulate their religious conduct. The establishing of the final rules for religious and legal practice after careful consideration of the arguments *pro* and *con* conferred upon the post-

Amoraïc teachers the name of Sabureans (Saburaï). After the various opinions (Sebora) were reviewed, they were the ones that established the final, valid law. The activity of the Sabureans really began immediately after the completion of the Talmud, and Giza, Semuna and their associates merely worked along the same lines; their intention was to develop a practical code rather than the theory of the Law. They did not arrogate to themselves the authority to originate. First of all, Giza and Semuna, the presidents of the academies, engaged in the work of committing the Talmud to writing. They availed themselves partly of oral tradition, partly of written notes made by various persons as an aid to memory.

As everything which proceeded from the Amoraïc authorities appeared of importance to their successors, they gathered up every utterance, every anecdote which was current in learned circles, so that posterity might not be deprived of what they deemed to be the fulness of wisdom. They made additions for the purpose of explaining obscure passages. In this form, as edited by the Sabureans, the contemporary communities and posterity received the Talmud.

4

The Talmud: Abraham Weiss's Views

Meyer S. Feldblum

Dr. Weiss approached the study of the Talmud with some misgivings; scholarly research had not, apparently, progressed sufficiently to permit a comprehensive inquiry into the Talmud. For the Talmud is the product of neither one man nor one school, but rather of many lands, and embraces the spiritual work of an entire people. It is the literary product of centuries, a creation inextricably tied to the people that created it. Indeed, it is difficult to say whether the nation created the Talmud, or the Talmud produced the nation. Therefore, to approach the Talmud with comprehensiveness as an objective implies not only a study of the history of our people, in the broadest sense possible, in that particular period, but the understanding of the spiritual and cultural evolution of centuries. Such study must be based on original research into all aspects of the Talmud, and on the history of the Talmudic period.[1]

The researches of Dr. Weiss comprise both an analysis of Talmudic material and its literary history, from the *mimrah* to the Talmud in its entirety. Without them, other studies lack all foundation; often, it is impossible to understand the Talmudic material in the absence of such work. Our author attempts to discern the nature of the *mimrah* and its history as a unit on the basis of the material found in the Talmud. He then proceeds to the history of the *sugyah*, its origins and development, and from thence to the problem of the development of the Talmud in its entirety, with all its attendant difficulties.

As a preface to his inquiry into the *mimrah*, our author defines the

Reprinted by permission of the author from *Abraham Weiss Jubilee Volume*, by Meyer S. Feldblum, Abraham Weiss Jubilee Committee—Yeshiva University, New York, 1964.

nature of the Talmudic *sugyah*. The *sugyah*, essentially, is any Talmudic discussion (be it long or short) that exists as an independent unit. Such discussion attempts to clarify a particular problem. The sources which the discussants utilize are two: a) the Torah and other traditional sources, and b) logic. Tannaitic discussion relies almost exclusively upon the Torah as its authority, aside from logical argumentation. But the Talmudic *sugyah* uses Tannaitic and old-Amoraic material to a much greater degree than it utilizes verses of the Torah. Mishnah and *baraitha* are for the Amoraim what Torah is for Tannaim. Of course, this new attitude evolved over a number of generations. The first Amoraim still permit themselves to disregard a Tannaitic source, a practice destined to vanish in a later generation. However, it is interesting to note that while on the one hand tradition is fundamental, on the other adaptation and criticism are apparent.

Tradition and exegesis, logic and explanation: these sanctify and sustain the old sources. Also, each generation renews its creative power. Exegesis and analysis have as their object both the bolstering of known and accepted matters, and the founding of recent innovations on old sources. It is not always possible to discern with which function we are dealing, but generally the character of the derivative exegesis is self-revealing.

THE ORIGINS OF THE *SUGYAH*

The earliest Amoraic material appears to have consisted of either a short explanatory note to an older source, usually a Mishnah, or a short statement (Halachic or Aggadic) lacking all argument or discussion. From the explanatory note there evolved the explanatory *sugyah*, while the independent *sugyah* developed from the short statement *(mimrah)*. Our author indicates that we possess practically not a single *sugyah*, in the normal sense of the term, from the first Babylonian Amoraim. There is not in the entire Talmud a discussion between Rav and Samuel, or their contemporaries, that embraces a sequence of questions and answers clearly attributable to these early Amoraim. Even the second generation, that of R. Huna and R. Yehudah, has left us very little *sugyah* material containing an extended discussion or argument. Rather, the *sugyah* in the accepted sense of that term becomes a constant phenomenon only in the following Amoraic generations.[2]

Our author rejects the possibility that there were such *sugyot* extant in early Amoraic times, but that they were subsequently lost. The very fact that later *sugyot* are produced as a continuation of the earlier material in its short form indicates that only this terse material was at their disposal. This is also reflected by the fact that we do possess full, extended *sugyot* of the early Palestinian Amoraim, such as R. Yochanan and Resh Lakish. Furthermore, in a number of instances we find Talmudic material derived from Rabbi and his contemporaries that bears an Amoraic impress in terms of both content and form. Such material contains an explanation and analysis of an early Tannaitic source, as well as the introduction of an objection, raised through a source, by the typical Amoraic interrogatory term "Eiseve" or another similar term. It is therefore improbable that only the Babylonian *sugyot* of that generation should have been lost without leaving a trace of their existence.

Our author concludes, that the Land of Israel is then not only the birthplace of Tannaitic Talmudic material, but is also the place of origin of the Amoraic *sugyah*, in terms of both its content and form. The period that saw the transition from Rabbi (Judah I) and his generation to R. Yochanan and Resh Lakish also saw the transition from the Tannaitic method of study to the Amoraic. In conformity with this development there was also a shift in the formal nature of the material. Mishnah and *baraita* were succeeded by *mimrah* and *sugyah*.

THE ANONYMOUS *SUGYAH*

There are *sugyot* that are at first anonymous and whose later developments name Amoraic speakers. Since this second part is a continuation of the first, one feels that this first part was probably known by the Amoraim named in the second. Yet we sometimes find that the words of one Amorah comment upon the statement of a man who lived in the following generation.[3] It therefore appears that an organizer of the *sugyah* is responsible for this particular order; from this we conclude that even in those situations where Amoraim are apparently continuing anonymous material, there is no necessity to say that they were familiar with this material.[4]

It is possible to prove the antiquity of anonymous material (only) in those places where a given Amorah utilizes such an anonymous *sugyah* for his own purposes. Of course, one must proceed carefully, proving that the Amorah himself used this antecedent *sugyah*, and that later sages did not incorporate his words in this old material. Our author cites a number of *sugyot* to clarify this problem of the antiquity of a *sugyah*. From the material assembled one may conclude at the most that those Amoraim whose lives bridged the second and third Amoraic generations possessed a number of organized *sugyot*. Hence it seems that the students of Rav and Samuel organized the first *sugyot*. The literary formulation and stabilization of Amoraic material, it is true, begins at an earlier date; but the task of creating the Amoraic *sugyah,* the foundation of a Talmud-to-be, fell to the second Amoraic generation. Those sages who already possessed fixed Amoraic material (mainly of Rav and Samuel), and in whose time the Palestinian *sugyah*-form was transferred to Babylon, laid the literary foundations of our Babylonian Talmud.[5]

MIMRAH AND *SUGYAH*[6]

Tannaitic sources were already fixed and established (in terms of form) by the period of *sugyah*-development. These sources are explicated and analyzed in the *sugyah* and serve, in turn, to provoke new problems. The *mimrah* (an Amoraic statement) essentially functions in the same way, as a determinate and fixed source for later generations. But the developmental path of the *mimrah* differs from that of the Tannaitic source. For the Tannaitic source bears its literary imprint of the period that gave it birth, and no emendation or addition can blur this imprint. Thus, even a *baraita* into which later material has been inserted (sometimes the *baraita* was divided into its components and *sugyah*-comment appended to each component, while here and there emendations were made) still bears the essential literary character of Tannaitic source.

It is different with the *mimrah*. For it is an Amoraic creation taking form with the very development of the *sugyah,* and so any change or addition to the *mimrah* recasts its literary form. And so, if it be impossible to understand a Tannaitic source without recourse to Tannaitic literature and parallels, it is likewise impossible to understand an Amoraic source except through the *sugyah*. Conversely, the *mimrah* illumines the essence of the *sugyah* and its character.

DEVELOPMENT OF THE *MIMRAH*

Generally, the *mimrah* was uttered by its declared author. But there are *mimrot* with a history, and occasionally the Talmud itself poses the problem of the origins of a *mimrah,* as when it notes, *lav b'ferush ittamar elah mikh'lalah ittamar* ("this view is implied, rather than explicitly stated"), or when it asks, *b'ferush sh'miyah lach oh mikh'lalah* ("did you hear this actually stated, or do you infer it?"), etc.[7]

From such *sugyot* Professor Weiss deduces a number of basic postulates concerning many Amoraic *mimrot.*

There are *mimrot* that were never uttered by the sage in whose name they were presented: rather, they were inferred from other *mimrot* of the sage, or from some general rule he pronounced, or from an actual case in which he participated.[8]

On occasion, the situation under discussion was mistakenly evaluated, or the central point remained somewhat ambiguous, and so two contradictory *mimrot* were created.[9]

Mimrot created in this way were transformed into *mimrot* quoted as explicit statements by their author. In seven instances the Talmud comments, "this was inferred from another statement" *(hada mikh'lal havertah itamar);* in all seven instances this comment is anonymous. Elsewhere a *mimrah* is created *le-shitatoh* (to harmonize with an opinion stated or inferred elsewhere; cf. the discussion of R. Eleazar's statement, Sanhedrin 31b, and the formulation of that statement, Sanhedrin 23a).[10]

Since the Talmud often testifies to such development of *mimrot,* it is reasonable to assume that other *mimrot* developed in similar ways, though we do not possess Talmudic corroboration of such case.

Through the analysis of such *sugyot* our author exhibits some of the paths of literary development taken by the *mimrah,* the foundation of the Talmudic *sugyah.* The *mimrah* derived from an actual occurrence shows us life being transformed into literature; the "inferential" *sugyot* *(lav be-ferush ittamar elah mikh'lalah)* show us the opposite, literary material being transformed into experience. Those *mimrot* derived from other *mimrot,* or stated by sage A as harmonizing with the view of sage B, and later quoted in B's name, reveal to us the developmental process of the *mimrah.* One *mimrah* produces another, and discussion of one *mimrah* either creates a new one, or recasts the old.

THE RANGE OF THE *MIMRAH*

The *mimrah* is often composed of two parts: one expressing the body of the idea, and a second, explaining and defining this idea.

The relation of this second part to the first is that of *g'marah* to Mishna. On this basis, Prof. Weiss created the terms, "the Mishnaic part of the *mimrah*," and the "g'marah part."

In a number of places the two parts are joined by the expressions "why?" *(mai ta'amah)* and "because" *(mi-shum)*.

We have already concluded that sometimes the *mimrah* was not actually uttered by its declared author. Prof. Weiss proceeds to ask, even in the case of those *mimrot* certainly attributable to their declared author, whether the explicative part was also created by him as well as the part expressing the basic idea.

He concludes, on the basis of source-material, that: [11] a) occasionally sages possessed only the basic part of a *mimrah*, and knew nothing of the explicative part; b) in many *mimrot* the explicative part was not created by the Amorah named as author of the *mimrah*, and that often an Amorah created both parts and we possess the basic part only.

This phenomenon of subsequently appended explicative material has already been noted by *rishonim*, the Tosafists in particular.[12]

The question now is: does even the basic part of the *mimrah* contain material not created by the declared author? There is, of course, a large difference between the addition of explicative material and the extension of the basic material itself. For in the last analysis the explicative part merely analyzes and explains the material before it, the material created by its named author. But to assert that material was added to the basic component without being so indicated, is possible only on the basis of Talmudic illustration of such phenomenon. Our author cites and analyzes a number of *sugyot* in which there are clear traces of such phenomena.[13]

Occasionally the opposite is true: the *mimrah* was composed of a number of statements bearing on one matter, but only a single statement was transmitted, while other statements belonging to the basic *mimrah* were never cited.

THE *MIMRAH* AND ITS *SUGYAH*

The distinction between basic material and later, added, material becomes more complex when we speak of a *sugyah*, whether it be entirely anonymous or only partly so. When a *sugyah* discusses a *mimrah* the question is raised whether it—in *toto* or in part—was created in the presence and with the participation of the author of the *mimrah*, or rather was created at a later time by scholars who succeeded the *mimrah*-author and discussed his statement.

On many occasions a given *mimrah* is transmitted by one sage in the name of another, and then is followed by discussion. Here too the question is posed: did the Amorah transmitting the *mimrah* also transmit the attendant discussion, thus presenting an entire *sugyah*, or did he present only the *mimrah*, with the *sugyah* developing later?

Professor Weiss analyzes many Talmudic *sugyot* with regard to their entire complex of problems of literary development,[14] and demonstrates that each *sugyah* has its own character. In some places, it is clear that the sage presenting the *mimrah* also transmitted the *sugyah*. On other occasions, the Amorah transmitting material presented only the *mimrah*, and later sages discussed it, adding more material. Though it is impossible to exhibit fully the development of every *sugyah*, it is necessary to understand, at the very least, the various phenomena of *sugyah*-development in order to understand the Talmudic material.

TEXTUAL VARIATIONS IN THE *MIMRAH*

Such ancient texts as Talmudic manuscripts and Geonic and *Rishonic* literature are studded with textual variations. There are also many variations in the parallel passages in the Talmud itself; there is no parallel *sugyah* that is structurally and verbally identical in every place it is found. Generally these variations are purely textual problems, with no relevance for the development of the *mimrah*. They are not links in either the conceptual or literary development of the Talmudic *sugyah*. Such variations were produced in a period when the Amoraic Talmud was already concluded, with a fixed literary structure. But it is necessary to distinguish between various periods even in post-Amoraic times. The variations introduced at a late period, in the centuries immediately preceding the printing of the Talmud, are generally slight. Those variations, on the other hand, produced in the time of the great *Rishonim* are more substantial. Even these, however, fall into the category of verbal polishing and conceptual clarification. It is otherwise with the variations left us from Saboraic and early-Geonic times. In this period, particularly in the age of the Saboraim, entire Talmudic *sugyot* were created. Indeed, the activity of the period is much more significant than is generally assumed, and Professor Weiss deals with the nature of the Saboraic period and its contribution in some of his essays. We shall later present a summary view of this period and its relation to the Talmud.

We find variations of *mimrot* and of entire *sugyot* in the Talmud. Some concern the turning of a phrase or an elucidatory comment; others touch the very essence of the *mimrah* or *sugyah*. Our author distinguishes between these two types by terming the substantial variations *nuschaot;* the insubstantial, *girsaot*. Substantial variations are introduced in the Talmud by: *ikah d'amri, ikah d'matni,* or *p'loni matni. Ikah d'amri* ("some say") introduces variations to material not yet having a fixed literary formulation; *ikah d'matni* ("some learn") has reference to a source that already possesses this fixed formulation. Variations are present in the Talmud with no hint of their origin or development. But there are also Talmudic *sugyot* that bear witness to the origins of variations: these are those *sugyot* containing the expression *elah i itamar, hachi itamar* ("If it were said, it was said thus").

This expression reveals that the original form of the *mimrah* is not that which was transmitted, but that which is now presented. Our author cites all the *sugyot* in which this formula is found, and analyzes them in order to clarify the precise meaning of the phrase.[15] The problem is: did the bearers of this new version actually consider themselves to be re-instituting the original language of the author of the *mimrah*, or did they mean that the author should have said thus, and we would then agree with him. Our author also clarifies, in each *sugyah*, whether the problem raised concerning the original *mimrah* justifies the doubt expressed as to its authenticity.

Such analysis leads Professor Weiss to the conclusion that these *sugyot* have a developmental history of their own. At first the object was to re-introduce the original formulation of the *mimrah*, while in later times the term was used even where the *mimrah* is being emended, and its fixed form changed. There is no *sugyah*, however, in which it can clearly be shown that the true, pristine, form of the *mimrah* was actually re-introduced by the term, *elah i itamar*.

From these *sugyot*, which exhibit the entire developmental course of emendations and variations, our author turns to *sugyot* containing the expressions *ikah d'matni*, or *p'loni matni*.

In *sugyot* having a *matni* formula the variation is not introduced as the result of discussion. Nevertheless, our author is occasionally able to display the factors engendering the variant. Sometimes a conceptual problem has been raised, in previous discussion of the first form of the *mimrah;* on other occasions, the problem is not with the *mimrah* itself, but rather concerns a contradiction between the *mimrah* and another statement. Such are the factors causing the introduction of the second version.

We have seen that in Amoraic material the variant version is introduced by either *ikah d'matni* or *ikah d'amri.* Do these different technical expressions indicate a respective difference in the nature of the change they introduce? I have already noted that our author surmises, on the basis of the verbal difference between the two terms, that *matni* introduces another version that is formally fixed, while *amri* is used for material that is still fluid, in a literary sense.

Our author's characteristic method is again evident. In the place of mere conjecture, he assembles and analyzes all the *sugyot* in which these expressions are found, and arrives at conclusions concerning the nature of the material and the character of the variations and their development.

With regard to the development of variations, there is practically no difference indicated by the use of one phrase rather than the other. But with regard to the character of the material and its presentation, there are phenomena present here that are lacking there. Expressions such as *ikah d'amri ipchah* ("some say the opposite"), or . . . *l'kulah* (". . . a lenient view") are rarely found; rather, we have *ikah d'matni ipchah* ("some learn the opposite") and *ikah d'matni l'kulah* ("some learn, more leniently, . . .). The variations introduced by the first formula are close to the reading first offered, in both content and form; the latter formula introduces a variation derived from a totally different source. When the variations reside solely in relating the same statement to two different texts, *matni* is used; rarely is *amri* found in such situation. This phenomena is explained by our author on the basis of his aforementioned theory.

THE FIXING OF TALMUDIC MATERIAL

Prof. Weiss has made an important contribution to the understanding of the Talmud through his research into the problem of whether oral material has received fixed literary form by the Amoraic period, as well as whether oral discussion had become literary debate. Are any expressions found in the Talmud to indicate the presence of such literary activity?

Our author surmises, on the basis of Talmudic *sugyot*, that the expression *itamar* ("it is said") presents material that has already received fixed literary form, while the expression *kevah* is used by the Talmud to denote the process of fixing material literarily. Thus, both expressions relate to one matter: one is a statement of process; the other, of fact. Their conceptual meaning resembles their verbal meaning—*itamar* means "it is said," and so *itamar amar p'loni* means, "it is said that someone said." Obviously, "it is said" must add something to "someone said," or else it is a meaningless tautology. It appears, also, that *itamar* corresponds to the Tannaitic *tanya* ("it is learned"); just as *tanya* denotes a fixed literary form, so does *itamar*. The nature of this term becomes most apparent in the *sugyah* 'Erubin 32b.

"R. Hiyya b. Abba and Raba b. Nathan sat at their studies while R. Nahman was sitting beside them, and in the course of their session they discussed the following: Where could that TREE have been standing? . . . It may still be maintained that [the tree] stood in a public domain and that the man's intention was to acquire its Sabbath abode below but [this Mishnah] represents the view of Rabbi. . . . 'Well-spoken.' said R. Nahman to them, 'and so also did Samuel say.' . . . . they said to him: 'Did you embody it in the Gemarah?' 'Yes,' he answered them. So it was also stated *[itamar nammi]*: R. Nahman reporting Samuel said: Here we are dealing with a tree that stood in a public domain . . . and the man had the intention to acquire his Sabbath abode below, and the Mishnah represents the view of Rabbi. . . ."

Of special significance is the exchange, " 'Did you embody it in the Gemarah?' 'Yes,' he answered them," and its relation to the continuation, "So also was it stated: R. Nahman reporting Samuel said. . . ." What does this mean? R. Nahman has already said, "Well-spoken," and "So also did Samuel say." What does "So it was also stated" add? In the light of our author's aforementioned surmise, the text is to be read thus: They ask, "Did you embody it in the Gemarah?", or in other words, "Has the formulation of Samuel's statement been fixed as a literary unit?" To this is answered, "Yes." Samuel's statement has a fixed formulation, "So also was it stated. . . ." The function of this continuation is not to prove that Samuel really said what R. Nahman reported in his name, but rather to cite Samuel's words in their fixed literary formulation as a *mimrah*.

In the *sugyah* just cited, the term is used anonymously by the Talmud; elsewhere we find it used by R. Jeremiah b. Abba and R. Nahman b. Isaac. Apparently, the Jerusalem Talmud as well as the Babylonian utilized the term *kavah* ("fix") to indicate the linguistic formalization of material.[16]

This process did not occur only in texts labelled by *itamar,* for such material is scattered throughout the Talmud.

Though I shall present our author's view concerning the redaction of the Talmud further on in this essay, it may be noted here that this view is closely tied to his approach to the problem of literary fixing of Talmudic material. According to this approach, the material was created by study, and it was made Talmudic material by fixed literary formulation. Talmudic material grew through constant study and uninterrupted literary formulation. With such a developmental process functioning, there can be no problem of final redaction of the Talmud in the accepted sense of the term. Nor is there the problem of the reduction of the Talmud to writing in the normal sense of that term. For through an analysis of Talmudic *sugyot* and a portrayal of the Talmud as a literary product, our author gives us a totally different picture of the development of the Talmud in its entirety.[17]

Prof. Weiss insists that though the Talmudic sages were capable of presenting their thoughts in most successful and precise literary forms, they nevertheless did not create fictional dialogues, assigning parts to famous scholars; there is no doubt that the Talmudic discussion occurred as it is given. The Tosafot (B.B. 154b, *s.v. kerem;* Bechorot 4b, *s.v. elah*) are of the opinion that such fictional dialogues are contained in the Talmud. A contemporary student of the Talmud[18] concurs: "On many occasions certain statements were attributed to Amoraim who, it is later learned, never made them." Our author analyzes the *sugyot* cited to confirm this verdict, and concludes that there is no basis for such suspicion.

Similarly, our author proves the theory developed in *Dor Dor V'Dorshav,* that some of the *baraitot* in the Babylonian Talmud are of Amoraic origin, to be without foundation. This theory claims that the Amoraim falsified both *baraitot* and *mimrot,* on the one hand presenting their own *mimrot* as *baraitot,* and on the other hand presenting as their own *mimrot* what were in reality *baraitot*. The author of *Dor Dor* buttresses his allegations with Talmudic *sugyot*.

After an analysis of these *sugyot* our author concludes that the allegations lack all basis.[19] Of course, *sugyot* containing expressions such as *amar p'loni v'amri loh b'matnitah tanah* ("[Amorah] X said, and some say it is stated in a *baraita*"), or *tanya nammi hachi* ("so it is stated in a *baraita* as well"), demand explication—but the desired explication is not that of *Dor Dor*. On occasion such duplication of Amoraic and Tannaitic sources grew out of imprecise transmission of material. Amorah X quoted a Tannaitic source; some auditors recorded it as a *baraita*, others as the Amorah's own statement. Sometimes an Amorah would cite an older source and add his comment, and due to this addition the entire statement was credited to him; we, then, possess this source as both *baraita* and Amoraic statement. Finally, a *mimrah* received Tannaitic form because it grew from a Tannaite source. In this manner the phenomena of Biblical verses being presented as *mimrot*, and *mimrot* being given as verses, can be explained as well.

In addition, the fact that both Tannaitic and Amoraic material is introduced by common terms, such as *amar mar* and *tah shmah*, caused irregularities.

Generally, these errors and problems are rooted in an atmosphere of living debate using literary material. The scholar citing a source was immersed in the discussion, and did not bother to label its source, or such identification, though given, was later forgotten or elided. Thus, this source was preserved in the *sugyah* as the sage's own statement. Later, the source from which our sage quoted comes to the attention of students of the *sugyah*, and they add it as *tanya nammi hachi*, or *tanya kavvatai* ("a baraita agrees"), for after the statement had been accepted as the sage's own, it could not be changed or eliminated.

PARALLELS IN TEXTUAL VARIATIONS

The problem of the original form of a given *mimrah* is present not only in those situations where the Talmud itself calls attention to it, as in *elah i itamar*, *ikah d'matni*, or *v'ikah d'amri* materials, but also in those places where a parallel *mimrah* occurs (whether in the same tractate or in a different one) with textual variations. We should note that one must distinguish between the *mimrah* itself and its explanatory *g'marah* element, for the problem of textual variations in this section of the *mimrah* is a totally different one.

Indeed, the approach to textual variations present in parallel passages differs from the approach to variations noted by the Talmud itself. Our author classifies the various types of variations, and so penetrates further into the process of *mimrah*-formulation.[20]

THE *MIMRAH*

There are two fundamental types of Talmudic *mimrot*. Into one category fall those *mimrot* that explain or clarify an older source; they have the character of supplements. Other *mimrot* are independent, that is, they have no relation to any older source.

The central problem concerning any independent *mimrah* is whether its present location is its original one, or rather, it was originally placed elsewhere and later transferred to its present frame of reference. We shall return to this problem in our remarks on the *sugyah*.

The Talmud itself on occasion debates the original site of a *mimrah*, generally with reference to supplementary *mimrot*. The object of such discussion is the identification of the source supplemented by the *mimrah*. Even in those situations where the identity of the source is clear, the problem as to which section of the source is being commented upon still remains.

Our author sees this problem as a central one in the history of the *mimrah*, one that can shed much light upon the study of the *sugyah* and the Talmud; consequently he is comprehensive in its treatment. He analyzes all *sugyot* containing the formulae *elah i itamar a'. . . . itamar* ("if it was said, it was said concerning. . . .") and *ikah d'matni a. . . .* (*"some learn it with reference to. . . ."),* and all *sugyot* with parallels in which one *mimrah* is appended to different sources, or to different sections of the same source.

The importance of such an inquiry lies in the fact that our author was thereby able to understand more clearly the various phenomena in the development of different readings in the *mimrah* itself and in its explanatory portion, and to display the process whereby the parallel *mimrah* came into being.[21]

DEVELOPMENT OF VARIATIONS (*NUSCHAOT*)

I shall here note a number of rules established by our author:

1. Variations develop when a statement supplementing an older source is transmitted without being clearly assigned to a specific section of that source despite the fact that it is possibly relevent to either *resha* (first part) or *sefah* (latter part).

2. There was originally one reading, but because of some difficulty the *mimrah* was transferred to a different source, or to a different section of the same source.

3. A *mimrah* appended to one source suited, in one way or another, another source as well; the one *mimrah* was then used to explain two sources.

4. Variations arose when different sages explained the same basic material in contrasting ways.

5. Upon occasion what are seemingly variations of one source are in reality two different sources.

THE *SUGYAH* AND ITS FORMS

Talmudic material is formulated in various manners:

1. The most common structure is the citation of a source in its entirety, followed by a *sugyah*-analysis or its various elements. The two expressions used in this procedure are *amar mar* and *ka-tani* ("it is learned").

2. A contrasting formulation is the explanatory *sugyah* that is presented as a supplement. This structure is most apparent where Talmudic explanation or comment are integrated into the *baraita*.

Prof. Weiss shows that both forms are commonly utilized by the Talmud.[22]

In a number of instances both forms—*piskah* (citation)—analysis and integrative—are used simultaneously, as in Ketuboth 103ab: "Our Rabbis taught: When Rabbi (Judah I) was about to die he said, 'I require the presence of my sons.' When his sons entered into his presence he instructed them: 'Take care that you show due respect to your mother. The light shall continue to burn in its usual place, the table shall be laid in its usual place. . . . Joseph of Haifa and Simeon of Efroth who have attended on me in my lifetime shall attend on me when I am dead' '. . . respect to your mother.' Is not this instruction Pentateuchal? . . . 'The light . . .' What is the reason? . . . 'Joseph of Haifa. . . .' He was understood to mean. . . . 'I require,' he said to them, 'the presence of the sages of Israel. . . . Do not lament for me,' he said to them, 'in the smaller towns, . . . My son Simeon is wise, my son Gamliel Nasi and Ḥanina b. Ḥama preside [at the college].' 'Do not lament for me. . . .' He was understood to mean. . . . 'My son Simeon is wise. . . .' What is the reason? . . . He said to them 'I require the presence of my youngest son. . . .' "

"He said to them, 'I require the presence of the Sages of Israel,' " and "He said to them, 'I require the presence of my youngest son,' " are continuations of the *baraitha* "Our Rabbis taught: When Rabbi. . . ." The *baraitha* is divided into three parts, with each part having additional material in the form of a *sugyah* analyzing citations.

An analysis of the material shows the simultaneous utilization of both methods. It follows, then, that insertions into the body of the text were known in Amoraic times.

Our author finds these two forms functioning in yet another area, in the development of the *sugyah*. There too, later strata were sometimes inserted into the very body of an earlier *sugyah*-text, while in other instances, the later material was appended as a continuation. Indeed, the insertion as a literary form was practiced for centuries after the Talmudic age; comments, both explanatory and analytic, were inserted into the text of the Talmud until a late period.

FORMULATION OF MATERIAL AND ITS ARRANGEMENT

Though the *sugyah* or *mimrah* is generally placed where it is topically suited, there are instances where a similarity of idea, or a verse or term held in common, determined the location of material. We sometimes possess, therefore, a body of material composed of *mimrot* or *sugyot* whose relation is merely a formal one.

Such units are often older than the frame of reference in which they are presently found, for they are self-contained older sources; since a part of the unit is here relevent, the entire unit was placed here. But it is also possible that the entire unit is of later origin than its frame of reference, or that part of the unit is a self-enclosed older source while part evolved here. This last phenomenon is most apparent in those instances where a series of *mimrot* of one author is followed by similar *mimrot* of later authors.

Doubtless there existed, in the Talmudic period, *mimra*-collections of a given author, which were considered source-material and were inserted as complete units into the Talmud. Most such units are older than the frames of reference in which they are presently found.

Our author cites the sources upon which this conclusion rests. One supporting citation is particularly revealing. *B.K.* 11ab contains a collection of various *mimrot* transmitted by Ulla in the name of R. Eleazar, with no hint given as to the genesis of the collection. But the Jerusalem Talmud, *Kedushin* chap. 1, sec. 4, preserved a list of questions sent by R. Yehudah to R. Eleazar. The collection before us, then, seems to be the answers sent by R. Eleazar to R. Yehudah. Prof. Weiss notes in passing that here we have "perhaps the first *she-alah u-t'shuva* (responsum)."

Our author posed the question, concerning such collections, whether there are traces in the Talmud of collections that were broken down into their component *mimrot*, with each *mimrah* being placed where it was topically suited. Furthermore, were parts of such collections preserved in the Talmud, while the collections as a whole were lost?

The sources indicate that both phenomena exist. Sometimes the Talmud utilized part of a collection, the entire collection later being lost; on other occasions the collection was divided into its component parts, and only the discerning eye can identify in scattered *mimrot* an erstwhile unit.

Generally, it can be stated that the forms of literary sources in the Talmudic period were two. The dominant form is that of Talmudic material created as clarification of the Mishnah and its attendant *baraitot;* the second form is that of the collection organized on the basis of some common idea, or because all its material was the work of the same hand.

THE *SUGYAH*

Our author distinguished between "simple" and "complex" *sugyot.* The "simple" *sugyah* is presented straightforwardly, sometimes showing normal historical development.

Here, for example, is a "simple" *sugyah* with no historical development. *Gittin* 32b: "It was said, Before how many must he cancel (a bill of divorce)? R. Nachman said, before two. R. Sheshet said, before three, etc. Said R. Nachman, whence do I derive my view? From the Mishnah stating. . . ."

But in *Gittin* 15ab we read: "R. Hisdah said, . . . Rava objected . . . rather, said Rava. . . . R. Ashi objected . . . rather, said R. Ashi. . . ." In this *sugyah* we see successive generations of scholars commenting on the strata of their predecessors, and adding to it.

Our author shows that in such *sugyot* the literary fixing was also accompanied by strata, each strata's form being fixed as it was created.[23]

The "complex" *sugyah* is one that itself utilizes other *sugyot*, or fragments thereof. In some instances we possess the sources from which the fragments, or the complete *sugyot*, were drawn; in others we do not possess these sources; occasionally it is difficult to ascertain whether literary sources were used at all.

Our author recognized certain problems in the literary development of the "complex" *sugyah*. One such problem lies in those *sugyot* whose presentation of material does not adhere to the chronological succession of the authors of the material. In such cases, the conceptual development of the *sugyah* must certainly have been different than it presently appears before us, where the words of an early scholar are cited after the words of a later one. Prof. Weiss cites many such non-chronological *sugyot* and clarifies them, explaining their development till their present form.[24]

Another problematic phenomenon is the structure of added material, or of continuations of the *sugyah*. In many instances we find part of a *sugyah* to be not a direct continuation of the preceding material, but rather a logical continuation of an idea found in earlier sections of the *sugyah*. Through an analysis of a number of *sugyot* Prof. Weiss shows that the continuation of Amoraic material—as the explanation of Tannaitic material—possesses two forms. In one, the *sugyah* is preserved in its original form and the new material added at the *sugyah's* end, though this new material often refers to earlier sections of the *sugyah*. In the other, new material is inserted into the very body of the earlier *sugyah*.

BASIC AND NON-BASIC MATERIAL IN THE *SUGYAH*

Discussion of the development of the *sugyah* and its creation center on that body of material created in the Amoraic age. But the *sugyah* also contains material not of this basic stock. We must distinguish, in both conceptual and textual senses, between the building-blocks and the material joining them, that is, between the basic and the non-basic material in the *sugyah*.

As defined by our author, the basic material contains those parts of the *sugyah* that it is impossible to detach without causing grave damage to the *sugyah*. Non-basic material are those elements that it is possible to detach from the *sugyah* without damaging its conceptual scope and content. Of course, the nature of the relationship between the sections of basic material may be thereby changed, but the nature of the concepts and the scope of topical development are not damaged.

From this it follows that citation of a source in a *sugyah* (i.e., *l'chi'd'p'loni*, "according to X," followed by a source containing X's statement) is not a "basic" element of the *sugyah*. The Talmud uses three methods of source-citation:

1. The name of the sage is given, but his view is not even hinted at for it was, apparently, well-known; i.e., Ketuboth 35b: "According to whom is the Mishnah? If according to R. Meir, 'his daughter' is open to objection; if according to R. Nechuniah b. Hakaneh, 'his sister' . . .; if according to R. Isaac, *'mamzeret'*. . . .;" the views of R. Nehumiah b. Hakaneh and R. Isaac are not given.

2. The name of the sage is given, along with a short version of his view; i.e., *Gittin* 13b: ". . . to R. Me'ir who said one may transfer an object not yet existent."

3. The name of the sage and his view are given.

Our author analyzes the problem of source-citation fully: its structure, omissions, and the conceptual relationship between it and the *sugyah*.[25]

Especially interesting is the analysis of *sugyot* in which, according to Prof. Weiss, the cited source is conceptually unsuitable, either because it lacks the anticipated idea, or even because it contains an idea contrary to the one it is cited to support. R. Tam already deletes a source cited in a particular *sugyah*, claiming that another source was initially intended.[26] From this our author concludes that a large portion of texts serving as cited sources were introduced into the *sugyot* at a late date. Doubtless, there are *sugyot* where the cited source is part of the basic material, and was included when the *sugyah* was itself developed; but in many instances the sources were later introduced from marginal references.

THE LITERARY REFINEMENT OF THE *SUGYAH* IN THE TALMUDS

The deterioration of the text of the Jerusalem Talmud is generally offered as the chief difference between the two Talmuds. But our author notes that we must distinguish between difficulties that arise because of a corrupted text, and those that arise from the state and nature of the text before us. Textual errors are generally obvious, and are easily corrected. The more deeply-rooted difficulties in the understanding of the Jerusalem Talmud arise because we are ignorant of the nature of the material. Prof. Weiss thus summarizes these problems: "Material is sometimes presented which, judging by the progress of the *sugyah,* should contain a question or an answer, yet it is difficult to ascertain what is the question and what the answer . . . sometimes the material before us is in such an abbreviated and fragmentary form that it is most difficult to know how it functions in the *sugyah.* Such difficulties are met quite often in the Jerusalem Talmud, and are generally of significance. On occasion, it appears that the text is corrupted, full of errors, but such is not the case. The text is not corrupt at all; rather, it contains basic material lacking literary refinement, and hence our difficulties. It contains the building-blocks for a *sugyah,* but lacks explicative additions, connective material, citation of sources, and so on. Thus, many difficult places in the Jerusalem Talmud lack what is present in the Babylonian Talmud as literary refinement, which aids in our understanding of the *sugyah,* and in our orientation within it." [27] For this reason our author sees the text of the Jerusalem Talmud as more pristine, for it is present before us in an older literary state. With the continual study of the Babylonian Talmud there was added explanatory material, its style was improved, and it is therefore more understandable. But on the other hand, it is more difficult to perceive in it the form given it by its original creators. This is not so with the Jerusalem Talmud, where the basic material rests before us, never having been improved literally.

The phenomenon of the transfer of a source from one location to another is present in both Talmuds; the difficulties arising from this procedure are more apparent in the Jerusalem Talmud than in the Babylonian. In the latter, the transferred sources were adapted to their new framework. This was not the case, on the whole, in the Jerusalem Talmud. Sometimes, indeed, more was transferred than actually necessary, and this added material is not understood in its new location. And so, conclusions which, in the case of the *Babli,* can be reached only after a close analysis of the text and comparison with its parallel, can be reached in the *Yerushalmi* at first glance. In this difference between the two Talmuds our author sees further proof of his hypothesis concerning the original form of the Babylonian *sugyah,* namely that the original form of this *sugyah* resembled the present form of many *sugyot* in the Jerusalem Talmud that contain only the building-blocks for a *sugyah,* lacking all literary refinement.

THE SOURCES OF THE *SUGYAH*

The Torah and the Mishnah were the basic sources possessed by the creators of the Talmud. A problem that engages our author is the degree to which they were in possession of our *Tosefta* and of our *Midreshé Halacha* as well. This question is a field of research unto itself. I here wish to present Prof. Weiss' approach to a solution of this problem, since any conclusion reached in ignorance of this approach must perforce be a shallow one. "The Talmud . . . is not a unified literary whole. We cannot make any general statement concerning the sources of Talmud as a whole on the basis of what we know concerning the relation of certain *sugyot* to their sources. From all we have seen about the development of the *sugyah* and its history, we must conclude that every *sugyah* has its own history, and so that each has its own problem of sources. Thus it is not merely possible, but rather is actually the fact, that one *sugyah* will know a given source, and another be ignorant of it." [28]

More complex is the problem of the Amoraic sources before the creators of a given *sugyah.* Our author cites and analyzes three types of literary Amoraic sources used in Talmudic discussions:

1. Early strata of our Talmud, which are used as the source of a *sugyah,* or in its later continuation. Often, the older material is absorbed by the new *sugyah.*

2. The various Talmuds of the Yeshivot (for each apparently had its own Talmud), from which were drawn complete *sugyot,* individual *mimrot,* and sometimes fragments of *sugyot.*

3. The various collections containing either the *mimrot* of one sage, or material dealing with a specific topic.

FROM THE *SUGYAH* TO THE TALMUD IN ITS ENTIRETY

Each generation of the Amoraic period studied and created Talmudic material, and each yeshiva seemingly had a Talmud of its own. The first Amoraim systematically studied the Mishnah, and to a certain extent the *baraitot* as well.[29] Tannaitic material was the main object of their study and analysis. The following generations of Amoraim studied, in addition to the Tannaitic material, the material created by the earlier Amoraic generations; they themselves created material dealing with both earlier Amoraic and Tannaitic sources. And thus the amount of material extant grew in every generation, and in each yeshiva; this material took on a fixed literary formulation, and was generally arranged as explanation of the Mishnah.[30]

Of course, not each sage left *novellae* covering all the material he studied and taught; not all the material that was created took on a fixed literary formulation; not all material so formulated gained entrance to the Talmud. It is also quite clear that certain additions and continuations were created in other places and on various occasions, and were not set in their present places in the Talmud until a later time. Certainly, also, there was early Amoraic material that retained its original form for a number of generations, and was finally expanded and explicated only by sages living at the end of the Amoraic period.

The process of the development of Talmudic material was a many-faceted one, and so the Talmud has a unique literary quality. The question is: Is it possible to discover the various strata within Talmudic material, and so to reveal the stages of its development? For example, can we discover the nature and form of the Talmud during the second generation of Pumbeditanean Amoraim? Or Suranean Amoraim? This same problem can be posed in terms of every generation and of each yeshiva. Naturally, it is impossible to establish such outlines for the entire Talmud. But at the same time, there are many places in the Talmud where the markings of such strata are visible, or are merely slightly concealed and hence easily recoverable.

So towering a task demands a Talmudic genius who is at the same time a perceptive literary critic, a man who can analyze each *sugyah* in terms of its content, in the light of all its parallels and sources, with the aid of the entire later explicative literature. Prof. Weiss has succeeded in understanding the development of the Talmud, and in discovering its place of origin; by the use of his unique method he has revealed the relationship of such tractates as Tamid, Nedarim, Nazir, etc., to the Talmud in general; finally, he has solved the problem of whether there ever existed *gemarah* to those tractates which in our Talmud possess no *gemarah*.

Before presenting the conclusions of our author concerning these problems, I wish to cite from his preface to *"The Babylonian Talmud as a Literary Unit.* ". . . I approached the Talmud . . . with the view of fully understanding the words of our sages . . . and of seeing their opinions in their original form. . . . While engaged in such study I occasionally became aware of various phenomena in the development of the *sugyah* and of the Talmud that were not understandable in terms of the accepted approach. When I had assembled enough material for an analysis of a problem touching on the development of the *sugyah* and Talmud as literary phenomena, I felt an inner need to express myself publically. In my book, *History of the Development of the Babylonian Talmud,* and in my essays in *Hazofeh Le-Chochmat Yisrael,* the *Monatsschrift,* and other journals, I attempted to clarify a number of the many problems surrounding the development of the *sugyah* and the Talmud as a literary unit, on the basis of material possessing certain characteristics in common. Through a conceptual and formal analysis on the one hand, and research into the language and parallels of passages on the other, I attempted to explain certain strange phenomena that had their roots in the history of literary development.

"Of course, the solution of single problems and the explanation of isolated phenomena is a far cry from a comprehensive treatment of the entire question. It was only after many years of study and research that I arrived, I humbly believe, at results comprehending in whatever degree the entire problem of the literary development of the Talmud. . . ."

THE TALMUD OF EACH GENERATION, AND THE ORIGIN OF OUR TALMUD[31]

There is hardly a tractate in which an early stratum[32] extends throughout the entire tractate. There are certain tractates that contain no early stratum at all.

The stratum most often encountered in the Talmud is that of Abayye and Rava. In a number of places there is a stratum serving as transition between an earlier stratum and that of Abayye and Rava; such a stratum contains the statements of Raba and R. Joseph, followed by those of Abayye and Rava.

In the earliest stratum R. Yehudah, dean of the yeshiva of Pumbeditha and its founder, is the chief figure. He transmits the words of Samuel, and often those of Rav as well.

In the stratum of Abayye and Rava, Rava is often found in the company of sages with whom we never, or only rarely, find Abayye.[33] R. Yehudah links Rav and Samuel. Raba and R. Joseph bring to Pumbeditha the work of the students of Rav at Sura. R. Kahana appears to be such a link in the next generation. R. Papa links Abayye and Rava. Thus is it possible to understand the fact that we find sages belonging to different yeshivot seemingly on one stage, as we so find Abayye and R. Hisdah, for example.

It is to be expected that the later the stratum, the larger in scope and in quantity it would be, but this is not so. Only the stratum of Abayye and Rava is larger than its predecessors.

On the basis of an analysis of material found in the different strata of the entire Talmud, Prof. Weiss has reached the following general conclusions concerning the development of the Talmud and its strata.

1. The earliest Talmud, it appears from the material in our possession, is that of R. Yehudah, dean of the yeshiva of Pumbeditha. It contained explicative and other *mimrot* of Rav and Samuel and of R. Yehudah himself; this earliest Talmud also included, it would appear, a quantity of *mimrot* of other early Amoraim. Various *baraitot* taught by different sages were also included. This Talmud was created only for a number of tractates, and sometimes only for specific chapters within the tractate.

2. There are tractates whose first strata are late ones. Even when these tractates do contain material older than these strata, it is scattered over the entire tractate, and so cannot be considered a unified and homogeneous stratum.

3. Practically the entire Talmud contains a middle unified, homogeneous stratum deriving from Abayye and Rava.

4. This middle stratum is not the product of one study-session. Abayye's part in this stratum dates from two different periods: one, from his study with Raba or R. Joseph; the other, when he had R. Papa as a student. In addition, this stratum has two parts, that of Abayye, and that of Rava. Abayye's contribution was created in Pumbeditha, while Rava's

was created partly there and partly at Mahoza. Therefore, the literary history of even this stratum is a developmental one.

THE ORIGIN OF OUR TALMUD

Wherever it is possible to discover the first stratum of the Talmud, it is clear that it was created in Pumbeditha. We come to this conclusion concerning the middle stratum as well.

After our author presents four different alternative solutions to the problem of the place of origin of our Talmud, he concludes that our Talmud is primarily the Talmud of Pumbeditha, upon which was added, in certain places and chapters, material from other yeshivot.[34] With the death of Abayye, the Talmud of Pumbeditha was studied at the yeshiva of Rava in Mahoza, from whence it was transferred to Narsch by R. Papa; from Narsch it passed to Sura-Mata Mahasiah in the days of R. Ashi. As it progressed from home to home, the Talmud developed, material was added and continued, until the Amoraic material it contained reached its present quantity.

Prof. Weiss notes that the idea that ours was the only Talmud is incorrect. He proves that within our Talmud itself there are many indications that there did exist Talmuds other than ours. The problem of source-citation is understandable only on the assumption that other Talmuds did exist: sometimes a source is hinted at but is not brought, nor is it found elsewhere in our Talmud; on other occasions the source reproduced does not contain the anticipated proof, and is brought at all only because the desired source has been lost.[35] Such phenomena prove that there did exist some Talmudic material outside our Talmud. A number of *sugyot* are introduced *t'nan hatam* ("the Mishnah says there . . ."), and the impression is gained that these *sugyot* derive from the discussion of the Mishnah in a different Talmud. Similarly, *sugyot* that are found in our Talmud in unsuitable locations, and were not properly placed, prove that there were a number of Talmuds in the Amoraic period.

THE TALMUD TO TRACTATE TAMID [36]

Tractate Tamid possesses Talmud to only a number of chapters, and even in these chapters its Talmud differs in both quality and quantity from normal Talmudic material. Z. Frankel claimed that this Talmud is a Saboraic creation, while Z. H. Chajot held it dates from Geonic times.

Prof. Weiss analyzes all the material of tractate Tamid in terms of this unique method. He examines the various strata, and determines who are the sages engaged in the different *sugyot;* in like manner, he compares the material found in parallel passages in the Talmud, and thus arrives at decided conclusions concerning the development of the tractate. Practically none of the material in Tamid has a parallel in Talmudic literature; those few parallels found in Hullin and Yomah have their origins in *Tamid,* and were transferred to these other tractates. From this we conclude that the Talmud in tractate Tamid was created during Amoraic times.

The beginning of the development of the Talmud to this tractate occurred in the days of Abayye; we possess from him a stratum-unit throughout the entire tractate. The nature of the development of the Talmud to this tractate was similar to that of other tractates. Abayye taught the Mishnah of Tamid, and the first stratum of Talmud to this tractate is the *product of this study.* This stratum contained material coming from the yeshivah of Sura as well. Rava, R. Papa, and R. Ashi also contribute continuations to this stratum. Apparently, the tractate was relatively neglected, and so remained small in size. This explains the fact that not much transferring of material between other tractates and *Tamid* took place, despite its large incidence in other tractates. We may conclude, then, that Tamid is not a Saboraic or Geonic product; rather the opposite is true, for we have before us Talmudic material left in a more pristine form than in other tractates.

THE ORIGINS OF THE TALMUD TO TRACTATES NEDARIM, NAZIR, T'MURAH, KERITOT, AND M'ILAH[37]

Rishonim already noted that these tractates differ in many figures of speech from the rest of the tractates. On this basis they declared, "the language of this tractate is different (or strange)."[38] Sometimes they noted that the idiom was "Yerushalmi," by which they meant that it differed from the normal idiom of the Babylonian Talmud."[39] The scholars who studied this problem concluded that the Talmud of these tractates was produced in a different yeshiva, and was edited by a different hand.

Our author notes that it is impossible to solve this problem on the basis of stylistic variations alone, for there are many other factors relevant to the matter. First, we must know whether the sages quoted by name in these tractates are, generally, those cited in the rest of the Talmud. We must also understand the development of the *sugyot,* and the nature of the various strata in these tractates and their relation to the other tractates of the Talmud. Next, we must analyze the linguistic and conceptual relationship existing between these tractates. Finally, we must see whether entire tractates, or only portions thereof, bear the aforementioned stylistic peculiarities. Only on the basis of a comprehensive analysis of all the *sugyot* of a tractate, comparing them with all parallel material, is it possible to reach any conclusions concerning the genesis of these tractates.

Prof. Weiss followed this prescribed approach. His conclusions are: [40] From the point of view of strata and the names of sages, the Talmud to these tractates is of the same origin as the rest of the Talmud; in the Amoraic period these tractates differed not at all from the others. The basic contrast between these tractates and the rest of the Talmud lies in their different modes of development in the post-Amoraic period. The rest of the Talmud, it would appear, did not suffer any interruption between the creation of material and its stylistic enrichment, for it was always studied. These tractates, on the other hand, were neglected, for a given period, and were not studied, and the break between the creation of material and the improvement of its style and correlation of sources caused phenomena that are rarely found in the rest of the Talmud.

ORDERS AND TRACTATES POSSESSING NO *GEMARAH* IN BABYLONIAN TALMUD

The Babylonian Talmud has *gemarah* for the entire order Mo'ed save Sh'kalim; to all order Nashim; to the entire order Nezikin save Aboth and Eduyyoth; to all order Kodashim save Middoth and Kinnim. Orders Z'raim and Toharoth have *gemarah* only to tractates Berachoth and Niddah. There are, however, scattered throughout the Talmud, Mishnahs from the tractates possessing no *gemarah* and complete *sugyot* and *mimrot* explicating them. From where is this material derived, since these tractates have no *gemarah?* The quantity of such material is not as great as might be immediately assumed, as in this context we consider only material that was not created in its present framework; it is only rarely that we can say with assurance that material derives from a different source. We must consider, therefore, mainly material introduced *t'nan hatam* ("it was learned there . . .") or *v'amar* ("and he said . . ."), and so on.[41]

Prof. Weiss alone analyzes this problem in an exact, scientific, manner. He categorizes such material found in the Talmud according to the order of the Mishnah and the terms introducing it. Then he proceeds to analyze the character of each *sugyah,* and its development. On the basis of this inquiry, he arrives at an understanding of the nature of the material considered and at the solution to the problem in general.[42]

An important part of the material concerned with Mishnahs of tractates having no *gemarah* is of Pumbedithanean origin, but this material was created in its present framework. So, too, the *sugyot* and *mimrot* of Pumbedithanean origin concerned with these orders and tractates were created in the contexts where they are today found. Occasionally there is material derived from a different source, but the Pumbeditha-nean continuation was produced in its present context. Therefore, there is no basis for belief in the existence of a Talmud of Pumbedithanean origin to the tractates of orders Z'raim and Toraroth. There are, in the main, 13 *places* concerned with the tractates of order Toraroth whose material was not created in its present framework but was, rather, transferred from elsewhere; this, however, does not establish the exis-tence of a Pumbedithanean Talmud to this order. However, material derived in its totality from a different yeshiva serves as additional proof that other yeshivot had Talmuds of their own.

After an analysis of the matter, Prof. Weiss concludes that there is no proof for the existence of a Pumbedithanean Talmud to orders Z'raim and Toharoth. He surmises that our Talmud never contained more than what we now possess. Appositely, he believes that if his hypothesis concerning the creation of other Talmuds by other Babylonian yeshivot be correct, then some of these Talmuds contained *gemarah* to tractates to which there is no *gemarah* in our Talmud. These Talmuds were the sources from which the Babylonian material concerned with tractates Z'raim and Toharoth—material not created in its present context, nor at the yeshiva of Pumbeditha—was derived.

PALESTINIAN MATERIAL IN THE BABYLONIAN TALMUD AND OUR JERUSALEM TALMUD [43]

The Palestinian material dealing with Z'raim and Toharot found in the Babylonian Talmud is derived, apparently, almost totally from a different source. With regard to order Z'raim, for which there is Jerusalem Talmud, we find parallels in this Talmud to material in the Babylonian Talmud.

Prof. Weiss poses the question, From which Palestinian Talmud is this material derived? As it is reasonable to assume that there were created in Palestine, too, many Talmuds, the problem is, Does the Palestinian material in the Babylonian Talmud derive from our Jerusalem Talmud, or from some other Palestinian Talmud? We may note, in passing, our author's surmise that the Talmuds of Palestine were also not created at one time, but rather came into being through the activity of generations of sages and authors who participated in their conceptual and literary development.

There are parallel *sugyot* in the Babylonian and Jerusalem Talmuds which indicate that Palestinian material in our Talmud derives from our Jerusalem Talmud. On the other hand, there is parallel material indicating that such material does not have the Jerusalem Talmud for its source. Prof. Weiss concludes, on the basis of all available evidence, that the Palestinian material in the Babylonian Talmud has for its source a number of Palestinian Talmuds, our Jerusalem Talmud among them. This conclusion holds true for Babylonian material found in the Jerusalem Talmud, as well; it may well be stated that if such material was derived from a Babylonian Talmud, it was derived from many Babylonian Talmuds, ours among them. But it must be emphasized that the Babylonian material used by the Jerusalem Talmud is found in its most primitive, rather than its present, form.

It is our author's view that there was, apparently, a Palestinian Talmud which contained *gemarah* to order Toharot, for the quantity of Palestinian material dealing with this order found in the Babylonian Talmud nearly equals that dealing with Z'raim. However, his research leads him to believe, *our* Jerusalem Talmud never contained such material.

THE EDITING OF THE TALMUD

The problem of the editing of the Talmud is not merely a literary-historical one; it penetrates to the core of all Halachic and Aggadic concepts based upon Talmudic authority. The incisive research of Dr. Weiss into the development of the Talmud in its entirety, together with his identification of the various strata of the Talmud and conceptual analysis of Talmudic *sugyot,* proves that the Talmud is the result of a continuous process of development that began with the first Amoraic generation and continued until the Geonic period. Obviously, one cannot speak of a final redaction of the Talmud, nor of R. Ashi as its redactor. However, our author realizes the necessity of contending with the accepted opinion that the Talmud was redacted, and that this redactor was R. Ashi, as this opinion is universally believed and is an ancient one. Prof. Weiss discusses this proposition and analyzes the evidence cited by both *Rishonim* and later scholars.[44]

Prof. Weiss shows that there is no trace, in the Talmudic material itself, of a final redaction, or of a redactor. On the contrary, this material indicates that already in early Amoraic times there was a complete Talmud serving as the earliest stratum upon which are added later strata; the development of the Talmud and that of the *sugyah,* are one. In addition, parallel *sugyot* and their development show that there was never any comprehensive plan governing the transfer of parallel *sugyot* from place to place. The various phenomena in the literary enrichment of the Talmud prove that we have before us a process that stretched over a number of generations, and in which both scholars and copyists participated. Thus, we cannot credit any "editor" with even this literary function.

There are *sugyot* to parallel Mishnahs that are repeated wherever the Mishnah appears; sometimes, though, the *sugyah* is found in its entirety in one place, and only partially in another; sometimes it is found in only one place. Such phenomena indicate that the transfer of parallel *sugyot* was not effected according to any specific blueprint.

With regard to the dating of parallel material, some transfers were made in Amoraic times; others, by later scribes. Parallel material possessing different continuations in two places dates, of course, from the Talmudic period. On the other hand, material which has not even yet acclimated itself to its present location is certainly of later origin.

Much copying of parallel material has for its cause a cursory note or reference. In some of these places it is possible that the marginal reference was not intended to suggest the copying of material from one place to another, but simply to indicate either the formal or conceptual similarities of the two places; nevertheless, a scribe transferred the material. This phenomenon, it is certain, was the cause of many complex and problematic *sugyot* in which the explicators of the Talmud attempt, as far as is possible, to adapt the new material to its new context, or note that it should not be introduced here.

A basic piece of evidence introduced by *Rishonim* and other scholars to prove the validity of the accepted approach is that the Talmud itself mentions R. Ashi as its editor. They cite B.M. 86a: "R. Ashi and Ravinah are the last authoritative teachers *(sof hora'ah),*" and B.B. 157b: "Ravinah said, 'In the first cycle *(mahadurah)* R. Ashi said that the acquisition is valid; in the second, he said let them divide.' " The accepted approach understands by *sof hora'ah* the end of the Amoraic period; hence R. Ashi and Ravinah are the last teachers of this period, or the editors of the Talmud. The term *mahadurah* is taken, by these scholars, in its modern denotation of "edition," thus indicating that R. Ashi redacted two editions of the Talmud.

However, it should be noted that even in these instances there are *Rishonim* who explain these terms in their purely verbal sense.

It is also generally held that this accepted approach is already followed by the *Iggeret* of Rav Sherirah Gaon. Prof. Weiss, however, proves from the very body of the *Iggeret* that Rav Sherira was ignorant of such a theory; the Gaon's words show, to the contrary, the groundlessness of this approach. Rav Sherira is at great pains to emphasize the function of Rabbi (Judah I) in the composition of the Mishnah, but he never speaks of the editing of the Talmud, or of R. Ashi as its editor.

He does say twice, "Talmudic material was added generation after generation"; in a third place he writes, ". . . thus teaching was added generation after generation until the time of Ravinah, as Samuel saw in the book of Adam: 'Ashi and Ravinah are the last authoritative teachers' and after this though there were no authoritative teachers, certainly, there were explicators and elders who were near-authoritative, and these great ones were called *rabanan saborai.* . . . ." This is all that is found in the first half of the *Iggeret,* which contains the Gaon's general interpretation of the history of the oral law.

In the latter part of the *Iggeret,* which contains the Gaon's listing of the Amoraic sages and the deans of their *yeshivot,* he writes the following about R. Ashi: ". . . and R. Ashi was chief of the yeshiva for nearly sixty-two years, as is stated . . . in the first cycle R. Ashi said thus, and in the second cycle, thus, for the Rabbis instituted that two tractates, however large or small, should be studied every year; he died in the year 738." The Gaon then continues with his listing of the deans of *yeshivot:* ". . . after him reigned at Mata Mahasiah R. Yemar . . . and after him . . . and after him Rabah Tosfa'ah who died in 788, and on 13 Kislev 811 Ravinah b. R. Huna, the last authoritative teacher, died. In these years there ruled at Pumbeditha R. Geviha of Bey Kathil, who died in 744, and after him . . . and after him . . . in the year 787 died R. Sama . . . and after him ruled R. Assi, in whose day was the end of authoritative teaching and the Talmud was concluded, and there appeared the *rabbanan saborai,* most of whom died in a few years, as the ancients tell us in their memoirs. . . ."

After an analysis of these statements, Prof. Weiss reaches the following conclusions:[45]

1. According to Rav Sherira, the remark of the Talmud in Baba Meziah, "R. Ashi and Ravinah are the last authoritative teachers," does not refer to R. Ashi of Mata Mahasiah (who died in 738) but to R. Assi, the last dean of the Amoraic yeshiva of Pumbeditha, who was appointed in 787; "Ravinah" is Ravinah b. R. Hunna, the last dean of Sura (died in 811). Thus, they are the last two authoritative teachers; both were of the same generation, and both were the last Amoraic *roshei yeshivot.* Ravinah alone is cited in the first half of the *Iggeret* as *sof hora'ah* though the Talmudic statement mentions R. Ashi as well, because Rav Sherira knew the date of Ravinah's death, while of R. Assi-Ashi he knew only the date of his appointment; in the first half of the *Iggeret* he wished to pinpoint the end of the Amoraic period as the time when the creation of Amoraic material ended.

2. By the expression *sof hora'ah* is meant only the end of the Amoraic period as the age in which Amoraic Talmudic material was produced, and nothing more. This is clearly indicated in Rav Sherira's statements: "There was added Talmudic material generation after generation," and "there was added authoritative teaching *(hora'ah)* generation after generation." We see here that *hora'ah* and *talmudah* are one, both growing in each generation.

3. The expression *mahadurah* means a review of studies, and nothing else. Since Rav Sherirah possessed a tradition that the famous R. Ashi served as dean for nearly sixty years, and since, as is well known, a different tractate was studied during the *kallah* months in this period, he explained the Talmudic reference in Baba Bathra as meaning that R. Ashi completed two cycles of studying the entire Talmud.

Thus we see that not only does the *Iggeret* lack all reference to the final editing of the Talmud, or of R. Ashi as its editor—it proclaims that the reference in Baba Meziah does not speak of the renowned R. Ashi, the re-founder of the yeshiva at Sura-Mata Mahasiah. Rav Sherira's statement solves, in addition, a problem that has vexed many scholars and has germinated many theories concerning the editing of the Talmud. The chief difficulty lay in the identification of the Ravinah mentioned in B.M.: if we understand him to be Ravinah, an older colleague of R. Ashi, he cannot be called *sof horaʾah;* if we understand him to be the last Ravinah, he was not a contemporary of the renowned R. Ashi. Indeed, according to Prof. Weiss' conclusion that the R. Ashi of B.M. is the final R. Ashi of Pumbeditha[46] (who was a contemporary of the last Ravinah at Surah), the entire edifice of a final editing of our Talmud by R. Ashi, which is founded upon the sources in B.M., B.B., and the *Iggeret,* is toppled.

Most scholars attempted to solve the problem of the editing of the Talmud "from the outside in," that is to say, on the basis of some chance remark in the Talmud or Geonic literature. But Prof. Weiss approached the problem "from the inside out," through a comprehensive examination of the *sugyah* material; hence his conclusions are derived from a conceptual and literary analysis of the *sugyah,* chapter, tractate, and the entire Talmud.

His conclusion in this matter is that the Talmud grew generation after generation. The first base of Talmudic material is the literary product of the study of the Mishnah by the first Amoraic generations. Each succeeding generation added the results of its study, formulating its contribution in a fixed literary form. Some generations produced strata found consistently throughout the Talmud, while others produced only occasional strata or notes. Similarly, Talmudic material produced in various *yeshivot* was added. This process continued until about the end of the fifth century. At that time the creative powers weakened, and the Amoraic period, the creator of Talmudic material, ended. Decades of persecution followed, and this situation caused the end of the period of *hora'ah*. The sages of the new era see their main function in the explanation and improvement of the Talmudic *sugyah*, through adding explanations, presenting sources, providing connective material for the basic Talmudic material, transferring *sugyot*, and so on. Thus it is clear that the history of the creation of the Talmud is to be read in the various phenomena occurring in the Talmudic material itself.

Though Prof. Weiss contributed much to the understanding of the history of the Talmud and its development, the chief accomplishment of Prof. Weiss consists of his having shown the way in which to understand the words of the Talmudic sages according to their original meaning and signification.

OTHER LITERARY SOURCES IN THE TALMUD [47]

Prof. Weiss poses the following question with regard to the Amoraic literary activity: Did the creators of the Talmud create in literary forms other than the *mimrah* and the *sugyah?* To the solution of this problem Prof. Weiss brings to bear the analysis of the entire Talmud, incisively sees that which has lain unrecognized till now, and proves the existence of various literary forms in our Talmud. Once so recognized, the solution seems obvious.

Our author divides these additional literary sources into three categories: a) collections, b) tractates, and c) *midrashim* and *aggadot*. Of these sources, some were created outside the *sugyah*-framework and were later incorporated into their present context as finished material. Others were created by the creators of the Talmud in their present context.

COLLECTIONS

The most common type of collection contains the statements of a particular sage, generally has a distinctive literary form, and is incorporated into the Talmud as a finished source. After an examination of the various sorts of collections found in the Talmud, our author concludes: "The creators of the Talmud possessed, in the period that saw the creation of the Talmud, material in the form of collections organized principally according to the name of the author of the statements or the name of the sage transmitting the statements, in addition to their having normal *sugyah-* and *mimrah*-material."[48] Prof. Weiss also shows that here and there exist *mimrot* from collections that have not been preserved in their entirety.

Among collections organized around a particular sage, there exist some composed of statements and questions; two or more *mimrot* are followed by one or more questons. Sometimes the question is answered, and sometimes it is not *(taiku)*. In such a collection does Prof. Weiss see the basic structure of the *she'iltah*. "Doubtless, the literary form of the *she'iltah* is grounded in collections of this type. In its most primitive we have, apparently, a form that literarily and topically is a juxtaposition of clarified and unclarified matters, and nothing else; occasionally the problem was solved, and occasionally it was not. But in the *she'iltah* we generally find first a number of simple *halachot* followed by a problem that is solved: for its entire purpose was to serve as a halachic framework for a public lecture, a function that does not allow of answered questions."[49]

In addition to collections organized around one sage, there are those with different frameworks, such as questions *(r'miyyot)*, court decisions, responsa, and clarified problems. Our author discovers collections of decisions in various areas, created in different periods. He emphasizes that the collections of legal decisions contained in the *Halachot Gedolot*, *Halachot Pesukot* and *She'iltot*, all Saboraic works (generally speaking), are basically and structurally founded upon *sugyah*-material of the Talmudic period, for this period already saw Amoraic sources in the form of collections of halachic decisions.[50]

MIDRASHIM AND AGGADOT

Our author finds in the Talmud other literary sources, in either short or extended form, that form either a midrashic or aggadic unit. We find, in such sources, either an explicative midrash to a section of the Bible, or midrash and aggadah discussing one specific topic. This category comprehends sources our author names: Midrash on Prayer, A Midrash on *Ruth*, A Midrash on *Job*, Midrash on the Giving of the Torah, Midrash *Ma'aseh Merkabah*, and Aggadot of the Destruction. Each of these sources is analyzed from the point of view of its development, relation to its point of origin, and relationship among its components. Let me cite a number of his notes to "Aggadot on the Destruction":

"In Gittin 55b–58a we find Aggadot on the Destruction, composed of two basic parts. The first part is primarily Palestinian, and derives from R. Yochanan; the second part is, generally, Babylonian, and derives from R. Yehudah."[51] The *mimrah* of R. Yochanan serves as the frame for all the material in the first section, which is actually an extended explanation of his statement. The six *mimrot* of R. Yehudah serve as foundation and frame for the material in the second section.

In a number of instances, midrashic or aggadic material concerning a specific topic is collected into what is seemingly a tractate within a tractate. Prof. Weiss analyzes some such tractates, naming them Tractate Hannukah, on Dreams, and on Wonders. This type of source was created during the Talmudic period either as part of the creation of the Talmud itself, or as independent sources.

MIDRASH ESTHER

Among the other literary sources of the Talmudic period, "Midrash Esther" is of particular importance. Prof. Weiss proves that there is embodied within the Talmud a complete Aggadic midrash of the early Babylonian Amoraic period to a book of the Bible.

Our author shows that there is found, from page 12 of Tractate *Megillah* and following, a midrash of nine sections, which is "an expositive and aggadic midrash to the Book of Esther that follows the structure of the Book itself. Here and there are, seemingly, sections of Amoraic midrash to *Esther* that are presented as finished sources. But primarily we find here Tannaitic and early-Amoraic material organized as a unified midrash to the Book of Esther."[52] Our author closely analyzes the material: he finds at its beginning introductory material followed by midrashic explanations arranged according to the order of *Esther* itself; complete excision of the midrash from Megillah would have no effect at all upon the *sugyot* of this tractate. According to Prof. Weiss, this midrash is fundamentally of Pumbedithanean origin, and "developed as did the entire Talmud, through the adding of layer upon layer of material."[53] It is not clear, however, whether the midrash developed in its present location or was developed elsewhere and was inserted here as a completed source.

The conclusion drawn by our author from all this evidence is that the Amoraic builders of the Talmud created literary *genres* other than the *mimrah* and the *sugyah*. Thus we find in the Talmud various sorts of collections and also "tractates and homilies which, from the point of view of literary form, merit individual treatment. Some are apparently curios, such as the Tractate on Dreams or on Wonders. But among them we also find a significant Midrash to *Esther* that is not only a Babylonian Amoraic midrash but is also the earliest Amoraic aggadah to a complete book of the Bible." [54]

THE SABORAIC CONTRIBUTION [55]

Talmudic scholars are well aware that the Saboraim played a part in the creation of the Talmud; some consider their contribution more significant than do others. But even for these the work of the Saboraim is limited to occasional explanatory comments to the basic Talmudic material, and a number of *sugyot* at the beginnings of certain tractates.

Our author considers this problem through a detailed analysis of hundreds of Talmudic *sugyot* and the testimony of Geonim and Rishonim. He finds that the opening *sugyah* of almost every tractate is of late origin. However, the nature of these *sugyot* varies. Some contain notes on the style of the Mishnah: such are the opening *sugyot* of 'Eruvin, Sukkah, Ta'anith, Mo'ed Katan, Sotah, Nazir, Shevuoth, Makkoth, Zebachim, Menachot, and Bechorot. Others are complete Saboraic *sugyot:* these are Berachot, Yomah, Hagigah, Yebamoth, Nedarim, Kiddushin, and Me'ilah.

Other tractates possess an opening *sugyah* that is basically Amoraic, but has been expanded and re-worked at a later date. Thus, the *sugyah* now before us is not an Amoraic sugyah with the addenda of a later period, but is rather a post-Amoraic *sugyah* containing early Amoraic material. Such *sugyot* are at the beginnings of tractates Pesachim, Bezah, Megillah, Gittin, B.K., B.M., B.B., Sanhedrin, Chullin, Arachin, Temurah, and Keritoth. (In certain tractates, the second *sugyah* follows this pattern also; i.e., Berachot, 'Eruvin, Nazir, Shevuoth, Zebachim, Menachot, Bechorot, and others.)

The early Amoraic material in some of these *sugyot*, as the ones at the beginnings of B.M. and Arachin, is very scanty; upon it, or around it, has been built the later *sugyah*. In other tractates, such as Pesachim and Sanhedrin, the creators of the later *sugyah* possessed a large quantity of Amoraic material. Occasionally, the creators of the *sugyah* before us used an earlier *sugyah* in its entirety, as in the beginnings of Gittin and B.K. The character of these *sugyot* differs from that of the normal Amoraic *sugyah*, which is composed of significant discussion; these contain clarifications presented in a lecture style.

In addition, *sugyot* identifiable as late are found not only at the beginnings of tractates, but scattered throughout the Talmud. Our author analyzes many Talmudic *sugyot* in his books and essays and shows them to be of post-Amoraic origin; thus, he sees the post-Amoraic *sugyah* as a normal phenomenon appearing in all parts of the Talmud.

The literary and conceptual analysis of Talmudic *sugyot* in the light of their parallels reveals that the "literary enrichment" of the *sugyah* and the Talmud is, primarily, the work of post-Amoraic times. Transfer of parallels, explanatory additions, supplying of citations—all these are mostly Saboraic.

During the Saboraic period whole *sugyot* were created as well, and existing Amoraic *sugyot* were expanded and re-worked to the degree that they, in their new form, are also Saboraic products.

It is Prof Weiss' contention that the part played by the Saboraim in the creation of the Talmud is more significant than one is able to prove; were it possible to identify and analyze all the material they created, we would find that the Talmud created by the Amoraim is far different—both quantitatively and qualitatively—than the one we now possess. The transfer of parallels, supplying of cited material, and production of post-Amoraic *sugyot* noticeably increased the size of the Amoraic Talmud, and the addition of analytic and explanatory material sometimes functioned qualitatively as well.

It also appears that in addition to their work on the Talmud proper the Saboraim also created a literature of their own. The works of early Geonim, such as the *She'iltoth* and *Halachoth Gedoloth,* shows that they used earlier collections of decided Halachot. It is Prof. Weiss' opinion that these collections were created by the Saboraim. Thus, as the sages of this era bordered, on the one hand, on the great Amoraic period, some of their work was absorbed into the Talmud; and on the other hand, their independent creation, their collections of Halachic decisions, was absorbed into the literature of the Geonim, who followed them. And so the work of this transition period remains concealed in anonymity. But in reality it was a period that lasted some two centuries and was not less creative than the ones following and preceding it.

NOTES

1. A. Weiss, *Le-Heker Ha-Talmud*, New York, 1954, p. 15 ff.
2. Abraham Weiss, *The Literary Development of the Babylonian Talmud*, Warsaw, 1939, part II, p. 2 ff.
3. Cf. *ibid.*, p. 5, nn. 10–12; and *Le-Heker Ha-Talmud*, pp. 18–32, for a rebuttal of the view of the Tosafists and some moderns that these *sugyot* are fictional.
4. A. Weiss, in *Ha-Zofeh-Le-Hohmat Yisrael*, XII, edited by L. Blau, M. Guttman, S. Hevesi (Budapest, 1928), p. 207 ff.
5. Cf. *Studies in the Literature of the Amoraim*, New York, 1962, from p. 50; cf. especially from p. 33 and from p. 295.
6. *Le-Heker*, p. 111 ff.
7. For a clarification of the sources, cf. *ibid.*, p. 129 ff.
8. *Ibid.*, p. 131 ff.
9. Cf. Shabbat 146b, Ketuboth 80b, B.K. 20b, B.B. 121a.
10. For other examples, cf. *Le-Heker*, p. 139, and n. 93.
11. *Ibid.*, p. 141 ff.
12. For references, cf. *ibid.*, p. 28, n. 54.
13. *Ibid.*, p. 152 ff.
14. *Ibid.*, p. 164 ff.
15. *Ibid.*, p. 179 ff.
16. Cf. *ibid.*, pp. 64–107 for a full treatment of the matter.
17. Cf. text covered by our notes 44–6 for a discussion of the accepted approaches concerning the redaction of the Talmud and the unique approach of Dr. Weiss.
18. Y. Kaplan, *The Redaction of the Babylonian Talmud*, New York, 1933.
19. *Le-Heker*, pp. 18–32.
20. *Ibid.*, p. 261 ff.
21. *Ibid.*, p. 279 ff.
22. *The Literary Development of the Babylonian Talmud*, part II, p. 15 ff.
23. *Ibid.*, p. 34; cf. especially the characteristic proof through the parallel *sugyot* in Arachin, B.B., Kedushin.
24. *Ibid.*, p. 34 ff.; also, *Ha-Zofeh*, XII (1928), p. 219 ff.
25. *Ibid.*, p. 93 ff.
26. Ketuboth 31b, Tosafoth, *s.v.* Rav Ashi.
27. *The Literary Development*, part II, p. 132 ff.
28. *Ibid.*, p. 149 ff. Prof. Weiss deals with the full scope of this problem in his recent *Studies in the Literature of the Amoraim*, p. 166 ff.
29. Cf. *Ha-Zofeh*, IX, p. 181.
30. A. Weiss, *The Babylonian Talmud as a Literary Unit*, New York, 1943, p. 3 ff.
31. *Ibid.*, p. 34 ff.

32. Our author created the terms, "strata of the *sugyah*," and "strata of the Talmud." The first term is defined as the segments of the *sugyah* that were created generation by generation. He defines the second term (in *The Babylonian Talmud as a Literary Unit*, p. 2) thus: "The definition of a stratum is the existence of a body of material, homogeneous as to time and place of origin, that explicates a series of Mishnahs. In other words, material that is recognizable as forming a stratum in the Talmud that was created at a specific known time by a specific individual or school. When we find such an old stratum continued by another homogeneous body of material, we have before us a later stratum following an older one."

33. Cf. *Literary Unit*, p. 35, for a treatment of this phenomenon based on the lives of Abayye and Rava.

34. *Ibid.*, p. 41 ff.; cf. p. 44, n. 81, concerning the accepted opinion that our Talmud is the literary product, basically, of the school at Sura.

35. Cf. A. Weiss, "Studien zur Redaktion des Babylonischen Talmuds," *Monnatschrift*, LXXIII, 1929, p. 196.

36. *Literary Unit*, pp. 45–6.

37. *Ibid.*, pp. 57–128.

38. Cf. *ibid.*, p. 57, n. 2 for references.

39. Cf. *ibid.*, n. 3–4 for references.

40. Cf. "Conclusions," *ibid.*, pp. 123–8.

41. *Ibid.*, p. 129.

42. *Ibid.*, pp. 137–59; cf. "Conclusions," pp. 167–9.

43. *Ibid.*, p. 169 ff.; on the literary relationship of the Talmuds, cf. note 27 to this chapter.

44. *Literary Unit*, pp. 242–57; cf. *Le-Heker*, pp. 408–20.

45. *Ibid.*, p. 250, 254–7.

46. Cf. *ibid.*, p. 251, n. 108a for Talmudic references to this R. Assi-Ashi.

47. Cf. *Studies in the Literature of the Amoraim*, New York, 1962, pp. 166–294.

48. *Ibid.*, p. 231, and pp. 188 ff.

49. *Ibid.*, p. 238; on Prof. Weiss' approach to the *She-iltot* cf. text covered by notes 51–7.

50. *Ibid.*, p. 246 ff.

51. *Ibid.*, pp. 261.

52. *Ibid.*, p. 290.

53. *Ibid.*, p. 292.

54. *Ibid.*, p. 294.

55. Cf. "The Achievement of the Saboraim—Their Part in the Creation of the Talmud," Magnes Press, The Hebrew University, Jerusalem, 1953.

5

The Amoraic and Stammaitic Periods

David Weiss-Halivni

THE AMORAIC PERIOD

After R. Judah Hanassi's death began the slow, gradual process of abandoning the Mishnah and returning to some salient features of Midreshei Halakhah. This statement requires qualification, however. "Abandoning the Mishnah" is not meant to suggest that the Amoraim stopped studying the Mishnah and it was gradually forgotten;[1] on the contrary, the Amoraim never ceased studying and commenting on the Mishnah. Their erudition in the study of Mishnah was second only to their knowledge of the Bible (that is, total mastery).[2] Nor should the phrase "abandoning the Mishnah" be construed to mean that the Amoraim stopped formulating fixed laws. The surviving statements of Rav and Shmuel, first-generation Amoraim who flourished during the first half of the third century in Babylonia, primarily consist of fixed laws, very much akin to the Mishnaic form. Later generations of Amoraim, however, did move away from apodicity, indeed, dramatically so in some instances.[3] This tendency is clear even in the sayings of a younger colleague of Rab and Shmuel, R. Yochanan, who flourished during the second half of the third century in Palestine.

What is meant by "abandoning the Mishnah" is that the Amoraim discontinued its development, even when they formulated fixed laws. The fixed laws formulated by the Amoraim were not integrated into the Mishnah; they remained loosely strung along the Mishnaic structure but

Reprinted by permission of Harvard University Press from David Weiss-Halivni, *Midrash, Mishnah, and Gemara: The Jewish Predilection for Justified Law*, Cambridge, MA, 1986.

never became a part of the Mishnah. This is evident when one compares, for instance, the relationship of the fixed laws of R. Judah to the Mishnah of his teacher, R. Akiba, with those of Rav and Shmuel to the Mishnah of their teacher, Rabbi. While the fixed laws of R. Judah are integrated into the Mishnah of R. Akiba, flowing smoothly without visible seams, those of Rav and Shmuel are attendant upon Rabbi's Mishnah, hover over it, but do not interlock. The gates of the Mishnah, so to speak, were already closed to them; they could come close but not enter.

The closest approximation to the Mishnah in the time of the Amoraim was *hora'ah,* rendering practical decisions. There is evidence—albeit conjectural—that the Amoraim, like the Tannaim, collected their fixed laws into a separate corpus called the hora'ah. This is probably what R. Chananyah in the name of Shmuel was referring to when he said (P.T. Peah 2:4 [17a] and parallels), "one does not learn [practical behavior] from *horayah* [or *hora'ah*]". It is indeed so cited by R. Chananel, Chagigah 10b). This is contradicted, however, by R. Zeira, quoted in the Yerushalmi (ibid.) a few lines above. According to R. Zeira, Shmuel did not include hora'ah in his list of the things from which one does not learn practical behavior. Shmuel said only "One does not learn [practical behavior] from halakhoth [Mishnah], nor from aggadoth [Aggadic Midrashim], nor from additions [toseftoth]." This process of collecting fixed laws in a separate corpus probably continued throughout the Amoraic period until the death of R. Ashi (427 C.E., in Babylonia), who is called (B.T. Baba Metzia 86a) "the end of hora'ah."

The approximation of hora'ah to Mishnah is, for our purpose, not too instructive. True, both contain fixed laws, and both were collected in separate corpora. But whereas the Mishnah, at the center of Amoraic study, affected every facet of Jewish religious life by systematically reexamining each law in order to ascertain in what category of classification it belonged—anonymous opinion (with maximum authority), majority opinion (relative authority), or individual opinion—hora'ah consisted of a few meager decisions of a few Amoraim, each law bearing the name of the respective Amora without classifications. The Gemara never refers to the Amoraic fixed laws other than by saying "a certain Rabbi gave a practical decision," and even that rarely (in the Babylonian Talmud not more than twenty times). The authority of hora'ah is derived from that of the individual Amora whose name is attached to a particular hora'ah;

it bears no collective authority. The inclusion of a particular Amora's hora'ah in the collection of hora'ah, unlike that of the Mishnah, did not endow it with additional authority; in fact, a hora'ah is never explicitly quoted as coming from a collection. Moreover, there are no special terms associated with *hora'ah* as there are with the Mishnah, such as "we have learned [in the Mishnah]." Indeed, its very existence is only conjectural, a further indication of its insignificance. *Hora'ah* finally disappeared altogether after the death of R. Ashi.

Much the same can be said about collections of sayings by the same Amora, or by the same combination of Amoraim, or any similar collections that we encounter in the Talmud in the form of "said a certain Rabbi . . ." These collections were made in this manner when the sayings were relatively few, and stringing them together made them easier to remember. Their authority, again, is that of the individual name attached; they bear no collective authority, and no special terms are to be found in connection with quoting them.

Neither *hora'ah* nor these collections were intended to take the place of the Mishnah, to be a successor to Rabbi's collection. Mishnaic form was no longer dominant during the time of the Amoraim. The major task (one could say the major ambition) of the Amoraim, even the very early ones, was not to carry on R. Judah Hanassi's Mishnaic tradition but to interpret it. By that time the Mishnah was almost closed, canonized, if you please, matchless. If one were to ask the Amoraim "Why is the Mishnah matchless?" they would reply: "Because of the greatness of Rabbi and his predecessors." But if there had been a compelling need to have the Mishnah further developed and extended, they would have found ways to overcome their modesty. They did not do so because there was no such need. The time of the Mishnah was over. The Mishnah could not last too long; it was not indigenous to the Jewish apperception.

The success of the Mishnah in the second part of the second century caused the importance of Midreshei Halakhah to recede and withdraw to horizons that were not within everyone's perception. The Mishnah became the major representation of the oral law, eclipsing Midreshei Halakhah. Paradoxically, after the Mishnah won its battle with Midreshei Halakhah and law became detached from the Bible, whose product it was, a natural need arose to have the apodictic laws of the Mishnah rejustified, either biblically or logically. Jews cannot live by apodictic laws alone; sooner or later they demand justification for their laws. Obsessed with the Divine, Whose will, they believe, is manifested in the Bible, they naturally prefer biblical justification but have settled for logical justification[4] when the former was not available. This position is not entirely unmishnaic. Along with the biblical justification, using the formula "as it says," the Mishnah also employs logical justification, using the formula "because."

The Mishnah, however, remained basically apodictic. The formula "as it says" is not used very often in the Mishnah; there are some tractates where it does not occur at all, and sometimes it was undoubtedly added later. Nor is the logical justification a frequent occurrence in the Mishnah. The Amoraim, in contrast, gravitated more and more away from the apodictic toward the justificatory, toward the vindicatory. In the Bible, God is His own justification. In the post-biblical period, the Midrash served as the link to the Bible, to God's word. After the interruption by the apodictic Mishnah, which reached its pinnacle during Rabbi's lifetime, the Amoraim gradually (less noticeably during the first generation, but nevertheless it began then) reverted back to the vindicatory style, providing the Mishnah with either biblical justification, using the Midrashic equivalent of "From where do we know these things . . . Scripture said," or logical justification, using the formula "What is its reason? . . . because."

In this respect the Amoraim were closer to the Tannaim of the school of R. Ishmael, who concentrated mainly on biblical exegesis, than to the Tannaim of the school of R. Akiba. The latter, it appears, were functioning both as formulators of fixed laws in the Mishnah and as biblical exegetes in the Midreshei Halakhah—and one cannot escape the impression that their exegesis served primarily, though not exclusively, as a means of deriving fixed laws. To use R. Judah again as an example, he is mentioned almost twice as often in the Mishnah as he is in the Midreshei Halakhah.[5] The study of Mishnah was his primary concern.

When the Tannaim were interpreting an early Mishnah—not an infrequent activity even among early Tannaim—they generally did not assume the role of interpreters, quoting the old source and expounding it, but rather couched their interpretations in the form of fixed laws, which was their main medium of expression (so much so that scholars only recently[6] have begun to realize that many controversies among Tannaim in the form of fixed law are in fact controversies in the reading and interpretation of earlier sources). With the Amoraim, however, the impression is the reverse: their major function was the interpretation of the Mishnah, not the formulation of fixed laws. Laws are necessary in order to know how to behave—a necessity of life which the Amoraim could not ignore—but interpreting the Mishnah was their vocation.

Despite their divergence from the Mishnah, the Amoraim remained essentially oriented toward the apodictic. Even when they interpreted the Mishnah, they used a style that combined both the interpretive and the apodictic. Characteristic is the formula "They learned this only [in a case such as] ... but" employed by all Amoraim but hardly found among Tannaim (perhaps in no more than a few instances).[7] This terminology is not purely apodictic because it does not stand by itself; it is unintelligible without a connection to an earlier source (a Mishnah, sometimes a Braitha, and occasionally even a statement by an Amora).[8] On the other hand, its content is easily transformable into apodictic law. If one drops, lo shanu and adds the connecting line from the earlier source, the result is a perfect apodictic law.

Even more indicative of the Amoraim's basic apodictic orientation is their indifference, shared with the Tannaim, to recording for posterity the various steps of the discussions, the "give and take," that led them to arrive at the apodictic laws. Only the final decisions were bequeathed by them to posterity. We can assume a priori that these final decisions must have been preceded by intensive discussions that gave rise to disagreements. Occasionally we come across these discussions in Tannaitic literature; the Tosefta or a Braitha in the Talmuds sometimes contain a much more elaborate debate than the one preserved in the Mishnah.[9] Yet very few of these discussions have survived. We have very little discursive material from this entire period. We do have an explicit mention of "the deliberations of Rav and Shmuel," but they were not considered worthy enough to be transmitted to posterity[10]—and did not survive. The terms "he raised an objection" and "he asked" are typical ones for asking in-depth questions, questions that ask for more than the supplying of missing information. Those expressions are almost never found in connection with Rav and Shmuel.[11] The term "he asked" (iteiveih) is found, however, in connection with R. Yochanan and R. Shimon ben Lakish, younger contemporaries of Rav and Shmuel. But as already noted by the early medieval commentators,[12] some questions and answers supposedly raised by "he asked" are fictitious, a later construction of what R. Yochanan and R. Shimon ben Lakish could have asked and answered. I have reason to believe that all instances attributed to R. Yochanan and R. Shimon ben Lakish are fictitious.[13] During their time, as during the time of the Tannaim, the argumentational, the "give and take," was not officially transmitted to posterity.

One has to concede that discursive material is more difficult to transmit than apodictic material, since the former lends itself less easily to memorization. But the difficulty is commensurate with the interest. Because the Amoraim had no strong interest in preserving the discursive material, they found the difficulties insurmountable. As a result, we do not have from the Tannaim and early Amoraim *sugyoth,* a woven fabric of sustained discussion centered around, and interspersed with, fixed laws. The link of tradition was maintained exclusively through the preservation of apodictic laws.

The observation that the principal medium of transmission during the Amoraic period, particularly among the early Amoraim, was the apodictic form is useful not only to literary historians but also to exegetes. It helps to explain several puzzling passages in the Talmud, such as B.T. Shabbath 75 a-b:

He who slaughters an animal on the Sabbath—under which category—[referring to the 39 principal categories of work prohibited on the Sabbath (M. Shabbath 7:2)] is he culpable? Rav said: Under the category of dyeing . . . Rav said: to the statement I made [earlier] let me add a supplement so that later generations will not laugh at me. Wherein is one pleased with the dyeing [one is only culpable if he is pleased with the dyeing]? One is pleased that the throat should be stained with blood, so that people may see it [i.e., the stain, and believe the animal to be freshly killed] and buy meat from him.

Why was Rav more concerned about being laughed at by later generations than he was about being laughed at by his own contemporaries? Was their laughter less troublesome to him? The explanation that first comes to mind is that Rav was confident that his contemporaries would hear the supplement either from him or from his disciples, but expressed concern about the later generations who would not have access to him or to his disciples and would have no way of knowing about the supplement.

This explanation is deficient. If that was Rav's concern, how would merely repeating the supplement guarantee that it be remembered? Moreover, one can assume that Rav must have offered the supplement almost concomitantly with his original statement. The statement by itself is unintelligible (Rashi calls it "astonishing"); the audience would not have understood it without the explanation contained in the supplement. What sense is there, then, to Rav's saying later on "let me add a supplement?" He must have done so already.

The answer is that Rav was addressing the transmitter who formerly heard from Rav both the statement and the supplement, but who, in line with the accepted mode of transmission of his time, transmitted only the apodictic statement and not the discursive supplement. In other instances of a similar nature it is supposed that the later generations, who had no access to the debates that gave rise to the apodictic law, would discover them on their own. The case of the slaughterers was different, however. The law (the statement) was so astonishing that Rav feared that the later generations would not take him seriously, that they would laugh at him and never discover the underlying reason behind his statement. Therefore, he asked the transmitter to make an exception and add the discursive supplement. The need to do so apparently occurred to Rav later, after the statement itself was already committed to the transmitter. Hence the semi-dramatic appeal by him: "To the statement I made [earlier, which is now outside of my domain] let me add a supplement."

Of more general interest is the puzzling phenomenon that, in the Talmud, problems (in the form of questions) preceding Amoraic statements are preponderantly anonymous. Such is the case even when it is certain that an Amora addressed himself to the problem, as when he says: "There is no problem. One source follows Tanna X and one source follows Tanna Y." In such an instance it is clear that the problem the Amora was trying to resolve was a contradiction between two sources which he or another Amora before him had raised. Yet the contradiction is stated anonymously. Why? Because official transmission was responsible, as it were, only for the formulation of the apodictic resolution (or the apodictic statement and the like), not for the formulation of the discursive raising of the question. As a result, the formulation of the former was transmitted as closely as possible to the original, whereas the latter was often improvised. Each academy formulated the discursive as it saw fit. The language of the problem preceding an Amoraic statement is not necessarily that of the Amora; more often than not it is the language of the later redactors, who may have modified or completely changed the original language. Hence the anonymous form of these problems.

A word should be said about who we consider the Amoraim to be. R. Chiya, R. Oshayah, Bar Kaparah (second quarter of the third century), and other contemporary compilers of Braithoth are usually classified as Amoraim even though they did not abandon the Mishnaic form. They opposed Rabbi's "codificatory system,"[14] his order of arranging the material, but they did not break with his mode of presentation. They continued to employ the Mishnaic form. Nevertheless, since they were Rabbi's younger colleagues, they should be considered as belonging more to the end of the Tannaitic period than to the beginning of the Amoraic period. The standard beginning of the Amoraic period is a few decades later, with Rav, Shmuel, and R. Yochanan. With respect to them, our observations concerning the abandonment of the Mishnaic form are correct. Indeed, it is this characteristic more than anything else that sets the Amoraim apart from their predecessors, both Tannaim and the post-Tannaim like R. Chiyah and R. Oshayah. The Amoraim became interpreters rather than imitators of the Mishnah.

The standard definition of the root *drash*, "to inquire," "to seek out" and, derivatively, "to exposite [texts]," which is adequate for biblical, sectarian and Tannaitic literatures, is seemingly not adequate for Amoraic literature. There are numerous instances in both Talmuds where the root *drash* introduces fixed laws accompanied by neither biblical exposition nor logical inquiry. Even if one concedes the possibility (which to me is unlikely) that later editors omitted the supporting evidence for these fixed laws, evidence that initially justified the use of the root *drash*, one would still have to account for the seeming difference between Tannaitic and Amoraic literatures in this regard. Whereas in the Bible *drash* is used more generally, denoting almost any kind of inquiry, in Tannaitic literature (and to some extent also in sectarian literature) its use is limited exclusively to biblical exposition or to hermeneutic principles relevant to biblical exposition.[15] In Amoraic literature, on the other hand, the root *drash* is used in connection with laws that are entirely rabbinic, having no biblical support, such as the first instance of *drash* in the Babylonian Talmud, Berakhoth 38b:

Darash Rav Hisda . . . over boiled vegetables one recites the blessing of "he who created the fruit of the ground."

The designation of the blessing "he who created the fruit of the ground" over boiled vegetables is entirely rabbinic; it has no biblical support. Yet the word *darash* is used. Given the specific usage of the word *darash* in Tannaitic literature, how did the Amoraim justify applying it to fixed laws without scriptural proof text?

The answer perhaps lies in the distinction between the more common use of *amar* "he said," and the less common use of *darash* preceding a fixed law. That the two usages are not interchangeable can be seen, for instance, from the statement in the B.T. Chullin 14a: "Said Rav Huna '*darash* Chiyah the son of Rav . . .' " The same statement contains both usages, *amar* and *darash*. Rav Huna quotes a fixed law in the name of Chiyah, the son of Rav. Rav Huna's statement is introduced with the word *amar,* and Chiyah's fixed law with the word *darash.* The close proximity of the two words precludes the possibility that the two usages may be interchanged. The conventional form of quoting someone else's opinion is "Said Rabbi X or Rabbi Y" or "in the name of" or "in his name." The use of the word *darash* together with *amar* in the same sentence is significant in that it indicates difference.[16]

It is generally assumed that the word *darash* preceding a fixed law means that the law was promulgated in public.[17] After the phrase "The lecturer placed an Amora [mouthpiece] by his side"[18]—customary when an "official"[19] law is delivered to a large public audience—the word *darash* is employed. The difference between *amar* and *darash* is that the former represents the formulation given in the academy, whereas the latter refers to the same law being delivered to the public.[20] In the example given above, it means that R. Huna told his colleagues in the Academy that Chiyah, the son of Rav, has publically promulgated the following law; hence the difference in usage.

It is quite plausible, therefore, that the use of the word *darash* preceding fixed laws in Amoraic literature was justified on the basis of its public posture. In Tannaitic times biblical exposition, Midrash, was taught in public either as part of worship in the Synagogue following the reading of the Torah, or in some other manner. In the course of time the root *drash* became attached not only to biblical exposition but to any teaching done in public, so that later on with the emergence of Mishnah, when fixed laws were also taught in public, the use of the root *drash* was transferred to fixed laws announced in public as well. Thus in Amoraic times the root *drash* was employed both for scriptural exposition and for introducing fixed laws. The latter usage was justified on the grounds that, like Midrash of old, it too was public.

Paradoxically, the use of the root *drash* was not extended to the exposition of Tannaitic texts. When it came to exposition, the expression was used exclusively in connection with the Bible. This is true despite the phenomenon, noticed by many, that exegetically the Amoraim did with the Mishnah what the Tannaim did with the Bible:[21] they subjected both texts to detailed hermeneutical analysis. This analysis was called by different names: *darash* in relation to the Bible, *t'na* in relation to Tannaitic texts.[22] The Amoraim did not transfer the use of the root *drash* to the exposition of Tannaitic texts, apparently out of fear that a similar usage would blur the distinction between the two texts. They had to draw a line between the texts, and they chose to draw it with respect to the official terminology employed in the Academy rather than that in the public halls. The latter, they must have thought, would not endow Tannaitic text with the same respect accorded the Bible.

This offers further support to my thesis that the Mishnaic form—that of transmitting fixed laws without scriptural support—was a relatively late mode of Jewish learning. In Tannaitic times the root *drash* was not yet applied to it, and even in Amoraic times the root *drash* was used only as a means of introduction, not as a description of the expository activity of the Mishnah.

THE STAMMAITIC PERIOD

The quasi-apodictic approach of the Amoraim was radically altered after the death of R. Ashi (427 C.E.). The gradual process of "de-apodicta-tion" that began with the early Amoraim reached its climax with the Stammaim, who flourished between 427 and 501 or 520.[23] (Stammaim means simply anonymous authors; *stammoth* is the term for anonymous sections.) Some sages, like Mraimar, Rafram, Mar bar Rav Ashi, and Ravina the Second, continued more or less in the old tradition; they remained quasi-apodictic, though not to the same extent as the previous generation of Amoraim. In contrast, however, the overwhelming majority of sages of this period preferred to break completely with the Mishnaic mode of learning: they were almost totally non-apodictic, and very few fixed laws were attributed to them. The few anonymous fixed laws that we encounter in the Gemara in the form of *ve-hilkheta* "the law is" were determined by modern scholars[24] to be of Gaonic origin.

   The Stammaim were concerned almost exclusively with the "give and take," the discursive (to the extent that one wonders how they coped with practical halakhah that requires the formulation of fixed laws). They offered interpretation in depth for the opinions of the Shammaites, for instance: "whose teaching is not teaching [for practical purposes]",[25] as well as for the opinions of the Hillelites, whose views are generally followed. It is hard to ascertain from their discussions which view they wished to reject, since contrary views are equally justified. They must have drawn practical conclusions from their discussions, but no evident traces of them are left in the text. Page after page is filled with discursive material without any discernible trend to tell us what the final decision ought to be. To the Stammaim, theoretical learning was a main mode of worship, worth pursuing even if it does not lead to practical decision making.[26] Any decision, however, that is the result of honest discussion and an attempt to seek out the truth through discussion is acceptable. When there are conflicts, one must decide and select one point of view. The basis for the selection is a practical one:[27] one simply cannot simultaneously follow contradictory views. But even the rejected view is not false; it is no less justifiable than the view that is being accepted. This explains the enormous effort lavished by these sages on the justification of opinions that would ultimately be rejected. Rejection was more for practical reasons, for religiously, even the rejected view was acceptable.
   The concern of the Stammaim with the argumentation was most probably a consequence of their realization that the "give and take," the discursive, is no less—and perhaps even more—important than the apodictic and deserves to be preserved. Therefore, they set out to reclaim what was left of the argumentational material from previous generations and to redact it. Since the Amoraim did not deem it important enough to have the discursive material committed to the transmitters with the same exactitude and polish with which they committed the apodictic material, most of the discursive material did not survive, and what did survive was cryptic and truncated. The task of the Stammaim was to complete what was missing (usually through conjectural restoration) and to integrate the whole into a flowing discourse. They reserved for themselves the right to preface, conclude, and even interpolate the words of the Amoraim;[28] otherwise they could not have integrated and reconstructed them. The state of some of the argumentational material that

survived was such that it required the intervention of the Stammaim at almost every turn. As a result, it is often very difficult to distinguish between what belonged to the Amora and what was added by the Stammaim, since the two are often interwoven. I did not exaggerate, therefore, when I said elsewhere that between us and the Amoraim stand the Stammaim.[29] We know the non-apodictic parts of the Amoraim only through the intervention of the Stammaim.

This close interlocking between the Amoraim and the Stammaim is truer of the middle generation of Amoraim than it is of the early generation, particularly Rav and Shmuel (mid-third century, Babylonia). From these two sages hardly any argumentational material survived, despite the explicit testimony that speaks of "the deliberations of Rav and Shmuel."[30] The deliberations must have been lost by the time the Stammaim appeared on the scene. The situation is different, however, in relation to the middle generation of Amoraim, particularly Abaye and Rava (first half of the fourth century, Babylonia). Here too we have testimony that speaks of "the deliberations of Abaye and Rava,"[31] but, in contrast to Rav and Shmuel, the Babylonian Talmud is replete with their discussions on all aspects of rabbinic learning—so much so that "Abaye and Rava" became in later jargon a synonym for the Talmud itself.

We attribute the preservation of the argumentational material from Abaye and Rava more to the short amount of time that elapsed between them and the Stammaim than to a special awareness by Abaye and Rava of the need to transmit the discursive as well. In other words, it was the Stammaim who preserved for posterity the non-apodictic material of Abaye and Rava, and not Abaye and Rava themselves. Because the Stammaim lived closer to the time of Abaye and Rava, for example, than to the time of Rav and Shmuel, the non-apodictic literary remains of the former survived better. This is also true of the non-apodictic literary remains of Abaye and Rava's teachers Rabba and R. Joseph, and of their respective students R. Papa and R. Ashi, among others.

Of course, one has to take into consideration also the quantity of production. R. Papa, for instance, produced less than Abaye and Rava, and therefore less of his productivity remained even though he lived closer to the time of the Stammaim. All things being equal, of those who lived closer to the time of the Stammaitic redactors, less was lost in the interval and more was reclaimed. Since it is unlikely that the realization of the importance of the non-apodictic material came suddenly to the Stammaim without any antecedents, one may assume that an awakening interest in, a burgeoning appreciation of, the non-apodictic existed even prior to the Stammaim.

In this respect, the middle generation of Amoraim may have served as a transition between the Tannaim and early Amoraim, who did not transmit formally and carefully the discursive, and the Stammaim, who concentrated on the discursive. But even though the middle generation of Amoraim may have evinced an interest in preserving the discursive, the actual preservation (that is, the collecting, completing, and integrating) was done principally by the Stammaim. The evidence is overwhelming that the redaction of the discursive material (and occasionally even the apodictic) was not contemporaneous with the composition of the material; the redaction was done later. We know, through critical analysis of the forced reconstructions and explanations of the redactors, that they did not always have an exact and accurate text before them; they often had to complement and correct it.[32] This would not have happened if the redactors had been living at the same time as the authors, for then the redactors would have had a more accurate text, straight from the authors or from their school. The absence of an accurate text of the Talmud—the lack of faithful reproduction, as it were, of the sayings and statements of the sages as early as prior to the closing of the Talmudic period—is definite proof that the redactors of the Talmud were not contemporaries of the authors, that the redactors lived later (sometimes much later), at a time when first-hand information was difficult to obtain. They had to rely on conjecture (which gives the right to a later scholar to try his own hand at an alternate conjecture, to "re-redact," as it were, the Talmud).

The notion of non-contemporaneity is the foundation of modern higher textual criticism of the Talmud. Much of the discursive material that was circulating for a while in a non-redactive state was forgotten during the interval; what remained was in a precarious state. The Stammaim reclaimed it, complementing and integrating it. The luxurious and flowing texture of the Talmud is the achievement of the Stammaim; prior to them there were only short dialogues and comments strung along the Mishnah and Braithoth. The Stammaim created the *sugya*, a semi-independent, sustained, multi-tiered "give and take." They redacted the Gemara from incomplete and truncated traditions. This

explains the many almost incomprehensible instances where the argumentational proceeds along lines that seem to us totally unnecessary,
and seems to make assumptions that are not warranted by the material
at hand. This material could have been organized in a much simpler,
more poignant way than the one proposed by the redactors. The redactors apparently had bits of tradition whose original context they did not
quite know. They drafted these bits onto the material at hand, organizing their material not in accordance with its natural inclination but in a
manner that would make it more assimilative of the stranded bits of
tradition. A striking example is B.T. Baba Kama 14b–15a:

> On the evidence of witnesses [he pays the fine]—thus excepting a confession of
> a [wrongful act for which a] fine [is imposed] and subsequently there appeared
> witnesses. That would accord with the view that in the case of a confession of a
> fine for which subsequently there appeared witnesses, there is exemption, but
> according to the opposite view . . . What is the import of the Mishnah? The
> important point comes in the concluding clause—that free men and persons are
> under the jurisdiction of the law. Free men excludes slaves. Persons under the
> jurisdiction of the law excludes heathens.

There is absolutely no necessity to say that the phrase "on the evidence of witnesses" in the Mishnah is meant to exclude confession
where there subsequently appeared witnesses. It is amply sufficient to
say—as is indeed stated in the Tosefta Baba Kama 1:2, followed by the
P.T. Baba Kama 1:3 (2c)—that the phrase excludes confession without
witnesses subsequently appearing. Had the Gemara so stated, it would
not have had the problem of explaining the Mishnah according to the
opinion which holds that if witnesses appear after the confession, the
confession is not valid. Why did the Gemara complicate the meaning of
the Mishnah, adding that subsequently there appeared witnesses, which
in turn forced it to say, according to the view that witnesses cancel
confession, that the phrase "on the evidence of witnesses" is in apposition to what follows and should be read accordingly, namely, on the
evidence of witnesses (that are) "free men and under the jurisdiction of
the laws?"[33]

The Gemara did so because it had a tradition that there is such an
interpretation that the phrase is in apposition, but it did not quite know
what prompted that slightly unusual interpretation of making the phrase
technically dispensable. The best explanation it could come up with was
that the usual interpretation, that the phrase excludes confession, re-

quires the addition of having witnesses appearing after the confession, which makes this interpretation unacceptable according to the view that the witnesses cancel the confession. In fact, however, we have a better explanation as to why there existed two interpretations of this phrase of the Mishnah—one of the oldest Mishnayoth—without adding the coming of witnesses. There is an old debate among Tannaim[34] concerning whether money damages paid for tort liability are considered fines, so that if the perpetrator confesses he is exempt from paying the fine, or whether they are considered compensation, so that even if he confesses he is liable for payment. The two different interpretations of the phrase "on the evidence of a witness" reflect these two divergent opinions. The opinion that holds that all indemnities are fines interprets the phrase to exclude confession without a witness; if the perpetrator confesses, he is exempt. The opinion that holds that the indemnities are compensation, on the other hand, is compelled to interpret the phrase to be in apposition with what follows. The Gemara (that is, the Stammaim, the redactors) knew only of the opinion that indemnities for damages with a few exceptions are considered compensation. In order to explain the motives behind the two divergent interpretations of the phrase "on the evidence of witnesses," the Gemara had to add artificially the coming of witnesses after confession, involving it with another controversy, which in turn is made to account for the divergence of interpretations.

I consider it improbable that the Talmud's redaction took place piecemeal, that every second or third generation redacted the works of the forebears of their forebears. Rather, I assume, using Occam's razor, that the redaction of the Talmud was done at one time. And since I discern no difference in redactional treatment between the sayings belonging to R. Ashi and those belonging to Abaye and Rava, I conclude, in conjunction with other evidence, that the redaction of the whole Talmud was done after R. Ashi's death, reaching its greatest intensity in the last quarter of the fifth century.[35]

A brief argument should be made here concerning why I consider the beginning of the sixth century the period when the redaction of the Talmud (the composition of the anonymous parts) was completed, rather than extending the redaction into the era of the Saboraim (the middle or end of the sixth century, or even later). I do so because of two reasons, one impressionistic and one factual. The Geonim (from the seventh to the tenth century) and the Rishonim (tenth to fourteenth centuries), our sole sources for identifying Saboraic materials, speak of the Saboraim as having added texts to the Talmud, which creates the impression that the Talmud was more or less complete during the time of the Saboraim. Without the anonymous parts, the Talmud would not have been even half completed. Second, Amoraic quotations in the materials generally attributed to the Saboraim can be traced to other places in the Talmud and were undoubtedly taken from there, whereas Amoraic quotations in the anonymous parts of the Talmud often have no parallel anywhere else in the Talmud. The authors of the anonymous parts of the Talmud had access to original collections of Amoraic statements, while the Saboraim—like the Geonim and Rishonim after them—depended solely on the existing Talmud for Amoraic information (Braithoth circulated independently and were always better known in some circles than in others. A knowledge of Braitha or a lack of it is no indication of a particular age). The Saboraim, therefore, were not the authors of the anonymous parts, were not the redactors of the Talmud, and lived at a time when the anonymous parts were already integrated into the Talmud proper.

It should also be added that apodictic material has no distinct literary style other than being apodictic—that is, responding to the concern at hand in minimal, concise language. In contrast, the Stammaitic Gemara possesses a rich and varied literary style (I am referring to those places where it does more than merely comment on early sources or fill in textual lacunae—where it composes a flowing discussion of its own). At the time of the Stammaim, the Gemara, because of its vast accumulated material and qualitative difference from Mishnah and Braitha, was rapidly becoming a separate book, and in the process acquired a literary style of its own. A notable example is its attraction to symmetry, to the extent that it will sometimes pad the discussion artificially in order to provide literary balance to the respective points of view.[36]

It has often been pointed out that the Babylonian Talmud differs from the Palestinian Talmud in that the argumentational material of the former is more complex, more dialectical, richer and more variegated in content, more removed from the *peshat* (the simple meaning) of the texts it discusses.[37] This is true even when the same opinion of the same sage is discussed in both Talmuds. Indeed, the discussions are qualitatively different. Z. Frankel[38] has already noted that the argumentational, the "give and take" of the Palestinian Talmud is qualitatively not unlike that of the early generations of Amoraim (I would add also that of the middle generation Amoraim) in the Babylonian Talmud, in those instances where we can ascertain with a high degree of certainty that the "give and take" is actually from the Amoraim. Both are simple, narrow in focus, responding to the question at hand, and without a unique style, whereas the argumentational in the Gemara of the Babylonian Talmud is colorful, pulsating, outreaching, often presenting an interwoven and continuous discourse with a distinct, identifiable style of its own. For the purpose of tracing the various modes of Jewish learning, the Babylonian Talmud is more pivotal than the Palestinian Talmud; hence the heavy representation of examples in this chapter from the Gemara of the Babylonian Talmud.

The thesis bears restating. Even a cursory examination will show that the apodictic parts of the Talmud were better preserved than the "give and take," the argumentational, the discursive. Sometimes it is difficult to determine the exact extent of the apodictic material, to differentiate between substance and accretion. Nevertheless, the apodictic kernel frequently stands out. One has only to compare parallel sources to realize that the apodictic remained more or less the same throughout the literature,[39] whereas the argumentational material is almost always radically different in the parallel sources. It is my contention that the difference between the apodictic and the argumentational in this regard is due to the fact that until after the death of R. Ashi (427), the Amoraim did not deem the argumentational important enough to be transmitted. When it was deemed important enough to be transmitted, there was no longer any access to the original statements, and it was necessary to be content with conjectured reconstruction. I concede that the inherent difficulty in transmitting discursive material was a factor; but I maintain that it was not the major factor. These difficulties could have been overcome. In fact, they were overcome later; otherwise we would not have today a Gemara with its variegated "give and take."

To the best of our knowledge, the present Gemara was compiled and transmitted while still in an oral state. (Our first reliable record of a written Talmud dates no earlier than the eighth century.)[40] Transmission of discursive material did not present insurmountable problems then, and indeed the problems did not have to be insurmountable at an earlier period. What did change was the interest in and the attitude toward the "give and take."

As already noted, very little argumentational material survived from the period of the Tannaim and early Amoraim; so little, in fact, that it is clear that this lack of survival cannot be attributed to the inherent difficulty of transmitting non-apodictic material. It can only be attributed to the disregard of the Tannaim and early Amoraim for perpetuating the "give and take." Our Gemara is the result of a new interest in the argumentational. The question is, when did this interest arise— during the period of the middle generation of Amoraim, from whom much "give and take" survived, or during the period of the Stammaim, after the Amoraic period? Since the argumentational material stemming from the middle generation Amoraim and from the Amoraim that followed them (like R. Ashi and his colleagues) is basically not different with respect to reliability from the argumentational material of the Amoraim that preceded them, neither of which were redacted contemporaneously with the enunciation of the sayings, and since to the best of our knowledge during the time of the Saboraim (sixth century) the Gemara looked not unlike the way it looks today (minus, perhaps, terminological expressions and a few additions that the Saboraim added to the Gemara), we must conclude that the interest in the "give and take" arose after the Amoraic period, and that the redaction was done between the period of the Amoraim and that of the Saboraim.[41] This corresponds roughly to the period between 427 and 501 (or 520). Since we do not know exactly who these redactors were, I call them the Stammaim, the anonymous.

I have been arguing, on the basis of textual evidence, that the anonymous redactors of the Talmud did not live at the same time as the Amoraim. Further evidence can be seen in their different modes of thinking. If the Stammaim were contemporaneous with the Amoraim, they would have shared similar thought patterns. The fact that they do not is best accounted for by positing that they did not live at the same time—that they were the product of different periods, and that each period has its own thought patterns.

I will mention one intriguing example from the Talmud that is relevant to our discussion. It deals with the question, "What if it is by deduction?" This question comes after a statement to the effect that a previous opinion of an Amora "was not stated explicitly by him but was rather implicitly deduced." Sometimes the stam (an anonymous statement) will proceed to show that there is something wrong with the deduction. The Amoraim too occasionally observed that a given opinion by an earlier Amora was implicitly deduced, but they were apparently content with this observation and did not seek to find fault with the deduction. They asked no further questions. To the Amoraim, the observation that an opinion attributed to a sage was not stated by him explicitly was in itself worthy of transmission, requiring no further elaboration. To the Stammaim, however, such an observation was not worthy of transmission, and they therefore assumed that the observation must carry the additional negative purport that something was wrong with the deduction. By the time of the Stammaim, attributing a statement of an Amora on the basis of an inference was quite common; it was of no special significance to point this out unless it implied that the deduction was wrong. Such differences between the Amoraim and the Stammaim are evidence that the Stammaim lived after the Amoraim; they could not have been contemporaneous.

There is further support for a post-Amoraic dating of the anonymous redactors in passages in which they have added Amoraic statements to their own. The anonymous material of the Talmud is made up of passages that contain no names at all and passages that contain names attached to statements imported from elsewhere. These statements were imported from Amoraic material because they were thought to be relevant to the new subject as well. Their relevance, however, was determined not by the Amoraim themselves but by the anonymous importer. They are, therefore, no less stammoth than when no name is mentioned. The imported Amora often lived after (sometimes much after) the Amora whose statement initiated the anonymous discussion. That type of stam was certainly not composed by contemporaries of the Amora whose statement opened the discussion. It is not likely that there were two groups of Stammaim—that the stammoth containing no names were composed contemporaneously with the Amora who opened the discussion, whereas the stammoth with imported names were composed not earlier than the time of the latest Amora mentioned in the discussion.

One must, however, differentiate between various kinds of anonymous commentary in any discussion of dating. I make a distinction between simple, concise explanatory comments, which can be as old as the text itself, and complicated discursive explanations, which are late, after the time of R. Ashi. For instance, B.T. Ketuboth 47a comments on the Mishnah's saying (4,4) that the father has control over his minor daughter's findings "in order to avert ill feeling between father and daughter." The comment is anonymous, but it is quite old, as old as the Mishnah itself, and probably accompanied the text from the very beginning. The Mishnah and the comment were always studied together. Brief comments may appear anonymously in one place and in the name of a given sage in another place (both B.T. and P.T.).[42] Because they are taken for granted, such comments may appear with or without a name; the absence of a name does not in itself indicate age. It is the presence or absence of a name in a complicated argumentational passage that is a likely indicator of age.

Any discussion of the anonymous sections of the Talmud must look at the question of why they are there. Why would a society that proclaimed, among other sayings, "He that tells a thing in the name of him that said it brings deliverance into the world" (Braitha Aboth 6,6) transmit more than half of its oral literature anonymously? More specifically, why would an Amora (say of the mid-third century, a contemporary of Rav) who, breaking with the exclusive apodictic form of the Mishnah, was interested in preserving argumentational material insist that the "give and take" be anonymous to the extent that he would set a rigid pattern for future Amoraim to follow? What is the cause-and-effect relationship between "give and take" and anonymity? If we believed that the Stammaim were contemporaries of the Amoraim, we would presumably answer that the break with the Mishnaic form was not as complete as one assumes and that apodicity remained dominant even in Amoraic times. As in Tannaitic days, only the apodictic material was transmitted attributionally, associated with names, whereas the "give and take," the argumentational, though by now considered worthy of preservation, was nevertheless thought of as being of lesser importance. To set the argumentation apart from the more important fixed law, it was transmitted anonymously, indicating its inferior status.

I find this answer unpersuasive, however. The half-break with the past does not seem logical. Once the early Amoraim decided to preserve the "give and take" they really had no reason to do so halfheartedly, especially since an ample precedent existed in the Midreshei Halakhah for the preservation of attributionally discursive material. More serious is the fact that bits of attributed argumentational material survive from almost every generation of Amoraim (and Tannaim); we come across them frequently in the Talmud. If there was a conscious decision by the early Amoraim not to break fully with the Mishnaic form, to transmit the "give and take" anonymously only, why was the policy so frequently flaunted?

One certainly cannot consider all stammoth to be contemporaneous with the authors of the text they are expositing. In that case, to what period would the many anonymous discussions around Mishnah and Braitha belong? Not to the Tannaim, because the discussions are in Aramaic. If these passages were earlier than those commenting on Amoraic passages, there would be some signs in the text of an early origin. But no such signs exist. Whether a stam explains a Mishnah or a very late Amora, like R. Ashi, the stam is qualitatively the same.

Clearly the stammoth around the Mishnah and Braitha came from the same period as those around the Amora; they are all from the post-Amoraic period. This late dating helps to explain why there are stammoth. I am arguing that the interest to preserve the "give and take" arose only in the post-Amoraic period, after R. Ashi. Prior to that period, as in the time of the Tannaim, only the apodictic was deemed worthy of being preserved. The argumentational, of course, was necessary; without it there would have been no fixed and determined law. But once the law was arrived at, the argumentational that gave rise to it was neglected, left to each succeeding academy to formulate as its members saw fit. There was no official version of the argumentational. As a result, in the course of time most of the argumentational was forgotten, especially that of the Tannaim. Bits of it, however, survived. Some survived with names attached, albeit haphazardly. But the overwhelming majority of the arguments did not survive and were reconstructed by the Stammaim in the Post-Amoraic period.

When the Stammaim added their discursive additions to the Talmud of the Amoraim, they added them anonymously in order to distinguish their additions (which they considered of lesser worth) from the teachings of the Amoraim. In the ancient world, anonymous additions signified subordinate activity, an acknowledgment of the supremacy of the main text. By being anonymous, the Stammaim acknowledged the supremacy of the Amoraic text. That recognition was consistent with their view of themselves as rebuilders of the old rather than creators of the new, as explicators and not originators. They considered their work as an explicit restatement of what to earlier generations was self-evident, and sincerely believed that they were adding nothing new. Paradoxically, this distorted image was shared by future generations, who failed to appreciate the Stammaim's activity. The two classical historians of the Talmud, the author of *Seder Tannaim ve Amoraim* and R. Sherira Gaon in his famous *Epistle,* do not mention them. The notion that the Tannaim and Amoraim did not show interest in preserving the "give and take," whereas the post-Amoraic sages did, does not sit well with those whose perception of Jewish spiritual history is that of constant decline. According to R. Sherira Gaon (*Epistle,* pp. 31, 62–64), both the Mishnah and the Talmud arose because "with each succeeding generation the hearts were weakened" and "many things that were simple to the earlier generations . . . were now in this [later] generation a matter of doubt [in need of recording and clarification]". Following such a general view of history, the post-Amoraic sages were perforce inferior to the Tannaim and Amoraim. Their interest in argumentational material was not a burst of intuition lacking in previous generations but rather a sign of weakness, part of a general intellectual decline marked by difficulties in figuring out things that had seemed self-evident to earlier generations. The work of the Stammaim was a concession to those who, so to speak, needed to be coached. To the learned they offered little. The Stammaim therefore did not attach their names to their additions, and future generations did not bother to attribute them.

The zealousness of the Stammaim to preserve the "give and take" led them sometimes to pursue the discursive as an end in itself. A characteristic feature of the Stammaim is their indulgence in the rhetorical and in pseudo-dialogue. Among the Amoraim, it is rare to find rhetorical questions or transparently false answers. But such questions and answers, along with their refutation, are frequent in the anonymous sections of the Talmud. They are there as literary devices. A striking example is found in B.T. Erubin 76b. The Mishnah states:

> If a wall that is ten handbreadths high and four handbreadths thick was placed between two courtyards, the inhabitants of the two courtyards require two *erubim* [allotments of food]. One joint *erub* is not enough [a wall of that size makes them into two distinct dwellings and family members from one courtyard cannot carry objects during the Sabbath into the courtyard of the other]. If the wall was not four handbreadths wide, it is the opinion of R. Yochanan that the

area is considered one courtyard and the people can carry objects over the wall from one courtyard to the other.

The anonymous Gemara raises the question of whether R. Yochanan's opinion contradicts the Mishnah or not, and notes that the Mishnah states that they are considered two separate courtyards, whereas R. Yochanan says they are one. The answer to the anonymous Gemara is that the Mishnah is talking about a wall that is four handbreadths wide, while R. Yochanan is dealing with a wall that is not four handbreadths wide. The answer that the anonymous Gemara gives to its question is obvious: the text explicitly stipulates that R. Yochanan refers to a case where the wall is not four handbreadths wide. The early medieval commentators were hard put to explain the Gemara's question. The question does not need an explanation, however; it is there merely as a rhetorical device to emphasize clearly, though verbosely (another characteristic of the Stammaim), the difference between the cases of the Mishnah and of R. Yochanan.

A typical example of an example that is not seriously intended is found in B.T. Rosh Hashanah 16a. The Gemara there quotes R. Yitzchak "asking": "Why do we blow a *shofar* on the New Year?" (that is, why do we blow a *tekiah?*). The anonymous Gemara interrupts him and expresses wonderment: "Why do we blow *[tokin]* the *tekiah*—because God said so" (in the Bible). and continues: "R. Yitzchak must be asking: 'Why do we blow the *teruah?*' [but this is no question either]? Why do we blow the *teruah*—because God said *sichron teruah*" (Lev. 23:24). Therefore, the question of R. Yitzchak must be: "Why do we blow the *tekiah* and the *teruah* when we are sitting and again when we are standing?"[43] The first answer, that the meaning of R. Yitzchak's question was "Why do we blow the *teruah,*" was not intended to be a serious answer because the same objection that exists in connection with the *tekiah* exists in connection with the *teruah*. This is a rhetorical device, expressing in question and answer form the idea that even though R. Yitzchak uses the word *tokin,* he is not referring to the *tekiah* alone.

Another kind of rhetorical device appears when the entire discussion is unnecessary, as when the sage whose saying is being discussed has already explained himself, putting to rest the questions now needlessly raised. An example is found in B.T. Baba Kama 11b. Ulla says there, in the name of R. Eleazar (an early fourth-century scholar): "The law is that distraint may be made of slaves." R. Nachman says to Ulla: "Did R. Eleazar apply this statement even in the case of heirs [of the debtor]?" "No [replies Ulla], only to the debtor himself." "From the debtor himself [the Gemara, the stam, asks], could not a debt be collected even from the cloak upon his shoulders? [The Gemara answers]: We are dealing here with a case in which a slave was mortgaged [by the debtor who had meanwhile died] as in the case stated by Rava [who lived a generation after Ulla and R. Nachman], for Rava said . . ." The Talmud continues: "After R. Nachman went out, Ulla said to the audience: the statement made by R. Eleazar refers even to the case of heirs. R. Nachman said: Ulla escaped my criticism." As it turned out, as Ulla finally divulged, R. Eleazar intended the law to apply to heirs too (otherwise there is no significance to the law). R. Nachman apparently surmised that and understood Ulla to be saying the opposite in order to divert his (R. Nachman's) criticism. There is no historical or legal sense in defending the position that R. Eleazar meant to have the law apply only to the debtor himself. This, however, did not prevent the Gemara from positing that position (and connecting the rule of R. Eleazar with the saying of Rava, a later scholar), not out of historical necessity but out of love for logical discourse.

This is reminiscent of later *pilpul,* which also sometimes ignored the sages' explanations. A case in point is Maimonides' statement that whatever is not explicitly written in the Bible is termed "from the words of the scribes." This statement of Maimonides generated much discussion, and various explanations were offered as to its source and meaning. Fortunately, we have a responsum by Maimonides in which he explains what he meant and what the source was. But publication of this responsum did not put an end to all discussion, which continues to this day, often ignoring Maimonides' own explanation.[44] Maimonides' name in this context, after the publication of his responsum, is merely a holdover from earlier times; it bears no historical reality.

More important than the rhetorical quality of Stammaitic literature is its dialogical quality, the tendency to stylize simple statements in question and answer form, as if there were a debate. This proclivity for discussion on the part of the Stammaim often transforms even a simple statement into a discussion. The anonymous Gemara may interrupt a statement that contains a law and a reason, and add before the reason the words "What is its reason? because:"[45] as if indeed someone had interrupted the author of the statement asking him what his reason was, which he revealed only because of the prompting of the interlocutor. This, of course, was not the case; the author gave the reason without prompting. Nor did the Stammaim intend to convey that it was the case. It is merely an expression of their love for the dialectical.

Another example is that of B.T. Baba Metzia 21a (already noticed by the early medieval commentators, who, however, did not see it as a part of the overall style of the Stammaim). The Mishnah there states: "One who finds fruits scattered about may retain them [since they are lacking any specially identifiable characteristic, it may be assumed that the owner has abandoned them]." The Gemara inquires: "What is the proportion of the fruit to the space, before abandonment of the fruit is performed? Said R. Yitzchak: One *kav* [spread over] four cubits." The question "What is the proportion of the fruit to the space?" assumes that there is a proportion, whereas in fact, this does not have to be so. Fruit that does not have any specially identifiable characteristic, spread over any territory, large or small, could conceivably belong to the finder. The question raised here requires an unjustified assumption. It is the opinion of R. Yitzchak that there is such a proportion, and this anonymous question was added after he expressed his opinion in order to endow R. Yitzchak's statement with a dialogical quality. In their zeal for the discursive, the Stammaim occasionally overstepped and included also the rhetorical and the pseudo-dialogical.

One should also note that discursive material lends itself more to fictionalization than does fixed law. It is rare (though not unknown)[46] to have someone attribute a fixed law to a sage who did not say it, although it is generally frowned upon on moral grounds; whereas to attach a reason to a fixed law enunciated by a sage and pass them both on in the sage's name is common and acceptable. This is the case only as long as the reason carries logical force. The Stammaim, being more involved with the discursive material, were more given to fictionalization than the Amoraim or the Tannaim before them.

We have now come full circle. The very late Stammaim, through their complete break with the apodictic, have in a sense followed the very early Midrash. Though not as scripturally oriented as the Midrash (Stammaitic material contains, however, plenty of scriptural references), the Stammaim share—against the Mishnah—the vindicatory quality of the Midrash and the biblical motive clauses. This vindicatory quality appeared to take the position that Jewish law must be justified, if not biblically at least logically. It is not surprising that the Midrash and the Gemara (the Stammaitic Talmud) share some common terminology. For instance, instead of the Midrashic "You interpret it to mean . . . perhaps this is not so . . .", the Stammaim say "How do you know it is so . . . perhaps this is not so. . . ."

I have already noted that the Midrashic formulas, which may have had their origin in polemical discussion, with real adversaries later on had only rhetorical value. Their content could have been equally well expressed categorically. It might not be incorrect, therefore, to say that the Gemara is the successor of the Midrash, both having important features in common. During Rabbi's time, it seemed as if Mishnaic form was superseding Midrashic form; that Jewish law, like the laws of other peoples, would be mainly apodictic, not accompanied by justification, biblical or logical. But this did not happen. The Amoraim abandoned the Mishnaic form but remained apodictically oriented. It was the Stammaim, flourishing during most of the fifth century, particularly the last quarter, who broke radically with apodicity and concentrated almost exclusively on the discursive,[47] restoring to Jewish law its original justificatory nature. Like Midrash and like some parts of the Bible, the Gemara reaffirmed the principle that Jewish law cannot be categorical. Making law categorical leads to autocracy, which Jewish apperception instinctively rejects. It must be accompanied by justification, either biblically like the Midrash, or logically like the Gemara.

So pervasive was the influence of the Stammaitic proclivity for the "give and take" that post-Stammaitic codes (with the exception of Maimonides' code, to which we shall return later) consisted of abridged Gemara, a mixture of fixed law with "give and take," including occasionally even the rhetorical and the pseudo-dialogical. The classical post-Talmudic codes like the *Sheiltoth* (eighth century), *Halakhoth Gedoloth* (ninth century), *Rif* (eleventh century), and *Rosh* (thirteenth century) all display the complete break with the Mishnaic form stimulated by the Stammaim. Their laws, whether they follow the order of the Gemara (like the last two) or another order (like the first two), are embedded in a matrix of discursive material,[48] which is now indispensable for any book of Jewish learning. (Of a slightly different genre is the work of M. Hameiri, 1249–1316, who actually composed two different tracts, one dealing with the "give and take," *Chidushim,* and one summarizing the fixed laws of the Talmud, *Beth Habchirah*. As one would expect, the tracts intermingled.)

The Stammaim captured the Jewish imagination, which was prepared all along to become captive to them by its natural reluctance to accept categorical law. Jewish imagination insists on having a reason, a justification, even if this can be obtained only through dubious discursive means. This was especially true during and following late antiquity, when the law was vast and its origin was difficult to track down. Law by its nature had to be fixed; it could not go on for long following the model of the Stammaim of almost total concentration on the discursive. But neither could it, after the Stammaim, discard the discursive, the "give and take." The justificatory nature of Jewish law remains, to this day, the most unique characteristic of Jewish learning.[49]

NOTES

1. "The Braitha was not known to me," (B.T. Sabbath 19b and parallels) applies to both types of Braithoth, those found in the Tosefta and those found in the Midreshei Halakhah. Cf. B.T. Yebamoth 72b. R. Yochanan apparently did not know the contents of the Sifra until he was advanced in age, when an exchange with R. Shimon ben Lakish, his colleague and student, made him memorize and study the book.

2. J. N. Epstein, in his monumental book *Introduction to the Text of the Mishnah* (Hebrew), Magnes Press, Jerusalem 1948, has devoted a chapter (pp. 771–776) to the question of how extensive the Amoraim's erudition in the Mishnah was. His conclusion is that it was almost perfect: he finds few instances where the Amoraim either contradicted or ignored a Mishnah. It is possible, indeed likely, that those are instances in which the Amoraim in fact had a different reading of the Mishnah. In another chapter (pp. 946–979), Epstein meticulously collected all kinds of late additions to the Mishnah. Why not, then, attribute the few instances where it seems as if the Amoraim's knowledge of the Mishnah is deficient to variant readings of, or later additions to, the Mishnah?

3. D. Kraemer, who wrote a dissertation at the Jewish Theological Seminary, New York, entitled "The Literary Characteristics of Amoraim Literature," informs me that the ratio of apodictic to argumentational traditions of Rav and Shmuel approaches twenty-two to one. "Of the apodictic statements, twice as many prescribe fixed laws, according to the model of the Mishnah, as interpret earlier texts. By way of comparison, the ratio of apodictic to argumentational traditions of R. Yochanan and Resh Lakish is approximately two to one, still a significant margin. In contrast, however, more of

these apodictic statements are explanatory than halakhic. Significantly, in the next generation, the model of preserved traditions diverges still further from the earlier Mishnaic precedent, and by the generation of Abaye and Rava the ratio of apodictic over argumentational traditions is substantially less than two to one, while the majority of the former is now explanatory."

4. Some biblically justified (that is, hermeneutically deduced) laws have the same authority as explicitly written laws (see my *Sources and Traditions,* Jerusalem, 1975, Yoma, pp. 7–9), whereas logically justified laws may not have that same authority. Consider, for instance, "Punishment can not be decreed on the basis of a mere logical inference" (Mekhilta, Mishpatim, parshah 11 [p. 288] and parallels).

5. One may contest this, however, saying: had we had Midreshei Halakhah of the school of R. Akiba to the whole Pentateuch, the number of times R. Judah is mentioned in the Midreshei Halakhah would have been considerably higher. In the Sifra, the most typical Midrash of the school of R. Akiba, R. Judah is mentioned quite frequently. Nevertheless, it is doubtful that even then the number would have equaled that of the Mishnah.

6. See E. Z. Melamed, "Tannaitic Controversies Concerning the Interpretation and Text of Older Mishnaoth" (Hebrew), *Tarbiz,* vol. 21, 1950, p. 164.

7. B. T. Gittin 18a and P.T. Shabbath 6:3 (8c). Tannaitic statements cited by Amoraim using *lo shanu* are found in B. T. Shabbath 50a, Erubin 64b, Nedarim 53a–b, Chullin 123b, and P. T. Moed Katan, at the beginning.

8. First noted by R. Malachi Hakohen, *Yad Malachi,* Livorno 1768, passage 356.

9. See, for example, B.T. Pesachim 48a: "He was silent in our Mishnah but answered him in another Tractate *(Braitha).*"

10. By way of comparison, *The Records of the Federal Convention of 1787,* edited by M. Farrand, might be of interest. Both considered deliberations of lesser importance, not worthy to be preserved along with the conclusions. To quote the book jacket of 1937, revised edition, Yale University Press, New Haven: "The Federal Convention of 1787 engaged in the great and complex labor of framing the Constitution for the Union of the States. For many years afterwards, little was known of its deliberations and nothing official was published. The variety of versions which began to appear thereafter tended to confuse rather than clarify the situation." Of striking similarity to the modern critical Talmud scholar is Farrand's attempt to sift through different versions of the deliberations, none of which was fully reliable. Farrand tells us of his travails in the introduction.

11. The exceptions are B. T. Ketuboth 51b; Baba Kama 87b, 116a; Niddah 24a.

12. Principally by the Tosafoth Baba Bathra 150b, s.v. *beram.* The list is incomplete. See the indexes to the volumes of my *Sources and Traditions,* s.v. *iteiveih.*

13. See, however, B. T. Rosh Hashannah 15b: *Iteiveih Resh Lakish le Rabbi Yochanan* (Resh Lakish asks R. Yochanan), and R. Chananel (ad loc.): "Yerushalmi (at the beginning of the fifth chapter of Shebiith):" "Said R.

Abba . . . Why is it that R. Shimon the Son of Lakish asks [R. Yochanan] and R. Yochanan accepts it and is silent. . . ." This *iteiveih* seems to be real, though the exact form is in doubt.

14. See my article "The Reception Accorded to Rabbi Judah's Mishnah," in *Jewish and Christian Self-Definition,* ed. E. P. Sanders et al., Fortress Press, Philadelphia 1981, pp. 204–212.

15. With the exception of the language of contracts. This type of language, especially in marriage contracts, was treated with the same detailed attention as was the language of the Bible. This prompted P. T. Ketuboth 4:8 (28d–29a) to say of some rabbis (with an element of surprise) that they subjected contracts to Midrash.

16. See also P. T. Beitzah 2:1 (61b): "R. Chuna *darash* like [the opinion of] R. Shimon ben Elazar, R. Yochanan *darash* to the Tiberians like [the opinion of] R. Shimon ben Elazar . . . R. Abahu *horei* like [the opinion of] R. Shimon ben Elazar." Here the words *darash* and *horei* are used together, though not in the same sentence. The difference between the two is that whereas *darash* introduces a statement that was promulgated in public, *horei* refers to the rendering of a decision given to a practical question whether delivered in public or in private. See, however, Sifrei Deut., piska 155 p. 207: "one is culpable for action, not for *horayah* [theoretical teaching]." and Mishnah Sanhedrin 11:2: "He is not culpable unless he gives a decision concerning what should be done". *Horei* alone does not necessarily mean action.

17. This found its way into ʿ*Aruk Completum,* ed. Kohut and E. Ben Yehuda, *Thesaurus totuis hebraitatis* s.v. *darash.*

18. For references, see C. J. Kasowski, *Thesaurus Talmudis,* Ministry of Culture and Education (Israel) and Jewish Theological Seminary of America, Jerusalem 1959, 1961, vol. 5, p. 2438, and vol. 9, p. 446.

19. See J. M. Kosovsky, *Sinai* (Hebrew), Mossad Harav Kook, Jerusalem 1959, vol. 22, p. 234.

20. See also ibid., p. 235. That *amar* refers to a statement enunciated in the Academy was already stated by R. Shmuel Sir(ilyo) ca. 1530) in his *Killei Shmuel,* ed. S.B.D. Sofer, Divrei Soferim, Jerusalem 1972, s.v. *a'mar,* par. 22, p. 20: "Wherever it says *amar* Peloni, it means that it was said in the Academy".

21. See *Piskei HaRid,* Shabbath, Mossad Harav Kook, Jerusalem 1964, p. 229: "[Exegetically] the relationship of the Amoraim to the Mishnah is similar to that of the Tannaim to the Bible."

22. However, when simple textual reading is involved, the usual phrase is "kore' ba-torah, ve-shoneh mishnah" ("reads Torah and recites Mishnah"). See my *Sources and Traditions,* Kiddushin, pp. 671–673.

23. R. Ashi died in 427; 501 is the date of Ravina the Second's death; 520 is the date of the death of R. Assi or R. Yose (depending on whether one follows the French or Spanish recension of the Epistle, p. 97). The first two dates are directly taken from R. Sherira Gaon's (966–1065) famous Epistle,

ed. B. M. Lewin, Golda-Itskovski, Haifa 1921, pp. 94–95, whereas the third date follows I. Halevy's interpretation of R. Sherira (*Dorot Ha-Rishonim*, B. Harz, Berlin and Vienna 1923, vol. 3, p. 28). I have serious reservations about the accuracy of Halevy's date for R. Assi's or R. Yose's death. However, since any substitute date is less certain, I leave it unchallenged. The B. T. Baba Metzia 86a calls both R. Ashi and Ravina "the end of *hora'ah*." R. Sherira presumably, as already noticed by H. Graetz (see his *Geschichte der Jüden*, 3rd ed., O. Leiner, Leipzig 1895, book 5, n. 2, pp. 347ff.; see also N. Bruell, *Jahrbücher für Jüdische Geschichte und Literatur*, Wilhelm Erras, Frankfurt am Main 1876, p. 26, n. 2), identified the R. Ashi of "the end of hora'ah of the Talmud" with R. Assi or R. Yose, whom he indeed called "the end of hora'ah."

R. Sherira's understanding of "the end of hora'ah" is the end of the Talmud. My understanding is the opposite: it means the beginning of the Talmud, that is, the beginning of the preserving of the "give and take," the deliberations. I interject the period of the Stammaim between "the end of hora'ah" and the Saboraim, diverging from R. Sherira's chronicle, on the basis of evidence presented elsewhere (the introduction to my *Sources and Traditions*, Shabbath, pp. 14–22). However, with respect to the time when the period of the Saboraim began, as well as what happened during the period, I do not dare to diverge from R. Sherira's chronicle. We are totally dependent on him—the oldest and most classical historian of the Talmud—for the history of the Saboraim.

24. See B. M. Lewin, *Rabbanan Saborai veTalmudam*, Achiever, Jerusalem and Tel Aviv, 1937, pp. 46–54.

25. See B. T. Berakhoth 36b and parallels. See also my *Sources and Traditions*, Shabbath, pp. 361–362.

26. At least twice (Yoma 5b, Ketuboth 3a), in connection with discussions of past events, the Gemara asks: "[What difference does it make?] What's past is past!" (See also Tosafoth Chagigah 6b, s.v. *ma'y*.) But this should not be interpreted as indicating impatience with discussions that had no practical application. As already noticed by the medieval commentators, the same question could have been asked in many other places in the Talmud but was not. Apparently, the Stammaim asked this question rhetorically when they had an answer to it. When they had no answer, they simply ignored it. The same is true of other similar questions (see my *Sources and Traditions*, Erubin, p. 208 n. 1).

Cf. E. E. Urbach, *The Jews, Greeks and Christians*, ed. R. H. Kelly and R. Scroggs, E. J. Brill, Leiden 1976, p. 120. His reference in note 12 to P. T. Kila'im 1:3 (27a) is not pertinent. Its meaning is similar to the statement in the Babylonian Talmud (Rosh Hashannah 14b, Ketuboth 7a, 27a) that one cannot necessarily deduce from a story that the law would have been different had the story been different. See also B. T. Sanhedrin 51b and Zebachim 45a.

27. For instance, the rule that "the law is like Rav in ritual matters (*issurim*) and like Shmuel in civil matters (*dinim*)" (B. T. Bechoroth 49b), even though

Rav is not always right in *issurim* or Shmuel in *dinim*. A very instructive responsum on this subject is that of R. Y. Bachrach, *Chavath Yair*, Frankfurt 1699, no. 94, at the beginning.

28. For an example, see the introduction to my *Sources and Traditions*, Yoma to Chagigah, pp. 2–5, and ibid., Pesachim, pp. 477–480.

29. Introduction to my *Sources and Traditions*, Shabbath, p. 5.

30. B. T. Berakhoth 20a and parallels.

31. B. T. Sukkah 28a and parallels.

32. See the Introduction to my *Sources and Traditions*, Seder Nashim.

33. The question, of course, did not escape the attention of the medieval commentators. The Tosafoth (ad loc., s.v. *ella*) explain that the Gemara had to add "that subsequently there appeared witnesses" because without subsequent witnesses, the Mishnah here would not be adding to what it says later on in the tractate at Chapter 7:4. The mere law that confession exempts one from a fine is stated there too; there is no need for repetition. The Tosafoth raise the possibility (based on the Gemara, ibid. 13b) that the Mishnah first stated the law in general terms (befitting an old Mishnah that uses such anachronistic expressions as *hav* instead of *hayyav*; see ibid. 6b) and later on exposited it. But, say the Tosafoth, that would have required the exposition to be of greater length than the general term—which it is not. The Gemara, therefore, was forced to add the additional clause.

However, the Mishnah 7:4 is not reporting the law that confession exempts one from a fine as a law by itself, but as an example among many when a thief pays only twofold restitution, not fourfold or fivefold as required by the Torah. It is quite plausible that the Mishnah is first stating the law in general terms and then in 7:4, based on the first Mishnah, includes it among similar instances where the outcome is that the thief pays only twofold restitution. The Gemara's motive for adding the clause must be other than to avoid repetition.

34. C. Albeck, in his supplement to the Mishnah Baba Kama 1:3, s.v. *bifnei*, p. 408, has collected the sources on whether or not money damages are paid for tort.

35. L. Jacobs, *Teiku: The Unsolved Problem in the Babylonian Talmud*, Leo Baeck Publication, London, 1981, concludes from the stylistic uniformity of *teiku* that besides the bare posing of the problem, the discussion of the *teiku* is the working of later editors "who must have lived subsequently to all the propounders . . . not earlier than the latter part of the fifth century" (p. 294), which corresponds to the period of the Stammaim.

36. A beautiful example is B. T. Shabbath 52b. See my *Sources and Traditions*, ad loc.

37. Z. Frankel, *Introduction to the Palestinian Talmud* (Hebrew), Breslau 1870, pp. 32b ff.

38. Ibid., p. 35b. It should be noted that there are some layers of stam even in the Yerushalmi (less so—almost none—in the older parts of the Yerushalmi, that of Tractates Baba Kama, Baba Metzia, and Baba Bathra, generally referred to as Yerushalmi Nezikin). The custom in the academy was

that the speakers' own ideas were conveyed without specific authorship, without quoting themselves as authors, whereas the ideas of their teachers were quoted attributionally, in their respective names. When the editors of the Yerushalmi decided to close the development of the text and to "freeze" it into a book, they recorded what went on in the academy at that particular time. The ideas of the then "present speakers" were therefore recorded anonymously (hence the existence of stammoth in the Yerushalmi). Had the editors allowed the text to develop further, the then "present speakers' " ideas would have been transmitted by their disciples attributionally, in their names. By arresting the further development of the text, the editors created an anonymous ring around the attributional material. But the ring was thin and not always significant; it was the result of a technical decision to record the "present speakers' " ideas anonymously. In contrast, the anonymous sections of the Babylonian Talmud are rich, multitiered and comprehensive, the result of a new awareness of the importance of the "give and take" and a desire to preserve and develop it. The difference is a qualitative one.

39. With gradations, however. The Mishnah remained much the same, despite occasional significant variations, but this is less true of the Braithoth. Those found in the Palestinian Talmud are usually closer to the original language than those found in the Babylonian Talmud. On the other hand, the Babylonian Talmud had a richer knowledge of Braithoth than the Palestinian Talmud. The apodictic statements of the Amoraim are often considerably different in the parallel sources yet resemble each other enough to be recognized as similar.

40. See D. Rosenthal, introduction to *Babylonian Talmud, Codex Florence,* Makor Publishing, Jerusalem 1972. See especially the first two lines on p. 2.

41. The fact that many sugyoth conclude with a statement of R. Ashi should not be construed as evidence that he was the redactor of the Talmud (see J. Kaplan, *The Redaction of the Babylonian Talmud,* Bloch Publishing Company, New York 1933, chaps. 5–6, especially pp. 75–79). On the contrary, the fact that R. Ashi is mentioned by name indicates that the redaction took place after his death and that it used earlier materials, including material of R. Ashi (though this is not the case with Rabbi, the editor of Mishnah). Furthermore, in a number of instances (see, for instance, my *Sources and Traditions,* Nedarim, pp. 326–327, Erubin, p. 27, Pesachim, pp. 304–305) the redactor of the Gemara misunderstood R. Ashi because he did not have a complete or accurate version of R. Ashi's statement. If R. Ashi had also been a redactor, he most likely would not have lived much before the final redactor, and the latter would have been more thoroughly acquainted with his teachings. Those who maintain the semi-traditional position (aggressively defended by I. Halevy) that the redaction of the Talmud began with R. Ashi (died 427) and concluded with Ravina the Second (died 501) have the unenviable task of explaining why a literature of 200 years' duration (starting with Rav, who established this Academy or a semblance thereof in Sura around 220) needed more than seventy years for redaction.

It may be added that the statements of R. Ashi and subsequent discussions thereon do not display any recognizable difference from their predecessors. If he were a redactor, we would have expected his statements to betray traces of this activity. On the other hand, with the exception of Mar bar R. Ashi and Ravina the Second, the vast majority of the statements of the Amoraim who lived after R. Ashi are radically different from their predecessors. Little is recorded in their names, and it is of a different quality: it is simple, single-tiered, and does not form a link in the chain of a continuous sugya. Their statements are hardly ever followed by subsequent discussions. While their attributed contribution is best described as minor "touch-ups" to an already existing and organized Gemara, to whose anonymous redaction these Amoraim devoted most of their efforts, their overall literary activity must have been greater than these meager leftovers. Cf. N. Bruell, "Die Entstehungsgeschichte des babylonischen Talmuds als Schriftwerkes," in *Jahrbücher für Jüdische Geschichte und Literatur,* Wilhelm Erras, Frankfurt am Main 1876, pp. 67–68 nn. 106 and 107; and J. Kaplan, *Redaction of the Babylonian Talmud,* pp. 10–11.

42. See my *Sources and Traditions,* Rosh Hashanah, p. 358, n. 4.

43. This is a reconstruction by the Stam. Originally R. Yitzchak, an early fourth-century Palestinian scholar, most likely said only: "Why do we blow the *shofar* on Rosh Hashanah? In order to confound Satan." He, like some Tannaim before him and some Amoraim a bit after him, was in the habit of giving explanations of commandments (Cf. Z. Chajes' gloss, ad loc. His distinction between *lammah* and *mipnei mah* is not warranted. The Gaonim read here too *mipnei mah*. [See my *Sources and Traditions,* Rosh Hashanah, p. 380, n. 6.]) By the time of the Stammaim, this was no longer customary. They, therefore, interpreted R. Yitzchak's question to mean not why do we blow at all, but why do we blow twice, sitting and standing.

44. See my article, "Contemporary Methods of the Study of Talmud," *Journal of Jewish Studies,* vol. 30, no. 2, Autumn 1979, pp. 195–196. For an apologetic explanation, See *Tarbiz,* vol. 49, p. 192.

45. See my *Sources and Traditions,* Pesachim, pp. 477–480 (particularly note 11x).

46. I collected most of the instances in my *Sources and Traditions,* Nashim, Introduction, p. 14, n. 19.

47. For a beautiful example of the difference in the mode of learning between the pre-Stammaitic and post-Stammaitic periods, see B. T. Baba Kama 20a–b and 21a.

48. For some time it was thought that *Sefer Hayerushoth* by R. Saadiah Gaon (882–942) constituted an exception to this rule. Recently, however, S. Abramson, *Inyanoth Besifruth Hageonim,* Mossad Harav Kook, Jerusalem 1974, p. 232, has shown that the present edition of *Sefer Hayerushoth* is only a shortened copy of an earlier, fuller one that contained proofs from the Bible and Talmud.

49. If my thesis is correct, that the school of R. Ishmael opposed the innovation of the Mishnah and insisted on the old way of transmitting laws together with their scriptural support, one may say that ultimately the school of R. Ishmael triumphed over the school of R. Akiba. We are observing a phenomenon not uncommon in the annals of intellectual history: esteem does not correlate with adherence. Rabbinic literature esteems R. Akiba and his school far more than it does R. Ishmael and his school; yet the mode of learning it finally adopted is closer to the school of R. Ishmael than it is to the school of R. Akiba. The hallmark of rabbinic learning is not Mishnaic style, the style so intimately connected with R. Akiba and his school, but Midrashic style, the medium of R. Ishmael and his school.

6

Talmudic Form Criticism

Baruch Micah Bokser

Form criticism is not a new discipline. Scholars in diverse fields have employed it and adapted its methods to different types of literatures, including the Hebrew Bible and the New Testament. Recently, several scholars have applied it to rabbinic works. They focus on liturgical and midrashic texts and Mishnah and Tosefta. But form criticism provides an important tool in the analysis of talmudic, amoraic traditions, as well. Its methods and assumptions appropriately respond to the specific textual and literary problems posed by *gemara*.

The Babylonian Talmud is made up of the teachings of at least three centuries of named masters, and of two centuries of expansion, literary enrichment, and redaction. Different portions of *gemara* come from different circles and they have not been fully harmonized and levelled. Within the last fifty years scholars have demonstrated that the Talmud does not merely record "live debates" between *Amora'im* and that traditions do not represent direct quotations and discussions chronologically arranged in sequence. Rather *gemara* is the result of an ongoing process of teaching, interpretation, and application, of revision and expansion of earlier teachings, as well as of post-amoraic literary enrichment and recasting on the basis of often extraneous and later concerns. The more we learn, the greater we recognize the impact of the end processes. The Palestinian Talmud, in the main edited ca. 400 C.E. likewise went through aspects of these developments, though it lacked much of the later literary enrichment.[1] Changes thus occurred in both the process of

Reprinted by permission of *The Journal of Jewish Studies*, Oxford University, Cambridge, England, volume 31, number 1, 1980.

transmission, as demonstrated especially by David Weiss Halivni, and in the stage of redaction. As in Mishnah, Tosefta, and Midrashim, these factors affected the selection, formulation, content, and structure of materials.[2]

Accordingly, to evaluate the thought, concerns, and world view of different generations, circles, and individuals, we must transcend the finished product and separate Talmud into its component parts and strata and distinguish between what a person might have said and what was later attributed to him. In addition, once we have accomplished this task we will be better able to appreciate the literary nature of the final product of Talmud itself.

To accomplish these goals we must supplement standard textual-philological criticism with several additional tools.

First, we can look at the end product and employ *redaction criticism.* We thereby remove the redactional layers and additions and in the process focus on the contributions of the latter period and the concerns which motivated the expansion and revisions of the earlier materials.[3]

Second, we can focus on the *history of the traditions.* We trace the ways in which different generations modified the materials and we thereby focus on the world view reflected in each stage.[4]

Third, we may employ *source criticism* so as to isolate elements possibly borrowed from elsewhere. We inquire, for example, To what degree is the source adapted to its new context and which portions fulfil the need for which the source was cited? We can then explain the presence of certain parts and the formulation of material which may not be germane or exactly fit in the present context.[5]

Fourth, we can examine the forms, structure and genre of the larger and smaller units of the material, a method which scholars in other disciplines and fields call *form criticism.*[6]

The use of form criticism involves several assumptions. Within *gemara* we find recurrent use of certain literary structures and formulations along with very particular language individualized to the issue at hand. For example, one can analyze Mishnah and offer interpretations, questions, citations, challenges, and discussions in one of several standard patterns. Perhaps due to the very nature of language, regular formulaic means are used for specialized purposes to convey similar types of thoughts. But the precise language and content of a tradition varies to make up the specific thought.[7] Students of oral tradition point to the use of brief formulaic utterances to express certain types of thoughts. For example, a person, in a confession or in an emergency beseeches God in a prayer as if he or she stood before a judge and employs language appropriate to a court room.[8] But patterns are found in literary sources as well. Teachers and editors-compilers of works which contain teachings structure the materials to express specific points and overall notions. As a formulation and structure may originate with the initial teaching or at any stage of its redaction, it is up to the form critic to identify the first appearance of a formulation and pattern.[9]

Scholars have focused upon the forms of larger units of talmudic materials and have described them in broad terms. Abraham Weiss has pointed to patterns and structures by which a tradition and *sugya* are presented. These include, first, a brief teaching *(memra)*, and, second, discursive material *(sugya)*. Each of these, in turn, may be autonomous and independent or else supplementary and dependent, upon some earlier text, comment, or discussion.[10] Several scholars in one manner or another likewise pointed to the above categories.[11] But A. Weiss, in addition, supplements them with, first, collections of teachings arranged by formal traits, e.g., a series of three teachings attributed to the same master; second, a compilation of *midrashic* and *aggadic* materials, e.g., a series of consecutive comments which explain successive verses in the Book of Esther; and third, treatises on specific topics, e.g. dream interpretations. We still insufficiently know which of these patterns are literary conventions employed at the final stage to present material and which predate the final arrangement of *gemara* and constitute moulds in which the materials were transmitted to the final editors.[12] Shamma Friedman has found a more complex literary structure in which amoraic teachings often appear in a tripartite division and subdivision. For example, a series of three amoraic responses, each in three parts, may follow a tradition attributed to an early master.[13]

Smaller units of traditions also employ forms and patterns. Previous research here, however, has not taken *gemara* as its point of departure.[14] Joseph Heinemann has fruitfully isolated in public and private prayers different forms used regularly for specific purposes. For example, an individual's private prayer opens with the following formula, YHY RṢWN MLPNYK H' 'LHYNW . . . Š-. . , "May it be Thy will, Lord our God . . . That . . ," "which is indicative of the awe and hesitation felt by the individual who turns to God with his private requests."[15]

Sibley Towner identified, in Mekilta, the form used for "Enumeration of Scriptural Examples," which serves to lay out proof texts. He demonstrated how teachings employ this form or are recast to fit it.[16]

Jacob Neusner catalogued the forms of traditions attributed to Pharisees pre-70 C.E. and throughout Mishnah and Tosefta Tohorot. He has traced for example, the use and variations of the dispute and debate forms to set out opposing views on a given legal issue.[17]

One may adapt these concerns to amoraic sources and focus on the forms of the small units. Elsewhere I have done so with the teachings of Samuel, a third century Babylonian Amora, from the first generation of post-mishnaic masters. The fruitful results demonstrate that we should expand this effort to the teachings of all the masters. The traditions attributed to Samuel which deal with Mishnah make up part of 'Samuel's Commentary on Mishnah'.[18] Samuel's comments which explain Mishnah employ a series of fixed patterns recurrently used to express certain types of thoughts. They often are formulated as brief glosses which for comprehension depend upon Mishnah. Many are introduced by a specific prefix or phrase which delineates their relationship to Mishnah. For example, the B-prefix introduces a gloss which defines the conditions under which Mishnah's rule applies.[19]

An example of the B- form is a tradition which deals with a special case of the law of "gleaning," *leqet*, in M. Pe'ah 4:11. Lev. 19:9–10 and 23:22 prohibit a reaper from picking up sheaves that fall to the ground. But what is the status of grain found in ant holes situated in the field? Some ants were known to gather large amounts of grain and even "harvest" from standing stalks. Moreover, these ant holes might contain grain collected even prior to the year's reaping and thus not liable to the law of "gleaning." We cite the first part of M., an anonymous opinion on the matter:

1. [As to grain found in] ant holes [in the field].
2. [If the ant holes] are situated among the standing grain—
   Lo, the [grain found in the holes] belong to the householder.
3. Those [ant holes] that are situated at a point beyond which the reapers [have passed]—
   The upper [grain found in ant holes] belong to the poor
   [= The sheaves are considered "gleanings."]
   The lower [grain found in the ant holes] belong to the householder.
   (M. Pe'ah 4:11)

Samuel in y. Pe'ah 4:8, 18c, defines what constitutes the "upper" and the "lower" and employs one word glosses of BLBYNYM, "the white ones," and BYRWQYN, "the green ones," respectively.[20] Recognition of this B- form thus enables us accurately to understand the tradition.[21]

Another form consists of the phrase WHW' Š-, literally, "And he that." It sets out the conditions for a case and the prerequisite necessary for a rule to apply. It is used for traditions where the referent is male or female, in gender, and single or plural, in number.[22] For example, M. Kil. 5:5 deals with mixed growths, kila'yim, in particular the rendering of a vineyard prohibited by planting or maintaining growths in a forbidden proximity to a vine. Samuel's tradition in y. Kil. 5:5, 30a reads:

And it be such that the middle one should be encircled by vegetables (WHW' ŠTH' H'MS'YT 'GWLH YRQ).

The word for a "vine," GPN, is feminine while the pronoun, WHW', literally, "and he," is masculine. But WHW' along with the prefix on the next word, Š-, constitute a form. Together they make up a stereotyped formulation and as a unit serve to introduce the specific comment. Accordingly, the word WHW' does not follow its literal sense.[23]

A comment on Mishnah originally formulated as a gloss may become somewhat obscured by its later history. Tradents or editors of the pericope may apply it to a new context or problematic. Naturally as a gloss which depends for comprehension upon its referent, such a comment can be easily transferred without substantively revising its wording. Our sensitivity to the formal considerations may thereby enable us to trace the transformations of a tradition. Below we provide an example of this process.

Form criticism has both exegetical and historical purposes. As we indicated above, the use of a specific form reflects the context out of which a comment emerged. Specific patterns are used for fixed purposes and the purposes are determined by the particular human conditions and literary intentions.[24]

First, form criticism helps us understand a whole pericope. By identifying the referents of traditions we are aided in isolating component parts of the sugya. Thus a B- form which opens a tradition and which lacks a referent immediately signals us to see if the tradition refers to Mishnah, a baraita, or some other general rule, and not the immediately preceding comment. We may therefore have to lift the tradition out of its present context. At times, commentators recognized the correct sequence and associated such a tradition with its proper referent, but they often remained baffled as to the use of the form.[25]

Second, the knowledge of the form and its use enables one to understand the tradition's meaning, as in the above cited instances of the B- and WHW Š- forms. For example, in the above use of the WHW' Š- form, the scribe of one MS and several commentaries could not account for the use of the WHW, a male pronoun, for a female subject, the "vine," GPN, and emended the text. Being sensitive to this problem enables us to appreciate the problem they faced and the steps they employed to deal with it.[26] Form criticism may thus become useful even in lower textual criticism.

Third, form critical considerations assist in analyzing an unusual use of a form. In such instances we have to ask if the usage is normal and one we had previously just failed to recognize or has the tradition suffered revision or interpolation.[27]

Fourth, and related to the third use, form criticism helps isolate fundamental parts of a tradition and separate out secondary and tertiary additions. For example, where two versions of a tradition both employ the same form but differ in wording or length, the regular usage of the form may provide a criterion by which to identify the most fundamental elements of the comment.[28]

The above analysis assumes that the use of the form originated in an early stage of the tradition, even considerably prior to the post-amoraic enrichment and working over of *gemara*. At times we can demonstrate this. For example y., which lacks much of the post-amoraic expansion, cites traditions formulated with forms. When the same tradition appears in b. and y., often the y. version constitutes a more pristine formulation and approximately what we would have posited as the fundamental form.[29] In addition, where we can identify early recensions of y., we find therein instances of forms; they are thus not solely the products of the final redactors.[30] Moreover, within *gemara* another tradition may attest Samuel's comment. That is, a tradition which is not redacted into a single pericope with Samuel's but which responds to it and is based upon it, can provide attestation that Samuel's tradition casted in a form circulated already at the time of the composition of that second tradition. For example, we have two such traditions on M. Kil. 3:3, which rules that a person's field must not even appear to contain diverse kinds of growths as when the head of a row of vegetables enters a field of a different vegetable. Samuel's comment defines the situation. A tradition attributed to Yoḥanan and Simeon b. Laqish responds to it:

A. Samuel said, they taught that only (L' ŠNW 'L') one row [may enter another vegetable field]. Lo, two are forbidden.[31]
B. R. Yohanan and R. Simeon b. Laqish both said, It makes no difference whether [there are] one or two [rows, for either way it is permitted] (HY' ḤT HY' ŠTYM).

(y. Kil. 3:3; 28d)

Samuel's comment employs a pattern found already in tannaitic sources and used even when a tradition is not disputed by a second view, as in B. A thus glosses Mishnah and stands alone without B. As A requires Mishnah for comprehension, it is formulated so as to circulate along with Mishnah. This accords with the fact that Yoḥanan and Simeon b. Laqish are Palestinians with whom Samuel would not likely have had discussions. Their comment, though, disputes Samuel and claims that the law is not limited to the case of one row. The comment is phrased so as to respond to Samuel's, wording, "It makes no difference whether [there are] one or two." It thus does not employ the same pattern as Samuel's, "They taught only . . ." and is not redacted to form a balanced dispute with Samuel. B accordingly attests that already in the time of Yohnan and Simeon b. Laqish, Samuel's tradition circulated along with Mishnah so that the two masters could dispute it.[32]

The way Samuel's comments are presented in relationship to those of another master in effect indicates that the dispute form does not represent the primary stage of the tradition and that Samuel's comments have not been totally revised. In the immediately preceding analyzed tradition and at times elsewhere Samuel's tradition is juxtaposed with the teaching of another master but is not redacted into a dispute form with that tradition. That is, they do not make up balanced apodoses differing as to an issue stated in a preceding protasis. We further find juxtaposed comments that may not even relate to each other or that may not even dispute a single matter, though they employ a dispute form and even the same phrasing. On the other hand, we find a high proportion of comments which do not form a dispute pattern, though in fact they may differ. Thus the formulation as a dispute is not the primary stage of the materials but rather is imposed upon the traditions. As many of the resulting dispute forms are imperfect and traditions often appear out of phase with each other, clearly the early form, if not totally the formulation, of the tradition has remained intact.[33]

We find cases as well in which the formulation of the comment as a gloss without a referent explains how later Amoraʾim without revising the substance of the tradition might apply it to a new context. The form of the comment thus had an integrity of its own and was preserved though the transference might obfuscate or obliterate the meaning in the new context.[34]

Form criticism contributes also to the study of history. Its findings relate to the problem of the beginning of *gemara,* a central issue in talmudic studies and the history of Judaism. When we examine the forms of traditions attributed to early third century masters, we study the formulations of the basic building blocks of *gemara* and of what became its first stratum. This conclusion is based upon several arguments.

If traditions with their forms are preserved despite secondary and tertiary additions, then we have access, if only partial, to teachings at their initial stage. As particular forms may reflect a specific kind of teaching conducted in a certain setting, we may have a key even to the activity behind the teaching. Unfortunately, however, we cannot automatically translate the projected setting of a form into an actual *Sitz im Leben.* Nevertheless, we at least may know what those responsible for the earliest stage of the tradition projected as the fundamental function of teaching.

This inquiry brings us closer to bridging the gulf between literary sources and possible actual instructional activities. It is necessary to pursue such speculation because historical and literary research proves that the Talmud does not consist of a record of "talmudic debates" in Babylonian academies. As pointed out above, much of the talmudic discussions are a literary product of post-amoraic circles.[35] In addition, as David Goodblatt recently proved, academies as institutions which transcend the personality and life span of a single master and as places where several masters taught, did not exist among Sasanian Jewry. Rather masters interacted primarily with a small, individual, circle of disciples or apprentices. Accordingly, when we theorize as to the actual teaching which became the first stratum of *gemara,* we must correlate our data with an historically viable model.[36]

In the third century, the rabbinic movement which had centred in Palestine expanded to Babylonia and there the rabbinic masters applied Mishnah, a Palestinian document, edited ca. 200 C.E., to Babylonian Jewry.[37] Even when masters, including Samuel, differed with Mishnah, they might formulate their comments in terms of Mishnah's agendum.[38] The scope of mishnaic study attests that Mishnah held a central place among first generation Amora'im. Jacob Sussmann has argued that Samuel's and Rav's traditions on mishnayot in Zera'im originated on those texts and are not transferred from non-Zera'im contexts. Amora'im in subsequent generations, however, did not extensively study this order of Mishnah. They analyzed these sources only when they were raised in other contexts.[39]

Abraham Weiss earlier had suggested that Rav's and Samuel's teachings make up the earliest stratum of *gemara*.[40] Naturally, as these masters were the major teachers of the first generation of Babylonian Amora'im, we should expect that their comments played a significant role and set the rubric for the discussion of their disciples. But what constituted their role? How did that non-literary role become translated into the literary stratum of our *gemara*? Jacob Neusner accordingly suggested that Samuel originally taught a commentary on Mishnah.[41] *Samuel's Commentary on the Mishnah* took up this suggestion and found that Samuel's preserved traditions represent the remnants of a sustained effort at commentary and mediating Mishnah in Babylonia; they do not comment upon and explain merely individual mishnayot. A significant portion of the traditions especially the brief glosses are so phrased in their most fundamental formulations as to circulate along with Mishnah. In the initial sample we found a correlation between comments briefly formulated as a gloss, the use of one of the commentary forms, e.g., B-, and the lack of a tradent. If such traditions were intended originally to circulate along with Mishnah it would have been inappropriate to cite a long attributive formula. In addition, the spread of the traditions, not on a single group of *mishnayot* and not clustered together in one place in *gemara*, indicates that the comments are not limited to one part of Mishnah.[42] Thus Samuel's commentary on Mishnah undoubtedly played a key role in the formation of *gemara's* first stratum. A reciter or disciple might cite Mishnah along with Samuel's comment.

The argument from the forms of the traditions and the role of Mishnah in early third century Iran, receives support from an extant model of what a commentary in fact did resemble. Tosefta provides us with an example of a work structured around Mishnah and which glosses, complements, and supplements M. While Tosefta at present is a literary work, it contains numerous instances of glosses, definitions and other forms which deal with Mishnah.[43]

Form-critical considerations thus provide us with tools to judge what might have existed before the transmission and redaction activity worked over the teachings. On the other hand, in the process we gain a greater insight into the concerns and needs of the circles represented in the later stages.

Let me provide an example which demonstrates several of the phenomena mentioned above.

Mishnah Ber. 7:1–2 rules that three individuals who eat together must preface their Grace After Meals with an "Invitation" to say the Grace. The summons consists of a series of refrains between a leader who invites others to Praise God and say Grace and listeners who respond. Mishnah lists those eligible and those ineligible from consideration to make up the quorum of three. Samuel (cited below) defines the category of "minors," QTN, which Mishnah excludes and he in effect rules that it refers only to certain types of minors. The ineligible minor is one who does not know the character of the blessing or, alternatively, the Referent of the blessing.[44]

Samuel's tradition represents a standard type of Mishnah-comment. Mishnah and Tosefta references to a "minor" often elicit definitions which limit the category, and the definitions usually are formulated in terms of the specific law. We find these definitions within Mishnah and Tosefta as well as in *gemara*.[45] Tosefta Ber. 5:18 in particular deals with M.Ber 7:2 and defines its instance of "minor." While its concrete criteria differ from Samuel's, it agrees with his notion that a child who has reached a certain stage, even before physical maturity, may be counted:

A minor who is able to eat an olive's amount [= the minimum amount necessary to become liable to say Grace]—they summon Grace with him; . . .
(And) they are not exacting as to a minor . . .[46]
(Tosefta Ber. 5:18, Lieberman ed., p. 28, 1s. 36–38)

There are two versions of Samuel's comment:

A. 'From when' do they start to consider him an adjunct [to make up ten] (M'YMTY 'WŚYN 'WTW SNYP)?

B. R. Avina said, R. Huna and R. Yehudah, both of them in the name of Samuel, dispute [the matter]:
One says, When he knows the character of the blessing (KDY ŠYH' YWD' TYB BRKH).
And the other said, When he knows to whom he says a blessing (ŠYH' YWD' LMY MBRK).

(y. Ber. 7:2, 11b)

A'. And until when is he considered a minor (W'D 'YKN YHYH QTN)?
B'. Said R. Avina, R. Huna and R. Yehudah, both of them in the name of Samuel, dispute [the matter]:
One said—Until he knows how to say a blessing ('D ŠHW' YWD' LBRK).
And the other said—Until he knows the character of the blessing ('D ŠHW' YWD' TYB BRKH).[47]

(Genesis Rabba 9.14)

Yerushalmi Ber. 7:2, 11b presents Samuel's tradition not as a gloss on Mishnah, but within a *sugya* which rejects Samuel's principle. The structure and contents of the *sugya* make clear that a minor to be counted for the quorum of three must achieve physical maturity. Secondly, the question which introduces Samuel's tradition, A, relates it to a different though cognate issue raised by Palestinian *Amora'im:* When is a minor counted for the quorum of ten (which calls for a special version of the Invitation to Grace)? Thirdly, the conjunction opening Samuel's comment has been altered to make it accord with the new problematic. Internal analysis of the *sugya,* including the chronology of the masters, isolation of Babylonian and Palestinian concepts, and usage of terms, demonstrates that Samuel refers not to the ostensible referent (an "adjunct to ten") but to Mishnah.[48]

Genesis Rabba 91.4, Theodore and Albeck edition 3:1111–1118, contains a *sugya* parallel to y. Ber. 7:2. While they exhibit close similarities and share the same materials, they differ in wording, formulation, and sequence. The best manuscript to this portion of Genesis Rabba is Vatican MS 60.[49] It presents Samuel's comment as a gloss on M. Ber. 7:2, that is, in the form and formulation which we posited based upon the internal analysis of y.Ber. 7:2. As indicated above, such a comment represents a standard type of Mishnah exegesis.

Form criticism thus aids in the analysis of Talmud—and more. It sensitizes the reader to transcend the finished product of the text of *gemara* and has implications as to other wider historical and literary problems. Above we discussed some of these areas. The last example focuses on the additional problem of how to find an objective criterion to compare different recensions of a *sugya*. To take the works in that example, Genesis Rabba contains numerous parallels to Yerushalmi and scholars have compared the analogues and evaluated the variations. Form criticism offers the following criterion: The version which preserves a teaching in its pristine formulation, in which the contents accord with the tradition's form, and which has experienced fewer revisions to fit a later problematic or need, that version constitutes the earlier recension. In the aforementioned text, Genesis Rabba is characterized by the above elements, and, therefore, it derives from a recension of y. earlier than the one in our extant y. Ber. 7:2. But form criticism—in this case at least—is important not just so as to identify the nature of different recensions. As in this last case, it further helps date when the tradition was worked over and integrated into a Palestinian perspective. It must have occurred sometime after the formation of Gen. R.'s recension and before the completion of PT's redaction, thus at the latter stages of the redaction of y. This finding supports the theories that Gen. R., for the halakhic materials at least, drew upon a recension of y. earlier than the one incorporated in the extant Palestinian Talmud, and that different recensions of y. circulated in different circles.[50]

Finally, the greater the number of exegetical tools available the better we are able to evaluate the exegetical work of earlier post-Talmudic commentaries. At times these "pre-moderns" were quite aware of the dynamics of *gemara*. For example, medievalists and moderns analyze Maimonides to identify his sources and principles.[51] In his comments on M. Ber. 7:2, the context of Samuel's comment on a "minor" for the Invitation to Grace, Maimonides presents the substance of Samuel's comment as a gloss on Mishnah. We cannot know if Maimonides applied Samuel's principles to Mishnah or if he believed Samuel's tradition initially addressed Mishnah itself, as we claim. But equipped with form critical sensitivities we can better appreciate the way he may have read the text of Talmud.

Form criticism along with textual-philological, source, redaction, and history of traditions criticism, can thus play an important role in the study of the literature and history of late antique Judaism. It provides a powerful microscope to focus on the contents and formation of *gemara* and offers fresh means to evaluate numerous long-standing historical and literary issues.[52]

NOTES

1. See J. Kaplan. *The Redaction of the Babylonian Talmud* (New York, 1933); H. Klein, "*Gemara* and *Sebara*," *JQR* 38 (1947–48): 67–91, "*Gemara* Quotations in *Sebara*," *JQR* 43 (1952–53):341–363. "Some General Results of the Separation of *Gemara* from *Sebara* in the Babylonian Talmud," *JSS* 3 (1958): 363–372, and "Some Methods of *Sebara*," *JQR* 50 (1959–60):124–146; especially the works of Abraham Weiss, in particular, *The Talmud in its Development* (New York, 1954), and *Studies in the Literature of the Amoraim* (New York, 1962), and his other works listed in *The Abraham Weiss Jubilee Volume*, ed. M. S. Feldblum (New York, 1964), Hebrew Section, pp. 5–11, and supplemented by Abraham Weiss, *Studies in the Talmud* (Jerusalem, 1975), pp. 252–253; M. S. Feldblum, *Talmudic Law and Literature: Tractate Gittin* (New York, 1969), and "The Impact of the 'Anonymous Sugyah' on Halakic Concepts," *PAAJR* 38 (1969): 19–28; J. N. Epstein, "Śeride Sheiltot." *Tarbiz* 6 (1935): 460–497, 7 (1936): 1–30, 8 (1937): 5–54, 10 (1939): 283–308, 13 (1942): 25–36, and *Introduction to Amoraitic Literature* (Jerusalem, 1962) [= *IAL*]: E. S. Rosenthal, "Leshemuʿat Happetiḥah Shel Bavli Taʿanit," Y. *Friedman Memorial Volume* (Jerusalem, 1974), pp. 237–248; David Weiss Halivni, *Sources and Traditions*, 1–2 (Jerusalem, 1968–1975); esp. 2: "Introduction"; Baruch M. Bokser, *Samuel's Commentary on the Mishnah, Its Nature, Forms, and Content,* Part One, (Leiden, 1975); Israel Francus, "Additions and Parallels in T. B. Bava Qamma VII," *BIA* 12 (1974): 43–63 [see also *Tarbiz* 38 (1969): 338–353, 43 (1973–74): 34–45, and *Sinai* 36 (71) (1972): 32–45, 37 (73) (1973): 24–49]; and cp. Ch. Albeck, *Introduction to the Talmud, Babli and Yerushalmi* (Tel Aviv, 1969), pp. 452–596. See also Louis Jacobs, *Studies in Talmudic Logic and Methodology* (London, 1961), pp. 53–164, Jacob Ephrathi, *The Sevoraic Period and Its Literature* (Petach-Tikva, 1973), and the analyses of all the above and additional literature in Jacob Neusner, ed., *The Formation of the Babylonian Talmud* (Leiden, 1970); David Goodblatt, "The Babylonian Talmud," *Aufstieg und Niedergang der römischen Welt*, [*ANRW*] II.19.2 (Berlin, 1979).), especially Ch. 4; and Shamma Friedman, "A Critical Study of Yevamot X with a Methodological Introduction," in *Texts and Studies, Analecta Judaica* [of the Jewish Theological Seminary of America], vol. 1 (New York, 1977), pp. 275–441. On the Palestinian Talmud see the aforementioned works, esp. those by Abraham Weiss, David Weiss Halivni, J. N. Epstein, and the numerous studies by Saul Lieberman, especially, *Talmud of Caesarea* [= *Supl. to Tarbiz*, 2] (Jerusalem, 1931), and Baruch M. Bokser, "An Annotated Bibliographical Guide to the Study of the Palestinian Talmud," *ANRW* II.19.2 (Berlin, 1979), especially Chs. 8–13, and the literature cited there.

2. See e.g. Wayne Sibley Towner, *The Rabbinic "Enumeration of Scriptural*

Examples" (Leiden, 1973), Saul Lieberman, *Tosefta Ki-fshuṭah* [= *TK*] 1- (New York, 1955), passim; Jacob Neusner, *History of the Mishnaic Law of Purities*, 22 vols. (Leiden, 1974–77), especially vol. 22, and "History and Structure: The Case of Mishnah," *JAAR* 45 (1977): 161–192; William S. Green, "What's in a Name? The Problematic of Rabbinic 'Biography,' " in *Approaches to Ancient Judaism*, ed. William S. Green [= *Brown Judaic Studies*, 1] (Missoula, 1978); Goodblatt, *ANRW*, Ch. IV, esp. 3; Bokser, *ANRW*, and "Redaction Criticism of Rabbinic Literature: The Case of Hanina Ben Dosa," (in preparation), and the literature cited there.

3. See fns. 1–2, especially the works of J. N. Epstein, Abraham Weiss, David Weiss Halivni, and Lieberman. See Goodblatt, *ANRW*, and Bokser, *ANRW*.

4. See Towner; Joseph Heinemann, *Aggadah and Its Development* (Jerusalem, 1974); Jacob Neusner, *Development of a Legend* (Leiden, 1970), *Rabbinic Traditions about the Pharisees before 70*, 3 vols. (Leiden, 1971), *Eliezer Ben Hyrcanus*, 2 vols. (Leiden, 1973), and *Purities*, and "The Study of Religion as the Study of Tradition: Judaism," *History of Religions* 14 (1975): 191–206. Cp. Douglas A. Knight, *Discovering the Traditions of Israel* [SBL Dissertation Series 9] (Missoula, 1975).

5. See the works of J. N. Epstein, *Introduction to the Text of the Mishnah* [= *ITM*] (Jerusalem, 1948, 1964), *Introduction to Tannaitic Literature* (Jerusalem, 1957), and *IAL*; Lieberman, *TK*; the works of Neusner; Bokser, *Samuel's Commentary*; and especially Goodblatt, *ANRW*, IV.1, and Bokser *ANRW*, especially VIII.C and X.

6. See nn.7–17 and especially the reference to Saldarini.

7. Joseph Heinemann, *Prayer in the Period of the Tanna'im and the Amora'im* (Jerusalem, 1964), especially pp. 9–16, 29–51, in English rev. ed., *Prayer in the Talmud* (Berlin, 1977), esp. pp. 1–12, 37–68; Neusner, *Purities*, vol. 21, and "Form and Meaning in Mishnah," *JAAR* 45 (1977): 27–54.

8. Heinemann, *Prayer*, pp. 121–137, in English rev. ed., pp. 193–207; Neusner, "Form and Meaning"; and G. M. Tucker, "Form Criticism, OT," *Interpreter's Dictionary of the Bible, Supplementary Volume* (Nashville, 1976), pp. 342–344. See also Edgar V. McKnight, *What Is Form Criticism?* (Philadelphia, 1969, 1971); Gene M. Tucker, *Form Criticism of the Old Testament* (Philadelphia, 1971, 1976), esp. pp. 1–21, 54–57, 70–71; John H. Hayes, ed., *Old Testament Form Criticism* (San Antonio, 1974); and the literature cited in these works.

9. See especially Neusner, "Form and Meaning," e.g., p. 53, fn. 3, and "History and Structure"; Tucker, whose observations that a form does not necessarily reflect an actual life setting, accords with Neusner's analysis of the dispute form, in *Pharisees*, 3:80f.; Hayes, esp. pp. xviii, 54–55, 136; and see below and the text thereto. Our observation here somewhat differently applies to the use of talmudic terminology which has been extensively analyzed. See, e.g., Wilhelm Bacher, *Die exegetische Terminologie der jüd-*

ischen Traditionsliteratur (Leipzig, 1899. Repr. Darmstadt, 1965), and in Hebrew edition, as *Erchē Midrash*, 2 vols. (Tel Aviv, 1923. Repr. Jerusalem, 1970), and Epstein, *ITM*, e.g., pp. 246, fn. 1, and 249–251.

10. Weiss, *Literature of the Amoraim*. See Bokser, *Samuel's Commentary*, pp. 2–3; Goodblatt, *ANRW*, IV.2; David Weiss Halivni, "Talmudic Criticism," lecture delivered at the Max Richter Conversation, Providence, R.I. June, 1977, and *Sources*, vol. 3 (Jerusalem, 1982).

11. E.g., J. Kaplan, and H. Klein.

12. Weiss, *Literature of the Amoraim*. See Goodblatt, in Neusner, ed., *Formation of the Babylonian Talmud*, pp. 95–103, and *ANRW*, IV.2.

13. Shamma Friedman, "Some Structural Patterns of *Sugyot* in the Babylonian Talmud," Sixth World Congress of Jewish Studies. *Abstracts* (Jerusalem, 1975), p. C-31, and in "A Critical Study."

14. Cp. J. Florsheim, "Rav Ḥisda as Exegetor of Tannaitic Sources," *Tarbiz* 41 (1971): 24–48, and Bokser, *Samuel's Commentary*, pp. 3f., fn. 8. Thus Anthony J. Saldarini, " 'Form Criticism' of Rabbinic Literature," *JBL* 96 (1977): 257–274, does not focus on the application to *gemara*.

15. Heinemann, *Prayer*, especially pp. 101, 114–118, in English rev. ed. pp. 159–160, 182–189, and cp. Hayes, pp. 200–205. See also the references in n. 8.

16. See Towner.

17. Neusner, *Pharisees*, 3:5–179, *Purities*, especially vols. 21–22. See also Gary G. Porton, *The Traditions of Rabbi Ishmael*, I- (Leiden, 1976–); Charles Primus, *Aqiva's Contribution to the Law of Zera'im* (Leiden, 1977); Tzvee Zahavy, *The Tradition of Eleazar Ben Azariah* [= *Brown Judaic Studies*, 2] (Missoula, Montana, 1977); and William S. Green, *The Traditions of Joshua ben Hananiah*, 1 (Leiden 1981).

18. Bokser, *Samuel's Commentary*, and *Part Two* (Leiden 1975). See also Neusner, *Pharisees*, 3:101–179.

19. The initial sample, published in *Samuel's Commentary, Part One*, consists of Samuel's comments on M. Zera'im, less Berakhot. (Berakhot does not integrally belong to Zera'im. See Sussmann, "Babylonian Sugyot to the Orders Zera'im and Ṭohorot," (Ph.D. dissertation, Hebrew University, 1969) [In press, Israel Academy of Sciences and Humanities], pp. 71f., fn. 2.) The 51 items are from y. Zera'im and throughout BT, wherever b. cites *mishnayot* from Zera'im. On the nature of the sample, see p. 4. Pp. 13–162 extensively analyze the pericopae and traditions; Ch. 2, especially pp. 174–177, focuses on the spread of the traditions; Ch. 3, pp. 178–186, analyzes the types of comments; Ch. 4, pp. 187–206, examines the literary phrasing of the tradition; Ch. 5, pp. 207–215, focuses on the modes of presentation, juxtaposed or alone; and Ch. 6, pp. 216–238, traces the role of the tradents and the history of the transmission of Samuel's comments and then correlates the results of the several chapters. Samuel's *Commentary, Part Two*, encompasses Berakhot. On the B- form, see pp. 188–190. Note Baruch Levine, *In the Presence of the Lord* (Leiden, 1974), pp. 118–120, indepen-

dently identified this form in a fourth to third century BCE Punic inscription.

20. The Tradition reads: 'R. Yehudah in the name of Samuel, "The upper belong to the poor"—the white ones (BLBYNYM). "And the lower belong to the householder"—the green ones (BYRWQYN). "R. Meir says, All belong to the poor because doubtful gleanings are considered gleanings"—for a harvest cannot end without some green ones'. See *Samuel's Commentary*, pp. 28–31, especially fn. 61, on the attributive formula.

21. See also pp. 188–190.

22. Pp. 190–192.

23. See *Samuel's Commentary*, pp. 50–54, and below text to n. 26.

24. See above n. 9.

25. Pp. 97–101, esp. fn. 275; 142–145 (note the observation of Elijah Gaon of Vilna); and 190–192, and fn. 7. Note the surprise of Israel Francus, "Berurim UBeurim BeTalmud," *Sinai* 71 (1972): 34, fn. 9. Cp. *Samuel's Commentary*, pp. 34–38, 47–49.

26. Pp. 50–54, esp. fn. 127.

27. See n. 28. Cp. *Samuel's Commentary*, pp. 157–162.

28. E.g., pp. 21–25, 235–236, and fn. 18.

29. See H. Klein's various works, especially "Some Methods of *Sebara*," p. 146, cited in n. 1, to which add "The Significance of the Technical Expression 'l' 'y 'ttmr in the Babylonian Talmud," *Tarbiz* 31 (1961): 23–42; Abraham Goldberg, "The Sources and Development of the Sugya in the Babylonian Talmud," *Tarbiz*, 22 (1962–63): 143–152; Bokser, *Samuel's Commentary*, p. 236 and fn. 19; and Goodblatt, *ANRW*, IV.3.C.

30. See e.g. below, text to nn. 44–47.

31. *Samuel's Commentary*, pp. 41–44, esp. fns. 107–108.

32. See the full analysis, pp. 41–44, esp. 44, and 214, esp. fn. 6, and 235.

33. See also pp. 161–162, 213–215 (and the references there to additional analyses on pp. 31–34, 60–63), 213, fn. 5; and 235; and *Part Two*, Ch. 7, and Ch. 10, fn. 17.

34. Pp. 157–162; see also p. 234. Below we provide an example of a gloss on Mishnah which appears as a comment on an amoraic issue. See nn. 44–47 and text thereto.

35. See above, nn. 1–2. Note esp. Hayes, pp. 51–56, 67–69, 101, 144–148.

36. David Goodblatt, *Rabbinic Instruction in Sasanian Babylonia* (Leiden, 1975). See also Goodblatt, *ANRW*, IV.2.C. Cp. Knight, pp. 9–10, 27, 70–78, 153, 160, 172, 390, 397. In general compare the historical uses of form criticism in Rudolf Bultmann and Karl Kundsin, *Form Criticism* (New York, 1934, 1962), and in the numerous examples in Hayes.

37. See *Samuel's Commentary*, pp. 1–2. The early masters also taught autonomous teachings and at times relied upon sources other than the Mishnah of Rabbi Judah. See n. 38. At the completion of the comprehensive analysis of all of Samuel's traditions we will have exact data on Samuel's agendum. We will be able to compare, first, the nature of Samuel's comments in different

tractates and orders of Mishnah and, second, each of the latter with the number and nature of comments not generated by Mishnah. *Samuel's Commentary, Part Two*, treats this problem in terms of Berakhot. Cp. Bernard S. Jackson, "Review," *JSS* 23 (1978): 118.

38. Bokser, *Samuel's Commentary*, 237–238. Epstein, in the *Introduction to the Text of the Mishnah*, pp. 166–404, esp. 353 examines the role of Mishnah in Palestinian and Babylonian circles and how it became an unrivalled authoritative source by the third generation of Amoraim. See esp. pp. 165, 166–352, esp. 349, 352, and Baruch M. Bokser, "Jacob N. Epstein's *Introduction to the Text of the Mishnah*," in *The Modern Study of the Mishnah*, ed. Jacob Neusner (Leiden, 1973), pp. 13–36, esp. 22, 32f. Epstein, pp. 212–216, and others point to Samuel's *baraitot* which explain or gloss Mishnah. See Goodblatt, *Rabbinic Instruction*, pp. 132–135. Evidence suggests that in Palestine some masters did not immediately accept the authority of Mishnah. S. Lieberman, *Siphre Zuṭṭa* (New York, 1968) demonstrates that the Palestinian circles responsible for Sifre Zutta accepted the authority of a corpus other than that of Rabbi's Mishnah. David Weiss Halivni, "Talmudic Criticism: A Historical Review," lecture delivered at The Association for Jewish Studies, Fifth Annual Conference, Sunday, October 21, 1973, Harvard University, Cambridge, Mass., suggests that Palestinian *Amoraʾim*, who were disciples of earlier, Tannaitic masters, and who believed that their teacher's views were not sufficiently or properly represented in Mishnah, more freely differed with Mishnah than their counterparts in Babylonia. See also A. Goldberg, "The Use of the Tosefta and the *Baraitha* of the School of Samuel by the Babylonian Amora Rava," *Tarbiz* 40 (1971): 144–157, esp. 147–50, and fn. 11.

39. Sussmann, passim, esp. pp. 242, 273–277, 287, fn. 120. See Bokser, *Samuel's Commentary*, pp. 3f.

40. Abraham Weiss, *The Babylonian Talmud as a Literary Unit* (New York, 1943), pp. 1–44, especially 6–14. See his other works, references to which are in n. 1, above, and *Samuel's Commentary*, p. 3, fn. 6.

41. Jacob Neusner, *History of the Jews of Babylonia*, 5 vols. (Leiden, 1966–1970), 1^2: 162–163; 2: 88, 232–236, 284, fn. 2.

42. See n. 19, above.

43. See Moshe D. Herr, "Tosefta," *Encyclopaedia Judaica*, s.v., 15: 1283–1285; Jacob Neusner, *Purities*, esp. vol. 21, and "Form and Meaning," p. 30. See Baruch M. Bokser, *Samuel's Commentary, Part Two*, and "From Mishnah to *Gemara*."

44. For a comprehensive analysis of this text, see Baruch M. Bokser, "Minor For Zimmun And Recensions of Yerushalmi," *AJS Review* 4 (1979), and the literature cited there. M. Ber. 7: 3 gives the opening formulae for the Invitations. There are two recensions of Samuel's tradition, one in y. Ber. 7: 2, 11b, and the other in Gen. R. 91.4. Each contains two reports of Samuel's teaching. Apparently in the transmission one of the criteria became corrupted so that we have the two definitions in our text and a third, "Until he may know how to say a blessing." See below, text to n. 47.

45. E.g. M. Suk. 2: 18; 3: 15; M. Hag. 1: 1 and T. Hag. 1: 2–3, Lieberman edition, pp. 374–376, ll. 5–22.
46. On variants in Tosefta and a correlation of amoraic comments with both readings, see "Minor For Zimmun."
47. Gen. R. 91, in Theodore and Albeck ed. 3: 1113–14, though we follow the superior reading in Vatican Codex 60, p. 332. See n. 49.
48. For these and additional factors see "Minor For Zimmun."
49. *Midrash Bereshit Rabba, Codex Vatican 60* (Ms. Ebr. 60). *A Page Index* by A. P. Sherry (Jerusalem: Makor, 1972). Albeck in his edition of Gen. R. did not make use of this MS. Codex Vatican 30, in general the best MS, deletes this portion of Gen. R. On the textual history see "Minor For a Zimmun."
50. See Lewis M. Barth, *An Analysis of Vatican 30* (Cincinnati, 1973), pp. 61–62 and the literature cited there, and Bokser, "Minor For Zimmun."
51. See e.g. Isadore Twersky, *Rabad of Posquieres* (Cambridge, 1962); J. Levinger, *Darkhei hamaḥshavah hahilkhatit shel haRambam* (Jerusalem, 1965); and Jacob I. Dienstag, "Maimonides, Moses, As Halakhist," *EJ*, s.v. 11: 764–768, especially 765.
52. I thank Professors Joseph Dan, Hebrew University, Jacob Milgrom, University of California, Berkeley, Jacob Neusner, Brown University, and Gary G. Porton, University of Illinois, Champaign-Urbana for their critical comments on earlier drafts of this paper. I am appreciative, as well, of the improvements suggested by Professor Geza Vermes, University of Oxford.

III

THE PALESTINIAN TALMUD

7

The Palestinian Talmud

Louis Ginzberg

No student of the post-biblical literature of the Jews can fail to be struck by the fact that it is predominantly interpretative and commentative. At first sight this seems to be rather strange, for Israel's classic literature, the Bible, with all its richness and variety of literary forms, contains not the slightest trace of the form most favored by the writers of later periods. The literature of a people, however, is but a mirror of the ideas which rule that people, and in post-Biblical times the idea of "the Book" was all-powerful among the Jews. Nehemiah records a covenant entered into under the guidance of Ezra: "To walk in God's law which was given by Moses, the servant of God, and to observe and do all the commandments of the Lord our God and His ordinances and His statutes." Whether we accept the traditional view of Ezra as "the restorer of the Torah" or follow the opinion of some modern Biblical scholars who picture him as the creator of a new movement, the significance of this *covenant* cannot be overestimated. By this solemn act a "book"—the Pentateuch—became the written constitution of the new commonwealth, its code of laws, and its way of life. But the dead letter needs to be made living by interpretation. Hence the interpretative character of the post-Biblical writings.

Old Talmudic sources call the spiritual leaders of Israel in the centuries between Ezra (about 450) and the age of the Maccabeans (175) *Soferim,* which means "men of the Book," interpreters of sacred Scripture, and not, as it is usually translated, "scribes." The most momentous

Reprinted by permission of The Jewish Publication Society of America from *On Jewish Law and Lore*, Philadelphia, PA, 1955.

event in the century and a half after Ezra was the conquest of Palestine by the Greeks. Another century and a half had elapsed before the Maccabeans freed the Jews from the Macedonian tyrants. This victory was made possible by the work of the *Soferim,* who had succeeded in establishing a normative Judaism that was able to withstand the allure of Greek thought and the attraction of Hellenic life. These *Soferim* had not only safeguarded "The Book," but had, by their interpretations and comments, made it workable under the new conditions that arose in Palestine with the arrival of the Greeks.

The enormous mass of "interpretation" thus accumulated during the centuries of the *Soferim* was further augmented in the century of the Jewish free state under the Hasmoneans, and this for more than one reason. With the final victory of "the pious over the wicked" the pendulum swung in the opposite direction. The problem now was no longer how to adjust the new ideas of Hellas to the spiritual inheritance of Israel nor how to respond to the demands made by foreign ways of life; it was actually the reverse. The strong national feeling engendered by the victorious wars in defense of Jewish religion and Jewish morals led to ordinances and regulations aimed at the complete isolation of Israel from the surrounding world. At the same time, the development of commerce and trade under the Hasmonean rulers peremptorily called for the building up of a code of civil law. The few rules found in Scripture bearing on this branch of the law were not sufficient and could not be made so, not even by the most subtle reasoning or the cleverest interpretation.

The time was certainly ripe for legislation. Every student of the history of jurisprudence knows that great as are the possibilities of interpretation and commentation, an old code has limits beyond which it cannot be stretched. When the breaking-point is reached, legislation comes to the rescue, abrogating obsolete laws and adding new ones which conform to the demands of the age. But how dare one tamper with sacred Scripture, in which the Divine Will is revealed? The sages and scholars of that time—about the middle of the Hasmonean era—had the necessary temerity. They took a very important step towards formulating what might be called, *de facto* though not *de jure,* a new code—they created the *Mishnah.*

To estimate adequately the radical changes that the Mishnah introduced, it is best to compare the mishnaic method of study with the midrashic (exegetical) method of the *Soferim*. These earlier scholars knew only one subject of study—Scripture; their comments and interpretations were interwoven with the text interpreted and commented upon. The creators of the Mishnah detached the enormous bulk of unwieldy material from the Biblical passages and studied it independently. The new method was not only highly practical, since the numerous laws based on interpretations of Scriptural passages could now be studied in a concise and systematic way, but it also gave "the oral law" an independent existence. Hitherto the laws, practices, and customs that had no scriptural basis could only be studied by being connected in one way or another with some text in Scripture. Yet many of these orally transmitted laws and customs were as old as the oldest found in Scripture and were no less revered by the people. In the mishnaic method of study, a difference between the written Torah and the oral Torah hardly exists. The origins of the Mishnah and the rise at the same time of a militant Sadduceeism which reacted against over-emphasis of the oral law certainly stand in some causal nexus, though it is hard to tell which is cause and which effect.

The final compilation of the Mishnah toward the end of the second century C.E. by the Patriarch R. Judah completed a work at which scholars had labored for about three hundred years. While the Mishnah was in process of formation, two great national catastrophes overtook the Jews—the fall of the Jewish state in 70 C.E. and the Hadrianic persecutions after the defeat of Bar Kochba in 133 C.E. These sorrowful events were not without influence upon the final form of the Mishnah. One is safe in saying that had it not been for the political disorders and persecutions, the Mishnah would have been completed long before the time of R. Judah, and would have been a much closer approximation to a code. For it has been well said that truth becomes more liable to change as the distance from its origin across the ages lengthens. In the centuries that elapsed from the beginnings of the Mishnah until its completion, differences of opinion multiplied so greatly that the original aim of offering the doctors of law a norm for their decisions could be only partially realized. Of the sum total of five hundred and twenty-three chapters of the Mishnah, there are only six which contain no controversies. Is further proof needed of the uncertainty of tradition at the time of R. Judah?

The prolonged delay in codification had a further important bearing

on the character of the Mishnah. Almost one-fifth of *our* Mishnah
consists of laws and rulings concerning matters that at the time of its
completion no longer had any bearing on contemporary life—they were
studied but not practiced. This was true not only of the sections of the
Mishnah dealing with sacrifices and other Temple laws, all of which
became obsolete with the destruction of the Sanctuary, but also of that
part of the Mishnaic criminal code which dealt with capital punishment.
It is well-known that capital punishment had not been exercised by
Jewish courts after Palestine became a Roman province. An interesting
illustration of the difference between the practical and the merely
theoretical parts of the Mishnah is the following statement found in it.
"R. Tarfon and R. Akiba said: If we had been members of the Sanhedrin
nobody would ever have been executed." To which a very pertinent remark was made by one of their disciples to the effect that they
would have caused bloodshed in Israel; meaning that murder is prevented by fear of punishment, and that when fear disappears crime increases.

Of course, the severe criminal code of the Bible was interpreted in
later times in accordance with the humaneness of Pharisaic Judaism, but
it can be assumed that many Mishnaic modifications probably date from
a period when the problem had only academic importance. Since an
integral part of Jewish piety is the study of divine revelation in Scripture
and of the interpretation of revelation apart from its direct bearing
upon life, the more extensively parts of the divine revelation lost their
application, the more lovingly they were studied.

To speak of the Mishnah as a code would, as we have seen, not be
correct, but to consider it only as a text book of "the oral law" would
be still less accurate. The main purpose of the work is to teach the
authoritative norm. While differences of opinion are frequent in the
Mishnah, they are always presented in a way that clearly indicates
which is authoritative. The accepted view is either given anonymously
or introduced by the formula: "But the sages say." The most distinguishing mark of a code is that a people accept it as the authoritative statement of its *corpus juris*. The Mishnah might therefore be described as a
close approximation of a code. Its authority was never seriously challenged either during the lifetime of Rabbi Judah or in the succeeding
generations. This authority was due not only to personal distinction and
his high position as the Patriarch, political as well as religious head of

the Jews, but also to the fact that the Mishnah was, in the words of the Talmud, produced "by Rabbi Judah and his court," i. e., the cooperative work of all the prominent scholars of that period. It was not the product of a legislature but it was the work of judicial legislation.

With the proclamation of the Pentateuch as a code the *Soferim*—the interpreters—had arisen, and with the acceptance of the Mishnah as the norm of the oral law came the *Amoraim*—the expounders. The activity of the former had led to the creation of the Mishnah; that of the latter gave us the Talmud, or to be accurate, the Talmuds, Palestinian and Babylonian. Since the Babylonian Talmud, by virtue of its greater influence upon Judaism and the Jews, is the more important of the two, and is therefore usually spoken of as *the* Talmud, it shall engage our attention first.

The history of the Jews in Babylonia for almost seven centuries from the time of Ezra and Nehemiah, about the middle of the fifth century B.C.E., to the rise of the academies for Jewish learning about the first quarter of the third century of the common era, is shrouded in deep darkness. A few clay tablets of the first century after Ezra containing the names of Jewish farmers and craftsmen as parties or witnesses to documents of the Gentile banking house of Murashu Brothers; a report by Josephus of an attempt by Jews in the district of Nehardea to achieve independence; and the names of four native Babylonians who came to prominence in Palestine because of their learning and scholarship—that is all we know about Babylonian Jewry for many centuries. No trace whatsoever is to be found of any cultural or literary activity among them. We have not the slightest reason for the assumption that either Hillel the Babylonian, one of the most illustrious names in the history of post-Biblical Judaism, or Nahum the Mede, who filled the position of city magistrate in Jerusalem in the last years of the Jewish State, received their training in their native country. The first signs of spiritual and cultural life among Babylonian Jews become visible about the middle of the second century, and one can assume that this new life was infused into the Jewry of Babylon by the arrival there of the Palestinian emigrants who fled Palestine because of the Hadrianic persecutions then raging in the Holy Land, especially in the south, the home of Jewish culture and learning. For the understanding of the relation between the two Talmuds, their striking likeness, and their almost equally striking diversity, the pre-Amoraic activity of Palestinian scholars in Babylonia is of great importance.

The two Talmuds have much in common, both in form and content. Both are huge commentaries on the Mishnah, and of course contain a good deal of common matter. In addition, the personal relationships between the scholars of the two countries was a very close one. Interchange of opinions and ideas between them was carried on without interruption through the so-called "Travellers," emissaries sent from the Babylonian academies to those of Palestine and vice versa. Yet the dissimilarities between the two "Commentaries" are enormous, and as their likeness extends to form and content alike so also do their dissimilarities. The non-Hebrew portions of the Palestinian Talmud are in Western Aramaic; those of the Babylonian Talmud in Eastern Aramaic. The first has a large number of Greek words; the other a goodly number of Persian. The Palestinian Talmud is more concise; its discussions are much less diffuse. More important, however, than the differences in form, are those which reflect differences in traditions and in economic, political and cultural conditions that prevailed in the countries of their origin.

To understand adequately the relation between the two Talmuds, one must of course have a clear idea of the activity of the "Expounders" of the Mishnah, an activity that culminated in the creation of these two monumental compilations. Whether we consider the Mishnah a code or only an approach to a code, we must not lose sight of the pre-eminence of the written Torah which has never ceased to be the pivotal assumption of Judaism. The covenant of Sinai has remained the Magna Charta. For many—one might be inclined to say most—of the commandments in the Pentateuch, however, neither mode nor measure is laid down. This task was left to the recognized spiritual leaders of the people— called by different names at different periods: Soferim, Tannaim, or Amoraim; leaders, who sought to interpret and define the intention of the Divine will as expressed in revealed writings. Hence the "Expounders" did not limit their study of the Mishnah to interpretation and explanation. The tracing back of the contents of the Mishnah to its origin, Scripture, forms a principal, perhaps the essential, part of both Talmuds.

The main source for this branch of the Expounders' study was the collections of exegetical comments on the Pentateuch by the scholars of former generations, the Tannaim. These collections, some small, some large, were very numerous. None of them, however, attained the degree of authority achieved by the Mishnah of R. Judah. While the latter became the standard work of study in all academies, Palestinian as well as Babylonian, the study of the Midrashim, as these collections are called in talmudic sources, remained more or less a matter of individual choice. Some of them, and among them those that were brought to Babylonia by the Palestinian immigrants during the Hadrianic persecutions, became very popular in the Babylonian academies, others enjoyed no less popularity with the Palestinian scholars. The use of different sources for the elucidation of the Mishnah inevitably led to differences in interpretation of the laws contained in it.

The study of the Mishnah in the light of the Biblical exegesis of the Tannaim is in a sense an attempt at an historical approach, though chiefly dictated by dogmatic interest—to establish Biblical authority for many of the laws laid down in the Mishnah. Of much greater interest to us for the understanding of both Talmuds is another branch of amoraic study in connection with the Mishnah. R. Judah, for practical reasons, eliminated much material that had been available for inclusion in the Mishnah. Admiring disciples maintained that by sound reasoning any doubtful case of law might be inferred from the material included in the Mishnah by R. Judah. But it is nevertheless true that very important laws are not to be found there, and that furthermore, those which are included are often not given in their historical development. This omission was purposeful; much of the dicta of the Mishnah was presented anonymously in order that it might be given the weight and authority which individual opinions do not command. For a work designed to approximate a code this was, of course, the ideal manner of presentation, but to the student who is interested in the origin and development of law, the Mishnah does not offer what is desired. Several younger contemporaries of R. Judah tried to correct the omissions, not only collecting a huge mass of material which had been excluded from the Mishnah but often also giving us the historical development of many of its laws. These collections, like the Midrashim mentioned above, were very numerous and form a substantial part of both Talmuds. The study by the Amoraim of the *Barayyata,* as these collections are called in the Babylonian Talmud, i. e. of the "extraneous" teachings and dicta of the Tannaim not found in the Mishnah, not only enriched their knowledge but also gave them some degree of independence towards the Mishnah. An Amora would hardly dare to oppose the Mishnah without the support of an old authority found in a Baraita. The discrepancies between the Mishnah and the "extraneous" teachings also afforded subtle minds an opportunity to display their acumen in reconciling apparently conflicting views. It was true of both Midrashim and of much of "extraneous" teachings that their lack of universally acknowledged authority led to many differences between the two Talmuds. Some of the Baraitot were highly thought of in Palestine but given little attention in the Babylonian schools, and conversely, the Babylonian scholars had "extraneous" teachings that were almost unknown in Palestine.

Midrash and Baraita were the basic materials used in Palestine as well as in Babylonia upon which their respective Talmuds were built, but the fabrics, while very similar, were not identical; hence the differences in the final products.

Even the Mishnah, the nucleus of both Talmuds, was not identical in both countries. Its compiler labored at this work for a great part of his long life, hence, the Mishnah reached posterity in several versions. The one used in the Palestinian schools was not identical with that recognized by the Babylonian academies; and these primary textual divergences were bound to result in divergences of interpretation. Many others have their origin in secondary divergences of text. In oral transmission, explanations, amplifications, and suggested emendations are apt to creep in. Granted that the Mishnah was reduced to writing by its compiler—a very moot question still!—we know for certain that as late as the end of the Geonic period, about the beginning of the eleventh century, the *oral* law, comprising primarily Mishnah and Talmud, was still taught *orally*. Consequently the text "expounded" by the Palestinian scholars was not always the same as that employed by their Babylonian colleagues. As the two Talmuds are commentaries upon the Mishnah, they would of course differ in their comments wherever their texts differed.

"Search it (the Torah) and search it again" says an old sage, "for everything is in it." One sometimes finds what one seeks but scarcely ever that for which one does not look. Objective interpretation of laws and authoritative dicta is an ideal toward which honest interpreters strive—it can, however, never be achieved completely. It is conditioned by emotion as well as by intellect.

Ample evidence of this striving for an unobtainable ideal is found in both Talmuds. The Babylonian, however, was at a disadvantage inasmuch as the Mishnah, Midrash, and Baraita, the three pillars upon which both Talmuds rest, were constructed of Palestinian material. The time that elapsed between the completion of the Mishnah and the completion of the Palestinian Talmud, roughly about two centuries, did not witness any violent changes in the economic, political, or cultural conditions of Palestinian Jewry. Its adjustment to the set of laws and customs which gave us the Mishnah was comparatively easy. Quite different were the conditions in Babylonia. Not only had Babylonian Jewry to grapple with the problem of adapting itself to the Palestinian Mishnah, but while occupied with this difficult task it was subjected to a radical change of government which was to be of far-reaching consequences for Babylonian Jews. When the Sassanids came to power, Zoroastrianism became the ruling religion in Babylonia and its Jewry had to struggle not only for its economic existence but also for its religious life, which was threatened by a hostile and aggressive priesthood.

Whatever branch of talmudic law or doctrine we study, the observation is forced upon us that numerous differences between the two Talmuds reflect the differences between Palestinian and Babylonian life and thought. Here are a few concrete examples. Important in the economic and domestic life of the Jews were the taxes which were collected almost entirely from levies on the products of the soil, for the support of the Priests and Levites who were originally the sole ministers of religion. Though the Priests and Levites were gradually outnumbered by lay teachers and ministers, the Biblical laws concerning tithes and other priestly dues were not abolished but remained in force in Palestine throughout the talmudic period. In Babylonia, however, as the result of the fearful depression precipitated by the protracted wars between the Persians and Romans during the third century, this set of priestly laws was abrogated. R. Johanan, the famous leader of Palestinian Jewry at the middle of that century, informs us of the important change that took place in Babylonia during his lifetime with regard to the Levitical tithes and the priestly share in the crops. Less than a century later a Babylonian Amora states: "Now the people do not give to the priest the first wool shorn," and we may add, nor his other dues.

The same Babylonian Amora also mentions the prevailing opinion of his time, supported by authority of the Babylonian Tanna, Judah ben

Batira. This held that "The words of the Torah do not become impure"; thus an important element of Levitical purity was abolished. In Palestine vigorous insistence was placed upon a ritual bath after pollution preparatory to prayer or study. Similarly, the Palestinian authorities insisted upon washing the hands before prayer, while the Babylonians made light of it and strongly censured the delay of prayer on account of lack of water.

The disappearance of the Levitical laws of purity in Babylonia and their retention in Palestine can in part be explained by differences in the relationship between Jew and Gentile in these two countries. Palestinian law was largely war legislation, for Judaism and Paganism were locked in combat for many centuries. In Babylonia this state of war never existed. Says a Palestinian author of the second century, "Israel in the diaspora worships idols in all innocence; whenever there be a wedding among the pagans of the town, the entire Jewry participate in the wedding feast, easing their conscience by bringing with them their food and drinks." Less than a century later, a Babylonian Amora remarks "The Gentiles in the diaspora—Babylonia—are not to be considered idolators in the real sense of the word." Hence follows the rather lenient attitude of the Babylonian Talmud towards the old Palestinian laws which had their origin in the desire to avoid any dealings with a pagan which might encourage him in his idolatrous practices. From the Babylonian Nahum of Media to his countryman, Samuel, this tendency is marked. The Mishnah teaches that three days before a heathen holiday, no merchandise may be sold to the pagan since he might use it for idolatrous practices. Samuel limited the ban to the day of the festival. Certain old Palestinian regulations which had their origin in the economic self-defense of the Jews against the attempt of the Greco-Roman world to push them out of Palestine were transferred to Babylonia, but there they were interpreted on a purely religious basis. For instance, selling cattle to a heathen who would use them in tilling the ground was prohibited in Palestine, obviously for economic reasons. In Babylonia this law was regarded as a measure to insure the Biblical commandment that the animal world should rest on the Sabbath.

No other parts of the two Talmuds differ as much as those dealing with civil law—for lack of any better term I use "civil." These are the sections contained in the first three treatises of the fourth order of the Mishnah and Talmud. Theoretically, Rabbinic Judaism does not recognize a distinction between religious and secular law. Whatever law is found in the Pentateuch is Divine revelation and has supreme authority; it is inflexible and can never be abrogated. In practice, however, Jewish civil law in post-Biblical times shows in its very earliest stages the greatest independence of Scripture and hence the greatest possibilities for development. Without detailed examination of the principle that guided Jewish jurists in building up this branch of the law, there is one observation to be made. The distinction between religious law and civil law is to be found in the fact that the former expresses the permanent relation between God and man, the latter the changeable relation between man and man. It is true that private property is sanctioned by Divine Will as revealed in Scripture, but the concept of property in Jewish civil law is decidedly social. The Roman praetor constituted his praetorian law *propter utilitatem publicam* and similarly the Jewish jurists taught "that the entire Torah was given for the purpose of establishing harmony in human society." If for the welfare of society it becomes necessary to disregard the interest of the individual, "the court" has the power and the duty to act accordingly.

The potentialities for the free development of court-made legislation were enormous, and in both Palestine and Babylonia this development was closely linked with the prevailing economic and political conditions. Palestine retained its agricultural character throughout the talmudic period, while in Babylonia, commercial activity among the Jews expanded noticeably during the same period. Talmudic law in Palestine was therefore dictated by the interests of the farmer; whereas in Babylonia commerce was given due consideration. A few examples will illustrate the difference.

Children: Potestas patris, which in Biblical times must have been very strong, as shown in the law concerning the rebellious son, is not to be found in rabbinic law. The two exceptions are the father's right to the earnings of his minor daughter and that of giving her in marriage. The latter "right" was recognized but strongly objected to on ethical grounds and hence rarely exercised. The complete emancipation of the adult daughter from the jurisdiction of the father is taken for granted in Palestinian as well as Babylonian sources and was established centuries before the compilation of the Mishnah. With regard to males, Palestinian authorities recognized the right of the father to the earnings of his children, male and female, minor or adult, as long as they were supported by him, while the Babylonians denied the father's right to the earnings of his adult children even when they were supported by him. The small farmer in Palestine could not easily afford to pay for the labor supplied by his grown children who were still supported by him; the merchant in Babylonia did not find it too arduous to compensate them for their labor. Another difference is the right of the father to the compensation allotted to his minor daughter for bodily injury, a right which was recognized in Palestine but not in Babylonia. The conservative character of Palestinian law is herein indicated; the Biblical law was not easily over-ridden.

Slavery: The Bible speaks of Hebrew slaves—perhaps it would be more correct to say Hebrew serfs—and slaves "from among the children of strangers." Hebrew serfdom no longer existed during the second Commonwealth, surely not in the time following the destruction of the Temple. Babylonian Jewry, however, practiced Jewish serfdom *de facto* and *de jure,* in the case of Jews seized as slaves by the Persian Government for the non-payment of taxes. The poor Jew who was seized as a slave by the government for not paying taxes surely preferred to serve his fellow-Jew rather than the pagan until such time as his debt was paid. The status was somewhat similar to white labor servitude in America until about the beginning of the 19th century.

With regard to the non-Hebrew slave, note the following difference. About the beginning of the second century, leading scholars, following the Roman example, prohibited the emancipation of slaves. In Palestine this law subsequently lost its validity, but not so in Babylonia. The social position of emancipated slaves was very precarious in Babylonia, where great emphasis was laid upon purity of race, while in Palestine where the bulk of the Jewish population consisted of small farmers, slavery must have been practiced on a very limited scale, so that freedmen were too few to constitute a social problem.

Trade: Julius Paulus, the famous Roman jurist, remarks that it is quite natural for men "to cheat one another alternately and therefore, there is no reason for law to interfere." His Jewish contemporary, the compiler of the Mishnah, has elaborate legislation against over-reaching, most of which antedates him by centuries. *Onaah* (over-reaching or over-charging) in Rabbinic sources though etymologically connected with the biblical *lo tonu* (you shall not wrong one another) is really a piece of later legislation which transmuted an ethical conception into law. Over-reaching beyond a certain amount, according to Palestinian law, entitles the injured party to invalidate the transaction, or to sue for refund of the amount over-paid. In Babylonia, commercial conditions modified the old Palestinian law to the effect that only when the over-reaching exceeded one sixth, could the transaction be invalidated by the injured party. Palestinian authorities, toward the end of the third century, developed the law of *laesio enormis*, i. e., over-reaching exceeding one half, in cases where the general law of over-reaching could not be applied. Babylonian schools gradually accepted it, but not without some modification.

Usury: The Biblical precept against usury and increase not only was turned into law by the Rabbis but was developed to an extreme which made dealings in futures almost impossible, and thus a curb was put on speculation, a clear case of legislation for the benefit of the farmer. In Babylonia the development of commerce forced the scholars to modify the rigor of Palestinian laws. For instance, the *Mashkanah* was allowed; that is, the creditor was permitted to enjoy the use of landed property during the time the debtor had the privilege of redemption. A similar case is *Tarsha*, a sale on time at a price higher than the seller would take if he sold for cash; the Palestinians prohibited it, the Babylonians permitted it. The Babylonian practice of *'iska*, partial partnership—the capitalist to bear some small risk for part of the money he invested in the debtor's business and to be compensated by a considerable share in the profits of the investment—has the support of certain Palestinian scholars of the tannaitic period, but the accepted law in Palestine would consider such dealings illegal.

In one respect the Babylonian jurists seem to have applied the usury laws much more strictly than did their Palestinian colleagues. Mishnah and Palestinian Talmud disqualify any man who takes interest from testifying—greed of gain will make him commit perjury as it made him transgress the law prohibiting the taking of interest. The Babylonian Talmud goes a step further and disqualifies the borrower on interest from testifying. In the light of what has been said of the differences in the economic structure of the two countries, the stricter attitude of the Babylonians is easily explained. In Palestine the simple conditions of Biblical times continued, relatively unchanged, in talmudic times. The borrower, a small farmer or an artisan, asked for a loan on interest because of personal need, and while from a higher ethical point of view he too was considered a "violator of the law"—the Mishnah describes as such all persons involved in an usurious transaction including the witnesses and the scrivener who draws up the contract—yet his motive was surely not greed of gain, and hence he was not considered likely to commit perjury. In a commercial society, on the other hand, both lender and borrower on interest engage in a business transaction for the same purpose, i. e. for the sake of gain, the lender to obtain interest and the borrow to invest the loan in a profitable undertaking. There was no good reason for the law to distinguish between them; neither could be trusted to act in accordance with the commandments of Scripture, whenever "gain" of money was concerned. They would commit perjury for its sake just as they had disregarded the prohibition against taking or giving interest.

The remarks found in the Talmuds relating to a gift *causa mortis* clearly corroborate the statement that the civil law of Palestine in talmudic times mirrors an exclusively agricultural society, while that of Babylonia reflects a life greatly modified by commerce. Both Talmuds accept the mishnaic law that if the sick man gives away his entire estate, the act is revocable in the event of his recovery, and takes effect only on his death; but it also states that it is not revocable if he sets aside for himself sufficient land to enable him to earn his living. In comment upon this ruling of the Mishnah, the following remark is made by the Palestinian Talmud: "If he reserved for himself movable property it is as if he would give away his entire estate; for land even of a small size enables a man to support himself, but precious stones and pearls do not enable him to support himself." In contrast to this view of the Palestinian Talmud it is explicitly stated in the Babylonian Talmud that the kind of property the sick man reserved for himself is immaterial; it might be either real estate or personal property, so long as it sufficed to support him. The most valuable kind of personal property, such as precious stones and pearls, were not considered sufficient means of support in Palestine, since in an agricultural society consisting chiefly of small farmers and artisans, they were difficult to dispose of: in Babylonia, they were articles of commerce.

Jewish civil law being what it was, neither isolated nor independent, and developing as it did in connection with and relative to other manifestations of the socio-economic life of the people, it could not remain untouched by foreign influence. Greeks and Romans ruled Palestine,

Babylonians and Persians ruled Babylonia, and *a priori* we assume that the law of the ruler left its effect on those who were ruled. The problem of the influence of foreign law, however, is a very intricate and complicated one. It is still a moot question whether parallel developments of law cannot largely be explained by the theory that the same economic or cultural conditions produce the same institutions. The recent discovery of new sources of Hellenistic and oriental laws in the papyri has, however, cleared up one important point. Contrary to earlier opinion, it was not Roman law which exerted the greatest influence, but rather the Greco-Egyptian *Volksrecht* of the eastern provinces of the Roman empire. On the other hand, it is quite possible that the undeniable affinity between Greco-Egyptian *Volksrecht* and the Jewish civil law finds its explanation in their common origin, the cuneiform laws.

In support of this view, one might refer to the fact that there is scarcely any difference between the two Talmuds with regard to the use of these foreign elements of law. The beginnings of the Talmuds by the disciples and other younger contemporaries of the compiler of the Mishnah almost coincide with the issue of the famous *Constitutio* of Caracalla (212 of the common era), which bestowed Roman citizenship on every subject in the wide Roman empire. One might expect to see the effect of this radical change in the Palestinian Talmud, but actually one finds that Roman law, which now became the only law recognized in the empire, left no mark on the Talmud. The bulk of the Greco-Egyptian elements of law is found in the tannaitic sources, a fact which points to high antiquity as the time of their absorption into Jewish civil law. The strongly "isolationist" policy of Pharisaism was not conducive to the adoption of foreign elements of law and furthermore this exclusiveness increased rather than diminished with time.

In this connection it ought to be pointed out that the Babylonian Talmud does not furnish any tangible proof that its civil law had been more influenced by the Assyro-Babylonian law than was true of the Palestinian Talmud. Traces of that influence are found in the oldest strata of tannaitic tradition which, in all likelihood, date from the very earliest times, perhaps from the period of "the children of Israel that were come back out of the captivity." It should, however, be mentioned that some clauses of Jewish conveyances have only Babylonian parallels. It is true that these characteristic clauses are met with first in post-talmudic sources but there can be no doubt that they had their origin in talmudic times. As an illustration of the strong hold which the Babylonian style of official documents had upon the Jewish courts, one might quote a formula in the Babylonian Talmud for a bill of divorce which was drawn up by a scholar of the fourth century of the common era; in this formula the third person is used. From earliest times, as early as the Elphantine papyri which date from 520 B.C., Jewish deeds had been written in the first, not in the third person, as was true of the Babylonian deeds.

A theory favored by many is that one of the characteristic distinctions between the two Talmuds is that the Babylonian Talmud, in contrast to the Palestinian, was greatly influenced by Persian law. In view of the new light shed on this question by the recent discovery of a Sassanian *Book of Laws*—so far the only one of its kind known—this theory can hardly be maintained. Fragmentary and obscure as this Persian *Book of Laws* is, it contains enough material to enable us to form an opinion on the relation of Jewish civil law in Babylonia to the Persian law in use in that country. Here too the observation made above is valid: the foreign elements in Jewish law date back to pre-talmudic, even to pre-mishnaic times. The parallels in the Sassanian *Book of Laws* to Jewish civil law are chiefly related to those parts of the latter which are also found in Palestinian sources such as the Mishnah and the Palestinian Talmud. If those parallels mean anything, they prove that in very early times, when Palestine was still a Persian province, old Persian law was not without influence upon the Jews of that country.

There is only one legal institution which the Jews of Babylonia may accurately be said to have borrowed from the Persians and which is therefore found in the Babylonian but not in the Palestinian Talmud. At about the beginning of the fourth century, the leading jurist of Babylonian Jewry, R. Nahman, introduced the oath of exoneration—an oath taken by the defendant to refute a claim not supported by any evidence at all—which is surely of Persian origin.

This Babylonian innovation in legal procedure, though not of very great importance for the development of Jewish jurisprudence, throws an extremely interesting light upon the cultural life of Babylonian Jewry. In antiquity, an oath was in reality one of the numerous forms of the ordeal. No trace of this concept existed in Palestinian Jewry of talmudic times, but it continued in Babylonia long after the talmudic period. The Persian oath was essentially an "ordeal," hence the adoption of the

Persian "oath of exoneration" by the Jewish courts in Babylonia is understandable.

In one respect, however, the attitude of the authors of the Babylonian Talmud toward Persian law was radically different from that taken by their Palestinian colleagues with regard to "foreign" law in the Holy Land. The opprobrium attached in old Christian writings to the "publicans" has its origin not in the dishonesty or wickedness of the tax-collector but in the fact that Palestinian Jewry never recognized Roman rule in the Holy Land as legitimate, and looked upon the publican as an accomplice of robbers, not the servant of a legitimate government. In Babylonia, on the other hand, immediately after the conquest of the country by the Sassanids, the rule was laid down: The law of the government (Persian) is law. According to the Palestinian Talmud, therefore, a "publican" is automatically disqualified from testifying, while according to the Babylonian Talmud he is disqualified only if he is found to have discharged his office dishonestly, favoring the rich to the detriment of the poor.

Both Talmuds are commentaries on the Mishnah, a book of laws, and hence chiefly legal. Yet almost one-third of the Babylonian and about one sixth of the Palestinian Talmud consist of non-legal matter, of so-called *Haggadah,* a very comprehensive term which includes theology and religious philosophy, folklore and history, mathematics and astronomy, medicine and natural science, and many other subjects. Because of the encyclopedic character of these non-legal parts of the Talmuds, the task of determining their Palestinian and Babylonian characteristics is almost insurmountable, though nobody will deny that they do exist. We shall cite a few illustrations from theology, a field in which we should expect to find the fewest divergences between the two Talmuds.

The main topics of theology and morals were established long before the talmudic period; Scripture spoke plainly of them and the traditional understanding of them was fixed in its essentials. Where this was not the fact, there was free diversity of opinion among the Palestinian as well as Babylonian scholars and sages. However, even the wise and the learned are often influenced by the cultural conditions under which they live.

The chief difference between the two Talmuds in the field of theology is to be found in the fact that the Palestinian authors of the Talmud excluded, almost entirely, the popular fancies about angels and demons, while in Babylonia angelology and demonology, under popular pressure influenced by Zoroastrianism, gained scholastic recognition and with it entrance into the Talmud. Contrast these two sayings: The first, in the Palestinian Talmud, reads: "Cry not to Michael or Gabriel but to Me says the Lord." The second, found in the Babylonian Talmud, recommends: "One should never pray in Aramaic because the angels do not attend to him." An intermediary role for the angels is obviously assumed in the latter statement. In the Palestinian Talmud, angels are rarely mentioned and, with the exception of the passage just quoted from it, wherein Michael and Gabriel are but Biblical reminiscences, angels remain nameless—they have no individuality. The Babylonian Talmud, on the other hand, not only makes frequent reference to angels and their doings but knows some of them by name and describes their specific activities. The Palestinian Talmud intentionally avoids the use of the word *shed,* demon, though it is found in the Bible, and instead employs—three times in all—the designation "they who do damage." In the Babylonian Talmud demons are found as often as angels, and though most of them are nameless some have proper names and are assigned spheres of activity. It is of special significance that according to the Babylonian Talmud demons propagate their species by the union of males with females; while in the Palestinian Talmud they are sexless— spiritual beings.

The student of religion is often baffled by the problem of how to distinguish between the religious beliefs of a people and their fantasies, between religion and folklore. There can be no doubt that a great part, if not all, of the angelological and demonological material found in the Babylonian Talmud is folkloristic and has very little to do with the theology of its authors. It is nevertheless of importance to note that the compilers of the Talmud saw no objection to including the popular fancies, while their Palestinian colleagues ignored this branch of folklore almost completely. A certain chastity characterizes the Palestinian Talmud which, even when it relates a folk-tale, avoids the exaggerated role ascribed to supernatural beings by popular fancy. For instance, a legend in the Palestinian Talmud tells of Solomon's being deposed for his sins by an angel who impersonated him and ascended his throne. In the Babylonian Talmud, it is lustful Ashmedai (= Asmodeus) who became the occupant of Solomon's throne as well as the master of his harem. There is good reason to believe that the figure of Ashmedai, a being who combined most of the weaknesses of man with some of the superhuman qualities of the angels, was well-known to Palestinian folklore. The compilers of the Palestinian Talmud, however, were reluctant to accept the creations of popular fancies at their face value, and while they admitted some of them—not too many—into their Talmud, they used some discretion. The same cannot be said of the compilers of the Babylonian Talmud.

A similar observation can be made in regard to the difference in the attitudes of the two Talmuds toward sorcery, magic, astrology, and other kinds of superstition. There is very little of all this in the Palestinian Talmud and that little is cautiously stated. Not without a touch of humor is the following story, given there at the end of a number of folk-tales the purpose of which is to show the superiority of the sages of Israel who out-maneuvered their adversaries at their own game of witchcraft. I quote verbatim. "Said R. Hinanah son of R. Hananah, 'I saw while walking in Gobta near Sepphoris a sectarian (an adherent of gnosticism that consists of pagan, Jewish, and Christian beliefs and practices) who took a skull and threw it high up, and a calf came down. When I narrated it to my father he remarked: If you ate of the calf then, of course, it was a real one, but if not, what you saw was only a delusion.' " The Babylonian Talmud contains two opposing views. The one holds that magic and sorcery are vain efforts, for "the Lord, He is God, there is none else beside Him." The other, however, finds in the Hebrew word for sorcery an indication that it sometimes achieves its purpose against the powers on high. The magic bowls discovered in Babylonia which date from the talmudic period prove the popularity of the second view. Folk-medicine in the Talmud as well as the numerous stories about the effects of magic and witchcraft, and the remedies against them which it contains, are further evidence of the hold that these popular beliefs had on Babylonian Jewry.

With the recognition of the Mishnah in both Palestine and Babylonia as the "Book of Law" for student and judge alike, began the activity of its expounders. In less than two centuries this culminated in the Palestinian Talmud and a few generations later in the Babylonian. The problems connected with the compilations of the two Talmuds are numerous and very baffling, and they relate some to both of them, some to the one or the other. The Babylonian Talmud refers to R. Ashi (died 427) and Rabbina as the two last representatives of "talmudic" activity. The statement is very obscure and open to many interpretations, but at least we have a direct statement in the Babylonian Talmud itself as to the time and person (persons?) who participated in its compilation. The Palestinian Talmud maintains complete silence about its history. No editor is mentioned, no time of compilation is indicated, no editorial principle is given which would enable us to tell the process of elimination and selection of the vast body of material available. And yet in some respects our knowledge about the compilation of the Palestinian Talmud is more adequate than that relating to the Babylonian.

The few well-established facts concerning the compilation of the Palestinian Talmud are as follows. About the middle of the fourth century, the oldest part of the Talmud was compiled at Caesarea (Straton), which was then as it had been for some time, the seat of the Roman government of Palestine. This part of the Talmud consists of explanations and interpretations of the mishnaic sections on civil law, which are contained in the first three treatises of the fourth order. These three talmudic treatises not only differ in age from the rest of the Palestinian Talmud, and of course still more so from the Babylonian one, but also differ in form, style, terminology, and many other things. Two characteristics of this "oldest Talmud," its brevity and its almost exclusively legal contents, are of special interest. Its brevity is such that many passages would have remained unintelligible but for the parallels to them in the other parts of the Palestinian Talmud. The most likely explanation for this rather strange phenomenon is that this "old" Talmud was intended not for students but for teachers. The judiciary in Palestine during and preceding the talmudic period included many nobles, political leaders, and members of the *Boulé* of the town, who, since they were not learned in Jewish law, often applied non-Jewish law. Some among them, however, had their "rabbinical prompters," who aided them in their judicial functions by instructing them in the rudiments of Jewish civil law. Intended as a guide for the instruction of the unlearned judges, this talmudic digest of civil law is therefore extremely brief; it was more in the nature of memoranda to guide the teacher than a textbook for students or a book of laws for judges. While the compiler of the guide, in striving for extreme brevity, wisely excluded from it all non-legal matter—the so-called Haggadah that forms a very important part of the other sections of the Palestinian Talmud—he did, however, for practical, pedagogic reasons include a few telling stories which emphasize the ethical aspect of the law. The section on labor law, for example, closes with an anecdote about the Rabbi-judge who made a colleague cancel his claim against his laborers for breaking several kegs of wine, and in addition made him pay their wages. As reason for this decision, contrary to strict law, he quoted the verse of Proverbs: That thou mayest walk in the way of good men and keep the paths of the righteous. The Jewry of Caesarea was in part Hellenistic; in some of the synagogues Greek was the language used for prayers. One is therefore safe in assuming that many of the Jewish judges knew a good deal more about equity in Roman law than about the rabbinic admonition to act within the line of justice, i. e., that justice must be controlled by moral and social principles which often over-ride the strictness of the law. The non-legal matter in the "Caesarean" Talmud, consisting almost exclusively of stories about wise and kind judges, has no other purpose than to emphasize the rabbinic concept of equity.

Shortly after the completion of the "oldest" Talmud, a great calamity overtook Palestinian Israel. Because of local outbreaks between the Jews and the army, its commander, Ursicinus, in the year 351 wreaked vengeance on the three cities of Tiberias, Sepphoris, and Lydda, the seats of the three most famous academies in the Holy Land. The death knell had tolled for Jewish learning in the home of its origin. Some of the Palestinian scholars did what their forefathers had done under similar conditions about two centuries earlier when they had emigrated to Babylonia during the Hadrianic persecutions. Those who remained could read the signs of the times. Christianity had now become—in the second half of the fourth century—the established state religion of the Roman empire. Though Judaism continued to be a licit religion, in accordance with the edict of toleration issued by Constantin the Great, vexatious regulations interfering with the economic and religious life of the Jews increased daily. For centuries the Jew had to fight for his existence in his own home, first against the Greeks and later against the Romans. But with the exception of short periods like that of the Maccabean revolt and the Hadrianic persecutions, it was not Judaism but the Jew who was attacked. Now a militant church arose which, backed by the power of the state, undertook a war against Jew and Judaism alike. The academies in which the spirit of Judaism had been kept alive were forced to close. If the Jew were to retain his cultural and spiritual individuality, something had to be found to take the place of the living word that had been silenced—the Palestinian Talmud was the result.

It was compiled toward the end of the fourth century in Tiberias, yet it was not the exclusive work of one school, as is shown by the frequent references in it to the scholars of the other famous academy, that of Sepphoris. Less frequently are the scholars of Lydda and Caesarea mentioned, but their views were by no means ignored. It is this product of the Tiberian school that is called the Palestinian Talmud, a designation which is quite correct so long as we do not use it to convey the idea of unity for the entire compilation. The Tiberian scholars incorporated in their work the "Caesarean" Talmud on the three treatises of the Mishnah containing civil law. They certainly were not unaware of its many shortcomings pointed out above, but conditions were such that they could not spend their time in revising or supplementing the work of their predecessors. The work of the Tiberian scholars bears witness to the serious situation in which they found themselves, a situation that called for the utmost speed. If one compares the Palestinian with the Babylonian Talmud, one is struck by the relatively careful editing of the latter in contrast to the hasty compilation of the former. The closing of the Palestinian academies and the emigration of many scholars to Babylonia prevented the Palestinian compilers from doing their work as they would have liked to have it done. The critical position of Jewish scholarship in Palestine is chiefly responsible for the shortcomings of the Palestinian Talmud.

The superiority of the Babylonian Talmud over the Palestinian, from the point of view of system and arrangement cannot be doubted. It is, however, not quite correct to ascribe it to the fact that the Babylonian scholars improved on the method used by their predecessors in Palestine. There is no reason to doubt the tradition, well-supported by internal evidence, which declares R. Ashi, for fifty-two years the head of the academy at Sura (375–427), to have been the compiler of the Babylonian Talmud. But if this is so, one must question the dependence of that Talmud on the Palestinian. R. Ashi is said to have spent fifty years on his gigantic work, a statement which is not at all unlikely when one considers the enormously difficult task that he faced. By the time the Palestinian Talmud was compiled about 400, the Babylonian Talmud must have been far advanced. It is also very doubtful whether R. Ashi's compilation differed essentially in order or system from that produced by his contemporaries in Palestine. One must not forget that the "editorial" shaping of R. Ashi's compilation extended over nearly a century, and that if we consider the finishing touches of the Saboraim (the Babylonian scholars of the sixth century), one might say that two centuries were spent by the Babylonians on the final redaction of their Talmud.

The obvious shortcomings of the Palestinian Talmud are three—repetition, lack of continuity, and contradictions—but all three are not entirely missing from the Babylonian Talmud. Both Talmuds, since they were products of gradual growth over a period of about two centuries, betray their origins by these defects, which are more pronounced in the Palestinian than in the Babylonian. The work of the compilers in Palestine as well as Babylonia might be said to have consisted in making a Talmud out of numerous Talmuds. Each generation of the "expounders," each school of a generation had its Talmud, i.e., its comments upon the Mishnah. When the several Talmuds were combined into one, certain inconsistencies were overlooked and the Palestinian Talmud because of the necessity for haste shows less editorial efficiency. One must not, however, measure by our standards of system and arrangement. The repetitions in the Palestinian Talmud are not due to lack of system but to the conviction that for practical reasons it is preferable to repeat things whenever cognate matter is dealt with. Much of the lack of continuity is only apparent: The order of the Palestinian Mishnah was not always the same as that of the Babylonian one, and some passages of the Palestinian Talmud seem to be disconnected only because they comment on a text of the Mishnah that differed in sequence from the Babylonian Mishnah. It is further to be noted that the text of the Palestinian Talmud was often badly transmitted, so that what seems to be faulty editing is sometimes actually faulty copying.

The three volumes of the present work, consisting of about twelve hundred pages, cover little more than six folios of the text of the Palestinian Talmud in the first edition. The title: *Commentary on the Palestinian Talmud,* may therefore seem strange to many, the more so since the author does not comment either on those passages where he accepts the interpretation of his predecessors or on those where, though disagreeing with them, he has nothing better to offer. The only justification for the title is that the plethoric character of the book will give the student a clear idea of the problems confronting a commentator on the Palestinian Talmud. Apparently they are the same three problems which the commentator on any old document has to solve: the establishing of an accurate text, its philological interpretation, and its historical understanding. A closer acquaintance with our subject, however, reveals not only the extreme difficulty and intricacy of each of these three problems but also a large number of additional problems which must be solved before we approach our three important tasks.

The printed text—that of the first edition on which the later editions are mainly based—is a very poor one. There is scarcely a page without one or more misreadings, some due to inaccurate printing, others to the poor quality of the manuscript—or manuscripts—from which it was printed. The only complete manuscript of the Palestinian Talmud in existence (University Library of Leyden, Holland) was the chief of the four manuscripts used for the printed text, and while not entirely without value for establishing the correct text, is of little assistance to us. A manuscript in the Vatican Library contains a little more than a fourth of the Palestinian Talmud, giving in more or less complete form the first ten treatises and the treatise Sotah. It was, however, written by such a careless scribe that scarcely a line is free from the grossest mistakes, and though it contains here and there a better text than the printed one, such cases are very rare. One can judge the character of this manuscript by the variants given by me in *Yerushalmi Fragments* (New York 1909) and supplemented by Professor Saul Libermann in *'Al ha-Yerushalmi* (Jerusalem 1929), who succeeded in obtaining a complete photographic reproduction of the treatise Sotah of this manuscript which had not been available to me twenty years before. Of real value for the text of the Palestinian Talmud are the fragments of the Genizah published by me in the abovementioned work; but unfortunately they cover only a small part of it, about seven per cent.

The most important source for establishing a correct text is the numerous quotations from the Palestinian Talmud found in the works of the old authorities, especially those of the Spanish school, and one must be grateful to Baer Ratner (1852–1917) for collecting them in twelve volumes of his work *Ahabat Zion we-Yerushalaim*, Wilna, 1901–1917. The parallels must, however, be used with great caution for the following three reasons. First, the first editions of the works of the old authorities were not available to Ratner and hence the variants he offered are frequently only misprints of poor editions. Second, he does not always distinguish between a literal quotation and a paraphrase—between text and explanation. In many cases the old authorities had the same readings as the printed text but they were not always interested in quoting verbatim, and consequently the differences between our text and theirs assumed by Ratner are merely imaginary. Third, he overlooked the very important fact that the antiquity of a text is not a guaranty of its correctness. Quite often the printed text is preferable by far to that given by the old authorities. Ratner never doubts that any reading not agreeing with theirs is *eo ipso* faulty. Though in the present work I have had occasion to call attention to these shortcomings of Ratner's book, its merits can not be denied.

Useful as the manuscript readings and important as the quotations are for establishing a correct text, we should have to despair of ever achieving it unless we make ample use of emendations, since the help we can expect from the other two aids is quite limited. The danger of subjective emendations degenerating into arbitrariness is very great, hence the utmost care must be taken in making use of them for the reconstruction of the text. It is very significant that the old style talmudists, the great majority of whom would not dare to change a single letter of the printed text of the Babylonian Talmud, went to the other extreme in suggesting the most radical emendations for the Palestinian Talmud. A cautious commentator will do well to avoid emending the transmitted text even when its corruption is obvious, so long as he is not able to explain the genesis of the present text. Fortunately in many cases the cause of the corruption can easily be established. Single words, for example, frequently owe their corruption to the confusion of letters similar in form, of which the Hebrew alphabet has so many. Less frequent and therefore not always recognized is the confusion of letters similar in sound, especially the guttural and emphatic ones which were no longer distinguished among people who did not use a Semitic language in their daily speech. Entire sentences are often missing because of *homoioteleuton,* i. e., when two sentences following upon one another ended with the same phrase the copyists often omitted one of the sentences. On the other hand, single words or phrases sometimes came into the text because of association—in the words of the Palestinian Amoraim, because of the slip of the tongue. An interesting case of association in the Mishnah pointed out in the Palestinian Talmud is the statement: Deaf mutes, people of unsound mind, and minors are not allowed to officiate as readers in the synagogue. These three classes are often mentioned together in connection with the legal disability common to them, hence the rather queer sounding ruling of the Mishnah that deaf *mutes* are not to officiate as *readers!* Doublets, glosses, and interpolations, transpositions of entire paragraphs and many scribal misunderstandings are to be found in the text of the Palestinian Talmud, some easily recognized, some not. Attention should be called to the fact that poor as the text of the Palestinian Talmud is, it is superior in one respect to that of its counterpart, the Babylonian—it was not "doctored." For centuries the latter has been on the "table of the scholar," while the former was left lying in a corner; the latter was made palatable, the former was left to itself. In the entire Babylonian Talmud, huge work as it is, there is scarcely a passage which one would recognize immediately as corrupt; the Palestinian Talmud has many of them. And the consequence is that we are sometimes in a position to reconstruct the original text of the Palestinian Talmud but not that of the Babylonian; for the skillful hands of great artists have changed its form beyond recognition.

Great as are the difficulties connected with establishing the correct text of the Palestinian Talmud, its interpretation offers still greater difficulties. From the time of the Babylonian Amoraim, the authors of the Babylonian Talmud, down to the present day, we have an uninterrupted tradition for its interpretation. We may sometimes doubt and sometimes even refuse to accept a traditional interpretation; we must, however, admit that without this tradition which enabled us to penetrate into the Babylonian Talmud, our doubts about and our rejection of certain details would not have been possible. Tradition taught us when to trust it and when to distrust it. For the Palestinian Talmud we have only the bare, and as we have seen, very poorly transmitted text, and not the slightest tradition to guide us. Puzzled by the linguistic peculiarities of the Palestinian Talmud in its Aramaic as well as Hebrew parts and bewildered by the intricacies of its legal discussion, any commentator on this Talmud would be doomed to failure without the Babylonian Talmud to guide him. The subject matter of both Talmuds is so much akin that in a certain sense one is entitled to speak of the Babylonian as the best commentary on its Palestinian counterpart. The danger, however, is great and many great talmudists fell into the grave error of harmonization, i. e., of explaining the Palestinian Talmud from the point of view of the Babylonian. It must be emphasized again and again that striking as the likeness is between the two Talmuds, no less striking is their diversity. How careful one must be in this respect is best seen by the different meanings the same term may assume in both Talmuds. Interesting examples, in which some of the greatest masters of the Palestinian Talmud during the middle ages read the Babylonian meaning into a term in the Palestinian Talmud, should serve as a warning to all students.

The Palestinian Talmud is only one link in the long chain of a literature that extends from the pre-Mishnaic collections of the last century B.C.E. to the Babylonian Talmud that reached its final completion about 500. An historical understanding of the Palestinian Talmud is therefore possible only after one compares it and contrasts it with this vast literature. The Mishnah, the non-canonical tannaitic sources, the so-called Baraitot, and the Babylonian Talmud are not extraneous matter but serve to give us a deeper and finer understanding of the Palestinian Talmud; for a knowledge of the whole is indispensable to the understanding of the parts.

The most contradictory judgments have been passed on the Talmud — its theology, its ethics, its system of law, and its literary form. There can, however, be only one opinion on its great influence upon Jewish life and thought for almost two thousand years. Biblical Judaism was limited to one small country and to a time of cultural homogeneity in the Jewish people. The Talmud made it possible for Judaism to adapt itself to every time and place, to every state of society, and to every stage of civilization. When we speak of the Talmud we think primarily or even exclusively of the Babylonian and not of the Palestinian. Yet we must not forget, first, that in essentials both Talmuds are identical and, second, that the foundation for both of them was laid in Palestine. The Babylonian Talmud may well be described as the best commentary on the Palestinian, but we must keep in mind that an historical appreciation of the former is possible only with the aid of the latter.

Both Talmuds are most important sources for Jewish history in Palestine and Babylonia for many a century. There is no need to point out that the Palestinian Talmud is the more important of the two for the history of Palestinian Jewry. For archaeology, geography, for the customs, and cultural life of Palestine, the Palestinian Talmud is a veritable treasure, and the author has therefore considered it one of his tasks to discuss fully the passages bearing upon these subjects. To give only one illustration:

Archeologists have been greatly puzzled by the orientation of the recently discovered synagogues in Galilee. The synagogues of Capernaum and Chorazin have their doors towards Jerusalem while the synagogues in Beth Alpha and Naʿaran are of opposite orientation. There are other synagogues which clearly indicate that their doors had once faced Jerusalem but had later been closed and transferred to the opposite side. The solution to this puzzle is found in the passages of the Palestinian Talmud bearing on orientation at prayer. Public prayer originally meant recital of prayers by the reader, and hence his orientation at prayer was all important. As he had to face the congregation— this rule is often mentioned—it was considered desirable to have the people enter from the south side so that the reader faced them and at the same time the Holy City. Later, however, with the increasing knowledge of Hebrew, the language of prayer, public prayer among the Galileans consisted of simultaneous prayer by the congregation. Consequently though the reader would repeat the main prayers (eighteen benedictions on weekdays and seven benedictions on Sabbaths and Holy days) for the benefit "of the ignorant," it was of course the orientation of the congregation toward the Holy City that was of importance. The entrance was therefore transferred from the south to the north side.

The attitude of the authors of the Palestinian Talmud to the Greco-Roman culture of their time—roughly from 200 C.E. to 400—was on the whole very hostile. They, like the Christian writers of that period, found little to praise and much to blame. Their criticism is often a valuable source for the political and cultural history of the Eastern provinces of the Roman Empire. I know of no better characterization of the absolutism of the Roman emperors than the Greek proverb quoted in the Palestinian Talmud—the only one of its kind!—"for the king the law is unwritten." What the Palestinian Talmud has to tell us about Diocletian, the last of the emperors referred to by name, is of historical importance. Until comparatively recent times, some scholars denied the emperor's stay in Palestine, for there was no clear evidence of it except for the explicit statement in the Palestinian Talmud, which was not known to them. It is still the only source for the following inscription by the emperor: "I, King Diocletian, established this fair at Tyre for eight days in honor of the Tyché of my brother Heracles." The inscription is hardly quoted literally but there is no reason to doubt its contents. Heracles, the brother of Diocletian, is Maximian whom he had made joint emperor, and it is highly interesting to note the emperor's attempts to revive at Tyre the worship of the old Semitic Moloch—Heracles. Characteristic of the decay of Roman political life at that period are the following remarks found in the first treatise of the Palestinian Talmud, in a parable designed to illustrate the doctrine of the nearness of God to each human being: "If a man has a patron, when a time of trouble comes upon him, he does not at once enter into his patron's presence, but comes and stands at the door of his (the patron's) house and calls one of the servants or a member of his family, who brings word to him, 'So-and-so is standing at the entrance of your court.' Perhaps he will let him in; perhaps he will leave him standing at the door. Not so is God. If trouble comes upon a man, let him cry neither to Michael nor to Gabriel but unto Me, and I will answer him forthwith." One could only approach the patron with the assistance of his slaves or free men (members of his family), who of course did not give their services free. The client's devotion to the patron and the services rendered him counted for nothing so long as he could not procure by bribery the services of the patron's slaves. An awful indictment of Roman society, but, as non-Jewish sources show, not without good reason.

The Palestinian Talmud, however, serves as a source not only for the general history of the Roman world of the talmudic period but also for the understanding of later historical developments, i. e., the rise of Islam. Few would doubt the great influence Judaism exercised on the origins of this religion, though opinions may differ as to which contributions came from Judaism and which from Christianity. The two great centers of Jewish life at that time were Palestine and Babylonia, and the problem is not yet solved as to which of the two it was that helped create Islam. The five daily prayers, one of the essential institutions of Islam, is still puzzling historians since it is known neither to Jews nor Christians. We call attention however to the fact that, as we can see from the Palestinian Talmud, the Jews in the Talmudic period met five times daily for prayer in the synagogue. It was only later that the two in the morning were combined into one as were the two in the evening. This points to the influence of Palestinian Jewry on an important institution in Islam.

The author has attempted to solve many problems; many more have been left unsolved. Our old sages said: It is not for thee to finish the work but neither art thou free to desist therefrom.

8

The Talmud of the Land of Israel and the Mishnah

Jacob Neusner

THE STARTING POINT

To describe the Talmud we first take up the whole and proceed to ask about its principal components. Looking at the Talmud whole, we notice two totally distinct sorts of materials: statements of law, then discussions of and excursus on those statements. We bring no substantial presuppositions to the text, if we declare these two sorts of materials to be, respectively, primary and constitutive, secondary and derivative. Calling the former the declaration of laws, the Mishnah passage, and the latter the exegesis of these laws, the Talmud proper, imposes no *a priori* judgment formed independently of the literary evidence in hand. We might as well call the two "the code" and "the commentary." The result would be no different.

In fact, as we see everywhere, the Talmud is made up of two elements, each with its own literary traits and program of discussion. Since the Mishnah passage at the head of each set of Talmudic units of discourse defines the limits and determines the theme and, generally, the problematic of the whole, our attention is drawn to the traits of the Mishnah passages as a group. Here, of course, a certain measure of descriptive work has been done. But even if we for the first time saw these types of pericopes of the Mishnah (embedded as they are in the Talmud and separated from one another), we should discern that they adhere to a

Reprinted by permission of the author and The University of Chicago Press from *The Talmud of the Land of Israel*, volume 35, 1983.

separate and quite distinctive set of literary and conceptual canons from what follows and surrounds them. Hence at the outset, with no appreciable attention to anything beyond the text, we should distinguish two "layers" of the Talmud and recognize that one "layer" is formed in one way, the other in another way. (I use "layer" for convenience only; it is not an apt metaphor.)

As I just said, if then we were to join together all the Mishnah pericopes, we should notice that they are stylistically and formally coherent and also different from everything else in the compilation before us. Accordingly, for stylistic reasons alone we are on firm ground in designating the "layer" before us as the base point for all further inquiry. For the Mishnah "layer" has been shown to be uniform, while the Talmud "layer" is not demonstrably so. Hence, itself undifferentiated, the former—the Mishnah "layer"—provides the point of differentiation. The latter—the Talmud "layer"—presents the diverse materials subject to differentiation. In the first stage in the work of making sense of the Talmud and describing it whole, what is the initial criterion through which the Talmud's diverse types of units of discourse are differentiated? It is the varied relationships, to the Mishnah's rule, exhibited by the Talmud's several, diverse units of discourse. Let me now expand on and qualify this point, for it is the principle of the opening initiative in this exercise of taxonomy and typology.

To amplify what I have said: since the Palestinian Talmud carries forward and depends upon the Mishnah, to describe that Talmud we have to begin with its relationship to the Mishnah, which is the Talmud's own starting point. While the Mishnah admits to no antecedents and neither alludes to nor cites anything prior to its own materials, a passage of the Talmud is often incomprehensible without knowledge of the passage of the Mishnah around which the Talmud's discourse centers. Yet in describing and defining the Talmud, we should grossly err if we were to say it is only, or mainly, a step-by-step commentary on the Mishnah, defined solely by the Mishnah's interests. We may not even say—though it is a step closer to the truth—that the Talmud before us is a commentary on or secondary development of, the Mishnah and important passages of the Tosefta. Units of discourse which serve these sorts of materials stand side by side with many which in an immediate sense do not. Accordingly, while a description of the Talmud requires attention to the interplay between the Talmud and the Mishnah and

Tosefta, the diverse relationships between the Talmud and one or the other of those two documents constitute only one point of description and differentiation. For the Talmud is in full command of its own program of thought and inquiry. Its framers, responsible for the units of discourse, chose what in the Mishnah will be analyzed and what ignored. True, there could be no Talmud without the Mishnah and Tosefta. But knowing only those two works, we could never have predicted in a systematic way the character of the Talmud's discourse at any point.

The Mishnah nonetheless permits us at the outset to gain perspective on the character of Yerushalmi. For the Mishnah does exhibit a remarkable unity of literary and redactional traits. By that standard our Talmud presents none. Accordingly, while whatever materials reached the framers of the Mishnah—ca. 175–200—were revised by them in line with a single and simple literary and redactional program, the same is not the case for the Talmud of the Land of Israel. Whatever the stages of redaction of the document as a whole, let alone of its components, we may say with certainty that the people ultimately responsible for the document as we have it did not do to the materials in their hands what the framers of the Mishnah did to theirs. The ultimate redactors did not participate in the work of formulation. Units of discourse framed in some prior setting have been preserved as is (though we do not know to what extent as to detail). They were drawn together whole and complete with other such essentially fixed and final units of discourse. That is the principal result of what follows in this chapter.

It might be wise to present charts to prove the present proposition about the fundamental difference between the literary and redactional condition of the Mishnah and that of the Talmud. But the reader need only open to any passage of the Mishnah and set it side by side with any passage of the Talmud of the Land of Israel. The contrast then will be clear. The former is constructed out of a severely limited repertoire of syntactic and rhetorical forms. The latter is diffuse and stylistically promiscuous. The former is tight, the latter loose; the former amply articulated, the latter remarkably elliptical; the former uniform and stylistically coherent, the latter diverse and formally incoherent. The former speaks in whole sentences; the latter in shorthand, abbreviated, notes toward discourse never amply articulated. Accordingly, it suffices to state as fact that what the Mishnah's redactors did to the Mishnah, Yerushalmi's redactors did not do to Talmud Yerushalmi. Our first task is to attempt to describe what they did do. But before proceeding, let us review the principal traits of the composition of the Mishnah. That exercise permits us to gain perspective as we proceed to the work of describing the literary traits of the Talmud of the Land of Israel.

REDACTION AND FORMULATION: YERUSHALMI CONTRASTED WITH MISHNAH

We now ask about the formulation and redaction of the Talmud of the Land of Israel as we know it—the end product in our hands—and not the formation, in earlier times, of ideas or whole discussions now contained within the document. The nature of the antecedent materials can only be determined when we have described what must be deemed the work of ultimate redaction. We shall first determine whether the process also included systematic formulation, or reformulation, of units of discourse already completed.

When I undertook to ask about the role of redaction in the formulation of the Mishnah, working on the division of Purities as my sample (roughly 25% of the entire Mishnah), I began from the outside and worked my way in. To review the process and its principal results, I began by asking this question: If all we had were a mass of words, how should we know where one thing stops and another starts? The first question is easy to answer definitively. We know that the mass of words is broken up (for Mishnah's division of Purities) into twelve principal divisions (tractates), uneven in length, because the subject of one long sequence of undifferentiated words ends and a new subject begins. There are, accordingly, lines of demarcation clearly drawn by the shift in theme or primary topic of discussion. What is blocked out, moreover, is consistent in its devotion to that given theme or primary topic, rarely dealing with a subject wholly irrelevant to the theme. It follows that the principal mode of organization is thematic. As is clear, the principal lines of division will be into tractates devoted to their respective, diverse topics. What is important is that that fact is shown on the basis of the internal character of the document, not merely of the *post facto* way in which exegetes, copyists, and printers organized matters.

Having proved that the Mishnah is organized, in its principal divisions, in accord with the unfolding of thematic and logical principles, I proceeded to ask about the delineation of the Mishnah's intermediate divisions. I avoided the word "chapters" because it can only yield confusion with the extant chapters, which are the work of copyists and printers, perhaps even of the earliest exegetes. These tell us nothing whatsoever about the original intent of the people who come before and stand behind the document, but only about the exegetical perceptions of the people who come afterward. How on the basis of internal evidence are intermediate divisions to be discerned? Having shown that the redactors not only organize their materials topically but also lay out the discussion of each topic in accord with its logically sequential parts, I am on firm ground in maintaining that one criterion for a demarcation line of undifferentiated columns of words of a Mishnah tractate, or principal division, will be a shift in topic or theme. What applies to, and emerges from, the whole surely must be asked to serve as criterion for what pertains also to the parts. There is, moreover, a second important criterion of delineation, and that is recurrent grammatical patterns or arrangements of words. This entails inquiry into the large-scale interplay between theme and form, between what is said and how it is said.

The first thing we notice when we study a Mishnah tractate from its opening sentence onward is that, when the subject changes, the formulary pattern shifts too. A given subtopic of a topical unit—a principal division—will be expressed in a distinctive pattern of syntax. These syntactical patterns, moreover, are divisible into two broad categories, tight and loose. The tight syntactical pattern will govern the layout of words for each concept, thought, or rule devoted to a given subtopic. The loose pattern will not. Rather, it emerges chiefly at the commencement of every conceptual unit. The former is therefore called an "internally unitary formulary pattern," in that the paramount formulary pattern everywhere governs the internal construction and wording of what is expressed. The latter is named an "externally unitary formulary pattern," in that the formulary pattern is external to what is expressed, being imposed primarily upon the opening clauses of a conceptual unit, not on the later wording. The remainder of the unit then will proceed in unpatterned sentences or clauses. To put matters more descriptively, we are unable to discern, in sentences which follow the commencement of the matter, any systematic pattern at all.

These results impose the requirement of further definition, differentiation, and analysis of the recurrent patterns by which sentences are constructed. The reason is that, once we recognize intermediate divisions because of the congruence of form and theme within a group of sentences, we come to the stage of the analysis of form. The appropriate framework for form analysis is the redactionally sizable, intermediate unit. For it is within the setting of the intermediate unit that the patterning and formalization of language become self-evident. It ceases to be a subjective observation that things *seem* to be stereotyped only when we see that, within circumscribed but sizable sequences of sentences, things indeed *are* not random but recurrent. Within that same framework we discern precisely what patterning of language is undertaken, how thought is reduced not merely to words but to words laid out in distinctive, recurrent syntactical structures.

It is at this point that we must define the smallest unit of formal analysis, which for the Mishnah I call "the cognitive unit." A cognitive unit is the formal (and formalized) result of a single cogent process of cognition, that is, analysis of a situation and statement of a rule pertaining to it, or some other, similar intellectual process. The Mishnah's smallest whole and irreducible literary-conceptual units are the end result of a single sequence, or process, of thought. Formal or formulary traits of such a unit commonly occur at the outset or in the first element of the result of cognition to be set into words and given linguistically formal character. After that point in the unit, what follows commonly exhibits no equivalent formalization. The remainder of the cognitive unit will generally consist of simple declarative sentences exhibiting no recurrent pattern and lacking all syntactical distinctiveness. The cognitive unit rarely stands by itself but is grouped together with other such units, devoted to a single principle or theme and exhibiting a single, distinctive syntactical trait or preference. Accordingly, the form-analytical work yields the result that the cognitive unit is shaped within the processes of organization of the intermediate (and principal) divisions of the Mishnah. This means that the work of giving formalized verbal expression to cognitive units and the work of organizing them into groups go together and reciprocally govern one another's results.

To state the historical result simply: the Mishnah's formulation and its organization are the result of the work of a single generation of tradent-redactors—tradents, who formulate units of thought, and redactors, who organize aggregations of these units. The Mishnah is not the product of tradents *succeeded* by redactors. It is not possible upon the basis of objective, internal literary evidence revealed by the Mishnah itself to specify much in formulation which derives from the period before that of redaction itself.

We may now rapidly relate these results to the document at hand. In the case of the Palestinian Talmud, the principle of organization is provided by the Mishnah itself. Tractates begin and end where the Mishnah does. Accordingly, if all we had were a mass of words, we should know the beginning and end of a tractate of our Talmud precisely as we do in the case of the Mishnah, because the point of demarcation is identical.

When it comes to the unfolding of intermediate divisions—"units of discourse" in my earlier paragraphs—we are in a different situation entirely. The Talmud's discussion attached to a given pericope of the Mishnah runs through two or more completed units of discourse. In general, therefore, the principle of organizing a discussion is not supplied solely and completely by the logical, or other exegetical, requirements of a passage of the Mishnah. The principle by which a discussion is inaugurated, worked out, and concluded is different from that of the Mishnah in general. It also differs from that supplied by a given intermediate unit of the Mishnah in particular cases. Since the intermediate divisions of the Yerushalmi are not demarcated by the requirements of the Mishnah, we cannot attempt to relate the delineation of those units to formal traits of the Mishnah. Formal considerations do not come into play in the Talmud before us in so rigid and disciplined a way as they govern the formulation of the Mishnah's ideas. It must follow that the work of ultimate redaction of the Palestinian Talmud is wholly separate from the work of formulation of individual units of discourse.

The upshot is that while the framers of the Talmud of the Land of Israel refer constantly to the Mishnah, they do not see themselves as bound by its patterns of formulation or even of redaction, let alone by its program and problems. They have in hand, or have created, diverse sorts of units of discourse, some of them essentially exegetical and tied to the Mishnah, others doing the same for Tosefta, still others of a quite separate literary character and substantive purpose. That is why, to describe the Talmud as a whole, we have to develop a taxonomy of its several types of units of discourse, in comparison and contrast to those of the Mishnah.

YERUSHALMI'S REDACTIONAL PROGRAM

To develop a taxonomy of the units of discourse contained within the Talmud of the Land of Israel, we begin by describing gross redactional traits. These are visible to the naked eye. The question then is simple: What kinds of units of discourse does the document exhibit and how are they arranged? The answer to this question should yield a first glimpse of the redactional program of the ultimate framers of the Talmud. Once we differentiate by type among the materials in the hands of the arrangers of the whole, we also may observe what principles, if any, guide their work of arrangement. For the present purpose, seeking the most general traits of the whole, a modest probe suffices. I review five tractates, a small one (Niddah), a very large one (Sanhedrin), an egregious one (Baba Mesia), and two medium ones (Nedarim and Sukkah).

The egregious category is defined by Saul Lieberman's landmark study, "The Talmud of Caesarea" (*Supplement to Tarbis*, vol. 2 [Jerusalem, 1931]), in which the tractates of the civil law, Baba Qamma, Baba Mesia, and Baba Batra, are shown to be different from all others in the Talmud of the Land of Israel. There Lieberman maintains that these tractates were edited in Caesarea about A.D. 350, that is, half a century before the closure of the Yerushalmi as a whole. The point of interest is whether the rough procedures with which we begin substantiate Lieberman's basic judgment of the egregious character of these tractates.

By unit of discourse, as I said earlier, I mean simply a discussion on a single topic, beginning either at a pericope of the Mishnah or at the point at which that topic is raised, ending either at the next pericope of the Mishnah or at the point at which some other topic is introduced, respectively. While the divisions are in some measure subjective, or may occasionally appear arbitrary, the relationship of a given set of materials ("unit of discourse") to the Mishnah will remain constant. I do not propose that quantitative numbers of units of discourse materially change matters, and, accordingly, the indications of units of discourse will not greatly affect the argument.

What is more important from the redactional perspective is the sequence of these units. As we shall see in a moment, where there is direct analysis of the Mishnah, or, at the very least, inquiry into the Scriptural foundations of the pericope at hand, the unit of discourse presenting such analysis or inquiry normally is the opening one in a sequence.

Among 335 Mishnah pericopes studied only twenty-six units of discourse pertinent to the Mishnah rule at hand commence discussion of that rule other than as unit I, less than 8% of the whole. (I exclude reference to the handful of Mishnah pericopes in which there is no analysis of the Mishnah law at all; I also exclude reference to the passages in which Tosefta's complement to the Mishnah's rule stands at the commencement of the discussion.) Accordingly, it will become clear that the usual redactional practice was to take a unit of discourse closely pertinent to the Mishnah and to place it at the commencement of discourse on the passage of the Mishnah at hand.

There is a further tendency to include in that opening unit, or in the one(s) immediately following, materials now found in Tosefta pertinent to the Mishnah. These Toseftan passages are cited either to amplify and extend the Mishnah's rule or otherwise to facilitate discourse about (or around) it. In Baba Mesia, that is invariably the case. Since, as we shall see in a moment, our results show again that Lieberman is surely right, the Caesarean Talmud may show us what the Talmud of the Land of Israel looked like, at least in the estimation of some circles or schools, at the outset. In that case it consisted, in the main, of the Mishnah's rule followed by Tosefta's amplification, then some (rather desultory) discourse, more commonly on the latter than on the former. If that is how things looked at the beginning, then in the next fifty years the other kinds of materials now preeminent in our Talmud were added. If the original conception was to join Tosefta to the Mishnah, then the next program was to amplify and vastly augment discourse, both concerning these compilations and also independent of them. These comments, however, should not be misunderstood to represent a thesis of the history of the formation of the Yerushalmi. They simply point to striking phenomena, apparent at first glance, as soon as we differentiate among types of units of discourse and ask about how they are arranged.

I differentiate among six possible relationships to the Mishnah pericope at hand, hence six types of units of discourse.

1. *Mishnah exegesis.* Here I first list each unit of the Mishnah in the five tractates, as marked out by the printed text. Where the Talmud contains no discussion of the Mishnah at all, I leave the item blank. Where there is any citation of the Mishnah passage, or clear-cut reference to it without direct citation, I list the number of the unit of discourse in which such discussion is contained. There is reason, of course,

to differentiate among types of treatments of the Mishnah, e.g., citation and gloss, inquiry into Scriptural foundations for the Mishnah's rule, rephrasing or restatement of the rule, and so on. This I do in later classifications. But for the present purpose, there is no reason for such differentiation. All we want to know is whether those units of discourse that take up the systematic and direct exegesis of the Mishnah pericopes exhibit a redactional pattern. The answer, as I said, is that they do—all the time, and, normally, at the very starting point of the Talmud's discussion.

2. *Tosefta: citation and exegesis.* The Palestinian Talmud frequently cites verbatim, or nearly verbatim, statements which also are found in the Tosefta. Moreover, where there are differences in wording between what we find in the Talmud and what we find in the Tosefta as we now have it, time and again (as Pené Moshe indicates) we discover that the Talmud's discussion presupposes the text now found in Tosefta rather than that now found in the Talmud. For that reason I do not think I claim too much in regarding this sort of material as the Tosefta's contribution. (I hasten to add the qualification that much more work has to be done on the matter than, for my purposes, I have thought necessary.) When Tosefta does appear, it tends to appear fairly early in the unfolding of the Talmud's discourse. In a fair number of instances where there is no clear-cut discourse on the Mishnah passage itself, the Talmud will cite the Tosefta and discuss that. We note in my brief explanation, therefore, that the Talmud's contribution to the exegesis of the Mishnah consists in the elucidation of the Tosefta's complement to the Mishnah, an orderly procedure indeed. This is a tendency, not a fixed rule.

3. *Legal speculation and reflection primary to the Mishnah.* A unit of discourse may well carry forward a discussion superficially separate from the Mishnah. Yet upon close inspection we notice that the discussion at hand speculates on principles introduced, to begin with, in the Mishnah's rule or in Tosefta's complement to that rule. There is a marked tendency for this type of unit to be included only in sequence after the first and second types.

4. *Harmonization of distinct laws of the Mishnah.* One of the more interesting kinds of units of discourse is that in which principles are abstracted from utterly unrelated rules of the Mishnah (less commonly, of the Tosefta). These are then shown to intersect and to conflict; or opinions and principles of a given authority on one such matter will be

shown to differ from those of that same authority on another, inter-secting matter. These units tend to occur in several different tractates verbatim, since they serve equally well (or poorly) each Mishnah peric-ope cited therein. Items on this list stand side by side with those on the foregoing. Both sorts of units of discourse relate to the Mishnah in essentially the same way. They vastly amplify the principles of the Mish-nah. But they do not serve for a close exegesis of its wording or specific rule. These entries are few, but always substantial and difficult. The reason is that several different kinds of law have to be mastered, then the underlying principles made explicit and brought into juxtaposition with those of other laws on other topics.

5. *Legal speculation and reflection independent of the passage of the Mishnah at hand.* There are units of discourse essentially independent of the Mishnah pericope with which they are associated. These pursue questions not even indirectly generated by the law in hand. From time to time we may guess at why the redactor thought the discourse belonged where he placed it. While there are not a great many of these, as in the foregoing instance, they are long and involved, and always difficult and unusually interesting. They tend to occur not at the initial stages of a Talmudic passage attached to a pericope of the Mishnah, but rather late in the sequence of types of units of discourse. At Baba Mesia, for example, with its rather brief units of discourse, dominated by (mere) citation of Tosefta, they invariably occur in the second of two units. In Sanhedrin we find them at the higher end of the scale of numbers of units of discourse, and beyond, and the same is so, in general, at Niddah and Sukkah. But this is only a tendency, by no means a rule so fixed as the one governing placement fo units of discourse devoted to Mishnah exegesis.

6. *Anthology, relevant to the Mishnah only in theme.* There are sizable units of discourse joined together only by a common theme, and joined to the Mishnah pericope at which they occur only because, in some rather general way, someone supposed their themes to intersect with those of the Mishnah passage at hand. This type of unit of dis-course is especially common in tractate Sanhedrin. In particular, it pre-dominates in those chapters where the Mishnah's statements, for their part, pertain not to law but to lore. Most such anthologies are rich in citation of, and comment upon, verses of Scripture. But the present category includes by no means the bulk of the Talmud's Scriptural

exegeses and comments in the tractates at hand. There is a tendency for this type of unit of discourse to occur later in the unfolding of a Talmudic passage assigned to a given Mishnah pericope, just as is the case in the foregoing.

Let me proceed to generalization. The redactional program of the men responsible for laying out the materials of Yerushalmi may now be described in simple terms. Most important, we see that there was such a program. There is nothing random. That is clear because, within the differentiation of units of discourse I have defined, diverse types of units of discourse are not mixed together promiscuously. There is a pronounced tendency to move from close reading of the Mishnah and then Tosefta to more general inquiry into the principles of a Mishnah passage and their interplay with those of some other, superficially unrelated passage, and, finally, to more general reflections on law not self-evidently related to the Mishnah passage at hand or to anthologies intersecting only at a general topic. Now while that program may appear self-evident and logical, we must not assume there were no choices in how to lay things out. The program I have described exhibits sufficient variation to rule out the possibility that our Talmud's way is the better way of doing things. The case of Baba Mesia, moreover, different in program as is that tractate from the others we probed, leaves no doubt about the matter. *Things are the way they are because people wanted them to be this way and not some other way.* We know this because the paramount traits of several hundred Talmudic passages devoted to units of the Mishnah, are, if not everywhere uniform, then fairly constant and consistent.

It therefore follows that the redactors of our five tractates knew precisely how they wished to lay out the materials that they drew together into the Talmud. Accordingly, the work of redaction was active and followed a program. Whether or not that work was done in a single generation is unclear. Following Lieberman, we must concur that fifty years prior to the formation of the Palestinian Talmud as we know it, a previous Talmud, the one made in Caesarea, followed the program we have uncovered. It may have been that the redactors of the rest of the Talmud accepted the plan of the Caesarean authorities for the tractates they later undertook to create. Perhaps there was a shared program among the various schools, along these lines: "Since we are studying the Mishnah and Tosefta as our principal texts, we shall now lay out some permanent guidelines on how to read these texts and interpret and apply them." The one thing that is clear is that the redactors took full charge of the layout of whatever materials came to hand. They made significant decisions about the order in which diverse types of discourse were to be carried on: this, then that.

If therefore we now take as fact that the Talmud before us is the result of a generation, or several generations, of redaction, it is because we see the evidence of active participation in the formation of the document: a plan, a program. The contrary possibility, that this is just how things happened to come to hand, seems unlikely, given the disproportionate replication of a single logical, self-evident pattern. The second question flows from the first. If the redactors participated in the organization of units of discourse, did they also place their mark upon the formulation of those same units of discourse? It is to this question that we must now turn.

FROM REDACTION TO FORMULATION?

The facts we have reviewed point to a general uniformity, from one tractate to the next, in redactional processes, with the important exception of the Babas, the Talmud of Caesarea. Even there, strikingly, the differences in redactional policy from other, more "normal," tractates lie in what is omitted rather than what is included. Accordingly, we are on firm ground in maintaining that we may speak of the Talmud as a whole, even though our sample is only five tractates. We must always allow for variation here and there. But uniform work on the whole Talmud clearly was done and done systematically, since, as we have seen, the fundamental policy governing organization of materials is uniform for the tractates at hand.

It follows that we may turn from redaction to formulation. Once more, with all due respect for variation and diversity, we seek gross and general traits, affecting the whole of the Talmud under study.

Since the close interplay between redaction and formulation constitutes the sole firm result of our study of the Mishnah, we ask about the same matter for our Talmud. The issue is whether we can find evidence of systematic attention to formulating units of discourse in such a way as formally or syntactically to relate one to the next within a single redactional program or process. If there is such evidence, we must conclude that, even in the ultimate redactional stages of the formation of the Talmud, work went on not merely in minor correction, revision, or glossing of a passage. Such work pertained even to the very formulation of the statement of its main points, in the structure and wording by which those points would be expressed. It would then follow that, prior to the redaction of the whole, we are unable to posit the existence of units of discourse as we know them. If we find no points of correlation between redactional policies and problems of formulation of units of discourse, on the other hand, it must follow that, separate from (perhaps then, prior to) the redactional stages (though we do not know how long before) a process of formulation of units of discourse was underway.

Our question thus is, did the redactors work with essentially finished units of discourse? Or did they themselves participate in the formation of the completed units of discourse which they also organized and juxtaposed? The criterion for positive evidence for the second proposition—hence, also, negative evidence for the first—derives from comparison with the Mishnah. What we compare are units of discourse of our Talmud and the formulary traits of Mishnah pericopes. The latter indicate the hand of redaction and organization within the very phrasing of individual units of law of the Mishnah. Absence of equivalent traits then will signify for the Talmud a different relationship of redaction to formulation from that prevalent in the Mishnah. For the Mishnah, essential to the organization and layout of completed units of discourse is the very pattern of formulating those same units of discourse. The result, as I have now made clear, is proof, for the Mishnah, that redaction is prior and critical to formulation. In the Mishnah, redaction is not solely a process of joining together statements bearing no formal relationship to one another, hence existing before (we do not know how long before) the process of organization and layout we call redaction. A clear grasp of how the Mishnah works is then essential to a comparative inquiry into the Talmud's traits.

Now to spell out the interplay of formulation and redaction in the Mishnah. The principal result of my inquiry was to show constant and close relationship between the one and the other. Specifically, I found that when the Mishnah's redactors wished to indicate the formation of a unit of discourse (which I called, in that setting, "intermediate unit"), they would take up a distinctive formulary pattern or form, different from that which they had used beforehand and also from that which they would use in the following unit. They would carefully group their smallest whole statements ("smallest units of cognition") so that each one would repeat the same syntactic pattern, setting up (in general) groups of three or multiples of three, or groups of five or multiples of five, with such internally patterned statements of a single principle being applied to a single theme. This seemed to me definitive evidence that the whole could not have been formulated prior to the work of redaction, at which point—and not before—the larger program of arrangement of topics and principles expressed in connection with those topics was in hand. Only when the whole was fully in view was it possible to form the parts in the uniform way in which they were formed. There is no other economical way of explaining the facts I have discovered, since, as is clear, the whole was planned before the parts were laid out in their matching and distinctive syntactic patterns and in their little sets of three or five repetitions of such patterns.

CONCLUSION

That the Talmud of the Land of Israel reveals a clear-cut plan for organizing its component parts is beyond doubt. But knowing that fact helps very little in defining the work before us. For all we have accomplished is to differentiate the redaction from the formulation of the Talmud's units of discourse. No one need doubt that a repertoire of patterns governed the way in which language was shaped for the expression of ideas. But when the use of these patterns indicates a fact of social or historical significance is by no means clear. Sometimes a recurrent syntactic pattern shows us nothing more than how people said things "in general." We cannot discover from that fact anything consequential for the interpretation of the history of our document and the formation of its building blocks. Clearly, a brief probe into a single form turned up a few interesting facts. Most proved negative for our larger purpose. In all, the key issue for the use of the units of discourse for the study of important events in the history of Judaism in the third and fourth centuries in the Land of Israel has yet to be framed. If we want to know who is responsible for the formation of the units of discourse, all we now know is that it was not those who undertook redaction. Those at the point of formulation, on the one side, and in the framework of transmission and preservation to the time of redaction, on the other, stand behind the little "talmuds" of which our Talmud is composed.

It looks to me as if the point of formulation of a sizable proportion of units of discourse—in particular, those containing the names of two or more authorities—can be no earlier than the moment at which the opinions of those authorities were made to intersect and form the foundations of a larger inquiry. For the sake of convenience, we may say, therefore, that if two members of the same generation, not in constant association with one another, are represented in a unit of discourse as disputing a common point, that representation must be the work of people who flourished somewhat later than the moment at which the two authorities expressed themselves on the common point, on the one side, and at which interest in drawing together diverse views on that same point had developed, on the other. So, obviously, this is "afterward." But how long? It can have been a day later, or a century later. The *terminus a quo*—a given authority's lifetime—is not very helpful for our needs. We require a *terminus ad quem*—a point prior to which the unit of discourse as we know it, or a principal component thereof, simply must have reached its present formulation.

On the basis of literary analysis, so far as I am able to accomplish it, I can say no more than this: Yerushalmi's units of discourse and their components were formulated sometime, somewhere, prior to the processes of ultimate closure and redaction. The work of formulation and original closure was essentially distinct from those processes. But, as I just said, that can have been earlier by a day, a year, or a century. It can have happened one house down the block. We have no evidence as to where or how the work was done. All we have is the result: what people said various authorities had earlier said.

9

The Palestinian Talmud

Abraham Goldberg

TANNAIM AND AMORAIM

The literary formulation and exposition of Oral Tora as expressed in the corpus of Tannaic literature reached culmination in the mid-third century C.E. The final editing of the Mishnah, Tosefta and Tannaic midrash collections marked the end of a period. It was followed by two-and-a-half centuries of specialized commentary to the Tannaic corpus: the period of the Talmud. The literal meaning of the word *talmud* is 'teaching', and indeed the talmudic period is marked by intense commentary to, and extended teaching of, all that went before it.

The period of the Talmud is also known as the Amoraic period, after the teachers of this period who are designated *Amoraim*. This term derives from the verb *amar* which means 'to say'. The Amora 'says' or 'explains', and his teachings are called *memra*, 'saying'. Thus this period is differentiated from the previous period whose teachers do not 'say' but 'teach' and are called Tannaim (from the Aramaic *tana*, to teach); their teachings are called *matnita*, 'teaching', in Aramaic, or in the Hebrew parallel: *mishna*. The Tanna 'teaches'; the Amora 'says'. The distinction between Tanna and Amora is clearly made in the Talmud itself. Thus Rav Papa refers to 'two Tannaim or two Amoraim who differ with one another'.[1]

Yet despite these distinctions, the transition from the Tannaic to the

Amoraic period is not clearly marked. The first generation of Babylonian Amoraim, for example, resemble in many ways the last generations of Palestinian Tannaim such as R. Hiya and R. Hoshaya, and their teachings are often indicated in the same way as Tannaic traditions.[2] Of the first-century Babylonian Amora Rav it is stated explicitly: 'Rav is a Tanna and may dispute a mishna or baraita.'[3] In other respects too, the Talmud is not just commentary to the Mishna which itself belongs to a clearly different period, but also an extension of the Mishna. In the course of its commentary on the Mishna it brings in almost every relevant Tannaic teaching, whether it be found in the extant Tannaic collections or in baraitot otherwise unknown. Regarding the last category, both Talmudim are very important sources for our knowledge of Tannaic teaching. Furthermore, the prime aim, especially of the Palestinian Talmud, is a further discussion of mishnayot in relation to other Tannaic halakhot, and in doing so it keeps very close to the direct meaning of the Mishna text.[4]

PALESTINIAN AND BABYLONIAN TALMUD

The Talmud is an extension of Tannaic teaching not only in time, but also in place. Simultaneously, two parallel processes of post-mishnaic teaching began, in Palestine and in Babylonia. While the Palestinian Talmud had its final editing at the end of the fourth century, the Babylonian Talmud was to grow for another century. Both Talmudim contain the edited discussions and halakhic decisions of the Sages of the various academies in Palestine and in Babylonia.

Although the two Talmudim emerged from two independent teaching traditions, these did not remain separate. They drew upon one another and have much material in common.[5] Thus many a completely Babylonian discussion will be included in the Palestinian Talmud, and, to a much greater extent, Palestinian teaching is found in the Babylonian Talmud, albeit often with characteristic changes.[6] The dependence of the Babylonian Talmud upon Palestinian teachings is especially marked in topics belonging to the Orders *Zeraim* and *Toharot*.[7] These close relations between both Talmudim are explained in part by the interchange of Sages between Palestine and Babylonia. In almost every generation, some of the greatest Palestinian Sages were Babylonians who had come to Palestine to study.[8] Most brought their own traditions with them and undoubtedly influenced the tone of Palestinian teaching.[9] At the same time, many Palestinian scholars for one reason or another left for Babylonia. A famous name in the early period is Ulla.[10] The causes for this exodus of Sages may not have been the disastrous outcome of an anti-Roman revolt in the mid-fourth century, as was supposed by historians following Graetz, but rather the difficult economic situation and the detoriorating position of the Patriarchate.[11]

In addition, in all periods special emissaries were appointed by the Palestinian academies to bring Palestinian teachings to their Babylonian colleagues. These emissaries were known as *nehutai,* 'those going down', i.e. from Palestine to Babylonia. In addition to Ulla, who also functioned as such an emissary, other important names are the early fourth-century Babylonian Amoraim Rav Dimi, Rav Abin, Rav Shmuel bar Yehuda and Rav Yitshak bar Yosef.[12]

Yet for all the similarity between the two Talmudim, a world of difference remains. This is reflected both in external form and in content. Externally, the language and the form of editing differ considerably. The non-Hebrew portions of the Palestinian Talmud are in the western Aramaic dialect, whereas in the Babylonian Talmud these are in Eastern Aramaic. Greek words appear quite frequently in the Palestinian Talmud, in contrast to the Persian often found in its Babylonian counterpart. As for editing, the Babylonian Talmud underwent a post-talmudic re-editing which gave it its polished and consistent literary form. It also included additional discussions by the Sages living between the talmudic and Gaonic periods who are known by the name of Savoraim. Compared with this highly developed form, the Palestinian Talmud is much simpler. Differences of content are also quite extensive, although, as stated, both Talmudim have much in common. One of these differences is in the interpretation of the Tannaic sources on which both Talmudim rely. This is related not only to differences in the traditions of interpretation, but also reflects a range of differences in the political, cultural and economic conditions peculiar to each country.[13]

Another difference between both Talmudim is in the aggada they contain. It accounts for about one-sixth of the Palestinian Talmud; the Babylonian Talmud has almost a third. The aggada is often interwoven with the halakha, or may serve as a signature to extended halakhic discussions. Thus it does much to reveal the deep spirituality of seemingly dry halakha. Taken as a literary device, it serves as a variation from the purely intellectual halakhic style. This material goes by the name aggada which is, as Louis Ginzberg wrote, 'a very comprehensive term which includes theology and religious philosophy, folklore and history, mathematics and astronomy, medicine and natural science, and many other subjects.' In this respect, however, there is not only a difference in proportion of material between both Talmudim. Angelology and demonology figure prominently in the Babylonian Talmud, but are almost entirely absent in the Palestinian. Angels, with the exception of Michael and Gabriel who are already mentioned in the Bible, are rarely mentioned, nor do those which appear have names, individuality and specific spheres of activity as they do in the Babylonian Talmud. There is also comparatively little of sorcery, magic, astrology and other popular beliefs in the Palestinian Talmud.[14]

There are differences as well in coverage of the Mishna. There is no Babylonian Talmud to the first Order, *Zeraim,* except for the special first tractate, *Berakhot.* The Palestinian Talmud, however, covers the whole Order of *Zeraim.* Conversely, there is no Palestinian Talmud to the fifth Order, *Kodashim,* while there is Babylonian Talmud to it, except for the tractates *Middot* and *Kinnim.* As for the last Order, *Toharot,* both Talmudim are equal: they have only the tractate *Nidda.* The Babylonian Talmud, furthermore, has no coverage of tractate *Shekalim* in the Order of *Moed;* the Talmud tractate printed in traditional Babylonian Talmud editions in reality is taken from the Palestinian Talmud. Again, both Talmudim are equal in not covering tractates *Avot* and *Eduyot;* these have a special character.[15]

IMPORTANCE OF THE PALESTINIAN TALMUD

It is not because the Palestinian Talmud came first, that we begin our discussion with it. The literary creation process out of which the Talmudim emerged, started simultaneously in Palestine and in Babylonia. The Palestinian Talmud, however, does have a primacy in that it is closest in literary tradition and material conditions to Tannaic literature, which was created almost exclusively in Palestine. This is also what its name implies: the Talmud of those in Palestine.[16] This is the one reason why the Tosefta and Tannaic midrashim are quoted in the Palestinian Talmud almost without change in wording, whereas the Babylonian Talmud often introduces major or minor changes.[17] For the understanding of Tannaic literature, therefore, the Palestinian Talmud is of prime importance. The same is reflected in the difference between Babylonian and Palestinian versions of the same narrative. In most cases, the Palestinian version should be given historical priority.[18]

The distinctive literary unit created in the talmudic discussion and characterizing it, is called the *sugya* (lit. course, lesson). It is a unique arrangement of sources and comments. It attains a fully developed literary form in the Babylonian Talmud, to such an extent that sometimes the literary brilliance obscures the sources on which it is based. In the Palestinian Talmud, the sugya is much simpler; this is another reason why it is much truer to the Tannaic sources. The Palestinian sugya is usually short and concise, with scarce editorial introductions and connections, often to the point of being enigmatic. It may consist of no more than the juxtaposition of a Tannaic text in seeming variance with a mishna, and a reconciliation of the two. Or it may begin with an Amoraic statement to which Tannaic sources or other Amoraic statements are found to relate either in support or in opposition; if the latter, there may be an attempt to smooth out the differences.[19]

The Palestinian Talmud represents a literary creation process of close to two centuries, during which development in literary form was inevitable. This development, however, is but modest when compared to that of the Babylonian Talmud which, even apart from its post-talmudic re-editing, lasted for at least a century after the completion of the Palestinian. A comparison of those sugyot in which only the early generations of Babylonian Sages figure will show that the Babylonian sugya at this time was not substantially different from the Palestinian one.[20] Moreover, development of the sugya in the Palestinian Talmud is especially marked in its later generations of Amoraim, who correspond in time to the middle generations of Amoraim in Babylonia (350–400 C.E.). Thus it is understandable that we find Babylonian sugyot in the Palestinian Talmud.[21] Less surprising is, that the Babylonian Talmud contains many Palestinian sugyot.[22]

In this respect, the special value of the Palestinian Talmud, with all its enigmatic brevity, comes out once again. The sugya is a literary form which develops from generation to generation, and some sugyot reveal the contributions of all the generations. The sugya then becomes a chain of several links, usually independent of one another. Often, however, the chain was shortened in the final editing, the middle link or links being eliminated, and the sugya in its present form retaining only the first and last links of the chain. Where such a sugya from the Babylonian Talmud appears in the Palestinian as well, the chain will end somewhere parallel to the middle of the Babylonian chain, in accordance with the earlier completion date. In these cases, the Palestinian sugya helps us to reconstruct the missing middle links of the Babylonian sugya.[23]

THE PALESTINIAN AMORAIM AND THE MISHNA

We now address ourselves to the question of how the Palestinian Amoraim related to the Mishna. Did they accept all its teachings, or did they differ with it; or, alternatively, did they try to emend its text? Here, however, we come up to a serious methodical problem.

The Mishna of the Palestinian Talmud is not always identical with that of the Babylonian; there is little doubt that it is closer to the version edited by Rabbi Yehuda the Patriarch. We are referring here, however, to the Mishna text which the Palestinian Talmud itself presupposes. The version which appears chapter by chapter as the heading of each respective Talmud chapter does not always correspond with the text on which the Palestinian *sugya* seems to have been based. It was appended by the printers from available manuscripts which were already influenced by Babylonian textual traditions. It is only the careful study of the Palestinian Talmud itself which can determine the exact Mishna reading which the Palestinian Amoraim had before them.[24]

The leading Sage of the first generation of Amoraim in Palestine, i.e. middle third century C.E., and indeed the most important figure in the entire Palestinian Talmud, is R. Yohanan.[25] His long life spanned the last Tannaic generation and three of the Amoraim. His prime teacher was R. Yannai, a pupil of R. Yehuda the Patriarch, but he also learned from several others of that generation: Hizkia, R. Hanina, R. Hoshaya and R. Shimon ben Yehotsadak. He was most familiar with the baraitot, i.e. the 'extraneous' halakhot not incorporated in the Mishna, and he himself was a *tanna* whose task it was to recite the baraitot in the sessions of the academy.[26]

R. Yohanan regarded the Mishna as a halakhic code rather than a text-book of halakha. However, while he usually follows its teaching, he does not necessarily do so always.[27] He saw the Tosefta and other baraitot as the prime source for a proper understanding of the Mishna, and he almost invariably interpreted the Mishna in harmony with them, even if that implied forcing the meaning of the Mishna.[28] Very remarkable, and almost modern, is his awareness of conflicting opinions within anonymous mishnayot, and he did not attempt to reconcile them even where this seemed most natural.[29] Other Amoraim would try to explain contradictions between different anonymous mishnayot, or even within a single mishna, by positing different situations. But here, R. Yohanan was not prepared to harmonize and preferred to assume different sources, following the principle laid down by his great teacher R. Hoshaya: 'He who taught this (anonymous section) did not teach that one.'[30] In another formulation this maxim reads: 'Two different teachers taught here.'[31] Viewing the Mishna as a halakhic code, he established the important principle that its editor gave the anonymous opinion or that of 'the Sages' as the accepted halakha.[32] Thus one mishna will teach the opinion of one Sage anonymously and another will give the differing view of another Sage, also anonymously, even though the underlying principle in both mishnayot seems to be the same.[33]

The great contemporary of R. Yohanan was his friend (in the Babylonian aggada, his brother-in-law)[34] R. Shimon ben Lakish.[35] Originally from the South of Palestine, he was attracted, like many from his area, to the Galilee, the greatest center of learning as well as the seat of the Patriarch. Yet he never gave up the traditions of his native area.[36] He is the chief opponent of R. Yohanan in halakhic discussions, differing with him not only on particular questions but in general principles as well.

Whereas R. Yohanan interpreted the Mishna on the basis of the baraita, R. Shimon ben Lakish insisted that the Mishna be interpreted only on what could be inferred from the Mishna itself. He had almost a contempt for the extra-mishnaic collections: 'If Rabbi did not teach such (in his Mishna), how could R. Hiya (Rabbi's chief pupil and compiler of baraitot) know it?'[37] On the contrary, it is only the Mishna which can be used to confirm the teachings of the baraita: 'This is like what Rabbi taught . . .'[38] Wherever possible, he preferred to explain away seeming contradictions within a mishna by positing different situations as necessitating different rules.[39] Yet he, too, upon occasion would not accept an anonymous teaching as binding, arguing, as sometimes did R. Yohanan himself, that the anonymous teaching in various mishnayot was only an individual point of view.[40]

The chief pupil of R. Yohanan and the leading scholar of the next generation in Palestine (later third century C.E.) was a Babylonian by birth, R. Elazar ben Pedat.[41] He followed R. Yohanan's general approach to the Mishna, but also brought with him elements of Babylonian teaching. With the passing of the generations, much Babylonian teaching was taken over in Palestine, especially since many of the leading scholars in almost every generation were Babylonian in origin. In this respect the name of R. Zeira is outstanding, for he cleverly tried to show (what he probably believed honestly) that the great Palestinian Sage, R. Yohanan, really taught Babylonian halakha![42]

Five generations of Sages, counting the generation of R. Yohanan and R. Shimon ben Lakish as the first, make their appearance in the Palestinian Talmud.[43] Many scholars date the decline of the Palestinian academies from 351 C.E., when the three important cities Tiberias, Sepphoris and Lydda, seats of the academies, are believed to have suffered greatly in the outbreaks against the Roman commander Ursicinus.[44] Many of the Sages emigrated to Babylonia. The extinction of the Patriarchate in 425 C.E. marks as well a final date for the Palestinian Talmud.[45]

RELATIONSHIP TO MISHNA, TOSEFTA AND BARAITOT

After the Tosefta, the Palestinian Talmud is considered the most important source in all that concerns a basic interpretation of the Mishna. As we have pointed out above, the *sugya* of the Palestinian Talmud, unlike that of the Babylonian, is in most cases very brief, and it is also closely related to the Tosefta. Very characteristic is the opening of a *sugya* on the Mishna with a quotation from the Tosefta, either with the introductory term *teni* or without.

The Tosefta is for the most part quoted literally in the Palestinian Talmud, and if there are occasional changes, they are minor. In many ways the Palestinian Talmud is a kind of extension of the Tosefta, as the Tosefta is of the Mishna. It will continue debates of the Tannaim begun in the Tosefta.[46] Again, just as the Tosefta will add to a topic taken up in the Mishna by a discussion of situations not brought up in the Mishna, so, too, will the Palestinian Talmud discuss situations not brought up in the Tosefta.[47]

The Tosefta serves the Palestinian Talmud as the prime source for the interpretation of the Mishna, and its interpretations of the Mishna are much closer, therefore, than those in the Babylonian Talmud; and although the latter does make use of the Tosefta, it is not to the same extent.[48] Questions in the Palestinian Talmud are often resolved by recourse to the Tosefta.[49]

Occasionally, however, the Palestinian Talmud will differ with the Tosefta[50] and may even 'correct' the language of the Tosefta in accordance with its own interpretation of the Mishna.[51]

The Palestinian Talmud also shows an attitude of relative independence in its interpretation of the Mishna. This is indicated in several ways: a correction given to the Mishna without recourse to the Tosefta;[52] independent interpretations to seemingly redundant language in the Mishna;[53] limitations to the teaching in the Mishna;[54] or independent definitions.[55]

The Tosefta, of course, is not the only source of extra-mishnaic Tannaic teaching in the Palestinian Talmud. The Tannaic midrash is quoted extensively, as it is in the Babylonian Talmud. So, too, are collections of baraitot, attributed to the School of Rabbi, Bar Kappara, R. Hiya, R. Oshaya, the School of R. Yishmael, the School of R. Akiva and the School of R. Shmuel (first generation Babylonian Amora). Most baraitot, even if their source can be determined, are quoted anonymously. A listing of baraitot of R. Hiya and those of R. Oshaya is given by the late American scholar Michael Higger, who collected and classified all the baraitot in both Talmudim.[56]

EDITING

Four great centers of learning existed during the Amoraic period in Palestine: Tiberias and Sepphoris in Galilee, Lydda and Caesarea in the South. All of these figure to some extent in the Tannaic period.[57]

The oldest part of the Palestinian Talmud was edited in Caesarea, the seat of the Roman government in Palestine, in the middle of the fourth century.[58] This 'oldest' Talmud consists of short comments, of almost exclusively halakhic content, to the first three tractates of *Nezikin*. Not only in its brevity does it differ from the rest of the Talmud, but also in style and terminology.[59] Although the differences in place and time of compilation have left their imprint, it is conceivable that the Talmud which at the same time was taught at Tiberias might have resembled in many ways the 'primitive' character of this oldest section.

This oldest part, *Bava Kamma, Bava Metsia* and *Bava Batra*, goes now by the name *Talmuda shel Kisrin*, the Talmud of Caesarea, as Lieberman termed it, in contrast to the later editing of the Palestinian Talmud which he called 'The Talmud of Tiberias'.[60] In many ways, it represents the tradition of Judea, as opposed to that of Galilee, and the names of the Amoraim which appear are primarily of the early generations.[61] There are special affinities to the Babylonian Talmud, which in general seems to be closer to Judean than to Galilean tradition.[62]

This theory found confirmation in the Palestinian Talmud contained in the Escorial MS., one of the most fascinating discoveries made recently by the late E. S. Rosenthal (see below). This superior manuscript (the Geniza fragments included) preserves the Palestinian Aramaic more closely than the Leiden MS. which is already influenced by the Babylonian Talmud; Greek words are much less mutilated. The Escorial MS. confirms Lieberman's theory of the Caesarean redaction, although some details now require revision. It can be shown, for example, that terms which he took to be uniquely characteristic of the Caesarean edition are only variations in the textual tradition.

The rest of the Palestinian Talmud—namely, the first three Orders and the remaining tractates of the Fourth plus *Nidda* of the Fifth—were edited at Tiberias. Some scholars see the Palestinian Talmud as simply a jotting down of academic discussion without organization or final reworking.[63] However, it should be emphasized that there was a conscious editing, expressed among other things in a definite plan and arrangement, although it is certainly true that it did not reach the degree of perfection of the Babylonian Talmud. Those attuned to the latter do not often fully appreciate the individual character of the Palestinian Talmud.

Although the greater part of the Palestinian Talmud was edited in Tiberias, it is not the work of one school. Frequent references are made to the scholars of Sepphoris, and to those of Lydda and Caesarea, although the last-mentioned occur somewhat less frequently. The Tiberian editors, of course, incorporated in their work the three treatises of the Caesarean Talmud. And, as we have pointed out in detail, many discussions of the Babylonian academies are introduced as well.

AUTHORITY

The Palestinian Talmud remained the Talmud of the Jews in Palestine for a great many years after the editing of the Babylonian Talmud, even though the latter was superior in range and literary quality. The same situation prevailed in adjacent Egypt; and in Kairwan and even as far as Southern Italy, the Palestinian Talmud was of great influence. A work from the mid-seventh century which was discovered fairly recently among the Cairo Geniza fragments, *Sefer ha-Maasim*,[64] indicates that in its day Palestinian Jewry still had one Talmud, i.e. the Palestinian.

This was the situation until the establishment of the caliphate in Baghdad in the eighth century, when Abassid Babylonia became the center not only of Arabic but also of Jewish culture. From then on, the influence of the Babylonian Talmud began to suppress the Palestinian Talmud. However, in Kairwan it continued to be studied; R. Nissim ibn Shahin and R. Hananael maintained it in the curriculum at an equal place with the Babylonian Talmud. Alfasi, the eleventh century scholar from Northern Africa who became the leading authority of Spanish Jewry, incorporated much Palestinian material in his digest of the Babylonian Talmud, most of it as it was already found in the commentary to the Babylonian Talmud of his great teacher, R. Hananael. Even Maimonides, two generations later, used the Palestinian Talmud for his commentary to the Mishna,[65] and occasionally, when deciding contrary to the Babylonian Talmud, in his Code;[66] he even composed a digest to the Palestinian Talmud on the pattern of Alfasi's digest to the Babylonian.[67] Although students from the Byzantine empire and from all parts of Europe—Italy, Spain, Provence—came to study in the Babylonian center in Baghdad, and subsequently brought its Talmud back home with them, the Palestinian Talmud was not entirely displaced. It continued to be well known in Spain and the Provence, and the first known commentary, now lost, to the Palestinian Talmud was by R. Yitshak ha-Kohen, a younger contemporary of Maimonides from the Provence. Although Rashi in eleventh century France knew it only second hand in all probability, the spreading influence of R. Hananael's commentary and his frequent mention of the Palestine Talmud, brought with it a desire to know the original. The French Tosafists of the twelfth and thirteenth centuries as well as their contemporaries in Germany had a thorough familiarity with it.[68]

It is paradoxical that Alfasi, who did incorporate much from the Palestinian Talmud in his halakhic compendium, was in a way responsible for its later decline. Following a Gaonic tradition, he laid down the rule that where the two Talmudim are in conflict decisions are to be made in accordance with the Babylonian. The Babylonian Talmud is to be considered authoritative, he wrote, since it was later, and its Sages undoubtedly knew of the Palestinian teaching, yet were convinced that their own point of view was the more correct one.[69]

The sufferings and persecutions of Jews in Europe during the fourteenth and fifteenth centuries made Talmud study difficult. It was hard enough to hold to even one Talmud, and the study of another one of lesser authority seemed too much of a luxury for those times. The one exception was in Spain where the Palestinian Talmud continued to be studied. It is not surprising, therefore, that our first extant commentary to the Palestinian Talmud was written by R. Shlomo Syrileio, a native of Spain who emigrated to Palestine after the expulsion of 1492, where he composed his commentary to the Order of *Zeraim* and tractate *Shekalim* in the first third of the sixteenth century.

BIBLIOGRAPHY

Commentaries

There is nothing for the Palestinian Talmud comparable to the Babylonian Talmud commentaries of Rashi and the Tosafists. We have just made mention of the first extant commentary to the Order *Zeraim* and Tractate *Shekalim* written by R. Shlomo Syrileio. Only one really full commentary exists, however, and that is the eighteenth century double commentary *Penei Moshe* and *Mare ha-Penim* by R. Moshe Margoliot, incorporated fully for the first time in the Zhitomir edition, 1860–67. A brief and rather fragmentary commentary to the entire Palestinian Talmud, written by R. David Darshan, had already appeared in the Cracow edition of 1609 and was reprinted later in the Krotoshin edition.[70] Next in importance to the *Penei Moshe* is the *Korban ha-Eda* (with a supplement entitled *Sheyarei Korban*) of R. David Fraenkel of Berlin (1704–62) on the Orders of *Moed, Nashim, and part of Nezikin*. This commentary was intended in a way to supplement the commentary of R. Eliyahu Fulda, which was limited to fifteen tractates.[71] Another important commentary is that of R. Yoshua Benveniste on eighteen tractates.[72]

Although all these larger commentaries undoubtedly help much in understanding the Palestinian Talmud, they all suffer from a Babylonian bias in their interpretation. Where the two Talmudim differ, a reconciliation is often attempted, usually without success. It is only in relatively modern times that the principle has been established that each Talmud should be explained in terms of its own individuality.

Perhaps the greatest impetus to the renewed interest in the Palestinian Talmud during the last two centuries was the work of R. Eliyahu Gaon of Wilna (1720–97). Indeed, the most intensive study of the Palestinian Talmud during the nineteenth century was carried out by his pupils. R. Eliyahu's commentary to Order *Zeraim* was published, however, only in the 1926 Wilna edition. Of almost equal importance in this connection is his commentary to the Mishna Order *Zeraim*, called *Shenot Eliyahu*, which is based primarily on the Palestinian Talmud. His commentary to the *Shulhan Arukh* contains as well many explanations of passages in the Palestinian Talmud.

A really critical approach basing itself upon philological-historical method is less than a century old. It really begins with Israel Lewy's commentary to the first six chapters of the treatise *Bava Kamma*.[73] The twentieth century has seen the publication of GINZBERG's four-volume *Commentary*, covering the first five chapters of *Berakhot*. In spite of its limited span in actual commentary to the Palestinian Talmud, it is of great importance because of its wide philological and historical interests.

The greatest modern-day authority on the Palestinian Talmud is the late Lieberman, whose *Hayerushalmi Kiphshuto* covering tractates *Shabbat, Eruvin* and *Pesahim* is outstanding. It is not a full running commentary but elucidates a great number of *sugyot* in the three tractates. Important is also his *Hilkhot Ha-Yerushalmi;* while it relates especially to Maimonides (see above), its prime importance is the insight it gives into the sections of the Palestinian Talmud it covers. Yet, and again, most of his contributions to the establishment of correct readings and interpretations to the Palestinian Talmud are scattered throughout the monumental *Tosefta ki-Fshutah* and *Talmuda shel Kisrin*. Noteworthy is his essay 'The Old Commentators' in which he gives detailed discussion of the early commentators down to the sixteenth century.

A focus of new and intensified critical study of the Palestinian Talmud has recently emerged in Jerusalem. Outstanding are Sussman, *Babylonian Sugyot;* Assis, *Parallel Sugyot,* and *id. 'Yerushalmi Sanhedrin'.*

Text

On the manuscripts see below.

In addition to the extant manuscripts, a valuable source for the textual criticism is the mosaic inscription found in 1974 at Tel-Rehov. In fact it represents the most ancient extant copy of rabbinic literature. Its content closely parallels *P.T. Dem.* 2, 22c–d and *P.T Shev.* 7, 36c. Despite the deviations it is clear that the text of the Palestinian Talmud served as the prototype for the inscription. See the penetrating analysis by Sussman, 'Halakhic Inscription'; *id.* Additional Notes'; *id.* 'Boundaries'. See also Lieberman, 'Halakhic Inscription'; and Z. Safrai, 'Rehov Inscription'.

Important for the establishment of correct readings is Ratner, *Ahavat Tsion* which culls variant readings and explanations of early authorities to all tractates of the first two Orders except *Eruvin.*

While parts of the Babylonian Talmud began to appear in print since 1482 (Portugal) and 1484 (Italy), the Palestinian Talmud had to wait until 1522–23. Bomberg in Venice, after completing his edition of the Babylonian Talmud, did the same for the entire Palestinian Talmud, basing his edition in the main upon the poor Leiden MS. This text was further corrupted by the editor of the printed text, who claimed to have had three additional manuscripts, but made many incorrect changes. The Venice edition was reprinted in facsimile in Berlin (1925) and this reprint was re-published in a smaller format.

A poor reprint of the Venice edition was made in Cracow 1609, with the addition of the small marginal commentary of R. David Darshan; it was followed in both respects by the Krotoschin 1886 edition.

A landmark edition was that printed in Zhitomir 1860–67. It contains on the page the commentaries of R. David Fraenkel and R. Moses Margoliot (see above) which subsequently became 'standard'.

The Petrokow edition of 1900–02 set the tone for the high quality of all future editions. It included many shorter commentaries in addition to the 'standard' Zhitomir commentaries. The most comprehensive edition is that published in Wilna 1922 which contains many new and relatively new commentaries as well as selections of variant readings; it serves as the source for all reproductions since.

There have been many editions of single Orders, such as *Zeraim* in the Amsterdam 1710 edition, which contains the commentary of R. Eliyahu Fulda (see above), as well as of single tractates, such as that of *Beitsa* with the first printing from manuscript of the commentary of R. Elazar Azeari together with introduction and critical notes by Israel Francus, New York 1967.[74]

Translations

Translations of the Palestinian Talmud have been very few and not helpful. The only full translation so far is the French by Schwab, *Talmud de Jérusalem;* it is very undependable. A Latin translation to twenty tractates was given by B. Ugolino, in his *Thesaurus antiquitatum sacrum* vols. 17–30, Venice 1755–65. For translations on individual tractates into English and German and further itemized listing see Bokser, 'Guide', 164–5; Strack-Stemberger, *Einleitung,* 181.

A complete English translation was undertaken by Neusner, *Talmud of the Land of Israel.* As was decidedly pointed out by Lieberman in one of his last written works, 'A Tragedy or a Comedy?', this translation is devoid of any value for scholarship and shockingly demonstrates the translator's ignorance of the textual criticism, languages, idiom and subject matter of the Palestinian Talmud. The German translation appearing under the editorship of Hengel *et al., Übersetzung,* is quite reliable.

Introductions and Auxiliary Works

The first real introduction is Frankel, *Mavo ha-Yerushalmi* (1870), which is still of importance today. A very readable and quite full introduction is given by Ginzberg in his *Commentary,* both in English and, more fully, in Hebrew.

Of unequalled importance are Lieberman's various books on the Palestinian Talmud and related literature. *Talmuda shel Kisrin* establishes the special nature of the first three tractates of Order *Nezikin* and on the redaction of the Palestinian Talmud in general. His important essay 'Al ha-Yerushalmi' deals with the criteria of the establishment of a correct text, with the importance of readings found in early authorities, and describes the attitude of the latter to the Palestinian Talmud as such.

Epstein, *Amoraitic Literature* gives full attention to the Palestinian Talmud, including a general introduction and a collection of variant readings to the first Order. Albeck, *Babli and Yerushalmi* is devoted to both Talmudim, though more so to the Babylonian. Yet no other book so far contains so succinct and complete a listing of Palestinian (and Babylonian) Amoraim and so helpful a guide to their characteristic teachings.

A most valuable bibliography is Bokser, 'Guide'. It refers to almost everything written on the Palestinian Talmud, either directly or indirectly, including such aids to the study as geography, inscriptions, legal studies and liturgical works. While one may sometimes disagree on the value of a particular work, his judgment in general is fair and to the point. More limited and without discrimination between the good and the mediocre is the bibliography in Strack-Stemberger, *Einleitung*, 163 and in the course of the chapter on the Palestinian Talmud which follows. This chapter, incidentally, is very helpful and one of the best in the book.

A great help in the study of the Palestinian Talmud will be Kosovsky, *Concordance,* a computer-produced production appearing under the auspices of the Israel Academy of Sciences and Humanities and the Jewish Theological Seminary of America. Upon completion it will have three sections: a thesaurus of the language with citations from all relevant passages; a thesaurus of names of persons and localities; and a thesaurus of midrash parallels, containing also all scriptural verses referred to. The concordance is based upon the Venice 1524 edition; a supplement will very likely be published containing textual variants from the various MSS.

MANUSCRIPTS OF THE PALESTINIAN TALMUD (BY MICHAEL KRUPP)

The title *Talmud Yerushalmi,* i.e. 'of Jerusalem', has been current since the first printing, but it was never taught in Jerusalem or edited there. It was taught in the schools of Galilee and Caesarea. Only the first four Orders and part of the tractate *Nidda* of the Mishna were commented upon in the Yerushalmi. The fifth and sixth Orders—in spite of medieval affirmations—were not lost, but never existed there (at least in writing). In contrast to the first four Orders, no fragments of nos. 5 and 6 were found in the Cairo Geniza.

Unlike the Bavli (Babylonian Talmud), the Yerushalmi did not originally contain the successive Mishna sections in full. It was inserted later from other sources, as the numerous Geniza fragments show.

When the Bavli was acknowledged as authoritative in North Africa and Spain in the tenth century, the Yerushalmi lost its importance and was probably transmitted and respected only in Italy and Ashkenaz, classically lands depending on Palestine, even though the Bavli was the supreme authority here. It is somewhat miraculous that under these circumstances the Yerushalmi survived at all: there was only one complete manuscript of it (MS. Leiden), which was then used as a basis for the first printed edition, Venice 1523–25.

Ms. Leiden, Scalinger no. 3. It was published in a poor facsimile edition (Jerusalem 1971) with an introduction by Lieberman and a list of variants from the Venice printing. The manuscript was the work of Yehiel ben Yekutiel ben Benyamin ha-Rofe, 1289, also well known as scholar, poet and copyist, and especially as author of a book of piety, *Maalot ha-Middot*. He lived in Rome in the 13th century, and the manuscript may have been written there.

The script is rabbinical, very legible, in one column. There is no commentary. In the colophon, the copyist complains that his prototype is corrupt and frequently unintelligible, and says that he had to emend it at times. But Lieberman says in his introduction that this verdict is rather to be referred to the inexperience of the copyist, unacquainted with the Yerushalmi. The prototype was better than the copyist judged it, whose emendations were unimportant and did no damage elsewhere. The real damage was done by the 'improvements' and arbitrary changes, additions and omissions of the compositor of the Bomberg edition, who had even less idea of the special traits of the Yerushalmi. The compositor put some of these emendations into the manuscript in handwriting, mostly on his own initiative and not, as he claimed in the colophon, on the basis of other manuscripts. There may well have been no complete manuscript of the Yerushalmi at the time of printing, apart from the Leiden.

Ms. Vatican 133, published in facsimile, Jerusalem 1970. It contains *Sota* and the Order *Zeraim* minus *Bikkurim*. The manuscript is from several hands, probably from Italy in the 13th century, two columns a page till nearly the end, without a commentary. The manuscript is very corrupt and has, according to Lieberman, hardly a line without several faults. On the other hand, the manuscript offers some good readings, up to sixty according to Lieberman, which show understanding of difficult texts which in the Leiden version are unintelligible. The Mishna text in *Sota* is prefixed chapter by chapter to the Gemara, as in the Leiden manuscript. The tractates of the Order *Zeraim* contain no complete Mishna text but only short *piskaot* at best, as in the Geniza fragments.

Ms. Escorial G-1-3 had been known for decades as a MS. of the Babylonian Talmud; it was listed by P. Blanco in 'Los manuscritos hebreos de la Bibliotheca de El-escorial', 1926. It was the late E. S. Rosenthal who first discovered, in the seventies, that the almost illegible small script in the upper margin of the first three tractates of *Nezikin* contains practically all of the Palestinian Talmud to that part. It is close to the Kokovtsev Geniza fragment containing five middle chaps. of *Bava Kamma* (Ginzberg, *Yerushalmi Fragments*, 240–53). After Rosenthal's death, the text was published by Lieberman, Jerusalem 1983, not in facsimile, which was inadvisable on account of the difficulties of deciphering the text. The introduction to the MS. was compiled from Rosenthal's notes by his sons A. and D. Rosenthal.

This is the only manuscript of the Yerushalmi from Spain. It is in rabbinical script of the 15th century and displays all the advantages of Spanish correctness. It contains hundreds of readings which are the only key to certain parts of *Nezikin*, a particularly difficult tractate. Apart from its being more exact and complete than the Leiden MS.—it provides the text in the 23 lacunae of the Leiden MS.—its importance consists in its representing another type of text than the Leiden, displaying major departures from the known text. This Escorial text has affinities with some of the oldest Geniza fragments, but is more correct than most of them. The division into chapters is uneven. It partly follows through all the thirty chapters of the whole tractate *Nezikin*, partly displays some *Bavot* numbers and often has both enumerations. In *Bava Kama*, and to some extent in *Bava Metsia*, the Mishna is given in full within the Gemara, where it is divided into parts of unequal length. Some parts occur in abbreviated form as *piska*, as in the printed editions of the Babylonian Talmud, while further on only short *piskaot* are found or no Mishna at all, like most of the Geniza fragments.

The manuscripts with the commentary of Solomon Syrileio must be numbered among the Yerushalmi MSS. His text of the Yerushalmi rests mainly on manuscripts and contains, along with additions from the Bavli and the midrashim, some valuable variants. Two versions must be distinguished, the first in MS. Paris 1389 and the other in the London 403 to 405, which are regarded as autograph. At least in the second, Syrileio had the printed edition before him in the beginning of the 16th century. The texts comprise the whole Order *Zeraim* and the tractate *Shekalim.*

The Yerushalmi *Shekalim* is also found in the Munich codex 95, which contains the whole Babylonian Talmud. As there is no Bavli on *Shekalim,* the scribe copied the Yerushalmi here, but assimilated to the Bavli in idioms. The Yerushalmi *Shekalim* is also given in the Babylonian Talmud MSS. Oxford 366 and 370 (with the commentary of R. Meshulam).

Doubtless, the Geniza Fragments are once more a great help for study of the Yerushalmi, representing as they do its text in numerous samples. This is especially true where the Leiden MS. is the only witness. A collection of the Geniza fragments was published by Ginzberg, *Yerushalmi Fragments.* Many further fragments have since been published, more have been discovered, and a complete edition is awaited.

NOTES

1. *B. T. Sanh.* 33a. A more specific use of the title Amora is to be found in *B. T. Sanh.* 17b, where it seems to indicate teachers of later generations. Thus Rav Huna and Rav Hisda, both of the second generation (250–300 C.E.) are designated *Sabei,* 'elders', of Sura, whereas Rabba and Rav Yosef of the following generation, are called 'Amoraim of Pumbedita' and Rav Hama is called 'Amora of Nehardea'. A third, and very different, meaning of the term *Amora* is implied in its use to indicate the *meturgeman* who interprets in loud voice the soft-spoken words of the Sage in the academy or synagogue.

2. Both Rav and Shmuel, and their schools, teach baraitot which originate with them. Thus we find: 'The *matnita* (= baraita) of Rav differs with him' (*P. T. Ber.* 2, 4c); 'Said R. Zeira, it has been taught (= a baraita) in *Ketuvot*

of the school of Rav . . .' (*P. T. Ket.* 2, 26c). The phrase 'Shmuel taught' occurs scores of times (e.g. *B. T. Yoma* 70a; *Sukka* 56b). The verb used in this expression, *teni* in the Palestine Talmud and *tena* in the Babylonian, indicates a Tannaic teaching or baraita. Moreover, the very common 'the school of R. Yishmael taught' is very often a corruption of 'the school of Shmuel taught', as Epstein, *Nosah,* 213 pointed out. On the other hand, late Palestinian Tannaim such as R. Hiya and R. Hoshaya are often indicated as belonging to a 'transition generation'. Albeck, *Babli and Yerushalmi,* 144–63 even lists them as the first generation of Palestinian Amoraim.

3. E.g. *B. T. Er.* 3b. This is not said explicitly of Shmuel, but his authority against a mishna or baraita is hardly less.

4. Cf. Frankel, *Mavo ha-Yerushalmi,* 28b–31a.

5. E.g. the leniencies of Palestinian Amoraim, and of their Babylonian colleagues, regarding work forbidden on intermediate festival days: compare *P. T. Moed K.* 2, 81b and *B. T. Moed K.* 12a–b. Again, Rav's exposition of the anonymous position and that of R. Yehuda in *M. Er.* 1:1, is found in both Talmudim (*P. T. Er.* 1, 18b; *B. T. Er.* 2a) and the parallel sugyot have many literary features in common.

6. For example, many differences of opinion between the first generation Amoraim R. Yohanan and R. Shimon ben Lakish as recorded in the Palestinian Talmud are reversed in the Babylonian. Even individual statements in the name of R. Yohanan (e.g. *P. T. Ket.* 8, 32b) are ascribed to R. Shimon ben Lakish (*B. T. Ket.* 82a). The exigencies of the Babylonian *sugya* may often make far-reaching changes in the content of the Palestinian tradition.

7. See Sussman, *Babylonian Sugyot,* who argues forcefully that in all cases where topics from *Zeraim* or *Toharot* are discussed, the Babylonian Talmud bases itself upon a primary Palestinian discussion.

8. R. Hiya, a Babylonian, studied at Rabbi's academy: so did Rav, but he returned to Babylonia. The outstanding pupil of R. Yohanan was the Babylonian R. Elazar ben Pedat. So were the great scholars of the next generation, R. Yirmeyahu and R. Zeira.

9. In this respect, R. Zeira stands out. See Goldberg, 'R. Zeira'.

10. Rav Hisda (2nd half 3d cent.) refers to him as 'our teacher who came down from Palestine', *B. T. Ber.* 38b.

11. Lieberman, 'Palestine', having thoroughly examined the talmudic and other sources, states that there is no evidence for a Jewish rebellion in the 3rd or 4th cents. The abolition of the Patriarchate in the early 5th cent. was probably the main cause for the 'completion' of the Palestinian Talmud (thus, among others, G. Stemberger in a public lecture, Hebrew University, January 1987; see below n. 44).

12. These find mention in the Palestinian Talmud as well, except that Rav Dimi goes by the name Rav Avdimi (Abduma) *nahuta* (*P. T. Er.* 1, 19b *et al.*). The phrase 'when Rav Dimi came' (and brought a Palestinian teaching) occurs several hundred times in the Babylonian Talmud, most frequently together with Rav Abin, both bringing variant traditions from Palestine (e.g.

B. T. Shabb 72a. 134a, 147a). All four are mentioned together in *B. T. Av.* 73a.

13. See Ginzberg, *Commentary*, 23–36 for a list of such differences reflected in Babylonian and Palestinian halakha.

14. Ginzberg, *Commentary*, 34–6, although the absence of these matters from the Palestinian Talmud is somewhat exaggerated.

15. The question why certain Orders and tractates lack Talmud has occupied many scholars. Especially intriguing is *Kodashim* which has Babylonian Talmud but no Palestinian. Moreover, many believed that even as late as the Middle Ages, Palestinian Talmud to *Kodashim* was still extant. The best discussion of the entire question, including a full critique of all previous writing on the subject, is Sussman, *Babylonian Sugyot*. See also the discussion of the missing tractates, and especially of the Order *Kodashim*, in Strack-Stemberger, *Einleitung*, 165–8: Bokser, 'Guide', 165–8.

16. While the current Hebrew designation is *Talmud Yerushalmi* (descending from the medieval practice of naming the main city for the land) it is known among early authorities as 'Talmud of the Land of Israel'. 'Talmud of the West' and the like. See Strack, *Introduction*, 65; Bokser, 'Guide', 149–51.

17. Epstein, *Tannaitic Literature*, 246; Frankel, *Mavo ha-Yerushalmi*, 22a–23a.

18. Cf. Safrai, 'Tales of the Sages'.

19. Cf. Frankel, *Mavo ha-Yerushalmi*, 31a–37a.

20. See Klein, 'Gemara and Sebara'; 'Gemara Quotations'; 'Some Methods'; 'Significance'.

21. Epstein, *Tannaitic Literature*, 312–4; Frankel, *Mavo ha-Yerushalmi*, 40a–45a.

22. Frankel, *Mavo ha-Yerushalmi*, 41a–b.

23. For examples see Goldberg, *Eruvin*, 44 n. 23; 102 and n. 16; 287 n. 17.

24. Schachter, *Babylonian and Jerusalem Mishnah*, deals with this problem but not in a sufficiently scientific way. The book covers only a selection of less than 150 mishnayot; the author's tendency to accept the Babylonian Mishna readings as primary is entirely unacceptable. Truly critical and of much value is Feintuch, 'Mishna of the MS. Leiden'. A comprehensive and fully detailed treatment of the whole problem is a prior aim of Epstein's main work, *Nosah*.

25. Outstanding in scope and depth is the discussion of R. Yohanan's attitude to the Mishna and his contribution to the formulation of the Palestinian Talmud in Epstein, *Nosah*, 234–85.

26. The set phrase 'R. Yohanan taught' (e.g.. *P. T. Kidd.* 1, 58c; *B. T. Pes.* 118a) refers to his teaching a baraita. So does the phrase 'I teach' (*B. T. Shabb*, 66b) and forms of the verb *shanah*. See Epstein, *Nosah*, 239f.

27. Cf. his phrase: 'I have only the Mishna to go by', *P. T. Ter.* 2, 41c. Occasionally, he rejects an anonymous teaching with the phrase, 'This is no (authoritative) mishna (being an individual opinion)' (*B. T. Yev.* 43a with reference to *M. Kel.* 13:8). See Epstein, *Nosah*, 241–4, 262–73.

28. See Epstein, *Nosah*, 47, 68, 160, 223, 244f. In accordance with a baraita he interprets, e.g., the 'dough prepared for dogs' (*M. Halla* 1:6) as being prepared in amorphous form (*P. T. Halla* 1, 58a), even though the Mishna itself seems to define it in terms of quality: 'as long as shepherds can eat of it'.

29. The first half of *M. Bava M.* 3:9 he takes as giving the view of R. Yishmael and the second as that of R. Akiva, stating: 'Anyone who will explain to me (this mishna of) "jug" according to only one Tanna, I shall be willing to carry his clothes after him to the bath-house.' Other Amoraim, however, offer harmonizing explanations by positing different situations (*B. T. Bava M.* 41a).

30. His approach is well-put in *B. T. Sanh.* 62b; 'R. Yohanan does not explain the first part (of a mishna) by one situation and the last part by another.' See Epstein, *Nosah*, 241f.

31. *P. T. Halla* 1, 58a.

32. See *P. T. Yev.* 4, 6b; *B. T. Shabb.* 46a.

33. E.g. *B. T. Hull*, 85a.

34. Cf. Safrai, 'Tales of the Sages', 229–32.

35. See Epstein, *Nosah*, 285–92.

36. His first teachers were in Judea: In Lydda, Bar Kappara whom he quotes frequently *(P. T. Pes.* 1, 28a *et al.)*; in Caesarea, R. Hoshaya whom he asks for a teaching (*B. T. Yev.* 57a) and whose teachings he quotes (*B. T. Pes.* 34b *et al.*). Of him it is said that he 'went into exile to study' (*P. T. Kil.* 9, 32d) from his native Judea to Galilee.

37. *B. T. Nidda* 62b.

38. *B. T. Yev.* 41a.

39. It is he who remarks with reference to R. Yannai's 'forced' interpretation of *M. Kidd.* 3:6. 'We give a forced explanation, positing different situations, rather than posit different sources' (*B. T. Kidd.* 63b).

40. *B. T. Yoma* 81a *et al.* See Epstein, *Nosah*, 287f.

41. See Epstein, *Nosah*, 292–307.

42. See Goldberg, 'R. Zeira'.

43. A full list of Palestinian Amoraim, arranged alphabetically, and commented upon, is given by Frankel, *Mavo ha-Yerushalmi*, 53–132. An even better presentation, according to the generations, is found in Albeck, *Babli and Yerushalmi*, 144–451.

44. See Ginzberg, *Commentary*, 38; Marx-Margolis, *History*, 229.

45. See Marx-Margolis, *History*, 230. Epstein, *Amoraitic Literature*, 274 points out that two generations of Amoraim (those of R. Mana and R. Yose be-R. Bun and of R. Shmuel be-R. Yose be-R. Bun) find mention after the generation contemporary with Ursicinus (that of R. Yona and R. Yose), and he estimates this to be a period of about fifty years. The end of the Palestinian Talmud he places, therefore, at 410–420 C.E.

46. See e.g. Goldberg, *Eruvin*, 255.

47. Goldberg, *Eruvin*, 11, 25, 35, 60, 127.

48. *Ib.* 189, 221, 282.
49. *Ib.* 196.
50. *Ib.* 31.
51. *Ib.* 124.
52. *Ib.* 155.
53. *Ib.* 198.
54. *Ib.* 230.
55. *Ib.* 239.
56. *Otsar ha-Baraitot* 2, 141f.; 204f.
57. Two of these were prime centres at the end of the Tannaic period: Sepphoris and Lydda. The centre at Lydda is generally referred to as 'the South', as in the phrases: 'a *matnita* of Bar Kappara from the South' (*P. T. Shev.* 4, 35d *et al.*); 'our Masters in the South' (*B. T. Er.* 66b; *P. T. Er.* 6, 23c); 'the elders of the South' (*B. T. Hull,* 132b). Sepphoris had long been established as the spiritual centre of the Galilee, leadership of which was handed down from father to son: R. Halafta (a contemporary of R. Akiva), R. Yose (R. Akiva's well-known pupil) and R. Yishmael (a contemporary of Rabbi).
58. Here we follow Lieberman, *Talmuda shel Kisrin.* Epstein, *Amoraitic Literature,* 279–86 does recognize the strong Caesarean influence in the first three tractates of *Nezikin,* but strongly rejects Lieberman's theory of the prior editing of these tractates. In the 1968 re-capitulation of his *Talmuda shel Kisrin,* 125–36, Lieberman rebuts Epstein's arguments.
59. The otherwise common phrase *heikhi 'Avida* 'how can it happen', for example, does not occur here. On the other hand, terms otherwise unknown in the Palestinian Talmud occur, such as *heikhi* 'and how', i.e. in which situation; and *ve-'inun d'amrin ken* 'and those say thusly', introducing a Babylonian teaching, instead of the usual *taman 'amrin* 'there they say'. See Lieberman, *Talmuda shel Kisrin,* 7f.
60. *Talmuda shel Kisrin,* viif.
61. E.g. 'The school of Levi', which is mentioned four times in these tractates, but not once elsewhere in the Palestinian Talmud (but 'The school of Levi taught' does appear in the Babylonian Talmud). On the other hand, the names of later Amoraim hardly occur. See Lieberman, *Talmuda shel Kisrin,* 6. *Ib.* 9–10, Lieberman gives a list of Amoraim born in Caesarea or otherwise connected with it.
62. See especially the traditions ascribed to 'The rabbis of Caesarea'. Goldberg, *Shabbat,* 22, 182 emphasizes this parallel.
63. See Strack-Stemberger, *Einleitung,* 169f.
64. See Safrai, ed., *Literature of the Sages,* 405–7.
65. Especially to the Order *Zeraim,* to which there is no Babylonian Talmud apart from *Berakhot.*
66. Again, the seventh book of his Code, *Sefer Zeraim* relies heavily on the Palestinian Talmud.
67. Two fragments are extant, one to *Berakhot* chs. 1–6 (published by Ginzberg in *Yerushalni Fragments,* 29–36) and another to sections of *Ketubot* chs. 1–

8 (published in *Tarbiz* 3 [1931] 21–36). These have been republished with introduction and full commentary by Lieberman, *Hilkhot Ha-Ye-rushalmi*. Lieberman points to the definite pattern of this digest. Maimonides omits all laws already found in the Babylonian Talmud, and for the most part those which contradict the conclusions of the latter, except for certain cases where the Palestinian discussion can also shed light on the accepted Babylonian halakha.

68. Two of the latter are R. Eliezer ben Natan of Mayence (1090–1170) and R. Eliezer ben R. Yoel Halevi (1140–1220). As for Italy, the most important figure who has reference to the Palestinian Talmud is R. Natan, author of the prime dictionary, the *Arukh*, in the twelfth century.

69. Alfasi, end of *Eruvin*, 104b. An extensive discussion of the vicissitudes of the Palestinian Talmud and its influence over the generations is to be found in Ginzberg, *Commentary*, introd., 41–50.

70. This author was identified only in recent years. For a listing of existing commentaries see Strack, *Introduction*, 70f.; Strack-Stemberger, *Einleitung*, 182–4; Ginzberg, *Commentary*, introd. 51–64; Frankel, *Mavo ha-Yerushalmi*, 132–6. Full discussion of the early commentaries is given by Lieberman, 'The Old Commentators'. See especially Bokser, 'Guide', 225–50.

71. This commentary appeared in different places: Tractate *Shekalim* in Frankfurt, 1689; the entire Order *Zeraim* in the 1710 Amsterdam edition; tractates *Bava Kamma* and *Bava Metsia*. Offenbach 1725; *Bava Batra*, Frankfurt, 1742.

72. Called *Sedei Yehoshua*, in three volumes. Constantinople 1662, 1749.

73. Published in the Year Book of the Breslau Seminary, 1895–1914, and now reproduced in book form, Jerusalem 1974.

74. For further references on editions see the exhaustive and detailed chapter on the Palestinian Talmud by Haberman in his re-edition of Rabbinovicz, *Maamar*, 203–222. Ginzberg, *Commentary*, introd. 51–64 is important for his critique of editions and commentaries. See also Bokser, 'Guide', 151–3; Strack-Stemberger, *Einleitung*, 180f.

IV

THE TALMUD AND INTERDISCIPLINARY STUDIES

A

History

10

In Quest of the Historical Rabban Yohanan ben Zakkai

Jacob Neusner

Concerning the effort to recover rabbinic biographies, Professor Judah Goldin writes:

... Such works are hardly biographies in the serious sense of the word, ... for not only do the primary sources disappoint us deeply in the amount of reliable *historical* detail they provide, but even as regards the opinions and teachings of the Sages, one is left to guess what is early and what is late. In short, there is practically no way to get at *development*, surely and desperately necessary for the historian and biographer. These books therefore are filled with speculation, sometimes plausible, sometimes not. As reflections of the author's own imagination and interpretation, however, and as *collections* of data about the specific sage, they are informative exercises.[1]

My research[2] exhibits, alas, the deplorable qualities to which Goldin points. At the same time, I have continued to reflect on what we know about Rabban Yohanan ben Zakkai. Here are some of the results.

LITERARY SOURCES AND PHILOLOGICAL FUNDAMENTALISM

We have no clear idea of the relationship between the forms in which rabbinic logia were transmitted and their historical or even academic origin. I have noted a number of obvious forms in which Yohanan's words were handed down.[3] Having recognized the existence of such forms, however, I cannot offer further judgments of a historical nature.

Reprinted by permission of the *Harvard Theological Review*, volume 59, 1966.

I do not know whether one form was used earlier than another, or whether any originated in a specific setting or for an identifiable purpose. It follows that one can do little to discover the living situation which underlay the rendition of a given saying into a literary form for the purposes of transmission. Both Louis Finkelstein and Y. N. Epstein[4] made it quite clear that some of Yohanan's sayings were carefully shaped for such purposes, but, so far, I cannot see any consequence for historical knowledge.

The kind of evidence we have for later Tannaitic and Amoraic times moreover is simply *not* available about rabbis who lived before 70 A.D., as did Yohanan.[5] After 70, academies were reestablished, and the traditions cultivated in them were handed down, orally or in notes, without substantial interruption, except for the Bar Kokhba war, until they were redacted. The Bar Kokhba War caused no drastic break in the transmission of either Akiban or Ishmaelean traditions, for some of the students of the two great rabbis escaped from Palestine, and preserved their traditions in Mesopotamia and Babylonia. (The Akibans returned to Palestine ca. 145.) By contrast, for the period before 70, we have no direct lines of transmission whatever. The destruction of Jerusalem marks a great break, and the paucity of information about Gamaliel I, Simeon b. Gamaliel I, their colleagues, not to mention Yohanan himself, is by no means accidental. We do not know much because not much was transmitted or survived the destruction, and what we do know underwent drastic revisions in the post-70 academies. *Even* if one grants, therefore, that some close relationship exists between event and tradition, or between a saying and the person to whom it is attributed, the necessary conditions for preserving the tradition did not pertain to the data emerging from pre-70 academies.

But one can hardly grant it. It is by no means clear quite how a given event was cast into literary form. No one seriously supposes that the rabbinic sources supply either eyewitness accounts of great events, or stenographic records of men's speeches or lectures. By the time we hear of a speech or an event before 70, it has already been recast, and it is rarely possible to know what happened originally. We sometimes have an obvious interjection which provides clearcut evidence that a given tradition originated very early, before the date of that interjection, and quite close, in fact, to the time it purports to discuss. The most striking example is the comment of Rabbi Akiba on the alleged conversation between R. Yohanan ben Zakkai and Vespasian. Vespasian asked, "Now ask me what I may grant you," to which R. Yohanan replied, "Give me Yavneh and its sages, and the chain of Rabban Gamaliel, and a physician to heal Rabbi Zadok." The source continues:

> Rabbi Joseph said, and some say, Rabbi Akiba said, 'He turneth the wise backward' (Is. 44.25). For he should have asked him to leave them alone that time, but he thought that perhaps so much he would not grant, and then there would be no relief whatever.
>
> (Bab. Talmud Gittin 56b)

Still later, Lamentations Rabbati i.5.31 was corrected to conform to the criticism of R. Akiba, or of the fourth-century Babylonian Amora, R. Joseph. This account contains criticism which would have been said sometime before 120. At the same time, it occurs in a much later document, the Babylonian Gemara, than that in The Fathers According to Rabbi Nathan, chapter four, which preserves an "earlier," but an utterly different, view of what happened and why. I have analyzed these accounts, following the perceptive views of G. Allon, in my book.[6] My purpose in treating them here is to point out two facts. First of all, if a tradition occurs in a later text, that does not mean it is less reliable, for in this instance, the later text, namely the Babylonian Gemara, contains a detail which may be very early, and yet is omitted in the account we have from Tannaitic times. Second, it is quite obvious that two accounts of the same event, the escape of R. Yohanan ben Zakkai from Jerusalem and his encounter with Vespasian, represent extraordinarily different versions of the event; both cannot be right; and since the accounts differ precisely on what happened and why, it is quite evident that neither provides the kind of factual information historians need and do not have for this period. They tell us, rather, what differing schools of thought chose to recall about a controversial event.

It might be tempting, also, to suppose that, whatever happened, the *actual* words ascribed to a given rabbi were actually said by him, as I assumed in my studies of R. Yohanan ben Zakkai. It was only later on that I found evidence to contradict it. Certain sayings of Rav and Samuel, cast into precisely the form one would expect, were never said by them at all. Their students observed a certain court-decision, and supposed upon that basis that the master held a given position upon the law. They then transmitted it in the form, "Rav says . . . Samuel says

. . ." as if the men had actually so dictated. The discussion of R. Ḥisda, in the next generation, suggests, however, that the master had said no such thing, but that the students merely presumed it. They observed a practical decision, and proposed a legal principle in the name of the masters to generalize upon it. What is of special interest to us, however, is that we should never have known it, were it not for further analysis of the case.[7] But the cases of R. Yohanan ben Zakkai undergo no such nearly contemporary analysis. The reports are extremely limited.[8] Extended discussion of the master's actions and words by his *immediate* disciples, so characteristic of later times, is rarely accorded to pre-70 figures. *Later* rabbis analyze their dicta, but almost never their immediate disciples. We have, therefore, no certainty that things he supposedly said were actually spoken by him. If one contrasts the varying accounts of his escape from Jerusalem, moreover, we find whole conversations attributed to him and Vespasian in one account which the other knows nothing about. Someone, and perhaps everyone, is providing pseudepigraphic dicta, and that is all we shall ever know for certain.

The relevance of *which* particular document contains a given source is rendered still more doubtful by the fact that none preserves a specific *Tendenz*. We know that Yohanan was subjected to criticism after his death, and probably during his lifetime as well, by his opponents.[9] R. Akiba's saying—if it was his—would reflect such opposition. No document was *edited,* so far as I can see, from the viewpoint either of his friends or of his enemies. The story cited in Bab. Talmud Gittin is not part of a collection edited to discredit R. Yohanan ben Zakkai. It is cited quite tangentially.

Omissions are highly noteworthy, on the other hand, for it was by suppressing data that the rabbis expressed their opinion of their opponents. I think it very likely that numerous sayings of Yohanan were not merely lost or forgotten, but rather suppressed. The most striking instance concerns what he thought about the revolt of 66 and the conduct of the war. Apart from the contradictory escape stories, we know nothing. About a quarter of a century earlier, he apparently commented upon the destruction of a pagan altar in Jamnia, concerning which the embassy to Gaius was sent. We have some generalized counsels of caution, indicating that some time in his life, Yohanan said that the biblical regulations on draft exemptions were sensible; and Cecil Roth quite reasonably has suggested that his sayings on the Temple as a source of peace and not war are most probably relevant to the "debate on the loyal sacrifices" which took place at the beginning of the revolt.[10] It would be unfair to him to suppose this was all he had to say at such a crucial time, when he was supposedly high in the councils of the Pharisaic party and of the Jerusalem administration as well. What he said and did his successors did not preserve. It seems reasonable to suppose that he not only predicted, a long time earlier, that "Lebanon," meaning the Temple, would be destroyed, but actively opposed the war, and had warned people that if they fought, they would lose. Those anxious to denigrate him would have done well to suppress the facts of his wise counsel, even though they were unable to wipe out the memory of his exegetical prophecy and providential escape from Jerusalem. Similarly we know only a few of his teachings and court-actions at Yavneh, nine decrees in all. One must wonder whether these were the only actions he took after the war, for most of them dealt only with the appropriation for the synagogue of rites formerly reserved to the Temple, with a few details about receiving testimony about the New Moon, the proselyte's offering, four-year-fruits, and the like.[11] To suppose that his teachings and acts at Yavneh were limited to the handful reported by rabbinic tradition is hardly reasonable. What is preserved of the legal record is clearly what the members of the court of Gamaliel II saw fit to recall. Yohanan probably envisaged a legal reconstruction of Judaism along lines which were subsequently modified. He may have proposed to declare in abeyance all those parts of the law which depended on the Temple for their performance or importance; modified those laws still useful to the synagogue; and rejected priestly privileges out of hand. Such a policy would have been utterly unacceptable to the priests, and disappearance of other references to his enactments as legally valid *precedent*—for that is the issue—may have been the price Gamaliel II later had to pay to secure their cooperation. But all of this is truly post-facto conjecture. Such speculation is necessary because the literary sources reveal almost nothing of the opposition he must have met, or of the viewpoints of groups that opposed him. Edited long after the great issues of Yohanan's day were settled, the sources may contain remnants of traditions handed on by opposing schools, but these occur mainly in legal matters, and even there, in a context of substantial agreement on basic political and social issues.

We have, therefore, almost no way of knowing what an editor

thought of any great issue, whether legal, historical, or theological, because, for the most part, we know very little about what he omitted, neglected, or suppressed. The only exception to this rule is the Mishnah, for we do have access to a rich body of Tannaitic data *not* included in it; but the Mishnah reveals nothing in particular about what its editor thought of R. Yohanan ben Zakkai, who is cited 24 times. At least one of the citations, Sanhedrin 5.2, refers to R. Yohanan as "ben Zakkai," which Allon plausibly took to be the name he bore within his opponents' traditions.[12] But numerous other sayings (e.g., Shabbat 16.7, 22.3) refer to him respectfully, and preserve important laws in his name. R. Judah the Prince as an editor did not therefore reveal his opinions of Yohanan one way or the other. He had available many sayings, some formulated in a manner thought to be disrespectful. He used what he found relevant. On the basis of these selections, we know only what he thought important for his own ends, but not how to evaluate his information.

Although traditions were accurately transmitted, they were not originally shaped by eyewitness observers nor revised by historians. The rabbis did not produce critical or any other kind of history in the manner of Josephus, Tacitus, or others.[13] Rabbinic data are mainly legal and theological. Facts on men or events emerge only occasionally, and then for other than (merely) historical reasons. An example drawn from later times will be of interest.

> The story is told about R. Judah b. Bathyra, R. Mattiah b. Heresh, R. Hananiah nephew of R. Joshua, and R. Jonathan, that they were going abroad, and when they reached Puteoli, they recalled Palestine. Their eyes filled up with tears . . . and they tore their clothes, and said, "And you will inherit it and dwell therein" (Deut. 11.31). They returned home, saying, "Dwelling in the land of Israel is considered equivalent to all the commandments in the Torah."
>
> Sifré Deuteronomy 80

The four second-century rabbis did emigrate, but only R. Mattiah went to Italy. They left Palestine at different times. And they never returned. So the "story" reflects only the fact that several rabbis went abroad, but it was told to make a homiletical point, and no serious interest in facts characterizes the telling.[14] One could duplicate this example many times. When, furthermore, we have two accounts of the same event, as of the escape from Jerusalem, the differences are so vast that comparison is not meaningful. It matters little, therefore, which story comes earlier, and which later. Much is made of the dating of various texts, with the presupposition that a tradition in an earlier collection more accurately reflects what happened than one first found later on. It is supposed also that once we have established a correct text and properly interpreted it then we know a historical fact. The *facticity* will be proportionately greater the earlier the text and the better its condition. Neither of these presuppositions is congruent to the nature of rabbinic sources. The former is simply unproven, and the latter preposterous. Philological fundamentalism offers a sterile approach for the historian.

"SPECULATION"

Speculation is not a naughty word for historians, but the very heart of the historical enterprise. Plausibility is another matter. One can urge the plausibility of a reconstruction by reasoned inquiry into the available sources, limited though they are, and by comparison of one's conjecture with those few incontrovertible facts we do have. If a conjecture contradicts no facts, helps to explain data in a sound and reasonable manner, and leads to an understanding of matters in a more comprehensive and sophisticated way than before, then it has a strong claim to plausibility. The historian, once he leaves his evidence and begins to reflect upon it, naturally must enter the realm of speculation and conjecture. If not, he merely repeats in elegant paraphrase the texts everyone knows, or has available. He would be better off to edit texts. Anyone who thinks that history, at least for Jewish antiquity, is more than an amalgam of the author's imagination and collections of data has simply not tried *critically* to write it. Furthermore, if the historian does not have to speculate about just *what* happened, then he conjectures upon *why* things happened; or interprets the "meaning" of events; or finds the connections or parallels between one event and another. Whether this is a wholly logical enterprise or not I cannot say; but it is what historians do who *have* vast bodies of sources available.

Upon what basis, however, do we form our speculation? We have many facts about the *background* of any first-century figure. We know that the Temple was destroyed. The literature of Qumran, the New Testament, Philo, certain apocryphal and pseudepigraphical books, and the like testify about ideas prevalent in specific circles. Rabbinic literature includes many traditions relating to the first century, some of questionable value, but some, such as Tractate Tamid, clearly edited in final

form not long after the destruction of Jerusalem, and still others, analyzed by Epstein and others, mostly redacted by then. We have, therefore, a substantial body of information by reference to which we may
understand and explain data about R. Yohanan ben Zakkai and the
setting of his life. Most recently, Goldin has shown the interesting connections between the logia of R. Yohanan's students and those of the
Stoa, which suggests the heuristic relevance of data coming from non-
Jewish sources as well.[15]

Concerning Yohanan, on the other hand, we know for certain very
little. I take it as a matter of fact that he survived the destruction of
Jerusalem by escaping from the city. The reason is not only that the
rabbinic sources say so. Josephus makes it clear very few escaped the
massive slaughter unleashed in August of 70. It is likely that someone
who survived was not in Jerusalem that month. Furthermore, the saying
attributed to R. Akiba, or to R. Joseph, and the existence of other hostile
sayings, suggest that R. Yohanan survived Jerusalem's fall by doing
something of which others disapproved. That is not much certainty.
When, however, we refer to "imagination" and "conjecture," it is
worthwhile noting precisely *how* conjectural our conjectures really are. I
also assumed that, as a matter of fact, he spent part of his life in
Jerusalem, part in Yavneh (Jamnia) afterward, and part in Galilee. The
Galilee years came either before Jerusalem, or after Yavneh. The sources
that say he was in Galilee say also that he then had a young son. It is
more reasonable to suppose he had a young son before ca. 50 than after
ca. 75–80. The contrary would have elicited a measure of surprise,
perhaps even ascription of some kind of unusual power. The story of the
Galilee years involves the disciple Hanina ben Dosa, who was never
mentioned in the traditions about the Jerusalem circle, preserved in
Avot, Avot de R. Natan, and elsewhere. I reasoned that Hanina-tradi-
tions referred to Galilee, and not to Jerusalem; and that Hanina himself
never studied in Yohanan's Jerusalem circle.[16] Two possibilities emerge.
One is that Hanina studied in Galilee and not in Jerusalem. The second
is that Hanina studied in Jerusalem, but that the record of his studies
there was suppressed. To assume the latter requires an explanation for
why Hanina's presence in the Jerusalem circle was consistently and
everywhere suppressed. I can think of none. Hence I suppose it was the
former. A third possibility exists, that the whole tradition of Yohanan's
disciples is a fabrication, and that the stories about his conversations

with his students were invented for, one might guess, aretological purposes. To suppose so, one would have to show that such was the case in other disciple-master stories. I regard it as possible but improbable in the absence of more comprehensive proof.

The larger question is, how we shall evaluate literary sources? In the foregoing paragraphs, I have supposed they do contain some historical facts. To think the contrary requires the supposition that all the literary evidence is a complete fabrication. I choose to think not. But we need not succumb to literary fundamentalism if we assert they are not. What is necessary is *historical* criticism of the texts which literary critics provide. Such criticism is at both lower and higher levels. Lower criticism will require us to assess sources by the measure of our knowledge of realities. The stories about R. Eleazar b. 'Arakh's *Merkavah* sermon include supernatural details which we may prefer to discount or to explain naturalistically.[17] We may discount the historicity of miracles, but we cannot discount the fact that they were told and believed. They do not prove Eleazar's sermon had any effect upon nature at all, but they provide very strong evidence that the *Merkavah* tradition was handed on in Yohanan's school. If we find stories which contradict facts of history, such as those about how R. Yohanan ben Zakkai directed Temple rites, we may discount them too, and, more properly, interpret them to be later and imaginary views of what happened a long while ago. If, again, we have reason to believe a story was invented for later, polemical purposes, such as those of R. Yohanan's debates with the Sadducees, we may thus explain such accounts.[18] Great inconsistencies among several accounts of one event are obviously noteworthy. If we find selfconsistent, literary accounts which in no way challenge reason or common sense, or contradict what we know from other more reliable evidence, then we may use these for historical purposes, and suppose that they approximate the truth, though perhaps remotely. Lower criticism facilitates the historical presentation of the major or most exemplary sources, along with our interpretation of them, in a chronologically sensible context.

A measure of higher criticism is also possible, through which one may transcend the limits of given, specific texts, by composing a theory making sense of several texts, though proved by none of them. A striking example pertains to R. Eleazar b. 'Arakh. We know that R. Yohanan dearly loved him, for he was quoted as praising his words above those of the rest of the students. Whether he said any such thing or not we do not know; but that the best "saying" was ascribed to him is a fact. We also know that in later life he separated himself from the main body of disciples, who went to Yavneh, and settled in Emmaus.[19] He was criticized by later generations for doing so. At the same time, we have the following:

> He [Rabban Yohanan] used to say, If all the sages of Israel were in one scale of the balance, and Rabbi Eliezer ben Hyrcanus were in the other scale, he would outweigh them all. Abba Shaul says in his name, If all the sages of Israel were in one scale of the balance, and even if Rabbi Eliezer ben Hyrcanus were with them, and Rabbi Eleazar ben ʿArakh were in the other scale, he would outweigh them all.[20]

Of those attributed to Yohanan, Abba Shaul's saying and the earlier one cannot both have been said by him. Either Eleazar b. ʿArakh outweighed in Yohanan's mind all the disciples or he did not. What we have therefore are two traditions, Abba Shaul's, dating from a time when Eleazar b. ʿArakh was in special favor, and another, reflecting the time that Eliezer b. Hyrcanus was preferred. I imagine that Eleazar b. ʿArakh could not have been in good grace after he went to Emmaus, in 70, and therefore suppose that Abba Shaul's saying reflects the earlier situation. Many other sayings, in fact, the whole collection of logia about "the good way" and "the evil way," in which Eleazar figures as the favorite student, must therefore have been edited before 70, while he was still in good grace. All of these logia were redacted before Eleazar b. ʿArakh lost his reputation for great learning, certainly during Yohanan's own lifetime. Sources which place Eliezer b. Hyrcanus at the climax of the discussion would date from the later period. We have, therefore, an example of internal criticism. But even here we have *presupposed* the historical accuracy of the texts dealing with R. Eleazar's biography in *criticizing* other texts relating to his position in R. Yohanan's circle of disciples. Such a circular procedure merely supposes that the sources were not so constituted as to *prove* the point which criticism yields. To reject it one should show that the sources were shaped by the editor for just this purpose, and he should want a reason to explain it.

Most sources do not yield the possibility of this sort of literary-historical criticism. Another kind of higher criticism, commonplace elsewhere but not in studies of Talmudic history, seeks meaningful and useful patterns within the sources, so that we may, after collecting them, present them in a fruitful and historically relevant structure. It should be abundantly clear by now that one cannot confuse such a presentation with what really happened. We shall never know, upon the basis of our current data, much of what actually took place. But we can attempt to explain the data we do have by composing a theory based upon but intended to transcend them. One obvious "theory" will be chronological. Stories clearly relating to R. Yohanan's death belong at the end; to early years and education at the beginning; and to the various events of his fruitful years in the order in which these events most likely took place, those relating to the Temple, for instance, in chronological order before the Jamnia period. I see nothing speculative or conjectural in all this. A second critical theory emerged from sociology of religion. I analyzed the religious ideas and encounters attributed to Yohanan according to the insights of Max Weber, which I found useful analytical tools, concerning the tension between charisma and routine within the religious life. As I saw it, Yohanan encountered a highly pneumatic kind of Judaism in his Galilean years. This was clear not merely from the content of the sources, which tell us that Yohanan had only one student and felt neglected, and that the one student he had was a miracle worker; but also from other sources relating to the same place and time. If Yohanan was in Galilee, it is most likely he would have seen a different kind of religious emphasis from that of his academic background. In fact, the sources specifically relate that he did.[21] In Jerusalem he encountered a mostly routinized religious life, embodied in the Temple rites and officials. Here, again, two sources of information were available: first, the stories of his bitter encounters with priests and Temple officials;[22] and second, the facts, available from other places, of what the Temple was like, and how its affairs were conducted. The Pharisaic "religion of Torah" seemed to me to synthesize the two polar principles, routine being imposed by the requirement regularly to study a given text, spontaneity and charisma emerging in two ways, first, from the very content of the Scriptural texts Yohanan studied, which in part embodied the highly charismatic experiences of earlier ages, and second, in the unexpected and unpredictable intellectual response of the student to the text. This synthesis was described and its social and exegetical accidents located. From this perspective, the discussion of Yohanan's active years took on sociological significance. I thus formed the data into an ideal paradigmatic structure for religious-sociological investigation. In so doing I probably forced them to conform to a much too neat "ideal type." But this provided the possibility of *interpreting* the corpus of relevant texts in some more meaningful way than a mere recitation of their content, in historical language, would have permitted. It is the author's "imagination" that placed the Galilee and Jerusalem years at opposite poles, that saw them as encounters with antithetical principles in religious life, and interpreted the subsequent career in teaching and leadership as a synthesis of them. This tentative interpretation of the literary data imposed structure, brought a measure of order to chaos, and offered an opportunity to use a fruitful sociological theory in studying otherwise discrete and arcane stories and sayings.

On the other hand, I found it relatively fruitless to engage in extended explication of texts, in part because I did not believe that the texts provided such accurate information about what R. Yohanan said, thought, and did that further explication, even exegesis, would prove *historically* illuminating. What is of interest to the theologian or the literary critic is not necessarily valuable to the historian. Since I do not believe we really know what, if anything, transpired when (if) Yohanan met Vespasian, I saw very little merit in elaborate exegeses of his conversation with him. For a theologian, the record of his words rightly represents an established fact, which permits elaborate discussion of ideas *ascribed* to him, but most certainly held by the tradent. For a literary or text critic, these words themselves, possessing a facticity of their own, permit extended elaboration, comparison with other ideas on the same matter, exegesis of what they imply. But since I could not be certain Yohanan really said them, I could not penetrate into *his* thought or motivation by explicating them. So long as the theologian does not use historical language, saying that R. Yohanan ben Zakkai actually thought what words ascribed to him suggest, the historian can have no quarrel with him. The literary critic can only contribute to the historian's enterprise, by helping him to establish the correct texts and to understand what they mean. When he identifies the text with what, if anything, happened, however, he will find in the historian a troubled and doubting student.

Goldin's judgment [23] is completely sound. Our sources are not extensive. Talmudic traditions do not tell us much about Yohanan, or anybody else before 70. If we had to depend upon them alone, about Jesus,

Paul, Philo, the Qumran group, and others we should have not a word, or, in the case of Jesus, nothing congruent to more reliable data. To Gamaliel I are ascribed a few legal sayings, revealing practically nothing about the extent of his authority or the society for which he legislated and some not too original ethical dicta.[24] Hillel, surely the most enigmatic figure of all, was supposedly Yohanan's master; yet we find only the most generalized reflections of his ideas in Yohanan's thought, apart from the *Merkavah* material. Other historical figures are preserved only as the Pharisees chose to remember them; for instance, Agrippa and the Adiabenian royal family cultivated their friendship, so they were recalled with great respect in Pharisaic lore.

The sources are formed in such a way that, whether early or late, they do not command unquestioning belief. Josephus wrote history; the rabbis did not. However accurately we may understand their words, however early are the sources that preserve them, we can never be sanguine that what happened and what the rabbis thought happened were quite the same thing. The sources are not, however, historically useless. Lower criticism can establish the greater *prima facie* credibility of some traditions over others. These may not forthwith be transmuted into history, but they may provide the basis for a historical reconstruction. Such a reconstruction presents several useful kinds of truth. It will, first, provide a survey and evaluation of the sources themselves. That evaluation may be implicit, rather than fully articulated. If one merely cites a report reflecting a fourth-century milieu, he does so because it is of interest, not because it offers evidence about what actually took place three hundred years earlier. In this category, for example, are the reports of Yohanan's unusual devotion to study.[25] I see no reason to doubt that he was an exceptionally brilliant person. The datum at hand does not prove it, but rather shows that the rabbinical conventions about the early years of great teachers were applied to whatever material the rabbis had about Yohanan himself. Second, reconstruction will presuppose that whether the details of the sources are accurate or not, their point sometimes has a sound basis in fact. That presupposition is illustrated by the stories about Yohanan's quarrel with the priesthood and the Sadducees.[26] They are demonstrably late and inaccurate. It stands to reason, however, that a major Pharisaic leader did oppose, though with what effectiveness we do not know, the priesthood and the Sadducees. The specific accounts of Yohanan's opposition reflect a historical fact, even though they do not necessarily give us accurate details about it. They record accurately how later generations recalled the earlier situation. They help us, moreover, to understand the meaning of some of his otherwise arcane legal sayings and decrees. The stories of his encounters with the Sadducees and Temple authorities together with his legal dicta do prove that he fought with the priesthood, though no one source is adequate, nor all of them together, to tell us more than that. They are fully consistent with other available data about the relations between Pharisees and the Temple. This is not the only fact we can attain, but it illustrates how some facts can be established.

CONCLUSION

The effort to recover such facts and to organize them into meaningful patterns constitutes the historical inquiry into periods far more richly endowed with sources, though less pivotal in the history of Judaism and Christianity, than the first century. Our choice is not between unquestioning belief that everything the sources say actually happened, and nihilistic and skeptical rejection of all literary evidence as historically useless. We may know much less than the sources tell us, but we know number of facts, and these facts can lead to a deeper understanding of Jewish, and Christian, history in the first century. With the facts supposedly established here, what do we understand about Rabban Yohanan ben Zakkai? Most striking is his paradigmatic exemplification of biblical figures. Even with the meager facts at hand, we know that he acted in 70 A.D. very much as had Jeremiah in 586. He reflected upon events much as had Ezekiel and Hosea (whom he probably believed to have lived before the fall of Northern Israel). Yohanan thus embodied major elements of Scriptural experience, citing at length biblical sayings exactly relevant to the crisis of his own day, and thus provided a living *midrash*, as he reenacted a moment of biblical history in his own age and idiom.

If the form of this quest is subject to criticism, it is not therefore that the data are insufficient to the task. They provide limited but illuminating information. I should criticize my approach quite differently. It is far too early, given the primitive state of our knowledge of Talmudic and cognate literature and of form-criticism of that literature, to raise the historical question at all. I have asked whether such-and-such really happened, whether under a given set of circumstances Yohanan actually said so-and-so. The answers to these questions, however, derive from a literature which has undergone no very searching form-criticism. What is decisive is the history of the tradition about Yohanan ben Zakkai, for, knowing more of that history, we can better assess the value of the facts it purports to provide. I have referred to the certainty that later generations *believed* Yohanan said this or did that. But without clearer knowledge of why it may later have been important so to believe, one can say little or nothing about whether that belief was wholly fabricated, or possibly based upon something really said or done. A history of traditions on Yohanan ben Zakkai cannot be separated from wider studies about the attitudes of later generations toward early figures. Such inquiries represent a formidable task, for little has been done to spell out the historical consequences even of the data we now have, for instance, those provided by W. Bacher's Tradition und Tradenten in den Schulen Palästinas und Babyloniens (Leipzig, 1914). A history of the tradition reciprocally depends, however, upon a prior reconstruction of the history of the academies, upon a study of which documents emerged from a given school,[27] of the ideas and attitudes of each successive age. That history requires a statement, even within the limits of present knowledge and methodology, of Babylonian and Palestinian events and issues. Such a statement will demand many revisions, as our knowledge of the history of the Jews deepens into an understanding of the history of rabbinic tradition. Among these revisions will have to come a renewal of the search, surely more satisfactory than this one, for the historical Yohanan ben Zakkai.[28]

ADDENDUM

In "The First Christian Century as Jewish History,"[29] Professor Martin A. Cohen raises the question of the relationship between Rabban Yohanan ben Zakkai and Rabban Gamaliel II, as follows: "The relationship of Gamaliel II to John [sic!] ben Zakkai has been the subject of numerous scholarly conjectures. Some of the questions posed include: 1) Was Gamaliel a pupil of John's? (cf. b. Baba Bathra 10b) 2) Is the account in Gittin 56b which tells of John's request to Vespasian to save the family of Gamaliel a fact or a legend? 3) Could John have been deposed by Gamaliel?"[30]

If R. Gamaliel studied with R. Yohanan b. Zakkai, the sources do not indicate it. All the stories about R. Yohanan's Jerusalem circle omit his name. The only reference which suggests otherwise, occurring as Cohen notes, and in addition in the Pesikta de Rav Kahana, Sheqalim ed. S. Buber 12b, and Yalkut Shimiᶜoni II 952, is quite equivocal. I have reconstructed[31] what I believe to be the original structure of R. Yohanan's academy's exegesis of Prov. 14.34, following the normal form of the *Avot* materials, that is, R. Yohanan asks a question, and his several students, R. Joshua, R. Eliʾezer, and finally, R. Eleᶜazar b. ᶜArakh, each provide an answer, to which R. Yohanan invariably comments, I like R. Eleᶜazar's answer better than anyone else's, because . . . It seems to me the several renditions of the incident are garbled. The one of special interest here is b. B.B. 10b, in which the main elements are as follows:

R. Yohanan asks the meaning of Prov. 14.34

R. Eliʾezer answers

R. Joshua answers

And then:

Rabbi Gamaliel answered and said, Righteousness exalteth a nation . . .

Said Rabbi Gamaliel, We still have to hear the opinion of the Modite.

R. Eliezer the Modite says . . .

R. Nehuniah b. HaKaneh said . . .

Said Rabban Yohanan ben Zakkai, The answer of Rabbi Nehuniah ben HaKaneh is superior . . .

The Pesikta and Yalkut accounts are garbled. In any event, the replies are as follows:

The reply in the *Bavli* of	=	in the *Pesikta*
Nehuniah b. HaKaneh	=	R. Eleᶜazar b. ᶜArakh
Joshua b. Hananiah	=	Gamaliel
Eliʾezer b. Hyrkanus	=	very close to Gamaliel's
Eliʾezer the Modite	=	Abin b. Judah.

As Bacher noted[32] the appearance of Gamaliel and Eliʾezer the Modite among the students of R. Yohanan is surprising. I should suppose that two stories are confused. In one R. Yohanan speaks with his students, and that story would have been transmitted in the normal form in which such stories usually were told, and in a second, Gamaliel presided, and eventually asked the opinion of the Modite, a common conclusion to such stories, as in b. Berahot 40a, Hullin 92b. Eliʾezer the Modite appears in a similar relationship with Gamaliel, never with R. Yohanan.

It is fairly easy to account for the garbled transmission of a story about R. Yoḥanan b. Zakkai's comment on Prov. 14.34. He actually made two such comments, as the text makes quite clear, one before the destruction, in which R. Yoḥanan said that just as sin-offering makes atonement for Israel, so charity does for the pagans, and the other afterward, in which he said that righteousness and kindness belong to Israel, but sin to the nations of the world. The former comment would have antedated the destruction of the Temple in 70, and the latter followed it. The only remnant of the former comment appears in b. B.B. 10b as follows, "R. Yoḥanan ben Zakkai said to them, Just as the sin-offering makes atonement for Israel, so charity . . ." That is all we have left of his earlier remarks, which probably included the usual discourse with the students.

So I do not think there is any literary tradition which unequivocally testifies to the discipleship of R. Gamaliel II. I think it reasonable to suppose that Gamaliel did study with R. Yoḥanan b. Zakkai before the destruction, when the master was closely associated with his father, Simeᶜon b. Gamaliel in the leadership of the Pharisaic party. The evidence of such study would have been suppressed by those eager to eliminate any suggestion that Gamaliel II was *ever* a disciple of someone they so disliked as R. Yoḥanan b. Zakkai. Who were these?

We shall never know what happened if or when R. Yoḥanan b. Zakkai and Vespasian came face to face. All we know are what three obviously different groups of people chose to say about the 'event'.[33] But the b. Git. 56b account to which Cohen refers says *nothing* whatever about R. Yoḥanan's *trying to save the family* of Gamaliel. It says that he asked, among other things, for the chain of Rabban Gamaliel. Whatever the narrator means by that, I do not think he means to say that R. Yoḥanan was asking to save his life. He did, the same account tells, ask for a physician to heal Rabbi Zadok, and that life-saving request is quite explicit.

The Talmudic account is on the whole unfavorable toward R. Yoḥanan. It preserves the details of the Avot de Rabbi Natan story about how R. Yoḥanan escaped by subterfuge from Jerusalem, adds a few concerning his conversation with Vespasian, and finally, the detail, which was probably the kernel of all such lore, about R. Yoḥanan's exegesis of Isaiah 10.34. All this I think is quite neutral. But the account continues by stressing R. Yoḥanan's ineptitude in this conversation. Vespasian supposedly said that he should not have waited so long to defect, to which R. Yoḥanan replied that he could not help himself. Vespasian then answered, "If one has a cask of honey and a reptile is curled about it, would one not break the cask in order to get rid of the reptile." Whereupon, R. Yoḥanan fell silent. The supposedly great rabbi could not think of anything to reply. The account continues:

Rabbi Joseph, and some say, Rabbi 'Akiba, applied to him the Scripture, 'He turned the wise backward and marked their knowledge futile (Is. 44.25).'
He should have answered him, One takes a pair of tongs, removes the serpent, and kills it, and saves the cask.

There follows the legend of how R. Yoḥanan's medical knowledge proved useful to Vespasian, whereupon he asked what he could give to the rabbi. The answer cited above follows, again with the comment of R. Joseph or R. 'Akiba, "he should have asked them to leave them alone that time, but he was afraid Vespasian would not give so much, and there would have been no relief whatever," with the proof-text for R. Yoḥanan's stupidity once again being Is. 44.25.

What is the intent of the ascription to R. Yoḥanan of the request for Gamaliel's chain? Rashi says that he was asking for the family of the *Nasi*, that they not be put to death so that the Davidic house would not cease in Israel. That is one way of looking at things. Another way would take into account the narrative's critical view of R. Yohanan, and lead to the supposition that he was alleged to have asked for the *authority* of Rabban Gamaliel. That the account is very late is quite obvious, and so the issue is, What would a party favorable to the 'Akiban viewpoint have thought R. Yoḥanan b. Zakkai, supposedly a doltish and easily confused man, was likely to have asked for? I think such an antipathetic view would have ascribed to R. Yohanan the request to take over the Jewish government by an act which the Messianist followers of R. Akiba would have regarded to begin with as treason.

In any event, it should be evident that the Talmudic account says nothing whatever about saving the life of R. Gamaliel, so it is futile to speculate on whether it is "a fact or a legend."

Could R. Yoḥanan have been deposed by Gamaliel?

I think it likely that he was deposed, and since R. Gamaliel was his successor, restoring the rule of the Hillelite house, I suppose he was involved in the deposition. R. Yoḥanan faced considerable opposition at Yavneh, and when one considers the policy implied by his legal reforms there, he can hardly be surprised. He attempted to endow his institution with the prerogatives hitherto reserved for the Temple.[34] He wanted to preserve its memory and sanctity, declaring in abeyance all those parts of the law which depended on the Temple for their observance. He modified those laws which might still be useful in the synagogue, and rejected priestly privileges. Such a policy, in which, from the priestly viewpoint, R. Yoḥanan wrongfully *arrogated* powers the priests had formerly exercised and disinherited the rightful authorities, would have been quite abhorrent to the remnants of the priestly and Temple classes, as we know was the case with the Bne Bathyra whom R. Yoḥanan outwitted. So one group eager to see him gone was surely the priesthood. A second was clearly the Hillelite family and followers, who would have regarded a scion of David as the only legitimate Jewish ruler. The third was that zealot segment of the Pharisaic party which both supported *and* survived the war, small though I suspect it was. The later, bitter relationships between R. Joshua and R. Eli°ezer, on the one hand, and R. Gamaliel II on the other, suggests that both sides were very sensitive and not averse to quarrel with one another.

And having set the precedent, Gamaliel II himself was probably deposed after the diasporic wars against Trajan, I should guess about 120–125. R. Gamaliel, like R. Yoḥanan, could stay in power only with Roman approval, and that depended upon willingness to keep the peace in Palestine. This he did with substantial success when the diaspora from Cyrenaica to Parthia arose in a vast rebellion. Gamaliel probably prevented serious trouble in Palestine. When the extent of the disaster became apparent, a reaction set in, in which °Akiba, who had earlier reassured the rabbis that the fulfillment of the eschatological promises would not be long postponed, came to power in the Pharisaic party. The recollection of Gamaliel's actions survived in both Roman and Jewish circles. As soon as they could, after the Bar Kokhba war, the Romans turned once again to a member of the Hillelite house. Simeon b. Gamaliel was installed to preside over the reorganized academy, which was dominated by—°Akiba's students! Herein lay one of the causes of the growing tension between sage and *Nasi* at the end of the second century and afterward. But someone else remembered too, for Gamaliel's grandson, Judah later called *Nasi,* was not given his grandfather's name, in spite of the former custom of the Hillelite house. If, therefore, Gamaliel did depose R. Yohanan ben Zakkai, it was not a happy precedent.

NOTES

1. C. J. Adams, ed., A Reader's Guide to the Great Religions (N.Y., 1965), 223.
2. A Life of Rabban Yohanan ben Zakkai, Ca. 1–80 C. E. (Leiden, 1962).
3. Ibid., 3–4, n.1.
4. Louis Finkelstein, M'vo LeMasekhet Avot veAvot de Rabbi Natan (N.Y., 1950), 38–43, 60–61, and Y. N. Epstein, M'vo-ot leSifrut HaTannaim (Jerusalem, 1957), 40–41, 295–96, 399–401.
5. Birger Gerhardsson (Memory and Manuscript, Oral Tradition and Written Transmission in Rabbinic Judaism and Early Christianity [Uppsala, 1961]), completely ignores this fact. We do not have adequate evidence to determine the methods of transmission used either in the early churches or in pre-70 Pharisaism. Gerhardsson admits that rabbinic Judaism differed from pre-70 Pharisaism, as the latter differed from the rest of pre-70 Judaism, but holds that the educational systems may have been substantially the same. His evidence is utterly inadequate to prove it. His view of Jesus as a kind of Pharisaic-rabbinic teacher, ignoring express statements to the contrary, suggests that we know more about the Pharisaic rabbis from Hillel to the destruction of Jerusalem than we do.
6. Life, 120–29.
7. See Bab. Talmud Bava Meẓi'ah 36a, and my History of the Jews in Babylonia, II: The Early Sasanian Period (Leiden, 1966), 249–85.
8. E.g., Mishnah Shabbat 16.7, recovering a scorpion on the Sabbath so that it shall not bite. "R. Judah said, Such a case once came before R. Yohanan ben Zakkai in Arav, and he said, I doubt whether he is not liable to a sin-offering." See also 22.3. R. Judah never knew R. Yohanan ben Zakkai, of course. The data in 16.7 and 22.3 may well have been in a collection of Arav sayings, which R. Judah or his teachers revised for their own purposes in compiling the Mishnah. A similar, fragmentary collection of Jerusalem sayings is clearly in Mishnah Ketuvot 13.1 and 13.2, as well as the sayings in Avot 2.8–9, which reflect the conditions of the Jerusalem circle, as we shall note below.
9. Life, 147–72.
10. "Debate on the Loyal Sacrifices," HTR 53, 93f., and Life, 104f.
11. Life, 147f.
12. G. Alon, Mehkarim beToldot Yisrael (Tel Aviv, 1957), I, 273, n. 86.
13. I have tried to explain why they did not in "Religious Uses of History: Judaism in First-Century A.D. Palestine and Third-Century A.D. Babylonia," History and Theory V, 2, 1966.

14. The same story, in the same form, is told about R. Eleazar b. Shamu'a and R. Yohanan HaSandlar, in the same passage of Sifre Deut. We have a formal narrative applied first to four men, and then to two, the occasions of whose migrations from Palestine were remembered. See my History of the Jews in Babylonia, I: The Parthian Period (Leiden, 1965), 122–23, n. 1.
15. Judah Goldin, "Mashehu ʿal Bet Midrasho shel Rabban Yoḥanan ben Zakkai," Harry A. Wolfson Jubilee Volume (N.Y. 1965), Hebrew Section, 69–92.
16. Life, 27f.
17. Life, 96–104.
18. Ibid., 44–58.
19. Ibid., 70f., 175.
20. Avot de R. Natan, ch. 14.
21. Life, 28f.; see especially the saying, "Oh Galilee! Galilee! You hate Torah," Pal. Talmud Shabbat 16.8.
22. Ibid., 33f.
23. Cited above, n. 1.
24. Life, 33–34, 41–43.
25. Ibid., 24–25.
26. Ibid., 49–57.
27. Y. N. Epstein's Mʾvo-ot leSifrut HaTannaim, cited above n. 4, and his Mʾvo-ot leSifrut HaAmoraim (Jerusalem, 1962), S. Lieberman's Talmud of Caesarea (in Hebrew, Supplement to Tarbiz II, 4 [Jerusalem, 1931]), Louis Ginzberg's "The Mishnah Tamid," Journal of Jewish Lore and Philosphy, I, 33f., as well as Lieberman's Tosefta Kifshuta (N.Y., 1955f., 10 vols. to date), provide the obvious starting-points for such literary studies.
28. Professor Jonathan Z. Smith, University of California, Santa Barbara, provided extensive criticism. Professor Brevard S. Childs, Yale University, offered the comments upon which the final paragraph is based. I am grateful to both for their kindly interest in this paper, though alone responsible for its limitations.
29. In J. Philip Hyatt, ed., The Bible in Modern Scholarship, Papers Read at the 100th Meeting of the Society of Biblical Literature, Dec. 28–30, 1964. (Nashville, 1965), 227–51.
30. Ibid., 242, n. 41.
31. Life, 135–38.
32. 'Agadot Tanna'e 'Ereẓ Yisra'el, I, i, 26, n. 4.
33. Life, 115–20.
34. Life, 115–67.

11

On the Reliability of Attributions in the Babylonian Talmud

David Kraemer

Historical scholarship of classical Babylonian Jewry has credulously assumed the accuracy of attributions in its primary source of evidence—the Babylonian Talmud. Jacob Neusner has properly criticized such methodological complacency, and consequently has insisted that we have access only to the Judaism attested in the final document. But Neusner himself has suggested a variety of tests by which attributed traditions could be *verified,* and despite his assumption that given the nature of the evidence, such tests have nothing to yield, two of the tests will, in fact, serve to verify traditions recorded in the Bavli. First, because the Yerushalmi and the Bavli may be spoken of as being "external" to (that is, independent of) one another, commonly attested traditions may be assumed to have emerged from the circle of disciples of the sage or sages with whom they are associated. Second, because traditions of different generations of sages in the Bavli are distinguished by characteristic and "superficial" literary features, these traditions may be assumed to have taken their present form within a relatively brief period after the generation to which they are attributed. Thus, histories, though not biographies, based upon this material may indeed be written.

The composition of histories of the Jews in third-to-fifth century C.E. Babylonia depends upon the reliability of attributions in the Babylonian Talmud. This document, virtually the only significant source of information on the Jews of that period and place, claims to record traditions that were authored by rabbinic sages who flourished in those centuries. If these claims can be accepted, then we have some record of the views expressed in those Jewish communities, generation by generation. If, on

Reprinted by permission of Hebrew Union College—Jewish Institute of Religion from *Hebrew Union College Annual,* volume 60, Cincinnati, 1989.

the other hand, the Bavli's claims for the authorship of individual traditions cannot be accepted, we will be forced to admit that those centuries are essentially invisible to us, and that the only picture we may truly have is that recorded in the document at its completion, that is, in the fifth-to-sixth century.

Despite the obviously crucial nature of this determination, those whose work depends upon the reliability of such attributions have merely assumed that they are generally accurate, without articulating the defensibility of that assumption. The only ones to have diverged meaningfully from this methodological complacency are Jacob Neusner and his students, who rightly criticize this approach as being overly naive and uncritical.[1] The question they ask is this: why, just because a document asks us to believe that a certain authority made a certain statement at a certain time, should we grant that it is so? The Bible claims to record the words of Abraham. Would we admit that such reports are historically accurate? The Zohar wants us to believe that it contains the words of the second-century sage, R. Shimon b. Yoḥai and his circle. Would we on that basis represent its ideologies as really second-century phenomena?[2]

Having articulated this critique, Neusner and those who follow him have been forced to accept the consequences: detailed histories of the centuries in question are now illegitimate. The admission of this condition is explicit. In the introduction to the third printing of his *A History of the Jews in Babylonia* (reprint Chico, California, 1984), Neusner makes clear that the methodological assumptions on the basis of which he composed that history must now be recognized as fatally flawed. He writes, both simply and to the point: "By the criteria laid out in the preceding sections, the book has some merits, but not many . . . The twin-pillars of fundamentalism stand firm and tall here (p. xxx)." In several other books which trace the development of certain central rabbinic concepts, we similarly see the consequences of Neusner's methodological skepticism.[3] In those works, he claims that we may only know of the existence of a concept at the final stage of the development of a document in which it is attested. No matter that the same idea might be attributed to a sage of the third century (or even earlier); if it appears for the first time in the Bavli, then we can only verify its currency in the sixth century, not before (the issue is 'verification', not assumption).

Let me illustrate the historiographic difference that this methodological assumption will make. Speaking of the relation between the written and oral Torah, the Yerushalmi (Hagigah 1:7, 76d) records the following traditions:

> R. Zeira in the name of R. Eleazar: "Though I write for him the great things (translate here: "most") of my Torah . . . (Hos. 8:12)." And is most of the Torah written? [Surely not!] Rather, more abundant are those things that are derived from the written [Torah] than those derived from the oral . . .

> R. Yohanan and R. Yudan b. R. Shimon—One said: If you have kept that which is oral and have kept that which is written, I shall make a covenant with you, but if not, I will not make a covenant with you . . .

Neusner notes that the myth of the dual-Torah (written and oral) is nowhere fully articulated prior to the Yerushalmi, as this text testifies.[4] According to his approach, therefore, we should conclude that the myth was only fully conceptualized in rabbinic circles by ca. C.E. 400, that is, the closing of the Yerushalmi. If he were to lend credence to the attestations, on the other hand, then the same myth would be evidenced by ca. 250.

What is at stake here is more than a mere difference of ca. 150 years. If the myth of the dual-Torah may only be pinned down to the end of the fourth century, then it is the experience of Judaism under early Christian Rome within which we must seek its roots. Moreover, as an apologia for rabbinic tradition, we will have to see it as a relatively late development. If, on the other hand, the myth is to be associated with R. Yohanan, R. Eleazar, and their circle, then we will have linked this same apologia with sages who stood in close relation to the Mishnah and its author. In that case, the response will be understood as being more or less from the same period, and the historical context will be that of the pagan Roman Empire.

But how, short of uncritical credulity, can we go beyond the final redaction of a given rabbinic text? In what way could we judge that attributions give us access to the generations that they claim to represent?

Neusner suggests the following reasonable tests by which attributions could be affirmed.[5]

1. A tradition may be cited in a source "entirely external to the rabbinic tradition." By "external," I believe what is intended is a text that could not be dependent upon the rabbinic text that we seek to verify, or which itself could not be the source of that same text. If the texts could be dependent, we would have gained nothing. If it was "external" to any such dependence, on the other hand, then we would

have gained a great deal. Such an external citation would of course demonstrate that the rabbinic document was not merely inventing the tradition for its own purposes. Neusner contends that no such external sources are available to us.

2. "The final date of compiling a collection in which a story (or here, tradition—D.K.) first occurs commonly supplies the final date for the present form of all the materials in that collection. . . ." This is the skeptical view which, as we saw above, Neusner presently employs. For purposes of the present discussion, therefore, it adds nothing.

3. Internal evidence may help us to confirm an earlier dating. If later traditions are clearly dependent upon earlier traditions, then the earlier traditions may be considered to be verified.

This approach, potentially, is of immense value in the dating of Yerushalmi and, in particular, Bavli traditions, because of the frequency with which this phenomenon is found in those documents. However, though Neusner was willing to use this test in his work on the Mishnah,[6] he has been unwilling to apply it in work on the Bavli and Yerushalmi. Why so? Apparently, if one is willing to take the skeptical approach to the extreme, then no attributed tradition may be taken to verify any other attributed tradition. Since there is no reason to give credence to any such tradition, the whole corpus becomes subject to the same doubt.

4. Though not included explicitly in his list, Neusner (still, in *The Pharisees*) clearly goes on to consider what "reason" will dictate. It may be that such a criterion is rendered meaningless in a confrontation with extreme skepticism, but in combination with other verifications it may, nonetheless, have a place.

5. Finally, Neusner adds the following test[7]: "*If . . . we knew that there was a characteristic mode of formulating ideas,* always particular to one authority or school, and never utilized by some other authority or school, *we should have a solid, because superficial, criterion for sorting out valid from invalid attributions* (my emphasis—D.K.)." This, we will see, is a test that holds immense promise.

Test #2 (the final composition of a text) will, as we said, not be useful in considering the possible verification of Amoraic attributions, because it already grants that such verifications are impossible. Tests #3 and #4 also are of little use as primary verifications because they might easily be criticized as being overly credulous. We will return to them, therefore, only in combination with other, more certain tests. Tests #1 and #5, on the other hand, do provide a key to verifying attributions, and if evidence of the sort that they describe is available, then we will be able to retreat from the position that critical skepticism has now demanded that we occupy.

In seeking a source that is "external" enough to be of some benefit, it is not necessary, as we have already implied, that such a source be external to the rabbinic tradition as a whole. It is only necessary that the source be demonstrably independent of the text in question. If, for example, both the Bavli and the Yerushalmi quote a Mishnah, we have discovered nothing that we did not know previously. Both documents are obviously dependent upon the Mishnah, and so the fact that they both quote a Mishnah adds nothing. If, on the other hand, both these documents quote a common Amoraic source, and if we could demonstrate that the Bavli was not dependent upon the Yerushalmi (as the Yerushalmi, having come to closure one to two centuries before,[8] was obviously not dependent on the Bavli), then we will have shown each document to be "external" to the other, and to be available as a source for verification of a mutually preserved tradition.

That "externality" (independence) is an accurate description of the relationship of the Bavli and Yerushalmi is a virtually undisputed conclusion in contemporary scholarship.[9] Neusner himself makes this argument persuasively and at length in his *The Bavli and Its Sources: The Question of Tradition in the Case of Tractate Sukkah*.[10] There he demonstrates that, while the Bavli and Yerushalmi might have shared common sources—the Mishnah, Tosefta, and some brief Amoraic traditions—"The Bavli and the Yerushalmi assuredly stand autonomous from one another." (p. 50). The expository programs of each are entirely independent, and all evidence indicates that the latter document, the Bavli, was in no way dependent upon the former. Even if the Yerushalmi were available to the authors of the Bavli—and, aside from chronology, there is no evidence that it was[11]—the fact that shared Amoraic traditions almost never correspond exactly points to the fact that the framers of the Bavli were independent of the Yerushalmi in all respects, even with respect to common Palestinian traditions.

This being the case, we may rightly speak of these documents as sources for the verification of commonly recorded Amoraic traditions. Since they did not derive these traditions from one another, they must have drawn them from a common third source, that being the circle of the sage to which the common tradition is attributed. Because early communication between the Palestinian and Babylonian communities is widely attested, whereas significant later communication is, as we saw, denied by available evidence, it is only a source such as this (the circle of the sage) that may reasonably be claimed to have supplied the tradition to both independent documents.

To see what sort of conclusions this verification test would yield, I examined all traditions attributed to R. Yoḥanan in the Bavli, tractate Shabbat, and compared these traditions to the record of the Yerushalmi. Of a total of 113 such traditions, I found that 75 have no parallel whatsoever in the Yerushalmi. Nine record the same opinion in the name of a different authority, while three record the same attribution dealing with the same issue but with a different legal ruling. 26 are, to one degree or another, closely parallel, and in these instances it is generally impossible to imagine that the independent documents could have shaped these traditions without a common source. An example of such a parallel follows:

Yerushalmi Berakhot 1:5 (3b) R. Yoḥanan in the name of R. Shimon b. Yoḥai: [people] such as ourselves who are involved in the study of Torah, even to recite the Shema we do not interrupt (our activity, i.e., our study). R. Yoḥanan said about himself: [People] such as ourselves who are not [properly] engaged in the study of Torah, even for Prayer we interrupt.	Bavli Shabbat 11a R. Yoḥanan said: they taught it only with respect to [people] like R. Shimon b. Yoḥai and his colleagues, for Torah [study] is their livelihood, but [people] like ourselves, we interrupt for reciting the Shema and for Prayer.

To be sure, there are important differences between these two versions. But the parallels are also unmistakable, and it is inconceivable that these two traditions are totally independent of one another. Rather, both the similarities and differences are what might reasonably be expected of an original oral tradition which came to be repeated and deliberated upon in what later became two independent traditions. There is little doubt, therefore, that this Bavli tradition, as a text that derives in basic content from the circle of R. Yoḥanan, may be considered to be *verified*.

The same may be suggested, though with less confidence, for traditions that record different legal rulings or that are attributed to different, though commonly associated sages (e.g., Yoḥanan, Eleazar, R. Shimon

b. Laqish). Particularly in the former instances, mistakes of this sort are typical of independently preserved oral traditions. The Mishnah itself is not infrequently preserved with such differences by the Bavli and Yerushalmi.[12] Of course, mere superficial parallels should be disregarded, but where similarities reasonably require a common source, even when differences are significant, the source for a tradition (if only in essence) should be sought in the circle of the sage or sages to whom it is attributed.

But what is the meaning of the whole sample in which less than 25% may be verified with confidence? We may note, to begin with, that the literary record of the Bavli is more comprehensive than that of the Yerushalmi, even with regard to prominent Palestinian sages. Parts of that "more comprehensive record" might be the product of artificial attributions, that is, invented traditions that were later attributed to R. Yohanan. But just because there is no Yerushalmi parallel does not mean that this is necessarily the case. Even unparalleled traditions might in fact derive from the circle of R. Yohanan; we simply have no evidence for this. Caution would, in any case, bid that we not grant any presumptive reliability to such traditions; other confirming evidence would be necessary before this presumption could be made.

Of course, it is not only the traditions of R. Yohanan that find expression in both Talmuds. Prominent early Amoraic sages of each major rabbinic community are represented in the document of the other. The same tests and reservations may, therefore, be extended to a good number of Amoraic traditions. Granted, we may still speak with confidence regarding only a relatively small minority of all Amoraic traditions. We have, nevertheless, begun to establish a foothold in the process of historical verification.

The second verification test that will yield positive results is that which seeks a mode of formulating ideas that characterizes one group of sages but not another (#5 above). Such a test may be deemed reliable because it uncovers patterns that are not essential to the subject at hand—they are "superficial." Of course, to isolate such patterns one must begin by presuming that the attributions are "accurate." It is only by examining together all traditions attributed to a certain sage or group of sages (united, for example, by presumed chronological proximity) that one may ascertain whether such patterns exist in the first place. If, after presuming accuracy, one discovers no patterns, then it is necessary to conclude that the attributions have not been verified. However, if one uncovers such patterns of formulating ideas, it is safe to assume that they are not the product of an artificial, final formulation. Precisely because such patterns are, at first glance, hidden, it is extremely unlikely that they could have been imposed on a broad scale by some later hand. The system for identifying traditions (that is, the attributions) in which such patterns are embedded may, therefore, be understood to convey a reasonably reliable confirmation.

Moreover, this test does not require that these "characteristic mode[s] of formulating ideas" be "always particular to one authority or school and never utilized by some other authority or school." To the contrary, such exclusivity is suspect precisely because it might easily be identified by a reader. Furthermore, it is those patterns that cannot be so identified, and which cannot, therefore, be thought to be the product of artifice, that are more reliable sources of verification. It is for this reason that this test should seek "patterns," that is, broad but significant differences that distinguish one group from another. If such patterns are discovered, then a "presumptive reliability" will have been established. Unlike the test examined above, this will not actually "verify" individual traditions. But attributions as a whole will no longer require the same skepticism. Again, as we will see, the circle of the sage under discussion will emerge as the most reasonable source for the particular Amoraic traditions.

With respect to these traditions in the Bavli, at least, such patterns may be shown to exist. In earlier research (which I supplement here), I examined the stylistic characteristics of Amoraic traditions in detail.[13] I discovered that, while there are only occasional features that characterize the traditions of one Amora in particular,[14] there are patterns that quite clearly characterize the traditions of a generation of Amoraim as a whole. These patterns are, as I pointed out, particularly persuasive in the present context, because there is no room for suspicion that they were imposed by a later author to create a unique individual characterization. Unless we were to consider the possibility that the whole literature of the Bavli is the product of a cunning, intentional deception, these patterns must be considered significant evidence in support of the attributional record of the document as a whole.

What follows is only a review of the most salient characterizing features that I have identified. These features are true of the traditions of the most prolific sages of each generation (Rav and Samuel; R. Yoḥanan and Resh Laqish; R. Judah and R. Huna; R. Sheshet, R. Ḥisda, R. Naḥman, R. Joseph and Rabba; Abbaye and Rava) and so may be said to be representative of the generation as a whole.

The earliest Amoraic generations barely diverged from the stylistic model of the Mishnah. The traditions of Rav and Samuel are over-whelmingly brief,[15] and these statements more often prescribe halakha (like the Mishnah itself) than suggest interpretation. They are also, like the Mishnah, overwhelmingly in rabbinic Hebrew[16] (the predominance of Hebrew over Aramaic in Rav's traditions is 4.56:1, and in those of Samuel 4.88:1). The same tendencies are apparent in the next generation with the production of R. Judah and R. Huna,[17] and, with minor excep-tions, also with that of the early Palestinian Amoraim, R. Yoḥanan (whose traditions prefer Hebrew over Aramaic by a ratio of 5.78:1) and Resh Laqish[18] (according to the record of the Bavli).[19]

In contrast, the argumentation of the first two Amoraic generations is extremely limited. Most cases are short and simple, extending for only one or two steps. Overwhelmingly, it was the brief, formulated conclu-sions that were preserved in these generations, and not the debates that produced them.

The stylistic development exhibited in traditions of the third Amoraic generation is substantial. The preference for Hebrew expression in this generation is either substantially reduced (in the traditions of Rabba, Hebrew is preferred by a ratio of 1.22:1) or altogether eliminated (the traditions of R. Joseph prefer Aramaic over Hebrew by a ratio of 1.54:1). There is still a preference for brief formulation, but the predom-inance of such traditions over argumentation is now significantly dimin-ished.[20] In fact, for the later sages of this generation, the record of their argumentational production equals that of their briefer traditions. Moreover, the brief traditions of this period exhibit a self-consciousness and a rhetorical edge not witnessed before. Self-justification is not un-common.[21] Reasoning, and not only the conclusion that results from it, is now a common subject of expression. The tone of many statements shifts from simple exposition of earlier traditions to a clear indication that what is being said is in *response* to what preceded. Clearly, the earlier preferred models are being supplemented and displaced.

Furthermore, all manners of argumentation are more commonly rep-resented in this generation. This includes objections from tannaitic sources, objections from logic alone (which appear in great number for the first time in this generation), and simple dialogues. It also includes occasional argumentational texts of great length and sophistication. The profile of traditions from this (the third) Amoraic generation characterizes it as one of great creativity and innovation.

This is even more the case in the next generation, that of Abbaye and Rava. Statistically speaking, the trends witnessed earlier come to fruition at this time.[22] Aramaic is preferred above Hebrew in the traditions of both Abbaye (1.79:1) and Rava (1.18:1). Though on a one-to-one basis brief traditions maintain a large plurality over argumentational texts, if one considers the sheer literary bulk of each, argumentation for the first time approaches brief formulations in quantity.[23] Moreover, the majority of brief traditions are now explanatory, confirming a trend evidenced in the previous generation, in which prescriptive traditions dominated earlier on, whereas explanatory comments were more common at a later stage. Also, like the immediately preceding record, self-consciousness in expression is widespread,[24] and even argumentation has finally taken its place as the object for detailed comment.

Most noteworthy is the quantity of argumentation attributed to sages of this generation. The number of argumentational traditions in the names of Abbaye and Rava far exceeds that of any other generation. This quantitative growth is evident, moreover, for exchanges of all lengths, including those that persist for many steps.[25]

We have shown, then, that the traditions of each Amoraic generation are characterized by a certain literary pattern, and that the patterns serve to distinguish one generation from another (or one productive period from another) in significant ways. Because these patterns differ, and because they are "superficial" to specific subjects of deliberation, these data may be said to offer "verification" of the presumptive reliability of attributed Amoraic traditions.

This verification is supported by application of the first test discussed above (the "externality" of the Bavli and Yerushalmi with relation to one another) to the language statistic (Hebrew/Aramaic) of R. Yoḥanan. (We apply this test to his traditions because his is the only name recorded in such significant numbers in both the Bavli and the Yerushalmi.) As we indicated above, the traditions of R. Yoḥanan, according to the record of the Bavli, prefer Hebrew over Aramaic by a ratio of 5.78:1. According to the Yerushalmi's record, the ratio is 4.6:1. While there is clearly a slight discrepancy in these numbers (a discrepancy which could, in any case, be explained by a number of factors, including the precise body of traditions selected for preservation, the stereotyped expectation in Babylonia that R. Yoḥanan, a Palestinian, would be more likely to express himself in Hebrew, and so forth), what is more significant is the fact that both documents record an overwhelming preference for Hebrew expression. Such a preference is not replicated in the Bavli except in the case of the earliest Amoraim. Independently, therefore, both the Bavli and the Yerushalmi attest to the same picture of R. Yoḥanan's traditions, and this, in turn, supports the reliability of the language statistic as a whole. By the criteria established in the test discussed most recently, this and other such factors would already have provided verification of the traditions as a whole. This independent support suggests that such a conclusion is not in error.

The nature of the verification, however, may only extend as far as the evidence will allow. How, precisely, should this "presumptive reliability" be defined?

The patterns that have been discerned characterize, as we said, only one generation from another, but not individuals. This suggests that conventions of formulation and preservation were shared by the sages of each generation (or by the redactors of the traditions of that generation who, nevertheless, redacted those traditions not long after they had originally been formulated), mostly eliminating uniqueness in expression as it might relate to individual personalities. This being so, traditions attributed to the sages of a given generation may be presumed to accurately reflect a view held in that generation, but not necessarily by that individual. What might have been unique to an individual was blurred by convention, but generations as a whole preserved their distinct personalities.

Even given this limitation, we have gone a significant distance beyond the paralysis with which we began. Based upon this latter test, we may presume that Bavli traditions record views that reflect the age in which they are claimed to have been formulated. Unless our task is to compose biographies, therefore, we have gained a useful tool. Histories of ideas may, in fact, be written, and developments between one generation and the next may be duly noted.

In combination with the earlier test, presumptions of reliability may be defined even more precisely. If a Bavli tradition is closely paralleled in the Yerushalmi, then we must assume that the tradition in question originated in the circle of the sage to whom it is attributed. Again, this does not confirm that the sage actually expressed the recorded opinion, let alone the words themselves. But it does confirm that his immediate circle believed he did. So, again, if it is history that we want to write, the data may be confidently employed. It is only biography to which we have little access.

Building upon these two tests, the other tests now take on some significance. To begin with, because traditions may now be said to be grounded in given generations, those later traditions that clearly depend upon prior traditions may be understood to strengthen their presumptive reliability. This is particularly true where these traditions exhibit the patterns by which their generation is characterized. In addition, building upon the foundation laid by this variety of mutually reinforcing tests, there is also now a place to ask whether it is reasonable to imagine "that the whole literature is pseudepigraphic in an extreme sense"?[26] Given the fact that differences between the generations are not flattened, and the fact, admitted by all, that the Bavli and Yerushalmi clearly depended upon earlier traditions in their composition, it seems impossible to support such a conclusion. To the contrary, evidence supports a view that traditions were formulated in relative chronological proximity with the sages to whom they are attributed,[27] and the final document (the Bavli and, most likely, the Yerushalmi) did not, for the most part, eliminate the uniqueness of the sources that it employed.

There are some who would want to claim that verifications can be made even more specific. Lieberman[28] understands that the *baraita* at B. Eruv. 54b, describing Moses' repetition of oral traditions to the priests and the elders, encapsulates the process by which rabbinic traditions were "published." Since the process begins with a single authority figure, it is tempting to claim that later rabbinic attributions were accurate to this extent as well. But the relation of the legend to purported later models is too transparent to accept uncritically. All we know from this text is that the rabbis claimed to publish traditions in a manner similar to Moses, lending authority and credence to the rabbinic procedures. However, just as we would reject a literal reading of the text as it applies to Moses, so too must we be dubious about its implied claims. The author of this text has too much to gain by convincing us.

In a similar way, Halivni believes that the gemara at B. Eruv. 32b alludes to the process by which Amoraic traditions were published.[29] There, after a lengthy deliberation, several sages ask R. Naḥman whether a given conclusion has been "fixed as *gemara*?" After an affirmative answer, the conclusion is repeated as a brief "apodictic" tradition in typical Amoraic form. In other words, after debating different sides of an issue, a given authority would see to it that the conclusion of the debate was formulated as a brief, easily repeated tradition. Again, if we take this text at its word (as interpreted by Halivni), we will be tempted to connect traditions with the authority to whom they are attributed.

But there are two difficulties with such a step. First, we would have to grant that this particular interpretation is the correct one. Given our distance from the source, and the alternative interpretations that have been proposed,[30] we must at least admit that the matter is not settled. Second, even if Halivni's reading of this text is the most convincing,[31] this does not mean that what is "reported" here is representative of the whole. If this were the precise process by which Amoraic traditions were published, then why is this the only example of such a report? If, on the other hand, this text was meant to act as a general illustration of the Amoraic process of publication, then why was it not more explicit? In either instance, enough questions remain to make this an inadequate foundation upon which to build a structure.

Single cases of any kind are insufficient evidence upon which to build. A far more extensive kind of evidence would be necessary before presumptive reliability could be granted to individual attributions. Unfortunately, I do not see that such evidence is available. We are at present unable, therefore, to go beyond the general circle of the sage to which a tradition is attributed. Thus, as we noted above, biography remains off-limits to historians of classical rabbinic society.[32] On the other hand, other matters of history, dependent though they might be on the dates supplied by rabbinic attributions, may legitimately (though cautiously) be pursued.

Given these conclusions, let us return to our original illustration to see how the history we now write will be altered. As we noted then, because the myth of the dual Torah is fully conceptualized in rabbinic literature for the first time only in the Yerushalmi, Neusner assumes that it originated at about the time of the closure of that document (ca. 400). But compare, now, the related Bavli version (Giṭṭin 60b):

R. Eleazar said: The majority of the Torah is in writing and the minority oral, as it says, "Though I write for him the great things (= "most") of my Torah, they are reckoned a strange thing (Hos. 8:12)." . . .

R. Yoḥanan said: The Holy One, blessed be He, made a covenant with Israel only on account of the things preserved orally, as it says . . .

The relation of the traditions in the two versions is striking and unmistakable. In both instances the name of R. Yoḥanan is associated with the opinion that claims that God's covenant with Israel was in some way dependent upon the oral Torah. In both instances R. Eleazar is connected with an opinion that emphasizes the primacy of written Torah, if only as the source for derivation. The biblical text quoted in both versions is the same as well.

Based upon the verification tests reviewed earlier, we may be confident that these opinions originated in the circles of the sages to whom they are attributed. This being so, then we may affirm that the myth of the dual Torah originated by at least the middle of the third century in the Palestine of pagan Rome. The sages in whose circle these views were current were early Amoraim, and R. Yoḥanan had in his youth even been—or so the Talmud reports—a student of R. Judah Ha-Nasi. It was, of course, this same Judah whose Mishnah they revered and—if this myth is to serve as evidence—whose legitimacy they self-consciously sought to defend.[33] The rabbinic sages did not wait for nearly two centuries to recognize that the Mishnah required some kind of explicit mythical empowerment. On the contrary, these sages saw fit to articulate an explicit empowering myth for the Mishnah at a relatively early stage. It was, moreover, a myth of incomparable power—one that would become the single most prevalent Torah-myth in rabbinic Judaism for all centuries to follow.[34]

NOTES

1. Several of Neusner's many statements of this critique are spoken of below. To these should be added, in particular, William Scott Green, "What's in a Name? The Problematic of Talmudic 'Biography'," in W. S. Green (ed.), *Approaches to Ancient Judaism: Theory and Practice* (Missoula, 1978).

2. Neusner has expressed this critique on numerous occasions, including in the introduction to the third edition of his *History of the Jews in Babylonia*. His most extensive statement of this view is to be found in *Reading and Believing: Ancient Judaism and Contemporary Gullibility* (Atlanta, 1986).

3. See *Messiah in Context: Israel's History and Destiny in Formative Judaism*

(Philadelphia, 1984) and *Torah: From Scroll to Symbol in Formative Judaism* (Philadelphia, 1985).

4. *Torah: From Scroll to Symbol in Formative Judaism*, pp. 75–77.
5. See *The Pharisees, Rabbinic Perspectives*, pp. 233–235.
6. See e.g., *Eliezer ben Hyrcanus: The Tradition and the Man* (Leiden, 1973), v. II, pp. 63–169, and *The Mishnah Before 70* (Atlanta, 1987).
7. See *Judaism in Society*, p. 31.
8. The Yerushalmi is generally assumed to have come to a close ca. 400 C.E. Present debate about the Bavli puts its closure somewhere between 427 and 600.
9. See J. N. Epstein, *M'vo'ot l'sifrut ha-amoraim* (Jerusalem, 1962), pp. 290–2, and Y. Greenwald, *Ha-ra'u m'sadrei ha-bavli et ha-yerushalmi?* (New York, 1954), pp. 56–70.
10. Atlanta, 1987.
11. See now Martin Jaffee, "The Babylonian Appropriation of the Talmud Yerushalmi: Redactional Studies in the Horayot Tractates," in *New Perspectives on Ancient Judaism*, vol. 4, *The Literature of Early Rabbinic Judaism: Issues in Talmudic Redaction and Interpretation*, ed. by Alan J. Avery-Peck (Lanham, 1989), pp. 3–27. Jaffee notes certain redactional similarities between Yerushalmi and Bavli tractate Horayot, and suggests that the latter document has been influenced by the former in its redactional choices. He admits that any influence is limited to redaction alone (see p. 6, n. 9). Even if Jaffee is correct, the fact that the authors of the Bavli did not amend their Palestinian traditions on the basis of the Yerushalmi record only strengthens the conclusion that they possessed their own earlier, independent tradition to which they were willing to give priority. This will therefore not affect our conclusion.
12. See M. Schachter, *Ha-Mishnah b'Bavli u-viYerushalmi* (Jerusalem, 1959).
13. David Kraemer, *Stylistic Characteristics of Amoraic Literature* [hereafter, SCAL] (Ph.D. dissertation, Jewish Theological Seminary, 1984).
14. SCAL, p. 87 and n. 11.
15. SCAL, pp. 49–53, 57.
16. My study of the language of expression of Amoraic traditions was conducted subsequent to my SCAL research, and so the specifics are included below. I did not examine the traditions of all sages who had earlier been the subject of study, but only of a smaller representative sample (as the presence or absence of statistics below will reveal). To arrive at these figures, I first examined all "brief" traditions attributed to Rav and Abbaye. Discovering that the ratio does not vary significantly over the whole sample, I restricted my examination, in the case of other sages, to smaller parts of their corpus, but in no case did I examine less than half of all "brief" traditions attributed to a given sage. Furthermore, I did not examine "argumentational" traditions. My sense, though, is that such traditions would tend, more than brief traditions, to prefer Aramaic (the opposite is certainly not the case). Since earlier Amoraim are associated with relatively little argumentation, this

omission will not affect their ratios significantly. For later Amoraim, on the other hand, this will mean that their preference for Aramaic should be slightly increased.

17. SCAL, pp. 62–4.

18. SCAL, pp. 69–70, 72.

19. A preliminary review of the frequency and scope of argumentation in the Yerushalmi supports the same conclusion. In the Yerushalmi, *Seder Zeraim* and tractates Shabbat, Eruvin, and Pesaḥim, I counted only forty argumentational sequences that persisted for three steps or more (most were four steps, a few extended to up to a dozen). This is the total number of such sequences, involving the participation of any sage. This is a relatively small number, of course, and there are clearly a far larger number of brief traditions attributed to the same sages. I have not examined those traditions to determine whether they prefer halakha or interpretation. See also below on the testimony of the linguistic record in traditions attributed to R. Yoḥanan, as it supports the general reliability of the Bavli's record of Palestinian Amoraic traditions.

20. SCAL, p. 80f.

21. SCAL, p. 81f.

22. SCAL, p. 109f.

23. In SCAL, I counted 1366 argumentational sequences that involved Abbaye and Rava, and 2125 brief (apodictic) traditions in their names. If one includes brief traditions that are followed by a single response in this number (what I called one-step argumentation) then the total number of apodictic traditions attributed to these sages is 2318. However, if each responsive step of an argumentational sequence is counted (being that each such step is more or less equivalent in length to an apodictic statement), then the number of argumentational statements attributed to these sages is ca. 1800 and the total number of steps in the argumentation in which these sages participate is at least 2821. (I say "at least" because I grouped all sequences of five steps or more into a single category, and for purposes of this counting I considered each to be only five steps, though some were considerably longer.)

24. SCAL, p. 110.

25. SCAL, p. 132.

26. Neusner, *The Pharisees*, p. 235.

27. Though, to be sure, they were often "re-formulated" in the course of transmission, as Halivni has demonstrated extensively in his *Meqorot umesorot*. As a general observation, it is necessary to caution that even with the presumed reliability that I have demonstrated, what we have at best is still a working presumption. All traditions must still be subjected to the variety of critical tests that Halivni and others have employed.

28. *Hellenism in Jewish Palestine* (New York, 1950), pp. 83–99.

29. *Meqorot umesorot* (Jerusalem, 1982), pp. 91–95.

30. See Albeck, *Mavo la-talmudim* (Tel-Aviv, 1969), pp. 576–7.

31. This reading is supported, indirectly, by J. Kaplan in *The Redaction of the Talmud* (New York, 1933), p. 196.

32. That is, in this we continue to agree with the conclusions of Neusner and Green; see above, n. 1.

33. This observation is found abundantly in Neusner's works on the Mishnah. In connection with R. Yoḥanan and his relationship to the Mishnah, see also D. Halivni, "The Reception Accorded to Rabbi Judah's Mishnah," in E. P. Sanders (ed.), *Jewish and Christian Self-Definition* (Philadelphia, 1981), p. 209.

34. My thanks to Burt Visotsky, Shaye Cohen, and Ruth Fagen for their kind suggestions in the preparation of this article.

B

Economics

12

Supply-Side Economics

Aaron Levine

INTRODUCTION

Ronald Reagan's succession to the presidency of the United States in
1980 marked not only a dramatic shift to the right in political power,
but a watershed in economic policy-making as well. Reagan's economic
policy adopted many of the tenets of the supply-side school of economics.[1] It will be our purpose in this chapter to describe two of the prescrip-
tions of this school of economics, namely, its advocacy of a reduction in
taxes and deregulation of industry. These ideas will then be examined
from the perspective of Jewish law.

SUPPLY-SIDE ECONOMICS

One of the basic tenets of supply-side economics is that government tax
policy can play an important role in promoting economic incentives in
the marketplace. Specifically, work effort can dramatically be increased
by reducing the tax liability associated with it. Similarly, a lower tax
rate for investment income encourages increased investment activity.
Increased investment, in turn, enhances society's capacity to produce
goods and services, hence raising its standard of living.

Increasing the cost of an undesirable activity can also be done directly
through taxation. Idleness, supply-siders claim, can be discouraged by

Reprinted by permission of the author and KTAV Publishing House, Inc., from *Economics
and Jewish Law*, New York, 1987.

linking unemployment compensation and welfare programs more imaginatively with work effort.

Another proposition of the supply-siders designed to increase the efficiency of the marketplace is their call for deregulation of industry. Supply-siders maintain that government regulation of the private marketplace has resulted in massive inefficiencies and increased costs; costs which far exceed any benefits which might be associated with such government interference. Thus, they are confident that as these regulations are relaxed, the business community will respond with an increase in supply.

Government regulation of the marketplace today is very extensive and is rooted in a variety of motivations. For the purpose of elucidating the supply-side position in respect to government regulation, we will draw upon the taxonomy Hailstones and Mastrianna have devised in categorizing government intervention in the marketplace.[2] Supply-siders have most stridently objected to government interference in the marketplace when its motivation is the prevention of excessive competition and the provision of better information to market participants. Much less vehemence is voiced in the areas of natural monopoly and market failure due to ill-defined property rights. Nonetheless, to the supply-sider, government regulation should only be carried to the point where the incremental costs equal the incremental benefits.

Preventing Excessive Competition

When an industry is characterized by a cost structure largely comprising variable rather than fixed cost, entry and exit into the industry by many small producers is relatively easy. This can produce wide swings in industry output and great instability in prices and profit in both the short and long run. These conditions create a maximum of uncertainty on the part of producers and consumers. The case for government regulation rests on the presence of excessive competition rather than excessive monopoly power and is justified to provide industrywide stability.

Supply-siders' advocacy of deregulation of the marketplace has scored its greatest success in those industries where government intervention is rooted in a desire to prevent excessive competition. Evidencing this success was the passage of the Airline Deregulation Act of 1978 and the Motor Carrier Act of 1980.

The most outstanding case of deregulation in the early 1980s has been that of the airlines.

Economic regulation of the airline industry dates back to 1938, with the creation of the Civil Aeronautics Board (CAB). The stated objectives of the CAB were to assure adequate, economical, and efficient air service at reasonable charges. To achieve these goals it acted to control entry and exit of domestic trunk lines to prevent excessive competition, and it supervised air fares to protect the public.

Under CAB regulations, airlines were prohibited from engaging in competitive pricing. Consequently, airlines were compelled to compete vigorously on the basis of customer service.

The most injurious form of service competition entailed flight scheduling in heavily trafficked markets. Individual airlines sought consumer identification by providing the largest number of daily flights between major cities so that customers would contact that airline first in making reservations to any destination. Many of these flights were duplicative, since the passengers they carried could have been accommodated easily by fewer flights. The resulting proliferation of flights created a chronic problem of excess capacity on these routes.

To compound the problem, airlines also competed heavily in other areas of costly nonprice competition. Over the years, airlines sought to attract passengers by providing greater comfort and more exotic foods and drinks than competitors. Such attempts to differentiate service also tended to increase the costs of providing passenger service.

The Airline Deregulation Act of 1978, which called for a gradual decrease in the control of routes and fares by CAB, has drastically changed that sector of the U.S. economy.

Deregulation has allowed airlines to utilize their aircraft more intensively. As anticipated, passenger comfort and costly service amenities have been curtailed. Market chaos has not resulted, but the scramble to reconstruct airline routes has created problems.

Route competition has intensified on many heavily traveled corridors, such as New York to California, where new entry has brought about price wars on discount fares. In lightly traveled markets, sharp declines in service have been recorded. However, commuter and regional airlines are expanding rapidly and are expected to pick up any slack.[3]

Regulation to Provide Better Information to Market Participants

Government intervenes in the marketplace for the purpose of protecting the consumer. An example of this form of social regulation is the Federal Trade Commission Act (1914). This act, as amended by the Wheeler-Lea Amendment of 1938, protects the consumer from false advertising claims and deceptive packaging. Similar protection is afforded the consumer in the drug market by the Pure Food and Drug Act.

The philosophy behind this regulation is the belief that consumers are unable to judge quality in advance of purchase. Because search costs for consumers are expensive, and the information gathered by individuals is difficult to disseminate, government intervention to improve the flow of information is appropriate.

On the factor-resource side, the same rationale has been applied to justify intervention in protecting laborers from unsafe working conditions in factories, mines, offices, and on construction sites.

The creation of government agencies for the purpose of protecting the consumer from fraud and misleading advertising is opposed by supply-siders. This position reflects a faith in the self-regulating nature of the marketplace. Fear of losing a customer to a competitor will restrain the seller from charging above the competitive norm, inhibit him from misrepresenting his product, and discourage him from adulterating it. Likewise, enterprises which fail to protect their labor force against accidents or industrial diseases or which work them unusually hard are penalized by the refusal of workers to work for them except at a higher wage than other employers pay.

The growing complexity of the products of the modern industrial economy has not dampened the faith of those believing in the self-regulating nature of the marketplace. While individuals may not be capable of judging the quality of complex products, specialists capable of making such assessments do exist. The success of these specialists, such as major retailers and other middlemen, hinges heavily upon the reputation for reliability they build up among their customers.

Product Safety

In the area of product safety, supply-siders are decidedly opposed to government regulation.

Given that safety is not a free good, the utility-maximizing consumer is well aware that the more safety he demands in the products and services he buys, the less other goods and services will be available to him. For this reason, the typical well-informed consumer would not be expected to demand the highest level of safety in the various goods and services he buys. Instead, the typical consumer is seen as constantly comparing the benefits of additional safety to the costs of that safety in terms of time, money, and effort. When the costs and benefits change, the level of safety the consumer desires also changes.

While government promulgation of safety standards has the effect of increasing the safety of the regulated products, it also increases their costs. Automobile safety legislation provides a case in point. Some estimates of the costs of automobile safety legislation have been made by Murray Weidenbaum and Robert DeFina of the Center for the Study of American Business at Washington University in St. Louis. The two economists reported that safety regulations enacted between 1968 and 1978 have added at least $450 to the price of a new car.

Higher prices, of course, lead to still other indirect effects. Other things being equal, as the price of a regulated product rises, fewer purchases will be made. Some consumers will turn to substitute products, which may be less safe than the regulated product. As a result, safety regulations can have the wholly unintended effect of reducing the overall level of safety.

In the face of higher prices for new cars, for example, potential buyers are encouraged to seek out alternatives. They may continue driving the cars they have; they may purchase used cars; or they may turn to less expensive forms of transportation, such as motorcycles, mopeds, or even bicycles. These are the kinds of indirect effects that are likely to decrease the level of safety. Working in the opposite direction to produce a higher overall level of transportation safety is the possibility of some shifting to public transportation.

Another indirect effect of safety regulation may be to induce consumers to exercise less caution in the use of the regulated products. The adverse effect of safer product design in product use was identified by Peltzman in his investigation of the effects of automobile safety legislation on traffic accidents and highway deaths. In particular, Peltzman found that a disproportionate share of accidents occurred in cars that had the new safety equipment as compared to those that did not have it.

He also found that, after adjusting for other factors, the new safety standards had no overall effect on the highway death rate. In fact, the only major result of safety regulation was a change in the way people died. The death rate went down for the occupants of automobiles, but it went up, by an offsetting amount, for pedestrians, bicyclists, and motorcyclists.

Certification

As an alternative to government regulation in the area of product safety, supply-siders favor government certification. Through certification the government simply provides information to the consumer regarding the safety features and risks of products. Its aim is to prevent mistakes, not to coerce, and the ultimate choice is left to the consumers themselves.

The health hazard posed by cigarettes is an example of one problem handled through certification. Cigarettes are not outlawed, even though the surgeon general believes that smoking is hazardous to health. Instead, manufacturers are required to post warnings on cigarette packages and in cigarette advertisements. Consumers are, however, left free to smoke as many cigarettes as they want.[4]

Ill-Defined Property Rights

The workings of a market economy are predicated on recognizable private property rights, but where property rights are unassigned or indefinite, anyone can use the property without paying for it, so long as no one else is using it. As a result, social costs may differ from private costs, since users will not bear the full costs and are likely to overuse the property. Ill-defined property rights justify environmental regulation in the form of controlling air and water pollution.

Exemplifying the supply-siders' approach to environmental pollution is Ruff's *effluent fee scheme*. The plan calls for those who produce and consume goods which cause pollution to pay the costs involved. All that is needed to implement such a plan is a mechanism for estimating the pollution output of all polluters, together with a means of collecting fees. Under such a system, anyone could emit any amount of pollution as long as he pays the price which the government sets to approximate the marginal social cost of pollution. If pollution consists of many components, each with its own social cost, there would be different prices for each component. Prohibitive prices would be set for pollutants that endanger human life. Once the prices are set, polluters could adjust to them in any way they choose. Because they act in self-interest, they will reduce their pollution by every means possible, up to the point where further reduction would cost more than the price. Should the initial price prove to be too low to accomplish the desired amount of pollution abatement, the price could be increased to effect the desired reduction.[5]

Natural Monopoly

Natural monopoly occurs when one firm is capable of providing for the entire market at decreasing costs. Under these conditions the first firm to establish sufficient output to achieve very low production costs could drive out competing firms with higher costs, leaving a monopoly situation. The cost structure of the industry, therefore, serves as a barrier to entry; and the unregulated monopolist may be in a position to charge excessive prices, restrict output, and reap monopoly profits. Thus, the government awards monopoly franchises to such firms, protecting them from competition. In return for monopoly privileges, the government regulates services, prices, and profits. Cases of natural monopoly are few, with public utilities being the major example.

Recent research has suggested that even if a market is a natural monopoly, it may still not be a good candidate for regulation. This occurs when the subject market is contestable, i.e., entry and exit are relatively easy to achieve. When the market is contestable, potential competition will keep a monopoly from charging high prices. To illustrate, it may be efficient for only a single airline to provide passenger service between two specific cities. Yet this monopoly firm need not be regulated if other airlines have access to the same market (route). If the airline flying between these two cities charges a monopoly price, another airline can easily enter this route, and can do so very successfully by offering somewhat lower prices.[6]

SUPPLY-SIDE ECONOMICS: A HALAKHIC PERSPECTIVE

Underlying the supply-siders' preoccupation with designing a tax system that would work to maximize society's wealth is the premium they put on marketplace activity. Encouraging people to devote more of their time to activities that generate for themselves an economic reward represents to the supply-sider an unqualified social gain. It will be our purpose in this section to demonstrate that while Judaism regards the efficiency aspect of economic incentives as a positive good, designing an economic system to maximally encourage people to spend their time in the marketplace is not desirable.

ECONOMIC INCENTIVES AND EFFICIENT WORK EFFORT IN THE RABBINIC LITERATURE

The talmudic insight into the paramount role economic incentives play in bringing forth efficient work effort is seen in connection with the rights of an assault victim to medical treatment: "If the offender says to him [the victim], 'I will bring you a physician who will heal you for nothing,' he might object, saying, 'A physician who heals for nothing is worth nothing' " (*Bava Kamma* 85a).

Commenting on this talmudic text, R. Solomon b. Isaac (France, 1040–1105) and others understand the case to refer to a situation where the physician is a relative of the offender. Presumably, the physician normally commands a fee for his medical services, but in this instance, as a favor to the offender, he is willing to render his services gratis.[7] Why the offer may be rejected by the victim is explained by R. Asher b. Jehiel (Germany, 1250–1327) on the grounds that anticipation of reward generates responsibility and diligence on the part of the party who obligates himself to render a service. A certain amount of potential diligence and responsibility will be lost when the service is rendered gratis.[8]

It should be noted that the adverse effect of noncompensation on work effort could very well be subliminal, as Jewish law presumes that a professional will do nothing consciously to ruin his reputation (*uman lo meira umnateih*).[9]

Further evidencing Judaism's recognition of the efficiency advantage inherent in economic incentives is R. Solomon b. Abraham Adret's (Spain, ca. 1235–1310) analysis of the appropriate method of filling the communal position of cantor. Rather than fill this position on a voluntary basis, R. Adret preferred the community to hire an individual specifically for this purpose. Defending his ruling, R. Adret points out that the former method suffers from the disadvantage of inevitably producing incessant disputes as to who should serve as cantor. Hiring an individual to serve as cantor avoids such disputes, as only the designated person may assume the role. Moreover, hired status pressures the employee to approach his cantorial duties more conscientiously than would be the case if he provided his services on a voluntary basis.[10]

Another example of Judaism's insight into the advantage of economic incentives is seen from the polemic that R. Eliezer b. Isaac of Böhman (12th cent.) directed against a proposal to deny religious functionaries compensation for their services. Building his case for compensation, R. Eliezer points out that during the time of the *Mishkan* (Tabernacle) and the First and Second Temples, Kohanim and Levites were entitled to support in return for the Temple service they rendered. Compensation was called for despite the fact that competition to officiate in the Temple was fierce and intense. What follows is a background description of how the Temple service was organized and the nature of the rivalry among the Kohanim. For the purpose of establishing a rotation system, the Kohanim and Levites were divided into twenty-four guards, or *mishmarot*. Each week a different *mishmar* would officiate in the Temple on a rotating basis. *Mishmarot* were further subdivided into daily groupings, called *batei avot*. Generally, Kohanim and Levites were permitted to officiate only during the period their *beit av* served. Daily Temple service requirements were assigned to individual Kohanim on the basis of an allotment system. Originally, the first service of the day, i.e., the removal of the ashes from the altar, was not assigned by means of allotment, since those interested in performing this service would have to arise close to the crack of dawn, and vigorous competition was not expected. The sages provided, however, that if there was competition, the contending Kohanim would have to run a foot race up the thirty-two cubits of the ramp of the altar to determine who would officiate. Surprisingly, fierce competition did arise for the honor of removing the ashes. Indeed, the Talmud records an incident where the losing contestant of the foot race, venting his extreme frustration, fatally stabbed the winner. The occurrence of a subsequent incident where the foot race resulted in one of the contestants breaking his leg convinced the sages that the previous bloodshedding episode could not be dismissed as a mere quirk. Consequently, an allotment system was instituted for the assigning of the removal of ashes service as well.[11]

Given the intense rivalry to officiate in the Temple service, the call for compensation, argues R. Eliezer b. Isaac, can only be understood in terms of the debilitating long-term effect a system of voluntarism would produce. Without economic incentive, enthusiasm for the Temple service would eventually wane and possibly be subject to gross neglect.

While the destruction of the Sanctuary brought with it the disruption of the Temple service, Torah study and prayer, according to tradition, substitute for it. Maintaining the viability of the Torah and public prayer institutions requires the community to provide its religious functionaries with adequate compensation.

Providing sufficient economic incentives for religious functionaries proved to be an enormous burden for the poverty-stricken Jewish communities in the time of R. Isaac. The communal burden was lightened somewhat by the practice of making gifts to such functionaries at weddings and various other festivities. The joyous mood on such occasions helped to engender a spirit of generosity. Corresponding loosely to the prescribed method of supporting the Kohanim, this system of voluntary gifts, which provided a good part of the income of religious functionaries, enabled the community to avoid the burden of making relatively high payments to them at regular intervals.[12]

A similar, albeit less detailed rationale for compensating religious scholars is provided by R. Joseph Caro (Safed, 1488–1575). This decisor brings into play the significant link between productivity and compensation. For Torah scholarship to flourish, the Jewish community must be prepared to adequately compensate those who dedicate themselves to the holy work.[13]

Another dimension of Jewish law's recognition of the efficiency implication of economic incentives is its treatment of fees for medical services rendered on the Shabbat.

Normally, demanding or offering a fee for work rendered on the Shabbat is rabbinically prohibited (sekhar shabbat).[14] Out of concern that the sekhar shabbat prohibition might cause a physician to hesitate in responding to a call for assistance on the Shabbat, the sages suspended the sekhar shabbat interdict in connection with medical fees.[15] On similar grounds the sages refrained from proclaiming that physicians taking sekhar shabbat would see no "sign of blessing" from the fee. Such a harsh pronouncement would surely deter physicians from demanding *sekhar shabbat,* but would at the same time remove the economic incentive for them to respond to a call for assistance on the Shabbat.[16]

While Judaism appreciates the efficiency aspect of economic incentives, it would decidedly disapprove of an economic incentive system designed to *maximally* encourage work effort. Analysis of the following tannaic dispute bears this out:

> Our rabbis taught: *that you may gather in your grain* [Deuteronomy 11:14]. What is to be learnt from these words? Since it says, *This book of the Law shall not depart out of your mouth* [Joshua 1:8], I might think that this injunction is to be taken literally. Therefore it says, *that you may gather in your grain,* which implies that you are to combine the study of them [the words of the Torah] with a worldly occupation. This is the view of R. Ishmael. R. Shimon b. Yoḥai says: Is that possible? If a man plows in the plowing season, and sows in the sowing season, and reaps in the reaping season, and winnows in the season of wind, what is to become of the Torah? No, but when Israel performs the will of the Omnipresent, their work is performed by others, as it says, *And strangers shall stand and feed your flocks* [Isaiah 61:5], and when Israel does not perform the will of the Omnipresent, their work is carried out by themselves, as it says, *that you may gather in your grain* [Deuteronomy 11:14]. Nor is this all, but the work of others also is done by them, as it says, *And you shall serve your enemy* [Deuteronomy 28:48].[17]

The apparent diametric opposition between the views of R. Shimon b. Yoḥai and R. Ishmael is somewhat narrowed by R. Edels' interpretation of this dispute. Pointing out that the phrase *that you may gather in your grain* is immediately preceded by the verse *And if you will carefully obey My commands which I give you today, to love the Lord your God and to serve Him with all your heart and with all your soul,* why then, asks R. Edels, does R. Shimon b. Yoḥai interpret verse 14 as referring to the circumstance where Israel does *not* perform the will of the Almighty? Noting that verse 13 curiously omits the phrase *and with all your wealth,* R. Edels, following the Tosafot's lead, posits that *you may gather in your grain* indeed refers to the circumstance where Israel does perform the will of the Almighty, albeit not with perfect righteousness. What follows is that R. Shimon b. Yoḥai's prescription for complete immersion in Torah study to the exclusion of worldly occupation is directed only to the perfectly righteous. Only this elite group has the right to rely on others to provide it with its material needs. This restrictive interpretation of R. Shimon b. Yoḥai's view is supported by Abaya's observation: "Many have followed the advice of R. Ishmael, and it has worked well; others have followed R. Shimon b. Yoḥai, and it has not been successful." With reliance on the support of others permitted only for the perfectly righteous, it is no wonder that out of the many that followed R. Shimon b. Yoḥai's lifestyle, few succeeded.[18]

Proceeding from R. Edels' analysis is the universally held principle that for the great majority of men pursuit of a livelihood is a positive duty.

Judaism apparently rejects disengagement from worldly occupation even as an ideal for the perfectly righteous. Strongly evidencing this rejection is the teaching of Rabban Gamaliel III (first half of the 3rd cent.), the son of R. Judah ha-Nasi: "It is seemly to combine the study of Torah with an occupation, for the wearying labor of both keep sin forgotten. All Torah study that does not have work accompanying it must in the end come to nothing and bring sin in its wake.[19]

R. Gamaliel's teaching is understood by the Polish decisor R. Joel Sirkes (1561–1650) to be directed at two distinct groups. Speaking in the first clause to people primarily immersed in occupational pursuits, R. Gamaliel warns that if they are to become God-fearing, Torah study must enter their lives. Addressing himself next to Torah scholars, R. Gamaliel cautions that preservation of their spiritual status requires them to combine an occupation with their Torah study.[20]

Another popular talmudic teaching which implicitly rejects the notion that complete disengagement from worldly occupation is an ideal is Ulla's dictum: "A man who lives from the labor [of his hands] is greater than the one who fears heaven."[21]

Further illustrating the importance Judaism attaches to gainful employment is the obligation it imposes on a father to prepare his son for a livelihood. This obligation, according to R. Meir,[22] may be satisfied by teaching the son either a trade or business skills.[23] Out of concern that business enterprises are prone to periodic slumps, R. Judah holds that the father cannot fulfill his obligation by teaching his son business management, for during slack periods, lacking capital or merchandise to transact with, the son may turn to crime.[24]

Apparently disputing both authorities is R. Nehorai's teaching:

I abandon every trade in the world and teach my son Torah only, for man enjoys the reward thereof in this world while the principal remains to him for the world-to-come. But all other professions are not so; for when a man comes to sickness or old age or suffering and cannot engage in his craft, he must die of starvation, whereas the Torah is not so, for it guards him from all evil in his youth and gives him a future and hope in his old age.[25]

Reconciling R. Nehorai's view with R. Meir and R. Judah, R. Edels posits that R. Nehorai's intention was not to say that he entirely discarded teaching his son a trade, but merely that he refused to prepare him for a trade that would make a major claim on his time and energy. Instead, R. Nehorai concentrated on teaching his son Torah, with the faith that the merit of Torah study would allow his son to make ends meet from his meager source of livelihood.[26]

Another approach for reconciling R. Nehorai's dictum with the obligation of the father to prepare his son for a livelihood is advanced by R. Eliyahu b. Hayyim (Constantinople, ca. 1530–1610). Taking note that both of the opposing opinions are recorded by R. Asher b. Jehiel, R. Eliyahu posits that R. Nehorai's dictum relates only to the childhood years. Once the son reaches maturity and must begin thinking of earning a livelihood, his father is obligated to prepare him for this by teaching him a trade or business skill.[27]

THE SUBSIDIARY ROLE OF LIVELIHOOD ACTIVITIES

While Judaism takes a very positive attitude toward the pursuit of a livelihood, excessive preoccupation with the acquisition of wealth is looked upon very dimly. Judaism teaches that man must give primacy to the spiritual domain. Worldly pursuits are permitted only a minor and subsidiary claim on man's time and energy. Epitomizing Judaism's view of the role that pursuit of material needs should play in the total life experience is R. Judah b. Ila'i's pithy observation:

See what a difference there is between the earlier and later generations. The earlier generations made the study of the Torah their main concern and their ordinary work subsidiary to it, and both prospered in their hands. The later generations made their ordinary work their main concern and their study of the Torah subsidiary, and neither prospered in their hands.[28]

Further clarification of the nature of the claim that livelihood activities may have on man's energies is provided by R. Judah Loew b. Bezalel (Worms, ca. 1525–1600). Material pursuits may claim man's energies only to the extent necessary to adequately support himself and his family. To avoid becoming a public charge, one should not regard any type of honest work as beneath him. In this vein Rav advised R. Kahana: "Flay carcasses in the marketplace and earn wages, and do not say, I am a priest and a great man, and it is beneath my dignity." [29]

Once subsistence needs have been met, however, King Solomon's admonishment, *Weary not yourself to become rich* (Proverbs 23:4), becomes applicable. At this point the spiritual domain must be given rein over man's energies and time. [30]

Economic Incentives and the Humane Impulse

Increasing the economic incentive to engage in work effort automatically increases the penalty for spending time on activity which produces no economic reward. Gearing society to maximally respond to economic incentives may therefore have the impact of shifting benevolent activity heavily in the direction of financial contribution and away from altruism in the form of personal involvement. Any significant reduction in benevolence of the personal-involvement variety has the effect of blunting society's humane impulse. Since the fostering of a humane climate represents one of the most important social welfare functions of the public sector of the halakhic society, increasing economic incentives to promote additional marketplace activity must be evaluated in light of its impact on this goal.

Economic Disincentives for Idleness and Halakhah

While Halakhah opposes government policies that have the effect of skewing society's energies away from Torah study and personal benevolence, it enthusiastically embraces methods of discouraging idleness by means of increasing the penalties it entails.

Indicative of the disdain Judaism has for idleness is its teaching that idleness brings on immorality. [31] Discouragement of idleness follows also from the halakhic disapproval of the "welfare mentality," as enunciated in Rav's advice to R. Kahana: "Flay carcasses in the marketplace and earn wages, and do not say, I am a priest and a great man, and it is beneath my dignity." [32]

Suggestive of halakhic approval of an unemployment compensation and welfare system designed with the aim of penalizing idleness among the employable members of society is one aspect of the halakhic definition of poverty. In talmudic times, an individual was not eligible to receive a stipend from the weekly disbursement of the public charity chest *(kuppah)* unless he did not have funds for fourteen meals. Having funds for fourteen meals makes an individual self-sufficient for at least a week and hence disqualifies him from becoming a public charge. Liberalization of the eligibility requirement to fifteen meals by dint of the religious duty to eat *three* meals on the Shabbat is rejected by the Talmud by invoking R. Akiva's dictum: "Treat your Shabbat like a weekday rather than be dependent on your fellow-beings."[33] Now, if the poverty standard of living implicit in the below-fourteen-meal crite- rion is not expanded to cover an additional food expenditure which is required as a religious duty,[34] then, *a fortiori,* the poverty standard is not expanded to include any amenities above bare subsistence.

What rejection of the third Shabbat meal in the eligibility requirement amounts to, in our view, is a definition of poverty in terms of bare subsistence. The discouragement of idleness inherent in this formulation can, of course, be expected to be significant.

REGULATION OF THE MARKETPLACE AND JEWISH LAW

In this section we will develop the case that Judaism calls for government regulation of the marketplace in the form of protecting the consumer against defective and harmful products as well as against false and misleading advertising claims. Also indicated is government intervention to protect the laborer against unsafe working conditions. Finally, gov- ernment regulation of environmental pollution is called for in the halak- hic society.

Pointing to this conclusion are: (1) Judaism's conceptualization of the nature of the information channels of the marketplace; (2) the disclosure obligation it imposes on the seller; (3) the method Halakhah prescribes to assure that proper disclosure takes place; and (4) certain aspects of Jewish tort law. We will discuss each of these elements in turn.

The Nature of the Information Channels and Halakhah

Halakhah rejects the notion that the marketplace is permeated by any semblance of perfect knowledge. This assertion follows from an exami- nation of the laws of *ona'ah* (price fraud).

The ethics of the price terms of transactions concluded within the framework of a competitive norm are governed in Jewish law by the laws of *ona'ah*. These regulations provide a taxonomy of grounds for invalidating or otherwise modifying transactions concluded at a price that diverges from the prevailing norm.

Individuals freely entering into market transactions are presumed, by Jewish law, to have an *approximate* notion of the value of the article involved. Hence, price agreements which diverge enormously from the prevailing norm are not regarded as having occurred as a result of ignorance of market conditions on the part of the participants. Divergent price agreements are, quite to the contrary, interpreted as representing a tacit understanding between buyer and seller to treat the price differential as a voluntary gift transfer.[35] Credence is given to a complainant's *ona'ah* claim only when the discrepancy between the sale price and the market price is more than one-sixth. Here, grounds exist for invalidating the original sale.[36]

Second-degree *ona'ah* occurs when the sale price differs from the market price by exactly one-sixth. Here, the transaction remains binding. Neither of the parties may subsequently void the transaction on account of the price discrimination. The plaintiff, however, is entitled to full restitution of the *ona'ah* involved.[37]

Finally, third-degree *ona'ah* occurs when the sale price differs from the market price by less than one-sixth. Here, the transaction not only remains binding, but in addition, the complainant has no legal claim to the price differential.[38]

We have demonstrated elsewhere that what stands at the basis of the *ona'ah* claim is the opportunity cost the plaintiff incurred at the moment he entered into the transaction. If the article of transfer was available at that time at a lower (higher) price, credence is given to the plaintiff's claim that he would either have insisted on an adjustment or walked away from the proposed deal, as the case may be. What follows is that the *ona'ah* claim is, in the final analysis, based on the imperfect knowledge of market conditions that Halakhah ascribes to market participants.[39]

Disclosure Obligations in Jewish Law

Jewish law requires the parties to a transaction to deal with each other in an open and forthright manner. Conveying a false impression (*genevat da'at*) by means of word or action is strictly prohibited.[40]

Proceeding from the *genevat da'at* interdict is a disclosure obligation for the seller. Proper disclosure requires the seller to divulge to his prospective buyer all defects in his product which are not visibly[41] evident.[42] The disclosure obligation extends even to a flaw whose presence does not depreciate the article sufficiently to allow the vendee an *ona'ah* claim.[43]

What constitutes a defect may depend upon the buyer's intended use of the product. The sale of a vicious ox illustrates the point. If the buyer intends to butcher the ox, its vicious nature would make no difference to him. If, on the other hand, the vendee intends to use the ox for plowing, its vicious character would render it unfit, as the ox would be regarded as a menace to society and the vendee would be prohibited from keeping it alive.[44] If the buyer discloses his intent to use the ox for plowing prior to the consummation of the transaction, he is entitled to cancel the sale on the basis of his discovery of the vicious character of the ox.[45] Seller awareness that the vendee is a farmer, according to R. Samuel b. Meir (Ramerupt, ca. 1080–1174), establishes a presumption that the latter's intent is to use the ox for plowing. Given this indirect awareness of the plowing-use intent, the vendee is entitled to cancel the sale on the basis of his discovery of the vicious nature of the ox.[46]

Discovery of a flaw not properly disclosed at the time of the sale may allow the buyer to void the original transaction. This occurs when the defect involved is objectionable to the extent that common practice would be to return the flawed article to the seller.[47]

The remedy available to the vendee when the product proves to be defective is confined to a recision right. The Jewish court will not, however, sustain the complainant's demand for a price adjustment on the basis of the defect he discovered. The latter's options consist of either demanding a refund or accepting the transaction as originally concluded.[48]

Forthright Disclosure

Disclosure of defects must be made in an open and forthright manner and not in a manner that deludes the vendee into discrediting the seller's declaration.[49]

Disclosure of the nonforthright variety, according to Maimonides (Egypt, 1135–1204), occurs when, for instance, a vendor (A) of an animal enumerates to his prospective buyer (B) a number of flaws in his beast, which, if present, would be readily apparent to him, e.g., lameness. Along with these defects, A admits to the presence of some specific *hidden* faults in his animal as well. Now, in the event that the readily apparent flaws were in actuality not present in the animal, subsequent discovery of the hidden flaw may allow B to void the original transaction. Credence is given to B's claim that he did not take seriously A's disclosure of the hidden flaw. Since the readily visible flaws mentioned by A were obviously nonexistent, B was presumably deluded into discrediting the existence of the real defect as well. B's claim of delusive disclosure is, however, not accepted when *one* of the readily visible flaws A mentioned was actually present in the animal. Here, B should have taken seriously A's disclosure of the hidden flaw.[50]

A variant of the latter case, according to R. Jacob b. Asher (Germany, 1270–1343) and R. Joseph Caro (Safed, 1488–1575), allows B to void the sale on the basis of the delusive disclosure. This occurs when A takes pains to *demonstratively point out only one* of the number of readily visible flaws he mentions. His failure to do likewise in regard to the other plainly visible flaws he mentions presumably leads B to discredit his disclosure of the hidden flaw. Subsequent discovery of the hidden defect may therefore allow B to void the original sale.[51]

The buyer's agreement to the vendor's demand not to void the sale on the basis of product defect does not nullify his recision right in the event he does subsequently find a defect in the article.

Why the recision right remains intact here is explained by Maimonides and others on the ground that acquiescence to a general disclaimer lacks specificity. For a waiver to be legally binding, the person making it must be aware of *specifically* what he is waiving. Now, since the seller here makes no mention either of specific defects that he is not responsible for nor of a specific depreciation in value that he is not responsible for, the vendee does not forfeit his recision right by accepting the disclaimer.[52]

Why the right to cancel the sale remains intact here is, however, explained by R. Joshua ha-Kohen Falk (Poland, 1555–1614) and others on the basis of the false impression such a disclaimer conveys to the vendee. The seller's insistence that the sale remain intact even if a flaw is discovered is interpreted by the buyer as conveying the message that the article at hand is such an extraordinary bargain that even if a defect is hypothetically present the article would still be a good buy. Since the buyer does not interpret the seller's disclaimer as an admission of the presence of any defects in the product, his acquiescence to it does not amount to an implicit waiver of his recision right.[53]

Vendee acquiescence not to void the sale on the basis of specific product defects does, however, nullify his right of cancellation in respect to the specific defects mentioned. The specificity requirement is met when the disclaimer clause either (1) details the defects the seller is not responsible for or (2) sets a limit to the depreciation in value from the sale price that the buyer must absorb on account of discovery of defects in the product.[54]

Seller Rights in the Defective Product Case

While the preceding discussion makes it clear that Jewish law rejects the doctrine of caveat emptor, a certain degree of mental alertness is expected of the buyer in a sales transaction. This expectation along with the various rights Jewish law confers on the vendor in product-defect cases, as discussed below, effectively qualify the disclosure obligation and limit the buyer's recision right.

1. The buyer's recision right—right of cancellation—is not recognized when the defect he bases his refund claim on is *visibly evident*. Since the defect is in plain view, the buyer was presumably aware of it at the time he entered into the transaction, and consequently he was agreeable to the terms of trade despite its presence. Buyer protest that the visibly evident flaw did not register in his mind at the time of the sale is greeted with incredulity.[55] Following this line, R. Eliezer of Toule (d. before 1234) denies the refund even on the strength of the buyer's sworn testimony that he did not notice the defect at the time he entered into the sale.[56]

It follows, in our view, from the denial of the recision right in cases where the defect is visibly evident, that forthright disclosure does not require the seller to point out to a would-be buyer the evident flaws in his article. Since the defects are plainly visible, the buyer is presumably aware of them at the time he enters into the sale. The vendor's failure to make mention of them or to point them out, therefore, does not amount to creating a false impression.

2. Another limitation on the buyer's recision right occurs in instances where the defect involved can be repaired or removed. The following real estate case recorded by R. Asher b. Jeḥiel illustrates this point: A returns from an out-of-town inspection of a house B has put up for sale.

Operating under the assumption that the house is in the same condition as he left it, A proceeds to purchase B's house. Before the sale went into effect, however, vandals entered the house, breaking the door and windows and smoking the walls. When A learns of this, he wants to void the sale on the basis of the vandalized condition of the house. B, however, demands that the sale remain intact, conceding only that A should be allowed a deduction from the original price to cover the expense of renovating the house. The Jewish court will here sustain the seller's position. Since the act of vandalism did not destroy the original identity of the article of transfer, it cannot be said that A actually acquired something essentially different than what he contracted for. The presence of a defect does not cause the transaction to be classified as one concluded in error, and rectification of the defect by the seller allows the sale to remain intact.[57]

Should the defect render the article something essentially different than what was contracted for, recognition would be given to the buyer's recision right. The following real estate case recorded by R. Moses Isserles (Poland, 1525 or 1530–1572) illustrates this point: A contracts to buy B's out-of-town house. Upon inspection he discovers that its walls are deteriorated. On the basis of this defect, A wants to void the transaction. B, however, insists that the sale remain intact, conceding only that A should be allowed a deduction from the purchase price to cover the expense of renovating the walls. The court here will sustain the buyer's position. Given the fact that a house with deteriorated walls loses its identity as a house, what A actually acquired is not what he contracted for. Since the defect here renders the original transaction as one concluded in error, recognition is given to the buyer's recision right, despite the seller's willingness to renovate the walls.[58]

3. Another limitation on the buyer's recision right occurs in the case of a standardized product. Here, the seller may insist on exchanging the defective product for a flawless model. If the market price of the standardized product went down in the interim, the buyer would, however, retain his recision right.[59]

The Seller's Testing Obligation

The seller's responsibility to his customer in the halakhic society clearly goes beyond forthright disclosure. Various halakhic norms point to various *testing* obligations for the seller before he can market his product.

Media advertising provides a case in point. Since media advertising reaches a very wide audience, the seller cannot rely upon his own conviction that his message is not misleading. Avoiding violation of the *genevat da'at* interdict requires that advertising messages be pilot-tested before being put into commercial use. Scientifically designed, a pilot-test can ascertain what impressions the advertising message makes on the targeted group, as well as the inferences this group draws from it. Should these sets of expectations fail to coincide with the actual properties of the product, revision of the message would be in order.

The seller's responsibility to test his product before he markets it to ensure that it is not defective or harmful proceeds, in our view, from the biblical prohibition against offering ill-suited advice *(lifnei ivver)*.[60] Without premarketing testing, the seller's implicit claim that his product will serve the customer's need amounts to a possible violation of the *lifnei ivver* interdict. A case in point is the pharmaceutical manufacturer who fails to properly test his drugs for their effectiveness and possible side-effects before marketing them.

It should be noted that talmudic decisors differ as to whether the *mere offer* of ill-suited advice constitutes a violation of the *lifnei ivver* interdict. *Halakhot Gedolot* takes this view.[61] Maimonides, however, does not regard the interdict as being violated until the individual who received the ill-suited advice actually follows it.[62] What follows from our application of the *lifnei-ivver* interdict to the sale of a product without proper premarketing testing is that the mere offer for sale of an untested product, according to *Halakhot Gedolot,* constitutes a possible violation of *lifnei ivver.*

Marketing a product which is possibly harmful without prior testing may violate the interdicts cited in connection with the obligation the Torah imposes on the homeowner to construct a parapet around his roof: *When you build a new house, you shall make a parapet for your roof, so that you will not bring the guilt of bloodshed on your house if anyone should fall from it* (Deuteronomy 22:8).

Exegetical interpretation of this verse extends the positive duty *(aseh),*[63] *you shall make a parapet,* and the negative duty *(lo ta'aseh),*[64] *so that you will not bring the guilt of bloodshed,* to the requirement for the individual to properly *remove* from his property any object that may cause someone damage.[65] Now, argues Rabbi Jeruham Fishel Perla (Poland, 1846–1934), if the Torah forewarns us to clear our property of dangerous objects, then, *a fortiori*, it forbids us to *place* a possibly harmful object anywhere it may cause injury.[66] Following this line, another application of the parapet interdict would be the sale of untested drugs.

Just as the parapet interdict is violated by the *mere* placing of an object which is possibly dangerous,[67] the *mere offer* for sale of an untested drug constitutes a possible violation of this prohibition.

Similarly prohibited under the parapet interdict, in our view, is the dumping of noxious chemicals and wastes in lakes and streams. Since water pollution of this type has been linked to genetic diseases and cancer, such action constitutes the "placing" of a harmful object in the public domain.

Safe Working Conditions

By dint of the parapet interdict, Rabbi Ben Zion Meir Hai Ouziel (Israel, 1880–1953) obligates the employer both to provide his worker with safe working conditions and to make restitution to him in the event of injury in consequence of his neglect to do so. Nonetheless, since the parapet interdict merely adjures the removal from one's property of objects which might cause injury, monetary claims by the worker for injuries he suffers as a result of his employer's failure to provide him with safe working conditions are denied by the Jewish court.[68]

The Enforcement Mechanism for Judaism's Disclosure and Testing Obligations

The preceding discussion has demonstrated that Halakhah imposes on the seller an extensive disclosure obligation as well as a premarketing testing responsibility. Would Halakhah rely on a system of voluntary enforcement to ensure that these responsibilities are carried out? Indicative that Halakhah would insist on public-sector involvement here is its call[69] for the appointment of public inspectors to ensure the honesty of commercial weights and measures. Why voluntary self-enforcement is not relied upon to ensure the integrity of commercial weights and measures is explained by Rabbi Jehiel Michel Epstein (Belorussia, 1829–

1908) as stemming from the unconscious, distorting impact the profit motive exerts on vendors. Rabbi Epstein uses this rationale to explain Maimonides' ruling[70] that in matters of Kashrut one may only patronize a vendor who is known to be reliable.[71] It follows that in the halakhic society, a voluntaristic system for enforcing proper disclosure and pre-marketing testing would be regarded as unreliable.

Certification and Regulation in Jewish Law

While the unconscious bias stemming from the profit motive necessitates government involvement in the area of product safety in the halakhic society, the form this intervention takes remains to be clarified. Certification and regulation present themselves as alternative approaches. Banning the product rather than just certifying the risks it imposes to users is clearly the indicated course when the premarketing testing determines that normal use of the product entails an imminent health risk to the typical consumer. Since Halakhah does not recognize the right of the individual to expose himself to an imminent health risk,[72] the public sector has no choice other than to ban the health-endangering product in the above instance.

Certification does, however, present itself as a viable alternative means of promoting product safety when the relevant health risk is assessed to be potential rather than imminent. This follows from R. Jacob Ettlinger's (Germany, 1798–1871) ruling that Halakhah only prohibits exposure to an imminent health risk, but not to a reasonable health risk which is assessed to be only potential. He derives this principle from an analysis of the Thanksgiving sacrifice *(korban todah)*. During the times of the Temple, this sacrifice was prescribed as an expression of gratitude when an individual was delivered from danger. Two qualifying circumstances consist of the safe return from a sea journey and the safe return from a trip across the desert. Since these safe returns are characterized as "deliverances from danger," sea voyages and desert trips were obviously regarded by the sages as fraught with danger. Given the prohibition of exposing oneself to danger, why, queries R. Ettlinger, didn't the sages prohibit these adventures in the first place? This dilemma leads R. Ettlinger to posit that Halakhah does not prohibit exposure to a reasonable risk when the danger is assessed to be only potential. Since most people who embark upon a sea journey or go on a desert trip return safely and, in addition, are not subject to immediate danger at the outset, the risk exposure is both reasonable and potential and hence is permissible.[73]

Validation of the certification approach as a means for the public sector to meet its responsibility to ensure product safety follows from R. Ettlinger's line in instances where the risk exposure involved is reasonable and the relevant danger is potential rather than immediate. While the distinction between immediate and potential danger cannot be precisely defined, the auto-safety area represents one clear-cut instance of a potential rather than an immediate risk.

Basing himself on R. Ettlinger's criterion, Rabbi Bleich posits that Halakhah does not prohibit cigarette smoking. Since the physiological changes caused by smoking are reversible, the risk involved should be characterized as potential rather than immediate. What follows is a halakhic approach which is in consonance with the current government certification approach to cigarette smoking.[74] Mounting recent scientific evidence in regard to the health dangers of smoking may, however, force this indulgence to be characterized as an "unreasonable" health-risk exposure and hence as halakhically prohibited.[75]

Another instance where a danger should be halakhically classified as potential rather than immediate occurs, as it appears to us, when a product exposes the consumer to an immediate danger only when it is used in an abnormal manner, but presents no danger when it is used in the conventional manner. Rotary lawn mowers provide a case in point. Using a lawn mower to cut hedges generates an immediate danger to the consumer, but in the halakhic society, it would be unwarranted to ban lawn mowers for this reason. Since cutting hedges with a lawn mower is clearly an abnormal use of the product, it can, at worst, be classified as only potentially dangerous. The certification approach, therefore, suffices here.

Elimination of Unnecessary Risks

Since exposure to potential danger is permissible only when the risk involved is a reasonable one, subjecting oneself to an unnecessary safety or health risk should be prohibited. An unnecessary risk is defined as a risk a well-informed individual would willingly spend money to eliminate. Given the average consumer's imperfect knowledge of the marketplace, the above line confers on the public sector the responsibility to promulgate design safety features for products when it assesses that the typical consumer, equipped with the necessary facts, would willingly spend money to secure those features. Auto safety provides a case in point. Since designing a car so that it can sustain a rear-end collision and requiring seat belts as a standard feature significantly reduce the probability of death or severe injury for the motorist, a presumption exists that the motorist would spend money to secure these features. Meeting its responsibility in the area of product safety requires the public sector, therefore, to mandate these provisions. Once the safety of product design reaches a certain level, we may no longer presume that the typical informed consumer would willingly expend more money to secure additional safety. Air bags provide a case in point. Installing this safety feature will add from $800 to $1,200 to the price of a car. Moreover, each time a bag is inflated the owner may have to pay twice that amount to have it replaced.[76] Given the present level of auto safety and the cost of achieving additional safety by means of installing air bags, mandating this safety feature cannot be said to eliminate an unnecessary risk. Since automobile use represents a potential rather than an immediate danger, mandating the elimination of a risk which cannot be characterized as unnecessary, e.g., the installation of air bags, would not fall within the purview of a product safety commission of the halakhic society.

Ill-Defined Property Rights and Jewish Law

Ill-defined property rights, as discussed earlier, justify environmental regulation in the form of controlling air and water pollution. Environmental pollution represents an example of a negative externality, i.e., an unintended negative side-effect of economic activity. Judaism's analogue to the negative-externality case is the law in circumstances where an individual conducts an activity on his own premises and this activity generates harm outside his premises. Involving many nuances, a negative externality is generally not subject to restraint unless two main criteria are met: (1) a direct link between the adverse effect and the action of the initiator must be established;[77] (2) the harm the plaintiff stands to sustain as a result of the defendant's activity must consist of actual or potential bodily harm or property damage.[78]

When an adverse side-effect is halakhically classified as a negative externality, the initiator, by force of a biblical interdict, must refrain from the activity generating it. R. Meir Abulafia (Spain, ca. 1170–1244) bases the interdict either on the verse *you shall not place an obstacle in front of the blind* (Leviticus 19:4) or on the verse *you shall love your neighbor as yourself* (Leviticus 19:18).[79] R. Asher b. Jeḥiel, however, bases the prohibition on the verse *Her ways are ways of pleasantness, and all her paths are peace* (Proverbs 3:17).[80]

In the absence of voluntary compliance, the courts will enjoin the activity by petition of the party that stands to be injured.[81]

Though the use of a restraining order does not preclude a *negotiated* change in the initial distribution of rights, the plaintiff would be within his rights to reject a scheme wherein he is compensated for damages actually sustained. Such a scheme amounts to licensing the defendant to inflict damage if he so chooses and only face penalties after the damage is already done. Jewish law clearly prohibits an individual from damaging his neighbor's property even if he promises to compensate the victim for losses sustained.[82] What follows is that unless the arrangement is voluntarily negotiated, the plaintiff may insist that the court impose a restraining order on an actionable negative externality.

The Reciprocal Nature of the Externality Problem

Economic theory has uncovered the truth that the externality problem is reciprocal in nature. Restraining the defendant gives primacy to the interests of the plaintiff. Nonintervention, however, favors the defendant's interests over the plaintiff's. When those adversely affected by the negative externality constitute an entire community, the reciprocal nature of the problem at hand assumes the proportions of a vexing social issue. Restraining a factory from polluting the atmosphere, for example, may force it to substitute more costly methods of production, placing it at a competitive disadvantage. Thus, the elimination of environmental pollution may take place at the cost of increased unemployment and a reduced standard of living.[83]

Given the reciprocal nature of the negative-externality problem, can a minority veto a majority-approved scheme that allows the industrial polluter to continue his enterprise and face only a schedule of fines for damage actually caused? From the perspective of the approving majority, the arrangement represents the most efficient means of allowing the community to maximize its economic interests: The enterprise, with its favorable impact on community employment, is allowed to continue, and at the same time its owners are made to pay, at least partially, for the damage it inflicts. Objecting to the arrangement on the ground that it effectively licenses the factory to inflict harm, the minority press for the relocation of the factory. What rights do the majority enjoy here?

Clarification of minority rights in a legislative matter requires an investigation of the halakhic view of both the parameters and the nature of the legislative process.

It should be noted at the outset that communal legislation enjoys no halakhic sanction when it comes into conflict with ritual prohibitions and permissions.[84] In matters of civil and criminal law, communal enactments are, however, generally recognized even if they come into conflict with a particular rule of Halakhah.[85]

Providing a basic source for the analysis of the halakhic view of the communal legislative process is the following *baraita* quoted in *Bava Batra* 8b: "The townspeople are also at liberty to fix weights and measures, prices and wages, and to inflict penalties for infringement of their rules."

Espousing the majority view, R. Isaac b. Jacob Alfasi (Algeria, 1013–1103) and others understand the communal legislative authority the *baraita* speaks of to become effective by means of a majority-decision rule.[86] Indicative that the coercive power of the majority over the minority is limited is the observation that all the actions the *baraita* speaks of are a communitywide welfare basis. What may therefore be inferred is that in matters not pertaining to a communitywide interest, the majority may not pass legislation that favors one group at the expense of another. Clearly enunciating this principle is the fifteenth-century decisor R. Joseph Colon (Italy, ca. 1420–1480).[87]

In this vein R. Solomon b. Abraham Adret ruled invalid a communal edict calling for the taxation of a resident on the basis of his ownership of assets located in a different town. Majority decision, as R. Adret points out, cannot legitimize robbery. Since the edict effectively subjected a segment of the community to "double taxation," the provision amounted to outright robbery.[88]

Further limitation of the coercive power of the majority in legislative matters follows from R. Meir b. Baruch of Rothenburg's (ca. 1215–1293) comments on the *baraita* quoted earlier.

Taking the position that unanimous consent is required before legislative proposals become operative, R. Meir posits that the *baraita* implies that *verbal* consent alone suffices to make town ordinances effective law. Though verbal consent alone normally does not constitute a *kinyan*, and hence does not make a commitment legally binding, unanimously approved legislation becomes binding by means of verbal consent alone. By dint of the pleasure each member of the community derives from the knowledge that his fellows have consented to enter into a mutually advantageous agreement with him, he resolutely binds himself to the commitment.[89]

Notwithstanding the halakhic rejection of the unanimous-decision rule in favor of a majority-decision rule, R. Meir's interpretation of the *baraita* as describing proposed actions of mutual benefit has evoked much discussion. Such actions as fixing weights and measures, prices, and wages are of mixed effect, i.e., some of the townspeople will gain while others will lose. Why, then, did R. Meir characterize these actions as mutually advantageous?

Espousing majority rule, R. Moses b. Joseph Trani (Safed, 1500–1580) posits that R. Meir's characterization of the actions described in the *baraita* as mutually advantageous is essentially correct. Rather than imposing absolute gains and losses on the townspeople, the fixing of weights and measures, prices, and wages merely determines the *relative* gains of economic activity. Amounting to an implementation of the townspeople's concept of *equity* in the distribution of the relative gains of economic activity, these measures must be characterized as mutually advantageous.[90]

Characterization of the actions recorded in the *baraita* as mutually advantageous is also justified, according to R. Trani, on the grounds that the relative impact of these measures often changes over time.[91] To illustrate, economic growth and inflation may very well work to reverse an earlier prolabor characterization of a legislated wage structure as now favoring employers vis-à-vis workers.

The aforementioned has many implications for the design of an effluent-charge plan to effect pollution abatement. Given the underlying motive of maximizing wealth, such a plan would clearly qualify as a measure for communitywide welfare. Minority opposition to the plan would therefore not cause rejection of it in a Jewish court.

Making concessions to the industrial polluter in the name of advancing the goal of community wealth is, however, subject to a constraint. Communal legislation, by means of majority rule, can only renounce those rights which Halakhah regards as subject to waiver but may not contract out of the law of the Torah entirely.[92]

Proceeding from the above is the legitimacy of a majority-sponsored effluent-charge scheme which calls for the industrial polluter only to partially compensate society for damages actually inflicted. Since it is within the halakhic rights of an individual to waive his right to compensation due him, a majority decision to this effect requires everyone to renounce his rights to full compensation in accordance with the plan adopted.

Moreover, since an individual may expose himself to some degree of risk to his health and even to his life for the purpose of earning a livelihood,[93] a majority-approved effluent-charge scheme entailing some small degree of health- and life-threatening risk is fully valid.

Clearly contrary to Torah law, however, is an effluent-charge scheme which exposes the townspeople to extraordinary health- and life-threatening risk. Since the plan violates the biblical injunction of *Take you therefore good heed unto yourself* (Deuteronomy 4:15),[94] the legislation is, in our view, invalid, despite majority or even unanimous approval.

R. Trani's remarks, presented earlier, indicate another limitation on effluent-charge legislation. Careful attention must be given to ensure that the plan does not generate a discriminatory effect on certain segments of the community. Typically, residents located close to the industrial polluter will bear the brunt of any effluent-charge plan which entails property damage and health hazards for the townspeople. Provision for special compensation and relocation expenses for those we anticipate will suffer disproportionately from implementation of the effluent-charge plan represents a halakhic approach to this problem in line with the previous discussion.

Another important implication of the preceding discussion is that cost-benefit analysis is an invalid criterion for the halakhic society in determining whether a plant should be required to install pollution-abatement equipment. Though the cost-benefit criterion can be universally applied, it contains an inherent bias against the poor and the old. Because valuation of life is based on earnings potential, the lives and health of those who can expect little or no future earnings, like the unskilled, the handicapped, or the elderly, are valued at next to nothing.

When benefits are measured in terms of anticipated health and longevity gains, the dollar value of the benefits proceeding from pollution abatement for a disadvantaged area would be calculated to be lower than the corresponding value in an affluent area. As a result, if a cost-benefit criterion is applied, plants located in disadvantaged areas would be more likely to continue to generate pollution than plants located in affluent areas. Amounting to a discriminatory license to injure people and damage property, such a scheme is halakhically invalid, even if approved by the majority.

It follows from the preceding analysis that the approach to pollution abatement in the halakhic society would stress cost-effectiveness rather than cost-benefit criteria. Specifically, goals in the form of pollution-abatement standards would be set, and these goals would then be pursued by means of the least-cost method. Any pollution-abatement plan in the halakhic society, as discussed above, would have certain special compensation provisions for the discriminatory impact it may impose on society.

ECONOMIC REGULATION OF THE MARKETPLACE AND HALAKHAH

While the aforementioned indicates that there is a sharp division between Halakhah and supply-side economics in regard to government intervention to protect the consumer and worker, general convergence can be found in respect to the issue of economic regulation.

Convergence on the issue of economic regulation of the marketplace follows from the halakhic preference for a system of freedom of entry. Protectionist pleas by an established firm to enjoin a new entrant are given consideration only when the impact of competition would *ruin* the established firm. To be sure, another school of thought rejects the protectionist pleas of the established firm even in this instance.

Moreover, protecting an established firm against a seller of a substitute product finds no sympathy in the Jewish court even when the competitive presence of the substitute product threatens to *ruin* the established firm. Similarly, established firms are not afforded protection against substitute products embodying new technology. The Jewish court would not sympathize, for example, with a protectionist plea by the horse and buggy industry that it enjoin the entry of the automobile.

NATURAL MONOPOLY IN JEWISH LAW

The concept of natural monopoly has explicit halakhic approval, according to the Hungarian decisor R. Mosheh Sofer (1762–1839), in the form of an ancient rabbinic edict prohibiting the publication of a religious work while copies of an earlier printing by another publisher were still available for sale. Within the spirit of this ancient ordinance, it became customary for prospective authors of religious works to secure from a rabbinic authority a formal ban on the publication of the same work by others for a specified period of time. The text of the ban was usually published in the preface of the work. Once conferred, the ban was effective not only in the jurisdiction of the issuing authority, but upon all of Israel as well.

Since the purpose of the edict was to promote the widest possible dissemination of Torah works, the ban, posits R. Sofer, does not extend beyond the sale of the earlier printing. Extension of the ban beyond this period would merely serve to create a commercial property right for the publisher of the previous printing, a windfall unintended by the ancient edict. Notwithstanding its lack of force, a ban extending beyond the sale of the previous printing remains operative within the jurisdiction of the issuing authority.

Promoting the social interest by means of conferring monopoly privilege apparently runs counter to Ezra's ancient ordinance. To afford Jewish women with easy access to beautification aids, Ezra (5th cent. b.c.e.) allowed itinerant cosmetics salesmen to peddle their wares from door to door, despite the competition this would create for local storekeepers. Encouraging free entry evidently represented for Ezra a more efficient means of promoting the social interest than protecting local tradesmen.

Defending the protectionist approach for the case at hand, R. Sofer posits that sufficient economic incentive would be lacking to motivate investors to undertake the publication of religious works without the expectation of monopoly status. Without this privilege entrepreneurs would direct their investments elsewhere. In sharp contrast, local stores, which carry, besides cosmetics, a whole line of other products, would not be likely to close down on account of the competition of cosmetics peddlers.[95]

Disputing R. Sofer's view, R. Mordecai Banet (Moravia, 1753–1829) argues, in effect, that the ancient decree described above could not have been promulgated. Drawing an analogy from Ezra's decree, R. Banet posits that promoting the widest dissemination of religious works calls for a free-entry rather than a protectionist approach.[96]

The dispute between R. Sofer and R. Banet, as it appears to us, is an empirical one. Rising standards of living and levels of education and religious observance may very well make competition feasible in a marketplace previously characterized as a natural monopoly. Moreover, identification of a natural-monopoly-product market may require the rabbinic authority, at times, to extend the ban on a new printing beyond the sale of the extant printing. This occurs when only multiple printings of the subject religious works are deemed sufficient to recoup for the publishers a reasonable return on their investment.[97] What constitutes a reasonable profit would, in turn, be determined by the opportunity cost of the publisher. Economic analysis is therefore of critical importance in determining whether, and under what conditions, it would be appropriate for the halakhic authority to impose the ban.

NOTES

1. For a presentation and critique of supply-side economics, see Thomas R. Swartz, Frank J. Bonello, and Andrew F. Kozak, *The Supply Side: Debating Current Economic Policies* (Guilford, Conn.: Duskhin Publishing Group, 1983).
2. Thomas J. Hailstones and Frank V. Mastrianna, *Contemporary Economic Problems and Issues,* 6th ed. (Cincinnati: South-Western Publishing Co., 1982), pp. 120–122.
3. Ibid., pp. 131–133.
4. John C. Goodman and Edwin G. Dolan, *Economics of Public Policy: The Micro View,* 3d ed. (St. Paul: West Publishing Company, 1985), pp. 39–57.
5. Larry E. Ruff, "The Economic Common Sense of Pollution," *Public Interest,* no. 19 (Spring 1970): 69–85.
6. William J. Baumol, John C. Panzar, and Robert D. Willag, *Contestable Markets and the Theory of Industry Structure* (San Diego: Harcourt Brace Jovanovich, 1982).
7. R. Soloman b. Isaac, *Rashi, Bava Kamma* 85a; R. Asher b. Jehiel (Germany, ca. 1250–1327), *Rosh, Bava Kamma* 8:1.
8. *Rosh,* loc. cit.
9. *Rashi, Menahot* 43a.
10. R. Solomon b. Abraham Adret, *Responsa Rashba* 1:450, quoted by R. Joseph Caro (Safed, 1488–1575), *Beit Yosef, Tur, Orah Hayyim* 53.

11. *Yoma* 22a, 23a.
12. R. Eliezer b. Isaac, quoted by R. Isaac b. Moses of Vienna (ca. 1180–ca. 1250), *Responsa Or Za'rua*, vol. 1, no. 113.
13. R. Joseph Caro, *Kesef Mishneh, Yad, Talmud Torah* 3:10.
14. *Tosefta Shabbat* 18:16; Maimonides (Egypt, 1135–1204), *Yad*, Shabbat 6:25; R. Jacob b. Asher (German, 1270–1340), *Tur, Oraḥ Ḥayyim* 306:5; R. Joseph Caro, *Shulḥan Arukh, Oraḥ Ḥayyim* 306:4; R. Jehiel Michel Epstein (Belorussia, 1829–1908), *Arukh haShulḥan, Oraḥ Ḥayyim* 306:9.
15. R. Ḥayyim Isaac Algazi (Smyrna, late 18th cent.), *Derekh Eẓ ha-Ḥayyim*, responsum no. 2; R. Ḥayyim Modai (Turkey, 1700–1784), *Ḥayyim L'olam*, p. 130; Rabbi Yehoshu'a Yesha'yah Neuwirth (contemp.), *Shmirat Shabbat ki-Hilkhata*, p. 164, n. 135.
16. *Ḥayyim L'olam*, loc. cit.
17. *Berakhot* 36b.
18. R. Samuel Eliezer b. Judah ha-Levi Edels (Poland, 1555–1631), *Ma-harsha, Berakhot* 35b.
19. *Avot* 11:2.
20. R. Joel Sirkes, *Baḥ Tur, Oraḥ Ḥayyim* 154.
21. *Berakhot* 8a.
22. The teaching is recorded in the Mishnah anonymously. R. Yoḥanan (*Sanhedrin* 86a), however, identifies R. Meir as the author of an anonymous mishnaic teaching.
23. *Baraita, Kiddushin* 29a.
24. *Baraita, Kiddushin* 29a, *Kiddushin* 30b, and *Rashi* ad loc.
25. R. Nehorai, *Mishnah Kiddushin* 4:14.
26. *Maharsha, Kiddushin* 82a.
27. R. Eliyahu b. Ḥayyim, *Imrei Shefer* 52.
28. R. Judah Ila'i, *Berakhot* 35b.
29. *Pesaḥim* 113a.
30. R. Judah Loew b. Bezalel, *N'tivot Olam*, vol 2; *N'tiv h'Osher*, chaps. 1–2.
31. R. Shimon, *Mishnah Ketubbot* 5:5.
32. *Pesaḥim* 113a.
33. *Shabbat* 118a; *Yad, Mattenot Aniyyim* 9:13; *Tur, Yoreh De'ah*, 253:1; *Sh. Ar., Yoreh De'ah*, op. cit. 253:1; *Ar. haSh., Yoreh De'ah* 253:1.
34. *Shabbat* 117b; R. Isaac b. Jacob Alfasi (Algeria, 1013–1103), *Rif* ad loc.; *Yad, Shabbat* 30:9; *Rosh, Shabbat* 16:15; *Tur, Oraḥ Ḥayyim* 291:1; *Sh. Ar., Oraḥ Ḥayyim* 291:1; *Ar. haSh., Oraḥ Ḥayyim* 291:1–2.
35. *Bava Batra* 78a and *Rashi* ad loc.; *Rif* ad loc.; *Yad, Mekhirah* 27:5; *Rosh, Bava Batra* 5:7; *Tur, Ḥoshen Mishpat* 220:5; *Sh. Ar., Ḥoshen Mishpat* 220:8; *Ar. haSh., Ḥoshen Mishpat* 220:7.
36. *Bava Meẓia* 50b; *Rif* ad loc.; *Yad*, op. cit. 12:4; *Rosh*, op. cit. 4:15; *Tur*, op. cit. 227:6; *Sh. Ar.*, op. cit. 227:4; *Ar. haSh.*, op. cit. 227:3.
37. *Bava Meẓia* 50b; *Rif* ad loc.; *Yad*, op. cit. 12:2; *Rosh*, op. cit. 4:15; *Tur*, op. cit. 227:3; *Sh. Ar.*, op. cit. 227:2; *Ar. haSh.*, loc. cit.
38. *Bava Meẓia* 50b; *Rif* ad loc.; *Yad*, op. cit. 12:3, *Tur*, op. cit. 227:4; *Sh. Ar.*, loc. cit.; *Ar. haSh.*, loc. cit.

39. See Aaron Levine, *Free Enterprise and Jewish Law* (New York: KTAV Publishing House and Yeshiva University Press, 1980), pp. 105–109.
40. *Yad,* op. cit. 18:1; *Tur,* op. cit. 228:5; *Sh. Ar.,* op. cit. 228:6; *Ar. haSh.,* op. cit. 228:3.
41. Rabbi Binyamin Rabinowitz-Teomim, *Ḥukat Mishpat* (Jerusalem: Harry Fishel Foundation, 1957), p. 90.
42. *Yad,* op. cit.; *Tur,* op. cit.; *Sh. Ar.,* op. cit.; *Ar. haSh.,* op. cit.
43. See R. Joshua ha-Kohen Falk (Poland, 1555–1614) *Sma,* Sh. Ar., op. cit. 228, n. 7; *Ar. haSh.,* op. cit. 228:3.
44. *Sma, Sh. Ar.,* op. cit. 232, n. 57.
45. *Bava Batra* 92a; *Rif* ad loc.; *Yad,* op. cit., 16:5; *Rosh, Bava Batra* 6:1; *Tur,* op. cit. 232:21; *Sh. Ar.,* op. cit. 232:23; *Ar. haSh.,* op. cit. 232:36.
46. R. Samuel b. Meir, *Rashbam,* Bava Batra 92a.
47. *Yad,* op. cit. 15:5, quoted in *Tur,* op. cit. 232:6; *Sh. Ar.,* op. cit. 232:6; *Ar. haSh.,* op. cit. 232:7.
48. *Yad,* op. cit. 15:4; *Tur,* loc. cit.; *Sh. Ar.,* op. cit. 232:4; *Ar. haSh.,* op. cit. 232:6.
49. See *Sma, Sh. Ar.,* op. cit. 228, no. 7; *Ar. haSh.,* op. cit. 228:3.
50. *Yad,* op. cit. 15:7–9.
51. *Tur,* op. cit. 232:8; *Sh. Ar.,* op. cit. 232:8, both on interpretation of R. Jeḥiel Michel Epstein, *Ar. haSh.,* op. cit. 232:13.
52. *Yad,* op. cit. 15:6; *Sh. Ar.,* op. cit. 232:7.
53. *Sma, Sh. Ar.,* op. cit. 232, n. 15; *Ar. haSh.,* op. cit. 232:11.
54. *Yad,* loc. cit.; *Tur,* op. cit. 232:7; *Sh. Ar.,* op. cit. 232:6; *Ar. haSh.,* loc. cit.
55. *Kiddushin* 11a; *Yad,* op. cit. 15:12; *Tur,* op. cit. 232:10; R. Joseph Caro, *Kesef Mishneh, Yad, Zekhiyyah* 1:1; *Ar. haSh.,* op. cit. 232:16; *Ḥukat Mishpat,* op. cit., p. 90.
56. R. Eliezer of Toule (d. before 1234), quoted in R. Ḥayyim b. Israel Benveniste (Smyrna, 1603–1673), *Kenesset ha-Gedolah, Ḥoshen Mishpat* 232 comments on *Tur,* n. 21.
57. R. Asher b. Jeḥiel, *Responsa Rosh K'lal* 96:6, quoted in *Tur,* op. cit. 232:5; *Sh. Ar.,* op. cit. 232:5; R. Moses Isserles (Poland, 1525–1572), *Rema, Sh. Ar.* ad loc.; *Ar. haSh.,* op. cit. 232:10.
58. *Rema,* loc. cit.; R. Jacob Lorberbaum (Poland, ca. 1760–1832), *N'tivot haMishpat, Sh. Ar.,* op. cit. 232, n. 7; *Ar. haSh.,* loc. cit.
59. Rabbi Ezra Basri, *Dinei Mamonot,* vol. 2 (Jerusalem: Sukkat David, 1976), p. 205.
60. *Torat Kohanim,* Leviticus 19:14; *Yad, Roẓeaḥ* 12:14.
61. *Halakhot Gedolot* on interpretation of R. Jeruḥam Fishel Perla, commentary on *Sefer ha Miẓvot* of R. Saadiah Gaon, *minyan ha-Lavin* 54. The authorship of this work is disputed, but it is generally dated to the geonic period. See *Encyclopaedia Judaica,* vol. 7, col. 1169.
62. Yad, loc. cit., on interpretation of R. Jeruḥam Fishel Perla, loc. cit.
63. *Sifre,* Deuteronomy 22:8.
64. Ibid.

65. Ibid.
66. Rabbi Jeruḥam Fishel Perla, loc. cit.
67. Maimonides, *Sefer haMizvot lavin* 298 on interpretation of R. Jeruḥam Fishel Perla, loc. cit.
68. Rabbi Zion Ouziel, *Mishpetei Uzzie'l*, vol. 3, *Ḥoshen Mishpat* 43.
69. Rami b. Ḥamma, reporting in the name of R. Yiẓḥak, *Bava Batra* 89a; *Rif* ad loc.; *Yad, Genevah* 8:20; *Rosh,* Bava Batra 5:22; *Tur,* op. cit. 231:2; *Sh. Ar.,* op. cit. 231:2; *Ar. haSh.,* op. cit. 232:3.
70. *Yad, Maakhalot Asurot* 11:25.
71. *Ar. haSh., Yoreh De'ah* 119:2.
72. Deuteronomy 4:15; *Shabbat* 32a; *Rif* ad loc.; *Yad, Roze'ah* 12:4–7; *Rosh, Shabbat* 2:21; *Sh. Ar., Oraḥ ḥayyim* 170: 16; *Rema, Sh. Ar., Yoreh De'ah* 116:5; *Ar. haSh., Yoreh De'ah* 116.
73. R. Jacob Ettlinger, *Binyan Ẓion* 137.
74. Rabbi J. David Bleich, *Tradition* 16, no. 4 (Summer 1977): 121–123; idem, *Tradition,* 17, no. 3 (Summer 1978): 140–142.
75. Dr. F. Rosner, "Cigarette Smoking and Jewish Law," *Journal of Halacha and Contemporary Society* 4 (Fall 1982): 33–45.
76. *Economics of Public Policy,* p. 43.
77. Ruling of R. Judah in the name of Samuel, *Bava Batra* 25b; *Rif* ad loc.; *Yad, Shekhenim* 10:5; *Rosh,* op. cit. 2:25; *Tur,* op. cit. 155:44–46; *Sh. Ar.,* op. cit. 155:32; *Ar. haSh., Ḥoshen Mishpat* 155:1.
78. R. Solomon b. Abraham Adret, quoted in *Shittah M'kubbeẓet, Bava Batra* 22a; *Tosafot, Bava Batra* 22a; Rabbi Aaron Kotler (1892–1962), *Mishnat Rabbi Aharon,* vol. 1, p. 68; Rabbi Yeḥezkel Abramsky (1886–1976), *Ḥazon Yeḥezkel, Tosefta Bava Batra* 1:5. For a treatment of the negative externality issue in Jewish law, see Levine, *Free Enterprise and Jewish Law,* pp. 58–77.
79. R. Meir Abulafia (Spain, 1170–1244), *Ramah, Bava Batra* 11:107.
80. R. Asher b. Jeḥiel, *Responsa Rosh, k'lal* 108, par. 10. A variant minority view on this matter is held by R. Moses b. Joseph Trani (Safed, 1500–1580). He regards the prohibition as only *rabbinical* in origin, since biblical law merely requires the defendant to *compensate* his victim for damage he is responsible for, but would not enjoin a harmful act with the objective of preventing damage from occurring (*Kiryat Sefer, Shekhenim* 9). *See* also R. Jacob Tam (Ramerupt, 1100–1171), *Sefer ha-Yashar, siman* 522.
81. *Bava Batra* 25b, 26a.
82. *Yad, Nizkei Mamon* 5:1; Naḥmanides, *Ramban, Bava Batra, dinei d'garme;* Rabbi Jacob Kanievsky (Israel, contemp.), *K'hilot Yaakov, Bava Batra, siman* 1.
83. For the seminal treatment of the reciprocal nature of the externality problem, see Ronald H. Coase, "The Problem of Social Cost," *Journal of Law and Economics,* October 1960, pp. 1–45.
84. *Responsa Rashba,* vol. 3:411; R. Simeon b. Ẓemaḥ Duran (Algeria, 1361–1444), *Tashbez* 2:132 and 239.
85. R. Gershom b. Judah (Germany, ca. 960–1028), Responsa R. Gershom

Me'or ha-Golah, ed. Eidelberg, no. 67; R. Joseph b. Samuel Bonfils (France, 11th cent.) quoted in Responsa *Maharam of Rothenburg* 423; *Responsa Rashba,* vol. 4, no. 311; R. Asher b. Jeḥiel, *Responsa Rosh* 101:1; R. Ẓemaḥ b. Solomon Duran (North Africa, 15th cent.), *Responsa Yakhin u-Vo'az,* pt. 2, no. 20.

86. R. Isaac b. Jacob Alfasi (Algeria, 1013–1103), *Responsa Rif,* ed. Leiter no. 13; R. Joseph b. Samuel Bonfils, quoted by R. Meir b. Baruch of Rothenburg (1215–1293), *Responsa Maharam* 423; R. Ḥayyim (Eliezer) b. Isaac (Germany, 13th cent.), Responsa *Ḥayyim Or Zaru'a,* no. 222; R. Eliezer b. Joel ha-Levi (Bonn, 1140–1225), quoted by R. Mordecai b. Hillel (Germany, 1240?–1298), *Mordecai, Bava Batra* 1:482; Naḥmanides (Spain, 1194–1270), *Responsa Rashba* (attributed to *Ramban*) 280; R. Solomon b. Abraham Adret (Spain, ca. 1235–ca. 1310), *Responsa Rashba,* vol. 2, no. 279; vol. 5, nos. 126, 270, 242.

87. R. Joseph Colon, *Responsa Maharik, shoresh* 14. See, however, R. Ḥayyim Halberstamm (Zanz, 1793–1876), *Divrei Ḥayyim* 2:60.

88. *Responsa Rashba,* vol. 1:788; see also *Responsa Rashba,* vol. 1:399.

89. R. Meir b. Baruch, *Responsa Maharam* (Prague ed.) 941.

90. R. Moses b. Joseph Trani, *Responsa Mabit* 1:237.

91. *Responsa Mabit* 1:307.

92. See *Responsa Rashba* 1:787, 4:185; R. Moses Isserles (Poland, 1525 or 1530–1572), *Responsa Rema* 73.

93. See R. Ezekiel b. Judah ha-Levi Landau (Prague, 1713–1793), *Noda bi-Yhudah, Mahadura Tinyana Yoreh De'ah* 10; Rabbi Mosheh Feinstein (1895–1986), *Iggerot Mosheh, Ḥoshen Mishpat* 104.

94. See *Berakhot* 32b; *Noda bi-Yhudah,* loc. cit.

95. R. Moses Sofer, *Responsa Ḥatam Sofer, Ḥoshen Mishpat,* nos. 41, 57, 79.

96. R. Mordecai Banet (Moravia, 1753–1829), *Perashat Mordecai,* no. 8.

97. See Rabbi J. David Bleich, *Contemporary Halakhic Problems,* vol. 2 (New York: KTAV Publishing House and Yeshiva University Press, 1983), pp. 126–127.

13

Unjust Enrichment

Naḥum Rakover

I. "ONE DERIVES A BENEFIT AND THE OTHER SUSTAINS NO LOSS"

1. Introduction

In Jewish law "unjust enrichment"[1] embraces all those situations in which one person derives a material benefit from another without being legally entitled thereto. The central question is whether and to what extent the person from whom the benefit is derived (the donor) may require something in return from the recipient of the benefit. Since no agreement exists on the matter, no action can lie in contract. Likewise an action in tort will not be available when the donor has not been injured by the recipient's enjoyment of the benefit. Is there no other way for the donor to assert a right to a *quid pro pro?*

The nature of the benefit and the manner in which it is obtained can vary considerably. It may or may not be accompanied by a loss sustained by the other party. A person who parks his car in a lot belonging to a neighbour may or may not have to pay a charge, depending first on whether he generally pays for parking his car,—for if he does not, he has derived no material benefit,—and secondly on whether the lot is intended for parking at a charge,—for if not, he may plead that the other has not sustained any loss.

Again, a benefit may be occasioned by an act not of the recipient but of the other party. A may make improvements to B's property either

Reprinted by permission of E. J. Brill from the *Jewish Law Annual,* volume 3 (1980).

through mistake or intentionally. If he does so without thought of receiving anything in return, he is certainly not entitled to be recompensed. If, however, he intended to get something in exchange, will he be entitled to be paid for the improvements? That B gave no thought to the matter may also be relevant. If B would himself have made the improvements in any event, A's act has saved him money. If not, B has gained nothing and to charge him with payment involves interference with his freedom to decide whether and when he will lay out money and for what purpose.

There may also be circumstances in which the outlay of money for another's benefit is of significant social and moral importance, for instance, in saving the life of a person or his property. Is the donor entitled to be reimbursed for his outgoings? Are such worthy acts of assistance to be encouraged by ensuring that the expenditure involved is recoverable? Moreover, in personal "rescue" cases, has the rescuer any claim to be reimbursed where the rescued person protests against the rescue and states that he will not make any payment? Is a person the master of his own fate to demand of others not to help him and so avoid payment?

From the viewpoint also of the recipient questions will arise about the amount he must pay. Is the criterion to be the benefit obtained or the money spent, which may be less or more than the benefit?

According to Jewish law four main categories of cases are distinguished: (1) where the one party derives no benefit and the other party sustains no loss; (2) where the one derives a benefit and the other sustains a loss; (3) where the one derives a benefit and the other sustains no loss; (4) where the one derives no benefit and the other sustains a loss.

As to the first two, the Gemara in Baba Kamma 20a—where the main Talmudic discussion of the subject occurs—states that the law is very simple: in the first no payment is required but in the second it is. The third category is the subject of extended debate, whilst the last is not dealt with expressly in the Gemara but is debated by the early post-Talmudic authorities.[2]

The Gemara as above elaborates a number of general rules in connection with the third category, along with definitions of "recipient" and "loss". The obligation to pay and the amount to be paid under the second category are treated elsewhere in the Talmud in reference to specific fact situations, such as improvements made to another's property, salvage and so on.

The first part of the present paper is concerned with an analysis of the principle embodied in the third category and its applicable rules. Other aspects, a discussion of which is necessary for an over-all view of unjust enrichment in Jewish law, have been considered in separate studies, and the conclusions are briefly summarized in the second part.[3]

The usual Common Law classification of obligations into contract and torts has led to "unjust enrichment" being treated under the rubric of quasi- or implied contract,[4] but there is a certain artificiality about this and in recent years a tendency has shown itself to regard it as an independent class. In Israeli law until 1979 the subject was not regulated by any particular statute. Several enactments—for instance the Guarantee Law, 1967 (section 9), the Land Law, 1969 (section 21), and the Agency Law, 1975 (section 10)—make provision for their respective purposes.

So long as there was no single enactment devoted to the subject, Israeli case law in the main drew upon English law in reliance on article 46 of the Palestine Order in Council.[5] No clear criteria exist in English Law for the right to claim in unjust enrichment. The view taken by Lord Mansfield, the father of quasi-contract, that the principles of natural justice and equity require restitution,[6] is very general in import. The Israeli Ministry of Justice published a bill on unjust enrichment,[7] the Explanatory Note to which states that in a number of respects Jewish law has been followed: a person who makes improvements to the property of another is entitled to restitution; the principle of "one derives a benefit and the other sustains no loss" serves as a consideration to exempt from payment for the benefit; and the right of the salvor to indemnity.[8, 9]

2. The Talmudic Discussion

Where one person's benefit is involved in another's loss the Talmud found no difficulty in holding that the recipient must make restitution. But where benefit and no loss occur the question of paying for the benefit is more complicated.

The discussion begins with R. Yohanan's attribution to the Tanna

R. Yehudah of the view that in three instances a person is prohibited[10] from deriving benefit from another's property and must pay for the benefit he obtains.[11] According to the *Tosafot ad locum* the basis for this rule is a rabbinical regulation *(takanah):* "although it would seem right to say that a person may enjoy a benefit if another does not thereby sustain any loss, the Rabbis nevertheless instituted the rule that the first must pay since no one may enjoy the property of another without agreement." The requirement to pay, it appears, does not follow from any rule of law but from a desire generally to discourage the use of another's property without his consent. The *Gemara,* however, rejects R. Yohanan's attribution of the rule and says that there is no evidence that R. Yehudah stated it, since each of the three instances mentioned may rest on different grounds.[12]

The basic discussion of various aspects of the problem is, however, to be found in *Baba Kamma* 20a–21a, from which it appears that the rabbis were considerably exercised in reaching a solution. There the question is whether rent must be paid for occupying another person's premises without his agreement. The *Gemara* analyses the different possibilities and concludes that the question will only arise with regard to premises not intended for letting, whether the occupier usually rents property. The argument proceeds as follows. Where the premises are not for letting and the person concerned would not rent another place, he has no benefit and the owner loses nothing; hence no payment is exigible. Where the premises are for letting and the person might rent elsewhere, he benefits and the owner loses; hence payment must be made. Several views are cited on the point and then an attempt to attribute these to Tannaim is dismissed and the question therefore is held to have been an open one in the Tannaitic period. Thereafter the *Gemara* proceeds to cite various traditions from which it emerges that most Amoraim held that a person occupying premises without agreement is to be treated in accordance with the principle (hereinafter called "the exemptive principle") that where "the one derives a benefit and the other sustains no loss", no payment for the benefit need be made.

Neither Maimonides nor Karo expressly lays down a generalised rule based on the exemptive principle; they confine themselves to the particular factual situation discussed in the *Gemara.*[13] As Maimonides puts it, "a person who occupies without agreement the premises of another, which are not for letting, does not have to pay rent although he normally rents property, since the one benefits and the other does not lose."

3. The "Manner of Sodom"

The exemptive principle and the rule that "one may be compelled not to act in the manner of Sodom" (i.e. not to adopt a dog-in-the-manger attitude) are often treated in association. It may be noticed that the rule is mentioned in a number of places in the *Talmud*[14] where the question of acting or not acting in relation to another's property occurs before anything is actually done, whereas the exemptive principle is applied where an act has already been effected. The difference is apparent in the fact that the Talmudic references to the one never mention the other.

The earlier post-Talmudic authorities, however, stress that the circumstances in which the rule will apply are those which give rise to the exemptive principle.[15]

4. The Legal Basis of the Exemptive Principle

Is it to be inferred that the exemptive principle will operate by reason of the rule? According to several scholars the answer is in the affirmative.[16] It is possible to show that the early authorities[17] speak of the rule and the exemptive principle in one breath, as it were. But what they really say is that the rule applies because of the exemptive principle and not vice versa.[18] All that the early post-Talmudic authorities aver is simply that the rule will apply where one benefits and the other does not lose. It may well be that the exemptive principle operates not because of the Manner of Sodom Rule, but because a party suffering no loss has no cause of action at all against the person who benefits, and it is unnecessary to call the rule in aid. Where, however, it is desired to prevent *ab initio* an offending act, the rule may have to be invoked.[19]

The exemptive principle can also be explained in other ways without recourse to the rule. Where there is no loss, there is nothing, it may be said, to which an obligation to pay can attach.[20] Or it may be urged that although in strict law a duty to pay may exist,[21] a waiver is deemed to be imported because no loss has been suffered.[22]

5. Protesting the Benefit

One important limitation on the exemptive principle occurs where a person declares that no one should benefit from his property.

In the *Gemara* the duty to make payment for any benefit obtained from Temple property is derived from the principle that because of the special nature of the property involved any benefit derived therefrom without knowledge is treated in the same manner as private property used with the owner's knowledge. The *Toṣafot ad locum* explain that the Divine wish is that no one should benefit in the course of committing sacrilege.[23] For that reason, the recipient must pay. There are commentators, however, who explain the ruling by arguing that the use of Temple property effected without protest from the competent authority is like the use of private property with protest.[24] Hence where the owner makes protest, the recipient of the benefit must pay although no loss has been suffered. Others again understand the phrase "use of property with knowledge" as meaning an implied agreement to pay.[25] Accordingly if no such agreement can be implied (even if protest is made) payment will not be required.

The rule in the Codes is that if the owner tells the occupier to leave and the latter refuses, he must pay rent.[26] Karo, basing the rule on *Tur*, says that this is obvious. This rule has been extended even to property not for letting and to an occupier who would otherwise not rent property.[27]

6. Intention to Pay for Benefit

(a) Another limitation on the exemptive principle arises when the recipient discloses an intention to pay for the benefit he obtains.

The *Toṣafot ad locum* derive this rule from the case where a person whose property encircles that of a neighbour puts up fences which run along three sides of the neighbour's property and then the latter erects a fence on the fourth side. R. Jose said that the neighbour must pay for his share in the entire fencing. The *Gemara* tries to infer the exemptive principle from this case on the ground that had the first person erected the fourth fence, the neighbour would inferentially have been exempt from payment. The *Toṣafot* query the inference since the erection of the fourth fence by the first person does not affect the exemptive principle:

Why should the neighbour pay if he erected the fence? In erecting that fence the neighbour has indicated that he is satisfied with the expenditure for the fencing. Hence the situation is different from that where a person occupies another's property and has not indicated that he is prepared to pay.[28]

The reasoning and conclusion of the *Toṣafot* were challenged in the 16th century by R. Shlomo Luria[29] on the ground that disclosure of one's readiness to pay is immaterial in the circumstances, since no loss has been occasioned to the other. Luria reasons that payment for the fencing arises because the burden on the first person is increased by the extension of the fencing, and therefore only in such circumstances will the disclosure of an intention to pay have effect.

A still later authority[30] is critical of the *Toṣafot* and holds that the reason for the obligation to pay in the fencing case is the financial gain of having a fully fenced property, whereas the exemptive principle is concerned with some indeterminate benefit.[31]

(b) Various explanations have been advanced for the obligation to pay where an intention to do so is present, as decided by the *Toṣafot*. A 19th century *responsum*[32] deals with the case of a person who bottled scent water and affixed a label which another person was using for production under government licence. After arguing that the defendant was to be charged because he had shown that the plaintiff's expenditure in obtaining the licence suited his own interests, the conclusion is reached that as long as "there are outgoings and acts beneficial to both parties, they are partners and can compel each other to contribute" — but only where the outgoings and acts were essential and for the common good. In any other situation, either may refuse to contribute to a benefit which he does not want. Hence where a recipient shows an intention to pay outgoings, he cannot plead that they were against his wishes and he therefore becomes a partner therein.

When a claim is made in respect of a unilateral benefit, no obligation to pay will arise *ab initio,* but if an intention to pay is disclosed that is equivalent to a legal undertaking to do so.

Another modern authority, R. Shimon Shkop,[33] explains the obligation to pay in the fencing case in two different ways. First, if the recipient has shown his readiness to share the outgoings, the other suffers a loss if payment is not enforceable. That is particularly so in the case of occupying premises where the owner could let the premises to the occupier at a rent and where the premises are not for letting. Another explanation is that the indication makes the recipient not merely a recipient of a benefit but enriches him. These two explanations are meant to demonstrate that the exemptive principle is not involved. Whilst the first stresses the loss of the one party, the second is based on the distinction between a mere recipient of a benefit and one who is financially enriched by the amount he had in mind to pay.

(c) The *Shulḥan Arukh* rules in accordance with the view of the *Toṣafot:* "where premises not for letting are involved, no rent need be paid provided the occupant has not disclosed that he would pay rent, were he not allowed to take up full occupation. Where he does disclose such an intention, he must pay." [34]

Manifestation of intention will only have this effect if it is made to the true owner, as may be gathered from the case mentioned in the *Gemara* of A who rents (lettable) property from B, which is found to belong to C. A must pay C the rent. If therefore the property were not for letting, A would not be bound, although he had disclosed to B (not C, the owner) a readiness to pay. [35] The *Shulḥan Arukh* adds that the rent paid to B, on the mistaken impression that he is the owner, is recoverable by A, [36] but this view has been disputed. [37]

7. Prevention of Foreseeable Profit

For the exemptive principle not to apply, must the loss of the other party be actual or is it enough if he is prevented from obtaining a profit which he anticipated?

For the *Gemara* the answer is simple: "loss" includes the prevention of an anticipated profit. When R. Ḥisda posed the problem whether one who occupied premises unbeknown to the owner must pay rent, the *Gemara* asks whether the premises were for letting and the occupier generally rents premises. If so, the occupier derives a benefit and the owner sustains a loss,—and payment must be made.

The criterion of anticipated profit was not, however, determined objectively. Thus a person who does not usually derive a profit from his property, where for example he does not normally let, will not be deemed to have suffered any loss, although others generally let property of the kind in question. Moreover, even if he had in the past let the property but no longer does so, the situation is treated as at the time when the recipient derives his benefit; thus the owner suffers no loss.[38]

The concept of "loss" is also limited by prescribing that prevention of anticipated profit will only occur when the owner could actually obtain it but not where he or his agent are for instance absent and cannot in fact let the property, for then no question of anticipated profit will arise. The same applies where the owner is available and wishes to let the property but there are no people wishing to rent, in which event the property is deemed not to be for letting.[39]

The category of lettable property is, however, significantly broadened by R. Eliᶜezer Bar Natan (Raʾavan) holding that a person who does not personally need some property of his will normally let it out, and by the more generalised presumption that today houses are deemed to be for letting, whether or not they are in fact let at the material time.[40]

8. Loss Preceding Enjoyment of Benefit

(a) A benefit may become possible initially by a preceding loss which has ceased when the benefit is enjoyed. Is the initial loss a relevant element? The Toṣafot to our Gemara cites a case from Ketubot 30b of a person who has stuffed food into the throat of another, the rule being that although no loss has been sustained (since if the food is "returned" it would be unpalatable and valueless) payment must be made. The Toṣafot to our Gemara explain the inconsistency on the ground that the other has benefited by reason of the first person's original loss, which brings into operation the principle of "the one benefits and the other loses" and therefore payment for what has actually been consumed must be made. The Toṣafot in Ketubot, however, offer another explanation. Since the food retains some value, payment must be made because of the partial loss sustained. Another view is that the two acts are treated as occurring simultaneously.

(b) It would seem from the Toṣafot in Baba Kamma that a preceding loss will create an obligation to pay for any subsequent benefit. That, however, is inconsistent with the decision of a later medieval authority[41] in the following case. A feudal lord after expropriating the house of A, a Jew who had fled from the lord's domain, allowed B, another Jew to occupy it. A claimed rent from B. The exemptive principle was held to apply since the house must be treated as not for letting since, if B were to vacate it, it might be given over to a non-Jew and no rent could then be obtained. According to the *Toṣafot* in *Baba Kamma*, B should have had to pay rent since his benefit was preceded by A's loss (the expropriation).[42] A suggestion to remove the inconsistency has been made by interpreting the *Toṣafot* to have distinguished the forced feeding case, where the two acts presumptively occurred together (as suggested above) from the expropriation case, where that was not so, A's loss occurring irrespective of B's benefit, for which reason B would not have to make payment.[43]

(c) The *Shulḥan Arukh* deals with a case where A has deposited a pledge with a non-Jewish money-lender and B who is in need of funds gets A to allow him to borrow on the security of the pledge.[44] If the pledge is destroyed, B will not, it is held, have to pay A its value. *Prima facie* B's benefit (release from his debt to the money-lender) arises because of A's loss (destruction of the pledge) and he ought to pay according to the *Toṣafot* in *Baba Kamma*. B's benefit, however, occurred after A's property no longer existed and therefore the ruling is to exempt B from payment.[45]

9. Benefit Involving Lesser Loss

(a) Will the recipient of the benefit have to pay the value of the benefit or the value of the loss, where the loss is less than the benefit?

Our *Gemara* cites a *Mishnah*[46] dealing with a house of which the upper part is owned by A and the lower part by B. The house collapses and A asks B to rebuild his part so as to enable him to rebuild the upper storey. B refuses. The *Mishnah* decides that A is entitled to rebuild the lower part and occupy it until B reimburses him for the outlay. R. Judah,[47] however, observes "one who occupied another's property without his agreement must pay rent", inferring that A will have to pay B rent although B has suffered no loss in the circumstances (because of his refusal to rebuild his part). The *Gemara* seeks to treat R. Judah's view as contradicting the exemptive principle but eventually distinguishes this case because the alteration ("the blackening of the walls") of the rebuilt part entails a loss and renders A liable to pay rent.

On this basis most of the earlier authorities decide that the value of the benefit and not merely that of the loss must be paid.[48] And that is also the ruling in the *Shulḥan Arukh*.[49]

(b) An 18th century authority[50] explains this last ruling on the ground that the exemptive principle rests on the rule that a person may be compelled not to act in the manner of Sodom and the rule is not applicable where there is a loss, even a minor one. Another explanation[51] is based on the view that where there is a loss a person will always be diligent in protesting against the use which another makes of his property, however small the loss he thereby sustains. Even when he does not know of the use, he is presumed to have protested, and this presumption brings the case into the rule discussed in para. 5 above.

10. Benefit Involving Loss to Other Property

Does the recipient of a benefit pay only where the loss is in respect of the property he has used or does his obligation extend to other property which is affected?

A 19th century scholar[52] had the following case put to him. A stole a book containing instructions how to paint and copied its contents. Apart from the question of copyright, the application of the exemptive principle is discussed in the *responsum*. If the book was new and was damaged in the course of the "theft", then the rule regarding lesser loss as above will apply. If the book is not damaged but the owner sustained loss by A now being able to compete with him in painting, it is problematic whether A must pay. A comparison is made with the case where one uses a shop of another without agreement and the shop is not for letting, but the owner does business from another shop, which may be affected. Is the damage too remote for liability to arise or is the owner's concern over the loss caused to him sufficient ground for charging the "guilty" party?[53]

The tendency is to make the recipient liable. Our *Gemara* itself asks: "What has he done to him? What loss or injury has he caused him?", the inference being that irrespective of the place of the loss the recipient is chargeable. Some of the authorities also take for granted the view that the loss need not arise in connection with the same property, but without going into the matter. In one 18th century case,[54] a writer sent to printers a commentary of his on two Orders of the Talmud. He complained that the printer had used the type set for his work to print a text with the commentaries of Rashi and the Toṣafot. The printer was adjudged to pay for the benefit he had obtained from using the type on the grounds that had he not acted as he did, the writer may have sold more copies of his own book without the competition presented by the printer's publication.

A somewhat similar case is that of the bottled water labels, already mentioned, where the defendant was ordered to pay on the principle that in the event of a lesser loss the entire benefit reaped must be accounted for. In the instant case, moreover, the whole question of passing-off was also a vital consideration. The damage caused concerns also increase of tax payments, and possible damage to commercial reputation.[55]

11. Recipient Providing a Benefit

Towards the end of our *Gemara* the argument takes a new line. A further reason for exemption is reported in the name of Rav. Unoccupied premises are apt to fall into decay and a person who goes into occupation even without agreement will prevent this and may even according to R. Yoṣef[56] put the premises into good condition.

This argument bases the exemptive principle on the benefit which the owner may derive from the recipient. It constitutes a revolutionary turn because, if that were so, the application of the exemptive principle would be severely limited; and some authorities do indeed draw this conclusion.[57] But neither Maimonides nor Karo mention this aspect of the matter and thus inferentially do not accept the limitation.[58]

12. Causation of Benefit

The benefit derived may be the result of an act by the recipient or the donor or a third element. It is clear from the examples given in the *Gemara* that the exemptive principle applied even when the recipient's own act brings about the benefit and that the charging principle of "the one benefits and the other loses" operates even when the benefit comes from the donor's act: in the fencing case an attempt is made to show that the exemptive principle does not operate when the owner puts up the fence on the four sides so that the recipient has to pay (but the attempt fails on the ground that the other party is deemed to suffer a loss). On the other hand the classic example of the exemptive principle is the occupation of premises without agreement where the recipient benefits entirely from his own act.

The above rules, however, are not confined to the acts of the two parties immediately concerned. They extend to benefits due to an extraneous element, as in the forced feeding case,[59] except that on one view the recipient will only be chargeable if his person and not merely his property is affected.[60] This view is stated in connection with the question whether when wool is dyed the improvement due to the dyeing is independent of the wool. Rabina poses the question where the wool belongs to one person and the dyes to another whilst an ape does the dyeing.[61] Is the improvement treated as a separate item from the wool, in which case the person to whom the dyes belong may ask the person to whom the wool belongs to give him back the dyes, or is the improvement not a separate item and the owner of the wool may say that he has nothing belonging to the owner of the dyes. The *Toṣafot ad locum* ask how it is possible to press the second of these alternatives and exempt the owner of the wool from payment, unlike other cases of enrichment, whereas in the feeding case although the benefit was not occasioned by the recipient, he engaged in it in his person. An alternative answer is that the dyeing of the wool is not deemed to be a benefit since it is only decorative. The answer is that in the instant case the wool is not improved by the act of the recipient or his "agent" but by a third party. Accordingly a distinction is made as to whether the benefit accrues or does not accrue to the person of the recipient.

The distinction in most explanations is challenged by the authorities.[62] *Shakh* rejects it since it is not mentioned in the Talmud and confines the exemption to cases where a third party intervenes, but where the benefit comes about from the donor alone the recipient will have to pay because of the general rule that a person who improves the property of another is entitled to have his expenses reimbursed.

13. Conclusions

The question whether the principle "the one gains and the other does not lose" is exemptive or not is treated in the *Gemara* as being without Mishnaic precedent and open to varying views. In holding that the principle is exemptive, the authorities do not lay down a general rule but one confined to the specific fact situation discussed—unauthorised occupation of premises. In addition the principle is circumscribed and its application beyond the limits indicated may yield results which differ considerably from those which emerge from the Talmud and the authorities.

The legal foundations for the exemptive principle vary: that the donor has no cause of action at all; or that even though he may have a cause of action, he will be restrained from acting in the manner of Sodom.

In applying the principle the "no loss" circumstances must be carefully defined. Whilst the loss of an anticipated profit is sufficient to remove the exemption, where the property concerned is such that normally it is not a source of profit, though it might be and though other people might treat it so, no loss will occur; the same is true where the profit is not practically possible.

The kind of property from which a profit may be derived is extended by the presumption that today houses are generally for letting, without the burden of proof being on the owner.

The loss need not be co-extensive with the benefit. Even if it is less the donor is entitled to all the benefit the recipient may obtain.

Two further rules of importance are established. If the donor protests the recipient's benefit, it must be paid for. If the recipient indicates any intention to pay for the benefit should he not be allowed to enjoy it freely, an obligation to pay will arise.

Thus the exemptive principle is limited and all cases in which the recipient should rightly pay for his advantage are excluded.[63]

II. OTHER ASPECTS OF UNJUST ENRICHMENT

In addition to the exemptive principle of "one derives benefit and the other sustains no loss", discussed in part I, there are other aspects of Jewish law on unjust enrichment.

Some of these aspects have been dealt with by the present writer in publications of the Ministry of Justice of Israel, Research in Jewish Law series: "Transacting business with another's property" (No. 45), "Agent who receives benefit in consequence of his agency" (No. 46), "Indemnity for salvage of property" (No. 50), "Indemnity for rescue of a person" (No. 51) and "Compensation for withholding another's money" (No. 52).

1. Transacting Business with Another's Property

There are various situations where, whilst the owner of property may suffer no loss from another's use of it, he is nevertheless entitled to recompense. One of these situations occurs when a person lets the property of another and receives the rent. The source of the rule is to be found in the observations of R. Jose in *Mishnah B.M.* 3:2, regarding the man who hires an ox from his neighbour and then lends it to another and the ox dies. The hirer may have made a profit from lending the ox, and R. Jose asks, "How can one do business with his neighbour's ox? The ox must be returned to its owner."

The legal basis for R. Jose's rule is sometimes explained by reference to the injustice of hiring out another's property and depriving the other of his property; and sometimes to quasi-agency, the person who obtains the benefit acting as it were as agent of the owner. The latter approach is characteristic of the rabbis who are not satisfied with merely deciding that the rights of one person pass to another but attempt to give the matter a legal complexion.

Whilst R. Jose was concerned with a specific situation, the earlier post-Talmudic authorities extended his rule by analogy to the case of a person who hires out another's property, holding that the hire price belongs to the owner, and also to the case of the unauthorised subletting of land, although some authorities sought to limit the latter to where the owner actually suffers some loss from the subletting.

Later authorities do not appear to extend the rule substantially further but more recently the possibility has been considered of applying it to the case where a stranger has effected insurance at his own cost and the question of the destination of the insurance money arises. The similarity between insurance and the lending of the ox is twofold. First, just as in the latter case the profit arises from the act of the hirer lending the ox, so with insurance the profit arises from the act of a tenant in insuring the property. Secondly, in both instances the profit derives from the monetary loss of the person involved—the hirer in having to pay the hire money to the owner without receiving anything from the borrower, and the tenant in having paid the insurance premiums.

The parallel has nevertheless been held not to apply. The owner's right to the insurance money does not rest on R. Jose's rule. The distinctive features of the ox-hiring case are not present in the insurance case.

In the former, the owner's right to the hire money arises out of the hirer's obligation or the sub-hirer's use or possession of the ox; in the insurance case the person paying the premiums enters into a personal transaction with the insurance company quite distinct from the hiring of the thing hired and therefore does not transact any business directly with the owner's property. The latter therefore has no call on the insurance money. Alternatively, whilst in the ox-hiring case it may be unjust to do business with another's property, in insurance it is unjust for one to pay the premiums and for another to reap the benefit therefrom.

In applying R. Jose's rule to modern problems, a number of distinctions are made, some substantive, emphasising unjust enrichment aspects, and some formal. Where the owner claims all the profit made from his property, it is essential, for instance, to establish whether indeed the property is the source of the profit. Analysis of R. Jose's rule has taken it out of the conceptual realm of abstract justice and prevented its over-extension involving injustice to others.

2. Agent Who Receives Benefit in Consequence of His Agency

Here the question is—how should the benefit arising from the act of a person representing another be treated? To whom does the benefit belong? Is the fact that the benefit arose out of agency activity determinative of the rights of the parties? Although possibly in agency law, the agent's act may not give any right to the principal, the latter is nevertheless entitled to receive or participate in the benefit because it is he who has been the "cause" of it. Alternatively, whilst the principal has a right to the benefit, the agent also has a right since but for his action the principal would have nothing, the benefit not being an integral part of the agency activity. If the right of the one in the benefit the other has received is recognised, there falls to be determined when he is deemed to be the "cause" to entitle him to the benefit. Juridically the problem falls within the bounds of unjust enrichment.

The rule that has emerged is that, irrespective of agency law, where a person has been the "cause" of a benefit he is entitled to enjoy it. First elaborated in the Palestinian Talmud, the rule was adopted by some of the earlier post-Talmudic authorities. Its history in the Shulḥan Arukh and the glossators is interesting. Whilst it did not receive explicit mention in the basic text, the glossators give it prominence as a point to be considered in the appropriate circumstances, in particular where the third party gives additional consideration, or where an agent has varied his agency. Reflection led to a number of distinctions depending on the connection between the benefit and the agency activity. The possibility of applying the rule to a benefit occasioned by mistake was also examined.

Some of the later rabbis held that the principal's right did not arise in strict law but resulted from rabbinical *takanah*.

The solution of sharing the benefit was not proposed under the exemptive principle—when the recipient would take all—nor under the rule relating to doing business with another's property—when the owner would get all. In the present context the agent not only enjoys a benefit from his agency but makes a profit. Accordingly, his obligation is greater than that of a person who only enjoys a benefit. On the other hand, he does not make his profit at the expense of the principal and therefore all of it cannot be said to be due to the latter. Thus the agent and principal have equally strong rights; both have contributed to creating the profit, the one by his activity and the other by his property.

The broadening of the rule would have far-reaching consequences, but beyond the situation where the third party gives additional consideration or where the agent varies his agency, no broadening of the rule was undertaken.

The law relating to the agent who obtains a benefit from his agency is examined from the viewpoint both of agency law and of unjust enrichment. In certain circumstances, an agent so benefiting may be in breach of trust or even criminally liable and be deprived of the advantage.

3. Indemnity for Salvage of Property

Is the voluntary nature of salvage significant to the salvor's right to indemnity? On the one hand, in doing what he did the salvor has acted piously in observance of a *mitsvah* (precept), unlike one who simply intervenes with regard to another's property and unasked enhances its value. Perhaps for this reason his rights are superior. Salvage should moreover be encouraged, and if the rules of law do not allow for proper compensation, they call for amendment. On the other hand, the doing of a pious act is its own reward and further monetary payment is superfluous. What connection is there between the pious act of the salvor and his monetary rights? His rights may be lesser than that of one who unasked improves another's property, since the latter presumably acted as he did in anticipation of being rewarded, whilst the former did not or waived any such right.

Regard must also be had to whether or not the owner was present when the salvage occurred and the salvor made any stipulation with him. What, further, is the position where the salvor is unsuccessful either because his efforts end in failure or because the property was salvaged without his effort? Does a person who whilst salvaging his own property salvages also his neighbour's, have any right to be paid in full or proportionately? Still another question is whether the salvor's right must be distinguished as between payment for his efforts and reimbursement of his outgoings and losses.

The source of the law is a *Mishnah* in B.K. 10:4: "If one was coming along with a barrel of wine and another with a jar of honey, and the jar of honey cracked, and the first emptied his wine and scooped up the honey in his barrel—he may only have the value of his services. But if he said, 'I am going to save your honey but you pay me for my wine', the other must pay him."

This Mishnaic rule that where a salvor makes no stipulation as to payment, he is only to be paid for the services he has rendered, is subject to significant reservations which make the rule exceptional, whereas the salvor's right is much wider.

The Talmud understands the Mishnah to be concerned not with the case where the property would be lost but for the salvor's action. If it is impossible to save the property, the salvor is entitled to all of it under the rule of *hefker* (renunciation of property), or at least to the value of what he lost in the course of the salvage.

The early post-Talmudic authorities introduced a further reservation—the Mishnaic rule does not apply where the owner is not present; in that event the salvor is entitled not only to payment for his services, but also to the value of his loss. His right is further extended to entitle him to full indemnity of his outgoings when, without his intervention, the owner would have used the salvor's property to effect his salvage.

The Mishnaic distinction between payment for services rendered and payment for losses incurred by the salvor requires clarification. The exemption as regards the latter when the owner is present and the salvor has made no stipulation is explained on the ground that the owner can argue that he could have salvaged his property with such expense. Thus, whenever this argument cannot be raised, the salvor is entitled to be paid for his losses, i.e. payment for services includes all the necessary outgoings, whereas the value of the property lost in the course of the salvage is confined to those outgoings which the owner might not have been ready to expend, for which reason stipulation must be made.

Accordingly the Mishnaic rule restrictive of the salvor's rights will apply where salvage was possible and effected in the owner's presence without his being consulted and the salvor acted freely of his own choice; he will then be entitled to payment for his services, i.e. his necessary outgoings as to which no stipulation need be made.

The owner may be exempt from payment if he voices opposition to the salvage. But where he knows that in any event the salvage will be carried out (because, for instance, it is involved in saving others) or his opposition is merely aimed at avoiding due payment for his outgoings, it will not be taken at its face value and have no effect.

The legal basis for salvage indemnity, as it emerges from a survey of the sources, lies on one view in *takanah* since in strict law, arguably, the salvor only acted to save the owner trouble and is not entitled to payment; and in order to encourage such acts a duty to pay was instituted by *takanah*. The "Rule of Court" *(tenai bet din)*, referred to in the *Tosefta B.K.* 4:26–27, which entitles a salvor to payment for his losses, may, it is suggested, be the source of the *takanah* as against the Mishnaic rule of law.

The connection between the rules relating to salvage and returning lost property has been one of reciprocal effect. The possibility in the case of lost property to stipulate payment in the presence of three persons is extended to salvage as an alternative to stipulation with the owner himself. Conversely, the importance of the owner's presence in salvage is extended to lost property.

The salvage rules illustrate the process whereby a deficiency in the law is remedied by *takanah* to obviate the possibility of one person enjoying a benefit at the expense of another. This regulation is in contrast to the law regarding improvements made to another's property without asking the owner.

4. Indemnity for Rescue of a Person

The rescue of persons is in Jewish law not merely a matter of moral sensibility. Very often the act will entail expenditure by the rescuer or damage to a third person's property. Rescue and salvage are similar in several respects. Both rest on religious precept and accordingly involve a voluntary act without any legal obligation between the parties to do the act or any agreement as to indemnifying the salvor or rescuer.

In contrast to salvage, however, an individual may not abandon his life or person. Again, salvage and rescue may be distinguished with regard to the obligation to incur expenses: whereas in salvage it is possible to set-off value against value, in rescue there is no measuring rod.

A guiding consideration is the encouragement of acts of rescue. The Talmud already prescribes under *takanah* that the rescuer is not bound to compensate any third person who has suffered a loss in the course of the rescue. Raba said (*Sanh.* 74a): "If one was pursuing another pursuer to save (the latter's victim) and broke some utensils, whether of the pursuer or the pursued or of any other person, he is not liable for them. This should not be so in law, but if you do not so rule, no man will save his neighbour from a pursuer."

As regards indemnity for the rescuer's expenses, the Talmud is not explicit but the early post-Talmudic authorities derived the rule in various ways. In order to encourage rescue, it was prescribed that the costs entailed must be paid immediately and without reservation. Opposition by the person rescued to payment was ignored. Similarly, where in the course of rescuing one person another is also rescued, the latter will not be heard to say that even had he himself not been rescued the rescuer would have incurred expenses, since every person could argue so and this might endanger people.

5. Compensation for Withholding Another's Money

The persistent fall in money value has sharpened problems concerning the unlawful taking of money and delay in payment of money due. Two purposes are served in providing for compensation in such cases—to make up for the owner's loss resulting from his inability to use his money and to impose sanctions for delay in payment. If profit is made, a further cause of action may be found in the rules regarding the transacting of business with another's property or under unjust enrichment.

On the other hand, a number of difficulties will occur if compensation is exigible. Under the law of theft, the value at the date of the theft is alone payable and any betterment belongs to the miscreant. Again, any compensation payable may fall within the prohibition of usury; in that case the fact that the money was not "lent" willingly must be borne in mind.

The rules here are also not based on strict law but on *takanah* and binding custom, having regard to the rabbis' awareness of the profitable use to which money can be put.

The observation in the Palestinian Talmud that a person can only complain but not more of another who renders "his pocket idle" is in conflict with and therefore restricted by other tannaitic and talmudic rules.

For the post-Talmudic authorities the discussion revolves around two questions—whether tort law applies to charge the "withholder" with damages and whether the additional payment partakes of usury. As to the first, the balance of authority is that compensation is payable for the loss entailed by preventing profitable use of the money. (Some authorities would charge the "withholder" on the principle of "the one benefits and the other suffers loss".)

As for usury, money withheld at the wish of the owner is distinguished from money forcibly withheld, as is also payment made for the right to retain money from payment made by way of "fine" or compensation for the loss incurred by the owner. Reference may be made to a formula, attributed to R. Jacob of Orleans, one of the Tosafists, which is incorporated in bills to provide *ab initio* for payment of a fine, which is indicative of rabbinical awareness of the need to resolve halakhically problems arising in trade and commerce.

A further distinction is made between "consumer" loans and money due in connection with employment, commerce and the like. This distinction is of current importance since most advances of money are today not in the nature of consumer loans but are made for other purposes, generally through banks, and are not "loans" in the halakhic sense. Even as regards loans, the view taken by some would permit compensation for withholding repayment.

The fall in money value, characteristic of our time, is an important consideration in respect not only of the hardship which delay in payment may entail but also of the legal basis of the obligation to indemnify. The traditional authorities concentrated on the question of compensation for loss of the prospective profitable use which the owner might have made of his money. Today it is not this loss only but the actual intrinsic loss from the fall in money value which is predominant, with its repercussions as to the tort and unjust enrichment liability of the "withholder" and as to usury. Thus the necessity arises for *takanot* to augment the strict law. Three centuries ago it became customary in Poland to compensate for market losses *(peseida deshuka)*. Although attempts were subsequently made to narrow the scope of this custom to the special circumstances in which it arose, modern conditions justify its wider application, since all and not only business men are affected. Thus the rabbis long ago treated the withholding of payment, which involves a loss of profit to the owner, as a form of theft.

NOTES

1. The Hebrew phrase for "unjust enrichment" was coined by Cheshin J. in reliance on *Jer.* 17:11 — "*he that getteth riches, and not by right,* shall leave them in the midst of his days."
2. Cases of actual damage were not dealt with, except such as are illustrated by that where lettable premises are occupied by persons who would not otherwise rent premises. Whilst the *Toṣafot* to *B. K.* 21a s.v. *Zeh* does not require him to pay for his occupation, *Rif* (*B. K. 9a*, Vilna ed.) *would make him pay because he causes financial loss.* *Rosh* explains that the obligation can be based on the fact that "he has eaten the other's loss", which is different from the case where a person closes up another's house and does not go into occupation (*Piṣke HaRosh* to *B. K.* 2: 6). See also the *Hagera* and *Naḥlat David* to *B. K., ibid.*
3. *Infra*, II. "Other Aspects of Unjust Enrichment."
4. For what follows, see D. Friedmann, *The Law of Unjust Enrichment* (Heb.) (Tel Aviv: Avukah Press, 1970), and regarding our present subject, *ibid.*, 41–48. See J. P. Dawson, *Unjust Enrichment* (Boston: Little Brown & Co., 1951) and Goff and Jones, *Law of Restitution* (London: Sweet and Maxwell, 1966), ch. 1.
5. Recently a Bill (No. 1361 of 31 July 1978, *Hatsaᶜot Ḥok* 307) has been tabled which proposes to abolish reliance on English law and replace it by reference to the Jewish sources of justice and equity.
6. See Friedmann, *supra* n. 4, at 8.
7. Bill No. 1353 of 5 July 1978, *Hatsaᶜot Ḥok,* 266.
8. See Silberg J. in *Zim v. Maziar* (1963) 17 P.D. 1319, 1933: "When the decisive question regarding a legal conclusion is one of philosophical outlook ... we may and indeed must draw upon our ancient sources since these alone truly reflect the basic conceptions of the Jewish people in 'its

entirety'." See also the judgments of Cohn J. and Kister J. in *Yekutiel v. Bergman* (1975) 29 P.D. (II) 764, 769.

9. For bibliography on the Jewish law of unjust enrichment, see N. Rakover, *Otsar Hamishpaṭ* (Jerusalem: Harry Fischel Institute, 1975), 436. See also I. Herzog, *The Main Institutions of Jewish Law* (London: Soncino, 1970), II. 49–59; J. Webber, "Observations on some Cases of Unjust Enrichment", *Diné Israel* 2 (1970), 24–42; Y. Rottenberg, "Unjust Enrichment", *Encyclopaedia Judaica*, XV. 1683–1687.

10. See *Maimonides, Responsa* (ed. Blau), 444, on the question how a prohibition arises in money matters.

11. *B.M.* 117b.

12. *Maimonides, loc. cit.*, also points out that R. Yehudah's alleged view is inconsistent with the rule that a person who occupies another's premises without agreement need not pay rent. See also *Ḥatam Ṣofer*, Responsa on *Ḥoshen Mishpaṭ*, para. 79. But see *Responsa Hare Beṣamim*, II. 245.

13. *Maimonides, Hilkhot Gezelah Va'avedah* 3: 9; *Shulḥan Arukh, Ḥoshen Mishpaṭ*, 363:6.

14. E.g. *Erub*, 49a, *Ket.* 103a, *B.B.* 12b, 59a, 168a. See the instructive contribution of A. Lichtenstein on the rule in *Hagut Ivrit Ba'Amerikah* 1 (1972), 362–382.

15. *Maimonides, Hilkhot Shekhenim* 7: 8; *Rashi* to *Ket.* 103a and to *B.B.* 12b; Commentary attributed to R. Gershon, *Or Zeru'a; Novellae Rashba* to *B.B.* 12b; *Rashbam* to *B.B.* 59a; *Yad Rama* to *B.B.* 168a.

16. See *Pene Yehoshu'a* to *B.K.* 20a, relying on the *Toṣafot*. See also *Novellae* of R. Ḥayyim of Telz to *B.K.* 39 and *B.B.* 109, and *Levush Mordekhai* to *B.K.*, para. 15. See also note 18 below.

17. See note 14 above.

18. The *Toṣafot* to *B.B.* 12b, s.v. *Kegon,* however, seems to imply that they held the exemption from payment arises under the principle that one may be compelled not to act in the manner of Sodom. *Encyclopaedia Talmudit, Zeh Neheneh*, note 8, also cites Maimonides (see note 15 above) to this effect but the matter is not clear. According to the *Toṣafot*, there are two forms of the rule, one arising under strict law and one by virtue of rabbinical regulation.

19. In the case of the unauthorised occupation of premises, the rule is not applied *ab initio* against the owner who has suffered no loss: *Toṣafot* to *B.K.* 20b; *Rema* in *Shulḥan Arukh, Ḥoshen Mishpaṭ*, para. 363, contrary to R. Eliezer b. R. Yoel Halevi, cited in *Mordekhai* to *B.K.* 2: 16. *Rema's* reason is that the owner might let the premises. See *Responsa Divre Malkhi'el*, III, 157, rejecting this last view and distinguishing the case where the owner can put an end to the occupation or use of his property at any time without the need for any act by the occupier from the case where the owner may be suffering loss because such an act is needed. In the latter case the rule does not apply.

20. As may be inferred from the reason given by R. Ammi in our Gemara for

exempting the recipient: "What harm has he done to the other? What loss has he caused him?" See *Novellae* of R. Shimon to *B.K.*, 19: 3, and *Levush Mordekhai, op. cit.*

21. Since the recipient holds something belonging to the donor and despite the absence of any agreement as to payment. See *Birkat Shmuʾel, B. K.* 14: 2–3, and *B.B.*, 7.

22. *Maḥane Efrayim, Hilkhot Gezelah* 10. See the discussion on the question whether minor orphans can make a valid waiver where *Nimuke Yosef* to *B.K.*, chapter 2, argues that as the exemptive principle applies to minors who cannot make a valid waiver the principle is not based on waiver. On the other hand *Toṣafot* to *B.B.* 143a holds that in some cases a waiver can be made by minors. And see also *Responsa Rashba*, II, 152. S. Albeck, *Dine Hamamanot Batalmud* (Tel Aviv: Dvir, 1976), chapter 4, seeks to rest the obligation to pay and the exemption from payment on the parties' resolve *(gemirat daʿat)* as to payment.

23. The *Toaṣafot* to *B.K.* 21a dispute the view they attribute to *Rashi* that occupation without knowledge involves payment. See *Responsa Terumot Hadeshen*, para. 317, where the explanation given of Rashi's view is difficult to reconcile with what he actually says.

24. This is the view of R. Yeshayahu in *Shiṭah Mekubetset* to *B.K. ibid.*

25. *Rashba* in *Shiṭah Mekubetset, ibid.*, and in his *Novellae*, in the name of R. Hananel.

26. *Ṭur, Ḥoshen Mishpaṭ* 363: 6; *Shulḥan Arukh, Ḥoshen Mishpaṭ*, 363: 6. *Minḥat Pitin ad loc.* points to an inconsistency between *Karo* and *Rema* on this matter and resolves it by saying that where it is wholly impossible to let the property, both would agree that the occupant is exempt even if told to vacate.

27. *Sema* to *Shulḥan Arukh, ibid.*, 14. See *Biʾur Hagera ad loc.* 13. But *Naḥlat David* opposes this view, relying on *Rashba*, note 25 above: the obligation to pay only arises where the owner has so stipulated but not where he has merely protested the occupation.

28. This also explains *M.B.B.* 1: 4, regarding an obligation to pay on the collapse of a wall dividing the premises of joint owners and the rebuilding of the wall by one of them (see *Toṣafot* to *B.B.* 5a, and *Yam Shel Shlomo* to *B.K.*, Chapter 16.)

29. *Yam shel Shlomo, ibid.* See *Encyclopaedia Talmudit, ibid*, note 67: *Ketsot Haḥoshen*, para. 158, 6.

30. *Ḥelkat Yoʾav, Ḥoshen Mishpaṭ*, para. 9.

31. See the distinction made by R. Ch. Eigash (*Markheshet* 2: 35) between the case where the benefit no longer exists, when the exemptive principle applies and where the benefit was created by the two parties and still exists and where the expenses should be shared and the exemptive principle is out of place.

32. *Responsa Divre Malkiʾel*, 3, 157.

33. *Novellae* to *B.K.* 19: 5 and 6; 20: 1–2.

34. *Hoshen Mishpat* 363: 8. *Arukh Hashulhan, Hoshen Mishpat* 373: 19, limits the rule: disclosure of intention will only be effective where the person would otherwise rent premises; otherwise the intention must be express. As to the date when the intention is to be disclosed, some take the view that it may occur during occupation (*Mahane Efrayim, op. cit.,* 9) and some even after the occupation has ended (*Perishah* to *Tur, Hoshen Mishpat,* 363, 7). See *Responsa Noda Biyehudah,* vol. 2, *Hoshen Mishpat* 24, distinguishing between a disclosure of intention as to partial payment and intention as to full payment; in the first instance, the duty to pay the value of the whole benefit will only arise if the expenses have been excessive, whereas in the second, payment must in any event be made.

35. See *Shitah Mekubetset* to *B.K.* 21a.

36. *Hoshen Mishpat* 363: 9. See *Novellae* of *Rashba* to *B.K.* 21a.

37. *Helkat Yo'av, Hoshen Mishpat* 9. See *Or Sameah, Hilkhot Gezelah* 3, 9; *Birkat Shmu'el, B.K.,* 14:2; *Novellae R. Sh. Shkopf, B.K.* 19: 5 and *B.B.* 4: 3.

38. *Nimuke Yosef, B.K.* Chapter 2, cited as the law by *Rema* in *Shulhan Arukh, Hoshen Mishpat* 363: 6.

39. See *Hagahot Asheri* to *B.K.* 3: 6 (in the name of *Ra'avia*) who followed *Rema* in *Shulhan Arukh, Hoshen Mishpat* 363: 10. But see the criticism of *Bet Aharon (Valkin)* to *B.K.* 21a, and its refutation by Y. Flakser, "Yishuv Piske Marama", *No'am* 13 (1970). 55–62. See also *Responsa, Terumot Hadeshen* 316, which needs explanation.

40. See *Ra'avan B.K.* 21a, cited as the law by *Rema, op. cit.,* 363: 6.

41. *Mordekhai* to *B.K.,* chapter 2, 17, cited by *Rema, op. cit.,* 363: 3.

42. *Mahane Efrayim, Hilkhot Gezelah* 13.

43. *Responsa Bet Shlomoh Hoshen Mishpat* 122.

44. *Shulhan Arukh, Hoshen Mishpat,* 72: 44.

45. See *Bet Shlomoh, op. cit.* The rule has been followed where a person insures his part of a house held jointly with another but mistakenly the insurance covers the entire house. The joint owner cannot claim any part of the insurance moneys if the house is burnt down. Recourse to the rule has also been made where one has paid insurance premiums for another's property: *Responsa, Erets Tsvi (Te'omim), Hoshen Mishpat* 15, and *Responsa Avne Tsedek, Hoshen Mishpat,* 7.

46. *M.B.M.* 10: 3.

47. The rabbis who oppose R. Yehudah admit that an obligation would occur for detriment due to "blackening" (see below) but give exemption for another reason,—the house is encumbered to the upper part.

48. R. Meir Halevi holds that only the sum of the loss should be paid. See *Nimuke Yosef B.K* Chapter 2. See *Responsa Noda Biyehudah* Vol. 2, Chapter *Hoshen Mishpat* 24, that this is all the view of Maimonides. Note the distinction made in *Responsa Amude Esh,* 67.

49. *Hoshen Mishpat* 363: 7. *See Tosafot* to *B.K* 21a; *Novellae ad loc.; Nimuke Yosef* to *B.K.,* chapter 2, in the name of *Ritba. Piske Harosh* to *B.K.,*

chapter 2, 6. See also *Responsa Yeshu'ot Ya'akov, Hoshen Mishpaṭ* 4. *Gidule Shmu'el* to *B.K.* chapter 2, deals with the question, whether he should pay the value of the benefit or the sum the owner could have got.

50. *Pene Yehoshuʿa* to *B.K.* 20b. A parallel question arises on the taking of property without intention to steal: *Shulḥan Arukh, Hoshen Mishpaṭ,* 363: 3 and *Sema, ibid.,* 7.8. See N. Rakover, "Fundamental Problems in the Jewish law of Theft", *Sinai* 49 (1961), 27–29; *Responsa, Amude Esh,* 66b; *Responsa, Divre Malkiʾel,* 3:157.

51. *Responsa, Amude Esh,* 67a.

52. *Ibid.,* 66b.

53. See text to note 51 above.

54. *Noda Biyehudah, Responsa,* Vol. 2, *Hoshen Mishpaṭ* 24. *Cf.* Kister J. in *Agudat Hakormim v. Yekev Hagalil* (1960) 22 P.M. 77.

55. See *Divre Malkiʾel* 3, 157.

56. The *Gemara* explains that if premises are not used for a residence, but for storing things, the reasoning of R. Yosef will not apply.

57. See *Shiṭah Meḳubetset* to *B.K.* 21a *per* R. Yeshayahu; *Aliyot Darkenu Yona* to *B.B.* 4b; *Or Zeruʿa, B.K.,* 120–121; *Raʾavan* to *B.B.* (ed. Ehrenreich, 28): *Torat Emet,* 129. For the reasons of those who oppose this conclusion, see *Novellae Rashba* to *B.K.* 21a; *Piṣke Harosh* to *B.K.,* chapter 2: 6; *Nimuḳe Yoṣef* to *B.K.,* chapter 2; *Yam shel Shlomoh* to *B.K.* 2: 16.

58. Maimonides, *Hilkhot Gezelah Vaʾavedah* 3: 9; *Shulḥan Arukh, Hoshen Mishpaṭ* 363: 6. See *Biʾure Hagera ad loc; Naḥlat David* to *B.K.* 21b. But *cf. Sema, op. cit.,* 15.

59. *Ket.* 30b and the *Tosafot ad loc.* See also *Piṣke Harosh* to *B.K.* 9: 17.

60. *B.K.* 101a and the *Tosafot ad loc.*

61. *B.K.* 19b; 55b; *Ket.* 30b.

62. *Shakh* to *Shulḥan Arukh, Hoshen Mishpaṭ* 391: 2. *Cf. Maḥane Efrayim, Hilkhot Niẓke Mamon* 2: 4; *Ḥelḳat Yoʾav, Hoshen Mishpaṭ* 9. See also *Markheshet* 2: 35; *Novellae* R. Sh. Shkop to *B.K.,* 19: 7; *Responsa, Bet Shlomoh, Hoshen Mishpaṭ* 122.

63. The view that the recipient is not exempt unless he also benefits the owner by the use he makes of the property would render the exemptive principle almost without effect, but it has not been accepted.

C

Ethics

14

Judaism and the Obligation to Die for the State

Geoffrey B. Levey

I

Dying in the state's behalf, and at its request, is a matter that one might expect to be of obvious concern to the Jews throughout their history. Twice in bygone eras (roughly, 1000–586 B.C.E. and 140–63 B.C.E.) they have been ensconced in their own sovereign land faced with preserving that sovereignty against hostile neighbors and ambitious empires. Elsewhere, in the diaspora, they have been forced to define their relations and responsibilities to the host powers under whose authority they have variously been classed as aliens, residents, and citizens. And now, again, they are reestablished in their own sovereign state of Israel, in whose short history the call to arms has been unfortunately all too frequent. Yet the obligation to die for the state is not a question which enjoys especial treatment or ready resolution in Jewish sources. In part, this is because the Jewish tradition is not in nature a philosophical tradition, given to abstract systematic treatises in the manner of the ancient Greeks, to whom Western thought has ever since been indebted. It is, rather, a legal tradition, given over to the interpretation and application of legal minutiae in keeping with divine edict. Still, it would be wrong to conclude that Judaism and the Jewish tradition lack a coherent position on there being (or not being) an obligation to die for the state. Such, anyway, is what I wish to argue in this essay.

Reprinted by permission of Barbara Cohen from *Jewish and Roman Law*, Jewish Theological Seminary of America, New York, 1966.

But I also want to argue that the Jewish approach to the question of dying for the state has wider importance for political theory. Classic Western treatments of the question of the obligation to die have typically been caught in an enduring dilemma. On the one hand, as has been said, any theory which, like Hobbes's, Locke's, and Kant's, begins with the absolute independence of freely willing individuals and goes on to treat politics and the state as instrumental to the achievement of individual purposes would seem incapable of justifying an obligation upon individuals to lay down their lives for the state.[1] So, too, would it seem incapable of providing a sense of active community. On the other hand, any theory which, like Rousseau's and Hegel's, begins with a notion of the state as an ethical institution representing shared values and common sacrifices over and above individual interests, and which goes on perhaps to regard the significance of war to be precisely that it enables the primacy of the state to be reasserted over private concerns, cannot hope, in turn, to preserve the individual's liberty to safeguard his life and property.[2] The Jewish approach to the question of dying for the state, I will contend, demonstrates *one* way this dilemma may be overcome.

At once, however, a possible confusion needs to be averted. It has often been noted that the concept of the state is problematical, if not alien, in relation to classical forms of Jewish government. Thus, Roland de Vaux, in his masterful study of ancient Israelite institutions, concludes:

Clearly we cannot speak of *one* Israelite idea of the State. The federation of the Twelve Tribes, the kingship of Saul, that of David and Solomon, the kingdoms of Israel and Judah, the post-exilic community, all these are so many different regimes. We may even go further and say that there never was any Israelite idea of the State.[3]

It may appear, therefore, that the very question of whether there is an obligation to die for the state according to and within Jewish tradition is ill-conceived. One, of course, may still want to inquire as to how Jews faced this question as communities in the diaspora, under foreign rule. But as regards how they did so under their own sovereignty, so goes the argument, the answer ought to be plain: there is no question of an obligation to die for the state in classical Jewish thought because there is no idea of the state governing classical Jewish life.

Now, the confusion here consists in the semantic use of the term "state." For in asking whether there can be an obligation to die *for the state*, the issue is not what constitutes a coherent conception or practice of statehood. The issue is whether one can be bound to sacrifice one's life for the security and well-being of *any* broad and inclusive political association of which one is a part because the political authority decrees it. That is, at stake is the nature and extent of individual obligation to the broader social unit or body politic. It is in this sense, then, that the convenient phrase "dying for the state" may be applied to the various regimes (as de Vaux puts it) characteristic of ancient Israel and Jewish self-government.

The precise nature and extent of an individual's obligation to the state may in turn, of course, depend upon the considered nature of the state itself. This is the approach characteristic of Western theorizing about the problem of political dying. By being (or not being) obligated to die for the state it is meant that one is (or is not) so bound by the state's general and acclaimed end or purpose, the act of its foundation or the relationship to it amongst its members.[4] Hobbes, for example, asserts the end of the state to be nothing else than the security and well-being of the individual, which, indeed, constitutes the individual's sole reason for contracting to form the state, and enthrone Leviathan, in the first place. For Hobbes, therefore, political obligation vanishes at the point at which an individual's security becomes compromised: there can be no obligation to die for the state.[5]

Rousseau, too, ultimately determines the case for the obligation to die for the state upon consideration of the state's basic purpose—though for him, unlike Hobbes, there *is* an obligation to die, since the state represents a shared moral life from which each citizen gains, and therefore owes his own. But Rousseau also suggests political dying to be obligatory in terms of the act of the state's foundation. The social contract includes, as it were, a "willingness to die" clause. "He who wishes to preserve his life at others' expense," states Rousseau, "should also, when it is necessary, be ready to give it up for their sake . . . and when the prince says to him: 'It is expedient for the State that you should die,' he ought to die, *because it is only on that condition* that he has been living in security up to the present."[6]

Again, Plato, in the trial of Socrates, suggests an additional reason, beyond the end and foundation of the state, generating an obligation to die. What leads Socrates to believe in the rightfulness of his drinking of the hemlock, as sentenced, is his long-standing acceptance of the state and its laws *as expressed* by his public commitments and prolonged participation.[7]

In classic Western treatments, then, the question of there being an obligation to die for the state typically turns upon a particular political theory. Now, this marks the point of departure for the Jewish approach to dying for the state. For in Judaism, one's obligations to the social compact, like one's obligations generally, are determined not according to political relations or some elaborated theory of the state but according to laws understood as divine commandments, or *mitsvot*. It is true that these commandments became binding for the Jews after they entered into a bilateral covenant with God, a founding act of consent resembling at least one of the ways Western theorists attempt to ground political obligation.[8] It may even be said that, because Jewish tradition understands the Sinaitic covenant as historical and literal (as it does the covenants of Abraham and David), the ancient Jewish commonwealths provide a more convincing case of political obligation than do the so-called liberal democratic states, for which liberal theorists have found it necessary to invoke the *fiction* of a social contract.[9]

Then, too, the similarities do not end with the founding act of consent. They also relate to the (problematical) fact that the Sinaitic commandments are undertaken by a particular community at a particular time and are yet considered obligatory for all who are born into the covenantal community. For there are commentaries in Scripture and elsewhere which seek to explain how succeeding generations can be bound to the covenant that very much resemble the modern liberal theories of tacit and hypothetical consent.[10] But for all the similarities, parallels, and historical connections, there is one difference unequivocally separating the Jewish and Western theoretical approaches to the issue of obligations to the body politic. The agents to whom consent is respectively rendered by the people in social contracts and in the biblical covenants are of completely different orders.

The "social contract" is generally formulated by political theorists to be an unwritten agreement among all contracting persons creating a sovereign. Consent, in this case, is rendered to *political* authority, and thus the institution of the state is central to the whole series of relationships binding citizen to sovereign and sovereign to citizen. The bilateral covenant at Sinai, on the other hand, is between a people, Israel, *and* the sovereign and creator of all things, God. In Judaism, if consent is meaningfully rendered at all, it is rendered to *divine* authority. The institution of the (Jewish) state, far from being the source of, and basis for, its members' obligations, is, according to Judaism, merely a necessary instrument in the fulfillment of obligations established elsewhere.[11] This fact, moreover, helps explain de Vaux's observation, cited above, that there never was any Israelite concept of the state but only a series of regimes governing Jewish collective existence. It is conformity to God's commandments that is the measure of a Jew's obligations and not any given political institution, structure, or arrangement.

The question of dying for the state in Jewish tradition is not therefore the question of political obligation it is for so many classic Western thinkers. There is no attempt in Judaism to ask (or to answer) in the abstract whether there can be an obligation to die for the state at all, under any circumstances. In Judaism, dying for the state is instead a question of what the commandments betoken in terms of an individual's relationship to the body politic when the supreme sacrifice may be involved.

In the remainder of this essay, I want to examine closely those commandments which are of direct relevance to the question of dying for the state. For the most part these are the commandments concerning the declaration and prosecution of wars. There are, in addition, some commandments dealing with self-sacrifice and self-defense which will require some treatment in passing. All of these various precepts I will consider only in the context of the biblical Jewish commonwealths (a context which, anyway, most of them presuppose). This is not to say that the "working principles" by which Jews traditionally determined their obligations to the foreign states in which they were resident are not instructive too. Only that, because such principles necessarily depart from the experience, and hence the challenges, of an authentic Jewish polity, they are best left to separate inquiry.[12]

Furthermore, we recognize here that there is a difference between fighting for the state and dying for the state, especially inasmuch as the subject is war. But to note the difference is to note that nothing much is changed by it either. Being bound to fight for one's country implies, in most cases, an unnaturally high risk of death (or, what is maybe worse, mutilation). And it is this implication and not the eventuality which is important in considering the question of ultimate obligation. Accordingly, "to fight" and "to die" will be used as synonymous expressions. It is important to recognize, too, that in Judaism, just what the commandments do indeed betoken is not always a straightforward matter. While Scripture constitutes the source and foundation of Jewish ethical teaching, it is in fact the exegeses supplied in the classical rabbinic material of the Talmud and other commentaries that represent normative Judaism as such. For this reason, we will begin first with an analysis of the relevant biblical passages before trying to elucidate the Jewish approach to the question of dying for the state implicit in the classical rabbinic literature.

II

The Bible contains numerous references to the nature of the expectation associated with the call to risk one's life in the service of communal goals.[13] Especially in the premonarchic period, the common feature of biblical wars is their sacred character. God marches along with the Israelites and is considered by Israel to be not only sovereign, but guardian. Thus the sacred character of biblical war ought not to be confused with the modern designation of "holy war." For, in de Vaux's words, "it was Yahweh who fought for Israel, not Israel which fought for its God. The holy war, in Israel, was not a war of religion," but of existence.[14]

Even so, it might be thought that the sacred quality of these biblical wars bore a distinct duty to participate in them. And in an important sense this is so. When the tribes of Gad and Reuben request of Moses that they be permitted to settle their cattle east of the Jordan rather than participate in the fight for Canaan, Moses rebukes them sharply: "Shall your brethren go to war, and shall ye sit here?" (Num. 32:6). He warns them that their proposed course of action would "augment the fierce anger of the Lord toward Israel" (Num. 32:14). Later, when the tribes of Gad and Reuben indicate their willingness to cross the Jordan in battle, Moses warns them that to refuse to participate in this war would be to sin against the Lord, and "be sure your sin will find you out" (Num. 32:20–23).

But the effect of the sacred quality of biblical wars with respect to a duty to participate is very much a two-edged sword. The fact that God is both the legitimator of Israel's wars and its guardian in battle meant that participation had to be infused with the requisite faith. "Fear not!" is the exhortation of God to Joshua and of Joshua to the people in the face of battle and danger (Josh. 8:1; 10:8, 25). Prior to battle against the Midianites, Gideon is commanded by God to go "Proclaim in the ears of the people, saying, Whosoever is fearful and afraid, let him return and depart early from mount Gilead" (Judg. 7:3). True, the reason God gives Gideon for this instruction is that the Israelite forces are too numerous, and hence there is a danger that in victory they shall pride themselves that "Mine own hand hath saved me" (Judg. 7:2). But it seems a mistake to see in this merely a device employed to reduce Israel's battle-strength: there is always the question why *this* means should be adopted, and adopted in the first instance.[15]

Perhaps more significant, though, is that this same emphasis on faith and consideration for the "fearful" is repeated and extended in Deuteronomy 20. Here, the sequence of events reveals dramatically the crucial regard in which a correct religious disposition is held as a condition for participating in Israel's wars. The chapter opens with a series of restatements of the need for having faith in God.

When thou goest out to battle against thine enemies, and seest horses, and chariots, and a people more than thou, be not afraid of them: for the Lord thy God is with thee, which brought thee up out of the land of Egypt. And it shall be, when ye are come nigh unto the battle, that the priest shall approach and speak unto the people, And shall say unto them, Hear, O Israel, ye approach this day unto battle against your enemies: let not your hearts faint, fear not, and do not tremble, neither be ye terrified because of them; For the Lord your God is he that goeth with you, to fight for you against your enemies, to save you. (20:1–4)

Next is specified a number of conditions of exemption from battle. However, surprisingly, the first exemptions have nothing obviously to do with a lack of faith in God or a fear of battle. They apply to individuals who, it seems, could well be ardent believers and accomplished warriors.

And the officers shall speak unto the people, saying, What man is there that hath built a new house, and hath not dedicated it? let him go and return to his house, lest he die in the battle, and another man dedicate it. And what man is he that hath planted a vineyard, and hath not yet eaten of it? let him also go and return unto his house, lest he die in the battle, and another man eat of it. And what man is there that hath betrothed a wife, and hath not taken her? let him go and return unto his house, lest he die in the battle and another man take her. (20:5–7)

It may be that having these other unrealized concerns on one's mind was taken to suggest that such an individual would naturally not be of the "right" religious temperament for battle. Or, more likely, it may be that against war such concerns simply represent conflicting duties and, as one commentator has put it, "a premature breach in a man's involvement in life was explicitly prohibited."[16] Whatever the case, the final exemption, explicitly referring to the "fearful," seems to take on extra force for having been preceded by other legitimate conditions of military exemption where any simple "crisis of faith" is *not* the issue.

And the officers shall speak further unto the people, and they shall say, What man is there that is fearful and fainthearted? let him go and return unto his house, lest his brethren's heart faint as well as his heart. (20:8)

The Bible, then, displays a central tension over the question of there being a duty on the part of the Israelites to risk their own lives in battle on behalf of their people. On the one hand, the sacred quality of Israel's mission and military pursuits suggests a responsibility of "equality of sacrifice" devolving upon each individual.[17] On the other, this very same sacred quality requires that the duty to fight be undertaken with "proper" faith or not be undertaken at all. Nowhere perhaps is this tension better played out in the Bible than in the Song of Deborah.

In this, one of the most poetic and dramatic of all biblical passages, there is the familiar call to arms, the familiar invocation of God as both witness and judge, the familiar and awesome pressure to plunge into battle. Yet Deborah exalts, not the fact of participation, but the fact that such participation was freely entered into. "Praise ye the Lord for the avenging of Israel, when the people *willingly* offered themselves" (Judg. 5:2). And again: "My heart is toward the governors of Israel, that offered themselves *willingly* among the people" (Judg. 5:9). But what, to bring the tension to the straining point, of those who exercise their will and opt not to fight? How shall they be judged? As independent souls due respect or as betrayers of duty? When the crunch comes the tension is resolved by Deborah in favor of the independence of those who refrained. There is certainly the expression of reproach and regret (though nothing stronger), as de Vaux notes.[18] "Why abodest thou among the sheepfolds, to hear the bleatings of the flocks?" chides Deborah (Judg. 5:16). But, more crucially, there is the ultimate deference to the integrity of conscience: "For the divisions of Reuben there were great searchings of heart" (Judg. 5:15–16).

On the face of it, the advent of the monarchy seems to confound this picture of "ultimate voluntarism" before any duty to risk one's life for the commonwealth. De Vaux has, characteristically, put the problem best:

. . . this strictly sacred character of war disappeared with the advent of the monarchy and the establishment of a professional army. It is no longer Yahweh who marches ahead of his people to fight the Wars of Yahweh, but the king who leads his people out and fights its wars (I Sam. 8:20). The combatants are no longer warriors who volunteer to fight, but professionals in the pay of the king, or conscripts recruited by his officials.[19]

The basis for the monarch being accorded these powers is found in a controversial passage in the First Book of Samuel:

And Samuel told all the words of the Lord unto the people that asked of him a king. And he said, This will be the manner of the king that shall reign over you: He will take your sons, and appoint them for himself, for his chariots, and to be his horsemen; and some shall run before his chariots. . . . And he will take your menservants and your maidservants, and your goodliest young men, and your asses, and put them to his work. . . . And ye shall cry out in that day because of your king which ye shall have chosen you; and the Lord will not hear you in that day. (8:10–18)

What ethical significance one attaches to these proffered royal prerogatives has tended to depend upon whether they are understood as divine dispensations, precipitated and agreed to by the people themselves, or rather, and only, as dire prophetic warnings of the sort of despotism a monarchy invites. Each interpretation has its notable protagonists.[20] It is perhaps reasonable, therefore, to see the merit in a third (although not necessarily exclusive) alternative: the Bible reveals a basic ambivalence toward the institution of the monarchy. After all, additional to the ambiguous passage cited above, there are others both evidently favorable to it (I Sam. 9 and 11) and suspicious of it (Hos. 7:3–7, 8:4, 13:9–11).[21] And yet, to highlight the ambivalence with which the kingship is regarded in the Bible can hardly be to sustain the view that its establishment preserved the on-balance, premonarchic value on individual willingness before one's life is put at risk doing battle. One side of the ambivalence is always that the king has the right to conscript for battle almost anyone he pleases.

The crucial consideration is not therefore the kind or degree of legitimacy which the Bible accords to the kingship. It is that the king, though he may obtain certain prerogatives (like initiating wars not necessarily part of the "Wars of Yahweh"), is nevertheless bound to abide by God's laws. Once he sitteth upon his throne, states Deuteronomy (17:18–20), the king

> . . . shall write him a copy of this law [which] he shall read therein all the days of his life: that he may learn to fear the Lord his God . . . That his heart be not lifted up above his brethren, and that he turn not aside from the commandment, to the right hand, or to the left.

The king of Israel remains God's agent, as do indeed all the people of Israel. It follows that even in the monarchic period respect must be accorded the Deuteronomic provisions exempting certain "classes" of individuals elaborated earlier. Of course, it may be argued that with the lack of sacredness associated with some of the king's military ventures goes too the relevance of the Deuteronomic stress on having faith in God as a precondition for participation in war. Nevertheless, the further Deuteronomic concern for those who are "afraid" and "fainthearted" effectively preserves into the monarchic period the principle that individual willingness *precedes* being duty-bound to fight.

The idea that the will to fight precedes the duty to do so is a radical one. Just how radical can be seen by reference to a contemporary political theorist. Michael Walzer has argued that "there is a crucially important sense in which the obligation to die can only be stated in the first person singular." Moreover, Walzer insists that this is so even though it "comes dangerously near to suggesting that a man is obligated to die only if he feels or thinks himself obligated." [22] Now, there is a crucially important sense in which this is precisely what the biblical concern for the fearful and the fainthearted does represent. For the fourth exemption effectively makes any obligation to die for the state self-constituting. Perhaps, then, the term "exemption" is not the best way of referring to or understanding the fourth Deuteronomic provision. With it, one is not so much excused from an obligation as there is no obligation until it is personally recognized. Yet, however one conceives of the fourth Deuteronomic provision, whether as dissolving a standing obligation or as helping create one, the conclusion remains the same. As the text stands, if the Bible advances any obligations to die for the state, they are "loose" obligations indeed.[23]

III

The significance of the Deuteronomic exemptions was not lost on the rabbis of the classical period. Nor, in particular, was the radical voluntarism implied by exempting from battle the "fearful" and "fainthearted." The Mishnah records that Rabbi Jose the Galilean understood the fourth exemption to refer to those fearful of having sinned and of having not yet repented.[24] This, he explains, is why it is juxtaposed with the exemptions of the newlywed man, the man who has built a house without dedicating it, and the man who has planted a vineyard but not redeemed it: they provide dignified pretenses under which a transgressor may discreetly return home. Rabbi Akiba, however, insists upon a literal interpretation of the fourth exemption: it refers to the coward, those "unable to stand in the battleranks and see a drawn sword."[25] But genuine cowardice is a condition not easily foretold: anyone may seemingly lay claim to it. Why then should the "coward" be so readily exempted? The Bible offers a psychological reason: "Lest his brethren's heart faint as his heart." This, however, assumes that genuine cowardice is involved, and does not treat the problem of decided noncowards abusing the provision.

An alternative, and more cogent, explanation is suggested by Rabbi Akiba himself. In another formulation, he maintains that the mention in the fourth exemption of *yareh,* or "fearful," refers to the coward, while the additional reference, *rakh halevav,* or "fainthearted," is to the compassionate. He who is "hero among heroes, powerful among the most powerful, but who at the same time is merciful—let him return."[26] There is some dispute among contemporary commentators as to whether this last entails something of the modern notion of conscientious objection.[27] Whatever the case, the inclusiveness of this formulation of the exemption effectively dismisses the need for determining genuine cowardice. Indeed, it seems to recognize the great difficulty in determining the real motivations of those not wanting to fight as against their stated reasons for not wanting to do so. Both the cowardly (or those fearful for their own lives) *and* the compassionate (or those fearful for the lives of others) are thus exempted. Such an argument, it may be noted, is even more radical than that of Hobbes. In his theory, only the genuinely cowardly—men of "feminine courage"—are esteemed to flee from fighting "without injustice." [28] As Rabbi Akiba appreciated, the fourth exemption is far more accommodating. It provides wide, almost open, opportunity to exempt oneself from duty on the battlefield.

But if the rabbinic interpreters recognized this, they were also moved to constrain its effects. This was done chiefly in the classification of biblical wars. The rabbis asked to which wars the exemptions applied. Except for one response where the terms are differently employed (entailing a peripheral dispute), the sages replied: "To discretionary wars [*milhamot reshut*], but in wars commanded by the Torah [*milhamot mitsvah*] all go forth, even a bridegroom from his chamber and a bride from her canopy." [29] This interpretation has stood as the more authoritative. But there are commentators who held differently. Maimonides and Rabbi Ishmael both ruled that the exemptions applied to all the wars engaged in by Israel. And the sixteenth-century talmudic scholar, Rabbi David ben Abi Zimra, maintained that while the first three Deuteronomic exemptions applied only to discretionary wars, the fourth, exempting the "fearful" and "fainthearted," applied to both discretionary and commanded wars. [30] Clearly, if the radical fourth exemption can be invoked in *both* commanded and discretionary wars, it is reasonable to conclude that there can never be an absolute obligation to fight for the state in Jewish law. If, on the other hand, the fourth exemption (along with the other three) were restricted solely to discretionary wars, it is possible that commanded wars constitute a class of war in which an absolute obligation to fight *might* exist. In either case, further questions must be faced before the full measure of any obligation to die for the state in Jewish law can be established. I propose therefore to broach the problem of the extensiveness of the exemptions according to the relative strength of case that can be made for any such obligation.

IV

It seems clear that the obligation to die for the state is most compelling in the context of *milhamot mitsvah*. Such wars are explicitly ordained by God, and, as we have seen, at least one authoritative rabbinic version claims that no exemptions are permissible here. The sages agreed that

the wars expressly mandated by God are those waged against the Amalekites and the idolatrous Seven Nations in the pursuit and conquest of
the land of Canaan. Some differences arise over whether the obligation
involved here attaches specifically to vanquishing the paganism of the
Seven Nations and not instead to the conquest of the land of Canaan,
the promised land, itself.[31] These issues, however, do not affect the
commanding or obligatory nature of the wars in question.

There is one ruling by Maimonides, though, which does importantly
qualify the nature of the obligation to fight with respect to war against
the Seven Nations. Maimonides posited that both a communal obligation to wage war against these nations and a personal obligation to
eliminate their members applied.[32] But, of course, a personal obligation
to fight is certainly not the same thing as being bound to fight for the
community (or state). One would be simply fighting, as it were, for one's
own sake. This difference is made no less significant by the claim of later
commentators that Maimonides meant the personal obligation to be
dependent upon the communal one: that an individual can be obligated
to endanger himself in the discharge of his personal obligation only if
the community has itself first fulfilled its obligation to wage war against
the Seven Nations.[33] For it remains that once war has been declared by
the community as a whole, the standing obligation to fight comes from
a commandment addressed *directly* and *specifically* to the individual.

Important discriminations must then be made among *milhamot mitsvah,* or commanded wars, before an obligation to die *for the state* is
asserted. In war against Amalek, where the individual's obligation to
fight derives from the general obligation of the community to wage war,
it is entirely fitting to speak of an obligation to die "for the state." But
in war against the Seven Nations, where individuals are bound to fight,
not through the community, but on account of a personal commandment, the notion of dying for the state is inappropriate.

Still another discrimination must be made. It arises, again, from an
important codification made by Maimonides and this time raises a more
general problem. In his *Mishneh Torah,* Maimonides posits another
variety of "commanded" war in addition to war against the Amalekites
and the Seven Nations. This is the defensive war, a war "to deliver Israel
from an enemy who has attacked them."[34] The difficulty is that, unlike
the wars against Amalek and the Seven Nations, no biblical injunction
or apparent talmudic reference exists for this kind of war. The question

is thus raised on what basis a defensive war can be deemed obligatory when no divine commandment warrants it.

One answer which seems possible from rabbinic sources is the so-called law of pursuit, or *rodef*. Under this law, a bystander is obliged to help save the life of an intended victim, although the life of the aggressor may only be taken if that is necessary for this purpose. Defensive wars might therefore be obligatory on the grounds that one must render assistance to victims of military aggression. The halakhic scholar J. David Bleich has recently put this explanation, but only to dismiss it.[35] Bleich offers a number of convincing objections to this use of the law of *rodef*, but certainly the most "damaging" is that "there is no obligation to eliminate a *rodef* [pursuer] if it is necessary to risk one's own life in order to do so." Since this risk is precisely what war entails for the individual combatant, the law of *rodef* can hardly serve as the basis for there being an obligation to participate in defensive wars.[36]

Of far more interest, therefore, is Bleich's own argument for the obligatory character of defensive wars. They are obligatory, he claims, because they are undertaken by the monarch. Indeed, such wars explain, in part, the very need for a monarch. While "Jewish law recognizes that society has inherent power, albeit limited in nature, with regard to the expropriation of the resources of its members," says Bleich, "only the sovereign enjoys the power to compel his subjects to endanger their lives."[37] Clearly, the issue of dying "for the state" is involved here. In the absence of a divine commandment sanctioning defensive war, the obligation to die, or to endanger oneself, is now linked to the power of the state, as represented in the sovereign.

Still, the state's having the legitimate power to conscript individuals does not necessarily mean that there is an obligation for them to "enlist." A right to induct is not necessarily correlative with a duty to fight. One commentator has pointed out, for example, that on the basis of the prophet Samuel's proclamation of the prerogatives of the king (as quoted earlier), "a citizen does not have to voluntarily pay his taxes or surrender to the military . . . [but rather] the king or government would be obligated to bear the burden for enforcing their taxation and draft regulations."[38] What is missing with Bleich's reliance upon the power of the sovereign is, then, an adequate explanation of why the individual should be obliged to fight in defensive wars.

In fact, the missing step is easily enough to be found in rabbinic sources. A number of commentaries assert not only that the king may compel his subjects to do his bidding but that his directions must be obeyed. Anyone not obeying a royal decree, or who rebels against it, was considered *mored bemalkhut,* or treasonous (strictly, "rebellious against the kingdom"), and could thereby incur the death penalty.[39] Of course, this in turn only raises the question of why one is obliged to obey the king's command. One rabbinic response, it may be recalled, is that the prophet Samuel's description of the king's rights represents divine commandments consented to by the people. And there are others.[40] But rather than rehearse them here, it is perhaps more apposite to reflect, for the moment, on a somewhat different literature.

It is often enough recognized among political theorists that the very nature of defensive war harbors its own imperatives. When a society's survival is threatened through no fault of its own, even the most liberal theorists, those championing the near-absolute freedom of the individual, seem to want to reserve for the state supremacy over the interests of its individual members. "When the Defence of the Common-wealth, requireth at once the help of all that are able to bear Arms, every one is obliged," writes Hobbes uncharacteristically, "because otherwise the Institution of the Common-wealth, which they have not the purpose, or the courage to preserve, was in vain."[41] One might easily suppose, then, that the same sort of concern is what led Maimonides to include defensive war within the obligatory category of *milhamot mitsvah.* Or, as Maurice Lamm has put it, "If the conquest of the land is an obligation, then it stands to reason that the protection of that land is also an obligation."[42] But then again, perhaps it need not stand to reason alone. Commenting upon the Deuteronomic verse (26:17–18), "Harass the Midianites and smite them; for they harass you," an oft-quoted Midrash states: "On the basis of this verse our sages said, 'If [someone] comes to slay you, arise and slay him.' "[43]

V

While the foregoing may explain why defensive wars are obligatory in the absence of a direct commandment by God, it remains the case that they fall within the category of *milhamot mitsvah* for no other reason than that Maimonides legislated them so. This is important to emphasize, since discretionary wars, too, may be waged only upon the initiative of the monarch and yet constitute a completely separate classification to that of commanded wars. Rabbinic sources agree that "discretionary" wars are in general those waged by the House of David for the purpose of territorial expansion.[44] Beyond this, they are variously characterized as wars to "eradicate pagan wickedness," wars to "enhance the monarch's greatness and prestige," and wars conducted for economic reasons.[45] But, as outlined earlier, the distinctive feature of discretionary wars is that all four of the Deuteronomic military exemptions are acknowledged to apply. Some rabbis contended that the exempt were nevertheless obliged to assist with noncombat duties in the service of the war effort, though here, as well, it is not entirely clear whether this also includes those exempted under the fourth provision.[46] But whatever the range of these other duties, it is clear that ultimate obligation, the obligation to sacrifice one's life, is, by virtue of the exemptions, severely and significantly circumscribed in discretionary wars.

A number of rabbinic authorities ruled that a war initially waged as a "discretionary" war could become "commanded" war under the threat of defeat. Accordingly, those who were previously exempted from fighting are no longer so and must take up arms with the rest.[47] Certainly the circumstance in which one's forces appear to be on the verge of being overwhelmed, and one's country vanquished, has the semblance of a defensive war, and it is easy to appreciate the logic of the rabbis' ruling. But it is also true that dire consequence, or its anticipation, is a feature common enough to any war, at least at some stage, in one or another battle. This ruling by the rabbis thus seems to seriously detract from the significance of the exemptions. It seems to suggest that even in discretionary war the presumption in Jewish law is in favor of the body politic over the life of the individual, insisting, so to speak, on an obligation to die for the state.

Thus it is important to see that such a presumption is actually less encompassing than it might appear. For the explicit elaboration of exemptions in connection with "discretionary" war carries with it an obligation on the part of the *monarch* to refrain from engaging in (discretionary) wars when he is not confident of victory and thus may require the conscription of persons who would ordinarily be exempt. It is, in part, for this reason that discretionary wars can only be embarked upon with the consent of the Sanhedrin, or Court of Seventy-One, and the confirmation of the *urim ve-tumim*, or "priestly oracles."[48] The task of the Sanhedrin was to assess the need and likelihood of success of a proposed war, while the role of the *urim ve-tumim* was to confirm or deny divine legitimization for the intended military activity. The net effect of these procedures is to safeguard that only "winnable" wars are attempted, thus ensuring that those exempt remain exempt. Only where a war has gone "badly wrong," confounding, as it were, all the intelligence reports, do the exemptions become legitimately waived.

The question remains whether apart from those exempted there is an obligation to die for the state in discretionary wars. After all, like defensive wars, discretionary wars require the initiative of the sovereign, and this suggests that the monarch's declaration of war might similarly generate an obligation on the part of most to fight. Now, if it were only for the first three Deuteronomic exemptions—exempting, as they do, certain objective and definite types of individual status—such a case might be made. But, of course, there is the fourth exemption; as we have seen, a radical and open-ended exemption to the extent that anyone may seemingly invoke it. It may well be asked, then, just how meaningful it is to speak of there being an obligation to die when virtually anyone can exempt himself from it. This is, of course, another way of putting our earlier point that application of the fourth exemption effectively means that the obligation to die for the state is self-constituting.

In any case, the way in which the so-called exemptions take force clarifies that there is no obligation to die as a result merely of the sovereign's declaration of (discretionary) war.[49] It needs to be remembered that prior to announcing the various military exemptions to the assembled people, the "priest anointed for war" spends some emphatic moments counseling them on the need for faith and against the need to be afraid (Deut. 20:1–4). Commenting on this address, Maimonides says that it is designed so that "their hearts be aroused to war and he bring them to endanger themselves."[50] Bleich, curiously, claims this passage as evidence for the contention that the king has the power to compel his subjects to risk their lives.[51] But, in fact, the function of the priest's address suggests not compulsion but persuasion: the people are *brought* to endanger *themselves*. What we find, then, is not the existence of an already standing obligation, the binding force of which the people are being told to remember, but rather the process whereby the commitment or obligation to fight is being made.

The proclamation of the exemptions, and the opportunity for the people to invoke one or another of them, is what constitutes this process. According to Maimonides, two stages are involved.[52] The first is "on the frontier, when they are about to set out, just before the battle is started," where those who have planted a vineyard and not yet enjoyed its fruit are asked to return home. The second opportunity to affirm a commitment to fight is presented to the people when "the battle lines are drawn up, and they are drawing near the attack." At this point, the "priest anointed for war" counsels further against being afraid but proclaims that the newlywed man, the man who has built a house without dedicating it, and anyone who *is* afraid may also return home. The consequential nature of these pronouncements is dramatized, moreover, by their successive repetition by officers assisting the priest. All told, in Maimonides' account, the people have impressed upon them the impending battle together with the opportunities for individual retreat no less than seven times.

Once the last condition of retreat has been issued, however, and "when all those entitled to return home have gone back from among the troops," those remaining on the field are presumed to have committed themselves to fight. An obligation to fight, if not to die, has been created. Accordingly, any soldier now seeking to withdraw from the military effort is considered to be reneging on an obligation that he himself willingly undertook. And, as the Mishnah and other commentaries agree,[53] at the moment of battle such an attempt poses an unpardonable threat to the success of the entire military operation.

And it shall be, when the officers have made an end of speaking unto the people, that they shall appoint captains of hosts at the head of the people. And at the rear of the people they station guards in front of them and others behind them, with iron axes in their hands, and should anyone wish to flee, they have permission to smite his thighs, because the beginning of flight is falling . . .

An obligation to risk one's life fighting for the state is thus neither automatic nor necessary in discretionary wars; it is contingent upon the individual's willingness to do so. But the process whereby the individual may indicate whether he will fight or not is not indefinite; it has limits. Beyond a certain point, the individual is deemed to have cast his lot, to fight or not to fight. After that, he who has elected to remain and fight is no longer free to indulge a change of heart or mind with impunity. In this, of course, the rabbinic formulation contrasts sharply with Hobbes's general theory, in which an individual may legitimately renounce a commitment to fight *whenever* he is so moved by fear.[54] Yet it is worth noting that, in practice, the rabbinic formulation is perhaps no more restrictive than Hobbes's. The people, after all, are not forewarned of battle and of the conditions for participation in the secure and removed environment of their homes or city. They are informed of such things on the edge of battle itself, where the clamor of shields and the ground-beating of horses' hoofs ought to impress upon all the deadly seriousness of what is in store.[55] The likelihood is increased, therefore, that those assuming a commitment to fight are those most prepared to carry it through to the end. The Hobbesian need of permissible individual retreat, mid-battle, is minimized.

VI

To complete our picture of the classical rabbinic varieties of war, consideration must finally be given to the case of preemptive war. First introduced in the Gemara as wars "to diminish the heathens so that they shall not march against them," preemptive wars were designated a form of "discretionary" war by the sages.[56] As such, most of what has been said about the nature and extent of the obligation to fight in discretionary war in general is true of preemptive war in particular. The applicability of all four of the military exemptions limits any obligation to fight by the process of its very creation. There are, however, a number of aspects peculiar to preemptive war that bear on the issue of the obligation to fight.[57]

One has to do with what actually constitutes a preemptive war in the rabbinic understanding. In Jewish law, a preemptive war is one that is waged solely as a preventive military operation. Whether this be to forestall an imminent or only future danger is of no consequence to its status of preemption. Yet a war that is solely conducted to prevent anticipated danger is not regarded as preemptive if it should be in response to a prior attack. This is so even if there has been an intermittent cessation of hostilities. Jewish law, rather, designates such a war to be of the order, "to deliver Israel from an enemy"; that is, a defensive war in the category of *milhamot mitsvah*. There thus exists the possibility that a war begun preemptively can become, through a conflation of enemy response and counterresponse, a strictly defensive war. The relative extent of the obligation to fight will then vary respective to the status of the war at any given time.

Certain preemptive military operations have warrant in Jewish law quite apart from the regulations and categories pertaining to war. In the face of imminent danger, and where innocent life is not put at risk, preemptive operations may be initiated on the basis of the principle, "If [someone] comes to slay you, arise and slay him."[58] The principle differs in this context from that of defensive war in that a preemptive war presupposes that no overt aggression has yet been visited by the enemy. Thus, however imminent such aggression may be or seem, preemptive action is deemed to be permissible only and not obligatory. That there is a difference between danger being imminent and danger seeming imminent helps to explain this halakhic ruling. The nonobligatory classification accorded preemptive war allows for the opportunity that alternative courses of action be tried, possibly averting the need for war or the exhibition of hostilities at all. Insofar, though, as preemptive action is deemed necessary, there is no obligation upon an individual to participate in it, just as the operation itself is not permitted should innocent lives be jeopardized.

All this changes should a preemptive action develop into a defensive war. As before, a preemptive action that is met by an aggressive enemy response has the effect of rendering any counterresponse a defensive, and no longer a preemptive, war. In these circumstances, the limiting conditions that attach to preemptive war sanctioned by the principle "If someone comes to slay you" will no longer apply. Instead, the war regulations as determined by the respective categories of "commanded" and "discretionary" war will, once again, come into play.

VII

In Jewish law, the type of war and the willingness of the individual are not all that is required for an obligation to fight for the state to be established. Such an obligation becomes truly binding only if certain conditions and institutions are fulfilled. Some of these have been mentioned already; for instance, the requirement that a discretionary war may be waged by the monarch only after the Sanhedrin and the *urim ve-tumim*, the priestly oracles, have, in their respective ways, determined that it is legitimate. Of course, in our day the Sanhedrin and the *urim ve-tumim* have no institutional existence. It thus follows that any obligation to fight requiring these institutions should be conceived in formal terms only.[59] Further such special provisions might now be noted.

While there is no need for the Sanhedrin in "commanded" wars (since such wars are divinely ordained and hence require no "independent" decision), there is need for the *urim ve-tumim* to pronounce upon their putative divine character.[60] Without the consultation of the *urim ve-tumim* or, what is perhaps less likely given their express sanction, without their confirmation, no obligation to fight in behalf of the state could exist. At least, no obligation could exist to fight the Amalekites and the idolatrous Seven Nations. For in defensive war, the third variety of *milhemet mitsvah*, the requirement of the *urim ve-tumim* does not apply. Just why defensive war should be exceptional in this regard is not all that clear, though Bleich, after elaborate consideration, suggests that it has to do with the role of the *urim ve-tumim* being to establish a state of war in which innocent lives are put at risk.[61] Because in defensive war innocent lives have already been endangered, and the harmony shattered, by the aggressor, the legitimating function of the *urim ve-tumim* is no longer necessary.

One way of understanding these various provisions at a more general level is as a kind of "covering law" which sanctions war "only when there is sound military reason to assume that Israel will be victorious."[62] In the case of the explicitly commanded wars against Amalek and the Seven Nations, "sound military reason" for expecting victory would presumably entail little more than popular expression of faith in God as the legitimator of, and guardian in, these wars. Hence the special requirement in these wars that the *urim ve-tumim* be consulted, an institution whereby divine sanction for the proposed war may be established and the individual's faith reassured. In the case of defensive war, where, of course, the aggression has been perpetrated by the enemy, the precaution for Israel's likelihood of victory becomes superfluous. Neither the *urim ve-tumim* nor the Sanhedrin, accordingly, need be consulted in defensive wars. Finally, in discretionary wars, because they are *discretionary*, "sound military reason" had to be "publicly" assessed. Along with the need for divine sanction mediated through the *urim ve-tumim*, therefore, an intended discretionary war had to be appraised and ultimately determined by decision of the Sanhedrin, a body independent of the monarchy and concerned with the life and welfare of the community.

Though the satisfaction of these special provisions is necessary for an obligation to fight to be established, it should not be thought that it is, in this respect, sufficient. What the respective provisions really determine is, in Jewish terms, the justice of an intended war venture. If the provisions are satisfied, Jewish law bestows legitimacy upon the intended war. But the justness of a given war is not, in Jewish law, what determines whether or not an *individual* is obligated to fight for the state. This reposes in a separate process. As elucidated earlier, it is that process whereby in relation to the proclamation of the so-called exemptions an obligation on the part of each individual to fight is either created or rejected. The sole possible exception to this separation of the justness of war and the obligation to fight occurs with "commanded" wars, precisely because, according to the sages, the exemptions do not apply here. Still, it bears reemphasizing that some notable rabbinic authorities disagreed on this. And this disagreement is significant enough to conclude that Jewish law understands the justness of war and the obligation to fight to be essentially separate, albeit related, issues.

VIII

Compared with that of the classic Western thinkers, the Jewish approach to the question of the obligation to die for the state undoubtedly appears complicated and involved. Most of the complexities, however, reduce to a few simple principles, and these are what lend the Jewish approach its coherence and importance. Of course, to isolate such principles from the amalgam of Jewish laws, conventions, and institutions for the purposes of theoretical elaboration is, in some sense, to part from one of the most fundamental of all principles animating the mode of traditional Jewish thought. There is certainly irony in this, perhaps even a paradox, but I do not see that any further implication follows from it. This being understood, it is perhaps not too bold to claim that the Jewish approach to the issue of the obligation to fight suggests a certain "theory," what might be called a theory of "graded ultimate obligation." At the general level are the gradations in obligation that Judaism posits *between* categories of war. These vary from "commanded" wars, in which the legal and conventional pressures upon the individual to fight are extremely compelling, to "discretionary" wars, where, because of the process by which the so-called military exemptions take effect, each individual determines for himself whether he will assume an obligation to fight.

At another, more specific, level Judaism asserts there to be gradations in the obligations to fight *within* each of the war categories. Within "commanded" wars, the most obligatory kind of war seems to be defensive war. Though lacking the express divine sanction in the manner of the wars against Amalek and the Seven Nations, the fact that they are yet included in the same category attests to their overriding power in their claim upon the military support of all members of society. That neither of the traditional Jewish checks upon the justice of a proposed war encounter, the Sanhedrin and the *urim ve-tumim,* are required in defensive wars, is further testimony to their compelling nature.

The wars against Amalek and the Seven Nations represent in Jewish history, if not the founding, then the "grounding" of a nation. Ordained, as they were, by God Himself, their obligatory character is commanding. Only in the case of wars against Amalek, however, is the obligation to fight actually in behalf of the state, the wars against the Seven Nations being properly the concern of a personal obligation, the duty, that is, of each individual qua individual in his direct relation to God. It may be that Maimonides' formulation of a personal obligation to fight against the Seven Nations is significant precisely in that the stakes in establishing the nation territorially are so high, and the historical and moral implications for the people so momentous, that it was held that an individual could not be bound to risk his life for any other reason than God's, and his own, sake. But it does not follow from this that the obligation to fight against the Seven Nations is any more or less "compelling" than the obligation to fight against Amalek. Both are, after all, divinely commanded, as both are, in our day, purely formal commitments. All that can be said is that while the latter represents an obligation to die for the state, the former does not.

As to "discretionary" wars, the undisputed applicability of all four types of military exemption makes differentiating the extent of the obligation to fight in such cases on the whole superfluous. The inclusiveness of the fourth exemption levels out any obligation to fight until, in the end, it is self-imposed. Yet Jewish law nevertheless insists upon one gradation when it comes to optional military ventures: certain preemptive actions, sanctioned insofar as they are in the face of danger and do not jeopardize innocent lives, cannot be obligatory at all. Outside of the formal regulations pertaining to war, such campaigns do not even witness the process whereby the exemptions are heralded and the obligation to fight can become self-assumed. They are completely voluntary throughout every stage of their execution.

Judaism, then, effectively grades the obligation to fight from its strongest to its weakest conditions. So whether or not there is an obligation to die for the state is a question not susceptible of decisive resolution in the sense of being either (and always) one way or the other: it is a question whose answer must depend on the context in which the problem presents itself. And the lines of division here do not, or do not only, fall between just and unjust wars. They also, and chiefly, fall between different kinds of just wars. The overall effect is to preserve the individual's freedom to protect his life and property in all but the most critical war situations. The first three Deuteronomic exemptions—treating of the man who has built a house, planted a vineyard, and newly married— represent, in this regard, quite explicit safeguards of the individual's property and life affairs. Beyond this, the radical fourth exemption acts as the final guarantee of an individual's liberty to choose whether to commit himself to battle-duty. Only where the very survival of the community is threatened can such individual liberties be overridden.

In this fashion does Judaism overcome the dilemma plaguing Western theories of the obligation to die. Against those liberal theorists who assert that the state exists for the sake of individual purposes, Judaism asserts that individuals can, at critical times, be rightly asked to subordinate their personal lives to the shared life and values of the community. And against those theorists who argue that, because the state represents a shared life and set of values, the individual owes his life to it, Judaism asserts that, in all but the most critical war situations, the individual has his own life to lead and his own choices to make. By not assuming the superiority of the individual or of the collective in terms of the state's foundation or purpose, Judaism is, consistently, able to safeguard the "lives" of both. The state gives way to the freedom of the individual, as the freedom of the individual gives way to the survival of the state. The individual, that is, may legitimately be called upon (as against volunteer) to risk his life for the state, not because the state so commands, but when it is genuinely imperiled. That leaves open the question of who is to decide such a matter, a function seemingly only performed by the state. But the distinction remains a crucial one nevertheless. For in a way that an obligation to die riding upon simple state decree does not, the condition of genuine state imperilment at least allows for the possibility of contention. And when individuals' lives are at stake, that possibility assumes the utmost importance.

NOTES

1. Michael Walzer, "The Obligation to Die for the State," in *Obligations: Essays on Disobedience, War and Citizenship* (Cambridge, Mass., 1970), p. 89.
2. The argument that it was Hegel's view that war "serves as a sort of civic education" by its ability to reassert state interests over private ones has recently been advanced by Steven B. Smith, "Hegel's Views on War, the State, and International Relations," *American Political Science Review* 77 (1983): 624–632.
3. Roland de Vaux, *Ancient Israel: Its Life and Institutions* (London, 1973), p. 98.
4. Walzer, "Obligation to Die," p. 77.
5. Thomas Hobbes, *Leviathan* (London, 1979), chap. 21. Hobbes does attempt to make certain exceptions to his principle that there cannot be an obligation to die, but with questionable success. See Walzer's discussion, "Obligation to Die," pp. 84–88.
6. Jean-Jacques Rousseau, *The Social Contract*, trans. G. D. H. Cole (London, 1975), bk. II, chap. V, p. 189 (emphasis added).
7. Plato, *Crito*, trans. Hugh Tredennick (Middlesex, 1969), pp. 90–94.
8. On the consensual aspects of the biblical covenant, see Daniel J. Elazar's essay, "Covenant as the Basis of the Jewish Political Tradition," in his edited volume *Kinship and Consent: The Jewish Political Tradition and Its Contemporary Uses* (Ramat Gan, 1981).
9. "The Biblical suggestion, for example, that covenant is the only moral, and, therefore, the most durable root for a political community has in the form of the social contract, become a dominant, if not *the* dominant, metaphor for Western theory since the medieval period. While important social contract theorists do not always emphasize the Sinai Covenant some (i.e. Spinoza) make it their central focus and others (i.e., Hobbes) refer to it often." David C. Rapoport, "Moses, Charisma, and Covenant," *Western Political Quarterly* 32 (1979): 124. This article provides a good list of sources dealing with the relation between biblical covenants and modern notions of social contract.
10. These are cited and discussed in Michael Walzer's book, *Exodus and Revolution* (New York, 1985), esp. pp. 83–88. See also Gordon Freeman, "The Rabbinic Understanding of Covenant as a Political Idea," in Elazar, *Kinship and Consent*, pp. 68–73.
11. Pinhas Rosenbluth, "Political Authority and State in Jewish Thought,"

Immanuel 7 (1977): 101–113. For a more general discussion, see Isadore Epstein, *The Jewish Way of Life* (London, 1947).

12. The basic principle in this regard is *dina d'malkhuta dina* (literally, "the law of the kingdom is the law"), attributed in the Talmud to the third-century amora, Samuel. There is now a growing corpus of work investigating the application of this principle, although the specific question of the obligation to die for the state is mostly only implicitly rather than directly addressed. See Gerald Bildstein, "A Note on the Function of 'The Law of the Kingdom Is Law,' " in the Medieval Jewish Community," *Jewish Journal of Sociology* 15 (1973): 213–219; Leo Landman, *Jewish Law in the Diaspora: Confrontation and Accommodation* (Philadelphia, 1968); idem, "Civil Disobedience: The Jewish View," *Tradition* 10 (1969): 5–14; idem, "Dina D'Malkhuta Dina: Solely a Diaspora Concept," *Tradition* 15 (1975): 89–96; idem, "A Further Note on the Function of 'The Law of the Kingdom Is the Law,' " *Jewish Journal of Sociology* 17 (1975): 37–41; Aaron Rakefet-Rothkoff, "Dina D'Malkhuta Dina—The Law of the Land in Halakhie Perspective," *Tradition* 13 (1972): 5–23; and Shmuel Shilo, "Maimonides on 'Dina D'Malkhuta Dina (The Law of the State is the Law),' " *Jewish Law Annual* 1 (1978): 146–167.

13. All biblical references are to the King James Version.

14. de Vaux, *Ancient Israel*, p. 262.

15. When it transpires that the people remaining are still too numerous, God instructs Gideon to further "sift them" according to how they drink at a stream (Judg. 7:4–8).

16. Everett E. Gendler, "War and the Jewish Tradition," in *Contemporary Jewish Ethics*, ed. Menachem Marc Kellner (New York, 1978), p. 208. See also Johannes Pedersen, *Israel: Its Life and Culture*, vols. 3–4 (London, 1963), pp. 9–10.

17. The phrase is from James E. Priest, *Governmental and Judicial Ethics in the Bible and Rabbinic Literature* (New York and Malibu, Calif., 1980), p. 179, who, though employing it in the same context, fails to note that it represents but one side of "principles in tension."

18. de Vaux, *Ancient Israel*, p. 215.

19. Ibid., p. 263.

20. Tosefta, *Sanhedrin* 4:3; and *Sanhedrin* 20b. References to later rabbinic views on this issue are cited in Leo Landman, "Law and Conscience: The Jewish View," *Judaism* 18 (1969): 24, n. 46. Two recent views claiming Samuel's speech to be an indictment of monarchy are Louis Jacobs, "The Concept of Power in the Jewish Tradition," *Conservative Judaism* 33 (1980): 24–25, and Bruce Vawter, "A Tale of Two Cities: The Old Testament and the Issue of Personal Freedom," *Journal of Ecumenical Studies* 15 (1978): 266–267.

21. Gendler, "War and the Jewish Tradition," pp. 191–192. Cf. R. F. Clements, "The Deuteronomic Interpretation of the Founding of the Monarchy in I Sam. VIII," *Vetus Testamentum* 24 (1974): 398–410.

22. Walzer, "Obligation to Die," pp. 97, 98.

23. The expression is borrowed from Barrington Moore, Jr., in his summary (but apt) description of military obligations in the Old Testament. See his *Privacy: Studies in Social and Cultural History* (Armonk, N.Y., 1984), p. 188.

24. *Sotah* 44a.

25. Ibid.

26. Tosefta, *Sotah* 7:14.

27. For a statement of the affirmative and critical views, see respectively, Landman, "Law and Conscience," pp. 25–26, and Maurice Lamm, "After the War—Another Look at Pacifism and Selective Conscientious Objection (SCO)," in Kellner, *Contemporary Jewish Ethics*, pp. 237–238.

28. Hobbes, *Leviathan*, chap. 21, p. 115.

29. *Sotah* 44b. The exceptional use of terms is Rabbi Judah's. The exemptions apply, he says, "to the wars commanded by the Torah *[milhamot mitsvah]*; but in obligatory wars *[milhamot hovah]* all go forth." The Gemara explains that there is no real dispute between the sages and R. Judah about the kinds of wars meant by these terms, the latter's novel use of terms representing rather a dispute about whether involvement in a given type of war exempts a soldier from the performance of other commandments.

   The suggestion here that in commanded wars women can be conscripted to fight ("even brides go forth") is actually a far more complicated issue. So, too, there are complicating rabbinic rulings about the valid age-limits within which males can be conscripted (the most commonly cited being ages twenty to sixty). In speaking throughout this article of "individuals" being obligated to fight, such conditions attaching to age and sex should thus be borne in mind.

30. See respectively *Maimonides' Mishneh Torah, Book XIV: Judges*, ed. and trans. Philip Birnbaum (New York, 1967), Kings 7:1; Rabbi Ishmael, quoted by *Midrash Tannaim* 20:1 and 20:19; and Rabbi Zimra (Radbaz), *Hilkhot Melakhim* 7:1.

31. Cf. *Sotah* 44b and Maimonides, Kings 5:1; idem, *Sefer ha-Mitsvot, mitsvot aseh*, addenda, no. 4.

32. The communal obligation is formulated by Maimonides in Kings 5:1 and in *Sefer ha-Hinnukh*, no. 425, and the personal obligation in Kings 5:4 as well as in *Sefer ha-Hinnukh*, no. 425.

33. See, for example, Shlomoh Goren, *Torat ha-Mo'dim* (Tel Aviv, 5714 [1954]), pp. 180 ff.

34. Maimonides, Kings 5:1. I have quoted the translation given in Bleich, n. 35 below, p. 7.

35. J. David Bleich, "Preemptive War in Jewish Law," *Tradition* 21 (1981): 23. The various talmudic references associated with the law of *rodef* are cited by Bleich, p. 39, nn. 32–37.

36. Ibid., p. 18.

37. Ibid., p. 23.

38. Rakefet-Rothkoff, "Dina D'Malkhuta Dina," p. 13.
39. *Sanhedrin* 49a; Maimonides, Kings 3:8–9.
40. These include the view that the king "owns" the land and has the right to expel noncompliant citizens (R. Asher ben Yechiel, R. Nissim Gerundi, and R. Shlomoh ben Aderes to *Nederim* 28a); the view that a pact exists between subjects and their king, whereby they agree to follow his ordinances (Rashbam's commentary to *Baba Bathra*); and the view that the Noachide precept of "Laws" ordains the "rule of law" and the king's right to execute it (*Even haEzer* to Maimonides, *Nizkei Mammon* 8:5, based upon Rashi's commentary to *Gittin* 9b). It must be noted, however, that these arguments are mainly addressed to the matter of obedience to non-Jewish kings.
41. Hobbes, *Leviathan*, chap. 21, p. 115.
42. Maurice Lamm, " 'Red or Dead?' An Attempt at Formulating a Jewish Attitude," *Tradition* 4 (1962): 185.
43. *Midrash Tanhuma, Parshat Pinhas*, sec. 3. See also *Sanhedrin* 72a and *Berakhot* 58a, 62b.
44. *Sotah* 44b.
45. See respectively Lamm, "Red or Dead?", p. 182; Maimonides, Kings 5:1; *Berakhot* 3b and *Sanhedrein* 16a.
46. Writes Maimonides: "All those who went back home from among the troops, after hearing the priest's proclamation, return now and provide water and food for their fellow soldiers and fix the roads" (Kings 7:9). See also *Sotah* 43a (in which there is also the statement that those returning home do *not* supply the army with noncombat assistance), and Tosefta, *Sotah* 7:15. Despite Maimonides' inclusive description, all mishnaic references are to variations only of the first three Deuteronomic exemptions; the fourth *appears* to be excluded.
47. R. Avraham Yeshaya Karelitz, and R. Haim ben Atar, *Moed* 114:2.
48. *Sanhedrin* 2a; *Berakhot* 3b and *Sanhedrin* 16a.
49. Cf. Maurice Lamm, "After the War," p. 237: "But there is a sleeper in this affirmation of Jewish selective conscientious objection. It is true only on a *national* level, not on a *personal* one. Determination of the justice of a war was never left to individual decision. That burden devolved upon the state . . ." (emphasis in original). Lamm is, of course, talking of conscientious objection and not directly of the obligation to fight. But he tends to assume that an individual is obligated to fight inasmuch as a war is pronounced (at the national level) just. Conscientious objection—and hence a judgment about the justice or morality of war (or selective conscientious objection—a judgment about the justice or morality of certain wars)—is not, however, the only ground upon which an individual may dispute the call by his country to enter battle. He may simply reject the state's command for him to risk his life, irrespective of his or the state's views about the justice of the proposed war. I discuss the distinction in Jewish law between the question of the justice of war and of the obligation to fight in Section VII below.

50. Maimonides, *Sefer ha-Mitsvot, mitsvot aseh,* no. 191.

51. Bleich, "Preemptive War," p. 23, and n. 47 (p. 40).

52. Maimonides, Kings 7:2–4, from which the following quotations are drawn. A similar account is given in the Gemara, *Sotah* 42a–b.

53. *Sotah* 44a–b. See also Maimonides, Kings 7:4; and *Pentateuch with Rashi's Commentary,* trans. M. Rosenbaum and A. M. Silbermann (London, 1934), at Deut. 20:9.

54. Hobbes, *Leviathan,* chap. 21.

55. Rashi comments that the four scriptural admonitions in the face of battle correspond "to four things which the kings of the nations do *in battle:* . . . LET NOT YOUR HEARTS FAINT—through the neighing of the horses . . . FEAR NOT from *the noise made* by the clashing of the shields, . . . AND HURRY NOT PRECIPITATELY at the sounds of the trumpets . . . NEITHER BE TERRIFIED by the noise of the shouting (Siphre: Sota 42a, b)" (*Rashi's Commentary,* trans. M. Rosenbaum and A. M. Silbermann, at Deut. 20:3).

56. *Sotah* 44b.

57. My discussion here is based on Bleich, "Preemptive War," esp. pp. 18–30.

58. Ibid., pp. 24–25, 29–30.

59. The respective obligations to fight against Amalek and the idolatrous Seven Nations would, in any case, appear nowadays to be purely formal ones, given the impossibility of identifying the descendants of these ancient peoples. See Maimonides, Kings 5:4–5, and the discussion of this issue in J. David Bleich, *Contemporary Halakhic Problems* (New York, 1977), pp. 17–18.

60. Ramban (Nahmanides) in his addenda to Maimonides' *Sefer ha-Mitsvot,* no. 17, and Maimonides, *Sefer ha-Mitsvot, shoresh* 14, cited in Bleich, *Contemporary Halakhic Problems,* p. 16. There is some question among commentators whether the war against Amalek requires the intervention of the *urim ve-tumim,* but this appears to relate to Amalek as a symbol of evil rather than to the Amalekites as a specific nation. See Bleich's discussion, ibid., pp. 16–18.

61. Bleich, "Preemptive War," pp. 28–29.

62. Ibid., p. 25.

15

Who Pays? The Talmudic Approach to Filial Responsibility

Michael Chernick

The Talmud is the great wellspring of the sources of Jewish life, learning, and spiritual values. Its style tends to be nonlinear and highly discursive. These features, no less than the Talmud's Aramaic text, have tended to close this marvelous work to many contemporary Jews. That this is a cultural and spiritual loss will become obvious, I believe, in the course of this examination of a Talmudic passage. Rather than bemoan this situation, I hope this presentation will encourage Jews to reclaim what is rightfully theirs: the values and life wisdom of the Jewish experience.

Secondly, the Jewish way has been to translate values into deeds. Therefore, Talmud's primary form of expression is cases, not high-sounding pronouncements. To discover the Talmud's spiritual message one must search between its lines, to analyze its case law and arguments for the underlying bases of the different opinions it presents. This will be our task in the next few pages, and here's how we will try to go about it. 1) We shall present the text in translation with a running commentary. 2) We will try to investigate the Jewish legal implications of the text. That is, what, under Jewish law, would be required of us? 3) We will try to discover what values and spiritual convictions caused the various rabbis who speak in the text to arrive at their opinions. This will take us into the area of Talmudic literature called *aggadah:* roughly, lore and religious philosophy.

Reprinted by permission of Plenum Press from *The Journal of Aging and Judaism,* volume 1, number 2, Spring/Summer 1987.

THE TEXT: TRACTATE KIDDUSHIN 31b–32a

Text: Our rabbis taught: What constitutes respect for parents and what constitutes honoring them?

Commentary: In Exodus 20:11 it states: "Honor your father and your mother that you may lengthen your days on the land which the Eternal, your God, has given you." In Leviticus 19:3 we find, "Each person shall respect (lit., fear) his/her mother and father, and you shall keep My sabbaths." These verses are the background for the question above.

Text: Respect is observed by not standing in the parent's usual place, nor sitting where they normally sit, by not contradicting the parent's words, and by not interfering in a parent's dispute with others.

Commentary: Noninterference in a dispute between a parent and others is interpreted differently by various commentators. Rashi, the Talmud's most famous interpreter, held that a child should not side against the parent. The Shulhan Arukh, the major code of Jewish law, suggests that a child should not even support the parent's position in an argument with others. This latter view was prompted by the sense that taking the opponent's side was not different from contradicting the parent. Hence, noninterference had to mean something other than siding against one's parent in a dispute. The view is very interesting, and we shall return to it in our analysis of this text as a whole.

Text: Honoring one's parents is observed by helping them to eat and drink, clothing and covering them, and helping them to go in and out.
  A question was raised by the Rabbis: Who pays for this? [lit., From whom?] R: Judah said, "The child." R. Nathan b. Oshaiah said, "The parent."

Commentary: The question relates to the commandment of honor since, as it was defined, it entails expenditures for food and clothing. Obviously, the parent who needs to be fed, clothed, and accompanied by another is of fairly advanced age. The "child" is an adult child since minors are not obliged to observe the commandments according to Jewish law.

Text: The Rabbis ruled according to the opinion that the parent must pay [in answer to a legal query raised by] R. Jeremiah. There are those that say [in answer] to R. Jeremiah's son.
  This ruling was challenged by the following source: The Torah states, "Honor your father and mother," and Proverbs states, "Honor the Eternal with

your wealth" (Prov. 3:9). Just as "honor" in regard to God means through monetary expenditure, so "honor" in regard to a parent means through monetary expenditure.

If the parent is to pay, in what way does the child observe the requirement to pay for his/her parent's honor? [The answer is:] through time given up from gainful pursuits.

Commentary: Though two opinions regarding who bears financial responsibility for an aged parent appear in the Talmud, the generally accepted preference was for the parent to pay for his/her food and clothing needs. This ruling stood in conflict with an older tradition which stated that children must honor their parents by spending on them. In order to maintain harmony between the two positions, the later Talmudic teachers claimed that the child's financial outlay took the form of loss of work time and the profits it might bring. The child, then, was expected to help feed and clothe the parent if that was necessary. The food and clothing, however, was paid for by the parent.

ANALYSIS OF THE TEXT AS A WHOLE

The Talmudic text has introduced us to a number of concepts. "Respect" and "honor," for example, are not emotions for the Talmud. Rather, they are concrete acts directed toward different aspects of the parent as human being. The acts which constitute "respect" are directed toward the parent's psyche. The acts subsumed under "honor" are directed to the physical needs of the parent. Thus, the emotional and physical well-being of the aged parent is the focus of Talmudic concern. Mere lip service to these issues is insufficient. Feeling respecful or feeling honor are not central to the Talmud. Rather, acting in a way which makes the parent feel that s/he is a significant and special person to the child is what Jewish law demands. Note, the Talmud does not preclude an internalized sense of respect and honor for one's parents. Indeed, it might even encourage it, but the central focus here is proper action, the most basically ethical behavior toward those who made one's life possible.

The Talmud's unwillingness to understand the Torah's commands of honor and respect as emotional is, I believe, greatly insightful. It recognizes that no one, not even God, can command the emotions of another. We feel what we feel. We can do little else. But appropriate and proper behavior, that is another matter. We can act as we should. It may take effort and will, but in the end we are the masters of our actions. Therefore, the realm of actions is the appropriate concern of *mitzvot*, commandments. To a great degree, this leaves the question of how one feels about one's parents out of the issue, and rightly so. All children feel ambivalent feelings towards their parents. How else can it be when the parent has been provider but also disciplinarian, compassionate supporter but also implacable judge? The Talmudic message is, in the face of this, that if one's parents were decent parents, complicated feelings about them do not provide excuses for inappropriate responses to their needs, emotional or physical. To no less a degree the Talmudic approach removes from children the burden of guilt for negative feelings about their parents. These may be inevitable, but, for Jewish law and thought, they are beside the point. In essence, what one actually does in the relationship between parent and child is ethically more significant than what one feels at any given moment.

The question "Who pays?" also leads to some consideration of the Talmudic way of doing things. Clearly, the Talmud is eminently pragmatic. If it determines that honor is observed by physical support in the forms of feeding, clothing, and accompanying, then its pragmatic thinkers and contributors ask the question "Who pays for this?" They knew that ethics cannot survive without realistic programs and "game plans" for carrying them out. This, too, is part of the rabbinic genius. The sages not only state the moral imperative, they also give some meaningful attention to the way such an imperative might be implemented.

Now to the argument over "Who pays?" itself. We note that there are two views, R. Judah's and R. Nathan b. Oshaiah's. On the face of the matter it would appear that R. Judah's view should prevail. After all the command to honor is directed toward the child! Therefore, let the child pay for the parent's honor. Indeed, one wonders what prompted R. Nathan b. Oshaiah to propound his position. Yet, in answering a question in regard to the final decision in this case, the prevailing rabbinic view was that a parent should pay for the physical elements of his or her honor. Why?

It is here that other elements of the passage come into play. We noted above that the Talmud found in the two different verses regarding the relationship of child to parent two different modes of the relationship, the psychological and the physical. "Respect," to reiterate, demands action which allows the parent to feel specially valued and revered. "Respect" from the child is meant to encourage a sense of worth, even power, in the parent. That is why the interpretation of the Shulhan Arukh regarding this passage is so striking. As noted above, it understands the noninterference of the child in the disputes of the parent as the child's resisting involvement *in support of the parent's position*. One wonders why, out of respect, one would be "nonsupportive" in such a case.

The answer lies in the result. Let us say the parent wins the dispute. There will always be that nagging doubt that it was not on his or her own merit that he or she won. Rather, the "win" might be due to the child's presence or strength or intelligence. In short, the parent has to contend with the possibility that he cannot fight his own battles. It may even be true, but how does this "supported" parent feel. The parental role is to support children, fight their battles, protect and defend them. The inversion of roles has to be painful for a parent, especially if he or she is factually in need of such support. Herein lies the point of juncture between the commandments of "respect" and "honor."

Let us again picture the parent who needs to be fed, clothed, and brought in and out by another person. That is the picture of a person whose physical capabilities are now extremely limited. An adult life of self-direction and self-support is no longer possible. One's sense of dignity in such a situation is frontally attacked. One is forcibly turned back into a child, at least at the physical level. The psychic degradation can be no less than horrendous. Now the question "Who pays?" points to more than the practical details of handling the commandment of "honor." It points to the facets of self-worth, control, and decision-making which are the components of independence, the very thing which the incapacitated aged lack.

Money is one of the most highly charged commodities known to humankind. It symbolizes value at more than the economic level. The Talmudic world understood that when it punned about money which is sometimes called *damim* in Hebrew. "*Damim* is a double-entendre," the sages said, because it means both money and blood. And "the blood is the life." This is not a statement which means that money is worth everything or that life is money. But it is a statement that money makes independence possible. Independence fosters a sense of self-worth, and self-worth makes life meaningful. For a child to say to a greatly diminished parent "I'll pay" when the parent still has personal assets is murderous. It kills the parental self. Here is the last framework in which the parent can be a self-directing, self-supporting person, and the child refuses to allow him or her that right and pleasure. "Who pays for accoutrements of honor?" If the *mitzvah* to revere one's parents means anything, then the parent pays if he or she can. This is what R. Nathan b. Oshaiah understood. This is what the Rabbis accepted as law.

But what is the child to do? The tradition demands that s/he give something tangible to the parent in order to fulfill the command to honor. Indeed the Talmudic answer is succinct and powerful: more than your money which is a mere external when all is said and done, give your time, your presence, your services. The moments taken from your own valuable time—and time, of all things, is truly life—share that with your parents if you wish to honor them. If they are not incapacitated physically, let them do for themselves, decide for themselves. They have been doing that for all their independent, adult lives. Remember that it is not our role, no matter how tempting in order to finally claim our independence, to diminish our parents in the guise of "caring for" them. Here, the Talmud's lore is most to the point: There are children who feed their parents pheasant and drive them from the world-that-is. And there are children who cause their parents to grind at the millstone and grant them the world-to-come (Kiddushin 31a–b).

SPIRITUAL AND PHILOSOPHICAL IMPLICATIONS

As we have seen, the question "Who pays." points to a Jewish concern for human dignity and self-worth. It asks people in positions of relative strength to remember that others once had that strength and to consider what its loss means. Once having done that, Jewish ethics demands that we act in light of the recognition of how hurtful such loss is. But why this concern for dignity? Is it not enough that the aged be cared for by whatever means? Here we enter the realm of the spiritual and philosophical background which leads to the question "Who pays?"

For a moment I would like to approach the issue of Jewish concerns negatively. The stake of Judaism in the value of the individual is not predicated on the pragmatic attitude of "What have you done for me lately? What can you do for me now?" Nor is the concern prophylactic in the sense that I must behave properly toward my aged parents lest my children learn how to deal with me improperly when I am old. Rather, the Jewish message of this Talmudic passage is something else. That something else is rooted in the Jewish conception of the creation of humanity in God's Image.

What do we mean when we speak of God's Image? Obviously, it does not mean "in God's form" since the Torah reminds Israel repeatedly that it saw no form when God revealed himself/herself at Sinai. Philosophers have sought to explain God's Image as the ability to reason. Yet, Judaism holds that mentally defective human beings are no less created in the Divine Image. That is why murdering such persons would call forth the full penalty of the law (see Gen. 9:6). No, the Image of God is more subtle. It rests in the characteristic of God which Jews proclaim twice daily as the central theological statement of Judaism: "Hear, Israel, the Eternal is our God, the Eternal is One!" That oneness is not merely unity, a thought that gained prominence only after trinitarian thinking became central to Christianity, but uniqueness. The exclamation of Israel after being saved from the Egyptians at the Sea, "Who is comparable to You among those revered as gods, Eternal God, who is like You, great in holiness?," is the finest commentary on the meaning of God's oneness and God's Image.

In light of this, when we speak of people being created in God's Image we mean that each person is absolutely unique and therefore endowed with inestimable worth. Who can replace the unique? Indeed, how can one begin to set its value? This is the core of the Jewish antipathy to counting people expressed both in Jewish lore and Jewish life. Yiddish speakers know how *"nisht eins, nisht tzvei,"* "not one, not two," becomes a circumlocution for "one person, two people, etc." For after all is said and done, Jewish values teach us that people can only be counted "one, one, one. . . ." Lowering a person's value in his or her own eyes, contributing to another's degradation in any way, these are crimes not only against the individual according to Jewish teaching, but affronts to God. Indeed, lowering oneself in one's own estimation is a failure to see oneself as what one really is: an Image of God, worth everything and worthy of everything.

What are the implications of all this for adult children and elderly parents? What is the meaning of these teachings for the care of the aged? First, the relationship of adult child to diminished parent cannot become one of inverted roles, not, at least, until it must. A parent who is old is still an adult. What life has taken away in terms of capabilities does not mean total incapacity until that state is truly reached. Whatever abilities remain which allow the aged to work, to do, to care for themselves and others must be given full rein. Any other attitude or ambience effaces the Divine Image and, thereby, destroys the life of the aged. "Who pays?" is answered by "The child" only when no choices exist. Then, knowingly, the Talmud calls the payment by its rightful name in terms of how it inevitably makes the parent feel: *tzedakah,* the closest that Hebrew can come to "charity." When choices exist, children and agencies must support independence in as many areas as possible for the aged.

Second, children are also created in God's Image. Their lives cannot be swallowed up by the crushing of their individuality under impossible burdens created by parents. Indeed, the commandments of respect and honor are incumbent upon children only when parents observe the commandments required of them. An attack upon the source of Jewish values, the Torah, by the parent invalidates the parent's rights provided by that source. Parents who have been irresponsible, cruel, neglectful, and harming to their children have failed to uphold their obligations in Jewish law and practice to their children. Hence they have forfeited the "honor" and "respect" with which Jewish law entitles them. Yet, there are cases of unforeseen and unintended tragedy between children and aging or aged parents. The legal codes of Judaism know this and deal with such circumstances thus:

One whose parent has become incompetent should try to deal with him/her according to his/her condition until s/he is healed. But if it is impossible for the child to bear because the parent is so radically changed, the child may go and leave the parent in the care of others.

The principle is clear. The child must do whatever is possible to carry out the requirements of "honor" and "respect" toward a decent parent. But when the parent begins to destroy the child, even in cases where the parent is not consciously doing so, the child may save himself or herself and observe the command to "honor ," that is, care for the parent, by proxy. In such a case, the child "respects" the parent best by warding off the development of such hostility toward the parent that breaches of filial responsibility will become inevitable, destroying both parties' sense of worth, love, and dignity.

In conclusion, it is clear that the relationship of parents and adult children is a complicated affair. The Talmudic sages knew this to be so, hinting that "honor" and "respect" for parents had to be commanded since they were not particularly natural responses on the part of children (Kiddushin 30b–31a). Rational use of parental prerogatives was not always gainsaid either. Hence, the Talmud placed those who struck their adult children under a ban, the equivalent of "shunning," for virtually tempting their children to sin by retaliating in kind (Mo'ed Katan 17a and Codes).

The so-called "generation gap" was not born yesterday. The intricacies of parent-child relations and appropriate and proper behavior in them were never less than complex. Because this is so, the ancient Talmud's reasonable, down-to-earth "Who pays?" and all the deep and rich spiritual background surrounding it, have much to teach us in this age of perplexed ethical and practical thinking about the aged and their care.

D

Classical Studies

16

Letter and Spirit in Jewish and Roman Law

Boaz Cohen

"No idea" said John Lightfoot[1] (1602–1675) "is more familiar to us than the distinction between the spirit and the letter . . . Yet, so far as I am aware, it occurs in St. Paul for the first time. No doubt the idea was floating in the air before. But he fixed it, he made it current coin." Lightfoot is referring to the celebrated epigram: "for the letter killeth, but the spirit giveth life."[2]

In trying to divine the meaning of an ancient writer, the trouble is, to use the words of Whitehead[3] "not with what the author does say, but with what he does not say. Also it is not with what he knows he has assumed, but with what he has unconsciously assumed. We do not doubt the author's honesty. It is his perspicacity which we are criticizing." It is Paul's unconscious assumptions[4] which we wish to bring out into the open in this brief study.

Speech is, as has been aptly said, a complication in nature. The sense and essence of a statement charged with an atmosphere of suggestion, by a mind as volatile as Paul's, can only be rightly apprehended by reverting to the environment in which it was first uttered. Before we proceed to disclose the nature of the dialectic which determined Paul's famous aphorism, let us examine the pattern into which Paul had designed the contrast between Letter and Spirit.

In an epistle to the Roman community, he justified the abolition of the rite of circumcision by the argument that the Scriptural command

Reprinted by permission of Barbara Cohen from *Jewish and Roman Law,* Jewish Theological Seminary of America, New York, 1966.

was only intended to be taken allegorically. To quote his own words:[5] "And shall not uncircumcision, which is by nature, if it fulfil the law, judge thee, who by the letter and circumcision dost transgress the law ... And circumcision is of the heart, in the spirit, and not in the letter." Paul's view that one who deliberately neglected circumcision, but otherwise fulfils the law, may criticize one who is circumcized, but otherwise transgresses the law, may result from a misunderstanding of the rabbinic ruling[6] that the ritual slaughter of an animal by an uncircumcized Jew is fit. According to one interpretation preserved in the Talmud,[7] this statement refers to one who defiantly violates the rite of circumcision.[8]

Paul justified the abolition of circumcision by the argument, first, that it is against nature,[9] and secondly, that Scripture itself by using the expression "and ye shall circumcise the foreskin of your heart"[10] implies that this command is to be understood in a spiritual sense. Paul was anticipated in this view by the radical Alexandrinian allegorists,[11] who interpreted away the literal sense of the law, and explained circumcision symbolically. The view of this group had been combatted by Philo who declared that "we have no right to annul the law which had been given regarding circumcision, and we must take heed of the words literally, in order to understand those things of which the laws are the symbols."

Secondly, in a letter to an audience in Rome, he proclaims[12] that the new Christians, exempt from adhering to the law, are required to observe the new dispensation[13] in spirit only, as the old dispensation was to have been observed in the letter. But now that we are set free from the law which is dead[14] wherein we were held down, that we should serve in the newness of spirit and not in the oldness of the letter.[15] In a missive to the people of Corinth,[16] he sets forth the thesis that he was divinely appointed to be a minister of the New Testament "not of the letter, but of the spirit, for the letter killeth, but the spirit giveth life."[17] As is well known, Paul made frequent allusions to Roman law in his writings.[18] In this passage, Paul is playing with the legal notion that a testament[19] (diatheke)[20] may be abrogated by a subsequent testament, and that a will is to be interpreted according to the spirit and not according to the letter. It is noteworthy that in the celebrated *Causa Curiana*, in 93 B.C.E., it was the jurist Quintus Scaevola, who defended the letter of the will[21] and the orator L. Crassus who insisted that it should be interpreted according to the spirit.[22]

Similarly, the Hebrew Scriptures or at least the ritual part was abrogated in the eyes of Paul, and the New Testament[23] was to be interpreted according to the spirit. This doctrine of Paul was known to the rabbis who combatted it in a very subtle manner. In an imaginary colloquy[24] between the Torah and the Deity, related by R. Simon ben Yoḥai, the Torah complains to God: King Solomon has challenged my plain meaning and fastened upon me the stigma of a forgery.[25] You have written in your Law, any Testament which is partly annulled, is entirely void.[26] Now Solomon has philosophized about the intent and purpose of your laws and reasoned thus: Why did God prohibit a king from marrying many wives, lest they turn aside his heart,[27] I can marry many wives without incurring this risk. But in his old age he did succumb to their temptation.[28] To this the Deity replied: Solomon and hundreds like him will pass away, but not a letter of the law will be abrogated.[29] The polemical tendency of this colloquy is obvious from the fact that the Torah is compared to a testament[30] just as was done by Paul.

The twofold argument of Paul that the Torah is a Testament that was annulled, and that a testament should be interpreted according to its spirit was answered as follows. First, there is the divine assurance that not a single letter of the law will ever be abolished, let alone the entire law. Secondly, the interpretation of the law according to the spirit was attempted by Solomon, the wisest of all men, and he went astray, how much more dangerous it is for mortals with less wisdom. Another attempt to counter Paul's argument may be detected in the statement of R. Abin b. Kahana, who explained that the new covenant (Jer. 31:10) refers to the new law implied in Isa. 51:4. God said: A new law will proceed from me, that is, new interpretations of the law will proceed in the time to come.[31]

Paul contradicted himself, when he claimed that the promise made to the seed of Abraham could not be annulled. Using the argument *a fortiori*,[32] he argued as follows: "Brethren, I speak after the manner of men. Though it be but a man's testament yet, if it be confirmed none disannulleth, or addeth thereto" (Galatians 3:15). How much more is it true, he argues, of the promise given to Abraham,[33] which was confirmed before God.[34]

The phrase contrasting the letter and the spirit of the law is original with Paul, but the terms of the antithesis were borrowed from Jewish sources. The conception underlying it may be traced to the early Greek writers antecedent to Aristotle, and was a commonplace[35] in the Greco-Roman world in the time of Paul.

The term spirit in connection with the law, not found in Greek and Roman sources, was unquestionably suggested to Paul by Isa. 28:5–6, where it is said that the Lord of Hosts will be a crown of glory and a diadem of beauty unto the remnant of his people and the spirit of the law (inspiring) him who sits in judgment.[36]

Similarly, the term letter with respect to law, Paul undoubtedly heard in Jewish circles. Commenting upon Deut. 12:2, "You should destroy the shrines of the nations whom you will dispossess," the rabbis say: Scripture should be interpreted according to the letter. Israel should not say, since we are required to destroy all the idols, then it behooves us to search every pit, well and cave, hence Scripture says: "Upon the high mountains and hills," only what is visible but not what is concealed.[37] Likewise, in the imaginary colloquy cited above, it is stated that not a single letter of the law will ever be abrogated.[38]

The letter of the law is used in several senses by the rabbis. First, it signifies that the law is to be understood literally, in its plain grammatical sense. Secondly, it means that a mere change of a letter in the text may alter the entire law. R. Meir, who was famed as a scribe as well as a scholar, was cautioned: If you omit or add one letter in copying the scroll of the law, you may destroy the whole world ('Er. 13a). Thirdly, it includes the interpretation of the redundancy of a single letter of the law. R. Akibah said to R. Ishmael: Brother,[39] I derive the rule from the pleonastic use of the letter Vav. To which R. Ishmael rejoined: Just because you find the letter Vav superfluous, shall we execute the adulterous daughter of the priest by burning (Sanh. 51b).

In the theory of the rabbis,[40] redundancy in Scripture was not accidental but deliberate, and is a form of emphasis, in the sense in which Quintilian defines the term, "emphasis succeeds in revealing a deeper meaning than is actually expressed by the words. There are two kinds of emphasis: the one means more than it says, the other often means something which it does not say."[41]

Paul therefore in this use of the terms letter and spirit of the Law drew upon contemporary Jewish tradition, but he invested them with significance derived from their equivalents *rhetos* and *dianoia*[42] in Greek rhetoric. Paul, who was as much concerned with gaining adherents among the Jews as among Gentiles,[43] coined the antithesis between letter and spirit instead of availing himself of the commonplaces of the rhetoric of his time.

The antithesis[44] between letter and spirit may be traced back to Protagoras (481–411 B.C.E.), who contrasted intent with literalness as Diogenes Laertius (IX.52) tells us, "In his argumentation, he by-passed the intention in favor of the literal meaning." Lysias too, argues before the judges that they should be concerned not with mere words but with the meaning.[45]

Aristotle, in his reflections upon the nature of law and its relation to justice, was attracted to the theory which contrasted the letter with the spirit of the Law.[46] According to him, considerations of equity should enter into the interpretation of the law, when it is defective because of its generality, or if it is a difficult case,[47] where the law is clear, but its application would result in injustice. This can be done by interpreting the law according to its spirit and not its letter.

With regard to the first instance, Aristotle[48] says: The law takes into its purview the majority of cases.[49] When therefore a case arrives which is an exception to the rule it is right to rectify the defect by deciding, as the lawgiver himself would decide, if he were present. Hence it follows logically that it is equitable to look not to the letter of the law, but to the intention of the legislator.[50] Secondly, with regard to the hard case, Aristotle[51] says: If the written law is counter to our case we must have recourse to the general law and equity, which are more in harmony with justice, and we must argue, that to decide according to the best of one's judgment[52] does not mean to abide entirely by the written law.[53] Equity is justice that goes beyond the written law.[54]

The antithesis between letter and spirit, which Aristotle has based on a philosophical understanding of the law, influenced all subsequent thinking on the subject. It is important to recall that the ancient Greeks were reluctant to alter their laws. This was partly due to their belief in its divine ancestry.[55] In any event, the possibility of interpreting the law according to its intention (*dianoia*) did help much.

Hermagoras, a rhetorician (about 150 B.C.E.), following in the footsteps of Aristotle, defines the contrast between the letter and the spirit, as the letter and the exception, or as Quintilian[56] puts it, *Legales autem quaestiones has fecit, scripti et voluntatis (quam ipse vocat kata rheton kai upexaires in) id est dictum et exceptionem.*[57] Hermogenes[58] (2nd century B.C.E.) seems to be the first author to use the antithesis *rhetos kai dianoia* to designate letter and spirit.

Aristeas,[59] too, is undoubtedly aware of the contrast between *rhetos* and *dianoia* as is implicit in his use of the term *dianoia* when he writes to Philocrates concerning the symbolical reason why calves, rams and he-goats are brought as sacrifices. He remarks: I have been induced by your love of learning to clarify the sanctity and the natural meaning of the law. Philo,[60] too, utilizes the contrast between *rhetos* and *dianoia* in the following passage: For each of these three individuals there is concealed in the narrative about them a literal as well as a symbolical meaning.[61]

Sextus Empiricus (who flourished during the second century C.E.) brings this contrast to the forefront in his criticism that rhetoricians are against the laws. For at one time they advise us to attend to the words of the lawgiver, at another time they advise to follow neither the ordinance nor the words but the intention. . . . Hence also, the Byzantine orator, when asked "How goes the Byzantian's law? replied "As I choose." [62] In Paul's time *rhetos* and *dianoia* was the usual Greek form of the antithesis between letter and spirit.

Greek rhetoric was introduced in Rome about the second century B.C.E. and its philosophical principles exercised some influence upon the lawyers in the time of Cicero. The task of the rhetoricians was to furnish the advocates with arguments *utramque partem disputare*.[63] In connection with the interpretation of laws, written documents, and oral agreements, five types of disputes were usually distinguished: namely those revolving on the question of ambiguity, letter and spirit, conflict of laws, syllogistic reasoning and definition.[64] We propose to summarize in the briefest possible manner the analysis of the question of letter and spirit as found in the rhetoricians. The Latin equivalents for *rhetos* and *dianoia* are *scriptum* and *sententia* or *voluntas* as Quintilian[65] informs us. In case of litigation, the question that first arises is: does the dispute concern the facts or the law.[66]

The main problems that occupied the rhetoricians were: first, how did a discrepancy arise between the letter and spirit of the law, and secondly, which should prevail.[67] As for the first question: First in importance is the element of ambiguity.[68] While calculated ambiguity serves a purpose in puns, politics and poetry, it is a perplexing problem in legal and logical discourse. Some writers were of the opinion that ambiguity was always involved in a dispute between letter and spirit,[69] for example, a thief should refund four times the amount of the theft.[70]

The question may arise even when the law is clear[71] *(ex manifesto)* e.g., children shall support their parents under penalty of imprisonment.[72] Jerome translated Deut. 17:8 ("If a case is too baffling for you . . .") *Si difficile et ambiguum apud te judicium.* There is no Hebrew word corresponding to *ambiguum*[73] in the text.

Secondly, contradictory laws which the Greeks call *antinomia* give rise to the question,[74] when one party may insist on the letter, the other on the intention[75] or both parties may attack the letter and raise the question of intention.[76] Thirdly, the *ratiocinatio*[77] provoked the question of letter versus spirit, that is where a gap in the law must be filled by a process of deduction which corresponds to the *casus omisus* in English law.

Fourthly, there is the matter of definition. Definition is the simplest way to exhibit the meaning of a word, but it must stop somewhere, and means nothing at all unless it does stop. Hence definitions must be of a general nature[78] and therefore constitute in themselves a form of ambiguity since they may bring out two meanings in the same term.[79] Consequently, the question arises, (1) when there is a doubt as to what a term includes, e.g. is a man, caught in a brothel with another man's wife, an adulterer?[80] (2) what term is to be applied, for instance, is the stealing of private property from the temple theft or sacrilege?[81] (3) What about the motive? Is he guilty of sacrilege who tore down arms dedicated to the temple to enable him to drive the enemy from the city?[82]

As for the problem, which should prevail, when there is a discrepancy between letter and spirit, the following should be noted. The abstract question whether to stand by the letter or the spirit could be argued indefinitely without reaching any conclusion.[83] The question very often was purely academic, being invented in the schools for a special purpose.[84] However, with respect to concrete cases, it may be said, that sometimes one follows the letter, and sometimes the spirit of the law.[85] The rhetorical writers furnished the advocates with arguments on both sides of the case, so that the latter could choose those that would best serve the interests of their clients.[86]

In the following, we merely note some of the principal arguments in favor of following the spirit rather than the letter of the law. First, when the letter of the law is contrary to equity and the public welfare.[87] There are some things which are not laudable *(laudibilum)* in themselves, but are permitted by the law.[88] Witness the passage in the Twelve Tables authorizing creditors to divide up a debtor's body among themselves,[89] a law which is repudiated by public custom *(mos publicus)*. There are certain things which are equitable but are prohibited by law, witness the restrictions placed on testamentary dispositions.[90]

Secondly, when it is against nature.[91] Thirdly when it is against custom.[92] Fourthly when a particular case should be regarded as an exception.[93] The *ius singulare* (D. I.3.16) is a form of an exception and may not serve as a precedent (D. 50.17.141).[94]

The Roman jurists were influenced to some extent by the rhetorical doctrine of *scriptum* and *voluntas* and their theory concerning ambiguity, as is evident from numerous passages in the Digest.[95] It is worthy of note that Ulpian employs the phrase *rhetos* and *dianoia*[96] as if it were a well known expression that needed no further explanation. Unlike the orators who were interested in victory, and could speak on either side of the case, *"ex utraque causae parte dicatur,"*[97] the jurists were interested in a just interpretation and decision. Hence, the jurist stigmatized as fraud the circumvention of the law by adhering to the letter of the law at the expense of its intention.[98]

Ulpian observes that the expression "according to the laws, refers to the spirit as well as to the letter of the law, *ex legibus sic accipiendum est: tam ex legum sententia quam ex verbis."*[99] According to Celsus, the laws should be interpreted liberally in order that their spirit be preserved.[100] Hence with respect to agreements[101] and the interpretation of wills,[102] the intention of the contracting parties or of the testator should be liberally construed.

With regard to ambiguity, the jurists expressed their views quite clearly. "Whenever a passage," says Julian, "has two meanings, we accept the one which is best adopted *(aptior)* to the case."[103] Celsus was of the opinion, that when the law was ambiguous, an interpretation that was in keeping with its intention should be put upon it.[104] Marcellus held that in case of ambiguity, we should adopt a liberal interpretation, which was no less just than safe.[105]

An oblique reference to the *ratiocinatio*[106] of the rhetoricians may be detected in Julian's[107] observation upon the specious syllogism. The kind of sophistry[108] which the Greeks[109] called *sorites*[110] consists in deducing from premises which are evidently true, by means of trifling changes, conclusions which are clearly false. The conflict between *scriptum* and *voluntas* ultimately became expressed in the antithesis between strict law and equity.[111] One of the tasks of *aequitas* is to preclude too strict an interpretation of the law, which was introduced for the public welfare *(pro utilitate hominum)* lest it result in hardship.[112]

In Biblical times, the laws pertaining to the rights and obligations of man in civil society were usually termed *mishpat*.[113] The lawgiver required that the judges be impartial and incorruptible (Lev. 19:15, Deut. 1:17) and render honest decisions (Deut. 16:19). In the earliest period it may be assumed that the judgments followed the strict line of the law. "I shall make the law[114] the line, and justice the plummet" (Isa. 28:17). As a Latin rhetorician[115] put it: it is useless to make laws if one can discuss their justice before a judge.

However, in the course of time it was realized that adhering to the strict law might not accomplish the purpose of the law which was justice and the welfare of society.[116] The prophet could envisage no worse punishment for Israel for their refusal to obey the divine law, than their forced submission to bad and intolerable laws (Ezek. 20:25).[117] Did not Scripture point with pride to the fact that Hebraic statutes and Laws were incomparably just (Deut. 4:8)?[118] The discrepancy between law and justice was duly noted by the prophets who continually stressed the importance of combining law and justice. David was extolled by the historical writers for his exemplary dispensation of justice.[119]

In order to combine law with justice the principle of equity came into being.[120] Equity is based on an understanding of the intent of the law.[121] In Scripture we recognize three terms which correspond to equity, each stressing a particular aspect. First *mishor*[122] and the plural form *mesharim*[123] are derived from *yashar*[124] to make straight,[125] to rectify. It is likely that this meaning of equity became attached to *mishor* because it denoted the rectification of the unevenness of the law, engendered by the application of the strict law.

Secondly, the term *mishpat 'emet*[126] the judgment of truth,[127] signifies laws which are truly just and morally right, in contradistinction to *mishpat* pure and simple, which is scrupulously correct and legal. Thirdly, the law of peace,[128] views the end[129] of law specifically to be the preservation of peace[130] in behalf of which a relaxation of the strict law is sometimes necessary. Isaiah portrays the future judicial activity of the Messiah as one in which equity plays the most significant role, "And he shall not judge after the sight of his eyes.[131] Neither decide after the hearing of his ears, but with justice shall he judge the poor, and decide with equity for the meek of the land." We have already noted before that the phrase "spirit of the law ", *ruaḥ mishpat*, is Biblical, and the term "letter of the law ", *'ot min ha-torah*, is rabbinic. Suffice it to say that the phrase spirit of the law has left its mark in rabbinic phraseology. There is a statement, that one who violates an oral pact, acts contrary to the spirit of rabbinical law.[132] The same phrase is used with respect to a person who bequeathes all his property to strangers, and thereby disinherits his children.[133]

The antithesis between letter and spirit does not form one of the rules of classical Jewish hermeneutics, yet it does figure prominently in the interpretation of the rabbis. The general rule is to follow the letter, and only in exceptional cases the spirit of the law.[134] R. Ishmael reported three instances where the traditional interpretation deviated from the letter of the law,[135] and three examples where he himself interpreted the law according to the spirit.[136] R. Judah maintained that one who translated Scripture literally, in opposition to the authorized Aramaic version, misrepresented the sense, and he who paraphrased it is as blameworthy as a blasphemer.[137] In other words, one who interprets the law, be it according to the letter or spirit, if it is at variance with tradition, is stigmatized as one who reveals facets of the Torah in contravention of the law.[138]

Interpretation according to the letter was usually indicated by such phrases, as (1) "the words are as they are written";[139] (2) "you have uprooted what is written in the Torah";[140] (3) "a decree of the text";[141] (4) "literally";[142] (5) "according to its plain sense";[143] (6) "exactly."[144] However, there was no corresponding phrase for interpretation according to the spirit. The rabbis could not formally admit an antithesis between letter and spirit, for such an admission could easily lead to an abolition of the ceremonial law, as was indeed attempted by the radical allegorists of Alexandria and later by Paul.[145] Departure from interpretation of the letter of the law was indicated by some circumlocution, such as (1) "One might imagine that the words should be taken as written, but the verse tells us . . ."[146] (2) "I might have thought to take this according to its plain meaning, but the verse tells . . ." and the like.[147]

While numerous hermeneutical rules are preserved in the Talmud, the overriding principles motivating their interpretations are rarely stated,[148] nevertheless we may distinguish two paramount attitudes that determined to a large extent their interpretation, that is strict law versus equity. There were times when the sages deemed it wise to accept the *ius strictum,* and the interpretation of the law was in keeping with the letter. In other instances equity was the supreme consideration and interpretation was in accordance with the spirit of the law. The problem confronting the rabbis was the same that faced the expounders of every other code of law. "A system of law must consist of a body of invariable rules or it will neither grow nor persist, at the same time it must do substantial justice." [149] Equity is denominated "within the line of the law" and contrasted with strict law." [150] The term "the line of the law " may be traced to Isa. 27:17,[151] " I shall make law the line, and justice the plummet." Equity is, in a way, a special rule, adapted to specific circumstances. Similarly Aristotle compares the special ordinance made to fit the circumstances of the case to the leaden rule used by the Lesbian builders.[152]

Instances are recorded in the Talmud of scholars who yielded in matters where the law was on their side, in accordance with the principle of " [going] beyond the limit of the law." [153] The equitable man, says Aristotle, is one who does not strain the law, but is content to receive a smaller share although he has the law on his side.[154] Other principles of equity are introduced in the Talmud in accordance with injunction of Deut. 6:18, "you shall do the just and good," such as *shuma hadar,* [155] which corresponds to the equity of redemption of English law,[156] and the *dina de-bar mezra* [157] or the right of pre-emption.[158]

While considerations of equity were undoubtedly the prime factors which actuated the rabbis to deviate from the letter or the *ius strictum,* there were other motives which were just as compelling, such as public welfare [159] or the interest in a peaceful society. On the whole, it should be remembered that the rabbis, like most jurists, do not ordinarily disclose their inner motivations but mostly give technical reasons for their interpretations. Consequently we are frequently left to our resources to conjecture the inner processes of their minds.

The rabbis developed a system of interpretation, but it can hardly be said that they had a real theory of construction. Rules such as were developed by the Greek and Roman rhetoricians played no minor role in Talmudic dialectics [160] which were primarily concerned with practical and academic questions. Books on Greek rhetoric [161] were in part handbooks on pleadings for advocates, whereas in Talmudic times, a legal representative empowered to *plead* in behalf of another was unknown except in the case where the High priest was a defendant, when it was assumed that the *entolarios,* pleader, might appear in his behalf;[162] hence the science of rhetoric[163] typical of the Greeks, with its emphasis upon devices and stratagems to help the client win his case, was not developed by the rabbis.

At a certain stage in the development of law, the inherent antithesis between the letter and spirit becomes more or less pronounced. Now it was the task of the rabbis to preserve a just balance between letter and spirit. The rabbinical jurists were fully aware of the fact that total law is total injustice,[164] yet they could not bend every law to the principle of equity. If they did, the traditional system of law would have disappeared. Yet their interpretation was a veritable triumph over the most contrary materials.[165] The rabbinic interpretation too, like that of other developed systems, was partly grammatical, partly logical, and partly technical, and casuistical. The rabbis made free use of analogy, and their interpretation was sometimes extensive, sometimes restrictive. Their sense of logic bade them to consider the reason for the law[166] as a basis of interpretation, or to look upon a Scriptural command as merely a typical case.[167] Paradoxically enough, the rabbis took deliberate advantage of the letter of the law to preserve its spirit. Logically speaking, says R. Simon, a wayward daughter should also be subject to the same law as the rebellious son, but we abide by the letter of the law which says a son and by implication rules out the daughter.[168] "Psychologists," says Santayana, "are not concerned with what an opinion asserts logically, but only with what it is existentially; they are asking what existential relations surround an idea when it is called true which are absent when it is called false. Their problem is frankly insoluble."[169] In law the jurist solves this problem by interpreting the statute according to the spirit rather than in conformity with the letter. Often the rabbis resort to technicalities in interpretation. A fruitful source was their conception of the total meaning of Scripture, which led to their discovery of legal notions and ideas embedded in the very economy of the Hebrew language of Scripture. They acted for the most part as if Scripture was not simple human discourse.[170] One word did duty for two.[171] In all cases, the technique of the interpretation of the law as well as the application of legal precepts were definitely determined by a combination of factors;

such as the ideals of a social order they envisaged, their ethical notions, received traditional values,[172] as well as the need for adjustment to individual circumstances.[173]

From the foregoing analysis it becomes clear that Paul's charming antithesis,[174] "the letter killeth and the spirit reviveth," is overdone. If it be taken literally, like any hyperbole,[175] it will be, at best, an elegant straining of the truth. When Paul said in effect, to use the words of Tennyson: "I broke the letter of it, to keep the sense," his Jewish contemporaries were saying to themselves, "He is like one who says: Break the jug but keep the wine,[176] and cut his head off, but keep him alive.[177]

Paul was eminently imbued with the culture of his day, and was undoubtedly familiar with the current doctrines of Greek rhetoric and Roman Law, which was natural for a man raised in Tarsus, the seat of a university where Stoic philosophy and Roman law were taught.

As a protagonist of a new religion,[178] Paul was as much interested in reaching the Jews as well as the Gentiles.[179] Consequently he used his Jewish[180] and Greek learning to discredit Jewish law, by methods employed by advocates in the law courts to win a case. Hence he coined the antithesis between letter and spirit, which is an amalgam of the familiar Greek antithesis of *rhetos* and *dianoia,* and dressed it in a Hebrew garb.

In conclusion, the rabbis were deeply concerned with preserving the spirit of the law,[181] in their own original manner,[182] without vain display. The jurists of the Talmud, like the Roman jurists, possessed, to borrow the language of Sir Henry Maine, "the same rectitude of moral view, the same sensibility to analogies, the same nice analysis of generals, and the same vast sweep of comprehension over particulars. If this be delusion, it can only be exposed by going step by step over the ground which these writers have traversed."[183]

NOTES

1. Quoted by A. Plummer in the *International Critical Commentary on 2 Corinthians,* p. 87, note *.
2. Corinthians 3:6. For Spinoza's interpretation of this passage, cf. *Tractatus Theologico-Politicus,* English translation, 2nd ed., London, 1868, ch. XII, P. 232; cf. also Isaacs, "Is Judaism Legalistic?" in *Menorah Journal,* VII, pp. 259–268.

3. *Science and the Modern World*. Pelican Mentor edition, p. 25.
4. Cf. his bold assertion, "We use great plainness of speech" 2 Corinthians 3:12.
5. Romans 2:5.
6. T. Ḥul. I.1.
7. Hul. 4b.
8. Cf. Bacher, *Z. f. H. B.*, XII, 1908, pp. 39–40.
9. Thus Antiochus recommends Eleazar to eat swine's flesh on the ground that it is given to us by nature (4 Maccabees 5:7). That law cannot be contrary to nature is implied in Aristotle's assertion that general laws are those based on nature (*Rhetoric*, I.13, [1373b]). Similarly the *Auctor ad Herrenium* II.10.14 and Quintilian VII.1.49 observe that *"Quod scriptum est"* cannot be contrary to nature. Spartianus in *De Vita Hadriani* XIV.2 speaks of circumcision as *mutilare genitalia*. (Cf. S. Solazzi, "Fra Norme Romane Antisemite" in *Bullettino Dell' Istituto di Diritto Romano* 44 (1937), pp. 396–406, and Zdzisław Zmigryder-Konopka, "Les Romains et la circoncision des Juifs," in *Festschrift Thaddaeus Zieliński*, Lemberg, 1931, pp. 334–350). The pagan view adopted by Paul that nature cannot be improved upon was resisted by the rabbis. Thus, in opposition to Cicero's remark: *non modo in homine sed etiam in arbore quidquid supervacaneum sit aut usum non habet obstare quam molestum est uno digito plus habere* (*De Natura Deorum*, I.99), R. Judan argued that circumcision made men perfect just as a fig loses its blemish when the stem is removed (Gen. Rab. 46.1), or as R. Levi put it, just as a matron became perfect when she, at the order of the king, removed the nail of her small finger, which was a little too large (*loc. cit.* 46.4). While Paul held that uncircumcision is, so to say, the natural state of man, yet he himself argues inconsistently that nature teaches us that a man's head ought to be uncovered but a woman's covered, 1 Cor. 11:14, cf. also Ginzberg, *Ginze Schechter*, I.3, note 18. Paul's argument from nature shows familiarity with similar arguments of the rhetoricians, see below, note 91.
10. Philo (*Spec. Leg.* I.6) anticipating the objections of the allegorists tries to explain away this figure of speech by asserting that it assimilates the circumcized member to the heart, cf. Heinemann, *Philons. jüdische Bildung*, p. 178, note 3, and Goodenough, *Jurisprudence of the Jewish Courts in Egypt*, p. 31, note 2.
11. Philo, *de Migratione*, I.16, 92, cf. Joel, *Blicke in die Religionsgeschichte*, I. 29, Heinemann, *loc. cit.*, pp. 177–178, and Wolfson, *Philo*, I.70, note 49.
12. Romans 7:6.
13. The term *diatheke kaine* is the Greek translation of "a new covenant", Jer. 31:30. The terms of the Septuagint when they were employed by those who came after them underwent a change in meaning (cf. Deissmann, *Bible Studies*, p. 78).
14. The term *katargeo* literally, idle or unemployed corresponds to the Hebrew *batel*, annulled. This reminds one of the view of R. Simon ben Gamaliel,

"When man dies, he is set free from the law." Using the rhetorical device *ex inversio verborum* (Cicero, *De Oratore*, 2.65.261), Paul spoke of man being set free when the law died. Likewise "she is legally free" (Romans 7:3) is an inversion of R. Johanan's statement (Shab. 151b, "When a person dies he becomes free from the commandments"). Löwy missed the point of Paul's rhetorical flourish, cf. *M. G. W. J.*, 47 (1903), p. 542, note 3, and p. 544, note 2.

15. Newness of spirit is a metaphorical expression for New spirit, cf. Ezek. 11:19 and Ps. 51:12; oldness of the letter is an elliptical expression for letter of the old and superannuated law.

16. 2 Cor. 3:6.

17. Paul was influenced by Deut. 32:39 and I Sam. 2:17.

18. Cf. Deissman, *Light from the Ancient East*, 3rd ed., p. 318, note 1, and M. Roberti, *La Lettera di S. Paolo a Filemone e la condizione giuridica dello schiavo fuggitivo*, Milan, 1933, and Verdam, "St. Paul et un serf fugitif," in *Symbolae van Oven*, Leiden, 1946, pp. 211–230.

19. The Roman rule is found in D. 28.3.1 and *Sententia Pauli*, 23.2.

20. The same is true in Jewish law, "a [later] will annuls a [prior] will," B. B. 152b. For the Athenian Law, cf. Lipsius, *Das Attische Recht*, 1908, p. 571, who states that a complete revocation of a will by a subsequent will is doubtful, whereas Greco-Egyptian testaments were revocable, but not merely by drawing up a new one. The revocation of the first had to be made either in the new testament or by a separate legal act, cf. Taubenschlag, *Law of Greco-Roman Egypt*, p. 153. In keeping with this figure of speech, Paul refers to Jesus as being appointed the heir of all things (Hebrews 1:2). For the difference between the *diatheke* and *Testamentum*, cf. Bonfante, "Le affinità giuridiche greco-romane Testamento greco," *Scritti*, I.337 ff., and Westrup, *Introduction to Early Roman Law*, II.137 ff.

21. Cicero, *De Oratore*, I.180, cf. Himmelschein, in *Symbolae Friburgenses in honorem Ottonis Lenel*, p. 387, note 1.

22. Cf. note 102.

23. Paul seems to have accepted the ethical laws contained in the Pentateuch, cf. Romans 3:31 and 13:8–10. On the other hand he says: "The Gentiles which have not the law, do by nature the things contained in the law," Romans 2:14. This seems to imply the rejection of the Pentateuch as a source of moral law too, cf. Moore, *Judaism*, II.10, and Davies, *Paul and Rabbinic Judaism*, pp. 69 ff. The difficulty in arriving at an understanding of Paul's attitude toward the law is partly based on the fact that he uses *nomos* in as many ways as Torah is used, cf. Dodd, *Bible and the Jews*, p. 35.

24. Cf. Ex. Rab. VI.1 and parallels. We are here presenting a composite of the various recensions of this colloquy.

25. Lev. Rab. 19.2. This term is quite common in the papyri, cf. Taubenschlag, *Law of Greco-Roman Egypt*, p. 237, note 13, and p. 351, note 204.

26. Yer. Sanh. II, 6 (20c) "a partly invalid testament is [considered] totally

invalid." This is based on the maxim, "partly invalidated testimony is [considered] totally invalid." Git. 33a and Yer. B. K. VIII.4, cf. also Mak. I.7, where the rule is stated that if one of a hundred witnesses is declared invalid, the entire testimony is rejected. For the maxim "Does there exist a decree which is partly invalid and partly valid?" cf. Boaz Cohen, "Peculium in Jewish and Roman Law," in the *Proceedings of the American Academy for Jewish Research,* vol. XX, 1951, p. 203, notes 360–361.

27. Ex. Rab. VI.1.

28. Sanh. 21b.

29. Lev. Rab. 19.2, cf. Yeb. 79a.

30. Cf. Bacher, *Agada der Tannaiten,* II.123, note 4. For *diatheke* in the New Testament, cf. Deissmann, *Light from the Ancient East,* 3rd ed., pp. 337–338.

31. Lev. Rab. 13.3, with reference to the slaying of the Leviathan, cf. also Ginzberg, *Legends of the Jews,* vol. V, p. 43, note 27 and Scheftelowitz, "Das Fisch-Symbol im Judentum," *Archiv für Religionswissenschaft,* vol. XIV, pp. 6 ff. In Sifra, ed. Weiss, 111a, Jer. 31:30 is explained as follows: God made a new covenant, because Israel annulled the first covenant, cf. I. Abrahams, *Studies in Pharisaism and the Gospels,* vol. II, pp. 125–126.

32. For the argument *a fortiori* and *a maiori ad minus,* cf. Cicero, *Topica* 23, Quintilian, *Inst. Or.* V.10.87–89, Digest, 50.17.21 and 26 and Schiller, *Virginia Law Review,* 27 (1941), p. 740, note 31. Cf. also U. Klug, *Juristische Logik,* Berlin, 1951.

33. Cf. Yer. Ber. V.2 (9b).

34. Galatians 3:15 and 17, cf. Deissmann, *Bible Studies,* p. 114. For classical Roman Law, cf. D. 28.4.1–4.

35. En passant, it may be noted that the celebrated medieval commonplace "Learn as though you were to live forever, live as though you were to die tomorrow" which occurs in Pierre Dubois, *De Recuperatione Terre Sancte* (1308), is taken from Isidore of Seville (c. 560–636) who wrote *"Disce ut semper victurus; vive ut cras moriturus."* Isidore, the author of *Contra Judaeos,* in turn was inspired by the saying of R. Eliezer ben Hyrcanus, "Repent a day before your death" (Mishnah Ab. II.10). When R. Eliezer was asked by his disciples, does a man know when he is going to die, he replied, therefore a man should repent every day lest he die tomorrow and consequently he will live all his life in a state of repentance (Shab. 153a and Ab. R. N., ed. Schechter, p. 62).

36. So Rashi interprets the verse. Kimhi cites Isa. 11:2 as a parallel; the spirit of God will rest upon him, so that he will execute true justice. The Septuagint has a slightly different text, "they shall be abandoned by spirits, condemned by judgment," cf. 1 Enoch 61:11 which speaks of the spirit of judgment and peace.

37. Cf. Midrash Tannaim, p. 60. The parallel passage in Mekilta, ed., Friedmann, f. 94b, is corrupt and was corrected according to the Midrash Tannaim by Horovitz in his edition of the Mekilta, pp. 310–11.

38. Cf. above note 29. See also Men. 29b and Matthew 5:17. Note that Philo speaks of the first commandment of the second table of the Decalogue as the first letter [writing] (*De Spec*. III.8) and again he speaks of the divine letter [writ] (Mig. Abr. 85). The phrase *kata grammata* according to the written laws or statute law is used by Plato and Aristotle in contrast to the unwritten law, or to custom, cf. Liddell and Scott, I.358 and Hirzel, *Agraphos Nomos*, p. 16, note 5.

39. For the use of the term *adelphos*, cf. Deissmann, *Bible Studies*, pp. 87–88.

40. For pleonasm in Scripture, cf. König, *Stilistik, Rhetorik, Poetik in Bezug auf die Biblische Literatur*, p. 173 ff. Useless pleonasm was criticized by Cicero, cf. Quintilian, *Inst. Or.*, 8.3, 53–54.

41. Cf. *Inst. Or.* 8.3.83. Confucius remarked that Language should be made such as fully to convey one's meaning but no more. Cf. also Volkmann, *Die Rhetorik der Griechen und Römer*, Leipzig, 2nd ed., 1885, pp. 445–446. For an example of a text which means something which it does not say, cf. B. M. 88b, and Bacher, *Exegetische Terminologie*, II, 150.

42. Pohlenz, *Die Stoa*, II.140. Neither is the term Spirit of the Law indigenous in Pehlevi Law. Bulsara in his English translation of the Sassanian code, *Matikan e Hazar Datastan*, Bombay 1937, pp. 90–91 translates paragraph 20 as follows: There was one who said that the charge must be drawn in accordance with the spirit of the law. Prof. Bernard Geiger informs me that "Both the transliteration as well as the translation of this paragraph are partly incorrect. The correct translation is: There was one who said thus: by lawfulness *(pat datakih)* he is condemned. In other words he is considered guilty in accordance with the law. The term Spirit does not appear in the original Pehlevi nor is it implied in the context." It seems to us that the term *pat datakih* corresponds to the Biblical term *ka-dat* Esth. 1.15. Noteworthy is the comment of R. Isaac in Midrash Esther *ad loc*. What shall be done according to the law to the sow that acted towards the holy people unlawfully, without mercy. R. Isaac takes *ka-dat* to mean strict Law.

43. Cf. Romans 1:15–16. I am ready to preach the Gospel to you that are at Rome also . . . to the Jew first, and also to the Greek.

44. Protagoras is said to be the inventor of the antithesis (*Diogenes Laertius* XI.51) which played such an important role in Greek rhetoric, cf. Norden, *Die Antike Kunstprosa*, I³, 16 ff. and 20 ff. Paul was influenced by the Greek antithesis of the rhetoricians rather than by the lapidary style of Heraclitus, cf. note 174.

45. *Against Theomnestus*, I.7, cf. Navarre, *Essai sur la rhetorique grècque avant Aristote*, 1900, p. 62.

46. This contrast is also found in Philo, *De Abrahamo*, 22 (ed. Cohn, IV.25). For Paul's literary contacts with Philo, cf. Jowett, "St. Paul and Philo," in his *Epistles of St. Paul*.

47. Cf. Ex. 18:26. The hard causes they brought unto Moses.

48. *Nichomachean Ethics* V.10 (1137b).

49. Pomponius (D. I.3.3) says, *Iura constitui oportet ut dixit Theophrastus in*

his quae *epi to pleiston* accedunt non quae *ek paralogou,* cf. similar statements by Celsus and Paulus in D. I.3, 4–6. Cicero says no one can include every case in one statement (*De Inventione* II.152), cf. 'Er. 63b.

50. Rhetoric, I.13 (1374b).
51. Rhetoric, I.15 (1375a).
52. Cf. Cicero's observation, "He did not think of you as mere reciters of documents in judicial proceedings but as interpreters of his wishes, *De Inventione,* II.139. The *recitatores,* mentioned by Cicero in this passage as well as that in *pro Cluentio* 51.141, remind one of the *"Tannaim,"* the professional class of scholars who committed to memory the traditional law (cf. Boaz Cohen, *Mishnah and Tosefta,* pp. 30–31). The statement in Sotah 22a, that the *"Tanna"* recites laws without being able to interpret them, does indeed call to mind a passage in *Auctor ad Herrenium* 2.10.4. *"Locus communis contra eum, qui scriptum recitel et scriptoris voluntatem non interpretur,"* cf. also Lieberman, *Hellenism in Jewish Palestine,* p. 88.
53. Rhetoric, I.13 (1374a).
54. Plato says that equity is contrary to strict justice, *Laws,* 757. D. Radin was of the view that *epieikeia* corresponded to *clementia,* cf. *Mnemosyna Pappulia,* Athens, 1934, pp. 213–220. Seneca notes that "Mercy has freedom in decision, it sentences not by the letter of the law, but in accordance with what is fair and good" (*De Clementia* II.7.3). In Yer. B. K. VIII.5 (6c) strict justice is similarly contrasted with mercy. It is noteworthy that the Septuagint translates "forgive" in Ps. 85 (86):5 by *epieikeia,* cf. also Hirzel, *Agraphos Nomos,* Leipzig, 1900, pp. 7 ff., and 60 ff., Cairns, *Legal Philosophy from Plato to Hegel,* p. 107, note 78, and M. Salomon, *Der Begriff der Gerechtigkeit bei Aristoteles,* Leiden, 1937, p. 139.
55. Cf. Bonner and Smith, *The Administration of Justice from Homer to Aristotle,* 1930, I, p. 75, cf. also Xenophon, *Memorabilia,* IV.4.14, and Sextus Empiricus, *Adversus Mathematicos,* II.34, and Westrup, *Introduction to Early Roman Law,* III, 69.
56. Inst. Or., III.6, 61.
57. In the Digest, strict law is opposed to exception, cf. D. 13.5.30 and D. 13.5.17, cf. the English legal maxim: The exception proves the rule. Not entirely irrelevant are Gilbert Murray's remarks: "As Dr. Freud has pointed out, our attitude towards the law, civil and moral, is always 'ambivalent'. We love it and uphold it as maintaining the wish or conscience of Society against wicked law-breakers who may do wrong to us and our community; but we feel, in our own *exceptional* case, a conscious or subconscious desire sometimes to escape from it." *Stoic, Christian and Humanist,* London, 1940, p. 161.
58. Cf. his *Peri ton staseon,* 2nd ed., H. Rabe, Leipzig, 1913, p. 82, cf. also Voigt, *Jus Naturale,* IV, p. 339, note 21, and p. 351, and Volkmann, *Die Rhetorik,* 1885, pp. 88–89.
59. Letter of Aristeas 171. There is a veiled allusion here to Aristotle, *Nichomachean Ethics,* V.7.1–2 (1134b), who in his discussion of justice opposes

the natural to the conventional. A rule of justice is natural that has the same validity everywhere. A rule is conventional that in the first instance may be settled in one way or the other indifferently, although once it is settled, it is not indifferent, e. g. a sacrifice shall consist of a goat and not of two sheep. Here Aristeas plays upon Aristotle's antithesis of natural and conventional and gives a new twist and symbolical meaning to dianoia, cf. F. Heinemann, *Nomas und Physis. Herkunft und Bedeutung einer Antithese im Griechischen Denken des 5ten Jahrhunderts,* Basle, 1945. The Malbim uses Aristotelian terms in his commentary upon Ps. 19:10, when he explains that in the divine law there is no conflict between the conventional and religious law and natural justice.

60. *De Praemiis et Poenis,* I.11, ed. Cohn, V.349. Cf. also Philo, *De Abrahamo,* XXXVIII, 217.

61. For *diegesis = narratio,* cf. the literature cited in Hadas, *Aristeas,* New York, 1951, p. 56. Philo contrasts literal account with real meaning or true intent, cf. *De Josepho,* VI.28, and *De Abrahamo,* XXIV, 119.

62. *Adversus Mathematicos,* II. 36, and 38.

63. Cf. Himmelschein, *Symbolae Friburgenses in honorem Ottonis Lenel,* p. 375. The person who provided the pleader with arguments was termed *pragmaticus* (*Inst. Or.,* XII.3.4) which was the Greek term for *jurisconsults* (*Inst. Or.* III.6.59). Cf. Wenger, *Institutes of the Roman Law of Procedure,* 1950, p. 88, note 26, and Friedländer, *Roman Life and Manners,* London, s. a. 7th ed., I.163 and IV.387. For scholars and jurists who were especially equipped to argue both sides of a question, cf. 'Er. 13b and Sanh. 17a.

64. Cicero, *De Inv.* II.116, *Topica,* I.96, and *Inst. Or.,* VII.5.6. The *Auctor ad Herrenium,* I.11.19 counts six, the additional one being *translatio;* for the latter, cf. Schwalbach, "Zur Geschichte der Lehre won den Prozesseinreden," in *Zeitschrift der Savigny-Stiftung,* vol. 2, 209 ff., and Wlassak, *Der Ursprung der römischen Einrede,* p. 11 ff.

65. *Inst. Or.,* III.6.46. Quintilian elsewhere uses *verba* and *sententia,* cf. also Voigt, *Das jus naturale, aequum et bonum und jus gentium der Römer,* IV, 339, note 21, and G. Segrè, *Atti del Congresso Internazionale di Diritto Romano, Roma.* I. Pavia, 1934, p. 225, note 1.

66. *Inst. Or.,* III.6.55, VII.1.13 and cf. *Digest,* 50.17.24, cf. B. M. 70a and Suk. 51a.

67. Cicero, *Topica,* 96, *Inv.* I.17, II.122.

68. Quintilian remarks: single words give rise to error, when the same noun applies to a number of things or persons (the Greeks call this homonymy): for example, it is uncertain with regard to the word *gallus,* whether it means a cock or a Gaul, (*Inst. Or.,* VII.9.2), cf. R. Yannai's statement: I do not know whether *kavul* means a slave's chain or a woolen cap, Shab. 57b.

69. *Inst. Or.,* VII.10.2.

70. *Inst. Or.,* VII.6.2.

71. Biondi, *Istituzioni di Diritto Romano,* Milan, 1946, p. 60.

72. *Inst. Or.*, VII.6.4–5. For the Jewish Law, cf. Yer. Peah I.15d, for the Roman Law, D. 25.3.5.1.

73. Jerome's translation calls to mind C. I.17.2.21 which reads, "If anything should appear ambiguous . . . it should be referred by the judge to the emperor for decision, for he is the only one who may legislate or interpret the laws." An obscure point of law is not the same as an ambiguous point of law (*Inst. Or.*, VII.10.2). Sometimes the term *obscuritas* corresponds in meaning to ambiguity, cf. the statement of Paulus in D. 18.1.21. The notion of ambiguity was expressed by the rabbis by different circumlocutions (Sotah V.5) which Rashi ('Ar. 4b) explains, Sifra, ed. Weiss 14b, cf. ps-Rashi to Gen. Rab. 18.5. For other passages, cf. also Bacher, *Die exegetische Terminologie*, I.196. Ohter circumlocutions are found in Giṭ. 32b, B. M. 32a, and Ket. 69a, cf. also Samuel ben Meir to B. B. 96a. Ambiguity is permitted in a special case of mourning, cf. Beer Heteb, Yoreh Deah, 402, n. 10. With regard to *Talak*, J. Schacht writes, the principle is unanimously affirmed, that in ambiguous expressions, the opinion of the speaker be considered ambiguous or not, cf. *Encyclopedia of Islam*, IV.638.

74. *Inst. Or.*, III.6.46 and VII.1.16.

75. *Inst. Or.*, VII.10.1.

76. *Inst. Or.*, VII.7.1.

77. *Inst. Or.*, VII.8.1, cf. J. Stroux, *Römische Rechtswissenschaft und Rhetorik*, 1949, pp. 39 ff., and Jolowicz, *Law Quarterly Review*, 48 (1932), p. 181, and *Gnomon*, 5 (1929), 65–87. In the Talmud the syllogistic reasoning has its counterpart in the oft recurring statement "This was not expressly stated, but rather derived by inference," Ber. 9a, cf. also Austin's observation that interpretation in the proper acceptation of the term should be distinguished from the induction of a rule from a judicial decision. *Lectures on Jurisprudence*, London, 1873, p. 1023.

78. *Inst. Or.*, II.5.10. For *Definitio*, cf. Pringsheim, in *Festschrift für Lenel*, pp. 251 ff., Schulz, *Principles of Roman Law*, p. 43, note 3, and Senn, *Les Origines de Jurisprudence*, 1926, p. 26, note 2.

79. *Inst. Or.*, VII.10.1, and William Empson, *Seven Types of Ambiguity*, London, 1930. From the very beginning, we are told, existentialism defined itself as a philosophy of ambiguity, cf. Simon de Beauvoir, *The Ethics of Ambiguity*, New York, 1948, p. 9.

80. *Inst. Or.*, VII.3.6.

81. *Loc. cit.*, IV.3, VII.3.21–22, cf. B. M. 57b the statement of R. Papa.

82. *Loc. cit.*, V.10.36.

83. *Loc. cit.*, VII.1.49.

84. *Loc. cit.*, VII.6.1.

85. *Loc. cit.*, III.6.87.

86. Cicero, *Inv.*, II.122. Philo speaks of hired advocates who have no thought nor care for justice, *Moses*, I.25 (Loeb Classics ed., p. 289). For the unscrupulousness of orators, cf. Gellius, I, 6, 4, and Schulz, *Classical Roman Law*, p. 278.

87. Cicero, *Inv.*, I.68, II.143 *ad Herrenium*, II.10.14, *Inst. Or.*, III.6.43.XII.3.6.
88. Cf. M. Ter. IV.6 and M. K. 22a and Yer. M. K. 8. The same idea is expressed by Paulus, *Non omne quod licet honestum est* (D. 50.17.144), cf. Kaser, *ZSS*, 60, p. 118, notes 1–2 and p. 138, note 1. A striking parallel is found in the view of Naḥmanides: One can be vile without violating any law (Commentary to Lev. 19:2). Note also the ancient proverb: *Honesta lex est temporis necessitas*, cited by Voigt, *Die XII Tafeln*, Leipzig, 1883, p. 16, note 1. A variation on this theme is given by Paul who asserted that not everything that is lawful is expedient (1 Cor. 6:12). In this connection, it may be well to recall Florentinus' definition of Liberty, *"Libertas est naturalis facultas eius quod cuique facere libet, nisi si quid vi aut iure prohibetur,"* D. I.5.4 pr., cf. Schulz, *Principles of Roman Law*, p. 140, note 2, Wirszubski, *Libertas as a Political Idea at Rome*, Cambridge 1950, p. 2, note 1, and Montesquieu, *Esprit des Lois*, XXVI.20.
89. Muirhead, *Historical Introduction to the Private Law of Rome*, London, 1916, p. 142, note 14.
90. *Inst. Or.*, III.6.84. For the conflict between law and morals, cf. Ames, *Harvard Law Review*, 22, p. 97.
91. *Auctor ad Herrenium*, II.10.14, *Inst. Or.*, VII.1.49. Cicero says that the first principles of justice proceed from nature, *Inv.* II.160, for this passage, cf. E. Costa, *Cicerone Giureconsulto*, I.20, note 6. Philo also taught that enacted ordinances are not inconsistent with nature, *De Abrahamo*, I.5.
92. *Auctor ad Herrenium*, II.10.14.
93. Cicero, *Inv.* II.130.131.140, *Inst. Or.*, VII.1.10.
94. Cf. Biondi, *Istituzioni di Diritto Romano*, 1946, p. 59, note 22. For a direct parallel in Jewish law to the *ius singulare*, cf. the principle "the [law of the] defamer is exceptional." Ket. 45a, and the statement "We do not learn from exceptions," Yer. Ter. VII.1.
95. Many of these passages in the Digest are of Byzantine origin, cf. Himmelschein, *Symbolae Friburgenses in honorem Ottonis Lenel*, p. 394, note 1. For the passages on *Scriptum et voluntas* and *ambiguitas*, cf. *loc. cit.*, pp. 398–417, and Alvaro D'Ors Perez-Peix, "La Actitud Legislativa del Emperador Justiniano," in *Orientalia Christiana Periodica*, Rome, 1947, XIII, nos. 1–2, pp. 125–132. The doctrine of ambiguity is fully expounded on the basis of the Digest in *Las Siete Partidas*, VII, 33.2–12. For the influence of rhetoric on Roman Law and Procedure, cf. also Wenger, *Institutes of the Roman Law of Procedure*, p. 140, note 18a and p. 195, note 16. For the Greco-Egyptian Law, cf. H. Schmidt, "Einfluss der Rhetorik auf die Gestaltung der richterlichen Entscheidung in den Papyri," in the *Journal of Juristic Papyrology*, IV, 1950, pp. 165–177.
96. D. 1.3.30. Cf. Steinwenter, *Studi Bonfante*, II, 433, note 80.
97. *Inst. Or.*, II.17.30, cf. Schulz, *Principles of Roman Law*, p. 130, note 3.
98. D. 1.3.29. "Attempts to evade the rules of law by keeping the letter while breaking the spirit were as common in Rome, as they have been in our courts," cf. Buckland, *Equity in Roman Law*, London, 1911, p. 112. An

instance of *"in fraudem legis"* in Jewish Law would be licit circumvention of the usury law, B. M. 62b, see also Giṭ. 54b.

99. D. 50.16.6.1. The statement of Paulus (D. 44.7.38) that we are not bound by the form of the letters *(Figura litterarum)* but by the meaning which they express, reminds one of R. Judah's statement, "one who translates a verse literally is a fabricator" (Kid. 49a).

100. *Benignius leges interpretandae sunt quo voluntas earum conservetur,* D. 1.3.18, Gaius (D. 50.17.56) remarks: *Semper in dubiis benigniora praeferenda sunt.* In 'Ab. Zarah 7a R. Joshua ben Korḥah formulated the principle, "Regarding pentateuchal law, follow the one who is stringent; regarding rabbinic law, follow the one who is lenient. The rabbis accepted the widely honored philosophy that doubts arising with respect to money claims should be resolved in favor of the claimants. Ket. 73b and parallels. For *benignus,* cf. Heumann-Seckel, s. v., and Savigny, *System des heutigen römischen Rechts,* vol. III, p. 28, note a. According to Albertario, the term is Byzantine, cf. *Studi di Diritto Romano,* I, p. 58, note 2. Berger in his article, *In dubiis benigniora* maintains the classical origin of the phrase, cf. Seminar, IX. (1951), pp. 36–49. Cf. also P. Laborderie-Boulon, "Benignitas, Essai sur la pensée charitable aux temps classiques," *R. H. D.,* 1948, pp. 137–144.

101. D. 50.16.219.

102. D. 50.17.12. *In testamentis plenius voluntates testantium interpretamur.* For this passage, cf. Maschi, *Studi Sull' Interpretazione dei Legati,* Milan, 1938, p. 17, and Koschaker in *Conferenze Romanistiche,* Milan, 1940, p. 153, note 202.

103. 50.17.67. For the view of Paulus, cf. D. 34.5.3.

104. D. 1.3.19. Ambiguity must be explained by conjecture and mainly according to the intention of the person who wrote or uttered the words. *Inst. Or.,* III.6.43 and VII.9.15, cf. Giṭ. 32b, with respect to ambiguity it says "the language which benefits one is what he said [intended]," cf. also C. TH. 1, 1, 6, 1, where it stated that the original texts were altered in order to remove superfluous words and to change ambiguous expressions *(mutandi ambigua).*

105. D. 50.17.192.1. If the point of law is doubtful, it must be examined in the light of equity. *Inst. Or.,* XII.3.6, VII.9.15.

106. Cf. Voigt, *Jus Naturale,* vol. IV, 1875, p. 364, note 60.

107. D. 50.17.65. This statement is wrongly ascribed to Ulpian in D. 50.16.177, cf. Lenel, *Palingenesia,* II, 1186, note 2.

108. *Ea est natura cavillationes, quam Graeci sorite appellant.* For *cavillatio,* cf. the use of the term in Quintilian 7.4.37: in these we meet with legal quibbles as to what is the meaning of action contrary to the interest of the state. *Hinc moventur quidem illae iuris cavillationes quid sit rem publicam laedere.* For the relation between sophistry and rhetoric, cf. Gomperz, *Sophistik und Rhetorik.*

109. For the question of interpolation, cf. Albertario, *Conferenze per il centen-*

ario delle Pandette, pp. 329 ff., Lenel, ZSS., 50 (1930), 15, and Scherillo, *Archivio Giuridico*, 109, (1933), p. 108.

110. Cicero's remark, "They call this argument '*sorites*' because by adding a single grain at a time they make a heap" (*Academica* II.16.49) reminds one of the comparison of R. Tarfon's dialectics to a heap of nuts, cf. Ab. R. N., ed. Schechter, pp. 66–67, and Rashi's explanation in Giṭ. 67a. Cf. also the phrase: he who heaps arguments against his opponent in litigation, Sifre, Deut. 16 (ed. Finkelstein, p. 27), cf. also Lieberman, *Kuntresim L'inyane ha-lashon ha-'Ivrit* (ed. Yalon), I.2, 1937, p. 47. According to Seneca's definition of *sorites* (*De Beneficiis* V.19.9) it is a chain argument in which the conclusion of one syllogism becomes the premise for the next *ad infinitum*. This is similar to the dialectical discussion of the Talmud in Yoma 13a and b.

111. Cf. Voigt, *Jus Naturale*, I.42, Pringsheim, "Jus aequum und ius strictum," ZSS., 42, pp. 643–668, for *Bonum et Aequum*, cf. ZSS., 52, 78 ff., and Jhering, *Geist des römischen Rechts*, II, 441, cf. also Schulz, *Principles of Roman Law*, p. 210, note 2. Westrup, *Introduction to Early Roman Law*, III.21–22, Wenger, *Canon in den römischen Rechtsquellen*, 1942, pp. 18–24, Jonker, "Aequitas," in *Reallexikon für Antike und Christentum*, Leipzig, 1942. (For the latter, cf. Steinwenter, ZSS., 62, p. 459). For Ferrini's view that the development of Roman private law is a continuous and more perfect victory of *aequitas* over *ius strictum*, cf. Pernice, ZSS., 7, p. 156. According to some scholars the question of *aequitas* versus *ius strictum* was one of the principles at issue between the school of Proculus and Sabinus, cf. Kübler in *Pauly-Wissowa*, zweite Reihe, vol. I, 1914, p. 384. In a Palestinian marriage contract published by Berliner, *Kobets al Yad*, vol. IX, and reprinted by Gulak, *Otsar ha-Shetarot*, pp. 35–36, the parties agree to the terms in accordance with Jewish and Gentile law, and the laws of equity. Here *aequalitas = aequitas*.

112. Modestinus, D. I.3.25. Maimonides (Commentary to M. Peah 1.1) divides all the commandments into two parts (1) religious, (2) civil law and ethics.

113. The term *mishpat* designates also "due measure," cf. Isa. 28:26, Jer. 30:11, 46:28.

114. The rabbis, too, understood *mishpat* to mean strict law, cf. R Haninah's remark. He who says God is lax in meting out justice, will shrivel up, B. K. 50a, Yer. Shek. V.1 and parallels. Livy (2.3) observes, the law knew no relaxation (*nihil laxamento*) for one who exceeded the bounds, cf. also Cicero, *Cluent*. 38.89 for *laxamentum legis*. For the expression *apo pantos toudikaiou*, in accordance with strict justice, cf. Bickerman, *Classical Philology* 42 (1947), p. 142, note 37, cf. also A. Deschamps, "La Justice de Dieu dans la Bible grecque," in *Studia Hellenistica*, vol. V, 1948.

115. Cf. Ps.-Quintilian, *Declamationes*, no. 264, ed. Ritter, Leipzig, 1884, p. 80. "*Nam si apud iudicium hoc semper quaeri de legibus oportet, quid in his iustum, quid aequum, quid conveniens sit civitati, supervacuum fuit*

scribi omnino leges." for this Declamation, cf. *ZSS.*, 41, p. 23 and Lanfranchi, *Il Diritto nei Retori Romani*, Milan, 1938, p. 143, note 7.

116. Similarly, Aristotle said that civil society was founded not merely to preserve the lives of its members, but that they might live well. *Politics*, III.9 (1280a), cf. also Maimonides, *Moreh*, I.42, and III.28, which Ibn Tibbon rendered "proper ordering of the affairs of society." This phrase in turn corresponds to the term "civil society," for the latter, cf. Hegel, *Philosophy of Right*, Oxford, 1949, p. X, and p. 122 ff.

117. As a punishment for their sins, God left them to follow their own ideas, which they eventually ascribed to Him, cf. Ps. 81:13, Spinoza's observation applies to this passage of Ezekiel, "If they (i. e., the Jews) desire anything, they say that God inclines their hearts thereto," *Tractatus Theologico-Politicus*, London, 1868, p. 33. For Spinoza's own interpretation of this baffling statement of Ezekiel, cf. *loc. cit.*, p. 310, and Montesquieu, *Esprit des Lois*, XIX.21. The rabbis too were puzzled by this verse, cf. e. g., Ex. Rab. 30.18.

118. Similarly Cicero extols the laws of the XII Tables precisely for *summa aequitas*, cf. *De Re Publica*, II.36, 61. Tacitus designates the laws of the XII Tables as *finis aequi juris*, cf. *Annals*, III.27.

119. II Sam. 8:15, cf. Sanh. 6b. King Solomon when he was in Gibeon, prayed to God that he be given wisdom to dispense law and justice, I Kings 3:9 ff., and his request was granted. For this incident, cf. Hildegard Lewy, *Archiv Orientalni*, vol. XVIII, no. 3, 1950 (*Hrozny Anniversary Volume*, part IV), p. 331–332.

120. The Greek *epieikeia*, the Roman *aequitas*, and the English equity are not synonymous, but have a basic notion in common, cf. Austin, *Lectures on Jurisprudence*, 1873, II, pp. 634 ff., Seagle, *The Quest for Law*, 1941, pp. 180 ff., 432–433, Diamond, *Primitive Law*, pp. 348–349, and F. W. Maitland, *Equity, Also the Forms of Actions at Common Law*, Cambridge, 1920, and Hazeltine, "The Early History of English Equity," in *Essays on Legal History*, edited by Vinogradoff, 1913. For *epieikis*, cf. Heinz-Horst Schrey, "Die Wiedergeburt des Naturrechts," *Theologische Rundschau*, 19 (1951), 28–29, and for *aequitas*, cf. E. M. Meyers, "Le Conflit entre l'equité et la loi chez les prémiers glossateurs," *Tijdschrift voor Rechtsgeschiedenis*, 17 (1941), 117–135, and Beseler, *Juristische Miniaturen*, Leipzig, 1929, p. 61.

121. I Kings 3:11, Prov. 2:9 and 28:5.

122. Isa. 11:4 and Mal. 2:6, where *mishor* is rendered by *aequitas*.

123. In Babylonian law, *Misârum* (equity) is opposed to *Kettum* (firm, strict law), cf. Koschaker, *Revue Historique de Droit Français*, 1935, pp. 424–425, and Price, *J A O S*, 52 (1932), p. 174. For equity in Islamic law, cf. Santillana, *Istituzioni di Diritto Musulmano Malichitto*, I, Rome, 1926, pp. 70–73.

124. Cf. Deut. 6.18, from which the rabbis derived certain rules of equity. Jerome translates this phrase by *placitum est et bonum*, perhaps he was

thinking of the Roman rule incorporated in D. I.4.1.1. *Quod principi placuit, legis habet vigorem,* (cf. Steinwenter, *Studi Bonfante,* II.423, note 11). Anyway "the fair and the good" (Deut. 6.18) does correspond to the Roman *bonum et aequum,* cf. note 111.

125. Cf. Isa. 40:5. In Prov. 11:5 there is an allusion to the fact that the justice of the upright is attained by the rectification of his path.

126. Ps. 19:10, Prov. 21:14, Ezek. 18:8, Zech. 7:9. Note that *Mishpat* in Micah 3:8 is rendered by the Targum as a law of truth. Observe also that the spirit of God is in *apposition* to law and strength.

127. Cf. also Mal. 2.6 and Cicero, *De Legibus,* II.11, *ut perspicuum esse possit in ipso nomine legis interpretando inesse vim et sententiam iusti et veri legendi.* On law and truth, cf. Hirzel, *Themis, Dike und Verwandtes,* 1907, p. 114, n. 4 and pp. 415–416.

128. Zech. 8:16. The rabbis explain it as arbitration, because, as they put it, "where there is [strict] law there is not peace," Sanh. 6b. Strict law is often incompatible with peace, cf. the remark of Steinwenter, "Nicht den Strafrichter sondern den Friedens- und Schiedrichter fordert die alte Zeit," cf. *Die Streitbeendigung durch Urteil, Schiedsspruch und Vergleich nach Griechischem Rechte,* 1925, p. 29, note 1.

129. Cf. Pound, "The End of Law as Developed in Juristic Thought," in *Harvard Law Review* 27 (1914), p. 605.

130. The rabbis derived their regulations "for the sake of harmony," from Prov. 3:17, cf. Giṭ. 59b and Yer. Ket. IX.4 (33a), cf. also Blackstone, *Commentaries on the Laws of England,* I. 349.

131. Isa. 11:3–4, cf. Ibn Ezra, *ad loc.,* and Sanh. 6b, "the judge only has what his eyes see [to direct his decision]." A judge who suspects that the witnesses are lying should not render a decision on the basis of their evidence, (Shebu. 30b–31a). In Roman law, a magistrate or one presiding in a criminal case who allows false testimony to be presented by which an innocent person may be prosecuted or convicted, is liable under the Cornelian law relating to assassins and poisoners (D. 48.8.1 pr.).

132. B. M. 48a, cf. also M. Sheb. X.9, T. Sheb. VIII.11 and parallels, Num. Rab. X.8 (ed. Vilna, f. 38c). This reminds one of the Roman rule, *nuda pactio obligationem non parit,* D. II.14.7.4, cf. M. Roberti, "L'influenza cristiana nello svolgimento storico dei patti nudi," in *Christianismo e Diritto Romano,* Milan, 1935, pp. 87ff.

133. B. B. VIII.5.

134. The principle formulated by the Amoraim, "a verse does not depart from its plain meaning," Shab. 63a, represented also the opinion of the Tannaim, cf. Boaz Cohen, "Towards a Philosophy of Jewish Law," in *Conservative Judaism,* vol. VI, no. 1, pp. 7–9. In Islam too every rule must be taken in its literal meaning *(Zahir)* unless there is an indication to the contrary, on the authority of the Prophet, or the consensus of the scholars, cf. Schacht, *The Origins of Muhammadan Jurisprudence,* p. 56, and Goldziher, *Die Zahiriten,* p. 122. The Moslem Fikh always strove, to use

the words of Goldziher, "den schroffen Buchstaben des Gesetzes durch spitzfindige Umdeutung mit der Praxis des Lebens auszusöhnen," cf. Z. D. M. G., 41 (1887), p. 96.

135. Sotah 16a, Yer. Kid. 59d, cf. Bacher, *Exegetische Terminologie*, I.44.
136. Mekilta, ed. Horovitz, p. 270 and parallels.
137. Kid. 49a, T. Meg., end.
138. Ab. III.11. An example is given in M. Meg. IV.9, cf. Büchler, *M. G. W. J.* 38, 1893, p. 108 and Margulis, *loc. cit.*, 39 (1894), 63–79.
139. Cf. e. g., Pes. 21b, Ket. 46a, Yer. Ket. IV.4, Ḳid. 17b, Sanh. 111a.
140. M. Pes. VI.2.
141. B. M. 11a, Sanh. 69b–70a.
142. B. K. 84a.
143. M. Sotah VIII.5.
144. Tem. 12b.
145. Cf. Ginzberg, *Jewish Encyclopedia*, s. v. Allegorical Interpretation. For the *doreshei reshumot*, cf. Levi, *REJ*, 60, 24 ff., and Lauterbach, *JQR*, N. S. V.291, and *Dictionary of Islam*, s. v. *Tawil.*
146. Ber. 35b, for this passage, cf. Azulai, *Birke Joseph, Yoreh Deah*, 246.1.
147. Mekilta, ed. Horovitz, p. 64. In contradistinction to the literal interpretation subsequently called *peshat,* Midrash attempts to fathom the Spirit of Scriptures. Neither was the consciousness of the divergence between Peshat and Midrash, which gradually increased, completely obliterated (cf. *J. E.,* VIII.548). Noteworthy is the statement of Raba, Scripture ordained forty stripes and the rabbis diminished the number by one, Mak. 22b.
148. Cf. B. B. 144a, Giṭ. 14a, where it is stated that only three rules are handed down without reason. With few exceptions, the Romans were not wont to give reason for their rules of law or legal institutions, cf. Schulz, *Principles of Roman Law,* pp. 98–100.
149. Cairns, *Legal Philosophy from Plato to Hegel,* p. 369. Hence many passages in Scripture and the Mishnah require a *duplex interpretatio* in view of the fact that the meaning which a passage had in its original context varied considerably from that given to it by the subsequent commentators. For the similar position of the Digest in the framework of Justinian's legislation, cf. Dernburg, *System des Römischen Rechts,* 1911, vol. I, p. 59, Windscheid, *Lehrbuch des Pandektenrechts,* I, 8th ed., 1900, p. 96, note 3, and Riccobono, "Interpretatio Duplex," reprinted from *Miscellanea Giovanni Mercati,* vol. V, 1946, pp. 1–5. The doctrine of the twofold truth, theological and philosophical, permeated the entire later medieval period, cf. M. Maywald, *Die Lehre von der zweifachen Wahrheit,* Berlin, 1871, and Windelband, *A History of Philosophy,* 1921, p. 320.
150. Mekilta, ed. Horovitz, p. 198, in the parallel passage in B. M. 30b, "[going] beyond the limit of the law" is contrasted with law, R. Yohanan, *loc. cit.,* contrasts it with "the law of the Torah." In M. Giṭ. IV.4 strict law is opposed to "the benefit of the world" with respect to the manumis-

sion of a pledged slave. For the Roman rule on this point, cf. Buckland, *Slavery in Roman Law*, p. 573. In Giṭ. 54b logic is opposed to law. The term *din* meaning strict law is found in the phrase "let the law *[din]* pierce the mountain," Sanh. 6b (where it is used in opposition to arbitration, cf. also Yeb. 92a), and in the phrase, "Do not be merciful [in the administration of] strict justice *[din]*," M. Ket. IX.2. For the latter, cf. Deut. 13:9, 19:13, 19:21, and 25:12. Sometimes *Torah* means a strict law, cf. the statement in Num. Rab. 21.5, man should not be more liberal than the law. Cf. also Zuri, *Mishpat ha-Talmud*, Warsaw, 1921, I.85–86. For the phrase "justice suffers," cf. B. K. 85b, T. Yeb. IX.8, Yer. Yeb. VII.4 (8b) and B. K. IV.1 (4a).

151. According to Rashi, 'Er. 51b, the phrase "his reasoning is flawless" was applied to R. Jose, because he was equitable in his decisions, i.e., "straight [fair] as a plumb-line."

152. *Nicomachean Ethics*, V.10, 7, (1137b).

153. Cf. B. M. 24b, 30b, B. K. 99b, Ket. 97a, Ber. 45b, cf. also Rashi to B. K. 108a–b and B. M. 33a, and Maimonides, *Hilkot Deot*, I.5. In B. M. 83a, the principle of equity is derived from Prov. 2:20, cf. Seneca, *De Ira*, II.28.2, Kaminka, *Mélanges Israel Levi*, p. 252, Güdemann, "Moralische Rechtseinschränkung im Mosaischrabbinischen Rechtssystem," in *MGWJ*, 61, pp. 422–443, and Eschelbacher, "Recht und Billigkeit in der Jurisprudenz des Talmud," in *Festschrift—Herman Cohen*, 501–514 and Abrahams, *Studies in Pharisaism and the Gospels*, II, 113, note 2. Occasionally it is stated that God acts in accordance with the principle of "beyond strict law," cf. Ber. 7b, and 'Ab. Zarah 4b. The principles of Law and Equity are personified in rabbinic metaphor: Elohim represents the attribute of justice, and the Tetragrammaton the Attribute of Mercy, cf. e. g., Gen. Rab. 33, 3, Yer. Ta'an. II.1, Cant. Rab. I.4. Ginzberg, *Legends of the Jews*, V, p. 4, note 6, and Vajda in *kovezz 'al yad*, V, 1951, Jerusalem, p. 134.

154. *Nicomachean Ethics*, V.10.8, (1138a).

155. B. M. 16b, 35a.

156. Blackstone, *Commentaries*, II, 158, Buckland and McNair, *Roman Law and Common Law*, p. 241.

157. B. M. 108a.

158. Cf. G. Ostrogorsky, "The Peasants' Preemption Right," *Journal of Roman Studies*, 37 (1947), 117–126. For the Muslim law, cf. Santillana, *Istituzioni di Diritto Musulmano Malichita*, I, p. 393 ff., and Bussi, *Ricerche intorno alle relazioni fra retratto bizantino e musulmano*, Milan, 1933, for the latter, cf. *ZSS*, 54:402 ff., and Roussier, *R. H. D.*, 1934, pp. 323–332, cf. also Volterra, *Diritto Romano e Diritti Orientali*, 1932, p. 62, note 2, cf. also Levy, *West Roman Vulgar Law*, Philadelphia, 1951, p. 119, notes 124–125.

159. For *tikken* note that one of the functions of the praetor was *corrigendi iuris civilis gratia* (*Digest* 1.1.7.1). With respect to the religious law, we

read that the Emperor Claudius as *Pontifex Maximus: Quaedam circa caerimonias . . . aut correxit,* cf. Gaston May, *Revue Historique de Droit Français,* 1938, p. 2, note 3.

160. Cf. Lieberman, *Hellenism in Jewish Palestine,* pp. 47 ff.

161. Cf. Schulz, *Roman Legal Science,* pp. 74–76, and Bonner, *Declamations,* pp. 46–49. Mitteis, *Reichsrecht und Volksrecht,* pp. 190 ff., and Steinwenter, "Rhetorik und römischer Zivilprozess," *ZSS.,* 65 (1947), 69–120.

162. Yer. Sanh. II, 19d, cf. Lieberman, *Greek in Jewish Palestine,* p. 13. For the law of representation, cf. Cohn, "Die Stellvertretung im jüdischen Rechte," *ZVR,* 36 (1920), 124–213, 354–460. For Greco-Egyptian Law, cf. Wenger, *Stellvertretung im Rechte der Papyri,* 1906, cf. Mitteis, *ZSS.,* 28 (1907), 475–483, and Taubenschlag, *The Law of Greco-Roman Egypt,* I.233–235.

163. Cf. Daube, "Rabbinic Methods of Interpretation and Hellenistic Rhetoric," *HUCA,* XXII, 239–64. For famous rhetoricians from the Roman near East, cf. Heichelheim, *An Economic Survey of Ancient Rome,* IV, 168, for the Jewish rhetorician Caecilius of Calacte, cf. Schürer, *Geschichte,* III (4th ed.), pp. 629–633. For the influence of Roman rhetoric upon later Jewish literature, cf. Brüll, "Zur Geschichte der rhetorischen Literatur bei den Juden," *Ben Chananja,* VI, (1863), 486–490, 509–513, 527–532, 568–573.

164. Cicero, *De Officiis,* I.10.33, cf. Moore, *Judaism,* III.187.

165. Cf. e. g., "How can both these verses be upheld?" Mekilta, ed. Horovitz, p. 64.

166. R. Simon interpreted the law according to its sense, Sanh. 21b, cf. also Bacher, *Agada der Tannaiten,* II.103–104. For the reason of the statute as a general ground of decision, cf. Austin, *Lectures on Jurisprudence,* 1873, p. 1026 For the *occasio legis,* cf. Dernburg, *System des Römischen Rechts,* 1911, I, 57.

167. Cf. Sifre Deut. 23:11 and Bacher, *Terminologie* I, 38, note 3.

168. Sanh. 69b–70a. Sometimes the interpretation of the law according to the letter or the spirit led to the same conclusion. Thus R. Judah excluded an Ammonitess and Moabitess from the prohibition in Deut. 23:4, because he took the verse literally. At the same time R. Simon interpreted the verse in the light of the reason given for the enactment. Scripture says, because they [Moabites and Ammonites] met you not with bread and water in the way (Deut. 23:5). This of course does not apply to the females, Yeb. 77a.

169. *Character and Opinion in the United States,* New York, 1920, p. 156.

170. Cf. Boaz Cohen, "Canons of Interpretation of Jewish Law," in *Proceedings of the Rabbinical Assembly,* 1933–38, p. 175, note 24.

171. Cf. e. g. Mak. 23a, B. K. 47b, 58b, 66a, B. M. 47b, Ḳid. 14a.

172. Cf. Yeb. 8.3.

173. Cf. Yeb. 16.3 and Aristotle's remarks: that the law having laid down the best rules possible, leaves the adjustment and application of particulars to

the discretion of the Magistrate, *Politics*, III. 16, (1287a). Elsewhere Aristotle notes that the laws should define the issue as far as possible and leave as little as possible to the discretion of the judges, *Rhetoric*, I.1.7 (1354a).

174. The antithesis of Paul was not inspired by the technique of thought of Heraclitus as H. Leisegang asserted (*Der Apostel Paulus als Denker*, Leipzig, 1923 p. 39), but by the Greek inventors of the antithesis, cf. Gomperz, *Griechische Denker*, I³, 370 ff., and W. Süss, *Studien zur älteren griechischen Rhetorik*, 1900, p. 3.

175. Quintilian tells us that the hyperbole is an elegant straining of the truth, *decens veri superiectio*, *Inst. Or.*, VIII.6.67. The rabbis too made use of the hyperbole, cf. Tamid 29a.

176. B. B. 16a.

177. Ket. 6a and parallels. These are proverbial expressions indicating that one is asking the impossible. The same idea underlies the Arabic proverb, "He threw him into the river and said take care, you do not get wet," to which Judah Ha-Levi alluded in the Kuzari III, 38 (ed. Hirschfeld, p. 188) as was first noted by Goldziher, *Z. D. M. G.*, 51 (1897), p. 472. It is to this very idea that Shakespeare gave expression in the *Merchant of Venice*, IV.1, 308.

> Take then by bond, take thou thy pound of flesh;
> But, in the cutting, if thou dost shed
> One drop of Christian blood, thy lands and goods
> Are, by the laws of Venice, confiscate
> Unto the state of Venice.

Jurists have sought in vain for some legal significance to this sarcastic and impossible decision, cf. Jhering, *The Struggle for Law*, Chicago, 1879, p. 81 and Griston, *Shaking the Dust from Shakespeare*, 1924, p. 137, 140–141, 146–148, 172–178. However, Shakespeare was not giving utterance to a legal concept but was playing with a proverbial expression that was considered merely as an ironical pleasantry in his time.

178. Cairns remarks that by the thirteenth century, the church fathers could be cited both for and against the thesis whether the Letter of the Law should prevail. On the basis of a sentence from St. Augustine it was held that the Letter of the Law should be followed, whereas St. Hilary, who was much influenced by Quintilian (cf. H. Kling, *De Hilario artis rhetoricae*, Freiburg in Br., 1909) was quoted in support of the view that the Spirit of the Law should dominate. Cf. *Legal Philosophy from Plato to Hegel*, p. 195. For the view of Canon Law on the subject, cf. Cicognani, *Canon Law*, Philadelphia, 1935, pp. 608 ff. Note that many of the Church Fathers were deeply versed in the doctrines of rhetoric, cf. Wilamowitz-Möllendorf, *Glaube der Hellenen*, II.452.

179. Cf. Daube, "Jewish Missionary Maxims in Paul," in *Studia Theologica*, Lund, I, 1947, pp. 158–169, and Davies, *Paul and Rabbinic Judaism*, London, 1948, p. 68.

180. As Prof. Ginzberg has written, "He (i. e. Paul) learnt the art of destroying the law by the law or as the author of Clementine writings has it, *ex lege discere quod nesciebat lex (Recognitiones,* II.54) from his Jewish masters," *Jewish Encyclopedia,* I.630, cf. also his remarks, *loc. cit.,* I.410, "Israel's history and legal enactments were construed (by Paul) as being in reality intimations of the realities of faith, concealing the spirit in the letter and reducing the Old Testament to mere shadows."

181. The purpose of Montesquieu in his classic *Esprit des Lois,* first published in Geneva, 1748, was to show that the diversity of laws was not the result of caprice but was the consequence of the operation of first principles upon the nature of things such as climate, religion, commerce, government and customs. Other books dealing with the spirit of law are: Jhering, *Geist des römischen Rechts,* vols. I–III which passed through several editions, A. Wagermann, *Der Geist des deutschen Rechts,* 1913 and Pound, *The Spirit of the Common Law,* 1921. The latter books purport to present characteristics, peculiarities, essence and temper of the legal systems they describe. For a criticism, cf. Seagle, *Quest of Law,* pp. 153–158. Seemingly influenced by Montesquieu is: I. E. Cellerier, *Esprit de la legislation Mosaique,* vols. I–II, Geneva-Paris, 1837 (non vidi).

182. "Durch 'Interessenjurisprudenz' erfüllt die Rechtswissenschaft ihre praktische Aufgabe, den Inhalt des Rechts zu finden: das Recht auszulegen, das Recht zu ergänzen, neuem Recht die Bahn zu brechen, den überlieferten *Buchstaben* mit dem *Geist* der Gegenwart zu erfüllen," cf. Sohm-Mitteis-Wenger, *Geschichte und System des Römischen Privatrechts,* 1933, p. 30. This is also an apt description of the aim of Rabbinic jurisprudence.

183. *Village Communities,* New York, 1880, p. 383.

17

Rabbinic Interpretation of Scripture

Saul Lieberman

The Rabbis never suggest a correction of the text of the Bible. In the entire rabbinic literature we never come across divergences of opinion regarding Biblical readings.[1] It is therefore obvious that the textual corrections of Greek classics practiced by the Alexandrian grammarians have no parallel in the rabbinic exegesis of Scripture.

In rabbinic tradition exceedingly few traces are left of the literary activity of the Soferim. The literal meaning of the word Soferim is scribes. The Rabbis interpreted it to mean "tellers"; the Soferim counted the letters of the Torah.[2] They probably knew the number of letters in every section.[3] In this they resembled the grammarian,[4] but they came much closer to his character in the rest of their literary activity. The word Sofer in Is. 33:18 was understood by the Septuagint in the same sense. They translated this verse: Where are the Grammarians?[5] Indeed the Soferim were grammarians,[6] and they engaged in the same activity which was pursued by the Alexandrian scholars. They elaborated the so called Midrash (interpretation) of the Bible. Although the word is already found in II Chron. (13:22 and 24:27) it is highly doubtful that it carries there the technical meaning of rabbinic times. The Septuagint translates it respectively: biblion, graphe.[7] However some copies of the Hexapla[8] translate midrash (in II Chron. 13:22), enquiry, which is the exact equivalent of our word. "Ezra has set his heart to inquire into the

Reprinted by permission of the Jewish Theological Seminary of America from *Hellenism in Jewish Palestine*, New York, 1950.

Law of the Lord" (Ezra 7:10). The Hebrew *lidrosh* is correctly translated by the Septuagint to inquire.

One of the first fundamentals of research is to ask "why," to inquire into the reasons of a given matter. "Why"[9] is the common term used by the Rabbis in their interpretation of Scripture. Similarly, Didymus the grammarian[10] likes to introduce his disquisitions with *zeteitai, diati* etc.,[11] and the *zetemata*[12] constituted a notable part of the philologic,[13] the philosophic and the juridic literature.[14] *Ekzetesis*, as found in some copies of the *Hexapla* (see above), is the correct rendering of *Midrash*.

But the first rudiment of the interpretation of a text is the *hermeneia*, the literal and exact equivalent of the Hebrew *targum*, which means both translation and interpretation.[15] The Rabbis derived[16] from the verse in Nehemiah (8:8) that Ezra performed the functions of a translator and interpreter and grammarian.[17]

The elementary task of the interpreter of the Bible was to explain the *realia* and to render the rare and difficult terms in a simpler Hebrew, or, sometimes, in Aramaic. The *Tannaitic Midrashim* swarm with such translations.[18] The Rabbis like to introduce such simple renderings with the term: *'ein . . . 'ela'*, "nothing else than."[19]

These translations are sometimes quite instructive. The Rabbis often explained the "Bible by the Bible,"[20] and their Hebrew translations are often quite illuminating. For instance, we read in *Sifra:*[21] " '*Ma'al*' (Lev. 5:15). '*Me'ilah*' is nothing but faithlessness, for it is written (I Chron. 5:25): *'And they broke faith (vayyim'alu) with the God of their fathers and they went a-whoring after the ba'alim'.*[22] *Similarly it is written (Num. 5:12): 'If any man's wife go astray and act unfaithfully (ma'al) against him'.*" Aquila translated *ma'al* (in Lev. 5:15) *parabasis*, transgression.[23] The Rabbis were more exact. They followed sound philological method and established its meaning from other places in the Bible where the word is explicitly associated with unfaithfulness. The Biblical *ma'al* was rendered *shinui* by the Rabbis, a word probably common in the current Hebrew of the time. Indeed, *Sifre Zuta*[24] also renders *"And acts unfaithfully against him"* (Num. 5:12) *shinat bo*.[25] It is likewise used in *Sifre*[26] with the same meaning.[27]

The Septuagint, the oldest of our preserved *Midrashim* often agrees with these simple interpretations of the Rabbis,[28] but the latter are sometimes more consistent. For instance, on Ex. 12:13 and 23 they remark:[29] "The word *pesiha* means nothing but protection,[30] as it is said

(Isa. 31:5): '*As birds hovering, so will the Lord of Hosts protect Jerusa-lem; He will guard and deliver it, He will protect and rescue it*'." The Rabbis prove the meaning of *pasaḥ* (passed over) from Isa. 31:5 where the context indicates that *pesiḥa* signifies protection.[31] The Septuagint translates Ex. 12:3 "and I shall protect you"[32] and ibid. 27 "protected." But *u-pasaḥ* (ibid. 23) is translated: :"And He will pass by." The latter agrees with R. Josia's interpretation[33] of the verb *pasaḥ*, which is ac-cepted by the Jewish commentaries.[34] Aquila also translates (Ex. 12:11 and 27) the name *pesaḥ* "skipping over," but Symmachus renders it:[35] "[The word] *faseḥ* means defence."[36]

Indeed the verb *pasaḥ* certainly means to step over, to skip,[37] but from the Prophets the Rabbis proved that it also signified to protect, and their translation makes much better sense of Ex. 12:23. Since the word has two meanings they preferred the one which suited the context best.

It appears that comments formulated " '*ein* . . . '*ela*' " which are incorporated in the *Halakhic Midrashim* have their origin in a very ancient commentary of the Law. Most of these comments undoubtedly provide the plain meaning of the text. In course of time this vigorous assertion (i.e., it is nothing but . . .) was extended even to *Midrashic* exposition,[38] but as such it was almost exclusively limited to the narra-tive parts of the Bible. The use of this emphatic formula for a *Midrashic* comment therefore becomes one of the characteristic exaggerations of the *Aggada*; it degenerates into a mere literary phrase, and the Rabbis themselves will not take a comment introduced by these words more seriously than any other *Midrashic* interpretation in the *Aggada*.[39]

The Rabbinic sages sought to understand the meaning of the difficult and rare words in Scripture not only through parallels in the Bible itself where the sense of the expression is clear. They also sometimes explained them with the aid of other languages, remarking that the given word is Phoenician,[40] or Coptic,[41] or Syriac,[42] or derived from some other tongues.[43]

Some of them travelled to the provinces for the sole purpose of discovering the meaning of some rare Biblical words in the dialects spoken there.[44]

In addition, they sometimes explained expressions of the Bible by the customary usage of the language,[45] although they were well aware that the meaning, or usage, of a given word in the Bible often differed from their own.[46]

There is no evidence that the Rabbis prepared special lexica of the Bible; they had no need of them. The entire rabbinic literature bears testimony to the fact that the Rabbis knew the Bible by heart.[47] Jerome[48] testifies that the Palestinian Jews of the fourth century were able to recite the Pentateuch and the Prophets[49] by heart.[50] The Jewish sages could well manipulate their explanations without the help of special vocabularies of the Bible.[51]

The early Jewish interpreters of Scripture did not have to embark for Alexandria in order to learn there the rudimentary methods of linguistic research. To make them travel to Egypt for this purpose would mean to do a cruel injustice to the intelligence and acumen of the Palestinian sages. Although they were not philologists in the modern sense of the word they nevertheless often adopted sound philological methods.

However, the Rabbis were confronted with a much more difficult problem than this simple linguistic research. They treated all of Scripture as one unit. They had to reconcile apparent contradictions in it. Moreover, the Bible, in addition to its narratives, contains the body of Jewish Law. No law book in the world explicitly encompasses all the possible cases. As life developed new legal questions arose which are not clearly stated in the Bible. It is only by way of comparison, inquiry into the spirit of the laws, and special interpretation that proper deductions could be made. Hence, the Rabbis had to introduce a complicated system of interpretation; the grammarians had sometimes to assume the functions of advocates and rhetors.

We learn from the *Tosefta*[52] that Hillel the Elder applied seven norms of interpretation in his discussion with the Bene Bathyra.[53] The seven rules are: 1. Inference *a minori ad majus*. 2. Inference by analogy (*Gezerah Shavah*, explained in detail, below). 3. Constructing a family on the basis of one passage.[54] 4. The same rule as the preceding, but based on two Biblical passages. 5. The General and the Particular, the Particular and the General. 6. Exposition by means of another similar passage. 7. Deduction from the Context.[55]

The context suggests that Hillel was not the author of these rules and norms;[56] he simply used recognized arguments to prove that the Paschal Lamb is offered on the Sabbath, if the fourteenth of Nissan happens to fall on that day.[57] He employed seven norms of interpretation to prove one particular law from the Torah.

A *Baraitha* ascribed to R. Ishmael[58] enumerated thirteen norms of interpretation[59] of the Torah. Schürer[60] calls these norms "a kind of rabbinic logic." Many modern scholars have investigated these rules in detail.[61] A. Schwarz devoted six books[62] to the analytics of these norms of interpretations. Neither he nor any of the other scholars has been able to discover definite Greek influence in them.[63]

However, we find this observation by Judah Hadassi[64] on the thirteen norms of interpretation: "And we also found that the sages of Greece have twelve norms in their rules and laws. They are called *ergasias kai epicheiremata* [executions and arguments].[65] They are *six and six*, together twelve. We examined them and we found them to be like those" (i.e. like the rabbinic rules).

Happily, we are in a position to verify the statement of the Karaite. We have no doubt that he refers to some mediaeval scholia to Hermogenes' *peri evreseos* (III. 7), i.e. to his chapter *peri ergasias epicheirematon*. Hermogenes counts[66] six arguments:[67] "[On] place, time, way (manner) person,[68] cause, fact."[69] He further teaches (ibid., p. 148): "Every argument is executed (or elaborated) . . . from a parable (an illustration), from an example,[70] from something smaller, from something bigger,[71] from something equal, from something opposite." Maximus Planudes[72] in his scholia to this chapter[73] mentions explicitly six arguments and six executions, exercises.[74] It is evident that these six executions and six arguments were well known in Constantinople in the time of Hadassi, and it is quite obvious that he refers to these rules.

The arguments have certainly nothing to do with the rabbinic rules; we therefore shall consider the executions only. A comparison between the executions and the thirteen hermeneutic rules of R. Ishmael will demonstrate that they have only the *kal va-homer*[75] and the analogy[76] in common.

Hadassi has found his followers in modern scholars who were unaware of their early predecessor. A. Kaminka[77] asserts: "At least one of the seven rules by which Hillel explained the Torah seems to be identical with a philological method known at the Alexandrian school . . . in the Halakah it is known as *gezerah shavah;* in Greek *dis legomena*. I believe this system was *not* originally used by Hillel in connection with the juridical or ritual questions but when commenting on Biblical passages in general." It was pointed out[78] that the early Rabbis resorted to this simple system of comparison of parallel words and passages in their

Targumim without making any mention of the term *gezerah shavah*. Moreover, etymologically this name has nothing to do with *dis legomena* (see below). The inference itself is so primitive that it could not escape any intelligent expounder of a text.

It goes without saying that any thinking person who was acquainted with Greek logic and who heard something of the nature of rabbinical exegesis of the Bible would be inclined to associate it in some way with the former. Indeed, Eusebius[79] remarks: "Verily they (i.e. the Jews) have certain *deuterotai*[80] of primary studies (for so it pleases them to name the expounders of their Scriptures) who by interpretation and explanation . . . made clear what was obscurely rendered in riddles." Obviously, he is referring to the elementary-school *Tanna* who taught the children *Mishnah* and *Midrash*. He adduces them as examples of those who employ the method of logic in Hebrew philosophy,[81] a logic which pursues the truth, unlike the clever sophistries of the Greeks. Eusebius, of course, is noncommital. His words only suggest that the Jews had their system of logic, a declaration which aroused the anger of Julian the Emperor.[82]

So far so good. We can safely assert that the Jews possessed their rules of logic for the interpretation of the Bible in the second half of the first century B.C.E.[83] The question is when were these rules organized in a system with a nomenclature, specific numbers and definite categories. It will be demonstrated below that interpretation in general is older than the revelation of the Law at Mount Sinai. A very great number of hermeneutic rules existed in antiquity many of which could not be applied to the interpretation of the Torah. The hermeneutics of dreams and oracles could not as a rule be applied to the legal sections of the Bible. Generally Scripture does not express itself ambiguously but states the laws in clear language.[84]

A Rabbi who maintained that a certain law could be deduced from Scripture had to demonstrate that the words of the Bible really imply the ruling in question, although it does not state it explicitly. Apparent contradictions in the Bible had to be reconciled by more or less plausible, and not fanciful, means. New laws could be derived from Scripture by comparison, especially by comparison with something more important, with something less important and with something equal. In this case the suggestion of Hadassi to compare the rabbinic hermeneutics to the executions of the rhetors deserves a closer analysis.

Let us first examine the terminology of the hermeneutic rules of the

Rabbis. The strangest term among them is *gezerah shavah*. No convincing explanation of the etymology and the exact meaning of the name has been suggested until now.[85] The word *gezerah* in both Biblical and rabbinic Hebrew means: *decisio,* decision, decree.[86] It corresponds to the Greek *syncrisis, decretum,* with which the Septuagint rendered the Hebrew *mishpat*[87] *Syncrisis* signifying *decretum,* decision, is already current in the Egyptian papyri of the third century B.C.E.[88]

Thus it is evident that *gezerah* is *syncrisis* both etymologically and logically. This word is also used in the sense of comparison by Aristotle and the Septuagint.[89] By the second century C.E., at the latest, it served as a technical term in the works of the Greek rhetors.[90] Aphtonius[91] defines this term.[92] "*Syncrisis* is a comparative term which by juxtaposition matches the greater or the equal with the thing compared." Ioannes Sardianus[93] summarizes it: "We use *syncrisis* [comparison] in a threefold manner: the equal with the equal, [the smaller] with the greater and [the greater] with the smaller." The term "*syncrisis* with the equal," is also employed by Hermogenes[94] who flourished in the second century C.E.[95]

Hence we unhesitatingly translate the term *gezerah shavah* as *syncrisis pros ison,* a comparison with the equal. The beginning of the *Baraitha* of R. Ishmael is certainly to be translated: The Torah is interpreted by thirteen hermeneutic rules: *apo meizonos kai elattou, apo syncriseos pros ison,* etc. The Greek rhetors counted them as three rules,[96] while the Rabbis considered them two norms.

Thus, originally, *gezerah shavah* was a simple analogy, a comparison of equals. In this sense it is employed by the School of Shammai[97] in the Mishnah:[98] "It is an analogy (i.e. comparison of equals): Dough-offering and [Priests'] Dues are a gift to the priest, and the Heave-offering is a gift to the priest etc."[99]

We also find this term in the same meaning applied by R. Eliezer (of the School of Shammai). In *Sifre Zuta*[100] he is quoted as saying: "One does not compare a voluntary and an obligatory or vice versa, but one may compare two voluntary acts or two obligatory acts for the purpose of analogy," i.e. a *syncrisis* (an analogy) can be drawn between equal categories only.[101]

The Rabbis also employ another term for analogy, viz. *hekesh.*[102] This word is the literal equivalent of the Greek *parathesis, adpositio, vicinitas* and comparison, juxtaposition, which is used in all these senses by Polybius.[103]

The school of R. Ishmael frequently employs the phrase.[104] "The word [in the Torah] is vacant [105] [for the purpose] of juxtaposing it and deducing a *gezerah shavah* from it." Polybius [106] expresses himself in similar style: [107] "Contemplated and compared by juxtaposition." [108] Again he employs the two terms together: [109] "by comparison and juxtaposition" which means literally from *hekesh* and *gezerah shavah*.

However in the official hermeneutic rules the term *gezerah shavah* was applied not to analogy of content but to identity of words (i.e. verbal congruities in the text), a manner of comparison which sometimes appears to be without logical basis. Rabbinic tradition therefore ruled [110] that "No one may on his own authority draw an analogy from verbal congruities in the text," i.e. this method can be applied only where authorized by tradition. The Palestinian Talmud [111] demonstrated the absurd conclusions which might be reached if the method of *gezerah shavah* were utilized by anyone on his own initiative and not by tradition.

We have no ground to assume that the method itself of both logical and verbal analogy was borrowed by the Jews from the Greeks. However, the method and the definition of the method—the terminology— are two different things. Unfortunately we have no means to decide who among the Rabbis used this term first. The *Tosefta* [112] maintains that Hillel applied the *gezerah shavah* in his discussion with the Bene Bathyra,[113] but it is very possible that this refers to the method alone and not to the term,[114] and it is the editor of the *Tosefta* who designated Hillel's arguments by the later terminology. The term *gezerah shavah* may thus be no older than the end of the first century C.E., or the beginning of the second,[115] the century when *syncrisis pros ison* was already a favorite tool in the preparatory exercises of the Greek rhetors in the Asiatic centers.

It has been pointed out that some of the hermeneutic rules found in the *Halakha* recur almost literally in the Roman legal classics (Sabinus, Celsus [116] and Gaius [117]). Hillel the Elder and the Rabbis of the following generations used to interpret not only the Torah but also secular legal documents.[118] Most likely general standards for the interpretation of legal texts were in vogue which dated back to high antiquity. But it was the Greeks who systematized, defined and gave definite form to the shapeless mass of interpretations.

The Rabbis were often confronted with the same problems as the Greek rhetors. The former sought to derive new laws from the Torah or to find support for old ones which were rooted in oral tradition. They were aware that in certain cases their interpretation is not borne out by the actual meaning of Scripture, and they accordingly termed such support *zekher la-davar* (allusion)[119] and *'asmakhta'* (support).[120] They went so far as to lay down the rule.[121] "For all laws which have no evident origin in Scripture support is adduced from *many* places [in the Bible]."[122]

But rabbinic literature abounds in such artificial and forced interpretations. They were merely a literary conceit. Rab[123] maintained[124] that no one is to be appointed a member of the high court *(Sanhedrin)* unless he is able to prove from Biblical texts the ritual cleanliness of a reptile (although reptiles are definitely declared unclean in Lev. 11:29). The reason for this requirement can be inferred from the statement of a younger contemporary of our Rabbi. R. Johanan asserted[125] that a man who is not qualified to offer hundred arguments for declaring a reptile ritually clean or unclean will not know how to open [the trial of capital cases] with reasons for acquital.[126] The judge must thus be a rhetor who can *disputare in utramque partem* and prove at one and the same time the two opposite points of view.[127] But the example given by the Rabbis is selected from the interpretation of the ritual part of the Torah. The methods of the rhetor[128] and the grammarian must sometimes be identical.

In their schools the Greek rhetors taught the art of twisting the law according to the required aim and purpose. The jurist had to be equipped with all the methods of the grammarian. In Rome the early grammarians were the teachers of rhetoric,[129] and the dialectical jurisprudence of the Romans is known to be a Greek product.[130] The Jews with their love and devotion to education would be much more susceptible than the Romans[131] to the sound contribution of the Greeks to learning. They would certainly not hesitate to borrow from them methods and systems which they could convert into a mechanism for the clarification and definition of their own teachings. The instruction and the works of the rhetors were most suitable for application in the hermeneutics of the *'asmakhta'* (support) type. For this purpose the art of grammar and the art of rhetoric were combined and fused into one device.[132]

The two basic works of Greek theology, the books of Homer and of Hesiod abound in atrocities, immoralities and abominable vices which they report of the Olympian gods. As is well known the Greek philosophers eventually began to interpret the works of Homer allegorically. In the fifth century B.C.E. Stesimbrotus founded a school in Athens where he sought to find the underlying, covert meaning all through the works of Homer.[133] According to Greek tradition, Anaxagoras[134] was the first to teach that in his poems Homer treats of virtue and justice, a thesis which is developed at greater length by his friend Metrodorus of Lampsacus.[135] The Stoic philosophers exploited this method of allegoric interpretation of Homer even more.[136] The Alexandrian grammarians forced Homer to conform to the behavior and manners of the Ptolemaic court in Egypt,[137] or to the Greek customs and habits of their own time and place.[138]

K. Lehrs[139] has convincingly shown the two tendencies of the grammarians with regard to Homer. One group, the so called *enstatikoi,* indulged in charges against his writings, the others, named *lutikoi* refuted the arguments of the accusers and came to his defence. The very terms of these grammarians prove their rhetorical methods.[140] We shall now consider one example of an *apologia* by one of the earliest Alexandrian grammarians, which is quite instructive.

We read in the Iliad (XI. 636 ff.):

Another man would hardly move the cup from the table
When it was full, but Nestor, that old man, raised it easily.

Sosibius[141] the *lutikos*[142] remarked:[143] Today the charge is brought against the Poet[144] that whereas he said all others raised the cup with difficulty, Nestor alone did it without difficulty. This statement of Homer seemed unreasonable *(alogos)* to some of the grammarians. It appeared senseless to them that in the presence of Achilles, Diomedes and Ajax, Nestor should be represented as more vigorous than they, though he was more advanced in years. To this Sosibius replied: "Of these accusations then, we can absolve the Poet by resorting to the *anastrophe.*"[145] He suggested that the word *geron* be transposed from line 637 to line 636 so that it will read:[146]

Another old man would hardly move the cup from the table
When it was full, but Nestor raised it easily.

The Poet is singling out Nestor from among the old men only. The difficulty is removed, and the Poet is acquitted of the charge of unreasonableness.

An exact parallel to this difficulty and solution is extant in rabbinic literature. It is stated in *Sifre:*[147] " '*And they came before Moses and before Aaron*[148] *on that day*' (Num. 9:6) R. Josiah said: If Moses did not know is it possible that Aaron would?[149] But the verse is to be *inverted*[150] and expounded," i. e. the men first came to Aaron who did not know and then they came to Moses. See above note 146.

The Rabbis encountered the same difficulty in Num. 9:6, that the Alexandrian grammarians traced in Il. XI. 636 ff. It seemed unreasonable *(alogos)* to them that the people whose question Moses failed to answer would consult Aaron on the same subject. They solved the problem by means of *anastrophe,* rearrangement of the verse, just as Sosibius did.

However, from the anecdote related by Athenaeus[151] we learn that the solution proposed by Sosibius seemed strange and ridiculous to his contemporaries,[152] which indicates that in the third century B.C.E. this method was not yet fully accepted. In the time of R. Josiah[153] this means of interpretation was very common in the rabbinic schools.[154]

The rhetor Theon[155] writes:[156] "We shall frequently make use of the inversion of the order." But he is really referring to the rhetoric scheme of "last first",[157] as is obvious from the examples he cites. This kind of *anastrophe* is also utilized by the Rabbis,[158] but the more common rabbinic *anastrophe* is that employed by Sosibius.

The solutions of the grammarians were not always complicated and artificial. They sometimes assumed much simpler forms. For instance, we read in the Iliad VIII. 555 ff. "Even as in heaven around the gleaming moon the stars shine very bright." It was asked: How now could the moon be gleaming when the stars [around it] were shining bright. To which Aristarchus solving this says:[159] It does not mean that the moon was gleaming at that time, but that by its nature it is gleaming."[160]

This kind of interpretation is common in rabbinic literature. The sages rule[161] that a man who takes a vow to derive no benefit from creatures that are born is forbidden to benefit from the creatures that are yet to be born. Creatures that are born means creatures whose nature it is to be born,[162] and not only those that have already been born.[163]

Literary problems were solved in a similar way in the schools of Alexandria and those of Palestine. The methods of the rhetors and their discussions had at least a stimulating effect on serious treatment of legal texts.[164] The following part of this chapter may shed more light on some aspects of text interpretation and its origin.

THE HERMENEUTIC RULES OF THE *AGGADAH*

Some of the hermeneutic rules used by the Rabbis to interpret the narrative parts of the Bible at first appear to us very artificial and far-fetched. These norms form part of the so called "thirty-two[165] hermeneutic rules of the *Aggadah*."[166] Let us consider a group of successive rules:

Rule 27. *Mashal*, i. e. parable or allegory or symbol. The *mashal* is already used in the Bible; as an allegory it is common in the *Midrash*.[167] Very often the interpretation by way of *mashal* is undoubtedly the only true explanation of the text. But some allegories are obviously far from the real meaning of the text.[168]

Rule 28. Paronomasia, amphiboly, i. e. playing with homonymous roots.[169]

Rule 29. *Gematria*,[170] *isopsepha*, i. e. computation of the numeric value of letters. Only a single instance is adduced in this *Midrash* to illustrate the *gematria*. The number 318 (servants of Abraham) in Gen. 14:14 has the numerical value of Eliezer, i. e. Abraham had only his servant Eliezer with him.[171] But rabbinic literature is replete with examples of *gematria*.[172]

Rule 30. Substitution of letters, the so called *Athbash* alphabet, i. e. ʾalef (the first letter) is written instead of *tav* (the last letter), *bet* (the second letter) instead of *shin* (the one before the last) etc. and vice versa. The *Midrash*[173] cites only one instance. *Leb-kamai* in Jer. 51:1 is nothing other than *kasdim* (Chaldeans), according to the *Athbash* alphabet.[174] But this method is quite common in the *Midrash* and Talmud.[175]

Rule 31. *Notaricon*,[176] i. e. the interpretation of every single letter (in a particular word) as the abbreviation of a series of words.[177] *Nimrezet* (outrageous) (I Kings 2:8) is explained as signifying *noʾef* (adulterer), *mamzer* (bastard), *rozeaḥ* (murderer), *zorer* (oppressor), *toʿevah* (abomination). The acrostic also belongs to this type, see below p. 445 ff.

Another kind of *notaricon* is the breaking of one word in two parts. Our *Midrash* cites as an illustration the word *karmel* (fresh grain) (Lev. 2:14) which is to be interpreted *rakh mal* (soft, easily crushed)[178] i.e. the word is broken in two parts, and the letters of the first part are transposed. The *notaricon* includes an *anagram* as well. The *Aggadah*[179] frequently resorts to the application of the anagram.[180]

Similarly *"Abrek!"* (Gen. 41:43) is interpreted by R. Judah[181] as *av rakh* (young father). The name of the Patriarch Reuben is dissolved[182] into *r'eu ben* ("see, a son").[183]

The artificiality of the last four hermeneutic rules is evident. An anonymous *Midrash* appended at the end of the thirty-two hermeneutic norms[184] remarks: "Behold it says: '*A dream carries much implication*' (Eccl. 5:2). Now by using the method of *kal vaḥomer (a minori ad maius)* we reason: If the contents of dreams which have no effect may yield a multitude of interpretations, how much more then should the important contents of the Torah imply many interpretations in every verse."

The author of the anonymous *Midrash* possibly felt that some similarity exists between the methods of the interpretation of dreams and some of the hermeneutic rules of the *Aggadah*. Indeed, we shall demonstrate the striking fact that the hermeneutic rules mentioned above are also applied to the solution of dreams. In this realm they are quite understandable. It lies in the very nature of some dreams and most of the oracles to make their revelations in a concealed and disguised way. Dreams and oracles lend themselves to many and various kinds of interpretation. They are, of course, always right. The expounder will show by the remotest ways possible that they did not lie. Necessity often compelled the priests and interpreters to invent the most clever devices for explaining the meanings of oracles and dreams. The cleverer the trick, the deeper the impression on the inquirer of the dreams and oracles. We shall now consider in order the application of the five above-mentioned rules to the elucidation of dreams and oracles.

1. Symbols[185] and allegories[186] are the most common means for the explanation of dreams.[187] We need not bring examples for it, the phenomenon being universally known.

2. Paronomasia, the playing with homonyms, is an important element in the interpretation of dreams. Artemidorus gives a number of instances[188] to this effect. Rabbinic literature[189] has preserved a lengthy catalogue of dream interpretations. H. Lewy[190] demonstrated the close parallel between Artemidorus' *Onirocriticon* and the dream interpretations of the Rabbis.[191] Paronomasia plays an important part in it.[192] In many places the style of the Talmudic passages (ibid.) makes the impres-

sion of being excerpts from a manual on dreams which contained general principles. The Rabbis frequently employ such general formulas[193] as "All . . . except." For instance they say: "All kinds of vegetables are of good omen in a dream except etc."[194] Dream books from all over the world and of all times have utilized similar methods.

3. The *gematria, isopsepha,* the numerical value of letters, is one of the most important components of the *onirocritica.*[195]

To see the weasel in a dream is a bad portent, because the letters of *gale* (weasel are of the same numerical value as *dike* (lawsuit or penalty).[196] Meeting a weasel on the way was believed in antiquity to be a bad portent,[197] and the Rabbis condemned this belief.[198] Nevertheless they saw in the weasel some sinister symbol. They said:[199] "Why does it[200] liken all inhabitants of the world to a weasel,[201] because just as this weasel drags and stores up and does not know for whom it stores, so the dwellers of the world drag and store, drag and store, not knowing for whom they store, [as it is written]:[202] '*He heapeth up riches, and knoweth not who shall gather them'.*"[203]

Artemidorus[204] similarly explains that the vision of a weasel in a dream is a bad omen because it spoils whatever it takes.[205] The latter interpreted the dream of a weasel by means of *gematria* and a symbol; the Rabbis apply it in the *Aggadah* with the help of paronomasia.

Although there is no evidence in early rabbinic literature for the use of *gematria (isopsepha)* in the interpretation of dreams[206] we can assume the Rabbis were not unaware of this method in the *onirocritica.* The wide use of the *gematria* in the magic and mystic literature[207] argues for its general application in all occult sciences of the time.[208]

4. Substitution of letters, *Athbash*[209] was widely practiced in antiquity.[210] No evidence is found for the application of *Athbash* in dream interpretations, but the common use of it suggests that the experts on dreams would not neglect this device when occasion arose. Rab[211] maintained[212] that Daniel had interpreted (Dan. 5:25) the oracle by the method of *Athbash.* This asserts its application in at least the interpretation of oracles.

5. *Notaricon* in all its forms and variations as it was employed by the Rabbis in the exposition of the *Aggadah*[213] is quite common in the interpretation of dreams among both Jews and Gentiles:

a. Every single letter is considered as an abbreviation of a word.[214] R. Joshua b. Levi said[215] that the vision of the letter *tet* in a dream is a good omen. "Is it because *tet* stands for *tov* (good)?"[216] Similarly, Artemidorus[217] relates that once a military commander saw the letters *iota, kappa,* and *theta* in a dream inscribed on his sword. The Jewish war in Cyrene[218] broke out, and the man who saw the dream died a hero's death. Consequently, the explanation of the dream was that the ι stood for *Ioudaiois* (Jews'), the κ for *Kyrenaiois* (Cyrenes') and the ϑ for *thanatos* (death).

b. The anagram[219] was a common device in the *onirocritica.* The Rabbis say:[220] "If a man sees barley in a dream it means that his sins were removed, as it is written (Isa. 6:7): '*And thine iniquity is taken away*'." The letters *sᵉorin* (barley) are transposed and made to signify *sar ʿavon* (sin is removed). It is a common procedure in the hermeneutic rules of the *Midrash.* TB[221] formulates it: "One may remove [a letter] and add [one] and then interpret." From Artemidorus[222] it is evident that this was the practice of the Greek interpreters of dreams. The anagram was also widely employed in mystic and magic literature.[223]

c. The dissolution of one word into two parts[224] was also generally practiced in the *onirocritica.* Ishmael is there interpreted[225] as *yishmaʿ ʾel,* "The Lord will hear [his prayers]," and *lulav* (palm branch) as *lo lev,* "To Him is [his] heart."[226] During his siege of Tyre Alexander the Great is said to have seen a satyr in a dream who mocked him at a distance. "The diviners, dividing the word 'satyros' in two parts (sa Tyros), said to him plausibly enough 'Tyre is to be thine'."[227]

We not only find the same methods employed in the *onirocritica* and in the *Aggadah,* but sometimes also come across the very same interpretations in both sources. The *Sifre*[228] playing on the word *morashah* (Deut. 33:4), heritage, interprets it as if it were written *mᵉorasah* (betrothed), and, deriving from it that the Torah is betrothed to Israel, it draws certain conclusions.[229] The identical exegesis is used in the solution of a dream.[230] In the *onirocriticon* the betrothed girl symbolizes the Torah. In the *Aggadah* the Torah is betrothed to Israel.

The methods applied in the understanding of dreams were invented neither by the Jews nor by the Greeks. They go back to hoary antiquity. The ingenuity of the diviner or seer produced the most complicated solutions of dreams, oracles and magic, which lent themselves to similar ways of interpretations; they borrow from each other and supplement one another.

"Seventy years, as the period of its (i. e. Babylon's) desolation, he

(i. e. Marduk) wrote down (in the Book of Fate). But the merciful Marduk in a moment his heart was at rest (appeased) turned it upside down and for the eleventh year ordered its restoration." [231] The Babylonian numeral "70" turned upside down, or reversed, becomes "11", just as our printed "9" turned upside down becomes "6".[232]

Writing or reading letters upside down was probably not limited to oracular interpretation only, but was practiced in magic as well. More than a thousand years later Plinius Medicus prescribed [233] as a "remedy" for a persistent haemorrhage the writing of the patient's own name on his forehead in letters inverted upside down.[234] The methods were the same at different times among different nations.

The Rabbis knew this truth. R. Abbahu [235] was once involved in a controversy with non-Jews about the survival of children born after seven or eight months of pregnancy.[236] The Rabbi remarked:[237] "From your own [alphabet] I will prove it to you $\zeta = epta$, $\eta = okto$." [238] The most plausible explanation was suggested by O. Crusius: [239] Since ζ equals 7 and η 8 the cryptogram has to be deciphered as: *ze ta epta* ⟨*mallon*⟩ *e ta okto,* i. e. "Infants of seven months are more likely to survive than those of eight." [240] R. Abbahu resorted here to the *notaricon,*[241] paronomasia and the numerical value of letters, and combined them together [242] for the purpose of investing letters of the Greek alphabet with mysterious significance. The method was well understood by Jew and Gentile alike.

To sum up, numberless methods for the interpretations of dreams, oracles and mystic writings existed in the ancient world from times immemorial. Very often the same phenomenon lent itself to various and even contradictory explanations.[243] The Rabbis who flourished at the end of the first and the beginning of the second centuries (and among them we find R. 'Akiba, the famous interpreter of the Torah) already employed the shrewd and complicated methods of the *onirocritica* in their dream interpretations.[244]

For the interpretation of sacred *legal* texts, which were not as a rule formulated in an ambiguous language, different means were undoubtedly in use among the priests. The Rabbis applied comparatively few rules to the elaboration of the legal part of the Torah. They were the result of choice, discrimination and crystallization out of many ways for the exposition of texts. In the *Aggadah* however and in the *asmakhtot* ("supports") for the *Halakha,* the Rabbis resorted to well established devices which were current in the literary world at that time. Had the Rabbis themselves invented these artificial rules in their interpretations, the "supports" from the Bible would be ineffective and strange to the public. But as the utilization of instruments accepted all over the civilized world of that time their rules of interpretation of the *Aggadah* (and their "supports" for the *Halakha* from Scripture) were a literary affectation which was understood and appreciated by their contemporaries.[245]

However, although we possess no evidence that the Rabbis borrowed their rules of interpretation from the Greeks, the situation is quite different when we deal with formulation, terms, categories and systematization of these rules. The latter were mainly created by the Greeks, and the Jews most probably did not hesitate to take them over and adapt them to their own rules and norms.

The name *Mekhilta, Mekhilata* (literally: measure, measures), for the *Tannaitic* treatises which interpret the Bible[246] corresponds exactly to *kanon, kanones*,[247] the treatise, or treatises, of logic.[248] Again the term *gezerah shavah* appears to be the literal translation of the Greek *synerisis pros ison*,[249] which indicates the influence of Greek terminology.

Hence we may go a step further. Although the Rabbis cannot be definitely said to have adopted a certain method from the Greeks, they may nevertheless have learned from them the *application* of that method to a particular question. We shall cite one interesting instance.

It appears that the device of an acrostic in a composition to indicate the name of the author was already employed in the Orient in the second millenium B.C.E.[250] According to Cicero[251] Ennius Quintus wove into some of his verses the acrostic:[252] Quae Q. Ennius fecit, "Quintus Ennius wrote it." In the view of modern scholars the Greek acrostic of this type[253] is not earlier than the second century B.C.E.[254]

Perhaps we may venture the conjecture that even the early Alexandrian grammarians sought acrostics in Homer's books for the purpose of establishing the authorship of certain poems found in our Iliad and Odyssey.[255] Athenaeus reports[256] that Sosibius[257] was a recipient of a royal stipend from Ptolemy Philadelphus. The latter once commanded his stewards to refuse Sosibius his stipend and to tell him that he had already received it. The stewards obeyed the order of the king and, consequently, Sosibius went to him and complained of their action. Ptolemy asked for the records and, upon examining them, affirmed that his stewards were right in their assertion that Sosibius had already received his stipend. The records had the following list of names of people who had already been paid their allowances: Soteros, Sosigenos, Bionos, Appolloniou. The king said: Take the *so* from Soteros, the *si* from Sosigenos, the first syllable from Bionos and the last letters from Appolloniou, and you have: So-si-bi-ou. "You will find that you yourself received your due according to your own devices,"[258] i. e. the way of your interpretation of Homer.

This anecdote makes good sense only if we suppose that Sosibius liked to look for acrostics in the poems of Homer which might contain the names (signatures) of their authors. Ptolemy argued that by Sosibius' own methods he could prove that the latter's name was found in his records indicating that he had already received his pay. If our conjecture is true, Sosibius was the first to introduce the search for an acrostic as a literary criterion for the establishment of the authorship of a given work. This innovation seemed ridiculous to his contemporaries, and he was accordingly given his own medicine.

In early rabbinic literature this kind of acrostic is not mentioned.[259] But the Rabbis were sometimes confronted with problems similar to the question of authorship in classic literature, and the possible discovery of an acrostic would be of some help.

For instance, the Rabbis differed as to the writer of the Second Tables. The Bible itself leaves room for doubt. Some verses imply (Ex. 34:1; Deut. 10:2, 4) that the Almighty wrote them (as He did the first ones). But other verses (Ex. 34:27, 28) indicate that Moses engraved the Second Tables. The prevalent rabbinic view is that both the First and the Second Tables were written by the Almighty Himself.[260] But some rabbinic sources suggest that the latter were the work of Moses.[261] Rabbi Isaiah the Younger (of Trani) states explicitly:[262] " *'And I will write'* (Ex. 34:1) is not meant in the literal sense, for it is said (ibid. 27): *'Write thou'*. Only the First Tables were of the Lord's own handwriting. The verse *'I will write'* means I shall order thee to write." Similarly Pseudo-Philo[263] records: "And the Lord said to him . . . write upon them the laws etc."

Consequently the opinions of the Rabbis were divided as to the handwriting of the Second Tables. Both parties found their evidence in *'anokhi* (I), the first word of the Tables, which they rated as an acrostic. The prevalent opinion read it[264] to mean: "I Myself wrote [and] gave [them]." In this view the first word of both the First and the

Second Tables indicates that they were both written by the Lord Himself.

However an anonymous statement preserved in the Yemenite *Midrash Haggadol*[265] records: "The Rabbis said *'anokhi* is to be resolved into: I *nomico* wrote [and] gave [them]." Here it is the *nomikos* (notary) who wrote and gave the Tables. There can be no doubt that the *nomikos* is none other than Moses. The Samaritan Marqah,[266] in enumerating the titles of Moses, calls him *misteh*,[267] *mesites*, middleman, and *nomikeh*, *nomikos, iuris prudens,* or scribe, notarius.[268] The Samaritans[269] and the Palestinian *Targumim*[270] call Moses *safar* (scribe). In the Greek of the Byzantine period *nomikos* was simply *tabellio*,[271] notary.[272] The Rabbis who maintained that the Second Tables were engraved by Moses explained that in these the letter *nun* in *'anokhi* stands not for *nafshi* (Myself) but for *nomikeh, nomikos,* Moses.

NOTES

1. The only questions sometimes raised by the Rabbis in this connection have to do with the *matres lectionis* or vocalization. See *Mishnah Sotah* V. 5; 'Abodah Zarah II. 5, passim. Comp. also *TP Kil'aim* III. 1, 28c; *Sanhedrin* VII. 11, 25v; *TB Kiddushin* 30a.
2. *TB Ḥagigah* 15b; *Kiddushin* 30a.
3. For the later *Massorah*, see C. D. Ginsburg, *Introduction to the Masoretico-Critical Edition of the Hebrew Bible* (London 1897), p. 113.
4. Concerning the number of letters in the Pentateuch, see A. Marx in *JBL* XXXVIII, 1919, p. 24 ff. On the counting of letters, see T. Birt, *Das antike Buchwesen* (Berlin 1882), p. 161.
5. Ezra the Scribe happened to be a grammarian as well.
6. Of course, not in the strict sense of our modern usage of the word.
7. See W. Bacher, *Die aelteste Terminologie der juedischen Schriftauslesung, ein Woerterbuch der bibelexigetischen Kunstsprache der Tannaiten* (Leipzig 1899), I, p. 104. Comp. also M. H. Segal in *Tarbiz* XVII, 1946, p. 194 ff.
8. See F. Field, *Hexapla* (Oxford 1867–1875), a. 1.
9. See Bacher, *Terminologie* etc. I, p. 113, s. v. *mipnei.*
10. Flourished in the first century B.C.E.
11. See G. Zuntz, *Byzantion* XIII, 1938, p. 647, n. 3.
12. In the Talmud *bᶜayot.*
13. See K. Lehrs, *de Aristarchi studiis Homericis* (Leipzig 1865), p. 217 ff. Comp. p. 213 ibid.
14. See F. Schulz, *History of Roman Legal Science* (Oxford 1946), p. 342, Note DD.

15. Comp. also Brockelmann, *Lexicon Syriacum* (Berlin 1895; Halle 1928), 834a.

16. *TP Megillah* IV. 1, 74d; *Bereshith Rabba* XXXVI. 8, p. 342; *TB Megillah* 3a and parallel.

17. Comp. A. Kaminka, *Encyclopaedia Judaica* IV, p. 622.

18. See *Mekhilta*, ed. Lauterbach (Philadelphia 1933–1935), I, p. 82₁₃; 204₂₃₁ passim. *Mekhilta deRashbi*, ed. Hoffmann (Frankfort-am-Main 1904), p. 12; *Sifra*, ed. Weiss (Vienna 1862), 108d (comp. Lieberman, *JQR* XXXVI, 1946, p. 352, n. 179); ibid. 111a–d; *Sifre Zuta*, ed. Horovitz (Leipzig 1917), p. 291₆; *Tarbiz* VI, 1934, 3, p. 105 and n. 3 ibid.; *Jubilee Volume in honor of Samuel Krauss*, Jerusalem 1937, p. 33, n. 16. Comp. also L. Dobschütz, *Die einfache Bibelexegese d. Tannaim*, pp. 20–25 and the instances quoted below.

19. See, for instance, *Mekhilta*, ed. Lauterbach I, pp. 276₈; 443, 5; 486₅; 498₃; 567₅; 679₅; 1104₂; 15920; 16041; 17013; 17470–73; 19147; 202200 22529; 245₂₅; ibid. II, pp. 225; 381₈; 885₂; 1514₁; 2694₂; 2896₆; ibid. III, p. 247₈; 259₀; 4556–58 and 6654–57. It is also very frequent in all the other *Halakhic Midrashim*, see Bacher, *Terminologie* etc. I and II, s. v. *'ein* and *lashon*. Comp. Gen. 28:19. It corresponds to the Greek: *ouden allo . . . e.*

20. See *TP Megillah* I. 13, 72b. For linguistic purposes the Rabbis considered the entire Bible as a unit. See *TB Baba Kamma* 2b.

21. *Vayyikra, Ḥoba* XI. 1, ed. Weiss 25c. Comp. *TB Meʿila* 18a.

22. This is also the reading of *TB* ibid. But our text of the Bible reads *"The gods of the peoples of the land."* The rabbinic scribes most probably completed the quotation from memory, according to the more familiar verse (Jud. 8:33).

23. On the rendering of the Septuagint, see J. F. Schleusner, *Lexicon in LXX* (Leipzig 1820–1821), s. v. *ianthano*.

24. Ed. Horovitz, p. 233₁₂.

25. See *Sifre* ibid., p. 117 ff. and comp. *Mekhilta Nezikin* III, ed. Lauterbach, vol. III, p. 259₀.

26. *Sifre*, vol. II, 306, ed. Finkelstein (Berlin-New York 1939), p. 330. The Rabbis explain Mal. 3:6 to mean "For I, the Lord, was not unfaithful." This is probably the true meaning of the verse, see below, n. 27.

27. H. Yalon in the Hebrew periodical *Melilah* II, 1946, p. 172, adduces post-*Tannaitic* sources which employ the verb *shanah* with a similar meaning. He correctly associated it with Prov. 24:21. According to the sources quoted above in the text, the verse should be rendered: *"Meddle not with traitors."* Comp. also H. G. Liddell and R. Scott, *A Greek–English Lexicon*, B. I. 4.

28. It can be ascertained by comparing the sources referred to above, n. 19, with the Septuagint.

29. *Mekhilta, Pisḥa* VII, ed. Lauterbach I, p. 567₅ (Comp. 578₇); ibid. XI, 879₀.

30. Variant reading for *ḥayyas* (pity): *ḥassut* (protection).

31. Comp. also *Tosefta Sotah* IV, 5, 29912; *Mekhilta*, ed. Lauterbach I, 185207.

The correct English translation of the verse ibid. is: "The Lord will *protect* the door."

32. "Take refuge" in Ps. 61:5 is translated by the Septuagint: *skepasthesomai.*
33. *Mekhilta* ibid., p. 5784.
34. Comp. also Field, *Hexapla* Ex. 12:11, n. 11, who refers to Philo and Josephus. See Riedel, *Zeitschrift fuer die altestamentliche Wissenschaft* XX, 1900, 320 ff.
35. Comp. Field ibid.
36. Comp. also the Aramaic *Targumim* a. l.
37. I Kings 18:21 and 26. See however Yonah Ibn Gānâh, *Sefer ha-Shorashim,* p.405.
38. See *Mekhilta,* ed. Lauterbach I, 151133; 1691; 19150; 19160; 20631; 20735; 21083; 22174 (in the variants); 22634; 22988; 23321; 241125; ibid. vol. II, 221–3; 2647; 6814; 13956; 169102; 186110 and so in the other *Halakhic Midrashim.*
39. See Lieberman *Sheqi'in* (Jerusalem 1938), p. 82 ff.
40. See *Sifre* II, 306, ed. Finkelstein, p. 33612 and notes ibid.
41. See *Pesikta deR. Kahana* XII, 109b. Comp. A. Brüll, *Fremdsprachliche Redensarten* (Leipzig 1869), p. 47.
42. *Mekhilta Pisha* III, ed. Lauterbach I, 28.
43. See Brüll ibid., p. 30 ff. Comp. also Samuel Rosenblatt, *The Interpretation of the Bible in the Mishnah* (Baltimore 1935), p. 33. This method was subsequently extended and pushed to the extreme by the *Aggadists;* they even tried to interpret certain expressions of the Pentateuch according to the Greek language, see Brüll ibid., p. 20 ff.
44. *Bereshith Rabba* LXXIX. 9, p. 946 ff. The Rabbis mentioned there flourished at the end of the second and the beginning of the third centuries.
45. *Mishnah Nega'im* X. 6, BR LXXV.6, p. 8927.
46. See *TB 'Abodah Zarah* 58b; *Hullin* 137b; *Esther Rabba* I.1 end, ed. Rom, 3d; *Pesikta Rabbathi* III, 7b. Comp. *TB Shabbath* 36a.
47. The exception in *TB Baba Kamma* 55a does not invalidate the general rule. Comp. J. Brüll in *Bet Talmud,* ed. Weiss I, p. 207.
48. *In Is.* 58:2.
49. Comp. also Eusebius, *Praep. Ev.* XI. 5, 513b–c.
50. *Libros Prophetarum ac Moysi memoriter revolventes,* quoted by Samuel Krauss in *JQR* 1894, p. 232. Krauss, however, committed a serious error in asserting (ibid., p. 233) that the Hebrew teacher of Jerome quoted Virgil in the original. He certainly misunderstood the church father. The latter reports (Praef. in Dan., Migne *PL* XXVIII. IX, 1292b) that the Jew convinced him to study Aramaic by quoting a passage in his tongue (*in sua lingua ingerente,* i.e. in the Jew's own language) that persistent labor will conquer everything. It is Jerome who associated it with Virgil (*Georg.* I. 145): *Labor omnia vicit improbus.* The Jew probably cited something like: "If a man says to you I have laboured but not found, do not believe him" (*TB Megillah* 6b).

51. On the rabbinic grammar of the Bible see L. Dobschütz, *Die einfache Bibelexegese d. Tannaim*, p. 25 ff.; S. Rosenblatt, *The Interpretation of the Bible in the Mishnah*, p. 10 ff.

52. *Sanhedrin* VII end, 4274. Comp. *Aboth deR. Nathan* ch. 37 and *Sifra*, Introduction, ed. Weiss, 3a.

53. In the second half of the first century B.C.E.

54. I. e. a specific regulation which is found in only one Biblical passage is extended and applied to a number of passages.

55. See on these norms Strack, *Introduction to the Talmud and Midrash* (Philadelphia 1931), p. 94 and notes ibid., pp. 284–285; E. Schürer, *Geschichte des jued. Volkes im Zeitalter Jesu* (Leipzig 1901–1909), 114, p. 397 and n. 20 ibid.

56. See H. Housdorff, *Jahrbuch d. jüd.-lit. Gesellschaft* (Frankf. a. M. 1907), p. 382 ff. and especially Sh. H. Kook in *Ha-zofeh le-Hokhmat Yisrael*, XIII, 1929, p. 91.

57. Hillel asserted (*Tosefta Pesaḥim* IV, 16228; *TP* ibid., VI, 33a; *TB* ibid. 66a) that his opinion was based on the authority of his teachers Shemaiah and Abtalion. It appears that his tradition went only as far as the law itself was concerned. The proofs were his own (Comp. the style in the *Tosefta* ibid.); he utilized the *Gezerah Shawah* on his own initiative, because it supported his tradition. R. Abba b. Memel (flourished in the third century) remarked (*TP* ibid.): "A man may utilize a *Gezerah Shawah* for the purpose of supporting his tradition."

58. Flourished in the beginning of the second century.

59. Introduction to the Sifra (Comp. M. Zucker, *Proceedings of the American Academy for Jewish Research* XVIII, 1949, p. 12, n. 15). See Strack, *Introduction* ibid. pp. 95 and 288, n. 8, where a list of selected literature and translations is given.

60. *Geschichte* II4, p. 397.

61. See Strack ibid.

62. *Die hermeneutische Analogie*, Wien 1897; *Der hermen. Syllogismus in d. talmud. Litteratur*, ibid. 1901; *Die hermeneut. Induktion* etc., ibid. 1909; *Die hermeneut. Antinomie*, ibid. 1913; *Die hermeneut. Quantitätsrelation*, ibid. 1916; *Der hermeneut. Kontext in d. Talm. Literatur*, ibid. 1921.

63. An article by D. Daube (*HUCA* XXII, 1949, p. 239 ff.) entitled "Rabbinic Methods of Interpretation and Hellenic Rhetoric" reached me when this chapter was already ready for the press. However, we found no reason to change anything in this chapter, as will be self evident from the comparison of Dr. Daube's article with this paper.

64. *Eshkol HaKofer*, 124b. He wrote his book in Constantinople in 1148.

65. This correct transliteration was made by P. F. Frankel in *MGWJ* XXXIII, 1884, p. 457. J. Perles (*Byzantinische Zeitschrift* II, 1893, p. 576) proposes: *orexeis kai apochremata*, or, as an alternative (according to cod. Leiden, see above n. 66), *ergasias kai epipeirismas*. Both eminent scholars were entirely unaware of what the author is referring to. They contented themselves with

the discussion of the two Greek words only without quoting the passage itself. We shall presently see that our text which is confirmed by two manuscripts must not be altered.

66. Ibid. 5, ed. H. Rabe, p. 140.

67. Comp. K. Lehrs, *de Aristarchi studiis Homericis*[3], p. 217.

68. Comp. the style in *Mishnah Sanhedrin* V. 1 and *Tosefta* ibid. IX. 1, 428₁₅ ff.

68. Comp. the style in *Mishnah Sanhedrin* V. 1 and *Tosefta* ibid. IX. 1, 428¹⁵ ff.

69. See R. Volkmann, *Rhetorik*, München 1901, p. 36.

70. An anonymous author in *Prologomena tes rhetorikes* (Ch. Walz, *Rhetores Graeci* (1832–1836; Osnabrueck 1968), VI, p. 34) gives the following definition: "The example is taken from facts which [actually] happened before; the parable is taken from the indeterminate and possible things which may happen." See also O. Schissel, *Rheinisches Museum* LXXV, 1926, p. 312, and Stegeman in *Pauly-Wissowa Real-Encyclopaedie der classischen Altertumswissenschaft* (Stuttgart 1894–1959), XV, s. v. Minuki-anos, p. 1987–8.

71. See the anonymous scholiast to Hermogenes a. l., ed. Walz ibid. VII, p. 759.

72. Flourished some two hundred years later than Hadassi, but he used earlier Byzantine scholia.

73. 365, ed. Walz ibid. V, p. 402.

74. Comp. also Joseph Rhacenditus, ed. Walz ibid. III, p. 479. He apparently flourished in Constantinople around the year 1300, see Walz ibid., p. 465.

75. *A minori ad majus*, from the light—less important—to the grave—more important—and vice versa.

76. Of R. Ishmael's rules the Karaite cited here only the first two, the *kal va-homer* and the *gezerah shavah* (analogy, see below), and added "etc.". Then he made his observation on the executions and arguments. Perhaps Hadassi was struck by the *verbal* similarity of the executions with some of the norms contained in the so called thirty-two hermeneutic rules of the *Aggadah*, which he reproduced in his book (58b). They include: the analogy (No. 7); something important which is elucidated by something trivial (No. 14); the parable (No. 26) and (No. 27), the opposite. These respectively correspond to: *apo isou, apo mikroteron, apo paravoles*, and *apo enantine*. But the similarity is only verbal, as can be seen from the instances given in the Hebrew source, and quoted by Hadassi himself, to illustrate the rules.

77. *Encyclopaedia Judaica* IV, p. 23 and *JQR*, N. S. XXX, 1939, p. 121. Comp. also Daube in *HUCA* XXII, p. 241, n. 7.

78. See above, nn. 18 and 19.

79. *Praep. Ev.*, 513c.

80. This is the literal translation of the Hebrew *mashneh*, or the Aramaic *matnĭin*—a teacher of *Mishnah*, see Bacher *Terminologie* I, p. 135, s. v. *sofer* I and no. 4 ibid.

81. Ibid. 513a: "the logical style of the Hebrew philosophers."

82. *Contra Gal.* 222a.

83. See above, no. 57.

84. *Sifra Mezora'* VII. V. 7, ed. Weiss 79a: "Scripture does not come to lock,

but to open." Comp. Bacher, *Terminologie* I. There were, of course, not a few exceptions, see *Shemoth Rabba* XV.22 beginning.

85. Blau (*REJ* XXXVI, 1898, p. 153) explains the expression *gezerah shavah* to mean "the same decision," "the same law." This is not exact. *Shavah* does not mean "the same" but "equal". The result of *Gezerah Shavah* is that the same law is applied to two situations. In rabbinic language we would expect in this case *gezerah aḥat*, and not *gezerah shavah*.

86. *gazar* means to cut.

87. See Schleusner, *Lexicon in LXX*, s. v. *syncrino* and *syncrisis*.

88. See Liddell and Scott, s. v. *syncrisis* III. 2. Comp. also M. Schwabe in *Sefer Yohanan Levi* (Jerusalem 1949), p. 229.

89. See Schleusner ibid.

90. See Ioannes Sardianus, *in Aphtonii progymnasmata* X, ed. Rabe (Leipzig 1928), p. 180. Comp. also F. Focke, *Hermes* LVIII, 1923, p. 331. However, its occurrence in Aristotle's works establishes it as a logical term in use in the fourth century B.C.E.

91. Flourished in the fourth century.

92. *Progymnasmata* X, in *Rhetores Graeci*, ed. Walz, I, p. 97.

93. Ed. Rabe ibid., p. 184.

94. *Progymn.* 8, ed. Rabe, p. 19.

95. It is a contracted form. Comp. *binyan av* instead of *binyan [bet] av*.

96. Comp. Cicero, *Top.* IV. 23, and Daube in *HUCA* XXII, pp. 251–253. The superior cogency of *kal va-ḥomer gezerah shavah* is indicated in *Tosefta Sanhedrin* VII. 7, 426₂₅. Both terms are frequently mentioned together (*Sifre* II, 313, ed. Finkelstein, p. 355₁₁; ibid. 317, p. 359₁₆; *TB Sukkah* 28a; *Temurah* 16a). Logically they may be characterized as one: *syncrisis*, comparison.

97. Probably in the end of the first or beginning of the second century.

98. *Mishnah Bezah* I. 6.

99. See Geiger, *Wissensch. Zeitschrift f. jüd. Theologie* V. 1844, p. 67, n. 1; Bacher, *Terminologie* I, p. 14, n. 1; ibid. p. 13, n. 1.

100. Ed. Horovitz, p. 257₁₉. So far as is known to me this text was not noticed by the students who treated the problem of *gezerah shavah*.

101. Comp. Bacher, *Terminologie* I, p. 23, s. v. *damah*. When Paul wrote (I Cor. II.13): "Comparing spiritual things to spiritual things," he used the legal terminology of the Jewish schools, i. e., you can apply the *syncrisis* to equal categories only.

102. See Bacher ibid. s. v. *hekesh*, p. 44 ff.; A. Schwarz, *Die hermeneutische Induktion*, p. 146 ff.

103. See J. Schweighaeuser, *Lexicon Polybianum* s. v. *parathesis*, p. 315 ff. and see below.

104. See Bacher ibid., s. v. *gezerah shavah*, p. 15.

105. Literally: emptied out.

106. Flourished in the second century B.C.E.

107. III. 32. 5.

108. Comp. Schweighaeuser ibid., p. 316.
109. XVI. 29. 5.
110. *TP Pesaḥim* VI. 1, 33a and parallels.
111. Ibid.
112. *Sanhedrin* VII, end, see above, n. 52.
113. In the second half of the first century B.C.E.
114. In *TP Pesaḥim* VI. 1, 33a, the term *gezerah shavah* is ascribed to the Bene Bathyra. But it is most likely the paraphrase of the editor, see *TB* ibid. 66a and *Tosefta* ibid. IV, p. 162. Our assumption is strengthened by the fact that *TP* ibid. ascribes to the Bene Bathyra the employment of the name *hekesh,* a term which occurs neither in the rules of Hillel nor in those of R. Ishmael (i. e. in the *Baraitha* attached to the *Sifra*). Only *kal va-ḥomer* appears to have been mentioned by name in this discussion (see *Tosefta* ibid.), but this norm (and perhaps also its name) is the oldest, and is intimated in the Bible itself, see Strack, *Introduction to the Talmud* etc., p. 285, n. 3.
115. See above, n. 100.
116. See David Daube, *Law Quarterly Review* LII, 1936, p. 265 ff.; idem, *Journal of Roman Studies* 1948, p. 115 ff.; idem, *HUCA* XXII, p. 252 ff.
117. See M. Joël, *Blicke in die Religionsgeschichte, etc.,* Vol. I (Breslau 1880), p. 39, n. 1.
118. See *Tosefta Kethuboth* IV, 9 ff., 264₃₀ ff. and parallels.
119. See Bacher, *Terminologie* I, s. v. *zekher,* p. 51 ff. and s. v. *samakh,* p. 133 ff.
120. See ibid. II, s. v. *asmakhta,* p. 13 and *samakh,* p. 143.
121. *TP Berakhoth* II. 3, 4c and parallel.
122. Comp. also Bacher ibid. II, s. v. *maḥvar,* p. 109.
123. Flourished in the beginning of the third century.
124. *TB Sanhedrin* 17a.
125. *TP* ibid. IV. 1, 22a.
126. Which is a *conditio sine qua non* in capital judicial procedure, see *Mishnah Sanhedrin* IV.1. Comp. also *TB* ibid. 17a, according to the reading of Maimonides, *Hilkhoth Sanhedrin* IX.1; Meʾiri a. l., p. 57. See the detailed evaluation of this reading in *Milḥemet Miẓvah,* (Leipzig 1856) by R. Solomon b. Simeon Duran, ed. pr., 33a.
127. See *TP* ibid. and *TB* ʿ*Erubin* 13b.
128. Comp. E. P. Parks, *The Roman Rhetorical Schools as a Preparation for the Courts under the Early Empire,* Baltimore 1945, p. 61 ff.; F. Schulz, *Principles of Roman Law* (Oxford 1946), p. 130, n. 3.
129. Sueton., *de grammat.* IV: veteres grammatici et rhetoricam docebant.
130. See F. Schulz, *History of Roman Legal Science* (Oxford 1951), p. 62 ff.
131. See Schulz ibid., p. 56 ff.
132. Comp. above nn. 69 and 70. See Octave Navarre, *Essai sur la rhétorique grecque,* p. 40 ff.

133. Comp. Laqueur in *Pauly-Wissowa Real-Encyclopaedie der classischen Altertumswissenschaft* (Stuttgart 1894–1959), III[2], p. 2463 ff.
134. Flourished in the fifth century B.C.E.
135. Diog. Laert. II. 11.
136. See C. Reinhardt, *De graecorum theologia capita duo*, 1910, p. 3 ff.
137. See C. G. Cobet, *Miscellanea critica* (Leiden 1878), p. 228.
138. See Athen. *Deipnos.* IV, 177b–f; ibid. 180c.
139. *De Aristarchi Studiis homericis*[3], p. 200, n. 122.
140. Lehrs ibid.
141. Flourished under Ptolemy Philadelphus, i. e. in the first half of the third century B.C.E.
142. See Lehrs ibid.
143. Athen. *deipn.* XI, 493d.
144. *Nyn to men epitimomenon esti to poiete.*
145. *Touton toinyn outus kategoroumenon te anastrophe Chresamenoi apolyomen ton poieten.*
146. I. e. mentally, but not literally, without destroying the meter.
147. I 68, ed. Horovitz, p. 63.
148. I. e., they brought the problem before Moses and before Aaron.
149. Comp. *Sifre* ibid. 133, p. 177, and the formulation in *TB Baba Bathra* 119b.
150. The verb *seres* means to turn upside down (Comp. *Mishnah Niddah* III. 5 and Rashi *TB* ibid. 28a. s. v. *mesoras*) which is the literal equivalent of *anastrephein*. In our case it has *no* relation to castrate, to distinguish (see Daube, *HUCA* XXII, p. 261). The latter may have some connection with the interpretation of *saris* (II Kings 25:19) by *Shir Rabba* (III. 7. Comp. *TP Sanhedrin* I. 2, 18c top). The *Midrash* states: " '*Saris*' (II Kings 25:19) refers to the *Mufla* (the head) of the court. Why is he called *Saris,* because he defines (literally: cuts) the *Halakha.*" Some years after the first publication of my book Daube independently discovered his mistakes. Comp. his article in *Festschrift Hans Lewald* (Basel, 1953), p. 28. See also ibid., p. 29.
151. Ibid. 494d.
152. See K. Lehrs, *De Aristarchi studiis homericus*[3], p. 218.
153. Flourished in the second century.
154. See Bacher, *Terminologie* I, p. 136, s. v. *saras;* ibid. II, p. 144.
155. Flourished in the second century.
156. *Progymnasmata* 193, Theon, ed. Spengel, p. 877₇.
157. See Cicero, *Ad At.* I. 16, beginning.
158. See *BR* LXX. 4, 800₆ and Bacher ibid.
159. *o Aristarchos touto dyon physi.*
160. *Alla ten physei lampran* (Apollonius Sophista, *Lexicon homericum,* ed. Bekker, Berlin 1833, p. 161.
161. *Mishnah Nedarim* III. 9.
162. This is the reading of the majority of mss. See also *Melekhet Shelomoh* a. l.

163. Comp. also ibid. 7; *TB Sotah* 25b passim.
164. See F. Schulz, *Principles of Roman Law*, p. 130, n. 3 end.
165. Some mediaeval authors quote "thirty-six rules" (See D. Cohen in *Tarbiz* II, 1931, p. 249). Joseph Rhacenditus (*Synopsis rhetorikes*, ed. Walz, *Rhetores Graeci* III, p. 479. See above, n. 76) repeats that the six executions can be applied to each argument forming together thirty-six rules.
166. The text is now available as an introduction to the *Midrash Mishnat R. Eliezer* discovered and published by H. G. Enelow, New York 1933, p. 10 ff. An English translation of these rules can be found in Strack's *Introduction to the Talmud and Midrash*, p. 96. For the time of its compilation see ibid., p. 95; for the sources, translation and literature, see ibid., p. 289, nn. 2–3.
167. See the abundant material collected by Einhorn in his *Midrash Tannaim* II, Wilno 1838, 30d ff. See also I. Heinemann, *Altjüdische Allegoristik* (1936), p. 15 ff.
168. See Heinemann ibid., p. 33 ff.
169. See Einhorn ibid. 33c; Bacher, *Terminologie* I, p. 111, s. v. *maʿal;* S. Lieberman, *Greek in Jewish Palestine* (New York 1942), p. 22 ff. Comp. *BR* XXXI. 8, 2815 and Field, *Hexapla* (to Jer. 1:11), p. 573, n. 13. Comp. I. Heinemann, *The Methods of the Aggadah*, (Jerusalem 1950), p. 257, n. 14.
170. I. e. *geometria* is used in the sense of manipulation with numbers. Comp. M. Cantor, *Vorlesungen über Geschichte der Mathematik* (Leipzig 1894–1908), I₃, p. 163.
171. See *BR* XLII. 2, 4168 and parallels referred to in the notes ibid. Comp. F. Dornseiff, *Das Alphabet in Mystik und Magie*, Berlin 1922, p. 107 and n. 5 ibid.
172. See Einhorn ibid. 34b; Bacher ibid. I, p. 127; II, p. 27 s. v. *gematria* and p. 69 s. v. *ḥushbana;* Dornseiff ibid., p. 110 ff. Comp. below n. 208.
173. *Midrash R. Eliezer,* ed. Enelow (New York 1933), p. 38.
174. Comp. the Septuagint (XXVIII. 1) and the Aramaic *Targum* a. 1.; Field, *Hexapla* p. 728, n. 1; *Jahrbücher* of N. Brüll, I, 1874, p. 61, n. 2 and M. Rahmer in *Jubelschrift . . . Graetz* (Breslau 1887), p. 324. See also below, n. 210.
175. See Bacher, *Terminologie* I, p. 127, n. 5; ibid. II, p. 27.
176. Shorthand, i. e. written according to the use of the *notarii.* See Krauss, *Byzantinische Zeitschrift* II, 1893, p. 512 ff. Comp. W. Schubart, *Das Buch bei den Griechen und Roemern* (Berlin-Leipzig 1921), pp. 78–80 and 180.
177. This kind of *notaricon* is very common in the *Aggadah,* see Bacher *Terminologie* I, p. 126; ibid. II, p. 124 and especially the rabbinic material adduced by Einhorn (see above n. 170) 34c ff.
178. This is taken from *Sifra* a. I., ed. Weiss 12d, ed. Friedmann, p. 123.
179. And in this category we count the *asmakhta* (see above p. 63) parts of the *Halakha* as well.

180. See *TP Nazir* VII. 2, 56b; *TB Mo'ed Katan* 9b; *Tanḥuma,* beginning etc. etc.
181. *Sifre* II. 1 (end), ed. Finkelstein, p. 8. See ibid. the strong objection raised by R. Jose of Damascus to this interpretation.
182. *Pirkei R. Eliezer* ch. 36, ed. Rabbi David Luria (Warsaw 1852), 84a, and comp. n. 36 ibid.
183. Comp. *TB Berakhoth* 7b.
184. *Midrash Haggadol Bereshith,* ed. Scheçhter (Cambridge 1904), p. XXV; *Midrash Haggadol Bereshith,* ed. Margulies (Jerusalem 1946), p. 39.
185. See A. Bouché-Leclerque, *L'histoire de la divination* (Paris 1879–1882), I, pp. 116 ff. and 312.
186. See Artemidorus, *Onirocriticon* I. 2; Bouché-Leclerque ibid., p. 302.
187. See Rabbinowicz *Dikdukei Soferim* to *Berakhoth,* p. 315.
188. Ibid. I. 68; II. 12, s. v. *aiges;* III. 28 passim. See Bouché-Leclerque ibid., p. 313 ff.
189. *TP Ma'aser Sheni* IV. 9, 55b, *Ekha Rabba* I, ed. Buber (Vilna 1898), 26a ff. and particularly *TB Berakhoth* 55a–57b.
190. *Rheinisches Museum f. Philologie* N. F. 48 (1893), pp. 398–419.
191. Comp. also I. Wiesner, *Scholien zum Babylonischen Talmud* (Prague 1859–1867), I, p. 124 ff.
192. See A. Kristianpoller, "Traum un Traumdeutung im Talmud," in *Monumenta Talmudica* IV (Vienna-Leipzig 1913–1923), p. 46 ff., Nos. 139–153; H. Lewy ibid.
193. *TB Berakhoth* 57b (many times).
194. Comp. Artemidorus ibid. I. 68: "All pulses are of a bad omen except peas."
195. See Artemidorus, *Onirocriticon,* ed. Hercher (Leipzig 1864), *Index rerum,* p. 303, s. v. *isopsepha;* Bouché-Leclerque ibid. I, pp. 313 and 318 ff.
196. Artem. III. 28.
197. See H. Lewy, *Zeitschrift des Vereins f. Volkskunde* III, 1893, pp. 135–136. Comp. also Lieberman *GJP,* p. 98, n. 19.
198. See Lieberman ibid.
199. *TP Shabbath* XIV. 1, 14c.
200. I. e. Scripture, Ps. 49:2.
201. A play on *ḥaled* (human) and *ḥuldah* (weasel).
202. Ps. 39:7. Comp. ibid. 6.
203. The Rabbis probably allude to the destruction of the weasel by the snake which then devours the food stored up by the former. See Arist. *Hist. anim.* IX. 1, 609b; ibid. 6, 612b.
204. Ibid. III. 28.
205. *o ti gar an lave, touto sepei.*
206. Comp. A. Loewinger, *Der Traum in der jüdischen Literatur,* p. 27, n. 7 and p. 30. See below n. 211.
207. See F. Dornseiff, *Das Alphabet* etc., pp. 91–118; Th. Hopfner, *Griechisch-*

Aegyptischer Offenbarungszauber, p. 181; R. Eisler, *Weltenmantel,* p. 789, s. v. Isopsephie; idem, *Archiv f. Religionswissenschaft* XVI, 1913, p. 305, n. 2.

208. The use of letters as numerals is apparently a Greek invention which was adopted by the Semites at a much later time, see Dornseiff, *Das Alphabet* etc., p. 11. (Comp. now H. L. Ginsberg, *Studies in Koheleth* [New York 1950], p. 32 ff.) At some time during the second commonwealth the Jews inscribed α, β, γ (signifying 1, 2, 3) on the several baskets in the temple of Jerusalem (See *Mishnah Shekalim* III. 2), i. e. the Jews availed themselves of the *Greek* alphabet to employ letters as numerals (In the *Mishnah* ibid. R. Ishmael is only explaining the statement of the first *Tanna*). Comp. however Tosefta *Ma'asser Sheni* V. 1.

The numerical value of *Greek* letters was also utilized in the rabbinic dream interpretations. R. Jose (*BR* ch. 68. 12, 785, see also the sources referred to above, n. 192) explains (the dream about the treasure in) Cappadocia to signify *kappa dokoi,* twenty beams. This is, of course, no *isopsephon.* The absence of the latter in early Jewish *onirocritica* may be quite indicative of its origin.

209. See above n. 174.

210. See Dornseiff, *Das Alphabet* etc., pp. 17 (and n. 2 ibid.), 125 and 136. Comp. also H. I. Marrou, *Histoire de l'éducation dans l'antiquité* (New York 1956), p. 212. For other ways of substitution of letters see Suetonius, *Jul.* LVI. 6 (A. Gellius, *Noct. Att.* XVII in Suetonius [reprint Oxford 1968] 9. 1–5); idem, *Aug.* LXXXVIII. Comp. *TB Sukkah* 52b.

211. Flourished at the beginning of the third century.

212. *TB Sanhedrin* 22a.

213. See above, nn. 177–182.

214. See above, n. 177. Comp. also the *Onirocriticon* of Rabbi Shlomoh Al-moli, Gate I, ch. 1 end.

215. *TB Baba Kamma* 55a, see *Dikdukei Soferim* ibid., p. 119.

216. *TB* ibid. For *tet* as an inauspicious sign, see Lieberman, *GJP,* p. 191. In the *Midrash* of the alphabet by the Samaritan Marqah (M. Heidenheim, *Der Kommentar Marqah's des Samaritaners* [Leipzig 1896], p. XI, n. 2) this letter is the symbol of the snake which brought destruction into the world. Comp. however, Rettig, *Memar Marqa,* p. 23. Dornseiff (*Das Alphabet* etc.) who collected the material on the exegesis of the alphabet overlooked Marqah's *Midrash.* See H. Baneth, *Des Samaritaners Marqah an die 22 Buchstaben,* Berlin 1888, p. 50 ff.

217. IV. 24.

218. The reference is probably to the Jewish war against Trajan, see Schürer, *Geschichte* I₃, p. 665.

219. See above n. 180.

220. *TB Berakhoth* 57a.

221. *Yoma* 48a; *Baba Bathra* 111b and parallels. Comp. *TP Sota* V. 1, 20a.

222. IV. 23: "Changing . . . removing and adding letters." Comp. ibid. I. 11.

223. See L. Blau, *Das altjüdische Zauberwesen* (Budapest 1898), pp. 147–148; Dornseiff, *Das Alphabet* etc., p. 63.
224. See above, nn. 178, 181–183.
225. *TB Berakhoth* 56b.
226. Ibid. 57a.
227. Plut. *vit Alex.* XXIV. Artemidorus (IV. 24) ascribes this analysis to the famous seer Aristandros of Telmessus in Lycia. See on him Bouché-Leclerque, *Histoire de la divination* II, p. 76 ff.
228. II, 345, ed. Finkelstein, p. 402. Comp. *Shemoth Rabba* XXXIII. 7.
229. See also *TB Sanhedrin* 59a and *Pesaḥim* 49b.
230. *TB Berakhoth* 57a.
231. The Black Stone of Esarhaddon of 680 B.C.E. (Luckenbill in *The American Journal of Semitic Languages* XLI, 1925, p. 242 ff.). Prof. H. L. Ginsberg has kindly drawn my attention to this inscription.
232. Luckenbill ibid.
233. I. 7, cited by Dornseiff, *Das Alphabet* etc., p. 56, n. 1.
234. Nomen ipsius, inversis literis, apices deorsum.
235. Died in the beginning of the fourth century.
236. According to a tradition quoted from an unknown source in the Yemenite *Midrash Haggadol* on Ex 2:2 (p. 13): "All the prophets were born after only seven months of pregnancy." *Protev. Jacobi* (V. 2) asserts (according to two manuscripts and the Armenian version) that Anna gave birth to Mary after seven months of pregnancy. The same was said about Dionysus and Apollo, see Th. Gaster, *The Joshua Bloch Memorial Volume* (New York 1960), p. 118, n. 4.

Rabbi Simeon Duran in his book (composed at the beginning of the fifteenth century in Algiers) *Keshet Umagen* relates: And they (i. e. the Gentiles) say that the reason a child born after eight months of pregnancy is not viable is that Jesus the Nazarene, who was born after eight months of pregnancy ordained that no child born after this period of pregnancy survive. Suspecting that the Rabbi drew his information from Moslem sources I inquired of Prof. Arthur Jeffery about this tradition in Arabic literature. Dr. Jeffery kindly supplied the following information: Ibrahim al-Thaʻlabi in his Ḳiṣaṣ al-Anbiā (i. e. *historiae prophetarum*), ed. Cairo 1921, p. 265 reports (The tradition goes back to Al-Kalbī): "The scholars differ as to the period of Mary's pregnancy and the time of her giving birth to Jesus. Some say that the measure of her pregnancy was the same as other women, namely nine months. Others say it was *eight* months, and that that was an added miracle, since no eight months child has ever lived save Jesus. Others say it was six months, others three hours, and others, that it was a single hour." In this source, however, there is no mention that it was Jesus who decreed that no child born after eight months of pregnancy should survive. The Rabbi denied the claim, pointing out that Hippocrate (See *de nutr.* XLII and the commentary of Sabinus quoted by A. Gellius, noctes Att. III. 16) and Aristotle (See *hist. anim.* VII. 4 584b) who lived hundreds of years before Jesus possessed knowledge of this rule. Consequently, it cannot be ascribed to the decree of Jesus.

237. BR XIV. 2, 1272 and parallels referred to by Theodor a. 1.

238. See A. Brüll, *Fremdsprachliche Redensarten*, Leipzig 1869, p. 16, n. 2; S. Krauss *Griechische und lateinische Lehnwörter Talmud* (Berlin 1898), I, p. 154.

239. *Apud* L. Cohn in *MGWJ* XLIV, 1900, p. 569; see Lieberman *GJP*, p. 23.

240. Comp. Galen, *Phil. hist.*, ed. Kühn p. 333; Oribasius, *collect. med.* XXII. 5, ed. Bussemaker and Daremberg III, p. 63. The latter remarks that the theory according to which children born after eight months of pregnancy are not able to live is false, for they do live. But the truth is that the number of surviving eight months infants is less than that of seven months children.

241. I. e. breaking the names of the letters in two parts.

242. It is the same device employed by R. Jose in his dream interpretation where he dissolved Cappadocia in *Kappa dokoi,* twenty beams, see above n. 211.

243. See Cicero, *de divinat.* II. 70.

244. *TP Ma'aser Sheni* IV, end, 55c.

245. We have suggested that some of the artificial rules in *Aggadic* hermeneutics were derived from the *onirocritica* rather than from the realm of oracles etc. because the former was in vogue among the Jews, whereas nothing of the latter was used by them in the rabbinic period save the "heavenly voice".

246. Or for collections of rabbinic law, see J. N. Epstein, *Tarbiz* VI. 3, 1935–1936, p. 102 ff.

247. See D. Hoffmann, *Zur Einleitung in die halachischen Midraschim* (Berlin 1887), p. 37 and Epstein ibid.

248. Comp. "the canon (kanon) of Epicurus", see Diog. Laert. X. 30 ff.

249. See above, p. 435 ff.

250. See B. Landsberger, *Zeitschrift f. Assyriologie* 1936, p. 33; R. Marcus, *Journal of Near Eastern Studies* VI, 1947, p. 109 and notes ibid.

251. *De divin.* II. LIV. 111, referred to by Graf in *Pauly-Wissowa Real-Encyclopaedie der classischen Altertumswissenschaft* (Stuttgart 1894–1959), I, p. 1200.

252. Quae *acrostichis* dicitur.

253. Notwithstanding the report of A. Gellius (*Noct. Att.* XIV. 6. 4) that some authors tried to find acrostics in the poems of Homer (see Graf ibid.).

254. I. e. not earlier than the previously mentioned Latin acrostic, see Graf ibid. and Dornseiff, *Das Alphabet* etc., p. 147.

255. Comp. Seneca, *epist.* 88. 40.

256. *Deipn.* XI, 493f.

257. See above n. 141.

258. *evreseis safton apeilnfonta kata tas sas epinoias.*

259. The only two instances are: *Pesikta Rabbathi* 46, ed. Friedmann, 187a which finds the acrostic *le-Mosheh* (by Moses) in Ps. 92:1 and *Tanhuma*

Ha'azinu 5 where a *gematria* derived from an acrostic forms the name *Mosheh*. In both cases we have apparently later interpolations.

260. See *Tosefta Baba Kamma* VII, 358₁ ff. and *Debarim Rabba* III. 17.

261. *Shemoth Rabba* XLVII. 9, end. Comp. ibid. 2 and *Tanḥuma* ibid., ed. Buber 59a and n. 123 ibid.

262. *Hebräische Beilage zum Magazin* of Berliner and Hoffmann, 1885, p. 16.

263. XII. 10, ed. Kisch, p. 149.

264. *TB Shabbath* 105a; *Pesikta Rabbathi* XXI, ed. Friedmann 105a; *Pesikta deR. Kahana* XII, 109a.

265. To Deut. 5:6 in *Hasegulah* XVIII, p. 53; *Midrasch Tannaïm*, ed. Hoffman, p. 20, note *.

266. M. Heidenheim, *Bibliotheca Samaritana* (Leipzig 1896), III, p. 114; H. Baneth, *Des Samaritaners Marqah an die 22 Buchstaben*, p. 48.

267. This was the surname of Moses in the Jewish Hellenistic writings, see W. Bauer, *Griechisch-deutsches Wörterbuch z. d. N. T.* (Giessen 1928), s. v. *mesites*. Likewise in *ascensio Mosis* (I. 14; III. 12) Moses is styled *arbiter*. The rabbinic writings as well term Moses "intermediary", see *TP Megillah* IV. 1, 77d; *Pesikta deR. Kahana* V, 45a (twice) and parallels; *Shemoth Rabba* III. 5: ibid. XXXIII. 1; *Debarim Rabba* III. 12 passim. Prof. Louis Finkelstein (*Tarbiz* XX, 1949, p. 96) discovered that Moses was also called *benai*, middleman. He is also termed *shaliah* (messenger) (*Sifre*, end, 115d), agent. See also *Pesikta Rabbathi* XV, ed. Friedmann 69a and *Shir Rabba* I. 4, ed. Rom 5a.

268. And not law-giver, as translated by A. E. Cowley, *The Samaritan Liturgy II* (Oxford 1909), Glossary, p. LXII, s. v. *nomikeh*. *Aggadath Bereshith* (XXXVI. ed. Buber, Krakau, 1903, p. 72) in referring to Is. 33:18 renders it: "Where are her *nomikoi*" (Comp. S. J. Miller, *The Samaritan Molad Moshe* [New York 1949] p. 60₁₂, where the plural is spelled *nomikim*.

269. See Marqah, ed. Baneth ibid., p. 42.

270. See ps.-Jonathan Num. 21:18 passim. He is also called *safra rabbah* (great scribe) (*TB Sota* 13b, Onkelos Deut. 33:21, passim) which corresponds to *Kataba rabbah* of the Samaritans, see Heidenheim, *op. c.* II, p. 138.

271. See G. Goetz, *Corpus Glossariorum Latinorum* (Leipzig 1888–1923), II, 1493; and F. Preisigke, *Fachwörter d. öffentlichen Verwaltungsdienstens Ägyptens*, p. 130, s. v. *nomikos*.

272. Comp. also Payne Smith. *Thesaurus Syriacus* (Oxford 1879–1901), p. 2232.

E

Literary Studies

18

The Torah as Love Goddess

Ari Elon

The Torah that was written by women has not been discovered yet. The Torah that we all know was written by men. Thousands of men participated in the construction of the written and oral Torah. Not a single woman that we know of participated in that construction. Therefore, even though I will write about the Torah as a woman, we will encounter only the world of men.

Generally, I divide the men who construct Torah into two groups: those who represent the commanding God by interpreting His supreme law, and those who study Torah *lishmah,* for her own sake—just because they are inspired by her. The former are the Torah's lawyers. The latter are her lovers. Here I intend to speak about the lovers.

Resh Lakish was one of the Torah's greatest lovers.[1] He was utterly devoted to her. He used to quote the verse, "He who commits adultery lacks a heart" (Prov. 6:32) and take it to mean, "This is the person who learns Torah only intermittently."[2] So devoted was he to his beloved Torah, so jealous of her honor, that he termed all who came to her only from time to time "adulterers, lacking in heart." He would even profane the sabbath rather than diminish his loving of the Torah:

Resh Lakish, while poring over the Torah, would unknowingly walk beyond the *tehum shabbat,* the sabbath boundary[3] in fulfillment of that which is written: "Find joy in the wife of your youth—a loving doe, a graceful hind. Let her breasts satisfy you at all times. Be infatuated with love of her always." (PT Berakhot 5:5)

Why is Resh Lakish's Torah compared to *ayelet ahavim,* a loving doe? Perhaps the following passage from BT 'Eruvin (54b) provides a clue:

R. Samuel b. Nahmani said, "Why was Torah compared to a doe? To tell you that just as a doe has a narrow womb, *rehem tzar,* and is desired by her mate each time as if it were the first time, so it is with Torah. She is desired by those who study her at all times as if it were the first time.

Resh Lakish was not the only rabbinic lover in perpetual thrall to the Torah of his desire, nor was he the only rabbinic lover tempted by his beloved to break the rules that she herself set forth. The Talmud contains similar tales of other *talmidei hakhamim* (sages)—R. Nehemiah and R. Rehumi, Yehudah, son of R. Hiyya, R. Meir, and many others.[4]

What I wish to do in this presentation is to embark on a journey in these lovers' footsteps. My approach, like that of the rabbis themselves, will be associative. I make no claim that the sources to be discussed are representative of the Bavli or rabbinic material more generally. Further, I have never been inclined to speak about the *talmidei hakhamim* in objective fashion, nor would I allow myself to do them that injustice. I would not do it, even if it were possible, because the mad and wonderful men we call *talmidei hakhamim* poured all their power into an associative, antisystematic enterprise driven by their love.

AYELET AHAVIM/AYELET HA-SHAHAR: THE LOVE DOE AND THE MORNING STAR

The "doe of love," *'ayelet 'ahavim,* is a love goddess. There are many sources, from many cultures, that teach us that gazelles, hinds, and does are all symbolic of eros. There are also idols and icons in many different pantheons, in which these beautiful and desirable creatures appear as erotic female divinities. Here I want to give only two examples of how the doe figures as a divinity from a text of deep concern to the rabbis.

In the Song of Songs we read three times the same oath of love uttered by the same lovesick young woman. "I adjure you, O maidens of Jerusalem, by gazelles or by hinds of the field: do not wake or rouse Love until it please!" (Cant. 2:7). An oath is normally binding because it invokes a divine power. In our case, too, the oath of love uttered by a lovesick woman invokes the names of her deities, the gazelle and the hind.

A second text in which the divinity of these creatures is even more apparent appears in Psalm 22. This psalm, the subject of enormous Jewish and Christian exegesis throughout the ages, states: "For the leader; upon *ayelet ha-shahar* [the doe of dawn or morning star], a psalm of David: My God, my God, why have you forsaken me?" Two rabbinic comments on the verse are especially relevant here. We read in several sources, including the Yerushalmi and Esther Rabba:

R. Hiyya and R. Shimon ben Halafta were walking in the Arbel valley at dawn when they saw the first rays of *ayelet ha-shahar*. Said R. Shimon, "My master, that is how the redemption of Israel will be. In the beginning the light will come little by little, and then it will come wider and wider. (PT Berakhot 1:1 [2c]; Esther Rabba 10:14)

A second passage in Midrash Shoher Tov 22 asks why Esther resembles *ayelet ha-shahar* and responds,

just as *ayelet ha-shahar* at first light comes little by little, and then will break forth swiftly, so does the redemption brought by Esther to Israel.

Indeed, Esther is compared many times in rabbinic literature to both redemption and *ayelet ha-shahar*. She, as the star of dawn, is the re-demptive light at the end of the night's darkness.

There is evidence from many cultures of rituals devoted to the star of dawn, many goddesses—particularly goddesses of love—who bear its name. Venus and Aphrodite, Hualu, Ashtoret, Ashtar, Estahar, and, of course, Esther. She is very much a love goddess in the book that bears her name. Like any love goddess, she brings redemption to those who give her their trust.

In a late rabbinic source we find the following midrash given here in shortened form. How did her name come to be Esther—is it not Hadas-sah? Indeed, her original name was Hadassah, but Ahasuerus gave her the new name because of this story. The icon (or picture) of Vashti hung on the wall of Ahasuerus's chamber. Whenever a new maiden entered the room, he would compare her to Vashti's image. The maiden, of course, always compared unfavorably. Until one night Hadassah ap-peared. "When Hadassah was brought to the king"—I now quote di-rectly—"and he looked at her, and then at the image of Vashti, he was astonished by her beauty and grace. He said, 'Your incredible beauty is greater than that of any daughter of man. Your name will no longer be called Hadassah, but rather Esther, because as one sees the glorious star Estahar, so I saw your face." [5]

In BT Yoma a different feature of Esther's anatomy is the subject of extravagant praise.

> Why was Esther compared to a doe [ayala]? R. Zera said: . . . to tell you that just as a doe has a narrow womb and is desired by her mate *[haviva 'al boa'alah]* time and again just as at the first time, so Esther was desired by Ahasuerus every time as the first time. (BT Yoma 29a)

Esther's beauty may have been a necessary condition for arousing Ahasuerus's love, but it was not a sufficient condition. We are speaking after all about a king who gave an order to bring to the palace harem every beautiful young virgin in all 127 countries of his empire. Each of them was to be prepared for their night in his bed for an entire year— six months with oil of myrrh, and six months with spices and beauty emolients—all for the one occasion on which the king would examine and explore the unique qualities of each one of them. Esther was only one more beautiful virgin from among a multitude of beautiful virgins in the lands between India and Ethiopia. And nevertheless, "The king loved Esther more than any other woman. None of the virgins found so much favor with him" (Esther 2:17). Why? Because, as we have just learned, she was the only sexual partner who remained a virgin even after her night with the king—and every night thereafter. As Rav says in tractate Megillah,

> If he (Ahasuerus) wanted the taste of virginity *(betulah)*, he tasted it. If he wished the taste of an experienced woman *(beulah)*, he tasted it. (BT Megillah 13a)

In short, Esther was perfect. She satisfied a male fantasy that Ahasuerus could find in no other "daughter of man." She was a superhuman lover—a veritable goddess. Only a divine woman can be sexual partner and eternal virgin, *betulah be'ulah*, at the same time, at all times. The Book of Esther, one of the wildest male fantasies ever written, is also known as the only biblical book that does not include the name of God. That is true, of course. But note that it is also the only biblical book that not only includes the name of a goddess, but is called by her name.

To review our journey thus far: Torah and Esther have a lot in common as love objects. The men who love them will never be satisfied with any mere human female being. They will rest content only with women like Torah and Esther, women of the "narrow womb," who remain desirable, *haviva*, as the first time.

There is an additional characteristic shared by Esther and the Torah: they both reveal and conceal. The interplay between covering and discovering may well be the sweet secret of their lovemaking. Esther is glamorous and shining. She is a star. (The English word *star*, in fact, shares the same etymological root as the Hebrew name *Esther*.) But Esther, as we saw earlier, is also a hidden goddess, esoteric in her nature. The Talmud notes "Where is Esther alluded to in the Torah? As it says, 'And I shall surely hide [Hebrew *haster 'astir*] My countenance from you on that day' (Deut. 31:18)." (BT Megillah 13a) According to the Gemara, who makes this statement? The revealed God, who announces that someday He will be the hidden God, i.e., *'Astir/'Esther*. Further, the Talmud explains her name thus, "Why is she called Esther (her original name being Hadassah)? Because she concealed *devareha*"—meaning, in Hebrew, not only the fact of her Jewishness (see Esther 2:20), but also the sexual parts of her body.

In sum, Esther contains in her name and presence both revelation and concealment. She is the light at the end of the tunnel and also the darkness concealing the light from view. Like any deep symbol, she signifies both the thing and its opposite. *Estahar* and *nistar* (the shining star and hiddenness), *galut* and *hitgalut* (exile and redemption). Turn her and turn her again, for all is found in her.

And the Torah is just like Esther. On one hand, she is light. For example, the combination "torah-orah" (Torah/light) appears several times. The word Torah contains associations of light. In the popular consciousness, the Torah shines with glorious rays. She shatters with lightning and thunderbolts. She shows the way. She brings light from darkness. But there is also the hidden, esoteric Torah. Her secrets are revealed only to those unique and exclusive men, the *talmidei hakhamim*, who are her lovers, the priests who devote their lives to their love goddess in her temple, the *bet midrash* (study house). The hidden Torah is the learned Torah. The learned Torah is loved in secret. The process of penetrating her secrets, *talmud Torah*, is very intimate.

TORAH STUDY AS SEXUAL INTIMACY

In the Song of Songs, in the midst of the lover's description of his beloved's body, we read, "Your rounded thighs are like jewels, the work of a master's hand" (Cant. 7:2). The Talmud comments on this verse in Sukkah 49a:

Why is it that the words of the Torah resemble the thighs [of a woman]? To tell you: as the thighs are hidden, so the words of the Torah.

Thus, Rabbi commanded his students not to study Torah in the marketplace, i.e., in public (Mo'ed Katan 16a), and R. Hiyya cited a tradition that

any *talmid hakham* who studies Torah in the presence of an *'am ha-aretz* [ignoramus] is compared to one who makes love to his betrothed in his presence. As it is said, "Moses commanded us the Torah, an inheritance [Hebrew *morashah*] for the congregation of Jacob" (Deut. 33:4). Do not read *morashah*, but rather *me'orasah*, betrothed. (Pesahim 49b)

For the same reason, according to BT Sanhedrin 59a, a heathen who studies the Torah is, at least according to one view, punished by stoning. The Talmud asks why such a person is punished by stoning, the most severe form of capital punishment used by ancient Jewish courts. It responds that this punishment is meted out because the Torah is *me'orasah*, a betrothed woman, and anyone who has sexual intercourse with a *me'orasah* is punished by stoning (Deut. 22:23–24). The offense is more severe than sex with any other forbidden woman. (The other opinion about a heathen who studies Torah, by the way, is that he is likened to the high priest—a very high status indeed. But that is not our subject here.)

Learning Torah is not the experience of intercourse with "just any woman." The Torah is not "just any woman." She is an eternal fiancée. And indeed, BT Berakhot says expressly: "If one dreams that he is having intercourse with a *me'orasah*, he may expect [imminently to merit] the Torah" (BT Berakhot 57a). In another comparison to eagerly anticipated lovemaking the Torah is compared to a bride. I will cite only three of many examples.

(1) When God gave the Torah to Israel she was *havivah* [beloved] to them as a bride under the wedding canopy is *havivah* to her groom. (Exodus Rabbah 41:6)

(2) Just as the bride is adorned with 24 ornaments,[6] so the *talmid hakham* must have facility with the 24 biblical books. (Exodus Rabbah 41:6)

(3) Anyone who says words of Torah that are not as delicious to those who hear them as a bride is delicious to her groom, it is better had he not said them. (Cant. Rabbah 4:22)

Thus the Torah is eternal virgin, eternal fiancée, eternal bride. The Torah studied in mystery is she of the narrow womb who gives eternal pleasure to her students. "Day in and day out the Torah is *havivah*, desirable, to her students as on the day of her giving at Sinai" (BT 'Eruvin 54b). At every hour she renews herself. At every hour the student uncovers her anew, discovers a new face. He turns her and turns her and finds that all is in her.

Shegal

Before we meet another love goddess who is *havivah*, let us note a passage in the Talmud that describes, for a change, a "normal" human woman who is *havivah*. The Talmud, seeking a rationale for the penta-teuchal prohibition of relations with a menstruant, cites R. Meir:

R. Meir said, "Why is it that the Torah imposed a seven day prohibition on relations with a mestruant woman? Because a man becomes accustomed to his wife and may come to detest her [Hebrew *ragil bah, v'katz bah*]. Consequently the Torah said, 'Let her be ritually impure for seven days so that she will be desirable [*havivah*] to her husband as she was when she entered beneath the *huppah*.' " (BT Niddah 31b)

The normal woman is not Esther, nor Venus, nor Torah. Her husband gets used to her and then tired of her. . . . The Torah is never subject to impurity (BT Berakhot 22a) for she is always *havivah*. Our next "superwoman" is also desirable—and available—at all times. Surprisingly, she is not well known. She is called *shegal*, and she appears in the Bible five times.[7]

A brief perusal of the sources will reveal that Shegal and Esther are, more or less, the same woman. Just as Esther is a sort of queen-goddess in Ahasuerus's oriental palace, so we find Shegal in the palaces of Artakhshashta (Ataxerxes) and Belshazzar. In two scenes described in Daniel and Nehemiah, we see two kings partaking in a royal feast. Beside them lie their Shegals. This Shegal is not a regular queen. She is rather a supreme queen, a point emphasized in Psalm 45, which describes a surrealistic wedding between a mysterious king (perhaps the messiah?) and Shegal.

For our purposes, the encounter with Shegal in tractate Rosh Ha-shanah is essential: "Because the Torah is *havivah* to Israel like Shegal is to idolaters, you have merited the *ketem 'ophir*" (BT Rosh Ha-shanah 4a).[8] Note that the passion for Torah is compared explicitly to the passion for a feminine idol. It is not a coincidence. I believe that the *yetzer* (urge) for idolatry and the *yetzer* for *talmud Torah* (Torah study) have a lot in common. I will return to this subject shortly, but first I wish to introduce yet another royal-divine couple.

GOD AND TORAH

974 generations before the world was created the Torah was lying in God's bosom singing with the heavenly angels, as it is written: "I was with him as a confidant, a source of delight every day, rejoicing before Him at all times" (Prov. 8:30). (Abot de-R. Nathan I, 31, ed. Schechter, 46a)

We recognize this scene from Daniel, Esther, and Nehemiah. The king and his advisers (or angels) are enjoying themselves in the palace, and while they do so the supreme queen lies in the king's bosom. Torah lay in God's bosom for 974 generations before the creation, and then, when it came time, God looked at his beloved Torah and through her created the world.[9] As He did so, the Torah repeated, "Bereshit bara Elohim," "At the beginning God created" (Gen. 1:1). In the thousandth generation—twenty-six after Father God and Mother Torah created the world—Torah was "revealed" at Sinai to the masses.[10] But the hidden Torah remained on Olympus with God, in the company of the *talmidei hakhamim*. There she continued to be their beloved, day in and day out as at the first day—the day of Sinai.

We all know that any teaching any *talmid hakham* discovers in the future was already given by God at Sinai (PT Pe'ah 2:6 [17a]). And we know that the Torah given at Sinai was already playing in God's bosom one thousand generations prior to Sinai. Time stops in the study of the Torah. Every day is the same as the day 974 generations before the creation; and every day will be the same 974 generations hence when a *talmid hakham*, the Torah in his bosom, explores her eternal delights. Every day the *talmid hakham*, like God, will look at his Torah and create worlds.

OBSESSION WITH TORAH AND THE *YETZER HA-RA'* OF IDOLATRY

There are two Torahs: the Torah that commands and the Torah that is studied. The first is the source of authority and reflects the male God. The second is the source of inspiration and reflects the female goddess. The first is directed to the entire people, the second to the small, exclusive group of *talmidei hakhamim* who isolate themselves in the Olympus of their *bet midrash*. Some of them are perpetually on the verge of addiction to their love goddess and on the verge of abandoning their obligation to the God who commands.

God, who commands unequivocally, conducts Himself according to *middat ha-din,* strict justice. He is not capable of bringing redemption to those *talmidei hakhamim* who have begun to devote themselves more and more to another god, or, more precisely, to a goddess. They have changed the Torah from a means to an end. That is,they have converted the male God's means of domination into an end that satisfies them and whose image is that of a goddess. Essentially, these *talmidei hakhamim* have forced the redemption before its time in order to redeem themselves.[11] Their private redemption is their *ayelet ha-shahar,* the redemptive dawn light, their Venus—the Torah they study. Every generation of *talmidei hakhamim* has invested a great deal of energy in concealing the fact that they are already redeemed. They pretend that they still are waiting with the rest of the remnant of Israel for the collective redemption to come. But their own redemption is their transformation of the distant past into the eternal present that is *havivah* every hour as it was the first hour. The Torah is *havivah* to them precisely as Shegal is *havivah* to idolaters. And just as the obsession with Shegal or any other love goddess constitutes a threat to the commitment to the God of the commandments, so obsession with the Torah constitutes the very same threat. Obsession with the Torah, as with any other idol, involves a flight from the real world to one of the worlds of infinite possibility in which redemption has already been accomplished. Hence, anyone who declares himself to be living in the midst of redemption is nothing less than an idolater.

There is a decisive difference between R. Hiyya and R. Shimon ben Halafta on the one hand and Resh Lakish on the other. R. Hiyya and R. Shimon look upon *ayelet ha-shahar* with desire and speak about the redemption she will bring one future day. Resh Lakish is actively obsessed with her. Idol-worshippers can be vulgar like Ahasuerus. They can also be refined like Resh Lakish and other *talmidei hakhamim* who are completely devoted to the Torah. When the latter place themselves in the existential situation of obsession—an obsession that costs their commitment to the commanding religious system—they are idol-worshippers, plain and simple.

The *talmidei hakhamim* themselves said that in their day the *yetzer ha-ra'* (evil inclination) of idolatry no longer existed, only the regular *yetzer ha-ra'* still survived. However, they knew enough to describe the *yetzer* of idolatry as a very powerful drive, which, if it had existed in their day, would have been beyond their resistance. Thus, at least, says Menasseh, king of Israel, to R. Ashi in the course of an astonishing and surrealistic story.

Menasseh, a greater *talmid hakham* than all the rabbis, appears to R. Ashi in a dream and teaches him wonderful interpretations concerning the blessing for bread that precedes a major meal. At the end of the lesson, R. Ashi asks him how he, such a great *talmid hakham,* could possibly have worshipped idols. According to the aggadah, Menasseh responded, "If you were alive in my time, you would have grasped hold of my cloak's hem and run after me to worship idols" (BT Sanhedrin 102b). Thus, distinguished *talmidei hakhamim* like Menasseh, Ahab, and Jeroboam were incapable of resisting the *yetzer* of idolatry. According to the aggadah—and fortunately for the amoraim—this *yetzer* was killed after the First Temple's destruction (BT Yoma 69b). Nevertheless, they did not, in fact, resist it.

We are informed by many talmudic sources about the *yetzer ha-ra'* of the *talmid hakham.* It is far stronger than that of ordinary people (BT Sukkah 52a). The *talmidei hakhamim* themselves admit it. For example, they tell us, "Whoever is greater than his fellow [in the Torah], his *yetzer* is greater than his fellow's" (ibid.) Abbaye testifies that the *yetzer ha-ra'* loves to visit a *talmid hakham* more than any other person (ibid.). Further, if one is a *talmid hakham* and the *yetzer ha-ra'* attacks, only dragging it to the *bet midrash* will provide any chance of warding off the assault (ibid.). Notably, average Jews can defend themselves against the *yetzer ha-ra'* through the observance of the commandments from which—equally notably—those *talmidei hakhamim* whose total occupation is Torah are exempt. Thus, for a *talmid hakham* only the attraction of Torah is capable of overcoming the sexual blandishments of the *yetzer ha-ra'*. Or, we might say, the erotic pull of Torah is stronger than the erotic pull of any merely human woman. That is why, if you are a *talmid hakham* enthralled with a woman forbidden to you, and you want to overcome this desire, run to the *bet midrash* and make love with the divine woman—the Torah. Your *yetzer* will be successfully repressed, and your *yezirah*, creativity, will remain intact, or even flower.

I would like to suggest a possible distinction between the normal *yetzer ha-ra'* and the *yetzer ha'ra'* of idolatry. The former, as depicted in our aggadic selections, is a sexual attraction to a forbidden human woman. The latter is sexual attraction to a forbidden divine woman. The former is ephemeral. The latter never ends. The former is capricious, dependent on passing stimuli. It is a nuisance, but it usually does not carry with it the danger of total addiction. The *yetzer* of idolatry is not a passing fancy. It is ongoing. It is a drug, and so is Torah, as R. Joshua b. Levi knew well:

R. Joshua b. Levi said, "And this is the Torah which Moses placed [Hebrew *sam*] before the people of Israel" (Deut. 4:44)—Do not read *sam*, placed, but rather *sam*, a drug.

If the *talmid hakham* merits it, the Torah will be a life-giving drug. If he does not, it will be a death-dealing one.[12] (BT Yoma 72b)

THE OBSESSION OF TORAH STUDY, EXEMPTION FROM *MITZVOT*, AND IDOLATRY

On the one hand, "talmud Torah k'neged kulam" (Torah study is equal to all the other *mitzvot* combined). It is the taste of life, a necessary drug to this fascinating group called *talmidei hakhamim*. They cannot rest satisfied with the boundaries of the commanding Torah that frustrate them. Thus they declare study equal to all the *mitzvot* and thereby relieve themselves of having to perform any of them.[13] Thereby they replaced the commanding Torah with a creative and redemptive one. Nevertheless, some of the *talmidei hakhamim* constantly fear that the ruling "talmud Torah k'neged kulam" (Torah study is equal to all other *mitzvot*) will boomerang on them, and the drug of life will prove fatal. Those *talmidei hakhamim* who feared this possibility constituted, I believe, the mature, responsible figures who stand behind the many stories and didactic sayings in the Talmud that point out the danger of addiction to Torah and warn against it. All the stories I analyzed in *'Alma Di*[14] were written, I believe, out of this sense of responsibility. Their cautionary words appear in the story of R. Rehumi, whose failure to keep his commitments to his wife as a result of his excessive attraction to the Torah caused his death (BT Ketubot 62b); in the tale of Yehudah, R. Hiyya's son, who failed to fulfill the *mitzvah* of satisfying his wife's sexual needs *('onah)* due to his enthrallment with Torah (ibid.); in the narrative about R. Shim'on b. Yohai and his son who looked with contempt on the "poor creatures" who fulfill the regular *mitzvot* but don't know the ecstacy of *talmud Torah* (BT Shabbat 33b); and in the report about R. Meir, who, because of his addiction to Torah, followed unwittingly his heretical teacher, Elisha b. Abuyyah, beyond the *tehum shabbat,* the sabbath limits. Thus, we have come full circle. We started with Resh Lakish, drunk with the love of Torah, passing the sabbath limits without noticing, and we end here with his predecessor, R. Meir, who does the same. In all these stories—and in many more like them— we find a great deal of empathy for these obsessed *talmidei hakhamim.* Along with the empathy, however, these stories issue a stern warning about the catastrophic dangers awaiting those obsessed with Torah.

LOST AND FOUND: *TALMIDEI HAKHAMIM,* NATIONAL CATASTROPHE, AND REDEMPTION

In BT Baba Mezi'a we read the following:

Rav Yehudah said in the name of Rav, " 'why was the Land [of Israel] lost?' (Jer. 9:12). . . . Because they did not pronounce the blessing for Torah study first [before engaging in study]." (BT B. Mezi'a 85a–b)

This comment seeks to explain Jeremiah's plaintive question, "What man is so wise that he understands this? To whom has the Eternal's mouth spoken, so that he can explain it: Why is the land in ruins, laid waste like a wilderness with none passing through?" God's response is, "Because they abandoned My Torah which I had set before them. They did not obey Me and they did not follow it, but followed their own willful heart and followed the Baalim, as their fathers had taught them."

The verse establishes essentially that the land was lost as a result of the abandonment of the Torah's commandments and the Israelites' turn to idol-worship. This is the plain meaning of the text appropriate to ordinary people. But in R. Yehudah's citation of Rav this verse is transformed and adapted to the exclusive circle of *talmidei hakhamim*. Why was the land lost? According to R. Yehudah, citing Rav, because those *talmidei hakhamim* who studied incessantly failed to precede their Torah study with the blessing thanking God for commanding Israel to learn Torah. The meaning of "talmud Torah k'neged kulam" is that the commandment of *talmud Torah* is weighed equal to all the other *mitzvot*. But when all is said and done, *talmud Torah* is a *mitzvah* and not just a creative joy. When one precedes *talmud Torah* with the appropriate *berakhah*, as is the case with all *mitzvot*, one consciously and publicly indicates that one views one's Torah study as a commandment. After all, the *berakhah* states, "Blessed are You, Eternal, ruler of the universe, who has sanctified us through His commandments and commanded us to occupy ourselves with the Torah's words." Viewed from this standpoint, there is no difference in principle between this *mitzvah* and putting on *tefillin* or lighting the sabbath candles. The one who recites the blessing ascribes the holiness of the act to come to the commanding God. In fact, it is just in this way that common people fulfill their obligations to Torah study: they recite the *birkat ha-Torah* and then say the *Shema'*. R. Yehudah, citing Rav, warns the elite society of *talmidei hakhamim* that study of the Torah all day long and then through the night will not properly fulfill the obligation of Torah study so long as they neglect to pronounce the Torah blessings. I believe we are dealing here with a reaction to those among the *talmidei hakhamim* who lost all ability to conform to the normative system of Jewish life due, paradoxically, to their obsession with the Torah. In essence, they declared that there is no god in their world except the Torah that they study—their love goddess. Hence, they could no longer dedicate their study to the God of the commandments.

Because of these *talmidei hakhamim* the people lost their homeland. And because the people found their homeland once again, they have lost these *talmidei hakhamim*.

NOTES

1. Resh Lakish, Palestinian amora, c. 250.
2. BT Sanhedrin 99b.

3. The sabbath boundary is a distance of 2,000 cubits beyond an inhabited area. One is not permitted to walk farther than this on the sabbath.

4. The stories about these figures appear in BT 'Eruvin 43; Hagigah 15; and Ketubot 62.

5. See Midrash Megillat Esther, sec. 2, in Aaron Jellinek's *Bet Hamidrash* (Leipzig 1853), p. 6; BT Megillah 13a; and *Encyclopedia Judaica*, s.v. "Esther."

6. See Isaiah 3:18–23.

7. Psalms 45:10; Daniel 5:2, 3, 23; Nehemiah 23.

8. *Ketem 'ophir* as used in the Bible means exceptionally fine gold.

9. See Bereshit Rabbah 1:2.

10. See Bereshit Rabbah 1:14.

11. This is the idea of *dehikat ha-ketz*, "forcing the end (of unredeemed history)." Generally speaking, the talmudic sages frowned on activities dedicated to bringing the redemption prematurely.

12. *Sam* meaning "placed" is spelled with the Hebrew letter *sin*. *Sam* meaning "drug" is spelled with a *samekh*.

13. See BT Shabbat 11a and Mo'ed Katan 9a–b. For a broader discussion of the issue of Torah study as an exemption from mitzvah-performance, see Ephraim E. Urbach, *The Sages: Their Concepts and Beliefs* (in Hebrew), Magnes Press, Jerusalem 1976, pp. 546–51.

14. Ari Elon, *'Alma Di, Shedemot* 114 (Spring/Summer 1990).

Glossary

LITERARY GENRE IN THE TALMUD

Aggadah: Jewish lore consisting of stories, homilies, parables touching on theology, ethics, philosophy, history, ancient science, and folk beliefs.

Baraita: (a) An "extra-canonical" *mishnah;* a source similar in form to a *mishnah* and from the same period that did not enter R. Judah ha-Nasi's Mishnah. (b) A collection of such sources. The best known collection of *baraitas* is *Tosefta.*

Gemara: A commentary to the Mishnah and *baraita* sources formulated from c. 200–525 C.E.

Halakhah: Lit., the way. (a) Jewish law. (b) A specific legal rule, as in "this halakhah was authored by R. Joshua." (c) A body of law on a given topic or rubric, e.g., "Sabbath halakhah." (d) Normative law, as in "the halakhah is that it is permissible."

Midrash: (a) Scriptural exposition. The interpretation of the Bible for the derivation of law *(halakhah)* or lore *(aggadah).* (b) Collections of such expositions, e.g., Midrash Rabbah.

Mishnah: A compilation of laws organized by R. Judah Ha-nasi (the Prince, head of the Sanhedrin) about 200 C.E. For the most part the laws are presented without reasons or scriptural proofs. The Mishnah is organized into large sections called *Sedarim* (orders), then into tractates, chapters, and, finally, into individual paragraphs called *mishnahs.*

Talmud: Any collection combining Mishnah and *gemara.* There are two Talmudim, the Palestinian or Jerusalem Talmud and the Babylonian Talmud. The term Talmud usually refers to the Babylonian Talmud.

477

TaNaKH: The twenty-four books of Jewish scripture. The word is an acronym that stands for Torah (Pentateuch), Nevi'im (Prophets), and Ketuvim (Writings).

PERIODS AND AUTHORITIES

Tanna, pl. *-im,* adj. *-itic:* (a) A teacher of the period from c. 30 B.C.E. to 220 C.E. (b) Having to do with the period of the *tannaim.*

Amora, pl. *-im;* adj. *-ic:* (a) A teacher of the period from 220 to 525 C.E. (b) Having to do with the period of the *amoraim.*

Sabora, pl. *-im,* adj. *-ic:* A teacher of the period from 500 to c. 680 C.E. (b) Having to do with the period of the *saboraim.*

Gaon, pl. *-im,* adj. *-ic:* The heads of the Babylonian and Palestinian academies after the saboraic period. The two most prominent academies were at Sura and Pumbeditha (Sassanian Iran). Each had its own Gaon. The Gaonic period extended from c. 750 to 1010 C.E.

Rishonim: Early commentators, active from 950 C.E. to the fifteenth century. Among the most famous Rishonim were: (1) Rashi, an eleventh-century commentator on the Talmud and Bible; (2) Tosafot, a group of scholars who criticized and added to Rashi's commentary; (3) Maimonides, a twelfth-century legalist and philosopher. He codified Talmudic law in his work, *Mishneh Torah.*

Aharonim: Late commentators, from the sixteenth century to the present.

GENRE OF THE RISHONIM AND AHARONIM

Codes: Digests of Jewish law distilled from the Talmud. They tend to formulate law in Mishnaic style, without rationales or proof-texts, although some have preserved portions of the Talmudic text. The most famous codes are Maimonides' *Mishnah Torah,* Jacob b. Asher's *Tur,* and Joseph Karo's *Shulhan 'Arukh,* which has become the legal standard for traditional Jewry.

Commentaries (Perush, pl. *-im):* Line by line explanations of a work, especially Mishnah and Talmud. When commentaries do not deal with each line, they tend to focus on a particularly difficult line or passage.

Responsa (sing. *responsum;* Heb. *she'elot u-teshuvot):* (a) Jewish legal literature created in response to questions about halakhic practice. (b) A particular question and response by a halakhic authority called a *posek* (pl. *posekim).*

SOME SPECIAL TERMS

Beth Din: A court. The lowest courts had three members and could not try capital cases. Between these courts and the supreme court (Sanhedrin) were courts of twenty-three members that had jurisdiction over capital cases. The Beth Din of three still exists both in Israel and the Diaspora. Its usual function today is issuing Jewish divorces and accepting converts. Some, however, are empowered to deal with suits.

D'oraita: Aramaic meaning "from the Torah." Its Hebrew equivalent is *min ha-Torah.* It is used to indicate Biblical law.

D'rabbanan: Aramaic meaning "from our Rabbis," hence, rabbinic law.

Gezerah: A rabbinic enactment, usually prohibitive. For example, the Bible prohibits working on the sabbath. The Rabbis prohibited handling work implements lest one use them on the sabbath. That prohibition is a *gezerah.*

Minhag: A custom. (a) A community custom given legal force by rabbinic authorities. (b) A rabbinic enactment with no basis in the Biblical text but reflecting the Torah's "spirit" and value system.

Sanhedrin: The supreme court of ancient Israel (Second Commonwealth). It consisted of seventy-one members and had judicial, legislative, and executive powers.

Takkanah: (a) A rabbinic enactment requiring or recommending an action. (b) A remedy or improvement of the law, e.g., carrying objects in public and semi-public domains is prohibited on the sabbath; the Talmudic rabbis worked out an arrangement that permitted carrying in semi-public areas. This arrangement was a *takkanah.*

Index

481

About the Editor

Michael Chernick is Deutsch Professor of Jewish Jurisprudence and Social Justice at Hebrew Union College–Jewish Institute of Religion. He is the author of *Hermeneutical Studies* (Lod, 1984) and *Gezerah Shavah* (forthcoming). He has written extensively on rabbinic interpretation of Scriptures, the relationship between early Judaism and Christianity, Jewish law and ethics, and the meaning of the Jewish legal tradition for contemporary issues such as the right to privacy and filial responsibility.